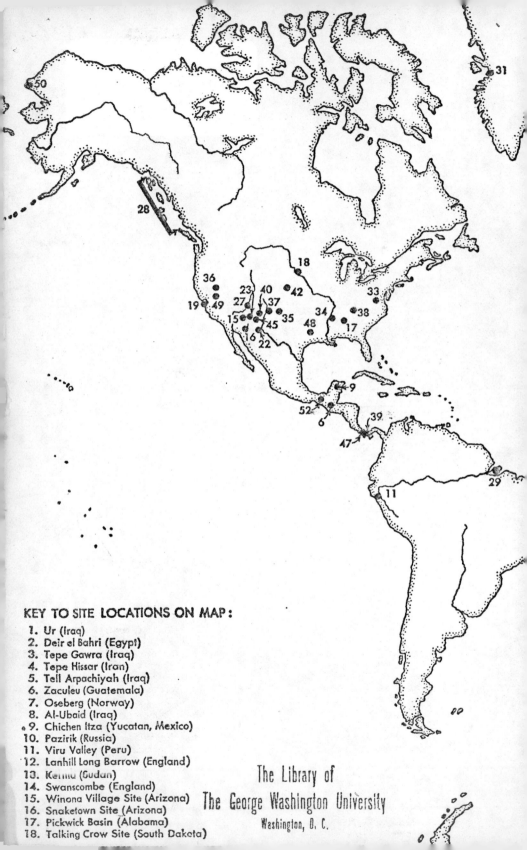

KEY TO SITE LOCATIONS ON MAP:

1. Ur (Iraq)
2. Deir el Bahri (Egypt)
3. Tepe Gawra (Iraq)
4. Tepe Hissar (Iran)
5. Tell Arpachiyah (Iraq)
6. Zaculeu (Guatemala)
7. Oseberg (Norway)
8. Al-Ubaid (Iraq)
9. Chichen Itza (Yucatan, Mexico)
10. Pazirik (Russia)
11. Viru Valley (Peru)
12. Lanhill Long Barrow (England)
13. Kerma (Sudan)
14. Swanscombe (England)
15. Winona Village Site (Arizona)
16. Snaketown Site (Arizona)
17. Pickwick Basin (Alabama)
18. Talking Crow Site (South Dakota)

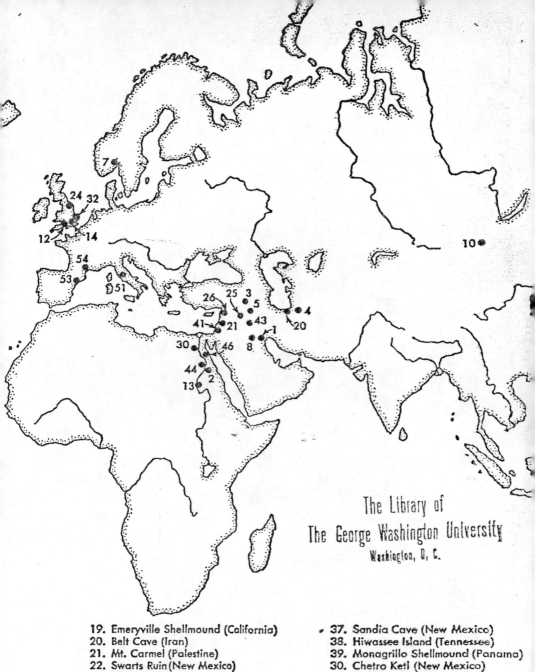

The Library of
The George Washington University
Washington, D. C.

THE ARCHAEOLOGIST AT WORK

EDITED BY ROBERT F. HEIZER

Professor of Anthropology
University of California at Berkeley

THE

ARCHÆOLOGIST AT WORK

A SOURCE BOOK IN ARCHAEOLOGICAL

METHOD AND INTERPRETATION

HARPER & BROTHERS, PUBLISHERS, NEW YORK

CONTENTS

v

REDUCTION OF POTSHERDS TO WHOLE-VESSEL COUNTS

CALCULATION OF THE NUMBER OF BASKETS FROM FRAGMENTS

12. Lithic and Metallic Sources   449

MATERIAL SOURCES OF BRITISH STONE AXES

USE OF SMELTED IRON BY PRECOLUMBIAN ESKIMO

COPPER BELLS FROM THE SNAKETOWN SITE

13. Art   465

MURALS IN ETRUSCAN TOMBS AT TARQUINIA

MURAL SCENES AT BONAMPAK, MEXICO

A LATE STONE AGE MURAL AT COGUL, SPAIN

AN ENGRAVED UPPER PALEOLITHIC PEBBLE

BATTLE SCENES FROM CHICHEN ITZA

PREFACE

IN THE COURSE of a decade of teaching anthropology the problem of choice and availability of reading selections for students has become progressively worse. This book of readings is an attempt to solve, in a practical way, this plaguing difficulty of too few books for too many students. Nearly all the original sources from which these selections have been abstracted are out of print or difficult for the average student to secure.

The selections in this volume are not ascribable solely to the capricious choice of the editor, but are, in part, the result of a joint (and pleasant) effort by the editor and a group of eight graduate students. This group met once a week for two semesters in the 1955–1956 academic year, and the members reported on their search for suitable materials, discussed the advisability of including excerpts which they had encountered, and reached decisions on these. As a guess, I would say that between three and four hundred selections were considered—part of what appears here is the residue of the screening process.

The thirteen chapters of the volume again represent an end product of classification into which the various selections could be fitted. The whole field of archaeological technique and method is not covered, as a casual reading of the chapter titles will show. No series of readings chosen by one person or even by a group can please everyone. We have tried to indicate in most cases why we believed the particular passages were worth including. The individuals chiefly responsible for organizing the different sections are: Martin A. Baumhoff (Chapter 5), James A. Bennyhoff (Chapter 1), Frank L. Bessac (Chapter 2), Sylvia M. Broadbent (Chapters 3 and 6), Albert B. Elsasser (Chapter 7), Gordon L. Grosscup (Chapter 12), Eugene A. Hammel (Chapter 4), Michael J. Harner (Chapters 10 and 11) and the editor (Chapters 8, 9, and 13). None of the persons listed above feels that he deserves any particular credit for his labors since the book was, literally, written by others.

In part we have attempted to select readings which are interesting and informative, and we hope that our brief introductory statements will not detract from the reader interest which the selections are intended to elicit. If there seems to be a certain lack of continuity between the different parts, this is in the nature of the materials, since they represent fairly specific, self-contained subjects. For this reason each chapter can be read independently of any other. The first four chapters deal largely with reconstruction and restoration of events or material items. Chapters 5 and 6 center mainly on man in nature. Chapters 7 and 8 are concerned with how archaeologists work and observe in the field. Chapters 9, 10, and 11 are the only concessions we have made to treating chronology or time-reckoning. This is a major subject in itself and deserves fuller treatment than that given here. Chapter 12 is concerned with some cultural inferences which have been achieved through laboratory inspection of raw materials used by prehistoric peoples. Chapter 13 touches briefly upon some evidences of artistic expression of prehistoric peoples. Each chapter is a sampling rather than a coverage of the topic.

As the subtitle indicates, there are two main warp threads in the contents, one of these being archaeological technique and the other being interpretation of data.

Internal bibliographical citation, except where deemed essential, has been deleted. Bibliographic sources of all citations which are given in the editorial prefaces or commentaries are collected at the end of the book. It was felt that such references might be of some pedagogical utility. Illustrations in the form of maps, charts, and the like, have been retained when they bear directly upon the subject discussed, for many of the passages are understandable only by consulting these illustrative materials. We believe that this minimal editing does no violence to the sense of the original passages and the authors' ideas.

To the nearly one hundred authors, both living and dead, represented in this volume, we express our thanks. Acknowledgments for permission to reprint are made in the text footnotes. It is a pleasure to record that the numerous authors and publishers, without exception, graciously granted permission for reprinting. Our thanks for assistance are extended to the following: Rexford Beckham, Albert Elsasser, Edna Flood, Alfred Kroeber, Eugene Prince, John Rowe, Mary Anne Whipple, and Richard Woodbury.

Throughout the pages which follow, the reader may detect what is implicit in the attitude of all archaeologists—a feeling of responsibility to and respect for the past. The archaeologist works to make the past live again in order to acknowledge the debt of the living to the uncounted generations of the dead who helped to fashion the world which we have inherited.

ROBERT F. HEIZER

No branch of anthropology requires more inference, or the weighting of imponderables; in short the exercise of the scientific imagination, than prehistory.

(M. J. Herskovits, *Man and His Works*,
Knopf, New York, 1948, p. 97.)

It is necessary that we [archaeologists] attempt to attain a measure of exactness in a study which deals so largely with the unknown and the shifting and the absent.

(J. A. Wilson, "Archaeology as a Tool in Humanistic
and Social Studies," *Journal of Near Eastern
Studies*, vol. 1 (1942), p. 4.)

Foremost among these [qualities required for archaeological field work] is the power to observe, and, moreover, to observe *critically*, to be able to distinguish the important from the trivial. Next comes the ability to record what is observed accurately and neatly and objectively: there is no place in archaeology, any more than in other sciences, for intellectual partiality in the choice of facts. Finally, the archaeologist needs both a broad and a scientific outlook: broad to understand his work not as a subject contained in itself, but as just one aspect of the wider study of man; and scientific to realize clearly the purpose and limitations of his methods, and meaning and value of his evidence.

(R. J. C. Atkinson, Field Archaeology,
Methuen, London, 1946, pp. 13–14.)

[The archaeologist] handles the actual things which helped men to pass their lives: the pots from which they ate and drank, the weapons with which they hunted or killed one another, their houses, their hearth-stones and their graves. Such material keeps him much closer [than the historian] to the essentials of history. He must be concerned with the lives and achievements of countless ordinary, anonymous people.

(C. and J. Hawkes, *Prehistoric Britain*, Penguin
Books, Harmondsworth Middlesex, 1949.)

The residue of possible findings [of prehistoric archaeology] is a sort of condensed social history.

(A. L. Kroeber, "An Anthropologist Looks
at History," *Pacific Historical Review*,
vol. 26 (1957), p. 281.)

1

RECONSTRUCTION OF SPECIFIC EVENTS

The archaeologist is forever seeking to reconstruct the past, to describe as much of a former culture as possible from the remains found in the ruins and refuse left by earlier inhabitants. Cultural change is of primary importance in the study of the development of culture and most archaeological reports are devoted in large part to an analysis of the successive alterations and trends which can be traced in architecture, pottery, and other cultural traits by means of stratigraphy and typological seriation. Such studies usually summarize relatively long time periods and must be phrased in broad generalities and are therefore not included in this topic of "specific" events.

Except in his study of graves the archaeologist is rarely able to limit his view to a moment of time, to distinguish a single event from the flowing continuum of life that produced the cultural deposit which he is excavating. The general pattern of living must often be reconstructed from discarded fragments mixed together in a refuse heap. However, occasional exceptions do occur, most frequently as a result of some catastrophic fire, earthquake, or battle, in which the event of an instant of time is captured and preserved. A burned building may often contain the associated objects which were used in it, victorious armies may force the hasty abandonment of a settlement before the defenders can collect their possessions, and occasionally the mortal remains of the defenders themselves are found where death overtook them. Examples of such captured moments form the bulk of this section. With careful excavation and observation, such associations frequently provide essential information on contemporaneous activities and aid greatly in the archaeologist's attempt to make the past live again.

1

The Royal Tombs of Ur

The excavation of the Royal Cemetery at Ur represents one of the classic achievements of archaeology. Five seasons of work were involved, carried out between 1926 and 1931 by the Joint Expedition of the British Museum and the Museum of the University of Pennsylvania. The project was directed by C. L. Woolley, one of the leading specialists in Near Eastern prehistory.

The following selection[1] presents a vivid reconstruction of the mortuary rites accorded to important personages of the Early Dynastic period in Mesopotamia, based on the analysis of the exceedingly complex stratigraphy and grave associations. Woolley would date these events as about 3500 B.C. For more recent data on Mesopotamian chronology see Childe (1953: chaps. 6–8) and Ehrich (1954). In addition to summarizing the complex sequence of events involved in the preparation of the tombs, the placement of the occupants, and the subsequent filling of the grave pit, with repeated offerings over a considerable length of time, Woolley presents stimulating interpretations of the status of the principal occupants of the tombs, and the function of the sacrificed attendants and the nature of their death.

Amongst the 1,850 graves unearthed in the cemetery there are sixteen which stand out from all the rest not simply because of their richness—indeed, most of them have been plundered and their wealth must be taken on credit, and few have produced such treasures as marked the grave of Mes-kalam-dug, itself not one of the sixteen—but for peculiarities of structure and ritual. All these graves belong to the Early Cemetery, and of most of them at least it can safely be affirmed that they belong to the earlier part of the period which that cemetery represents. In the majority of cases they underlie and are necessarily earlier than graves whose contents assign them to Cemetery A; where this is not the case the contents of the graves themselves are characteristically of the Cemetery A type; it is not a question of positive depth reckoned from the modern surface, though as a matter of fact most of them do lie at much more than the average depth; it is a relation which admits of no dispute. To the connexion between the sixteen graves and the rest I shall return later; it is necessary first to explain in what way they form a class apart.

The normal manner of burial, with its variants of wooden, wickerwork, or clay coffin or matting roll, will be described in Chapter V. In contrast to those interments which, whether rich or poor, were essentially simple, the so-called 'Royal Tombs' include a building of one or more chambers constructed in stone or brick, and the burial was marked by long-drawn ceremonies in which a great part was played by human sacrifices. In the de-

[1] C. L. Woolley, *Ur Excavations*, Publications of the Joint Expedition of the British Museum and of the Museum of the University of Pennsylvania to Mesopotamia, London, 1934, vol. II, "The Royal Cemetery," pp. 33–38, 41–42. By permission of the Trustees of the British Museum and of the Museum of the University of Pennsylvania.

tails of arrangements, etc., we find almost as many variants as there are tombs, but in all those which are well preserved the outstanding features of a built chamber and of a number of human victims are present; where, as in three instances, there is no chamber, the lack can be explained by the disturbance of the soil by later diggers and the consequent destruction of the masonry. In PG/1237 the chamber has gone, but enough of the stone-work survives to show that it was originally there; in PG/580, PG/1232, and PG/1332 no signs of a chamber were found, but the disturbance of the soil almost down to pit bottom was evident.

The principal body is always laid inside the tomb chamber, accompanied as a rule by a few attendants; then a place had to be provided for the bodies of the other victims, and this problem is solved in various ways. Sometimes the bodies were placed in separate chambers of the stone buildings, but more often they were in a 'death-pit,' a sunken court open to the sky which might be part of the pit in which the chamber was constructed or might be contiguous to it, or again they might be buried in the filling of the tomb shaft. The number of people sacrificed in a single tomb might vary from a mere half-dozen to between seventy and eighty.

The character of the tombs will best be understood from a description of the making of them.

To begin with, a shaft, generally rectangular, was dug down into the mixed soil of the old town rubbish-mounds to a depth of ten metres or more. It might measure as much as thirteen metres by nine; the walls were cut necessarily on a slope but as steeply as the nature of the soil allowed, and on one side an entrance was made by a sloping or stepped passage leading down from ground-level; the bottom of the pit was carefully levelled. At the bottom of this pit, as a general rule, the tomb was built. Sometimes the entire area of the pit was taken up by a building containing two or four rooms; there was a door facing the *dromos* passage and the rooms opened off each other; the walls were built of rough limestone faced with mud plaster or cement, the roofs, also of stone, were vaulted or domed; here the inner chamber served for the principal body, the outer chamber or chambers for victims of lesser standing. Sometimes the tomb, consisting of a single chamber built like the first of stone with a brick roof, occupies only part of the pit's area, lying in a corner or at one end of it or it may even be outside the pit proper, where it stood in a sort of annexe at a higher level; in that case the pit itself, its sides lined and its floor covered with matting, was the place for human sacrifice. In one instance the sacrifice took place before even the tomb was prepared for the great dead; the mat-lined pit was made ready and the victims were killed and the chamber was built over the earth that covered them, and it is likely that the same was true of PG/1332; but such was not the normal custom. As a rule the stone chamber was completed and the body of the dead king was brought down the sloping passage and laid in it; sometimes, perhaps generally, the body was enclosed in a wooden coffin, but the two queens whose bones we found undisturbed lay uncased, Shub-ad upon a wooden bier, the other apparently stretched on the floor of the tomb; in PG/789 there was a shallow depression in the floor clearly meant to take the coffin; in PG/1236 a similar coffin-trench had round it holes which seemed intended for the uprights of some sort of canopy; but here again there is no single pattern to which all the tombs conform.

Three or four of the personal attendants of the dead had their place with him in the chamber; two were crouched by Shub-ad's bier and one lay at a little distance; four shared the tomb with the nameless woman in PG/1054; in the plundered tombs scattered bones betrayed the presence of more than one body: these must have been killed before the door of the chamber was blocked up. The principal occupant of the tomb was decked with a wealth of finery befitting his or her station—in the case of Shub-ad the whole of the upper part of the body was covered with semi-precious stones and gold; the custom was the same as prevailed in the case of commoners, and there is in this nothing to support a theory that the 'royal' burials are anything more than the burials of people distinguished by their riches; the type of objects is uniform and it is only the costliness of the material or the quality of workmanship that sets them at all apart. The same is true for most at least of the other furniture in the chamber; the vessels containing food and drink are far more numerous and may be of gold and silver or of beautifully coloured stone instead of copper and clay, but this is merely the distinction of rank; the only object which is commonly present in 'royal' tombs and scarcely ever in others is a clay bottle of peculiar shape and unusual ware which is certainly foreign and presumably contained some expensive imported luxury reserved for the use of the court: even the silver boat in PG/789 has its counterpart in the bitumen models of many graves.

When the principal body had been laid in the tomb with the attendants about it—these not themselves laid out as for burial but crouched as for service and unprovided with any grave equipment—and when the offerings had been set on the floor or on the shelves which might line the chamber walls, the doorway was blocked with brick and stone and plastered smoothly over, and the first part of the ceremony was complete.

The next act is best illustrated by the graves PG/789 and PG/800, where the 'death-pit' lies outside the chamber and there is therefore a clearer distinction between the two parts of the ceremony; in the case of the tombs with several chambers these two parts must have been at any rate continuous, for the human sacrifice had to be concluded before the tomb as a whole could be closed. In these graves, that of 'the King' and of Shub-ad—and the same is true of PG/1237, PG/1232, and probably of PG/580—we must imagine the burial in the chamber to be complete and the door sealed; there remains the open pit with its mat-lined walls and mat-covered floor, empty and unfurnished. Now down the sloping passage comes a procession of people, the members of the court, soldiers, men-servants, and women, the latter in all their finery of brightly coloured garments and head-dresses of lapis lazuli and silver and gold, and with them musicians bearing harps or lyres, cymbals, and sistra; they take up their positions in the farther part of the pit and then there are driven or backed down the slope the chariots drawn by oxen or by asses, the drivers in the cars, the grooms holding the heads of the draught animals, and these too are marshalled in the pit. Each man and woman brought a little cup of clay or stone or metal, the only equipment required for the rite that was to follow. Some kind of service there must have been at the bottom of the shaft, at least it is evident that the musicians played up to the last, and then each drank from the cup; either they brought the potion with them or they found it prepared for them on the spot—in PG/1237 there was in the middle of the pit a great copper pot into which they could have dipped—and they composed themselves for death. Then some one came down and killed the animals and perhaps arranged the drugged bodies, and when that was done earth was flung from above on to them, and the filling-in of the grave-shaft was begun. The bones of the animals are found *above* those of the grooms and therefore they must have died later; similarly in PG/789 the lyres have been placed leaning against the wall on the top of the bodies of the women, and can only have been put there after those were dead.

The evidence for all this has become increasingly clear. From the first one could not but remark the peacefulness of the bodies; all were in order, not only set out in neat rows but individually peaceful; there was no sign of violence, not even such disturbance of the delicate head-dresses of the women as was almost bound to result did the wearer merely fall; they died lying or sitting. The bones are always so broken and decayed that nothing in them could show the manner of death, but the evidence of the ornaments would seem conclusive. In my first report I suggested that the killing might possibly have been done elsewhere and the corpses brought and laid in their positions, or that they were killed here and the bodies arranged after death, but again there is the difficulty of the intact head-dresses, for it is unlikely that sixty or seventy corpses could be carried down the slope and laid in place without any disarrangement of the elaborate crown of ribbons, wreaths, and combs. The idea, first put forward by my wife, that the victims quietly drank some deadly or soporific drug is borne out not only by those appearances on which we had at the outset to base our conclusions but by the fact that in every royal grave afterwards found a little cup seems the invariable and sole attribute of everybody; the big copper pot in PG/1237 is further confirmation. Owing to the decay of stone and metal the evidence is sometimes incomplete, and the cup is not always actually with the bones, for it could be dropped and roll away to some distance; but as the detailed accounts of the graves show, one can fairly deduce the cup's invariable presence. It is of course true that the cup is an invariable part of the furniture of every grave: but whereas in the private grave it is *part* of the regular furniture, the bodies in the royal graves have the cups and nothing else—e.g., they never have the water-jar which is the general rule elsewhere, nor any vessel for food. That a drug should be used is not surprising; *hashish* or opium suggest themselves as more or less local products having the desired effects, and whether immediate death or simply sleep were induced there can be no doubt as to the death of the victims being peaceful; that it was voluntary is another question to which I shall refer later.

The covering with earth of the bodies of the dead retinue was not the last act in the funeral ceremony. When the filling of the shaft had reached a certain height there was laid over it a floor of trodden clay, and on this new rites took place. Drink-offerings were poured to the dead—in PG/1054 there is a regular drain for the purpose, in PG/789 and PG/800 a hole sunk in the floor of the sloped *dromos* seems to have served the same end, and in PG/337 and PG/1237 there is a more elaborate construction with a proper offering-table into which the libation was poured and from it ran down into the filling of the shaft. Fires were lit and some kind of funeral feast was prepared, and there might be a 'table of god' also; on a piece of matting—the original 'table' of the nomad—were set out little cups and plates containing drink and bakemeats, and over them was inverted a great clay bowl which would keep them undefiled by earth, and then the filling-in of the shaft went on again. Higher up in the pit there was again a pause; the surface of the loose filling was smoothed and plastered with clay, and on it were built the mud-brick walls of a chamber or chambers. The space between the outer walls of the building and the sides of the grave-shaft was filled in promiscuously with soil, but inside the work went on by slow degrees and with a careful ritual; a layer of earth was followed by one of clay making a smooth floor, more earth and another clay floor, and so on, and on each floor offerings were placed, vessels of food, animal bones, and now and then a human victim; when this had been done a number of times the final floor of the chamber was made ready and a sacrifice on a larger scale was carried out; against the walls were set the coffins of retainers of a higher grade—and these were not mere chattels, like those below in the death-pit, but individuals provided with all the paraphernalia of death—and the whole floor was crowded with offerings, probably the last tokens of the mourners, for here we find (PG/1054) a box containing gold daggers and a king's signet, and hundreds of clay saucers thrown in one above the other, the gifts of the highest and of the humblest. Then the chamber was roofed with mats spread over rafters and daubed with clay, after the fashion of the ordinary house of that time and of to-day, and more earth was thrown in until the shaft was full. Probably some kind of chapel was built above ground, but of that we have no trace; that there was something above the shaft to preserve the sanctity of the spot is inherently likely, and it would seem that the tomb robbers who drove their shafts and tunnels with such accuracy underground must have been guided by something on the surface; but denudation and the activity of later diggers and builders have combined to destroy all the upper levels, and not even the foundations of such chapels have survived.

In the foregoing description of the ritual of the burials I have of course been obliged to draw my evidence impartially from different graves, assuming, what cannot always be proved, that what was true of one was also true of the rest. Actually the evidence for the later stages is tolerably complete only in two instances, but in the other more ruined graves there are often remains which can only be explained on this analogy, and if allowance be made for those differences which I have pointed out, e.g., between the graves with a single chamber and a separate death-pit and those with a two- or four-chambered building occupying the whole shaft, the generalized account will probably hold good. It is clear that we have to deal with a long-drawn ritual which required a number of days and may have been spread over months; the construction of the intermediate building half-way up the shaft marks a stage in the rite quite distinct from the actual burial in the tomb and the killing of the victims in the death-pit, and distinct also from the setting up of the funerary chapel which probably stood above the ground. To all this we find no parallel in the common graves; there, so far as the evidence goes, however rich the ordering of the grave, the rite ended with the burial and the filling-in of the shaft, and though a mound—almost inevitably—marked the place of interment, no sacrifice interrupted the simple replacement of the earth.

When we discovered the first of these tombs, so startlingly different from the hundreds of commoners' graves already known to us, I argued with some confidence that they must be royal tombs. My reasons were, first, that they were definitely graves and, in view of the presence of a stone-built chamber, as well as of the richness of their contents, graves of people pre-eminently important; secondly, that the principal occupant of the stone chamber was provided with just those things which are invariable in the private graves and seem to be the necessary furniture of the dead, whereas the subordinates have nothing of the kind; they are not even in the attitude in which the dead were always laid; he therefore retains his personality but they do not—they are as much his chattels as are the cups and the spears, the oxen and the harps; it is not their funeral, and therefore they do not require the provision which is his right: the principal person is buried; the rest are not buried but sacrificed in his honour. Sacrifice is the prerogative of godhead, and we know that in later times at any rate Sumerian kings were deified after their death and even in their lifetime; we do not know when that custom originated, but it may well have prevailed early; if it did so, the human sacrifice in these tombs becomes perfectly explicable on the assumption that the tombs are those of kings. There was nothing in Sumerian literature to prepare us for human sacrifice on this or on any other occasion, but parallels were easy to find; there is Herodotus' well-known description of the funeral rites of the Scythian kings, lately illustrated by archaeological discoveries in south Russia [see chap. 3], there are the First Dynasty royal graves of Egypt and graves of Ethiopian kings or Egyptian nobles in Nubia and the Sudan: the silence of the texts might be explained either by the custom having lapsed and been forgotten or by the reluctance of the historic writers to record a barbarous survival of which they were ashamed. Lastly, although the few inscriptions found in the graves were not conclusive, yet the title NIN given to Shub-ad might well denote 'queen'—'The Lady' *par excellence*—and the names compounded with *Lugal* might also be royal; and it was symptomatic that such names occurred only in connection with the stone chambers.

Human sacrifice, I would repeat, is only found in connexion with the chamber-tombs and with them is invariable. That it was not the prerogative of wealth is shown by the fact that Mes-kalam-dug's simple grave is much richer than, e.g., the domed tomb PG/1054, yet the former has no human victims and the later has eight: neither was it confined to one sex, as is proved by the same grave PG/1054 and by Shub-ad's grave PG/800, both of which are those of women, whereas PG/789, PG/1618, and PG/1648 are certainly and others probably those of men: it must be an attribute of kingship, and since sacrifice means godhead it implies that for the Sumerians there was in kingship, which, in the words of the King-lists, 'was sent down from on high,' an element of divinity: the deification of the rulers of the Third Dynasty of Ur was on the lines of a very ancient tradition. Do the tombs then simply establish this fact, or from their details can we learn anything more about the beliefs of the Sumerians, unattested as they are by any other evidence?

The first thing to notice is the character and to some extent even the position of the men and women sacrificed at the funeral. Quite evidently they have different ranks and functions; they are not merely so many victims gathered together to make up the necessary quota, as might well be the case in a 'fertility sacrifice' or anything of the sort, but they form a hierarchy or, more correctly, a household. Inside the chamber (I take the single-chambered tombs as giving the clearer evidence and as being less plundered) we find the two or three personal servants whose attitude shows them to be in direct attendance on their masters or mistresses; they have little in the way of finery and must rank as mere domestics. The soldiers are on guard at the door, the grooms hold the heads of the animals, and the drivers are in or by the chariots; the musicians are alongside their instruments, the ladies of the *harim*, distinguished by their rich attire, are grouped together and in PG/789 take their place as near as may be to the royal chamber; military officers of higher rank must be represented by those who have weapons of gold and silver; in PG/800 the man wearing a court head-dress who lies along the end of the great chest may well be the Keeper of the Queen's Wardrobe. In short, the king or queen go to the grave accompanied by the court which attended them in life. It is quite true, as Sidney Smith pointed out, that all this implies a view of the after-life which neither the surviving texts nor the evidence of later burial customs would warrant our attributing to the Sumerians; but if the King is at the same time God that difficulty ceases to exist. God does not die, and the death of a god-king is merely a translation to another sphere. He is to continue his life, and presumably with no diminution of status, rather the reverse, and therefore he takes with him his court, his chariots and animals, and the furniture of his palace which he will go on using as heretofore. Quite possibly the word 'sacrifice' is in this connexion misleading. I have pointed out that there seems to have been no violence done to the men and women who crowd the death-pit, but that they drank quietly of the drug provided and lay down to sleep. To me it appears more likely that they were not killed in honour of the dead king nor because their terms of service must end with his life, but were going with their divine master to continue their service under new conditions, possibly even assuring themselves thereby of a less nebulous and miserable existence in the afterworld than was the lot of men dying in the ordinary way: the degree of faith which would make death the gateway of life has not been unknown in primitive ages.

If it be true that the members of the king's court who went down with music into his grave did so more or less voluntarily, that it was a privilege rather than a doom pronounced on them, then it is a fact most important for our view of early Sumerian religion and culture. The material and artistic splendour of the age as represented by the treasures from the cemetery scarcely seems to harmonize with such brutal and wholesale massacres as the death-pits might be thought to attest; if we adopt the interpretation I have given above, the general picture is more consistent and more likely to be true. But even for the common people who took no followers with them to the next world but who were provided with a wealth of objects which sometimes rivals that of the kings, were the prospects as gloomy as later texts and the material remains of later periods suggest? The argument that they were is not necessarily sound. None of the religious texts on which our knowledge of Sumerian ideas of the other world are based is earlier than the period of the Larsa Dynasty, *c.*, 2170–1910 B.C. Under the Third Dynasty of Ur, from 2300 B.C. onwards, the burial customs of the Sumerians have undergone a remarkable change, and amongst other things the grave furniture has been reduced to a minimum; apart from the royal tombs, which must have been very rich but whose plundered state prevents our saying more than that, the graves are beggarly compared with those of the Predynastic Cemetery and very much poorer than the average grave of the Sargonid period. The change in custom must go hand in hand with a change in belief (assuredly in the prosperous times of the Third Dynasty there was no other excuse for such parsimony towards the dead) and the texts, themselves still later in date, must reflect the creed of their own day and would naturally give no accurate picture of what men had thought a thousand years before. Sumerian culture is so conservative, so static, that we are always tempted to argue from the better-known periods back to the unknown past, but the argument can be pressed too far, and where, as in this case, we have definite proof of a change in the outward manifestation we are not justified in assuming identity of spirit. It seems to me probable that those members of the royal court who went with their king were translated to a higher sphere of service and so had an advantage over common men; but that did not exclude the common man from an afterworld so far like this that the individual was well advised to take with him to it all that he habitually required for his use and his amusement. The vision grew more shadowy with the passing centuries and men took less thought for it, but at the end of the fourth millennium B.C. it was still a potent force.

Egyptian Warriors of the Eleventh Dynasty

H. E. Winlock, also the author of the next selection, treats here[2] the death and burial of a group of Eleventh Dynasty Theban soldiers, and a reconstruction of the battle in which they died. The dry Egyptian climate has sustained a fine state of preservation, so that a detailed analysis is possible. Indeed, were it not for the marked linen, preserved hair and skin, and the cane arrows (which lacked flint tips), the bodies could not have been dated nor could the full significance of their death in battle have been determined.

The month-long Mohammedan fast of Ramadān was upon us in March that year, and we had kept on only a small gang of men for just such jobs as this. The tomb was re-opened and all of its gruesome tenants brought outside while Hauser measured and planned the crypts and corridor within. Not a single object was discovered in the tomb and although about sixty bodies were in it, we found chips of no more than two or three cheap Eleventh Dynasty coffins. That the bodies were late seemed at first unquestionable. In the hot sun they were extraordinarily unpleasant—to put it mildly—and they had all the look of the dried-up

[2] H. E. Winlock, *Excavations at Deir el Bahri, 1911–1931,* Macmillan, New York, 1942, pp. 123–127. By permission of Helen C. Winlock.

corpses of Copts of whom many had been buried in the neighborhood. Still there was something not quite Coptic about the bandages, and the men were told to start early in the cool of the next morning, sorting out the linen which the thieves had ripped off of the bodies, to see if by any chance it was marked. It seemed unlikely, but to assure a conscientious search a bakshīsh was offered to any man who would discover a bit of inscription.

By seven o'clock next morning the men were down at the house with some thirty bits of marked linen, and by noon the number had been doubled. What we never expected had happened. Here were sixty-two absolutely typical examples of Eleventh Dynasty linen marks, with such familiar names as Amūny, Sebk-hotpe, Sebk-nakhte, In-tef, In-tef-oker, Mentu-hotpe and S'en-Wosret, and most striking—and also most numerous, for half of the marked bandages bore it—was a curious, enigmatic ideogram which we had already found on the bandages of 'Ashayet and the women of Neb-hepet-Rē''s harīm. Furthermore, only a few weeks before, we had recognized the same mark on a chisel dropped by some stone-cutter in the catacomb tomb at the bottom of the hill, and we had concluded that it must have denoted property of the royal necropolis, or of its dead, in the reign of Neb-hepet-Rē'. After all, then, the sixty corpses in the tomb were four thousand years old, preserved in that dry, hermetically sealed, underground corridor in an unbelievable way.

From the point of view of physical anthropology the find had attained an unexpected importance. Of all of the Eleventh Dynasty tombs that we had dug, nearly every one had been plundered, had been re-used in later times, and then been plundered again, until it was impossible, generally, to tell whether the bones we found in them were of the Eleventh Dynasty or later. The result was that we had obtained a disappointingly small amount of information on what physical manner of men had descended from Thebes about 2000 B.C., conquered Memphis, and started the second great period of Egyptian culture. Here, however, were sixty individuals definitely of the very race we wanted to know about, and an urgent telegram was sent off to Dr. Derry to come up from the medical school in Cairo to examine them.

As soon as Derry, Brewster, and I started in on our study, the first and most obvious thing which we remarked about these bodies was the simplicity in which they had been buried. As we had already seen, probably no more than two or three could have had coffins and in the crypts the rest must have been stacked up like cord-wood with no other covering than their linen wrappings. These last, where enough had been left by the thieves to judge, seem to have averaged no more than some twenty layers of sheets and bandages, which are less than one may expect to find on even a middle-class body of the period. As our examination went on, this same hurried cheapness became evident in the embalming

—or perhaps more accurately lack of embalming, for at the most little could have been done to these bodies beyond a scouring off with sand, and we differed among ourselves even as to that.

The second striking point was the absolute similarity these bodies bore, one to another. So far as we could see, all of them had been buried under identical conditions and all at the same time. Moreover, all were men, and as Derry's examination proceeded they turned out to be remarkably vigorous men, every one in the prime of life. We found none who showed any signs of immaturity and only one whose hair was even streaked with gray. Another curious point was that there did not seem to have been a single shaven head among the lot. On the contrary, every one of these men had a thick mop of hair, bobbed off square at the nape of the neck as on the contemporary statuettes of soldiers from Assiūt. Sometimes it was curled and oiled in tight little ringlets all over the head.

However, it was broiling hot; Derry's time was short; and ahead of us lay a long unpleasant task. We were wasting no time on theories, therefore, and had methodically measured the first nine bodies when the tenth was put on the table and Brewster noticed an arrow-tip sticking out of its chest.

Physical anthropology immediately lost its interest, and another unexpected chapter was added to the story of the tomb. Up to that time our work-tent had been a mere laboratory. From this moment onward it took on some of the gruesomeness of a field dressing station—only the front was four thousand years away.

Before we were done, we had identified a dozen arrow wounds and we felt certain that we had missed many others. So neat and small were they that they would easily pass unnoticed in the dried and shriveled skin except in those cases where some fragment of the arrow had been left in the bodies. Of head wounds we noted twenty-eight and again we felt that others were probably lost in the rough handling of the ancient thieves. But even so, we had seen two-thirds as many wounds as there were bodies and we felt justified in concluding that every one of these sixty men had met a violent end. This seemed especially likely when we discovered that six of the bodies on which no wound was visible to us had been torn by vultures or ravens, and that could hardly have happened except on a battlefield.

Obviously what we had found was a soldiers' tomb. To judge from the cheapness of their burial perhaps only the three who had had coffins were more than soldiers of the rank and file, and yet they had been given a catacomb presumably prepared for dependents of the royal household, next to the tomb of the Chancellor Khety. Clearly that was an especial honor. If we were right in supposing that all had been buried at once, they must have been slain in a single battle. Considering the especial honor paid them it would follow that this fight must have been one which meant much to the King Neb-ḥepet-Rē'. To us, unfortunately, lacking a single line of inscription from the tomb—for the linen marks tell us nothing beyond the date—it was only a nameless battle of the dim past.

And yet, without unduly stretching our imaginations, we can see how it was fought.

It was not a hand-to-hand encounter. We saw nothing that looked like dagger or spear stabs; none of the slashes which must have been inflicted by battleaxes, and no arms or collar bones smashed by clubs, as one might expect from fighting at close quarters. Many of the head wounds—for the moment we will omit a certain class of crushing blows on the left side of the skull—were small, depressed fractures in the forehead and face such as would be given by smallish missiles descending from above. From the same direction must have come several arrows which found their marks at the base of the neck and penetrated vertically downward through the chest, or one which entered the upper arm and passed down the whole length of the forearm to the wrist. Such would have been the wounds received by men storming a castle wall, and with this clue to guide us we had only to turn to the contemporary pictures of sieges at Deshāsheh and Beni Ḥasan. The defenders line the battlements armed with bows and arrows, with slings and with handfuls of stones. The attackers rush up to the walls with scaling ladders, or crouch beneath them with picks, endeavoring to sap the defenses under a rain of missiles falling on their heads and shoulders, only precariously protected by their companions' shields.

It must have been during an assault on a fortress, then, that our unknown soldiers fell, under a shower of sling-shots on heads protected by nothing but a mass of hair, or with lungs and heart pierced by arrows aimed at their uncovered shoulders. The fire had been too hot, and their fellows had scampered away out of range, but not without some of them being overtaken by a storm of arrows. One of them had been hit in the back just under the shoulder blade by an arrow which had transfixed his heart and projected some eight inches straight out in front of his chest. He had pitched forward, headlong on his face, breaking off the slender ebony arrow-tip in his fall, and the ragged end between his ribs was found by us all clotted with his blood. It was only after he was long dead that those who gathered up his body had broken off the reed shaft sticking out of his back, for that end had no trace of blood upon it.

With the attack beaten off there had followed the most barbarous part of an ancient battle. The monuments of Egyptian victories always show the king clubbing his captives in the presence of his god, and the battle pictures show the Egyptian soldiers searching out the enemy wounded to despatch them. Usually they grab the fallen by the hair and dragging them half upright, club or stab them, and as they swing their clubs with their right hands their blows fall upon the left sides of their victim's faces and heads. We recognized at least a dozen who had been mercilessly done to death in this way. One of the wounded had fallen unconscious from a sling-shot which had hit him over the eye; another had been stunned by an arrow which had all but penetrated one of the sutures of his skull; and a third probably lay helpless from loss of blood ebbing from the arteries in his arm torn by an arrow. None of these need have been fatal wounds, but evidently, as soon as the attackers had retired out of range, a party had made a sortie from the castle to mop up the battlefield, and when the last breathing being had been finished off, their bodies were left lying beneath the walls to be worried and torn by the waiting vultures and ravens. The ghastly evidence of their work was plain enough to see and the ancient pictures of the carrion birds devouring the slain were made only too real by these mangled corpses.

Unquestionably a second attack on the castle had been successful or these bodies never could have been recovered for burial in Thebes. Furthermore, the reed arrows with ebony tips used by the defenders show that the castle was in Egypt, and we know that no part of Egypt successfully resisted King Neb-ḥepet-Rē'.

Of Theban bows and arrows we have found a great number. Every one of the great nobles had enough to equip a whole bodyguard, piled up in the crypt of his tomb, and of the lesser fry buried at the bottom of the hill each had his single bow and set of arrows beside him in his coffin. The bow was always of the long type with a twisted gut cord simply hitched around either tip. The arrow had a shaft of reeds with three feathers, and a tip of ebony some eight or nine inches long, almost invariably pointed with a chisel edge of flint set in cement. Of the ebony arrow-tips used by the defenders of the castle, remarkably enough, not one had a flint point—and yet they had been driven as cleanly into a man's body as one drives a nail into a pine board. Perhaps, some day, we may discover whether there was any particular part of Egypt where it was usual to dispense with the flint points, and if so, we will be a long way toward knowing where this battle took place.

The Venality of Egyptian Undertakers

The excessively dry climate of Egypt has favored the preservation of perishable material and the archaeologist therefore has unusual opportunities in that area to observe more of the cultural remains of past centuries than is possible in most other regions. The following description[3] of the techniques and venality

[3] H. E. Winlock, *Excavations at Deir el Bahri, 1911–1931*, Macmillan, New York, 1942, pp. 110–114. By permission of Helen C. Winlock.

of embalmers during the Twenty-first Dynasty is an example of the specific reconstruction which can be done under these remarkable conditions.

H. E. Winlock participated in the excavations at Luxor, Lisht, and the Kharga Oasis, carried out by the Metropolitan Museum of Art between 1911 and 1939.

Only one abnormal circumstance was noted among all ten mummies. The girl Hent-towy—she was about eighteen years old—found in the tomb of Nin-mose, had not been subjected to the long process of embalming but had been merely bandaged up and buried alone in the abandoned tomb as soon as she had died. Haste had been shown but no particular economy, for her coffins were of the best and her shrouds of the most voluminous. Furthermore, on her wrists there were nine little bead bracelets, on her throat three strings of beads with gold lions hanging in front, and on her left hand two gold rings with green glazed scarabs. It is noticeable, though, that these were the little trinkets which Hent-towy wore in life and not the sepulchral amulets especially made for the dead. What her story may have been we can not guess. At least no such haste was shown in disposing of the young woman named Gau-sen, aged twenty, when she came to an untimely end at the hands of persons unknown, who struck her over the eye with a blunt instrument, fracturing her forehead and the left side of her face. However, poor Gau-sen had lived several agonizing weeks before she had died, and evidently there was then no concealment possible—even if it had been desirable—for her body had been put through the whole long preparation for burial and was finally laid to rest in the tomb of the three princesses.

When a Twenty-first Dynasty undertaker received the body of a person to be prepared for burial, his first operation was to make an incision in its left flank and to remove all of the internal organs except the heart—the seat of life. The organs were carefully preserved, and the body was put to soak in a brine vat for a period which probably ran into weeks. When the body was taken out of the bath again, it was emaciated beyond all recognition, and with what seems very doubtful taste, the undertaker then proceeded to give the body what was conceived to be a natural look. Salt, soda, ashes, and sawdust were rammed into the arms and legs and even into the cheeks of the corpse until it was literally stuffed into a travesty of the human form—an operation which left many evidences of rather rough handling, even necessitating an occasional leather patch to make good the damage done to the skin. False eyes of glass or little balls of white linen with black pupils painted on them were then pushed under the eyelids, the face was painted, and the eyebrows blackened . . .

The organs which had been preserved in brine were wrapped up into seven packages, in four of which were put small wax figures of the four children of the god Horus. These seven packages were then put back into the body through the incision in the flank, and the latter was covered over with a plate of metal or wax displaying the "Eye of Horus."

When the time came to return the organs into the body of one woman, it was discovered that they were lost or strayed—unless they had been willfully thrown away in the first place to save trouble. The embalmer thereupon made up some intestines with a coil of rope, a liver out of a piece of cowskin with the red hair still on it, and the other organs with bits of leather or rag, and solemnly bundled them up into the seven required parcels and put them in the poor lady's body with the four sacred figures. It seems rather a callous cheat.

The days had passed when the dead were decked in the ornaments of this life. In the Twenty-first Dynasty their whole equipment was more ghostly and more magically potent. Their only amulets were those which protected the dead from their natural enemies, the demons of the underworld. Djed-Mūt-es-'ankh had a little gold uraeus on her forehead and on her throat four little gold amulets which were, at the same time, hieroglyphs. In the order in which they were strung they spelled out, perhaps intentionally, a punning charm on her name. Djed-Mūt-es-'ankh may be translated "The Goddess Mūt says, 'She lives.'" The four little amulets may be read Djed-Mūt-djed-ib—"Mūt says, 'Let her heart endure!'" Two more important amulets were put upon the mummy's chest after the first layers of the bandages. One was the hawk with outstretched wings in metal, and the other, a large stone scarab, laid over the heart and inscribed with an old and potent charm which enlisted the aid of Mūt in the heart's protection. Another object to be regarded as an amulet was the papyrus placed between the mummy's legs at a slightly later stage in the bandaging. . . .

Meantime the bandaging had begun. There was a rigid system to be followed and probably an equally fixed ritual of recitations to accompany it. A well-defined and never varying order can be traced, of alternating bandages wound on the limbs and body spirally, and of sheets covering the body from head to foot. At a certain stage the head was always drawn forward with a strip of linen twisted from the back of the head over the face and under the ribs; the arms were lashed to the thighs at a stated moment, with a prescribed hitch; sawdust packing had its proper level to round the mummy out; and always twice in the course of the proceedings the bandages were made impervious with melted resin, poured on the first time, and smeared on by hand the second, as it chilled.

The amount of linen used on a single body was enormous, but there is one interesting side-light on the cost of the material. Almost all, if not quite all of it was old, worn linen, frequently darned and mended. Most of it was old shirts and some, old sheets and shawls, but closely as we might study it, we never could determine absolutely whether undertakers bought up old rags for their business or whether everybody saved their own old clothes for the purpose. Probably it was the latter. There was, however, at least one sheet made especially for the trade, to be put on the mummy when it was practically finished. It was a sheet of specially woven, coarse linen, spread over the bandages and tied in place by cords woven in for the purpose. On this sheet was drawn a figure of Osiris, life-sized, as if to make the body one with the god himself. A protective outer sheet was put over the whole body and stitched up the back, and a set of tapes applied outside, more for looks than anything else. The body was now ready for its coffins and the tomb.

Twice, above, the undertakers have been accused of venality. There was the case of the substitution of organs in one woman, and still further back, the vandalism done the coffins of the three princesses was laid to those who buried the later bodies in the tomb. This last case is a fairly clear one. No one could have got at the princesses' coffins after those of Nesit-Iset and Ta-beket-Mūt were put on top of them, and the robberies therefore must have been committed at least before these last two funerals were over. At a later date the professional necropolis thieves had been in the tomb, it is true, but they had only penetrated to an upper, later chamber and had never found the lower crypt where the princesses were buried. Hence . . . we laid the guilt to the ancient undertakers.

Apparently Ḥent-towy, daughter of King Pay-nūdjem, was the first person buried in the tomb, Djed-Mūt-es-'ankh was the second, and Ḥent-towy, daughter of Iset-em-kheb, the third. The mummy of this second, and Ḥent-towy, daughter of Iset-em-kheb, the third. The mummy of this second Ḥent-towy lay in its coffin, neatly wrapped in its bandages with the outer sheet sewed up the back and the tapes tied tightly above it. When we came to Djed-Mūt-es-'ankh and the first Ḥent-towy, however, the tapes simply lay upon the outer sheets which had been pulled up over the mummies, and when these sheets were turned back the bandages over the mummies' chests were found to be a mess of crumpled rags, through which some one had torn and cut his way, rummaging down to the place where jewelry might be found. On the mummy of Djed-Mūt-es-'ankh they had even slashed their way down to her left hand, which they had pulled up, searching for rings. The loot once seized, the bandages were hastily stuffed back and the outer sheet—purposely uncut in the first place—was drawn up again more or less neatly, to hide the theft. That the second Ḥent-towy had not suffered this treatment argues that it was her undertakers who had robbed the first two princesses. As for the pilfering of the gold-leaf from the coffins of all three princesses, suspicion for it falls, as we have seen, upon those who opened the tomb for the funeral of Men-kheper-Rē', and they too had hidden their theft by laying a linen sheet across all three mutilated faces. The ordinary ancient tomb robbers never displayed any such scruples.

Such venality is bad enough, but even if we have reconstructed the sequence of these robberies correctly, it might still be said that at least the undertakers had not robbed their own patrons. Further evidence came to light, however, that thefts often took place without even that much to be said by way of extenuation.

The mummies of Hent-towy, daughter of Iset-em-kheb, and of Nesit-Iset lay just as they had been placed in the grave, and we had every reason to believe that they were still intact. The tapes, the outer sheet, and the Osiris sheet were neatly and carefully folded on the bodies and stitched up the back. Everything was in perfect order at first, and then gradually, as we unwrapped them, we began to find more and more confusion among the bandages over the chest. The truth dawned on us when we found at last, on both mummies, casts in the resin of the metal pectoral hawks, but the pectoral hawks themselves gone. Then we noticed that the heart scarabs in both cases had been taken out and put back carelessly; that around the torn bandages on the chests there were the marks of fingers sticky with resin on layers of linen that should have been clean; and finally that the left hand of Nesit-Iset had been laid bare in a search for finger rings.

There can be little question as to what had happened here. The mummies had been rifled before they were even completely wrapped, and that must have taken place in the undertakers' own establishments. Fortunately for us, pieces of metal jewelry only were being sought, and papyri or heart scarabs were useless to the thieves. But what a picture do we get for the moralists!

Violence at Tepe Gawra

The following selection[4] presents evidence for the violent end of a cultural period at Tepe Gawra, an ancient site near Mosul, Iraq. Stratum XII represents the terminal phase of the Ubaid period at this site. An extensive settlement contained a larger population than the mound had ever supported before. The settlement appears to have been conquered by foreign intruders, for the succeeding stratum (XI-A) represents the beginning of the Late Prehistoric period, marked by a profound change in architecture, ceramics, and mortuary customs.

Tepe Gawra was excavated between 1931 and 1938 under the joint sponsorship of the American Schools of Oriental Research and the University Museum of the University of Pennsylvania; the different seasons of work were directed by E. A. Speiser and Charles Bache. The twenty strata revealed at Tepe Gawra have yielded essential information on the development of culture in northern Mesopotamia.

Wheeler (1950:30–31) presents a vivid reconstruction of a similar scene of the massacre of citizenry at Mohenjo-daro, West Pakistan, about 1500 B.C.

The excavated area of Stratum XII contained no religious structures, and only a single building which may have served as a watchtower, so

[4] Arthur J. Tobler, *Excavations at Tepe Gawra*, Museum Monographs, Museum of the University of Pennsylvania, Philadelphia, 1950, vol. II, pp. 25, 26. By permission of the Museum of the University of Pennsylvania.

that it is completely secular in character. In this respect it markedly differs from the succeeding occupations, where religious and military buildings were the dominant constructions. Moreover, Stratum XI–A has already been described as the earliest level of a period characterized by unpainted pottery, tombs, and a distinctive type of temple architecture. All these features are lacking in Stratum XII, which is thus representative of an earlier and different culture. In view of this cultural cleavage, the defensive precautions adopted by the builders of Stratum XI–A are surely significant, and may well indicate continued hostility between representatives of the old and new civilizations, even after the latter had become established at Gawra. The testimony of Stratum XII tends to support that view, for unlike the immediately succeeding occupations which were peacefully superseded, the present level seems to have come to a sudden and evidently violent end.

Evidence to this effect is restricted to the northern section of Stratum XII. Room 42 (the White Room—so called because of its white plastered walls), as well as Rooms 18, 43, and 49 bore clear signs of having been destroyed by fire. Room 18 was covered with forty centimetres of ashes and its walls were strongly fire-marked, while many objects were found scattered on the floors of the White Room and Rooms 32, 37, and 38 . . . "A very thick layer of ashes and charred refuse lay over the whole area [of the White Room complex], so it appears that it must have been destroyed by fire, which would account for the profusion of objects, left by people fleeing the destruction. We have other evidence of a hasty departure, in that one room had a small cooking-stove in a corner, in which nestled a cooking-pot with a lid. Inside it were the bones of the meat which may have been in the process of being prepared for some luckless person's dinner, at the time of the conflagration."

In addition to these signs of fire, Room 44 of the White Room building contained the skeleton of a baby lying on the floor, while at the rear of the White Room itself lay the remains of a child of about twelve or fourteen years. Furthermore, in Room 80 at the end of the curved street in Square 6–0, the skeleton of a child of approximately the same age was discovered, sprawled on its face, with a stone (perhaps thrown from a sling) in its back . . . The narrow, three-sided enclosure in Square 6–Q . . . contained similar evidence of a struggle, for there the skeleton of a youth was found, lying half-turned on his back, with arms outstretched.

On the other hand, the lack of further signs of fire in the remaining portions of Stratum XII, coupled with the fact that only these four skeletons were found on its floors, suggests that the settlement was quickly overrun after its main northern gate had been entered, perhaps by surprise. The two skeletons in the White Room and in Room 44 may have been accidental deaths as a result of the fire which destroyed the building, but the skeletons lying in Room 80, and in the enclosure in

Square 6–Q to the northwest are positive evidence of violence since those buildings were not included in the conflagration. It is even possible that more inhabitants of Stratum XII met their deaths before the capture of Gawra, and that their bodies had been thrown down the slopes of the mound, or hastily interred at its foot, but there is no proof for such a theory. Thus, while massacre and complete destruction do not seem to have accompanied the end of Stratum XII, it is plain that the occupation was terminated by other than peaceful means. Soon after the fire in the northern sector the stratum was deserted, for no attempt seems to have been made to re-use or rebuild the fire-consumed White Room building, while the corpses in Squares 6–0 and 6–Q were allowed to remain where they had fallen.

Armed Conquest at Tepe Hissar

Burned structures, charred skeletons, and the position of artifacts all provided clear evidence for the violent end of period IIIB at Tepe Hissar, a settlement in north-central Iran. Period IIIB cannot be dated with certainty as yet, but perhaps is contemporaneous with the Early Dynastic or Akkadian periods in Mesopotamia.

The excavations were carried out in 1931 and 1932 under the sponsorship of the University Museum of the University of Pennsylvania and the Pennsylvania Museum of Art in Philadelphia. Erich Schmidt, the author of this selection,[5] is a leading Iranian specialist who has also done field work in Asia Minor, Mesopotamia, and Arizona.

The dramatic story of the destruction is told, to a certain extent, by the contents of the building. We may attempt to reconstruct the event. The attackers had doubtless surrounded the building. The stubborn defense of the occupants is indicated by the numerous arrow points found in the vicinity of the building. We do not think that the enemy succeeded in taking the well-protected gate, but they seem to have gained the roof, driving the defenders down the stairs into Room 1, where they held the two exits to the roof. However, there may have been an opening into Rooms 4 or 2, where wheat and perhaps other inflammable stores were kept. From above, the attackers apparently threw firebrands into supplies of this kind and set the building afire, repelling at the same time the probably desperate attempts of the cornered defenders to rush the exits. The warriors among the occupants of the building were massed near the base of Stairway 1b, as was indicated by the fact that most daggers (all pointing toward the stairway) were found here, together

[5] Erich F. Schmidt, *Excavations at Tepe Hissar, Damghan*, Museum of the University of Pennsylvania, Philadelphia, 1937, p. 171. By permission of the Museum of the University of Pennsylvania.

with many charred skeletal remains. Some of the defenders may have been killed by the weapons of the attackers, but most occupants of the building presumably perished during the conflagration and the collapse of the roof. This refers particularly to those persons (presumably women, children and men incapable of fighting), crowded together in Chamber 5, but also to those who had apparently hidden in the storeroom (2) and in the "wheatroom" (4). We are sure that the enemy could not take the interior of Room 1. The defenders and the subsequent conflagration cheated them of their loot. Otherwise we would not have found a cup of gold, hundreds of ornaments of gold, silver, lapis lazuli and beautiful chalcedony, vessels of silver, or the copper daggers, particularly the dagger with silver grip. We do not know whether the victors were new-comers of Hissar IIIC. At any rate, houses, alabaster objects and typical burials of this last phase of the mound occupation are directly superim-posed on the debris of the burned building of Hissar IIIB.

The Sacking of an Artisan's Workshop

The excavators of Tall Arpachiyah were fortunate in finding a burned house which contained objects indicative of the function served by the structure and its inhabitants. The building dates from the Halaf period, representing the Chalcolithic Age in Mesopotamia. Arpachiyah is in northern Iraq, near the ancient city of Nineveh. Sponsored by the British School of Archaeology in Iraq and the British Museum, the excavations were carried out in 1933. Mallowan, whose account appears below,[6] has also participated in excavations at Nineveh, Brak, and Chagar Bazar.

This house proved to have been the workshop of a potter and a maker of stone vases of flint and obsidian tools. It seems that the building must have been inhabited by the headman of the village, for it lay in the very centre of the site and was more spacious in plan than any other found. Moreover, the rich and varied character of the objects which it contained proved that its occupant was a man of substance. The workshop contained in all more than 150 objects, the stock-in-trade of the potter and stone worker. Polychrome pottery, stone vases, jewellery, cult figu-rines and amulets, flint and obsidian tools were lying in confusion in a single room, and there were in addition thousands of flint and obsidian cores and chips characteristic of the debris in a stone-carver's shop. All the objects found in this house displayed that elegance of finish which is the hall-mark of the master craftsman. It is significant, therefore, that

[6] M. E. L. Mallowan and J. C. Rose, *Prehistoric Assyria; Excavations at Tall Arpachiyah, 1933*, London, 1935, pp. 16–17, 105–106. By permission of Professor M. E. L. Mallowan, Institute of Archaeology, University of London, and Dr. John C. Rose.

this place of manufacture lay in the very centre of Arpachiyah. From the fact that the most important site in the village was given over to the manufacture of *objets d'art* we may infer that the wealth of Arpachiyah came from these factories. Even the kilns lay in the centre of the site.

It is true that in the East the Bazaar, or *suq*, often lies in the middle of a town; but when in a comparatively small village we find the richest site given over to the manufacture of objects of luxury, rather than of mere utility, we may assume that the master craftsman enjoyed some special status, and that the prosperity of the village came from the pursuit of the handicrafts and not merely from agriculture and a pastoral life. We might, in fact, guess that the stone-carver and painter at Arpachiyah had as a class singled themselves out in a manner similar to the Amarah silver-worker of to-day. In the East the more specialized trades, remaining hereditary for so long, are often found to be in the hands of special communities. In Iraq at the present day the silver-workers are Subbis and the jewellers Armenians. Whether indeed the makers of the splendid polychrome pottery at Arpachiyah were of a different race and caste we have no means of determining, but it is at least certain that their skilled labours had brought them to a position of high importance in the community.

That the occupant was a potter and not merely a collector is proved by the discovery of a large lump of red ochre and of painters' palettes lying on the floor associated with the pottery. Many of these objects, in particular the pottery and jewellery, lay close to the walls of the room, on carbonized wood, suggesting that they had originally rested on shelves, or more probably, tables.

The fortunate chance which resulted in the discovery of so many superb examples of painted pottery was due ultimately to the fortunes of war. The sixth settlement had been sacked and burned by some invader —presumably the southern peoples who introduced the Al 'Ubaid ware found in all the upper settlements. When the enemy entered the potter's and stone-carver's shop he found it richly stocked with variegated wares, and his eye was attracted by the brilliantly painted plates which lay stacked on the tables or shelves with which the rooms seem to have been furnished. The first instinct of man in the heat of the fight is to destroy, and here was glorious material for destruction. After he had killed or driven out the occupants, the invader had indulged in an orgy of smashing; had deliberately hurled cups, saucers, bowls, plates, and dishes against the walls, sometimes irretrievably destroying large portions of the vessels, sometimes actually preserving them by this very act of vandalism. For when he had tired his arms with the breakage, he kindled a fire which burned more virulently in some parts than in others. The worst of the conflagration raged at the south end of the house: debris cast in that direction had therefore as a rule suffered terribly, whereas material that had chanced to fall at the opposite end had often hardly suffered at all.

A Possible Earthquake in Guatemala

Zaculeu, in the highlands of Guatemala, was the Mam Maya capital at the time of the Spanish Conquest in the sixteenth century. In 1946 the authors of this selection chose the site for excavation and reconstruction, sponsored by the United Fruit Company. Excavation revealed an occupation stretching from the historic period back to Early Classic times.

The following selection[7] illustrates the possibility of reconstructing past events if careful observations are made during an archaeological excavation. There would be a tendency to assume that a ruined structure at an abandoned site had merely collapsed from age and neglect. However, at Zaculeu, after noting the position of the debris as it was exposed and examining the construction still in place, the excavators concluded that the collapse had been sudden, perhaps caused by an earth tremor.

The reader may be interested to know that in the Near East, an area of seismic activity, an attempt has been made by Schaeffer (1948:1–5, 255–256, 560) to establish an "earthquake chronology" for the period 2400–1225 B.C. The chronology is based on what he interprets as major destructive quakes identifiable in the archaeologic record of destroyed cities. This ingenious theory has been criticized by Hanfmann (1951).

Evidence indicated that the temple had been destroyed by sudden collapse rather than by gradual deterioration. The entire west façade had toppled inward as a unit, turning about a line through the top of the columns which were kicked outward by the resultant thrust. Complete absence of debris between the fallen wall and the floor leads to the conclusion that the roof was in place when the wall overturned. Had a flat beam and rubble roof disintegrated first, mortar and rubble would have been deposited on the floor. In the case of a thatched covering, falling truss members would most certainly have dragged at least a small amount of wall materials into the room; and in addition, the most probable failures of a triangular truss would tend to exert an outward thrust, rather than an inward pull, on the supporting walls. At the north, south, and east sides of the substructure long round tenons from the upper part of the walls were found near the top of the debris, a position indicating that the end walls and the circular wing had not fallen outward, but had dropped vertically.

Turning to the substructure, the cause for such a wall failure may be seen in structural weakness where the walls rested close to the edge. At these points deep lines of cleavage existed between the conico-cylindrical

[7] R. B. Woodbury and A. S. Trik, *The Ruins of Zaculeu, Guatemala*, Richmond, Virginia, 1953, pp. 43–44. By permission of the United Fruit Company.

element and its inner core on the east, and between the upper zone of the platform and the walls of Structure 4-K on the north and south. Due to the weight of the walls alone, or induced by an earth tremor, the edge of the platform would readily tend to part along the lines of cleavage and vertically drop the superincumbent walls. In the event of a continuous flat roof over the entire building, the lowering of the round wing would develop a backward pull that would be transmitted through the beams. The front and medial walls, unsupported by the already fallen end walls, would be pulled over to the condition in which they were found. Remains of the roof itself would be left on top of the collapsed building where the pumice and mortar occurred.

2

RESTORATION

Often a well-preserved artifact faces destruction if left *in situ*. It may be destroyed by the dislodgment necessary for further excavation, or by defacement, or simply by exposure to the elements. In dealing with some objects such as stone axes no difficulty except that of collecting and cataloguing is usually encountered. In other instances, however, extreme care and ingenuity is necessary if the find is not to be destroyed either in the initial disengagement from the enclosing earth or in shipment to a museum or storage place. Each excavation poses a unique problem. The examples given here of similar problems and their solutions are meant not only to offer suggestions which may prove handy in analogous situations, but also to encourage the worker faced with a difficult situation to summon the patience and ingenuity necessary to recognize and preserve the interesting and unique objects found in the course of his work.

At times decomposition of parts of the artifact and the ensuing fragmentation demand attention of two types: first, care in dislodgment and preservation and second, observation of the original position of the parts so the find can be reconstructed.

In some excavations the unit, referring to a whole building or habitation site, cannot be moved or even assembled in its original form but must be reconstructed in small scale or presented as a diagram in the final report. In order to do this the arrangement of the objects and their relationships within the total unit must be known. It is for this reason that notes and photographs play such an important role in the course of an excavation. In the examples given here not only is the arrangement found by the archaeologist noted but an attempt is made to explain altered positions of elements by tracing the effects of decomposition, disturbance, or erosion. Functional interpretations are dealt with, not as an end in themselves, but as a means to a more exact exposition of the original form.

Chariots and the Queen's Harp from Ur

In the Royal Cemetery at Ur, which was excavated by Woolley, a tremendous quantity of gold objects and jewelry of semiprecious stones was discovered.

In the King's grave were found the vestiges of wheeled chariots, whose construction and dimensions were reconstructed on the basis of the position of metal fittings and imprints in the soil. The following excerpt[1] summarizes the reconstruction of their form.

Nearby was the grave of the King's wife, Queen Shub-ad. Among the remarkable finds in her tomb was the harp, whose ornaments alone remained. The sounding-box was a cavity, into which plaster of Paris was poured, producing, when the surrounding earth was removed, a cast of the interior of the harp with the ornamental inlays attached in their correct position.

CHARIOTS

In the shaft immediately in front of the [tomb] entrance were the remains of two chariots or wagons each drawn by three oxen; they had been backed down the slope and had taken up their position with the animals abreast facing the *dromos* and had been killed there: by the animal heads was the body of a groom, and by the side of one chariot and behind the second lay the skulls of their drivers (see Fig. 2.1).[2] The woodwork of the wagons had perished, but of certain parts of them a very clear imprint was left in the soil and could be photographed and measured; they were of the same type but not of the same size. The first, that in front of the entrance, had front wheels with a diameter of 0.60 m. and back wheels of 0.80 m. with an axle-hole 0.10 m. in diameter; the axle length was 0.70 m. and its diameter 0.14 m.; the body of the car was 0.56 m. wide and copper bolts 0.185 m. and 0.105 m. long secured it to the axle-box—unless indeed the wheels revolved on a fixed axle, in which case it was to the latter that the body was nailed. The second wagon had four wheels of the same size, 1.00 m. in diameter, and the axle was 1.00 m. long, but the body of the car seems to have been only 0.50 m. wide; the sides of it could be traced only as far as the axles, but it must have overlapped them to some extent. All the wheels were of solid wood, apparently made up of three pieces, and they had tyres; round the rim was a band of decayed white substance which seemed to have the texture of leather—this was very clear in the case of the first wagon and can be seen in the photograph; in

[1] C. L. Woolley, *Ur Excavations*, Publications of the Joint Expedition of the British Museum and of the Museum of the University of Pennsylvania to Mesopotamia, London, 1934, vol. II, "The Royal Cemetery," pp. 64–65, 74–75. By permission of the Trustees of the British Museum and of the Museum of the University of Pennsylvania.

[2] The illustrations reproduced throughout the book have been renumbered. In cases where illustrations are referred to in the text but not reproduced, the numbers remain as they appear in the original texts.

the second it was less obvious. I was at first inclined to think that the wheels were fixed to the axle which revolved with them but the fact that the axle-hole is circular is an argument against this, and although the traces in the ground were not enough to prove that the central part of the axle-tree was square, yet the position of the copper nails does rather suggest that the body of the car was fixed directly to the axle-tree itself.

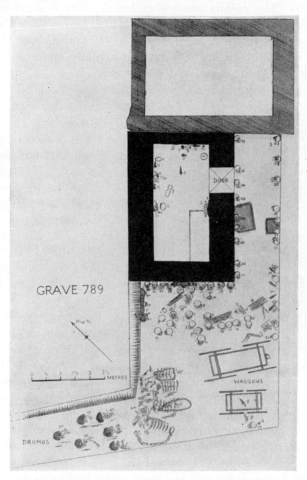

Fig. 2.1. Ground plan of King's grave (PG/789) at Ur.

From the front of each wagon projected a pole on which at a point 2.70 m. from the front axle was fixed a terret or rein-ring; one of these was of silver and was well preserved, the double ring surmounted by a mascot in the form of a standing ox; the other, which was of copper, was completely decayed but had been of the same form. Through the rings passed the reins, which were decorated with very large silver date-shaped beads (0.10 m. long) interspersed here and there by smaller beads of lapis lazuli; they were lying in order, but the silver beads, made of thin metal over a bitumen core, were too far decayed to be re-strung.

The draught oxen were rather small beasts but with a good horn span of 0.45 m. Each had a silver ring in its nostrils, for guidance, and a silver collar 0.09 m. wide decorated with a repoussé pattern of eyes in square compartments with a rayed border; the reins appeared to be made fast to the collars. The collars seemed to be more or less crescent-shaped, 0.09 m. being the greatest measurement, which narrowed at the ends, and judging from the remains on the two lowest animals the broad centre came in front of the chest—it was lying actually underneath the bones of the neck; the reins came to the narrow ends, which must have met over the back in front of the shoulders. The loop made by the reins was curiously short, coming only just behind the rump, and there was only one set for each car, not one for each animal; it is of course possible that they are not reins at all but an ornament of the harness.

Fig. 2.2.   Queen Shub-ad's harp (restored). Height 1.07 m.

THE HARP

At the south-west end of the shaft there lay a harp (see Fig. 2.2) and the bodies of ten women. The harp stood against the pit wall and one woman lay right against it with the bones of her hands actually in the place of the strings; she must have been the harpist and was playing almost to the last. The other nine women were ranged in two rows facing each other, three in one and six in the other; all wore the rich head-dress of the court.

The first thing to come to light was the gold cap of the upright, which seemed to be loose in the soil and gave us no hint as to what lay below. As the work went on there were found two or three gold-headed nails and, searching for their possible connexion, we found a hole running down into the earth across which could be seen the shafts of more nails obviously in position, i.e., the hole represented some wooden object which had decayed away altogether but the nails once fixed in it were being kept in place by the soil against their heads. A stick was therefore inserted into the hole for so far as it would go and plaster of Paris was poured in round it; measurement of the soil and the calculation of the distance apart of the dislodged nails gave the full length of the upright and enabled us to refix the gold cap at the original height. Below, the plaster had expanded into the "shoe" of the instrument and its flow had then been stopped by the not altogether decayed bitumen which had held the shoe to the base; this, with the line of shell and lapis inlay which emphasized its curve, was at once hardened with paraffin wax. This brought us to the sounding-box which, being of wood, had completely perished, but the broad band of mosaic along its edges was for the most part in position, though rather distorted, and could be cleared little by little and secured as it appeared by waxed muslin. The wood had apparently been painted black with a line of red paint running parallel to the edge a little inside the inlay border. The top edge was first treated and then the side could be laid bare and the form of it ascertained; as the second photograph shows, the rectangle of the near side was complete (it was indeed lifted in one piece) and the back of the inlay of the far side could also be cleaned and secured. The gold and lapis-lazuli calf's head which decorated the front of the instrument seemed to be in rather bad condition, for the whole of the top of the head, consisting of lapis tesserae representing hair, had fallen down into the hollow left by the decay of the wooden core, and the metal was a good deal bent, but nothing was missing; in the end it was restored without much difficulty.

Burial of a Viking Queen

One could scarcely find more exciting reading in archaeology than the description of the uncovering of one of the elaborate Viking ship burials, in which an entire ship with its last cargo of dead people and rich offerings was covered by an earth mound. The Oseberg ship described here[3] was 21.44 meters long and 5.10 meters wide. It is believed that when in use it carried a crew of 35 men, was propelled by sail and 30 oars, and displaced about 12 tons. It is concluded that the ship was built about 800 A.D., served as the private traveling vessel of the Oseberg queen, and had been out of use for some time when, 50 years after its construction, "it was brought out once more and equipped to carry the queen on her last voyage."

One humorous note is injected into the solemn occasion of the queen's burial when Schetelig says: "The burial-feast was probably as splendid as the grave, and several irregularities of the arrangement are explained by the influence of drink consumed on the occasion."

The Viking ship burial discovered earlier at Gokstad is described by Nicolaysen (1882). A recent article summarizes the Oseberg burial and illustrates additional grave finds (Sjøvold, 1958).

[3] A. W. Brøgger, H. Falk, and H. Schetelig, *Osebergfundet*, Kristiana, 1917, vol. I, pp. 369–394. By permission of the Universitetets Oldsaksamling.

PLANNING THE EXCAVATION

In August 1903 the proprietor of Oseberg farm (in Sem parish, Jarlsberg and Larvik) informed Professor Gustafson, then director of the University Collection of Antiquities, that he had discovered remains of some wooden construction by digging in a tumulus situated on his estate. Professor Gustafson immediately proceeded to a preliminary exploration, and was able to state at once that the tumulus contained an important ship-burial. The season being far advanced, the winter of 1903–1904 was spent in preparing for the complete excavation next summer. Many practical measures had to be taken beforehand. A contract was made with the proprietor to arrange for all eventualities; money had to be procured; skilled assistants were engaged for the work, and necessary equipment prepared.

It was decided that the excavation should be carried out on Government account, the direction of the work being confided to Professor Gustafson. Among his assistants should be mentioned H. Schetelig, now [1917] professor in Bergen, and Paul Johannessen, preparator at the University Collection of Antiquities.

The excavation was planned according to results obtained by the preliminary exploration that Gustafson had made in 1903. The tumulus was much damaged and not of imposing appearance. The ship was shewn to be lying north and south; the mast had been discovered, also part of the grave-chamber that was erected in the ship. Gustafson further succeeded in tracing the northern end of the vessel, afterwards found to be the stern.

The task consequently was to open a trench through the mound down to the level of the ship itself. The necessary technical arrangements, drainage, conduits, etc. were planned by the railway director Darre-Jensen.

The excavation of 1904 was started in the middle of June and continued till the end of September. The upper strata of the mound were removed, a passage-way being provisionally arranged for the purpose, and the drainage trench was opened (see Fig. 2.3). The stern was uncovered on July 5 and the stem on July 21. The gunwale was traced and the dimensions of the ship thus ascertained. The excavation was now confined to the ship according to the scheme shown by the sections and plans. First attention was concentrated upon a stratum left by an earlier plundering of the grave, then on the spoil-stratum situated at a level somewhat higher than the ship; next the grave-chamber was explored, then the after-part, and lastly the forepart of the ship. . . .

The ship was buried in a cairn of stones which covered the whole from stem to stern. All the tomb was placed under and between these stones.

Fig. 2.3. Original trench cut into burial mound of Viking ship.

THE SPOIL-STRATUM

At an early stage of the excavation it was discovered that the tumulus had been broken into some time after the interment. This had been done by opening a passage some 3 m. broad from the southern border of the mound in the direction of the mast. The robbers evidently aimed at the grave-chamber, and reached the roof of it close behind the mast. Here a hole had been cut in the roof and the chamber had been plundered of various objects, broken fragments of which were scattered in the spoil-stratum of the mound. The objects were bedded in a layer of sandy clay. Among the many fragments found here the following should be mentioned:

Fragments of the stem, of the planks adjoining it, of the carved ornaments of the gunwale, and of the dragon's head were scattered as far as the mast, and the position of these fragments proves that the robbers had cut off the top of the stem. A number of shovels left by the robbers were found. In the centre of the stratum is seen a barrow composed of oaken planks (excepting one of pine) and with long poles. In the same place a great quantity of down and fragments of woven stuff were found beside a piece of wood belonging to a bed in the grave-chamber.

Of much importance is the fact that practically all the remains discovered of human skeletons were found in the spoil-stratum. The robbers have, we may conclude, dragged out into the trench the two female bodies that rested in the grave-chamber, and have handled them with

shocking regardlessness. The anatomical examination of the fragments
has proved that two women were interred in the ship.

Among the objects originally deposited in the grave-chamber are noticed fragments of some chests, of a wooden saddle, of buckets, scoops
and dishes made of wood, fragments of small implements, awl, knife, etc.
Broken fragments of two beds and a single piece belonging to a loom
were also found in the spoil-stratum.

THE GRAVE-CHAMBER

In the beginning of August the work had so far advanced that the
grave-chamber was accessible for exploration. In Fig. 2.4 the chamber is

Fig. 2.4. Grave chamber of the Viking ship.

shown seen from the West uncovered but not yet excavated. The big
broken oak-trunk at the top is the ridgepole of the chamber, and the
hole the robbers had cut in the roof appears as a dark gap under the
ridge. The roof was built of heavy irregular oaken planks inclining against
the ridge and covered the greater part of the ship behind the mast. Owing
to displacements in the mound, the ridgepole had been broken and the
part of the bottom of the ship that was covered by the chamber had
been pressed upwards against the roof. This state of things added to the
difficulties of the excavation as the pressure had damaged that part of
the furniture in the chamber which had not been spoiled by the robbers.

The excavation of the chamber was executed in the manner that the planks were removed one by one and the objects found entered in the diagrams. Close to the mast were located the remains of an oaken chest containing crab apples, a quantity of wheat mingled with the seed of many weeds, and a single shell of a walnut. . . . In the interior [of the northeastern gable of the grave-chamber] two portable wooden posts are seen in hopeless confusion, tied up in the ropes for a rattle and a hook of iron that belong to them. They represent a remarkable type of portable posts terminating in animal heads and richly carved, five specimens of which were discovered in the ship. The eastern side of the chamber was the place for the remains of stuffs, many of which are woven with figural representations. . . . The fragments of [woven] stuff were to a great extent intermingled with down and feathers from the bed-clothes.

Fig. 2.5. Crushed wooden buckets.

Farther on the eastern side of the chamber two oaken chests appeared. The upper one had been broken and nothing was left in it but a bone-comb, a bit of leather, etc. The other chest was intact so that the cover still turned on the hinges. It contained various objects, two lamps made of iron, a wooden club, a thread box, a pair of scissors, a bone-comb, a number of horse's calks, etc.

A large bed . . . was placed in the grave-chamber, and not far from it the remarkable bucket with bronze mountings, two of which are enamelled (known as the Buddha-bucket). At the other end of the chamber [were] again two portable wooden posts equally carved and with their iron chains still in position.

In the south-eastern part of the chamber were deposited a great number of small square tablets of wood, being an apparatus for weaving narrow bands and on the opposite side fragments of a larger loom beside a common reel. At some distance were the remains of *different* buckets (see Fig. 2.5). At the north-western side of the chamber were discovered fragments of a carved head-post from one of the beds.

THE AFTER-PART OF THE SHIP

The excavation of the after-part turned out to be the easiest section of the work, the grave-chamber not having left sufficient space for depositing much of the tomb furniture here. The majority of the objects found in the after-part are ordinary kitchen furniture. An iron caldron with the upper side broken in was discovered close to the northern gable of the chamber and next to it three slender iron bars with trident terminations at the lower end, forming an apparatus for suspending the caldron. Further an iron kettle was found here, and into this had been put a kitchen-knife with wooden handle, two small troughs made of wood, and other small articles. A frying-pan, a pot-hanger, a wooden scoop, two light hatchets with wooden handles, and a kitchen-stool the seat of which is made of oak, were situated about the same spot, and close to these a hand-mill [quern]. On the starboard side in the middle of the after-part a young bull [was found] resting on its right side and with its mouth wide open. The contents of the stomach were partly preserved and have given samples of juniper, different sedges, heather, dog-rose, etc.

Some pieces belonging to the equipment of the ship were also arranged in the after-part. An oar was placed in position in a porthole.

THE FOREPART OF THE SHIP

The examination of the forepart was started immediately after the grave-chamber was cleared, and it was soon evident that the richest and most astonishing finds were stored in this part of the ship. The excavation here was made particularly exciting by the confused position of these very numerous articles which were to a great extent hopelessly smashed between the big stones of the covering cairn. Consequently this part of the ship presented by far the most difficult task to the explorer.

By the unearthing of the stem a coarse hawser appeared stretching along the carved part of the gunwale adjoining the stem; it turned round the stem-pole, and was fastened to a big stone on the starboard side outside the ship. In other words the ship was regularly moored in the mound (see Fig. 2.6). Some of the oars were placed in the portholes of the forepart.

The gang-way used as a landing-stage was also found here. It partly rested on two barrels made of wooden staves (see Fig. 2.7). The anchor of the ship was found under these barrels.

Fig. 2.6. Stern of Viking ship, with hawser and stone anchor.

Fig. 2.7. Wooden barrels.

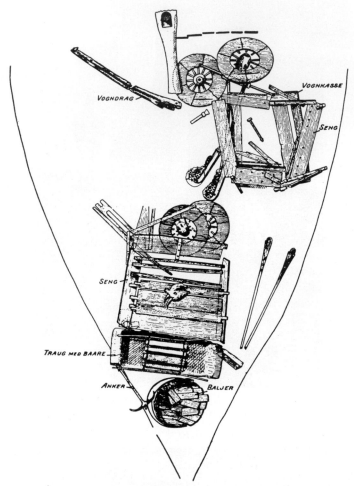

Fig. 2.8. Objects found on foredeck of Viking ship.

Fig. 2.9. Carriage after restoration.

Among the great number of objects found in the forepart, the carriage first of all claims our attention (see Fig. 2.8). It was situated with the hind-wheels close up to the southern gable of the grave-chamber and was in a very broken condition, pressed down by the cairn and the overlying mound. The various parts were forced out of position by displacements due to pressure. . . . The stones being removed, the body of the carriage soon appeared and at last the wheels. The complete carriage is figured in its present restored condition (see Fig. 2.9).

The carriage is one of the largest objects that were deposited in the forepart. It stood on the floor-boards, which were found in complete order in this part of the ship, in the direction North-South facing South. In the carriage were placed a bed and a loom, the remaining space being filled with stones.

THE SLEDGES

Four sledges were brought to light by the excavation and their position is seen at a glance in the plan (see Fig. 2.10). In front of the grave-chamber one sledge is situated with the forepart turned towards the south. The photographs show in what [fragmentary] condition it was found, and Fig. 2.11 gives an impression of how it looks now after restoration. During the excavation this sledge was called Gustafson's sledge as it was uncovered and entered in the plans by the professor himself. The name has stuck to it ever since and ought to be still preserved. To the west of the carriage on the starboard side of the ship, another sledge was deposited pointing in the same direction as the one first mentioned. It was discovered later, and the care of it being confided to Schetelig it was called at once Schetelig's sledge and that name is still attached to it. In Fig. 2.12A part of it is shown as photographed during the excavation, and its present state after restoration is given in Fig. 2.12B.

Farther forward in the ship still, a sledge with carved decorations was placed upside down. It is generally named the 4th sledge. . . . They are all profusely carved and provided with high detachable frames also carved and tied with ropes to the sledges. It is a curious fact that none of the frames was attached to the sledge for which it was originally designed.

The last sledge, generally known as the simple sledge, was found on the port side of the forepart in a position perpendicular to the axis of the ship and with a bifurcated shaft still attached to it.

The three sledges first mentioned possess richly decorated shafts which were however not found in position on the sledges. The shaft most exquisitely worked . . . was situated at the highest level.in the forepart of the ship and was so prominent that the robbers had cut off the end of it on their way from the stem towards the grave-chamber.

Another remarkable fact has yet to be mentioned. In spite of profuse

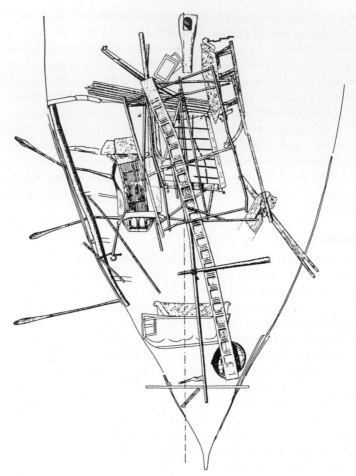

Fig. 2.10.   Wooden sledges in forepart of ship.

Fig. 2.11.   Gustafson's sledge after restoration.

Fig. 2.12A. Schetelig's sled as found.

Fig. 2.12B. Schetelig's sled restored.

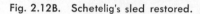

equipment of many horses, a carriage, and four sledges no trace was found of harnesses, bits, or horseshoes; in short all the belongings for the use of horses and vehicles were wanting. It is also worth noticing that several of the horses were buried with complete tethers, one of them with a halter, and some with calks. The skeletons indicate at least 15 horses in the ship, most of them being placed on the starboard side in the forepart (see Fig. 2.13). Here at least 10 horses were collected but some of the heads had been cut off and deposited separately at another place in the forepart. Outside the ship one of the horses was placed on the starboard side forward, and three horses on the port side close to the stem.

In addition to the remains of one or two beds discovered in the grave-

chamber, the forepart of the ship also contained three beds, all much
ruined partly by displacements in the mound and partly by pressure of
surrounding stones. Part of the large bed is seen in Fig. 2.13. The sketch
(Fig. 2.14) is a reconstruction of this bed. The two head-posts terminate
in carved animal heads and are covered with magic symbols painted on
the wood. In the bed a bull's head was deposited, the skeleton belonging

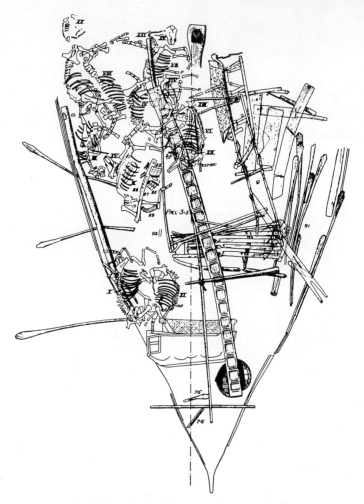

Fig. 2.13.   Horse skeletons in forepart of ship.

to it being found on the port side of the bow. The position of bed no. 2, in
the diary called Shetelig's bed, is indicated by the corner-posts, a, b, c, d,
on Fig. 2.10. A third bed was in extremely bad condition and partly covered the body of the carriage as mentioned above.

Close to the mast-partner and resting on the bottom of the ship were some fragments of a wooden structure interpreted as a chair (see Fig. 2.15). Further the forepart contained the frames of two large tents, the largest of them illustrated by the sketch (Fig. 2.16). It measures 5.70 m. along the ground-sill and is 3.50 m. high from the ground to the ridge.

Another set of frames also found in the forepart belongs to a very curious construction, possibly to be explained as a kind of canvas-house.

An apparatus for card-weaving was found between the stones that filled the carriage. It is provided with a complete set of 52 small square cards of wood, all of them with holes in the corners through which the threads are passed for weaving the ribbons and edge-bands. A band half finished was still attached to it when

Fig. 2.14. Reconstruction of bed.

it was found. Nos. 82 and 85 on Fig. 2.13 indicate the places of two wooden buckets containing some thread-balls, a number of curious wooden implements, a piece of wax intended for rubbing the thread, a buckle, a dog's chain of iron, a small box filled with the seeds of cress (*Lepidium sativum*, Lin.) and seeds of flax intermingled as a weed in the cress. Another small box found in the bucket contained a quantity of dyer's woad (native indigo). Among the contents of the bucket were further a good many crab apples and at the top of all a long and heavy comb of bone. The bucket no. 85 was less productive, containing chiefly 3 crab apples, the total number of apples found being thus more than 50. Most of the apples were ripe.

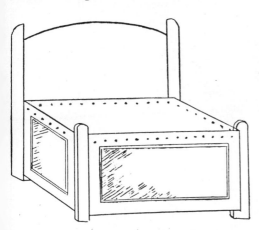

Fig. 2.15. Reconstruction of wooden chair.

Other objects discovered in the forepart deserve mention. A long pole inscribed with runes and a rather large trough were placed not far from the stem. Three shovels, a dish made of wood, a pair of shoes, etc. were found, and four dogs were deposited in the forepart among the horses.

The excavation of the forepart which had required so much hard work and had been so rich in surprising discoveries was completed in the middle of September. On Monday, September 19th the gunwale, prows, and rudder were finally uncovered. For the first time the whole ship was now visible, the examination during the summer having been concentrated upon details only. The sight of the ship when totally cleared (see Fig. 2.17) was striking and at the same time most depressing. Excepting the prows the greater part of the ship was very badly injured by displacements in the mound. The bottom was pressed upwards, the planks were broken, and their bands disjointed. The part of the ship that had been covered by the grave-chamber, was literally inverted, the bottom being here raised to the

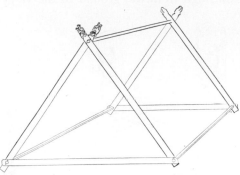

Fig. 2.16.   Wooden tent frame.

Fig. 2.17.   The ship fully exposed.

interior height of the chamber. It was evident that the ship could not be moved as a whole. The only way was to take up the single fragments. During the time required for preparation, the ship was measured and drawn by the marine engineer J. M. Glende whose drawings were later a most useful guide for the restoration of the ship.

THE PRESERVATION AND RESTORATION OF THE FIND

The history of the Oseberg find comprises three principal stages, first the excavation, then the restoration of the ship and last of all the preservation and restoration of all the various articles found in the ship. The last section was by far the longest and most difficult part of the task, the objects falling into two groups, viz., those made of wood and those of other materials. For the latter perfect methods of preservation were already known, but very different was the case regarding the wooden objects. Here Professor Gustafson had to face quite new problems and to work out methods of his own by experiment. The results obtained are of special interest to curators in general and deserve an extended notice here.

The many objects not made of wood have been subject to the usual treatment. Articles of iron were cleansed of rust and boiled in paraffin. Quite small iron objects were dressed with celluloid lac only, and the same method was used for the treatment of bronze and brass. All the iron objects from Oseberg were in a remarkably fine state of preservation.

Ropes from the Oseberg find are preserved in considerable quantity. The ropes kept in store-rooms and at present not exhibited in the museum represent alone a total length of at least 100 metres. The best method of preserving this material apparently is the glycerine-treatment by which the ropes are made soft and flexible and seem to be preserved in a very satisfactory manner.

Objects made of skin and leather comprising principally the shoes mentioned above, were soaked partly in whale-oil and partly in glycerine. Neither of these fluids produced quite satisfactory results, as they both contain fats of organic origin. The pieces were again cleaned and impregnated with chronometer-oil which is composed of mineral oils only.

The wooden objects were first washed in water on the spot during the excavation, wrapped in wet packcloths and stored in the cellars of the "Historisk Museum" at Kristiania. To understand the following process of preservation it should be kept in mind that all the wooden articles were broken and damaged by pressure and displacements in the mound to such a degree that most of them were completely ruined. When brought to light by the excavation the carriage, the sledges, and generally all the largest objects were reduced to fragments and had to be treated by a method to secure not only the preservation of single pieces, but their complete restoration. The wood had to be treated in such a way that it should keep its original volume and form and that the fractured surfaces should be fairly unchanged.

The work was started with long experiments to improve the methods already known, but the results being still doubtful, special precautions were taken regarding all the more important objects. All carved decorations on the sledges, the carriage, the poles, etc. were reproduced in full size drawings mostly executed by Mrs. Sophie Krafft after 1907.

Additional care was bestowed upon some things of prime importance. It was purposed to make exact copies in wood of unique specimens like the portable wooden-posts terminating in animal heads with delicate carvings that would be exposed to deterioration by any manner of preservation. For this work Gustafson had the good fortune to find a collaborator eminently competent for the task, the wood-carver Jørgen Eriksen who executed in wood most excellent copies of the said wooden posts, of one pole and some other pieces. The copies were made of pear-wood and possess a special value as the ornament is more distinct in the bright fresh wood, and as missing details were supplied in the copies, though so far only as the original design could be traced with absolute certainty. Of course the artistic value of the originals is unattainable as well as the finely patinated character of the surface, but the copies will be of lasting interest as scientific documents.

Other wooden objects were reproduced in plaster-casts before the process of preservation. Such precautions were naturally not intended to avoid an elaborate preservation of the priceless original objects. In the autumn of 1904, immediately after the excavation, Professor Gustafson accompanied by preparator Johannessen went to Denmark, Germany, and Switzerland to study the methods there known for the preservation of wooden antiquities. The Danish "moss-finds," the find of Oberflacht in Bavaria, the lake-dwellings of Switzerland have yielded considerable quantities of wooden objects which are preserved in the respective museums, but all these finds consisted exclusively of quite plain articles. The case of the Oseberg find was very different, as the wooden objects here were for the most part richly decorated and the treatment of the wood had principally to aim at the preservation of the ornaments.

The methods which Gustafson declared to be the most suitable were the glycerine-treatment used in Copenhagen, the impregnating process of Berlin, and the formol method of Berne, though none of these methods reached the high standard required for the Oseberg objects.

In the case of hard woods obvious methods answered the purpose. The oak, being the material most easily handled, was steamed, pressed in form, and then preserved by soaking in creosote or in a mixture of linseed-oil with karbolineum. Greater difficulties are presented by woods of a less degree of hardness, and in such cases different impregnating liquids were tried, as varnish, linseed-oil, etc. Some few objects turned out in a satisfactory manner without being subject to any complicated treatment, as the fine little bucket made of yew-wood (see Fig. 2.18), which was only pressed into form.

The really difficult problems were presented by the soft woods, beech, pine, fir, etc. Experiments were made for a long time starting with the methods already known, and the process finally arrived at was alum-boiling, which has proved a splendid success in the preservation of the Oseberg find. . . .

The principle of alum-boiling is as follows: the hot solution of alum immediately crystallizes by cooling, and a piece of wood boiled in such a solution for a time sufficient for the alum to penetrate, is prevented from shrinking by the sudden crystallization.

The treatment comprises three stages, the boiling, the drying and lastly the impregnation.

The boiling is done in a copper vessel and is in itself a very simple process. The difficulty is to determine the proper strength of the solution, to keep it at the exact temperature required, and to adjust the duration of the boiling according to the character of each piece.

By experience it was learned that the consistency of the wood is the chief thing

Fig. 2.18. Bucket of yew-wood.

to consider. The best results were obtained in the case of very soft woods, and the most difficult cases were the objects presenting different degrees of hardness.

The alum-solution must be made much stronger than in earlier experiments. It is found as a rule that the softer the wood the stronger must be the solution, and the very softest pieces required a solution as strong as possible. But no general direction can be given practice and experience being the only sure guide in this question. The temperature of the solution was generally kept at 80–90° Celsius.

A very important point is the duration of the process, and here also the question must be decided from experience. Regarding the softer woods a general rule may be stated that the longer the boiling is continued the better are the results obtained. The time normally required for the boiling of objects from Oseberg was 12 to 26 hours, but instances are noted of pieces being boiled for about 30 hours.

The primary result obtained by the alum-boiling is that the wood assumes a peculiar dull appearance, becoming hard and crisp and of a character similar to glass. A piece of wood in this state of preservation will crack by falling on the floor and it does not stand shaking or knocking.

A most important detail must be mentioned. The moment a piece is lifted from the boiling alum, it is washed at a tap with hot water to prevent the surface being spoilt by alum crystals.

The process of drying, beginning immediately after the boiling and washing is finished, takes place without any artificial means. The pieces are exposed on tables and kept at a constant temperature, and the time required for the drying of each piece is decided by noting the loss of weight. The pieces are weighed every day with the utmost exactitude and this is continued till the weight proves constant, and consequently the wood is subject to no more changes. Then only is the piece fit for impregnation. In exceptional cases the long process of drying may be omitted, but as a rule it is necessary for good preservation, and the objects of larger size require a long time for drying. For a good many objects exact weight-tables were kept during the drying.

The alum-boiling and the drying being finished, the pieces are impregnated with linseed-oil according to the Danish recipe. Small pieces are simply dressed with linseed-oil on the surface, but pieces of larger dimensions were provided with holes to facilitate penetration into the interior of the wood. For the same purpose the oil is mixed with turpentine during the first part of the treatment. The linseed-oil gives strength to the wood, thus in some degree counteracting the disadvantage of the alum.

The impregnation may begin as soon as the drying is tolerably well advanced and at first the oil is applied from one side only, so as to leave a free escape for moisture. The impregnation is continued till the surface becomes hard and shining by saturation with the linseed-oil. Here also the time required is decided by experience.

The process of preservation thus completed, the finished pieces may be lacquered as a necessary protection against atmospheric agencies. All the antiquities from Oseberg exhibited in the museum have been treated in this manner, in spite of the unattractive lustre produced by the lacquer. It is an unavoidable precaution.

A number of the wooden objects are decorated with silver buttons fixed on the wood by iron-rivets. In such cases the rivets were taken out before the alum-boiling and treated separately. After the process of preservation the rivets were restored in the original order.

This short summary may suffice to give an impression of the long and difficult work required for the preservation of the wood. As an example [note] the preservation of one of the wheels of the carriage consisting of 6 parts. The preservation was begun on November 6th 1905 and finished

January 27th 1906. The treatment of one wheel thus taking a time of about 3 months, it is easily understood that the preservation of all the various objects included in the find was continued for years.

The treatment of the single pieces of wood thus finished, the next problem was to assemble the fragments. To some extent a kind of restoration was necessary, though not in the usual sense, as in the case of ancient buildings, etc. In treating the Oseberg find, the plans and diagrams drawn during the excavation provided ample means for controlling every detail of the original construction of the objects. But all the large things, the carriage, the sledge, etc. had to be reconstructed from hundreds of fragments. It should be specially noticed that the restoration was made without filling in cracks in the wood, missing fragments, etc. and new pieces were not inserted except when absolutely necessary to support the construction. The additions thus made are executed in such a manner that an expert will see them at once and without any special examination. A few examples taken at hazard will illustrate the method.

Fig. 2.19A (*Above*). Fragments of wooden bucket. Fig. 2.19B (*Below*). Bucket restored from fragments shown in Fig. 2.19A.

The fragments of many objects were good and strong, with no parts missing so that the restoration caused little difficulty. A photograph (see Fig. 2.19A), shows in all 104 fragments of a bucket found in the forepart of the ship and the same bucket completely restored is illustrated (see Fig. 2.19B), every single fragment of it having been treated in the usual manner by alum, linseed-oil, and lacquer.

Far more difficult was the preservation of one of the sledges called the 4th sledge. The frame was in 225 fragments and the corner-post of the frame in 34. As the sledge is finally restored 87 of these fragments are left out as they could not be placed conveniently. The remaining 981 fragments are assembled as the finished sledge, the total work of preservation having required about one year. Naturally a reconstruction from so many fragments is possible only by means of special supports for which some fresh material was added. The only method possible for restoring the high frame of the sledge was to attach the original fragments to a new interior frame. The left length of the [original] frame is sufficient to prove that the fragments could not be mounted in any other way, and unfortunately iron-clasps and screws had to be applied at the corner-posts to keep the frame together. This brutal but necessary method is justified by the successful result.

Careful execution of this work naturally took a long time, and the objects could not be ready for exhibition all at the same time. Gustafson started with the preservation of the large things, the carriage, the sledges, and some other of the more prominent antiquities. Of all the rest the preservation of fragments is completed, but few of the things have not yet been restored. A number of them, the beds, the tents, etc. are injured and broken to such a degree that their restoration seems doubtful. A good many things of small and medium dimensions were completely restored by Gustafson, but the find being so comprehensive, a great number are still left for restoration.

We have still to mention the method of preservation used for five portable wooden posts and two poles, the most precious of the Oseberg antiquities and unique as works of art from that period in all Northern Europe. From the very beginning Gustafson contemplated having these pieces kept in a preserving liquid, as any other method of preservation would injure the delicate character of the surface. Experiments with this process were delayed till 1912, and preliminary trials had proved that by this method every piece requires individual treatment. Arrangements that suit one of them are not fit for another.

The best fluid for the preservation of the objects is water with a special admixture to kill possible organic germs in the wood, to prevent moisture, etc. The choice of a suitable mixture is confined to substances not affecting metals, as some of the wooden posts and both poles are decorated with silver-domed rivets. The best results obtained after trying many different substances were those produced by a mixture of formol, which is also recommended by other museums. The problem has not yet arrived at a final solution, but the initial results are in favour of the formol-mixture. A special case was made for each of the pieces.

The wooden post no. 1 is preserved in 122 litres of water mixed with 2 litres of formol and mounted on a celluloid stand. It has been in excellent condition for three years, the water being not once renewed all the time.

The second wooden post, also without any metal rivets, was exhibited in formol at the same time as the one first mentioned; at first some slimy moisture appeared, but after several experiments the piece is now (spring, 1917) in perfect condition.

The wooden post no. 3 profusely decorated with metal-mountings, sil ver-buttons, was exhibited in the autumn of 1916 in a case containing 72 litres of liquid paraffin as a substitute for the formol-treatment. Many difficulties ensued and the condition of the piece is now (spring, 1917) decidedly improved, the paraffin being replaced by formol-mixture.

The wooden post no. 4 was in the spring of 1916 treated by the process of alum-boiling, etc. as described above. Different considerations led to the experiment which will not be repeated. The illustrations [not reproduced here] representing part of the post before and after the process of preservation clearly show how the details are blurred by the alum-boiling, soaking in linseed oil, etc. Only when kept in water does the piece perfectly preserve the delicate modelling of the carvings and the exceedingly attractive patina.

THE MOUND AND THE FARM

The place where the mound is situated is part of the farm *Lille Oseberg* in Slagen parish, near Sem, Vestfold. It is a valley watered by a brook Slagen-boekken, which had during the Viking period a more considerable flow of water than at present. It flows from the North towards the South, the mouth being a little to the east of the town of Tønsberg, about 4 kilometres distant from the tumulus at Oseberg. During the Viking period the brook was probably navigable to such an extent that a ship could be sailed almost up to Oseberg farm. The farm is now rather distant from the sea but during the Viking period it may have possessed a harbour not far off. . . .

It is a remarkable fact that the early habitation of the district did not extend to the bottom of the valley which is now most fertile and well cultivated, but absolutely destitute of prehistoric monuments and antiquities. The tumulus at Oseberg is the only monument that ever existed in the bottom of the valley. The natural conditions explain why this level valley tract was not taken under cultivation before the historic period. Professor Jens Holmboe has made out that the plain where the tumulus was erected still at that period consisted of swampy marshes, and the interment with all its rich furniture was consequently on a site accessible to the sea at high water through the brook. A similar situation is noticed in the case of two more prominent monuments in Vestfold—the royal tumulus built on the grave of Bjørn Farmand at Tønsberg and Kongshaugen (the King's mound) in the neighbourhood of Sandefjord which contained the renowned Viking ship of Gokstad. This isolated situation being rather singular for monuments of the heathen period, raises the Oseberg tumulus to a higher rank than the average tombs of that time.

A survey of the antiquities and monuments in Slagen parish also proves that the richness of the Oseberg find is quite exceptional among the remains of the Viking period in the same district. All the other finds indicate a plain and uniform condition of the population with no traces of special wealth or magnificence. The parish was not a place of importance and none of the finds can be compared to that from Oseberg. The splendid equipment of this tomb is in striking contrast to the plain monuments of the neighbourhood.

The Oseberg farm existed during the Middle Ages and may well date from the Viking period. . . .

No local traditions are connected with the tumulus at Oseberg, and it is unknown in the earlier antiquarian literature. It is mentioned for the first time by N. Nicolaysen (*Norske Fornlevninger*, Kristiania 1867) but with no special distinction nor in preference to the common mounds of the district. This total lack of tradition is most remarkable in the case of a mound that contained the richest find of antiquities ever discovered in Norway, but the fact is partly accounted for by the reduced appearance of the mound. As mentioned below the mound had sunk during the historic period so that it did not seem to be of very large dimensions, at least when seen from a distance. It was rather by accident that the excavation was started in 1903. The tumulus was then called Raevehaugen (the fox's mound) a common name of no special interest, indicating only a foxearth.

THE TUMULUS AND INTERMENT

The tumulus is erected in the plain close to the broad old bed of the brook, the level of the plain being here about 15.5 metres above the sea. The diameter of the tumulus before excavation was about 40 metres. The height in 1904 did not exceed 2.5 m. but according to the statement of Professor W. C. Brøgger the tumulus has sunk so much that the original height may be calculated at about 6 metres.

The mound chiefly consisted of sods of good quality and dimensions, arranged horizontally. The sods are cut from the surface around the mound. Special mention is made of a peculiar disposition of the sods in the western wall of the trench, the contrasting dark and bright portions of the wall meeting in a sharp line. The explanation given is that the material covering the forepart of the ship was filled in after the rest of the mound was built.

The erection of the mound, the arrangement of the ship and of all the tomb furniture necessarily required some time in spite of the evident hurry in which all was done. The body of the queen was probably kept at another place during all this time, the interment itself certainly being the last and final act of the ceremonial as recorded by the Arab traveller Ibn Fadlan in the case of a Scandinavian Viking chief who was buried in Russia at the beginning of the 10th century.

The huge mass of sods forming the mound and acting as an hermetic cover, has been a powerful means of preserving the contents of the grave. The deliberate arrangement of the sods is a most prominent feature of the tomb as a whole, and prompts the question whether the mound was built intentionally in this manner to provide lasting protection for the contents.

The strata of sods rest on the central cairn surrounding the ship and the grave-chamber. Considerable labour was required for this great quantity of stone, the purpose of the cairn apparently being to prevent the dead from reappearing, according to the conceptions of the Old Northern pagan faith.

Around the ship the original surface of the soil is covered by a stratum of clay and the sections show that this material was obtained by digging out a bed for the ship, the soil all over the plain consisting of clay geologically determined as a post-glacial isocardia-clay.

The ship rested on transverse piles as already mentioned.

The damaged condition of all the objects in the mound is ascribed solely to automatic displacements. It is evident that e.g. the carriage was deposited in full working order, and no traces were found of the custom of spoiling or killing the tomb furniture which is otherwise well known during the Viking period in Norway.

THE BONDWOMAN

Attention has already been called to the remarkable fact that the Oseberg ship contained the fragments of two female skeletons. One of the skeletons (no. 1) is tolerably complete, the missing parts being the right hand, the left humerus and all the fingers of the left hand. In other words the missing parts are those wearing the most expensive ornaments, the chief object of the robbers. The skeleton is identified as a woman aged 40–50 years.

The other skeleton (no. 2) is represented by very scanty fragments, though sufficient to indicate a woman at the age of about 30.

It is stated that the one of these women probably was the queen of Oseberg, the other being the bondwoman who accompanied her mistress. A passage from Ibn Fadlan is quoted [elsewhere] relating how the deceased chieftain is accompanied on the pyre by a bondwoman chosen of her own free will to die with him. This custom no doubt was widely spread in Northern countries during the Viking period.

In the Oseberg find it is difficult to decide which of the two women was the queen, whether the one aged 30 or the other aged 45. A detailed discussion of this question is reserved for another volume of the work.

THE DATE OF THE FIND

The date of the find is decided by the style of the ornaments. The carved ornaments of the prows of the ship and several other details belong to the variety of Northern animal decorations which has been named Style III by Bernhard Salin. This style flourished about 800 A.D. But beside such specimens the grave contained carvings of a later style with new animal motives. All the different stages in this change of style are represented in the find and consequently a difference of age is shown of about 30–40 years between the oldest and the latest carvings. The foundation of the grave may be thus dated about 850 A.D.

THE PLUNDERING

Two questions are discussed: how and when the mound was broken into. It is shown that the mound was opened by a trench starting from the southern border, but to understand the whole proceeding it is necessary to study the reconstruction . . . [of] the original position of the ship. Arguments are given to prove that the inroad was made before any displacements of the mound had occurred, the grave-chamber having at this time probably still the undiminished height. The original level of the robbers' trench is known as it passes the stem which was cut off by the robbers, and reaches the roof of the grave-chamber, thus it rose somewhat from the border towards the centre of the mound. The trench was about 3 metres broad with sloping sides and passed from South to North.

To decide when the mound was broken into involves considerable difficulty as very vague indications only are given by the find itself. The fact that both the bodies were at that time reduced to skeletons is of little significance, and no more information is obtained by considering the time required for the sinking of the mound. The robbers evidently had no knowledge of the interior of the mound as they started the trench from the southern border, though the grave-chamber was accessible with much less trouble by the shorter way from the North.

More general considerations may possibly contribute to solve the problem, the most obvious question being whether the family to which the grave belonged and the population of the district during the pagan period would allow such a plundering of the grave. The question is most important as we have not only to date the breaking open of the Oseberg mound but at the same time to explain the remarkable fact that traces of ancient plunderings have been noticed in most of the great tumuli in Norway.

The literary sources are reviewed, especially the legal regulations concerning valuables found in the earth, and reasons are given for believing that most plunderings of tumuli date from the early Christian period, probably during the first half of the 11th century. According to this theory the plundering of the Oseberg mound should be dated some years after the interment. A special term in the laws of Magnus Lagerbøter is subjected to a closer examination, viz. *haugodelsmaor*, the man possessing "odel" of the mound, undoubtedly meaning a direct descendant of the person buried in the mound. The word thus proves that Norwegian families even in the 13th century still knew who rested in the ancient pagan tombs.

The facts drawn from the laws are supplemented by the Icelandic Sagas which contain many descriptions, more or less fabulous, of the plundering of ancient mounds. All of these early plunderings of graves were most probably occasioned by the change of religion, by the conversion from pagandom to the Christian faith.

THE SEASON OF THE ERECTION OF THE MOUND

A considerable part of the remains of plants preserved in the mound must be from the year the queen died, and some of the plants provide the means of deciding at what season the mound was built. The great quantity of grass on the sods is sufficient to show that the interment took place during the vegetation period of the year, comprising the spring, the summer, and the autumn. The wheat and other seeds found in the grave-chamber may have been preserved from a preceding year. The crab apples, on the contrary were certainly the fruits of the same year, and must have been gathered after the middle of August or in September. The supposition entirely agrees with the fact that *Leontodon autumnalis* was found with ripe fruits still on its receptacles. On the other hand the mound evidently was built some time before the leaf fell from the alder trees, branches with leaves of *Alnus incana* being found in the mound.

Indications in the same direction are given by the remains of the plants found in the stomach of domestic animals in the grave.

The Temple of Nin-khursag at Al-'Ubaid

For more than half a century Sir Leonard Woolley has devoted himself to Near Eastern archaeology. Since 1907 he has continually done research on or written about his subject, except for the war years when he served as an Intelligence officer and as archaeological advisor to the British War Office. From 1922 to 1934 he headed the excavations at Ur for the Trustees of the British Museum and the Museum of the University of Pennsylvania. H. R. Hall shared the responsibility both for excavation and preparation of the report.[4]

The task which Woolley undertook was not only to describe but to interpret and reconstruct the formal aspects of the temple at Al-'Ubaid in as much detail as possible. The resulting report has been quoted at length here because it shows an imaginative, controlled, and economic manner of conducting an excavation and, even more important, it indicates the scope and many-sidedness of Woolley's approach to the actual job of excavating.

THE AL-'UBAID SITE

A beginning was made at the south and south-east of the tell [mound]. Some pickmen were directed to deepen and widen the trench dug by

---

[4] H. R. Hall and C. L. Woolley, *Ur Excavations*, Publication of the Joint Expedition of the British Museum and of the Museum of the University of Pennsylvania to Mesopotamia, Oxford, 1927, vol. I, "Al-'Ubaid," pp. 58–61, 105–124. By permission of the Trustees of the British Museum and of the Museum of the University of Pennsylvania.

Dr. Hall from the east corner to the end of the wall of burnt brick, and to try to find the face of the crude brick projection into which the former workers had cut, and the rest of the men were lined up some fifteen metres away from the building with orders to work towards it, thus testing the area between the limit of Dr. Hall's excavations and the assumed south corner of the temple. The latter gangs at once found themselves scraping the weathered surface of a solid mass of mud bricks, dark grey in colour and obviously different from the mud brick of the projection from the temple, regularly laid in mud mortar: accordingly some of the men were made to face about and trace the same south-eastwards, with the result that at a distance of 39 metres from the temple front they came upon a retaining-wall of burnt brick—not the plano-convex bricks of the temple, but larger and squarer flat bricks having on one side the deeply-impressed finger-marks which characterize the plano-convex type and are here a survival into a later period. The rest of the line of diggers advanced towards the temple: before long the easternmost gangs began to lay bare a flight of stone steps, of which the surviving treads had been buried below the grey mud brick: the others, cutting into the now steeply rising slope of the mound, found that the grey brickwork rose with it, its upper surface weathered to the present contour, its lower laid in a series of steps over fallen brickwork of a different colour and texture—the debris of the temple which was our objective: the grey brickwork could be traced across the wall-line of the earlier building, and, as Dr. Hall had remarked, formed the cap of the existing mound: at one time it had completely buried the "first period" temple. As we began to remove this later brickwork on the south-west side of the staircase there came to light just such a hoard of precious objects as had been found by Dr. Hall on the north-east side of it—objects, that is, similar so far as regards their general type and date, but, as I shall have occasion to point out later, individually different—statues and reliefs of cattle in copper, mosaic friezes in shell and in stone, as well as copper-sheathed columns and columns in mosaic and artificial flowers like those from the earlier excavations. The whole of the area between the stairs and the south angle of the building was littered with these precious remains hidden below or mixed up with the masses of mud brick fallen from the wall above, and the removal of them was a matter of no small difficulty and kept us busy for a long while. All the debris in front of the south-east facade was removed for a distance of some sixteen metres from the wall, work going down to or below the original floor level: we then dug round the south corner, until here too we came upon mud brick forming a projection from the south-west face of the burnt-brick rectangle, and followed this round as well as might be—for its edges were completely destroyed—to the foot of the second flight of stone stairs whose upper treads had been cleared by Dr. Hall: the drain at the west angle of the projection was the only feature calling for mention. At the foot of these stairs, on both sides and in front of the buttress-like drain support on the north-west side, in the middle of the north-east side and against the east corner of the building we enlarged the narrow and shallow trench by which Dr. Hall had traced the retaining-wall and carried it down to floor level; but apart from the pipe-drains in front of the buttress and a patch of brick paving and another pipe drain by the middle of the north-east side, nothing was found: and so, having thus thoroughly tested the site and proved that there were no objects along three of its faces to make digging worth while, I decided to stop work. The plan of the building had been established so far as the state of its ruins permit—the only doubtful part is the exact extension of the mud-brick platform on the south-west— and all ground likely to contain antiquities had been thoroughly dug over: on the three sides where the walls had not been cleared down to their foundations along their whole length the accumulation of soil did not extend far from the face of the building, and represented for the most part the later grey-brick structure and not the original temple, and beyond this relatively narrow slope erosion had destroyed the original floor level, so that here there was no hope of further discoveries. But the south-east side had amply repaid us: not only had we got from it, as Dr. Hall had from its eastern corner, a collection of objects of art unrivalled from any early Babylonian site, but amongst these was one, the foundation-tablet of the temple, which fixed the date and authorship of the building and brought into Mesopotamian history a period which heretofore had been generally regarded as mythical.

The workmen were now brought back to the cemetery on the little hillock to the south, and a number of graves were dug; but as the excavations were pushed farther northwards and westwards over the brow of the hill and down the slope exposed to the prevailing winds, it was found that the surface of the ground was more and more eroded and the graves were in consequence more ruined: the fragments of pottery which strewed the ground here in far greater quantities than on the comparatively sheltered south-eastern side were in themselves evidence of the denudation of the soil. It is worth remarking here that in southern Mesopotamia, where the destruction of ancient monuments is due to two main causes, wind and rain, these two work in contrary directions. The dry north-west winds prevail during the greater part of the year, the winter rains generally come up on the south-east wind. A wall standing exposed suffers more from the brief action of driving rain than from mere wind however constant and violent; the north and western faces of walls are therefore as a rule the better preserved. But in the case of a mound consisting largely of light soil wind is the chief agent of destruction: when once a natural slope has been formed rain tends rather to consolidate the surface and washes very little down from it, whereas the wind is forever carrying away the fine alluvial dust and grit of crumbled brick, and will in the end produce a level;

at the same time, in the case of standing walls, the wind deposits this dust against their lee side and further protects their south and east faces.

THE FIRST PERIOD OF THE TEMPLE

The ruins of the temple mound belonged to three distinct periods. The lowest down and the earliest of these was that identified by the foundation-tablet already mentioned. This was a tablet of grey marble shaped like a plano-convex brick, measuring nine centimetres by six, and bore the inscription, "Nin-khursag: A-anni-padda king of Ur, son of Mesanni-padda king of Ur, has built a temple for Nin-khursag." The name of A-anni padda is new to us, but that of his father is given on the Sumerian king-lists as the first of the First Dynasty of Ur: there is no difficulty in fitting the new king's name into the list—on the contrary, his admission does away with what was a stumbling-block, the unlikely length of reign attributed to the founder of the Dynasty—and though the exact date of the dynasty must remain uncertain, we can at least assign our temple at Al-'Ubaid to a definite sequence-point in Sumerian history.

The site of the temple was a low natural hillock, an "island" rising above the alluvial plain: on the top of this was built by A-anni-padda a solid platform whose core was of crude mud brick and its walls of mud brick above and burnt brick below resting upon a foundation of limestone blocks two courses deep; the approach was by a flight of stone steps projecting from the south-east side, and on the south-west side there abutted a smaller platform built of crude brick throughout in which there was a second flight of steps. On the main platform stood the temple.

That the building was violently destroyed was evident from the condition of the ruins, for the objects found lowest down on the floor level at the foot of the platform were just those which could have been removed and flung there, and could not have fallen there of themselves, and on the top of these lay whole sections of the actual walls of the shrine, undermined and overthrown before the delicate ornament attached to the wall face had time to fall off or decay: it was also evident that the ruins had been long neglected and exposed to the weather, for not only was there no stump of the temple wall left in position, but the upper part of the supporting platform too had perished, worn away by rain and wind, so that by the time the site attracted the attention of a new builder the original structure was represented by a mound whose top, weathered to a gentle slope, was standing no more than three and a half metres above the First Dynasty pavement level.

THE RECONSTRUCTION OF THE TEMPLE

An account has now been given of the existing ruins and of the objects found in connexion with them, and on the basis of these it is tempting to venture on the reconstruction of a building of such extreme antiquity and

interest. But it must be emphasized that the ground-plan which we possess is that of the substructure only; of the temple which stood upon it
there is not a single brick left *in situ*, nothing remains to fix even its outline,
and any idea which we may form of its original appearance must needs be
largely theoretical. I feel that the attempt ought to be made, because in
the course of excavation there comes to light a number of facts which, perhaps unimportant in themselves, do when taken together constitute evidence pointing in particular directions, and it is only by using that evidence
that one can do justice to the facts: no amount of straightforward description can give them their proper value, and if the field-worker fails to give
due weight to the intangible impression which he receives from the condi-

Fig. 2.20. Reconstruction of the Nin-khursag Temple at Al-'Ubaid.

tions of his work, which only he can receive and which he cannot impart
as such to others, then he fails just where his work begins to be most scientific, and his record, however painstaking, is not a complete presentation of
the truth as he has seen it. If in what follows there is a certain amount of
repetition from previous chapters, it is because here the same facts are
looked at from a new point of view: no detail in the reconstruction should
be inserted without reasonable evidence, but that evidence must be carefully weighed in the light of the facts and in order to get the true implication of these their restatement may be essential. On Fig. 2.20 the original
temple is shown in the form of a sketch, because the scientific accuracy
implied by an architectural elevation is in the circumstances unobtain-

able; to restore, if only on paper, a building whose very foundations were rooted out nearly five thousand years ago is necessarily hazardous, but it need not be wholly fanciful, and to make the attempt is only to do justice to one's material.

We may begin with the platform. The height to which the existing ruins stand gives of course a minimum measurement for that of the original structure, but does no more than that; had the top preserved a moderately level surface one might have argued that this approximated more or less closely to the original terrace, but with the walls varying in height as they do from three and a half metres to zero, there is no intrinsic reason to suppose that even the highest point has not suffered seriously from denudation. Three features of the building help us to estimate its maximum height, namely the two staircases and the drain against the north-west face. If the slope of the drain front be produced upwards until it meets the line of the wall it gives 6.30 m. as the height of the platform: but as against this the terrace may have been lower and the top of the drain [may] have run out from it horizontally before beginning its slope, or, though this is inherently less likely, the terrace may have been higher, the inclined drain being carried up through a cut in the terrace edge: perhaps 6.30 m. is the safest measurement on which to reckon, but this is only a maximum figure and not necessarily the height of the building.

In dealing with the south-west stairs the length of the staircase has to be determined before its height can be fixed. The stairs lead on to the top of the mud-brick platform and we have to allow for a parapet wall round the edge of the platform, which being built of mud brick would have had not less than a metre's thickness, and for a landing between this wall and the stairhead wide enough to admit of a gateway on its north-east side communicating with the main platform, this requiring from one and a half to two metres: we are left with about 13.50 m. for the length of the flight, and since the remaining treads give a rise of 1.50 m. in 2.90 m. we have again a maximum height for the landing of about six metres above floor level.

If the south-east stairs ran up at their present slope to the line of the platform front it would make the terrace some ten metres high, a figure wholly inconsistent with the evidence of the other features; we must conclude that the steps did not extend the whole length of the ramp, but that there was at the stairhead a level approach or landing projecting from the terrace edge, and, since there is nothing to show what proportion of the ramp was taken up by this and what by the stairs, it is impossible on internal grounds to estimate the height of the latter.

The maximum height for the platform is therefore 6.00 m. approximately, and 3.50 m. its minimum; for the purposes of reconstruction I have arbitrarily taken a mean between these two and have drawn it as about 4.50 m. high. In assuming this comparatively low elevation I was influenced by aesthetic considerations: the decorative elements of the fa çade were attached, as the conditions in which they were found proved, I think, beyond question, to the wall of the temple and not to that of the platform, and judging from the order of their arrangement they must have occupied a very considerable vertical space on the wall; the lowest of them would be as much above eye-level as the base of the temple wall, and the highest much higher up; one could not imagine that they were "skied" to the extent of being invisible, and so, in order that due justice might be done to their small scale and delicate workmanship, I have brought them down as low as possible by reducing as far as seemed safe the height of the platform.

When I visited Al-'Ubaid in the spring of 1923 and saw the outline of the building in so far as it has been traced by Dr. Hall, I concluded that the wall was the containing-wall of a platform and that the greater part of this platform had been an open court, the only superstructure upon it being comparatively small and occupying the south-east side of the terrace, or, more probably, its south corner. This conclusion is worth recording because it was based on certain very obvious features of the site, namely that the highest point of the mound rose above just that part of the supposed rectangle which had not yet been excavated, i.e., its south corner, while from this highest point the levels fell away to the east, north, and west so steadily that there was virtually nothing to mark the [known] confines of the building. I had already suggested projections from the rectangle on its south-east and south-west faces, and was inclined to connect these with the superstructure, wherein I was in error, but on the main question of the position of the building on the platform the surface indications were fully borne out by the results of excavation. Along the north-east face of the platform all the upper courses of burnt brick had fallen and the north corner was ruined down to its foundation; the west corner and the south-west wall as far as the smaller staircase was preserved up to the top of the burnt brick, and the north-west wall also was in good condition; but along the south-east face, on each side of the main stairs, there remained crude brickwork which, though tilted forwards, still stood above the burnt brick to a total height of 3.50 m., running down to nothing at the east corner where only the burnt brick was left; consequently in the centre of this face the mound stood high; and at the south corner, though we found that the whole wall, crude and burnt brick alike, had been violently overthrown almost from ground level, and was leaning forwards at an acute angle, yet even so the accumulation of ancient debris was so great that the mound's highest point lay south-west of the main flight of stairs, and the high ground ran right out beyond the angle of the platform. And this was not merely a surface accident. When the builders of the second temple started to lay their brick terrace over the top of the old ruins the latter formed a mound of much the same shape as we see to-day; thus towards the north corner, which is now ruined down

almost to its foundations, the grey brickwork of the second period also is
carried down to a level much below that to which elsewhere the burnt
brick and the red mud brick of the earlier building are preserved; just by
the main staircase the old work was standing to about 3.50 m., and in
front of this the heaped rubbish against the south-east wall was virtually
as high, so that in order to lay their terrace bricks the Second Period
labourers trimmed the rubble slope into steps of which the first from the
top was 2.60 m. above the old floor level and extended 2.50 m. from the
face of the south-east wall of the platform, and then came steps 2.10 m.,
1.80 m., 1.20 m., and 0.90 m. high respectively, and giving a total extension
from the wall of nearly ten metres. On the north-west face on either side
of the stair projection the total deposit of rubbish, which was 2.35 m. high
against the wall, represented all three periods and sloped down rapidly
to nothing, and on the north-east face there was even less—the platform
wall stood only about 1.85 m. high above floor level, and when we ran a
trench out from this following the original ground level for a distance of
over 25.00 m. we found that the total amount of debris here was no more
than would be accounted for by the collapse of the platform and of the
later buildings, and did not at all support the theory of a contemporary
superstructure on this side of the platform itself. The natural processes of
detrition by weather will not suffice to explain this recurring feature of
the shape of the ruins. As I have said before a building with mud-brick
walls suffers more from the rain brought up by the south-east winds than
from the dry winds which prevail from the north-west, and therefore had
the oldest Nin-khursag temple occupied the whole of its platform we
should have expected its north-west part to be best preserved and its
south-east part to be most decayed; but the reverse is the case with the
platform itself, and of the temple we have the south-east wall fallen almost *en bloc*, whereas of the other walls there remains no trace whatsoever; and, though the temple was violently overthrown, yet the argument
is not without force, for had it occupied the whole platform and all its
walls been destroyed in the same way as that on the south-east, then solid
masses of mud brick and mortar such as we found there would have lain
also against the north-east and north-west faces of the platform and would
have resisted wind-erosion almost as effectually as would standing walls;
but we found nothing of the sort. So far as this evidence goes it certainly
looks as if the temple had been a small one standing in the south corner
of the platform court.

Another argument pointing in the same direction is that whereas
against the south-east face there lay under the fallen ruins of the wall a
mass of objects belonging to the mural decoration, nothing of the sort was
produced by our work along the three other faces.

It is true that we did not everywhere excavate down to floor level,
but the generalization made above holds good none the less. Dr. Hall had

merely traced the outline of the platform from the south-west stairs round by the north, west, and east corners to where the burnt brickwork of the south-east wall comes to an end against the crude brickwork of the main stair ramp; his trenches averaged 0.50 m. wide by 0.75 m. deep, and so reached floor level only at the north corner where the wall was ruined down to its foundations: while following along the south-east face he came upon the copper Imgig relief and the lions' heads, etc., and in order to extricate these had to widen his trench to about four metres, but did not work down to the original floor because the objects lay on the top of a stratum of debris a metre thick, which he had not time to remove. In 1923 we cleared on the south-east face between the stairs and the east corner out to a width of ten or twelve metres, going down through the stratum where Dr. Hall had found his objects to the white lime floor; on the south-west face a clearing on a similar scale between the south corner and the projection of the south-west staircase produced only one fragment of copper-sheathed timber; at the foot of the south-west stairs a clearing extending as far out as the drain and carried down to floor level yielded parts of one clay flower; on the north-east face we worked round the east corner for some metres and found nothing, and farther along the same wall a clearing some seven metres wide was equally barren; on the north-west face we went down to ground level on each side of the "spout" drain and out for ten metres from the wall, and again found no objects. These tests were so thorough that further excavation along the remaining lengths of wall was unnecessary.

We were justified in concluding that either the exterior mural decoration of the temple had been confined to the south-east facade, or, if the other walls had been decorated, they stood so far back on the platform that nothing from them fell over its edge when the building was destroyed. The latter alternative is supported by the relatively small quantity of debris found against these faces. Even so, since the platform is not so very large and the temple walls therefore cannot have been very far from the edge, we might have expected to find at least a few bits of wreckage from their ornament, if they were ornamented, flung out to a distance and lying near the corresponding walls of the platform, but this was not the case, and we may conclude that in all probability the north-west and south-west walls were bare of ornament; for the north-east wall the negative evidence is, as we shall see, less strong.

It is quite certain that all the objects found between the main stairs and the south angle of the platform adorned the south-east wall of the temple, for the latter had fallen forward in great masses, and the sections of friezes were found still adhering to these with their copper holdfasts embedded in the undisturbed brickwork. It was possible to trace the actual line of the fall; the upper parts of the wall had come down first and had smashed to pieces on the floor, over which their debris formed a layer about a metre thick burying the lower half of the burnt brickwork of the retaining wall; then the main part of the wall followed suit. Generally a goodly length of mud-brick wall sagged forwards as if it had been undermined and thrust out from behind and collapsed *en bloc* (thus at the south corner the standing stump of the burnt-brick wall of the platform itself was bent forwards in a curve, and a section cut through the rubbish in front of it showed its upper bricks forced apart and lying radially in a parabola), and might turn a half-somersault in its fall, with the result that, e.g., the three copper bulls . . . which had not been broken apart but formed still a single strip over 2.50 m. long secured by its holdfasts to the wall face, lay at an angle of forty-five degrees face downwards and parallel to the wall with their feet towards it, with the wall-mass to which they were attached on top of them and below them the rubble due to the earlier fall. Their original position on the wall-face could thus be determined within half a metre—it was exactly above where they lay. On the other hand, in the angle between the wall and the south-west side of the stair-ramp a large section of the temple wall had fallen quite differently, its footings had slipped outwards and downwards, while at the same time it broke across horizontally, so that the original outer face of the lower part of the wall still faced outwards and was nearly vertical, resting on the layer of rubble which covered the pavement, and leaning back slightly against the retaining wall of the platform, and the original upper part lay face downwards on the top of it. Here, too, there was no possible doubt as to the place from which the wall fragment had slipped and therefore none as to the real position of the decoration on it—in this case the inlay frieze with the milking scene, and, below it, bulls from the copper relief.

Clearly the position of the objects in the debris is a matter of the first importance for the reconstruction of the temple, but their original position on the building ought to be established before we can argue much more as to the plan.

There is no doubt at all that the copper reliefs of bulls lying down formed one continuous frieze, and that this was on the outside and not on the inside of the building; so much is clear from the position of the fragments. The same is true of the inlay frieze represented by the milking scene, the panels with rows of cattle, and the limestone panel of the bull and eagle, which was found actually attached to the milking scene, and by a few small fragments including parts of cattle, human figures, and another bull-and-eagle panel. The birds also formed a frieze which was probably not the same as that with the cattle. We therefore have certainly two and probably three friezes which have to be assigned to that part of the temple facade lying between the staircase and the south corner.

Of the copper bull reliefs we found twelve with their bodies more or less complete and two extra heads, fourteen animals in all. The length of each beast is 0.55 m., but there are blank spaces between them (where as a rule the holdfasts come), so that the average wall length occupied by each is 0.70 m.; in addition there were found fragments of plain panelling belonging to the same frieze, perhaps inserted in less conspicuous places (one such was attached to the long strip formed by reliefs 4, 5, and 6). Thus the extant remains represent sufficient length of frieze virtually to fill the whole wall space between the stairs and the south corner of the temple, especially if the latter building were set back somewhat on the platform and its front were consequently rather shorter.

These copper reliefs formed roughly speaking a line parallel with the wall of the platform, and most of them were face downwards and relatively high up in the productive stratum. This is because the wall masses to which they were attached had fallen forwards, turning as they fell, on to the other debris, fallen sooner, which was heaped up against the wall face and sloped away from it; when, therefore, a section of the wall collapsed, what had been its base generally lay highest and nearest to the platform, face downwards, and we are able to conclude that the copper reliefs had formed a frieze relatively low down on the temple façade. What the actual height was cannot, I think, be very accurately calculated from the line of fall of the brickwork, for this was naturally irregular and any calculation would be greatly complicated by the temple having been, as I believe it was, set back from the edge of the platform: but on the whole it seemed as if the frieze must have stood at not less than five and not more than eight metres above the level of the lime floor in front of the platform.

Of the inlay frieze of animals much less was found, a total length of 3.65 m. represented by more or less complete panels and scattered figures or parts of figures which together might account for another 2.30 m., i.e., only some 6.0 m. as against a wall length (supposing that this frieze also ran the whole length of the wall between corner and stairs) of about twelve metres. The best preserved examples lay in the corner by the stair-ramp, where, as has already been noticed, the temple wall had slipped forwards from its base instead of tumbling headlong, and here naturally they were high up in the debris. The smaller fragments were found farther away from the platform than were the copper-bull reliefs, and rather deeper down, closer that is to the floor, not necessarily under a greater accumulation of rubbish, for the modern surface of the mound sloped down eventually to floor level and below it, and a few scattered pieces of the inlay occurred in quite the top soil beyond the foot of the stairs; two small fragments were found by Dr. Hall on the east side of the stairs and one by us as far off as the "kitchen range." The reason for this is clearly that the inlay relief was higher up on the face of the temple wall than was the copper relief of bulls; when the wall fell the upper part of it naturally came down farther from the platform and crashed with greater violence, since it had farther to fall, on the hard floor which here was less protected by loose rubble; and so it broke up more completely and the inlay fragments from the frieze might be flung out to a considerable distance. Only where a section of the wall slid forwards base first instead of falling outwards was the inlay frieze well preserved.

The bird frieze was the most broken of all and the most incomplete; we found in all ten birds represented by complete figures or by fragments, and these give a frieze length of only 2.20 m. No section was found complete. Three bird figures were found together in a line, but with most of the background missing, and can be said to form a section. These lay comparatively close to the platform, the section upright on edge, made fast to a small block of mud brickwork which had fallen vertically though nearly at right angles to the platform; they were deep down, below the main masses of fallen brickwork and in the looser brick rubble which represented the upper part of the temple wall. One bird's head was found by Dr. Hall and a second by us east of the stairs, other fragments lay as much as 10.00 m. from the platform's foot. The facts certainly seem to show that the birds belonged to, or formed, a frieze distinct from that of the milking scene and set higher up on the temple façade; and the character of the frieze itself would point to the same conclusion, for the large scale on which the birds are rendered would harmonize ill with the little figures of men and animals if they were combined in a single composition, and again the simple outlines of the birds and their almost complete lack of internal detail, which contrasts strongly with the delicate modelling of the bulls carved in shell and, though in a less degree, with the limestone figures in the same frieze, is far more suited to a position higher up above eye-level.

So far then we have a scheme of mural decoration consisting of three friezes, the lowest of copper reliefs of bulls, the second of men and cattle, etc., in shell and stone inlay on a black background, and the third of birds also on a black ground; the order is practically sure, the intervals separating the bands are quite unknown. These friezes run the whole length of the wall from the south angle of the temple to the south-west side of the stair-ramp. All of the remains found come from this part of the wall, and none can have belonged to any eastern extension of it.

It is then the more surprising that just these elements of the decoration which we can with certainty attribute to this part of the façade should not be represented in the hoard of objects found by Dr. Hall on the other side of the stairs. It is true that the deposit which overlay and protected the productive stratum thinned off considerably towards the east corner of the platform, but in the angle by the stairs it was as deep on one side as on the other, and the objects on the east side were almost as numerous as on the west, but whereas it was in the angle that we found most of the frieze fragments, Dr. Hall in his angle found things of quite a

different sort. He found, as I have said, two small fragments from a limestone panel of men and cattle and one limestone bird's head, all three of
which, being here isolated and without context, it is fairly safe to attribute to the other side of the stairs: such scattering of stray fragments
from the higher friezes presents no difficulty, but is fully consistent with
the conditions observed by us. He also found three copper figures of
standing bulls in the round like ours. But the great Imgig relief, the four
life-size lions' heads, the smaller heads of two lions and two "leopards,"
the stone statue and the fragment of another, found by Dr. Hall, have no
counterpart in our finds; and to the long series of copper reliefs of bulls
which we discovered there was on the other side of the stairs nothing to
correspond but a single head of a bull, and even this was distinguished
from those of our series by having a crescent on its forehead. On both sides
of the staircase were found wooden beams sheathed with copper, and on
both sides columns of mosaic-work. Nearly all our wooden beams were
heavy timbers measuring up to 0.30 m. in diameter, whereas of Dr. Hall's
fragments two were of about the same size, one was slightly smaller, and
the rest so much more slender that he suggested they might have been
parts of a throne. Of the five mosaic columns found by Dr. Hall two were
of the same diameter as ours and made with tesserae of the same size,
three were slenderer and made with smaller tesserae and resembled the
fragment which we found against the east corner of the building. Even
here therefore the parallel between the discoveries made on the two sides
is not so close as a mere enumeration of the objects might imply. Either
we must suppose that from the line of the ramp eastwards the decoration
of the temple façade completely changed its character, or we must conclude that the temple itself did not run eastward beyond the ramp: but
the choice between these alternatives will be simpler if we can first establish positions for some of the other objects.

The four lions' heads present least difficulty. As Dr. Hall has stated,
two of these when found had attached to them the front parts of the
bodies, that is the chest, neck, and shoulders of each; the forelegs seem
vaguely indicated and can safely be assumed, but he is of the opinion
that no more of the body than this had ever existed. Dr. Hall at first suggested that the heads came from a throne, but they seem too large for
this, and again two beasts would be more appropriate than four to a construction of the sort. The most likely use for the foreparts of animals cut
off just beyond the shoulders is as architectural ornaments, the Greek
protomae, showing the beast issuing from the face of a wall. For such a
principle of ornament there is plenty of analogy in later Mesopotamian
art and in the art of the Hittites, and the general rule there is that the
animals flank the entrance of a doorway: it is more than probable that
the Hittite and Assyrian practice is based on a very ancient tradition. The
Assyrian parallel is valid for position rather than for type, since in Assyria

the whole flank of the beast was shown in relief on the inner face of the jamb: in Hittite art both the corner-relief (like the Assyrian) and the true *protomae* are employed. In my drawing (Fig. 2.20) I have followed Hittite analogies and have perhaps shown less of the body of the lions than the very fragmentary remains might warrant. (If it is considered that the remains of the lions' bodies really show that they were originally intended to represent the whole animal as far as the tail, not mere *protomae*, they must have been sitting up in the style of Greek lions, which is highly improbable. Personally, I agree with Mr. Woolley that they are long *protomae*. H. H.)

The monumental staircase which led to the top of the platform can scarcely have done otherwise than correspond to a door in the façade of the temple, and if amongst the objects found at the stairs' foot there are some which are peculiarly suited to the decoration of a doorway, this probability is practically confirmed; the lion *protomae* are so suited, and I shall show later that other of the objects found close by would also fit in best with a temple-entrance. Assuming, therefore, that there was a door at the head of the stairs, we may next inquire what the fashion of that door is likely to have been.

The only actual building of anything like contemporary date from which we can argue is the Sumerian palace at Kish, which is known to us from photographs, but the plan of it has not yet been published: here we have a doorway approached by a flight of steps set back in a double recess with deep reveals on either side of it. The front faces of the reveals are precisely the places where by later analogy we should restore the lion figures of Al-'Ubaid. In the Kish palace the sides of the reveals are deep enough for the whole flank of the animal to be shown in profile, like the man-headed bulls of an Assyrian palace; at Al-'Ubaid we should assume shallower reveals with the lion *protomae* set in the centre of the front face of each instead of at the angle as in Assyrian art.

In the milking scene from the inlay frieze (see Fig. 2.21) we see a building which obviously must be contemporary with the temple. This is a

Fig. 2.21.   Frieze showing milking scene from the temple at Al-'Ubaid.

byre made of a stockade of upright reeds fastened together with bands of rope, and it has a door flanked by two buckled spears and surmounted by a panel (or window?) having a crescent above; on each side of the door are heifers, of which, whether intentionally or by primitive convention in perspective, only the foreparts cut off behind the shoulders are shown. It might seem hazardous to argue from a country byre to a richly decorated temple built of brick, but there is much justification for so doing. The temple of Nin-khursag built by Ur-Nammu in the town of Kesh [not to be confused with Kish] is variously called the "Protection of the Divine Enclosure," the "Brilliant Grove," and the "Solid Reed Construction," and the names prove that the shrine of this patron goddess of the farmyard goes back to the primitive farm building. The byre of the inlay frieze is indeed something more than the shed of the ordinary farmer, for the men who work round it are not labourers but priests. The stela of Ur-Nammu found at Ur shows that certain distinctions of hair and dress which are noticeable on early figured scenes and have generally been taken to denote differences of race are in fact differences of social status; the gods have long hair and beards waved like running water and wear the horned caps of divinity; the king has long hair and a beard elaborately combed and curled, and wears a simple close-fitting skull-cap and a fillet or turban round it, and his dress is a skirted garment reaching from neck to ankles and a shawl or cloak which envelops his whole body; the common workman has his hair fairly short and brought down in a heavy curl over forehead and neck, a short natural beard, and a tunic dress; the priest is altogether clean-shaven and wears the apron-like skirt which is derived from the ancient "kaunakes." In the milking scene all the figures are on this analogy those of priests, though one isolated fragment giving the head of a man with short hair and beard proves that laymen also were represented on the frieze. We may conclude that the byre is at least the sacred farm attached to the temple (like the Drehem farm near Nippur in the time of the Third Ur Dynasty), if it is not a conventional rendering of the traditional temple itself. It is not wholly fanciful to see in the friezes of the Al-'Ubaid temple a decorative motive derived from the horizontal bands of rope binding which secured the primitive reed walls of the byre; indeed, in the building shown on the early steatite vases already cited which marks a more advanced stage of construction than the byre of the inlay panel in that its walls are a mixture of matting and brick, there is a frieze running along the façade on the level of the door lintel; the upright spears which flank the byre gate may well be represented by the columns of the temple porch, and the heifers on either side of the door offer an unmistakable parallel to the copper lions in the reveals of the temple gate.

In the inlay frieze it is quite clear, and on the steatite vases it is probable, that the door is set in a projecting gate-tower, and in the former we see above the door lintel a black panel inset in the wall, while in the latter there is something not altogether dissimilar, though here the proportions have been so far modified to fit the subject into the space that it would be rash to say exactly what is meant by the apparent panel divided by vertical bands into seven fields. In the Al-'Ubaid ruins we have in the Imgig relief a panel which might well have stood over the door, and there is reason to think that the door was set in a projecting tower.

In attempting to decide the height of the platform we found that the best evidence was given by the drain at the back and by the south-west stairs, which agreed well together, whereas to make the estimate so reached harmonize with the slope of the main stairs and the distance of the stair foot from the front of the platform it was necessary to assume that the steps did not occupy the whole length of the stair-ramp, but that there was a flat landing at the stair head on the level of the platform ter race and affording easy access to it. If the temple stood near to, though not actually upon, the edge of the terrace, and had corresponding to the platform steps a projecting entrance, the projection must have come forward over the top of the stair ramp, since there was no room for it elsewhere, and, conversely, the length of the ramp, which necessitates a flat space at the top of it, would be explained by the need to accommodate the projection planned for the temple entrance.

On both sides of the staircase there were found mosaic columns and palm-logs sheathed in copper, these being, as I have said before, of different sizes and dimensions. On the west side we found two complete mosaic columns lying one above the other parallel to the platform front and 3.00 m. from it, and with them two more broken copper-sheathed logs again almost parallel to the wall; all lay on the small rubble fallen first from the upper part of the temple building, and below the reliefs and great masses of brickwork which represented the lower part of the wall of the same; it was therefore certain that they had been thrown down here at a comparatively early stage of the temple's destruction, before the walls had fallen. This fact alone makes it practically impossible for the columns to have formed part of the interior decoration of the temple, for they could not have fallen over the wall while that was still standing, and it is equally absurd to suppose that the destroyers carried them from inside the building and threw them down, for apart from the pointlessness of such an act it would have been impossible to remove them without bringing the roof down on the workers' heads, nor, had they been carried to the doorway, could they have been flung from the ramp into the position in which we found them, for that would have meant an end-on throw which with the length and weight of the columns would have been an almost superhuman feat. To lie as they did, the columns must either have fallen from the edge of the platform immediately above, or have been standing upright on the top of the ramp and from there come to the ground turning a somersault as they fell. Either, therefore, there was a colonnade along the front of the temple, or there were columns at the door of it.

The discoveries at Kish prove that a colonnade was not at all an impossibility at this period, but here the evidence is not in favour of such a feature; only two mosaic columns were found on this side of the stairs, and they are so well preserved, and the other objects from this part of the facade are so thoroughly representative (thus the frieze of copper bulls is not far from complete) that it would be difficult to explain why all the other columns of the series, had it existed, should have disappeared and left not the least trace of themselves; moreover the length of the mosaic shafts at least is against a colonnade, for they measure only 2.30 m., and if there had been a colonnade the mural decoration must surely have been under and not above the roof of it, but under a roof only some two and a half metres high there is not room for the various decorative elements for which we have to account—the three friezes already described and the statues of bulls in the round and the flowers of which we have to speak later. On the other hand, 2.30 m. is a very reasonable height for a door.

The copper-sheathed palm-logs are of two or three sorts, distinguished by their different thicknesses; some are too slender for columns and may have been roofing timbers, others are as much as 0.30 m. in diameter and may well have been columns. All were broken, but one of the thickest shafts was almost complete, and its parts fitted together gave a total length of approximately 3.60 m., and all the other pieces of the same diameter found on the west of the stairs seemed to belong to one shaft, making thus a pair of similar dimensions. The arguments in favour of the mosaic columns having stood outside and not inside the temple and at the door rather than along the façade apply equally to the heavier copper-sheathed examples, and it is natural to suppose that they too came from the entrance of the building, but we can only do that if we can explain the disparity in the lengths of the two types. Now it has been suggested that the Im-dugud or Imgig relief stood over the lintel, and if it did so it presumably had some kind of support. The height of the Imgig relief is 1.07 m., and if to this we add enough for a timber frame enclosing the whole we shall get a total of about 1.30 m., which is just the difference between the lengths of the mosaic and the copper columns. Further we have to account for the many fragments of copper-sheathed wood found on both sides of the stairs which must be judged too thin for column shafts and more suited to have been roofing timbers—and for roofs of wood overlaid with metal we have analogies in plenty, in Solomon's temple and in the inscriptions of Mesopotamian kings going back to the days of the Third Dynasty of Ur. The simplest suggestion and one which accords best with the evidence appears to be that shown in the restoration in Fig. 2.20. There is a projecting tower in which is a door set between shallow reveals ornamented with the foreparts of lions in copper. Above the lintel is the copper Imgig relief in a wooden frame supported by the two mosaic columns which stand immediately in front of the door jambs: from above the top of the relief there projects from the face of the gate-tower a pent-house roof made of copper-sheathed timbers whose outer corners are supported by the two copper columns; tower and porch alike rest on the top of the ramp and fill up the greater part of the flat space between the top of the steps and the line of the temple frontage. Judging from certain remains of copper beading, L-shaped in section, which were found alongside the ramp, the door itself was probably of wood decorated with panels of which the frames were sheathed with copper. This restoration would in my opinion account better than any other for the position in which the lions and the Imgig relief were found. The latter stood on edge, right way up, facing outwards and almost vertical, leaning back slightly towards the wall but separated from it by some twenty centimetres, the left hand end of it only some 0.60 m. from the side of the ramp; it rested on the mixed rubble and the brickwork masses must have fallen later than it, though owing to its position close to the wall face they did not exactly cover it. The lions lay in front of it, roughly in a row, facing outwards. If the enemy who destroyed the temple first pulled out and toppled down on to the floor below the two copper columns supporting the pent-house roof, this would have collapsed on to the top of the ramp, and in order to clear the ground for further work they would naturally have tumbled its loosened timbers to this side and that off the ramp, where in fact we found them. If the mosaic columns were next wrenched from their places (the obvious way to do this would be by a rope tied high up round the shaft), and that on the right of the door came away first, then the Imgig relief could very easily have slipped and fallen into just the spot where Dr. Hall discovered it, falling sideways and so coming to ground vertically; the wooden frame would be leaning against the wall, and the decay of this would account for the interval between the copper and the brickwork. The lions must have been thrown down one by one, and their rough alignment in the rubbish is perhaps accidental, or possibly the spoilers meant to carry them away and stacked them side by side for removal, just as on the other side of the stairs they piled the bull statues one on top of the other, and then left them there: this might account for only four figures being found, for if Dr. Hall's three bulls belonged to the east side there ought to have been eleven on the west, whereas there was no trace of more than four.

Of the objects found on the west side of the stairs there remain to be considered the copper statues of bulls and the artificial flowers. The former were lying all in a heap, one on the top of the other, and had evidently been thrown or placed there, so that, though we may perhaps assume that they would not have been carried far, yet their exact position cannot be greatly stressed as evidence for their original place on the building. But it does seem to me legitimate to conclude that they too came from the outside of the temple, for otherwise they would scarcely have been brought out through the door and carried down the steps (for they were too far from these to have been flung from the top landing to their present position), and then heaped together as we found them; it is much more likely that they fell or were thrown from the wall immediately above and were then collected into a heap, perhaps to be carried off as trophies. Therefore I should assign the bulls also to the part of the façade between the stairs and the south corner of the temple. Now the four bulls were true statues in the round, faithfully worked on the back as well as on the front, but as in all of them the head was turned sharply round over the shoulder so as to be facing to the front when the body of the animal was seen in profile, it is clear that the animals stood sideways to the spectator and were meant to be looked at only from one side. This sharp turn of the head is a commonplace in Sumerian art and can be paralleled by a number of reliefs, of animals e.g. by the bulls in the lowest frieze of this same temple, by the bulls on the steatite vase found in the E-nun-makh temple at Ur, and by various other decorated vases; in all these the ornament is in relief and only the head of the animal projects in the round, and this fact in itself amounts to a proof that the bull statues, though completely in the round, were, so to speak, detached reliefs, standing against a background, and by their detachment from it gaining in freedom and realism. The natural place to which to assign them is the base of the temple wall; then we should have gradation in the successive bands of decoration on the temple front; at the bottom the standing bulls in the round, above them the continuous frieze of reclining bulls worked in high relief and with their heads boldly projecting from the background, above these the inlay panel carved in shell and limestone, its figures of beasts and men relieved only by very delicate modelling, and above these again the row of birds, mere silhouettes on a black ground. I think it highly probable that the limestone figures were painted; this would explain the difference of the materials employed in the milking-scene frieze, the shell figures being left white and the stone ones coloured, and would further justify the summary treatment of the birds and their almost complete lack of detail.

It is inherently probable that a building set upon a platform should be really set upon it, i.e., should stand back from the platform's edge far enough to make a distinction between the two elements of the whole scheme, rather than that the platform wall should be carried up into the superstructure without any apparent break; and in Sumerian architecture the stepped building is a familiar form and must depend upon a very old tradition; it is certainly not unreasonable to suppose that the terraced temple which in the time of the Second Dynasty (?) of Ur occupied the Al-'Ubaid site shared this feature in some degree with its predecessor. The manner in which the temple walls have fallen over the edge of the platform in great masses proves conclusively that the step along the south-east façade is not inconsistent with any of the evidence from the ruins. Both inherent probability and what we know of Sumerian style would therefore justify us in supposing that there was a step or ledge along the foot of the temple, and such a ledge is precisely what is required as a standing-place for the bull statues.

Of the artificial flowers we found on the west side of the stairs rather more than fifty complete or nearly complete examples and fragments representing at least as many more: on the east side there were perhaps fifteen. Dr. Hall, who found the first specimens, concluded that they were rosettes for wall decoration, the long stems being let into the wall and the flowers appearing in relief against the wall face; he compared them with the nail-like cones of baked clay which decorated with a mosaic pattern the mud-brick walls of the temple at Warka. This analogy would appear convincing enough, and it seems to derive further support from our own discovery at Ur of clay dedication-cones of Ur-Nammu let into the face of his terrace wall of E-temen-ni-gur with the smooth round heads exposed and making, with their more or less regular rows, a sort of pattern on the mud-brick wall. But the argument is not so strong as it looks at first sight. The Warka cones (similar cones are common, but have not yet been found in position, at Eridu (=Abu Shahrain), at Ur, and at Al-'Ubaid) were certainly purely decorative; they are slender, smooth, and sharp-pointed, and their length varies between four and (rarely) ten centimetres; they were set close to one another and were driven into a thick plaster of mud which was applied to the wall after that was built. The stems of the artificial flowers are from 0.20 to 0.35 m. long, thick and blunt-pointed, and in many there are near the point two small bars projecting from the stem; no mud plaster was ever thirty centimetres thick, and I defy any one to drive one of these flower-stems into a mud-brick wall half an hour after it was built without smashing the flower head; indeed it would be impossible to do it at all. Consequently, if the flowers were let into the wall as rosettes they at least were not used in the same way as were the Warka cones, and the analogy has to that extent broken down. The Ur-Nammu cones afford a better parallel in that they are thick-stemmed and blunt, and they were not driven into the wall after its completion but were laid between the bricks during the course of construction, which could have been done with the flowers; but the real object of the Ur-Nammu cones was not wall decoration (this was a very secondary motive even if the heads of the cones showed and were not covered with mud mortar, which is not quite certain) but the recording of the king's piety, and this record, which would have had no permanence if stamped on the mud bricks of which the wall was made, was inscribed on the stems of the cones; what mattered then was the stem which was concealed in the brickwork, not the head of the cone which may or may not have been visible—the reverse of what was the case with the flowers. Here, too, then the analogy based on the general resemblance of shape between flower and cone breaks down if we regard the motives behind their use; indeed, the same analogy might be used to show that the flowers were buried out of sight in the heart of the brickwork as were the cones of Werad-Sin at Ur or below the floor like those of Sin-balatsu-iqbi!

Every flower-stem has, near its point, a small hole drilled through the clay before baking, and every one has high up under the calyx, just where the wire fixing in the corolla comes out, a horizontal nick cut in the soft clay. These features (which do not occur on dedication-cones) must have a purpose. The hole is only large enough to allow a string or wire to pass through, and in some cases a copper wire was actually found in it; the obvious purpose for the nick, and the only one I can think of, is to prevent a string or wire looped round the tapering stem from slipping down it: both of these imply a use of the flowers very different from that suggested before, for two strings or wires attached to the stem at the bottom and at the top respectively could only be of service if the stems were free, and certainly were not wanted if they were embedded in brickwork. I venture to suggest that two strings were passed one through the holes and one round the top of the stems of a number of flowers and the ends made fast to uprights or to staples in the wall; in this case with the point of the stem resting on the ground the flowers would stand upright with their heads in the air or could lean this way and that according to the tightness with which the top string was tied; the small knobs on many of the stems I would explain as buds. Standing free in this way the flowers would have a very naturalistic appearance, and might be so arranged as to give the copper bulls the air of pasturing in a flowery meadow; they might even sway in the wind! For this the step along the base of the temple wall would have to be a double one, as the height of the flowers is disproportionate to that of the bulls and their solid heads would hide too much of the animals; in the restored drawing the flowers accordingly are made to occupy a lower ledge and the bulls appear just above them. I am aware that this theory as to the nature of the flowers is the most controversial point in the whole reconstruction of the temple, and I do not myself consider that it is proven, but it does receive support from the conditions in which they were found. Had they been embedded in the wall then, considering in what very large masses the sections of the wall had fallen, the chances were all in favour of some at least being still embedded in the brickwork, but not a single case of the kind was remarked. All were buried in broken debris, and for the most part they were scattered in complete disorder. The only exception was close to the great block of brickwork to which were attached the three copper bulls joined together in one strip; about a metre closer to the platform wall and at about the same level as the bulls there were five stems in a row (the heads were broken off) roughly twenty centimetres apart from one another, lying parallel to the bull frieze and tilted at exactly the same angle as it; had they originally been driven horizontally into the wall face they ought to have been lying at right angles to the face of the frieze; as it was, if their position means anything, it means that they stood upright, lower than the frieze, and on a more advanced plane, i.e., exactly as they are shown on the restored drawing. Moreover, had the flower stems been embedded in the brick-work then, since the latter fell in very large blocks, the flower-heads might well have been smashed, but one would have expected to find many of the stems intact, but actually we found more complete calyces than stems. This should mean that the stems were as much exposed to damage as the flowers, that, in other words, they were standing free.

We have accounted for virtually all the objects found on the west side of the stairs and for some of those from the east, and the decoration of the temple wall from the south corner of the building to the door, and of the door with its porch, has been restored with a greater or less degree of certainty. Now there arises the question whether the door was central to the temple façade or whether this was continued further towards the east.

It has already been stated that the contours of the mound's surface before digging started favoured the theory that the temple was confined to the south angle of the platform and did not extend far to the east, where there was no more debris underlying the Second Dynasty (?) terrace than would be accounted for by the collapse of the platform itself. It has also been remarked that the objects found on the east side of the stair-ramp did not by any means correspond to those found on the west, and now that so many of these objects have been eliminated from the discussion by being assigned to definite places on the temple, and a scheme of decoration has been worked out which in the case of the wall to the west of the door may be taken as correct at least in general principle, we are in a better position to appreciate the evidence afforded by the residue of the objects discovered by Dr. Hall. These are two small stone statues of seated men, two copper "leopard" heads, two copper heads of lions on a smaller scale than those assigned to the main door, fragments of mosaic columns, two similar to those assigned to the main door, and three others made with smaller tesserae and therefore not part of the same series, three copper-sheathed columns, four small copper heads of birds, one copper bull's head like those of our reclining bull-reliefs but distinguished from them by having a crescent on the forehead, and three copper figures of bulls. Only the last give any hint that the ornamental motives on that side had been repeated on the east like the bulls on the west side, they had been thrown down and were not simply fallen; the few little isolated fragments of inlay scattered here have been not unreasonably attributed to the western wall, and, since there is nothing to explain the total disappearance of all the rest of the mural decoration if it ever existed, we must conclude that either the wall did not run on much beyond the door, or, if it did, there was at the door a complete change in the decoration of the facade. If we incline to the latter alternative we have still to face the difficulty that there is practically no more in the remains to illustrate the fresh scheme of ornament than there was for the old; the mosaic columns and the copper-sheathed columns (Dr. Hall's larger pieces) can best be attributed to another door, and so too the lion "protomae"; we are left with only the "leopard" heads, one bull's head, and the three bulls for the whole length of the wall—a striking contrast to the wealth of objects found on the other side, where the conditions ought to have been the same. In favour of the view that the door was not central to the temple front but at its east end, perhaps some three metres from its east corner, we have besides the surface contours the following arguments: (1) such a wall-length between the door and the corner of the building explains the three copper bulls; (2) artificial flowers were found on this side of the stairs, showing that that particular motive was carried on on this part of the temple front, but there were far fewer here than on the west side, implying that the wall so decorated was shorter; (3) the copper bull's head with the crescent on its forehead might have come from a frieze of reclining bulls like that on the other side of the stairs, and if so the fact that it was the only one found here is an argument in favour of such a frieze having been short; (4) the existence of an open courtyard between the N.E. end of the temple and the N.E. edge of the platform would explain the finding at the foot of the S.E. platform wall of objects whose original position would seem to have been either along the N.E. side of the temple or inside it; if there was in the N.E. wall of the temple a doorway giving on to a court, it would have been easy for the destroyers to throw down over the S.E. platform edge objects which formed part of the door decoration or were stored inside the shrine; (5) the foundation tablet of A-anni-padda was found high up in the rubbish against the foot of the stairs by the south corner of the parapet; judging by the practice of later times it was originally embedded in the brickwork low down in a corner of the building (i.e. of the temple, not of the platform); the manner in which the temple wall had fallen, and particularly at the south corner, where it had been thrust straight forward, make it, I would not say impossible, but highly improbable, that the tablet came from this corner; I am not able to say how the wall east of the stairs fell, but if the east corner was only about three metres away from the stairs the tablet could far more easily have come from here; moreover the south corner fell early, at the time of the general destruction, as is shewn by the small amount of loss debris beneath it, whereas the tablet, lying ten metres away and high up, must have come here relatively late, and this too tends to connect it with the east corner of the building, whose lower stump (containing the foundation-deposit) may well have stood up from amongst the ruins for quite a long time.

I therefore hold that the temple façade ended a very short distance east of the doorway, and that beyond it there was an open court extending to the north-east side of the platform; and it is on the whole probable that the decoration of the west side was continued on the short length of wall east of the door. The total disappearance of the friezes would not present such very great difficulty if there had never been more than three metres' length of each: indeed we need only assume that this short stretch of wall was not wholly overthrown but remained standing and exposed for some little while.

There remain the other objects found by Dr. Hall, and in the third argument given above I have indicated the manner in which I should account for them. The temple must have had access to the courtyard lying to north-east and north-west of it, that is, it must have had a door in one of those two walls. Some of the mosaic columns and the copper lions repeat on a smaller scale the decorative motives of the main entrance, and one need have little hesitation in assigning them to the doorway whose existence we are bound to postulate. Dr. Hall found three fragments of mosaic columns, slender and made with small tesserae, against or close to the east end of the wall; we found a piece (the end of a shaft) 0.22 m. long standing on end and leaning against the east corner of the platform; if these belonged to the same column it had been broken before it was thrown down here, if they represent different columns both must have been broken before they came into their present positions, though the piece against the corner may have been a good deal longer than twenty-two centimetres, the upper part having perhaps decayed gradually with the denudation of the soil. Certainly this piece which we found had all the appearance of having been tipped over the edge of the platform from immediately above where it now stood, and if there was no building at that point it must have been dragged there to be flung over; Dr. Hall's columns also, since they did not form part of the south-east façade, must have been brought to the platform edge from some distance; if we have to find a common point of departure for them all it should be as near as possible to their finding-spot, and that would be somewhere on the north-east face of the temple. The theory is that these objects, since they could hardly have fallen here of themselves, were deliberately flung down by people engaged in destroying the temple; if the door whose porch they were demolishing stood at the back of the building they would scarcely carry its timbers all the way round to the front in order to throw them over from the terrace, whereas if it were on the north-east their easiest course would have been to throw them just where the column fragments were found. If the shafts were broken up beforehand and only some of the bits tossed over the platform edge, the rest would certainly have per ished, whether it was left on the platform or flung over the north-east wall, where there was no wreckage from the temple fabric to protect them. The same holds true for the lions. The statues and other votive objects must have been inside the shrine, and since they would be carried out for destruction by the same door, some at least of them were likely to have been thrown or tumbled over the south-east side of the platform: actually the two statues, the heavier objects, were lying east of the stairs under where the open terrace is assumed to have been, and the inscribed vase fragments were found thrown out as far as the foot of the staircase. Whether the north-east end of the temple was decorated otherwise than by the ornamental doorway, and if so whether the leopard heads belonged to this decoration or were part of the doorway scheme (e.g. heads of beasts in a copper relief panel above the door), or, as I have suggested to Dr. Hall, formed a double head of the Im-dugud or Imgig bird in the great copper relief, there is absolutely nothing to show.

The main weakness of my reconstruction, in my own opinion, is that it fails to account satisfactorily for the two fragments of mosaic columns found by Dr. Hall, which in diameter and in size of tesserae correspond to those discovered by us on the west side of the staircase. I have assigned the smaller columns to the supposed north-east door because they harmonize better with the smaller scale of the lions assigned to the same place, and in that case there is no room there for the larger columns. The position in which Dr. Hall's larger columns were discovered, relatively close to the east corner of the building and nearly vertical, scarcely connects them with the stairway entrance, and they certainly are not fragments broken off from our columns, for the latter were complete. One might suggest that at the doorway on the top of the stairs there were four mosaic columns, two on either side, set close together so as to give something of the effect of the façade at Warka with its half-columns decorated with a mosaic pattern of cone bases: but two columns could hardly be fitted into the narrow space of the jamb fronts, if these are correctly restored. The suggestion has certain advantages but would necessitate modifications of the plan which are not without serious objections, nor do I see quite how the fragments could have come into their actual positions if they really belonged to the stair-head. On the whole I have preferred to adopt the simpler scheme of restoration with single columns and to leave Dr. Hall's larger columns, like the bird's heads found by him, unexplained.

The temple is a rectangle measuring about eighteen metres in length by about eleven metres in width; the length is of course dictated by the distance between the east angle as fixed by the above arguments and the west corner of the platform, allowing for a set-back from the platform edge of anything up to one metre; the width allows for a similar set-back along the front and assumes that the gateway, which must have

provided communication between the main and the subsidiary platforms, opened on to the courtyard of the main platform and not into the
shrine; for obviously there must have been some means of direct access
from the ground to the terrace without passing through the shrine, and
since the south-east stairs must have led via the smaller mud-brick platform to the court behind the temple. The south-east doorway is shown as
described above, projecting over the landing at the head of the stairs, and
the smaller door from the shrine to the terrace court is put in the centre of
the north-east end of the building. About the internal arrangements of the
shrine and about the height of its walls or of the gate-tower it would be
unprofitable to speculate.

In the sketch of the restored temple on Fig. 2.20 the burnt brickwork
of the lower part of the platform wall is left exposed and the mud brick
above is shown as plastered and whitewashed. It is true that on the
masses of brickwork fallen from the platform and temple walls we observed no trace of whitewash, but this is not decisive, for with the wall
lying face downwards and with its surface much broken by its fall remains of whitewash if any remained at all would be very fragmentary
and might easily have escaped our notice; but the plastering and white-
washing of mud brick was so common a practice that we may safely assume it here. In the case of the temple wall I have suggested that the
lowest part, behind the standing bulls, was panelled with wood like the
parapet-wall of the stairs; the only justification for this is the finding of a
fair number of loose copper nails scattered along the floor below the wall
and the possibility that a conservative tradition might retain something
more definitely reminiscent than panelled brickwork of the primitive half-
timbered building which was the lineal descendant of the reed byre. The
upper part of the wall is shown as whitewashed.

If the facts observed in the course of the excavation of the ruins have
been rightly interpreted we can recover a fairly complete picture of the
temple of Nin-khursag as it stood in the days of A-anni-padda more than
five thousand years ago. At least I can say that no single detail has been
admitted which did not seem to be approved by such evidence as was
forthcoming, and that evidence I have endeavoured to state without
prejudice.

Restoration of a Mosaic Plaque from Chichen Itza

The events leading to the discovery and restoration of the turquoise mosaic
plaque are presented in an editorial foreword to Ichikawa's report[5]:

[5] S. Ichikawa, "The Maya of Middle America: Pt. III. Restoration of the Turquoise Mosaic Plaque," *News Service Bulletin,* Carnegie Institution of Washington,
1931, vol. II, no. 19, pp. 129–132. By permission of the Carnegie Institution.

In one of the rooms [of the Temple of Chac Mool upon which had been later built the Temple of the Warriors] clear evidence of an ancient altar that had disappeared had already been found. Cutting into the floor beneath the part assumed to have been covered by the altar tablets, the pick finally touched an object unlike the materials composing the floor. When uncovered this object proved to be the lid of a large stone bowl. Carefully opening it Morris found that it contained ornaments of jade, and below a thin stratum of dust and earth he caught the glint of turquoise and the faint outlines of a rare ornament of mosaic type.

With infinite patience Morris removed, grain by grain, enough of the obscuring film to reveal the true nature of the find. Many of the pieces of the beautiful mosaic were still held firmly in place by the original lacquer. Much of it lay loose upon a layer of dust which had once been the wooden backing to which it was cemented. With unsparing care Morris then removed the jar to a place of safety.

Restoration of the plaque was deemed of such importance that President Merriam, who was present when it was discovered, cabled to the American Museum of Natural History requesting the loan of their ablest artist-preparator. Accordingly Mr. Shoichi Ichikawa was sent to Chichen Itza. In speaking of the result of Ichikawa's work Morris has said:

"In the repair of the disk Mr. Ichikawa found a task worthy of his mettle. It called for all the skill and ingenuity at his command, but at the end of six weeks, the plaque appeared practically as of old, barbarically beautiful and in condition to last for centuries if properly cared for. . . ."

When I took the cover off the stone jar which contained the mosaic plaque, I saw the mosaic which was for the most part visible. I was very much disappointed, because the color of the mosaic was very ugly and it completely betrayed my expectation. I was told that it is beautiful beyond description, but now it had turned the color of half green to dried straw, due to the fact that some chemical substance thinly covered the entire surface of the plaque. I examined the contents of the jar minutely with the aid of a powerful magnifying glass and picked out all the suspicious tiny remains, which easily escape one's attention, with a pincher and kept them in the labeled boxes for future examination. The upper contents had already been removed by Mr. Morris, and the rest of the remains were a practically powdered substance, excepting the mosaic.

I brushed off the non-important remains carefully, using camel hair brushes for the purpose until the entire surface of the mosaic was exposed. I found two-thirds of the mosaic was held together by a pitch-like substance but that it was curled up by moisture and age-long pressure from above. One third of it had fallen to pieces.

The center was a yellowish concave sandstone disk with two large pieces of reddish brown mosaic stones. I took all necessary measurements for determining the exact size of the plaque in its original state by laying wet cotton thread in a straight line on the uneven surface of the

mosaic and stretching it out. I also made a careful sketch of the exact designs of the mosaic (see Fig. 2.22). These measurings and sketchings were
simply a matter of precaution in case of destruction of the shape and
design by removal.

From the edge of a fallen part of the mosaic, I could see underneath it
and noticed a differently colored powder from the other remains. This
proved to be the remains of a wooden disk on which the mosaic once was
laid. This powdered substance was very important to me as a reference

Fig. 2.22. Mosaic plaque from Chichen Itza.

in reconstructing the original form of the plaque, so that I decided to tak
the utmost care with it.

I gave a thin coat of liquid celluloid to the surface of the mosaic to pre
vent breakage. Up to this point, the work took me three days and no
I was facing the most difficult task, that of removing the fragile mosai
from the stone jar to my working table.

I thought it wise to work out a few good schemes before removing th
mosaic and to select the best practical one among them. So, I locked u
my working room, spent the whole day outside, thinking about th

process of removing the mosaic. That night at about one o'clock, when everybody was sleeping, I started the delicate enterprise as I was then safe from any unexpected interruption and the calmness of the night makes for better concentration.

I produced a spool of cotton thread and tied one end of the thread in a knot. I dipped the knot in liquid celluloid, glued it on the mosaic, drew the thread outside of the jar and cut it with the scissors. I repeated this until more than twenty threads were stuck at one end all over the mosaic. Then I took two small wooden sticks, placed them crosswise and from edge to edge over the mouth of [the] jar. Next I gathered all the loose ends of the threads over the crossed sticks in the center and secured them in a bunch.

The deck of my working table being cleared, I placed it as close to the stone jar as possible. Holding the bundle of threads in my left hand, discarding the sticks, I started pulling the mosaic upwards very cautiously, my right hand assisting, carefully and diligently working with a pinchers. Gradually, the mosaic lifted from its position without disturbing the contents below, and finally was removed safely to the table, then I cut off all threads very closely. Thus the most tense moment of my life passed.

I made a thorough examination of the powdered substance which was left under the mosaic. Measurements of the thickness of the powder at every point were then taken, and gradually brushing off the powder, I found a dark red powder at the bottom layer. This red powder proved to be the original color, painted on the back of the plaque.

Lastly, I removed the round sandstone disk which was left in the center, and found the same powdered substance in the same order with other parts. This proved that the sandstone disk was set into the wooden disk but not pushed through the wood. I also took measurements of this powdered substance as well as the sandstone disk. As a result of the measurement of this disintegrated wood, it was found that the original wooden backing of the mosaic was of decreasing thickness toward the circumference (see Fig. 2.23). It followed that the plaque must have been somewhat elliptical in section.

To find the exact variations of thickness as well as the shape of the outer edge, whether square or rounded, became the problem. Fortunately, I found among many of the fallen mosaic pieces, a small outer edge piece of the plaque which gave the angle of the incrassation from the outer edge to the center. Consequently I gathered all the factors for the reconstruction of the wooden disk on which the mosaic later was to be laid except the surface curvature for which all the data are lost, since the mosaic was out of its original shape as I have mentioned before, and also the exact nature of the original wood.

I had a consultation on this subject with Mr. Morris, and finally decided to take the surface curvature of a plain sandstone plaque, which was found on another temple site, now preserved in storage, as a sample and the wood of any available tree, but well seasoned. After quite difficult study, I drew the plan of the wooden disk to be made, based on the

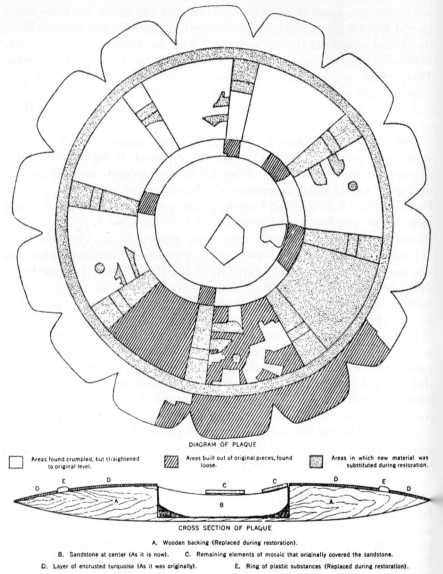

DIAGRAM OF PLAQUE

☐ Areas found crumpled, but straightened to original level.   ▨ Areas built out of original pieces, found loose.   ▨ Areas in which new material was substituted during restoration.

CROSS SECTION OF PLAQUE

A. Wooden backing (Replaced during restoration).
B. Sandstone at center (As it is now).   C. Remaining elements of mosaic that originally covered the sandstone.
D. Layer of encrusted turquoise (As it was originally).   E. Ring of plastic substances (Replaced during restoration).

Fig. 2.23. Plan and cross section of mosaic plaque, Chichen Itza.

above data and gave directions to the carpenter in the camp, for the making of the disk.

Following this I made an accurate plan of the mosaic on Japanese paper which I pasted with liquid celluloid on the wooden disk already made by the carpenter. The next step was making the mosaic in even surface: i.e. to flatten it. I had already tested the substance which held the stones with crude ether and found that it dissolved. I broke the mosaic off in pieces of convenient size and wetted them with ether and an alcohol mixture, putting each in a separate cigarette box matted with cloth soaked in the above chemical mixture, covered tight and let them stand for a few hours. I found them all to be pliable, made so by the fumes of the chemicals. I took them out, putting flat boards as a weight on the surface of each mosaic piece, and left them to dry.

I had sifted all the remaining powdered contents at the bottom of the jar with cheesecloth, picking up all loosened stones of the mosaic and cleaning them in chemicals. I also picked up all the suspicious looking objects and kept them for future examination as before. I did not know the real name of the substance which held the stones of mosaic, and thought it might be the sap from a tropical tree. So I went in the woods, spent a half day in gathering different kinds of tree sap, and tested them with the same chemicals which I applied to the above mentioned substance, but all failed to be of the same material.

Next I started to lay all the mosaic pieces on the wooden disk on which exact positions had already been drawn. It was a matter of patience from start to finish. The detail of reconstruction can be found from the explanatory drawings accompanying the colored plaque.

I can only add that the restoration of the original color of the mosaic was obtained by careful polishing, application of fine linseed oil and exposing it to the tropical sun.

The making of the water-color drawing of the mosaic plaque was comparatively simple work but required excellent judgment and infinite patience. There were nearly three thousand stones, and I sketched faithfully the color of each, without missing the stains and cracks.

The most difficult part of the drawing was the outlining of the stones in their exact size and position. This was done, after several failures, by transferring the outline impression by rubbing on the thin but strong Japanese paper.

3

RECONSTRUCTION OF LIFE AND CUSTOMS

More detail concerning the life of the people can be obtained from burials than from any other type of feature found by the archaeologist, except data incident to such major catastrophes as the destruction of Pompeii. The reason is simple: burials are almost the only major class of archaeological features that one can expect to find in the original complete condition, not worn down by use, and exactly as the people left them. Disturbance can result from the ruthless work of grave-robbers and from deterioration due to natural conditions. Even this last is minimized by the fact that burials are usually underground and are thereby protected from some aspects of weather damage. On the dry coast of Peru, where it rains at most once in a generation, this is especially true. It is no accident that a significant proportion of Peruvian archaeological interpretation, chronological and otherwise, is based on grave excavation.

The robbing of tombs in ancient times appears to have been a very common practice. This particular expression of human greed is described in this volume in the accounts of the Pazirik burial, of the Egyptian tombs of Giza necropolis, and of the Oseberg Viking ship burial.

Frozen Tombs in the Altai Mountains

The Pazirik burial, a log-lined earth tomb of some nomadic Scytho-Sarmatian or Scytho-Siberian chieftain, is one of the unique archaeological finds of all time. Dating of the tomb is placed in the fifth century B.C. The kurgans, or burial mounds, of the Altai Mountains have been known since the time of Radlov's investigations in 1865, but not until 1924 were further investigations made by the Ethnographical Section of the State Russian Museum in Leningrad. As will be seen from the extract printed below,[1] a great deal can be inferred concerning the equipment and mode of life of these ancient nomadic groups. An excellent survey of the culture of the nomadic Scythian tribes who occupied the Asiatic grasslands from China to the Danube River has recently been written by T. T. Rice (1957). This book is a remarkably successful attempt to reconstruct the culture content and history of a vanished people from documentary and archaeological records.

The expedition of 1929 excavated a second similar burial in the Eastern Altai near Pazirik (Yan-Ulaghan River). [The first burial, excavated in 1927 near Shiba on the Ursula River, is described in the *Wiener Prähistorische Zeitschrift*, Vol. 15, 1928.] Here also the burial was in a condition of perpetual frost. Thanks to the peculiar combination of circumstances all objects found in the grave were firmly cemented by the ice, in consequence of which the processes of decay were completely arrested. It seemed as if the hand of time had not touched the objects which had been lying in the grave more than two thousand years. The ten yellow mares which had been buried with the man were preserved so well that not only skin and hair, but muscles, and entrails with the remains of undigested food in them were found.

On the handle of an axe discovered there could be seen the shiny surface, polished by the hands of the man using it, as if this axe were left yesterday and not thousands of years ago. This exceptional state of preservation of the objects in the Pazirik burial puts it in a class by itself among all other burials found in Siberia. The materials of the Pazirik kurgan illuminate with unusual brilliancy the different sides of the economic and social life of the nomads, who buried their chiefs in the mountains of Altai.

The Pazirik kurgan is situated 1500 meters above sea level in the dry bed of an ancient glacier. It is one in the chain of five kurgans stretching from north to south. The investigated kurgan represents a stone-pile mound some two and one-half meters in height and fifty meters in diameter. The very indefinite form of the stone mound and the hardly perceptible depression on its top indicated an ancient robbery of the burial beneath, a supposition confirmed by excavation. Under the stone pile was discovered an earthen mound of similar form but of smaller dimensions, with a well-pronounced funnel-like pit on the site of the robbers' excavations. Finally under this earth mound, in the center of the reconstruction over the grave was a square grave-pit with vertical walls. Its area was 54 m. square (7.2 × 7.2) and 4 m. deep.

The enormous pile of stones over the burial has created the most favorable condition for its preservation, since the loose stones are bad conveyers

[1] M. P. Griaznov, "The Pazirik Burial of Altai," trans. E. Golomshtok, *American Journal of Archaeology*, vol. 37 (1933), pp. 32–43. By permission of the *American Journal of Archaeology*.

of heat, and at the same time the cold, heavy air easily penetrates the lowest layers of the pile. As a result, everything situated under the stone pile freezes during the first frost of winter, which begins in this locality about August and ends in June. In summer the frozen ground has no time to thaw, as the stone and earth mound has not been thoroughly heated through. Besides this, the cold lower layers of the stone pile serve as very strong condensers of the humidity from the air. Consequently, there was a large quantity of water both in the mound and in the grave pit proper. The Pazirik burial was found filled with water which was frozen, and the processes of decay were stopped in their very beginning. Thus it seems that large stone mounds in regions of high altitude create the best conditions for the conservation of objects against the actions of time. The inside appearance of the burial gave the impression that hardly a year had passed since its construction. The very timber out of which the burial chamber was built had not only preserved its original shape and quality but had retained its fresh smell of pitch (see Fig. 3.1).

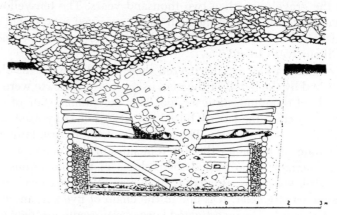

Fig. 3.1. Cross section of the Pazirik mound, showing construction of burial chamber and stone mound.

The wooden chamber of the deceased did not occupy all of the grave pit. It was situated in the southern larger half of the grave (see Fig. 3.2). The chamber, together with the floor was constructed of boards and although the room was spacious, the log ceiling was low. Over this chamber was another enclosure made of logs with a log ceiling. The space between the walls of this double chamber was filled with loose stones. All this construction occupied the southern part of the grave and contained the burial of the deceased and the grave furniture. In the northern smaller part were deposited the bodies of horses killed for the burial. Over the chamber and the bodies of the horses were placed about three hundred thick logs, evidently to prohibit robbers from entering. To prevent this mass of heavy logs and the layer of earth over them from crushing the wooden construction of the burial chamber there were three pairs of special pole-braces which supported the whole weight of the logs and earth.

In spite of all precautions on the part of the builders, the burial had been plundered. The robbers dug a shaft in the center of the kurgan mound and reached the pile of logs. There they cut a wide passage with axes and reached the ceiling (see Fig. 3.1). Here they made a small circular hole through which they took everything from the burial chamber that was in their opinion valuable. To make their work easier they apparently dragged the body itself outside, to be better able to strip it of its gold decorations. When they had finished, hardly anything was left. The sarcophagus hollowed from the trunk of an enormous fir tree was found empty with its lid overturned. It was covered with the bark of the "tcheremuha" tree glued to the surface and decorated by an appliqué of bird-figures cut out of leather. On the wall of the chambers here and there were copper and wooden nails and pieces of felt. The walls once were covered with a thick, black felt carpet decorated with a border of thin felt of many colors with representations of tigers' heads in profile done in appliqué work. Pieces of this felt were strewn on the floor among other rubbish. Here were found also several objects of undetermined purpose.

To judge by the size of the coffin and burial cham-

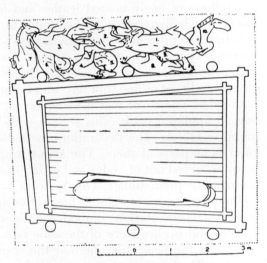

Fig. 3.2. Ground plan of Pazirik burial.

ber, many objects must have been placed with the body. Yet the robbers evidently penetrated there soon after the burial and found everything in such a state of preservation that they could take complete objects to the surface and there strip them of their valuables. This is the reason so few objects were found in the burial chamber itself.

The northern part of the grave escaped the robbers. Although they attempted to enter here, they were able to make only a small opening not large enough for a head to pass through. In the operation they apparently broke an axe, leaving behind the handle which was found near the entrance. The form of this handle is interesting as it was made out of a branch of a pine tree where it joined the trunk. Consequently they had a long handle with the trunk part on one end, well suited for the hafting. The celt itself was carried away by the robbers. This section of the grave was preserved exactly as it was left by the constructors of the kurgan. Under the thick layer of birch and fir bark were corpses of ten horses with a corresponding number of saddles and trappings. The horses were killed by a blow from a sharp axe on the forehead and were thrown into the bottom of the grave pit. In disorder, in various poses, they filled the narrow space between the outer wall and the northern side of the grave pit.

The exceptional state of preservation of the horses and the saddle trappings allows us to study not only the animals themselves, but many questions such as the technique of work on wood, leather, fur, and felt and the processes of dyeing, gilding, etc. The study of these in their interconnections makes possible a partial reconstruction of the picture of the social and economic life at the time of the Pazirik burial.

The construction of the saddles is very simple. They were made of two soft pillows of finely tanned leather and felt, stuffed with reindeer hair. There is a belly-strap, a breast-strap (to prevent backward sliding), a tail-strap (to prevent forward sliding). There was no wooden foundation for the seat and there were no stirrups. A square piece of felt was placed under the saddle to prevent chafing. Over the pillows were placed special covers made out of fine thin felt, with felt or leather trappings hanging on both sides. The cover was usually decorated with scenes of animal combats in appliqué work. This style is well known from the gold plaques found in Siberia. The decorations on the saddle trappings also represent animals or parts of them. The breast-straps and bridles are covered by plaques carved out of cedar and gilded or silvered. Here also animal representations predominate. One is struck by the diversity of subjects, the technique of execution and richness of design. Altogether more than forty different representations embodying the animal style were utilized. All saddles and bridles were of the same type. The bridle, besides the main strap over the head, has one over the nose and forehead and one under the chin. The bits are simple, one of bronze, the rest of iron. All bridles are of wood and were decorated with numerous designs carved in low relief and covered with gold or silver leaf.

This find is very important, since, up to the present time in Scythian burials we have found few remains of saddles, except those at Sebastopol. Only on some designs and on one plaque have we schematic representations of saddles, but owing to their small size it has been impossible to form an idea of their construction.

Especially rich were the decorations of two horses. Besides the saddles and bridles, near their heads were buried ornamented leather covers for the tails and similar covers for the manes and finally masks for the heads. The latter are of unusual interest.

On the head of one of the horses was a mask made of leather, felt, fur and gold leaf in the shape of a reindeer's head with horns of natural size. On the front part of it was placed a figure of a bear cut out of fur. The second mask has a composition of two animals, representing a bear and a griffin.

The latter has large wings and a sculptured head with bull's horns.

The gilded figure of the bear covered the upper lip, nose and forehead of the horse. The figure of the griffin covered the cheeks and its beautiful wings towered from the top of the horse's head. The wings occupied the place of the reindeer's horns on the first mask. All of this was colored, silvered and gilded.

These masks are interesting for us inasmuch as they tend to confirm the theory of N. Y. Marr concerning the order in which the domesticated animals were utilized for travel. On the basis of linguistic materials, Marr has sought to establish the fact that the reindeer as an animal for transportation purposes preceded the horse.

In a recently published work (1928) on the origin of the domestication of the reindeer, Professor Maximov agrees with Gann, Laufer and Hatt, that the Altai-Sayan region was the centre of distribution of the domesticated reindeer, but he thinks that reindeer breeding is a later acquisition of culture, being as it were, the result [i.e. imitation] of the domestication of horse and cattle. It is possible that in the Altai-Sayan region reindeer were used in antiquity for riding and that the type of saddle found in our kurgan or perhaps an even more primitive type originated for use with the reindeer and was only later used for the horse.

The mask with the reindeer horns in the burial ritual speaks in favor of the priority of the reindeer. The buried horses are the same animals which were used during the life of the master and his burial procession; they follow the master to the other world. If the reindeer was the basic means of transportation among the natives, it was necessary for him to follow them to the hereafter. With the substitution of the horse for the reindeer in economic life, the latter was preserved in the rituals. Later the conservative ritual demanded the masking of the horse as a reindeer. By the time of the kurgan in question, the horse had completely taken the place of the reindeer as a means of transportation and even the meaning of the participation of the reindeer in the burial ceremony is forgotten. While one mask has typical reindeer horns, the second deviates considerably from the original model. Under later cultural influences, appears the horned head of the griffin and the place of the reindeer horns are occupied now by the wings of the griffin. Considerable time must have elapsed for the change to have taken place in the ceremony. Here we have the material confirmation of the theory of Marr.

It is impossible in this short article to describe with any degree of completeness all the finds made in the part of the burial occupied by the horses. There are shields made out of sticks sewed together with interlacing strips of leather and hung on the right side of the saddles. In spite of their small size it is evident that we are dealing with armour. We recognize in them the shields known to us from representations of fighting Scythians on the gold of Greek manufacture from the kurgan, Solokha.

There were also found fur bags for provisions; one is made from the head of a lynx, having a corresponding form, the other is cylindrical in shape with a round leather bottom. Both are decorated and are made from pieces of leather and fur of different colours. They are in a beautiful state of preservation and form exceptional objects for archaeological museums.

The variety of technique and design is striking. Eagles and moose, reindeer and mountain goat, bears and griffins, birds and fish, figures in "flying gallop," single heads, peculiar combinations of animals, the head of one in the mouth of another, carnivorae attacking animals from mountains and forests with the characteristic bent back head, in numerous combinations and variations, disclose a very rich but so far little known culture.

The majority of decorations, with the exception of a comparatively small series with plant motifs, are adorned with a very characteristic and very peculiar animal style. In the decorations of saddle trappings, wool, leather, thin felt, fur and horse hair are employed, embellished with silver and gold, red, blue and yellow pigments. Absolutely unique examples of art were thus created.

It is necessary to mention the finds in the upper part of the grave pit. There, among the logs, were discovered two yokes for bulls and the parts for an arba [cart]. Evidently we are dealing here with the very widespread custom of leaving in the grave of the deceased the vehicle on which the body was carried. The arba, to judge by the well preserved upper longitudinal axis was of small dimensions and was very likely two-wheeled. The yoke was very simple, in the form of a stick with holes in the centre for fastening to the shaft and two pairs of holes on the ends, for the sticks placed on the sides of the bull's neck. It should be pointed out, that among the numerous objects found in the burial there is nothing which could indicate a foreign origin. The whole complex of finds is exclusively of local manufacture.

The main occupation of the constructors of Pazirik was herding. We are led to this conclusion by the natural conditions of the country, where agriculture was impossible to any large degree, as it is today. The whole complexion of the local industry indicates that we are dealing primarily with herding peoples. Of course this does not exclude hunting as an occupation. The moose, reindeer, mountain goat and bear, the favorite motives in decorative art, are executed with a knowledge possible only to people who have observed them directly in life. The horse and sheep of many colors (black, white and brown) were the main domesticated animals. The burial of horses with the deceased of all classes shows that we are dealing essentially with a horse-using people. The numerous felt objects made of sheep's wool of different colors and of different quality indicate very well developed sheep herding.

The material obtained gives us data about various technical processes and the comparatively rich and complex social structure. The Pazirik kurgan is a monumental structure, requiring a considerable number of workmen for the earth, stone and wood work, demanding organized means of transport to erect this structure in a short time. Hundreds of logs were used for the building. That both axes and adzes were used is seen from the traces of the tools on the numerous logs and thick boards. Wood carving was very highly perfected, perhaps with the use of special knives. The remains of textiles are insufficient to determine the place of origin. Though bone work is absent here, the technique of bone work and bone carving was well known and was well developed as can be seen from the beautiful examples of it in Katanda and Ursula kurgans. Felt making, leather tanning, and the preparation of furs were also very highly developed. We have examples of the different types of felt, from the thick and rough type to the thinnest, finest kind, rivaling the modern machine-made felt. The finer type was used mostly for decorative purposes. Quite as diverse was the leather work. It varies from the thick belts for the saddles to the thinnest leather cut out in various designs. Well tanned furs were well preserved in spite of the fact that they were for a considerable time in the water and then in the ice. There is no decoration of twined horse-hair but it was utilized as a medium of decoration. Dyeing methods were well known. Felt, fur, leather and hair were dyed with red, yellow and blue pigments. Both vegetable and mineral dyes were used in solution as well as on glue. Pottery was present, large vessels being well fired. There are reasons to think that metallurgy was developed. Mining may have been practiced, though we have found no actual mines as yet. From the complex excavations conducted in making burial pits seven and more meters deep, one might conclude that mining was possible. Bronze and iron tools were widely used and gold was most likely one of the main articles of import. In the burials of the ruling class many gold objects were found.

The population was well versed in the technique of silvering leather and wood; various objects were decorated with thin gold leaf, the designs being pressed out and glued. The perfection of the carved-out wood and cut-out leather objects, together with the jewelry, prove the existence of specialists and perhaps a separate class of artisans.

The people to whom the Pazirik burial belongs were a sedentary or semi-sedentary group, as is natural considering the geographical condition of the country where the herding even today is combined with a sedentary mode of life. This is also indicated by the presence of pottery, by the fundamental log structure in the grave, showing the knowledge of house construction. The details of the burial chamber tell us something about house construction.

The social organization was that of the clan type with the head of the clan as the leader, as far as it is possible to surmise on the basis of the domestication of animals as the economic base. More than likely, we are dealing here with a period leading to the decay of clan organization. The character of the burials allows us to surmise the existence of three economic groups—that of the rich, middle class and poor. Along with this we have indications of a well-formed concept of private property as is shown by the property marks on domesticated animals. The buried horses have cuts on the ears, some on the right, some on the left, one, two or three, showing that the horses belonged to different individuals. We know from Herodotus that Scythians carried the bodies of kings among conquered tribes and those of noblemen among friends, each place providing the funeral festivity. Food and presents were given to the deceased. Among those presents may have been horses.

The horse was the means of transportation. It was ridden and also used for carrying heavy objects. Logs were dragged by a method used today, *viz.*, by making a hole in one end of the log and fastening a rope through it to the horse. Boats may have been known, at least the dug-out type made in the same way as the sarcophagus.

Burials at the Huaca de la Cruz Site, Peru

The following account[2] is a good example of how much can be inferred from a single lot of materials found in a grave. This grave was a very rich one found in the course of excavations by Strong and Evans in the Virú Valley project, a multiple-phase program designed to provide as detailed a study as possible of one small north coastal Peruvian valley. Comparing this grave, called by the excavators the tomb of the Warrior-God (cf. Strong, 1947), with other burials of the same period and using historical evidence to support their interpretations, the authors are able to reconstruct a substantial segment of the religious and social life of these ancient Peruvians. Much of the interpretation is frankly hypothetical and not subject to rigid proof. But the authors have used their imaginations and have succeeded in providing a measured blend of fact and interpretation which successfully brings the past to life.

The reader who may be interested in pursuing the subject of the identification of the profession or trade of individuals as deduced from the items accompanying the corpse in the grave is referred to McGregor's detailed description of the contents of a prehistoric Southwestern medicine-man's grave (McGregor, 1943).

In regard to status differentials, the Huancaco period burials [*ca.* 1000 A.D.] we encountered at V-162 can most easily be placed in two classes, (a) individual burial (Burials 1–7, 9–11) and (b) group burial (Burials 12–16). The individual burials vary in elaboration, but they are simple in comparison with the group burial, that of the Warrior-Priest, which is complex and presents many unique features. We will first consider certain general and particular characteristics of the individual Huan-

[2] W. D. Strong and C. Evans, Jr., *Cultural Stratigraphy in the Virú Valley, Northern Peru*, Columbia Studies in Archaeology & Ethnology, Columbia University Press, New York, 1952, pp. 196–202. By permission of Columbia University Press.

caco period burials we encountered at V-162 and then do the same for the group burial.

Concerning the individual burials of the Huancaco period at V-162, the majority are extended and most often are oriented with the head to west regardless of sex or age. The only evidence suggesting sacrifice of any sort is the llama above the woman's body in Burial 5. No suggestions of human sacrifice or human trophies were noted in these single burials. Erect cane or algarroba posts at the head end of burials occur in six cases. These may be merely grave markers or may have had other symbolic purposes, such as permitting the dead to breathe or receive liquid offerings. The bodies of men, women, and children were first wrapped in cloth and then in cane mats. Infant burials wrapped only with cloth or without any wrappings were encountered. This lack, however, may well be due to the more rapid and complete decay generally characteristic of children's remains. Red pigment occurred on the body of one juvenile. Simple gourd bowls were used to cover the face and other parts of the body for both sexes and all ages. They were also used as containers for offerings but were not themselves decorated. Simple copper face masks occur on women and juveniles as well as on men. The same is true of folded copper, often wrapped in cotton, placed in the mouth cavity, and copper plates or ornaments under the feet and near the hands. A few burials lack such copper offerings. Both sexes, juveniles, and infants are usually accompanied by pottery vessels ranging in number from 16 to 2. The only figurine from these Huancaco burials came from an infant's grave. No "honored child" or unusually rich infant's burial was encountered. Women's graves often contained weaving equipment as well as cotton and food plants. Burial 10, an adult woman, had two weaving baskets and many gourds full of corn, beans, and cotton, as well as the remarkable carved wooden distaff showing an "honored" woman with her two pages. Burial 5, a younger woman, had similar weaving gear but, lacking the distaff, her grave was notable for a remarkable male portrait head, a pot showing a male drinking scene, and a goblet identical to those used in the drinking scene. With the exception of the central figure in the group burial men's bodies were usually accompanied by pottery but without weapons or other specifically male offerings.

From the foregoing, it would seem that individual burial rites during that portion of the Huancaco (Mochica) period represented by this group of graves at V-162 were much the same for men, women, and children. Indeed, the small sample shows more elaborate burials for women than for men. Considering the small consideration shown for women in the wide range of Mochica art, this appearance of sex equality in the ritual of the dead is unexpected.

. . . The occurrence of agricultural and textile products and implements in women's graves has already been stressed. Similarly, the occurrence in a young woman's grave of equipment suggesting ceremonial or merely pleasureful drinking is of interest, as is the fine aristocratic portrait jar in the same grave. The fact that the only figurine found in a grave occurs in that of an infant, like the occurrence of the well-known woman drummer with a mutilated mouth in another child's grave, may or may not prove to have significance. Two burials, those of a man and a woman, show a considerable emphasis on birds, the parrot, cranes, and mythical "cup-drinking" hawk. In addition to her other elaborate offerings, including the beautifully carved "distaff," the woman in Burial 10 has a remarkable *Gato de la Luna* pot which undoubtedly has lunar, solar, or other religious significance. Finally, in Burial 11, that of a child, is the beautiful polished black effigy vessel depicting the great tusked god of the Mochica, whose cult becomes so vivid in the next burials described.

Class B, the group burial (Burials 12–16) at Huaca de la Cruz, has many features in common with the Class A individual burials and these need not be stressed again. They include head orientation to the west, grave head post, llama sacrifice by beheading, reed mat and cloth wrappings, copper face mask, copper in mouth and at hands and feet, red pigment on body, and numbers of decorated vessels, gourds, and plant remains with the bodies.

The group burial, however, differs markedly in other respects. First, the inclusion of five persons in one grave shaft or tomb; the strong probability that two women and a boy represent human sacrifices; that Burial 12, a man, may have been either a sacrificial or a later interment; and, finally, the wide cultural range of the artifacts buried in the upper of the two compartments in the cane coffin containing the main protagonist in this grim but dramatic mortuary group.

Concerning human sacrifice, the evidence is inferential but highly suggestive. This is particularly true concerning the two adult women and the boy. The distorted position of the women crowded in at each end of the Warrior-Priest's coffin (see Fig. 3.3), their lack of mat wrappings or cloth ties, as well as the sash around the neck of Burial 14, all suggest voluntary or involuntary sacrifice to accompany the main, male figure in the tomb. The same is true in regard to the little boy with the deformed skull and abnormal facial features. His waist band decorated with plaques of gilt copper suggests a certain status, probably that of page for the old man below, but the inclusion of the boy's body with all the old man's other grave gifts and insignia of godhood, as well as temporal power, suggests deliberate sacrifice. The case for the mature man in the upper burial is somewhat different. He was fully wrapped and prepared for burial, with mortuary pottery, and with his knees and ankles bound with cloth as in the case of the old Warrior-Priest. It is quite possible that he was buried somewhat later, but in all probability intentionally, in the same grave shaft as the old man. That the others in the shaft were sacrificed cannot be proved, but the inferential evidence is strong. Thus, to animal (llama) sacrifice we can,

Fig. 3.3 (*Above*). Tomb of the Warrior-Priest, Huaca de la Cruz. Burial 12 had been removed, exposing the cane coffin and skeletons of two sacrificed women, seen in upper left and lower right corners of coffin. Fig. 3.4 (*Below*). Tomb of the Warrior-Priest, showing contents of cane coffin after removal of lid.

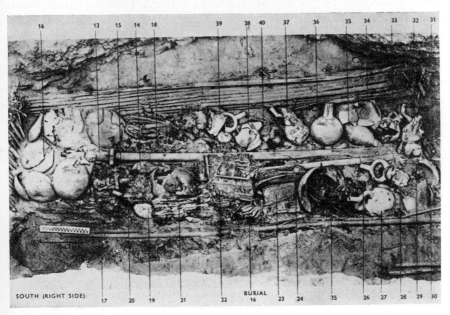

with a high degree of probability, add human sacrifice and status burial as mortuary practices in Huancaco (late Mochica) times at Huaca de la Cruz. It may be noted that as late as Inca times some of the noble's "wives and servants might be killed and buried with him." This would seem to be the case here at a much earlier date.

The fact that the entire burial complex within the cane coffin (see Fig. 3.4) was arranged to correspond with the carved effigy of the tusked god and his page (or son) as they stand on the top of the great ceremonial digging stick has already been stressed. Here we are concerned with wider interpretations concerning the probable role, or rather roles, of the old Warrior-Priest in actual Huancaco (Mochica) society, as depicted in the symbolic art which appears upon the three carved batons. That he represented in his own person the, even then, very ancient lineage of the tusked god seems certain. The basic concept of a great feline deity goes back to Chavin times and undoubtedly persisted on into Incaic times. In different periods and places he undoubtedly assumed many different aspects and names, but as a central divine symbol the great tusked feline deity is well depicted in the art of Chavin, Gallinazo, Mochica, Tiahuanaco, and later periods. . . .

The tusked-god effigy on the ceremonial digging stick indicates one thing most strongly, and that is, that he is the god of agriculture, opening up the ground with his digging stick while a small boy at his side plants the grain. The green bits of turquoise in the boy's hands may well symbolize maize kernels, and it is of interest that he too has a wide mouth which may formerly have been tusked. Whether this implied a father-son relationship can only be guessed at. The tusks of the god and the catlike heads on both headdress and digging stick all accentuate the deity's feline characteristics. Equally so does the actual headdress with the overlapping-fanged dog-fox on the front, which lay above the face of the actual man. Is it carrying symbolism too far to suggest that the three serpents twining down the god's back and, ultimately, across the furrows, represent water and irrigation? In any event, there is a clear resemblance here to Father Cobo's description of the later role of the divine Inca, or his representative, in opening the cultivation of new lands dedicated to the gods: "If the Inca himself, or his governor, or some high official happened to be present, he started the work with his golden taclla or plow, which they brought to the Inca, and, following his example, all the other officials and nobles who accompanied him did the same." Here, perhaps a thousand years earlier, we would seem to have the feline-anthropomorphic god of the Mochica opening the planting season.

The second large mace, or staff, with the owl carved on its top, had lost its point before it was placed in the burial, hence we can only surmise from its similarity to the first in size and form that it, too, was of copper and chisel-shaped. We can also only speculate as to the ceremonial aspect represented by either the owl staff or the remains of the elaborate imitation bird headdress. However, from their position just over the body of the old man, they obviously represented some aspect of his power in council or cult activities.

The third large wooden object, the knobbed and copper-pointed war mace, seems clear in both its use and major symbolism. This, for all its original ornateness, was a battered war weapon at the time it was buried, presumably with its Warrior-Priest owner. The scenes of conflict, council, and death leave no doubt as to its purpose. To presume that the smaller warriors fleeing from the Mochica conquerors were the defeated Gallinazo culture soldiers is a tempting but hardly verifiable hypothesis. That the battered war mace, however, represented the military role and prowess of the old man who lay beneath it and, perhaps, even that of his ancestors, seems a reasonable if not strictly verifiable conclusion. Thus, from these major artifacts alone, it can be concluded that the old man buried beneath these offerings not only represented in his own person the great tusked deity of the Mochica but that in this incarnation he had to assume the economic roles of an agricultural deity, a priest, a war leader, and a councillor as well. This combination of vital roles, plus many more, for the most-often depicted Mochica deity will surprise no one who has studied the very numerous ceramic and other portrayals of this god gathered together by Larco. However, to find direct evidence of a human being who, in his own lifetime, appears to have assumed these roles in the eyes of his people, makes the record written in ceramics and other portrayals even more vivid. Just as in earlier times the Cupisnique artist showed the man behind the jaguar mask of the god, so here we find the actual, old, old man who lived and acted behind the symbols of *Ai apaec* during the late Mochica occupation at Huaca de la Cruz. In Incaic times the creator-god has been assigned the name Wira-Kocha and, for Mochica times, Larco has employed the term *Ai apaec* for the tusked feline creator-god. . . .

[The old man's] gilded copper and turquoise mouth mask, found *in situ*, has unique interest since this decoration is not commonly shown on the almost innumerable portrait vessels of the Mochica period. The mouth mask, however, is commonly depicted on Nazca culture pottery, often in association with a feline deity.

Within the cane coffin (Burials 13 and 16) there were sixteen vessels. They include two bottles, two floreros, and two dippers or "corn poppers," all with geometric designs. Two, and possibly three, stirrup spout vessels have scenes in which *Ai apaec* participates with his lizard "servant." One is a sacrificial scene in which victims are thrown from the mountain peaks to the shore below, where the god sits. In this case the tusked head is missing (having formerly been broken off and temporarily fastened on with asphaltum), but the scene occurs on other vessels with *Ai apaec* and his animal servants clearly depicted. Another stirrup spout shows *Ai apaec* fishing from the mountain peaks. A third which may or may not be *Ai apaec,* represents a demon warrior seizing a fish. One vessel gives a very vivid depiction of a deer hunt, another anthropomorphizes the potato in a most grotesque manner; a third depicts a skull. No tusks are depicted here, but *Ai apaec* is sometimes shown as a skull. The cane-coffin offertory section also includes three male effigy stirrup spouts, all of which are of Huancaco Red, White, Black type, and all have elaborate black facial paintings. Unless the bedizened potato pot may represent a woman, it is interesting to note that no females are presented in any of the artistic products from the cane coffin or the tomb as a whole (Burials 12–16). Considering the realistic art depicted in wood carving, ceramics, and metalwork that is directly associated with this Warrior-Priest burial, the scenes represented fittingly include religion (mythology), sacrifice, warfare (conquest?), council, agriculture, hunting, fishing, noblemen (in elaborate costume), birds (on pottery, wood, and metal), mammals (particularly the feline), reptiles, death (the skull pot and dead warriors), and a strong mountain cult which always seems to have been important in Peru.

Because most of the vessels with Burial 12 and with sacrificial Burials 14 and 15 were outside the burial wrappings, their exact association is not so certain as those gifts inside the cane coffin. Considering the seven vessels immediately adjacent and under the middle-aged man (Burial 12), we find one florero and two bowls decorated with geometric designs. The other vessels include two rather crude, duplicate feline faces cast in the same mold and each marked on the bottom by an X; a "sea lion" effigy; and a vessel with war symbols. The ceramic mortuary complex here is interesting but seems to throw little light on the earthly role of the man whose body it accompanies (Burial 12). One presumed sacrificial victim, a woman (Burial 15), was associated with a broken stirrup spout bottle or pitcher with one sealed mouth, a broken stirrup spout jar in the form of a man's head with black face paint, and a most effective offering to the dead representing in stark simplicity a kneeling man dressed in white, raising his face to the skies. He is accompanied by two bowls of food and a jug of water. The other sacrificed woman (Burial 14) was associated with one broken stirrup spout vessel which, interestingly enough, also has one mouth sealed. The seal in this case is a strange, squatting, anthropomorphic figure with hands clasped across the mouth and face upraised to the skies. There is a strange suggestion of diving here, seeming almost to parallel the concept of the Maya "diving god." The fact that two unusual vessels, both with the erect spout sealed, were each placed by a presumably sacrificed woman may have significance. However, Burials 5 and 6, both those of women, contained stirrup spout bottles with sealed erect spouts. There was no suggestion of sacrifice in either of these cases, hence there may be some association between this particular type of vessel and female burial In any event, it is obvious that we need much more objective data on such associations not only for the Mochica, but for all other periods in Peru. The above associations, both in Class A (individual) and Class B (group) burials at Huaca de la Cruz are most interesting and throw considerable light upon many aspects of culture which can be obtained in no other way. Torn apart from their grave lot associations they would lose much of their finer temporal and cultural significance.

One other highly significant fact remains to be stressed concerning the nature of the Huancaco (late Mochica) culture at Huaca de la Cruz. This concerns the fact that whereas the carved wooden batons, the war mace (Burials 12–16), and the "distaff" (Burial 10) at V-162 represent the finest examples of wood carving known for the Mochica period as a whole, the objects themselves were very old, and had either been broken and mended in the course of time or left unrepaired (as in the cases of missing copper points and shell inlays) when they were deposited in the graves. On the other hand, the decorated pottery (including a high proportion of Huancaco Red, White, Black) which accompanies these finer objects in the burials, and in Huancaco living levels, is often elaborate, but is poorly made when compared to the preponderant and finely made Mochica White and Red vessels recovered by Uhle at Moche. There is reason to believe that the Huancaco Red, White, Black ceramic type marks a very late stage in Mochica development in the Virú Valley and probably elsewhere. Therefore, it seems the most logical explanation that the fine, but old and battered, ceremonial wood carvings from the tombs were heirlooms from an earlier and artistically finer stage of Mochica development than that represented by the Huancaco (late Mochica) occupation at Huaca de la Cruz. That objects bearing such important symbolic associations of religion, government, war, and agriculture were buried with the old, old Warrior-Priest at V-162 suggests, further that his demise represented the end of a dynasty (possibly that of the late Mochica conquerors of the Virú Valley), and for that reason these symbols of past glory and power were buried with him. . . .

Having outlined the major characteristics of Huancaco (late Mochica) mortuary practices, as we know them at present for the Virú Valley, a very brief comparison with those of earlier periods seems in order. Such a comparison will be more effective when the extensive data on Gallinazo and other period burial practices secured by Collier, Bennett, and Bird are available. However, we have already presented some similar evidence for the Gallinazo and Puerto Moorin (Salinar) mortuary complexes (sites V-66 and V-59). Concerning the former period there are certain striking similarities between the Gallinazo warrior and the Huancaco Warrior-Priest (Burial 13, V-162) discussed immediately above. First, the Gallinazo burial was that of a warrior accompanied by his weapons, a wooden mace, and an atlatl with copper hook and sea lion tusk handle, together with copper objects. It is interesting to note that this Gallinazo war mace is much lighter than that found with the Mochica Warrior-Priest, lacked the needle-sharp copper point, and must have been a far less effective weapon. Both men were attired in cloth to which were sewn small rectangles of gilded copper, both had folded gilded copper pieces in their mouths, and both were extended and laid on cotton pillows. We have discussed the probability that the remarkable wooden symbols and weapon buried with the Mochica Warrior-Priest represented an earlier Mochica art style. It is therefore especially interesting to note that with the Gallinazo warrior there was one fine vessel which is of the earlier Late Guañape (Cupisnique) style, although it was associated with other vessels of Gallinazo type. There is a suggestion here that heirlooms or symbolic pieces from earlier times may have been regarded as particularly suitable for burial with important personages. While the Gallinazo warrior burial lacks the richness as well as the sacrificial and other aspects of the Huancaco Warrior-Priest burial, it does present certain important similarities.

A Family Tomb of Neolithic Britain

Here is the description[3] of the contents of a stone chamber tomb in Great Britain which consist of an accumulation of remains of one family group, individuals of which had been buried seriatim.

Multiple burials presumably representing a family group interred at one moment in a single grave have been noted (e.g., Hooton, 1920:14–15, Pl. 4), but the long-continued use of a tomb by one lineage is quite another matter, since each opening and new body added introduces additional complexities of interpretation. Lothrop (1937:61) suggests that certain groups of graves at the Sitio Conté in Panama can be interpreted as those of a single family.

The chamber at first sight appeared to contain a heterogeneous and disordered mass of bones; careful examination, however, showed this to be by no means the case. No less than seven skulls could be observed, these being placed as follows. Three lay against the eastern side of the chamber; one of these (No. 7) being considerably nearer the portal than the other two. This skull was lying on its left side and faced to the west; the second and third skulls (Nos. 1 and 2) lay upside down and actually touched each other. A curious feature of these last was that each was furnished with a lower jaw placed in approximately the correct position, but it was subsequently proved that one of these jaws could not have originally belonged to the skull in association with which it was found. Skull No. 3, badly fractured, was close to the southern wall. The two larger portions of it were upside down, the face and frontal bones downwards, as was the occipital base

---

[3] A. Keiller and S. Piggott, *Excavation of an Untouched Chamber in the Lanhill Long Barrow*, Proceedings of the Prehistoric Society for 1938, Cambridge, 1938, vol. 4, n.s., pp. 125 ff., 147–148. By permission of the editor, J. G. D. Clark.

which lay close to it, while in this case the correct lower jaw was underneath the fragments. Skull No. 4 was lying on its left side in the southwestern corner and touching it was No. 5. Only the cranium of the latter
remained, the facial bones and both jaws being absent. The cranium rested
upside down. Touching this skull again was No. 6, lying on its left side.
The forehead was in an advanced state of decay and quite soft, and the
right facial bones had completely disappeared, while there was a large
hole in the right side of the skull and frontal bone where it had rotted
away, apparently through a constant dripping of water on it from a crack
in the roof above. Between these skulls was a mass of bones clearly not
articulated. Several long bones (3 femora; 2 tibiae; 2 fibulae; a humerus
and a radius) were lying side by side across the chamber from east to west,
the shorter bones being placed between the femora. Around and under
them again were pelvic and other bones scattered without any order, and
lower still, in a layer of reddish clay flecked with mildew 0.1 ft. in depth
which lay on the paving of the chamber, was a mass of smaller bones including metapodials intermingled with sections of vertebrae, ribs, etc.
Among these last were four instances of vertebrae definitely articulated;
two of two sections together, and two of three sections, showing that these
must have been united by ligaments when placed in their present position.
The majority of the exposed bones, as well as the skulls, were thickly encrusted with a calcareous accretion, a condition noted in the excavation of
some of the Long Barrows in the Cotswolds. On removal of this accretion
remains of gristle were disclosed on one humerus showing that the deposit
must have been formed with considerable rapidity. Subsequent examination of these skeletal remains disclosed the fact that bones representing an
eighth individual were present. No skull existed which could be allotted
to this skeleton. In addition to the above a single incomplete femur of an
infant was identified, thus bringing the total of individuals interred to nine.

Although skull No. 7 lay completely exposed, a deposit of earth was seen
to cover the floor in the vicinity of the portal. The removal of this earth disclosed the fact that it covered an articulated skeleton, to which this skull
belonged, resting in a crouched position upon the paving. The exact position of this body is of some importance. As may be seen from the plan [not
reproduced here], the skeleton was lying on its back with both the shoulder-
blades and the pelvic bones flat upon the floor. The legs were flexed, the
femora together, the knee joints within 0.3 ft. of the front of the skull. The
tibiae and fibulae of each leg were articulated and lay parallel to each
other. The feet were incomplete, a certain number of the digits having
disappeared. The vertebral column was slightly curved, and the left arm
lay across the chest. As to the right arm, however, the humerus lay parallel
to the eastern wall of the chamber, and 0.05 ft. from it, the space between
the bone and the wall being filled with reddish earth containing an admixture of a white mildew-like substance. The arm was flexed at the elbow,

so that the hand lay upon the chest. Beneath the left scapula was found a small flint flake, the sole artifact discovered in association with the burials.

In clearing out the antechamber and passage, a clavicle and a section of vertebra were found near the sill across the entrance, while a single cervical vertebra was found in the blocking of the passage at the north end.

The conditions described above admit of only one interpretation. It seems clear that the skeletal remains of the eight individuals occupying the rear of the tomb represent successive interments previous to the contracted burial, and that they must have been placed in the position in which they were found immediately prior to, and in order to leave room for, that interment. It is obvious that by this time the previous burials were in a skeletal condition, and it will have been observed that considerable care was taken in the symmetrical rearrangement of the bones, although no attempt at articulation was made save in the case of certain skulls where it has been shown that lower jaws were deliberately supplied, although not always to the correct skull. This goes to prove that more than one, if not all the skeletons were disturbed at the same time, but this does not render it impossible for the previous interments to have been successive ones, since it would appear that the primary, and indeed the sole, purpose of redistributing the skeletons was to make room for a newcomer in an already crowded chamber. This definite instance of a series of successive burials is of considerable importance, if only in view of the claims frequently put forward to account for the multiple interments in British megalithic tombs, namely that these represented a burial of a quantity of individuals made at one and the same time. The bodies of such individuals are thought of as having been previously stored elsewhere, so that most, if not all, would already be in a skeletal condition at the time of the ceremony. While this practice of "reserved" burials undoubtedly existed in antiquity, the evidence does not seem to warrant a belief in its normal employment in British megalithic tombs.

The total or partial absence of certain of the bones need not occasion surprise, since it is not uncommon, under conditions similar to those prevailing in this case, for skeletons to be found in an incomplete condition, although the interments had demonstrably taken place when the flesh was still present. A single parallel will suffice: that of the contracted burial in proximity to Stonehold 31 in the megalithic avenue leading from West Kennet to the Circles of Avebury. In this case, the destruction of parts of the skeleton had undoubtedly been due to the seeping of water through part of the filling of the grave. Some of the bones were in a remarkably good state of preservation, though others were partially decomposed while the ribs and most of the spinal column were represented only by discoloured smears upon the chalk on which they lay. Certain small bone had disappeared completely.

The singularly fortunate circumstances of the discovery of this un touched chamber at Lanhill render it possible to reconstruct the stages of the final burial. The passage having been opened, an individual crawled through the porthole into the chamber, and (a task impossible without some form of artificial lighting) rearranged the bones already there in the position in which they were discovered, thus clearing a sufficient area on the floor to take the forthcoming burial. The individual then retired from the chamber and the corpse was inserted upon its back into the passage-way. It was then manoeuvred head first through the porthole, in all proba-bility by pushing its legs. When the shoulders had passed the aperture, whoever was negotiating the burial—and there was only room in the pas-sage for one such—took the right hand of the corpse in his left, and con-tinued to press the body through the porthole. This resulted in a form of swivelling action on the right shoulder-blade, and simplified the body being placed transversely across the chamber. Experiments carried out by the writers with a full sized model of the chamber and porthole entrance, dem-onstrated that an individual of the same height as that estimated from the skeleton could be inserted through the aperture by tightly flexing his legs against his body, which accounts for the contracted position of the burial. On insertion into the tomb the corpse would still be lying upon its back, while the legs, if they did not naturally fall into the position in which they were found, would take this up as a result of a slight push from without. Finally the right arm of the corpse, bent at the elbow, was forced into the chamber and the upper arm pressed almost at right-angles to the body against the eastern wall. It should be noted that the space of 0.05 ft. be-tween the humerus and the wall of the chamber filled with mildewy soil, may be accounted for by that taken up originally by the skin and flesh prior to decomposition.

As regards the period of time after death during which such a burial took place, two alternatives are possible, but for various reasons only one probable. The interment might have taken place prior to the setting in of rigor mortis, but this presupposes that the transport of the body to the barrow and its insertion, to say nothing of the careful rearrangement of the bones already within the chamber, must have taken place within an almost incredibly short time after death. It would seem to be very much more likely that the burial was undertaken after rigidity had worn off—a matter, generally speaking, of forty-eight hours, but varying with climatic and individual conditions—while it should be understood that, actually, a dead body would be easier to manipulate, in the manner described sub-sequent to the cessation of rigor mortis than prior to the onset of that con-dition. After the body had been disposed in the manner described, it must have been covered by a thin layer of earth, the head, however, being left exposed. The next stage of which we have evidence consists of the final blocking of the outer portion of the passage by means of the rough stone-work described. In this regard it may be suggested that the bones, which, it should be recollected were of small size, found in the antechamber and passageway, were inadvertently dragged out from the chamber during the withdrawal either of whoever was responsible for the rearrangement of the other bones of the previous burials or, less probably, of the individual who had carried out the actual insertion of the corpse.

The above reconstruction of the final burial inevitably recalls the practices described by Dr. A. J. B. Wace in the Late Helladic Chambered Tombs of Mycenae (*Archaeologia*, Vol. LXXXII, 1932), where the favourable circumstances of careful excavation and record, no less than the relatively high material culture represented, enabled a more detailed restoration of the burial rites to be made than has elsewhere been possible. Although the Mycenaean tombs in question are chronologically later than the British chambered cairns, the burial rites, and indeed the details of the interior structure, are so similar as obviously to represent only slightly divergent specialisations from a common stock.

Wace is of the opinion that the tombs of Mycenae were "family sepulchres used by the same families over a considerable period of years" and there seems little reason to doubt that most, if not all, British chambered tombs are susceptible of a like explanation. As at Lanhill, when the Mycenaean tombs were reopened for a fresh burial the remains of the preceding burials were, when necessary, removed or more often "simply swept up in a heap to the sides and corners of the chamber" to make room for the later occupant. It should be noted, however, that no instance was recorded at Mycenae of the careful arrangement of the bones such as has been described above.

The similarities to Mycenaean practices presented by the final interment at Lanhill (No. 7) are almost startling. There "the dead when laid in the tomb seem to have been placed on their backs or slightly on one side. The knees were bent upwards and the head seems to have been slightly raised, for in one case a stone was found beneath the skull and in others the lower jaw was found among the ribs. The position of the hands varied. Sometimes the arms were bent upwards as in the contracted attitude of burial, sometimes they lay by the sides, but in many cases it was noted that one hand lay in the lap." The slightly raised skull is noteworthy, since at Lanhill the fact that the body was covered with earth, whereas the skull was left exposed, points to a similar practice. Wace observed that in some cases a layer of earth had been laid over a body. "This may have been done," he suggests, "just before the closing of a tomb after a burial, but it is more probable that it was done on re-opening the tomb as a purification to prepare for a new burial." The Lanhill evidence, however, implies that his first suggestion may be the more probable. . . .

[The report on the skeletal material by A. J. E. Cave reads, in part:]

That the Lanhill Long Barrow skeletons (1–9) belong all to one distinct racial type (the Mediterranean) is sufficiently obvious from the . . . [osteological analysis]. That, further, they represent the several members of one particular family group is equally obvious on various grounds. . . .

Moreover, a distinct family resemblance is anatomically apparent between certain members of this group, as study of the cranial drawings well reveal. It is very possible, although no certainty can be reached on the point, that skulls Nos. 1, 3 and 7 are those of brothers. The younger woman (No. 5) may well be the daughter of one aged female (No. 2), and further—though, again, no certain opinion is possible—it is quite likely that the youth of 20, the child of 12 and the year-old baby are her children. . . .

Another curious piece of evidence indicating familial relationship is the frequency of Wormian ossicles in the lambdoid [bones] in these Lanhill crania.

The Lanhill family, obviously people of importance in their day, were buried, as they died, in the family sepulchre, their remains being thereafter undisturbed, save to accommodate later burials.

Suttee Burial at Kerma

The following extract,[4] by G. A. Reisner, is taken from a long account of findings in the Eastern Cemetery at Kerma in the Sudan, along the Nile, in which Egyptian officials were buried. The type of sacrificial burial in which large numbers of retainers accompanied the chief personage is not typical of Egyptian funerary practice and reminds us of the retainer burial described by Woolley at the Mesopotamian site of Ur, and instances from the New World as at Coclé, Panama (Lothrop, 1937) and the southeastern United States (Sears, 1954).

When the facts presented by the large tumuli are taken under examination, they are found to be exactly the same as in the subsidiary and independent graves, but on a much larger scale. In these, the chief burial [was anciently] without exception entirely cleared out, and the accompaniments scattered in the debris. In [tombs] K III, K IV and K X, the chief body was in a separate room which, in [tombs] K III and K IV at least, was roofed with a vault of crude-bricks; in the other graves the separation was not so clear, although the tumuli, K XVI, K XVIII, and K XIX, each contained more than one main burial chamber. In K III, the fragments of a bed were found made of blue-glazed quartzite but of exactly the same form as the ordinary wooden bed; and the fragments of a slate bed, which I believe to have come from K IV, were found in the debris of the cemetery chapel K II. In K X, the body was buried in a box, a temporary variation of the ordinary custom which extended to a few subsidiary graves in that tumulus. In the other tumuli the beds were of wood and of the usual form. From the fragments found in the debris disturbed

---

[4] G. A. Reisner, "The Eastern Cemetery," *Excavations at Kerma,* Harvard African Studies, Peabody Museum, Harvard University, Cambridge, 1923, vol. 5, pt. 3, pp. 68–72, 77, 280. By permission of J. O. Brew, Director of the Peabody Museum, Harvard University.

by the plunderers, a series of unusual objects were recorded which I assign without hesitation to the chief burial and which show that the equipment of that body was of the same general character as that of the chief bodies in the subsidiary graves but much more expensive and of finer materials. The parallel is continued by the contents of the other rooms in these tumuli which, according to the form, I call sacrificial corridors or sacrificial chambers. These apartments contain a large number of bodies in the same variety of attitudes and positions as the extra bodies in the subsidiary graves and resting also on the floor of the room, sometimes in almost regular rows but more often in quite irregular groups. The number of the extra bodies were as follows. I give also the estimated original number, as all these sacrificial apartments had been more or less plundered, although many individual bodies were quite intact:

| | Number of Sacrificial Bodies | |
| | | Estimated original |
Tumulus	Actually found	number
K III A	45±	100±
K IV B	95	110–120
K X B [Fig. 3.5]	322	400
K XVI B, C	30±	100±
K XVIII B	42	80±
K XIX	none	80±
K XX, one chamber	12	50±

These numbers, although astonishingly large, correspond more or less to the proportions of the large tumuli as compared with other graves. Even in the graves, the number of sacrifices usually increased approximately in proportion to the size of the grave; which means that the graves were made of a size to contain the expected burials. It may be remarked that the estimated number of burials is based on the organic stains on the floor in plundered areas, and would by no means entirely fill these ample apartments. Nor is even the estimated number for K X, 400 bodies (based on concrete evidence of 322 bodies), too large for the size of the hareem of the family of the Egyptian governor of the Sudan. They include a large proportion of women and children, but also some males, no doubt bodyguards or hareem servants. That some of them were eunuchs is of course possible but indeterminable. The man was the governor of a country which controlled the main trade lines and the gold supply of Egypt, and at the distance of so many days' journey from Thebes and Memphis, must have held the position of a nearly independent but tribute-paying viceroy to the king of Egypt. Under such circumstances, a hareem with all its dependents, servants, and miscellaneous offspring would in the Orient easily amount to five hundred persons or more. Thus all the statements in regard to the extra bodies in the smaller graves apply in equal degree to those of the great tombs. These enormous burials also represent family interment made on one and the same day, differing only in scale which was pro-

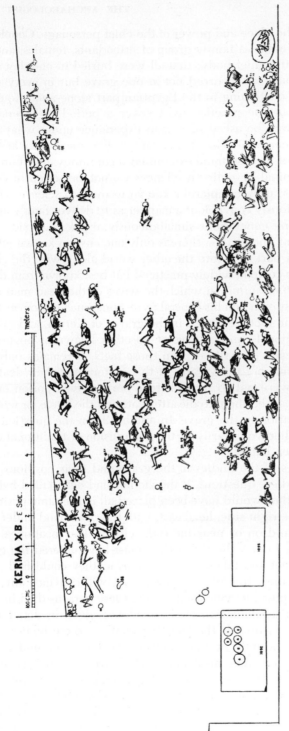

Fig. 3.5. Plan of Tomb X B at Kerma, showing remains of sacrificed individuals.

portionate to the place and power of the chief personage. Concluding that the burial represents a family group of attendants, females, and children together with the chief body; that all were buried in one day and in the same grave; that this occurred not in one grave but in every grave in a vast cemetery, containing in the Egyptian part alone about four hundred graves; and that the practice must cover a period of several hundred years; it may well be asked of human experience under what conditions such a custom can exist. The chances of war become at once an absurdity; the possibility of the continual extermination of family after family by execution for criminal or political offences cannot be seriously considered; and there is certainly no microbe known to modern science which could act in so maliciously convenient a manner as to deliver family after family through so many generations simultaneously at the grave-side. In all the range of present knowledge, there is only one custom known which sends the family or a part of it into the other world along with the chief member. That is the custom, widely practiced but best known from the Hindoo form called *satî* or *suttee,* in which the wives of the dead man cast themselves (or are thrown) on his funeral pyre. Some such custom as this would explain fully the facts recorded in the graves of Kerma, and after several years of reflection I can conceive of no other known or possible custom which would even partially explain those facts. It remains only to determine in what manner the victims of this custom met their death; that is, whether they were put to death before burial, given poison or a mortal wound which caused them to die after entering the grave, or whether they died by suffocation in the grave. In another form the question becomes: whether they died voluntarily by the compulsion of traditional duty or by the act of other hands.

The attitudes of the bodies in the grave and their positions answer at once a part of these questions. If the victims had been killed before entering the grave, they would have been placed all in the same position neatly arranged on the right side, head east, with the right hand under the cheek and the left hand on or near the right elbow. The location and various attitudes of the bodies show that they must have entered the grave alive on their own feet and taken their positions as they could find place. The most casual examination of the photographs will convince anyone of this fact. The only possible conclusion is that these persons died in the grave. A more careful examination of the evidence given in detail in the descriptive chapters reveals the fact that many of these bodies are in attitudes which could only be the result of fear, resolution under pain or its anticipation, or of other movements which would naturally arise in the body of perfectly well persons suffering a conscious death by suffocation. It must be remembered that in those cases where the body was covered directly, the close pressure of the earth would have prevented all but the smallest movements, even those produced by convulsion, and death, or a any rate unconsciousness, would have been a matter of a few minutes. Whatever movements took place would have been mainly the result of fear acting at the last moment before the living body was covered with earth. If a person had the fortitude to withstand the emotion of being covered with earth, subsequently little movement was possible and death came quickly. That there were such persons is clearly shown by a small number of bodies, usually of mature age, which lie approximately in the attitude of those who were buried as corpses. Then there were a few bodies, probably males, who lay in a similar attitude but with the left hand resting on the hilt or the scabbard of their dagger. Even under the hide, the pressure was quite as great, but slightly less close. Only very minor movements, such as those of the extremities, would have been possible after the filling in of the lower part of the grave, but owing to the very slightly greater amount of air, death would have been a little slower. The most unfortunate persons were those, usually younger females, who crept under the bed and being thus enclosed in an air-space of about 0.175 cubic meter died much more gradually by the exhaustion of the air. Thus in the great majority of cases, the movements to be expected are those of emotion in anticipation of death, stirred by the feel of the falling earth. The convulsive movements which take place in a body dying of suffocation will only have been possible in a few cases by accidents of position and chance inequalities in the process of filling the grave.

As a fact, the movements exhibited are largely those of emotion at the prospect of death by burial under earth. The most common thing was for the person to bury the face in the hands. It was also not unusual for one hand to be over the face and the other pressed between the thighs. But most of the better preserved graves presented a case or two of unusual attitudes. In K XX, three bodies have one arm passed around the breast clasping the back of the neck from the opposite side, and indeed that whole group is particularly worthy of attention. In K X B, the very well preserved body AC has the head bent down into the crook of the elbows in a manner most enlightening as an indication of her state of mind at the moment of being covered. Near that body is another lettered PB, which lies on the right side, head west, but with the shoulder turned on the back, while the right hand clutches and presses an ostrich-feather fan against the face which is bent down towards the breast; the left arm passes across the breast so that the left hand holds the right forearm. In K 444, the two bodies, G and H, lie with their foreheads pressed against each other as if for comfort. In K 1026, body B has the fingers of the right hand clenched in the strands of the bead head-circlet, and this was not uncommon. The more unusual conditions are presented by the following examples. In K 3501, the principal sacrifice, a woman who was on a bed under the hide, is turned on her back, legs spread wide apart (probably partly by pressure of filling), left hand half closed on breast, right grasping tightly the right pelvic bone, head bent down against left shoulder. In K 1000A, the woman B, who had been under the bed and is shown by the position of her legs to have been originally on her right side, head east, has turned her body over on the stomach with the head twisted around to lie on its left cheek, facing south instead of north; the arms are stretched down with the left hand on the buttocks and the right apparently grasping the left foot; owing to the lowness of the bed she was unable to turn her legs over without straightening them out and she could not straighten them because they projected beyond the foot of the bed and were held fast by the filling. Another most instructive example is body B in K 1047, a woman lying at the foot of the grave and under a hide; she has turned slightly on her back with the right hand against the right leg and clutches the thorax with the left hand as if in agony. But it is unnecessary to multiply these grewsome evidences further. No one of normal mentality who will read the detailed evidence in the descriptions will escape the conviction that these extra bodies are the remains of persons who died in the places where we found their bones, and who had been in fact buried alive.

Together with these human sacrifices, there were in almost all graves from one to a dozen rams also buried entire and often with the tips of their horns protected by knobs of ivory or wood to prevent goring. Towards the eastern part of the cemetery and in the Nubian graves, the rams become more numerous and the human sacrifices fewer, until in the northern Nubian Cemetery most of the graves have only ram sacrifices. In a few cases, the ram was clearly attached by a lead or thong. They were all buried under conditions similar to those of the human beings and therefore probably alive. But in their case the question has less importance. Whether buried alive as I believe or not, these rams are not ordinary food offerings such as were placed in Egyptian graves in all periods; nor have we more than a few similar cases in Egypt. Perhaps the presence of mummified animals in the tombs of human beings may be based on a similar idea.

Much must remain uncertain. It may be suggested that the human sacrifices were more or less stupefied at the great funeral feast, the remains of which I would see in the crescent of ox-skulls about the southern edge of the tumulus. But I judge that feast to have taken place after the burial. . . . I am personally convinced that these people died simply by suffocation. But the question is not of great importance as compared with the general and obvious features of the burial custom here revealed.

. . . But whether the spirit of Prince Hepzefa, [who was buried in tomb K III] for example, was setting out on the long journey to Egypt or was remaining to face the unknown spirit-world of the Sudan, his need for the company of his family was more urgent than in Egypt. The family itself was in a still more difficult situation. If they lived on and died singly whatever perils the after-life might bring, whether those of the journey to Egypt or those of a shadow-world filled with the spirits of the wild tribe and the raging gods of the south, all must face it alone without the aid and protection of their master. Only a few moments of present pain separated them from his familiar presence. Existence was not to cease. The fact of continued existence under the accustomed habits of life on earth was not a matter of doubt. From their point of view manifestly the safest and the most desirable act was to pay the small price and to enter the future life in their familiar family environment. . . . Thus self-sacrifice as practiced in the *sati*-burials at Kerma was not a cruel inhuman thing, but rather a kindly custom, an act of loyalty which provided both him who had died and those who offered themselves to a living death, with the assurance of the continuation of the long-accustomed family life in the other world.

Under such circumstances, the mind attempts to reconstruct the funeral of Prince Hepzefa, probably the first of the Egyptian governors to be buried in Ethiopia. Many of the preliminaries are quite beyond our ken— whether the chapel, K II, and the skeleton of the tumulus had been built before the actual death; to what extent the body was mummified or prepared for burial, whether it lay in state in the thick-walled chapel for some days with the funeral equipment gathered about it; and many similar details. It was entirely in accordance with Egyptian custom to slaughter cattle for a great funeral feast, and the skulls of over a hundred oxen laid on the surface and buried by drift sand around the southern circumference of the tumulus form ocular evidence of such a feast at the funeral of Hepzefa. The disposal of these skulls without rather than within the tumulus seems to indicate that the actual eating took place after the burial. A meat-feast was and remains among primitive people a rare occasion of which advantage was taken by every person within reach and such a ceremonial feast as was provided at the funeral of Hepzefa must have called together almost the whole population of the district for more than fifty miles around, if the delay between death and burial was greater than a few days. I imagine the procession filing out of the chapel, K II, and taking the short path to the western entrance of the long corridor of the tumulus, K III; the blue-glazed quartzite bed, on which the dead Hepzefa probably already lay covered with linen garments, his sword between his thighs, his pillow, his fan, his sandals in their places; the servants bearing alabaster jars of ointments, boxes of toilet articles and games, the great blue faience sailing boats with all their crews in place, the beautifully decorated faience vessels and the fine pottery of the prince's daily life; perhaps the porters straining at the ropes which drew the two great statues set on sledges, although these may have been taken to the tomb before this day; the bearers who had the easier burden of the statuettes; the crowd of women and attendants of the hareem decked in their most cherished finery, many carrying some necessary utensil or vessel. They proceed, not in the ceremonial silence of our funerals, but with all the "ululations" and wailings of the people of the Nile. The bed with the body is placed in Chamber C, the finer objects in that chamber and in the anteroom, the pottery among the statues and statuettes set in the corridor. The doors of the chambers are closed and sealed. The priests and officials withdraw. The women and attendants take their place jostling in the narrow corridor, perhaps still with shrill cries or speaking only such words as the selection of their places required. The cries and all movements cease. The signal is given. The crowd of people assembled for the feast, now waiting ready, cast the earth from their baskets upon the still, but living victims on the floor and rush away for more. The frantic confusion and haste of the assisting multitude is easy to imagine. The emotions of the victims may perhaps be exaggerated by ourselves; they were fortified and sustained by their religious beliefs, and had taken their places willingly, without doubt, but at that last moment, we know from their attitudes in death that a rustle of fear passed through them and that in some cases there was a spasm of physical agony.

The corridor was quickly filled. With earth conveniently placed, a few hundred men could do that work in a quarter of an hour; a few thousands with filled baskets could have accomplished the task in a few minutes. The assembled crowd turned then probably to the great feast. The oxen had been slaughtered ceremonially to send their spirits with the spirit of the prince. The meat must be eaten, as was ever the case. If I am right in my interpretation of the hearths, consisting of ashes and red-burned earth, which dot the plain to the west and south of the tumulus, the crowd received the meat in portions and dispersed over the adjacent ground in family or village groups to cook and eat it. No doubt the wailing and the feasting lasted for days, accompanied by games and dances.

The Culture of Swanscombe Man

Kenneth Page Oakley, the author of the following article, is a senior principal scientific officer in the Department of Geology of the British Museum (Natural History). Oakley's applications of the fluorine dating method have provided important additions to our knowledge of fossil man (Oakley, 1951). His study, made in collaboration with C. R. Hoskins, of the fluorine content of the Piltdown specimens led the way to the final exposure of Piltdown as a forgery (Oakley, 1955; Weiner, 1955). At the same time, Oakley's fluorine test of the Swanscombe fossils has established the contemporaneity of the human and animal remains at that site.

In the following excerpt[5] he attempts to utilize paleontological evidence in the reconstruction of the cultures of fossil man. Oakley's effort to reconstruct the culture of Swanscombe man is particularly interesting because Swanscombe man dates from the Second Interglacial phase of the Pleistocene (Ice Age) and thus existed at least 100,000 years ago.

[5] K. P. Oakley, "Swanscombe Man," *Proceedings of the Geologists' Association* 1952, vol. 63, pt. 4, pp. 283–290. By permission of the Geologists' Association.

Until recently most students of the Lower Palaeolithic were inclined to equate tool-type with culture and to say that, in gravels where certain forms of bifacial hand-axe represented the culture of Acheulian man, flakes of Clactonian or Levalloisian types from the same deposit were necessarily made by men of different cultures, or even of different species. Careful excavation of actual ateliers or workshop sites of Lower Palaeolithic age has shown, however, that simple rule-of-thumb correlation of this sort is not justified. Of course it cannot be denied that some assemblages of artifacts, such as those in the Swanscombe Lower Gravel and in the Clacton Elephant Bed, represent a culture (the true Clactonian) entirely distinct from the Acheulian *biface* or hand-axe culture which locally succeeded it. But there is also no doubt that Acheulian hand-axe industries include a number of primary waste-flakes of Clactonian form, and also a variable percentage of retouched flake-tools which, isolated from their context, would be regarded as "advanced Clactonian." At some sites industries occur which suggest a blending of the two traditions (e.g. the Acheulo-Clactonian industry at High Lodge in Suffolk).

Some groups of Acheulian hand-axe makers adopted the so-called Levalloisian technique of striking flakes from prepared cores. At one time this was regarded as a practice confined to the "Mousterian" group of cultures. But flake-blades and cores of Levalloisian type have recently been found on a Middle Acheulian workshop site in the 30-m. Terrace of the Somme at Cagny. Similarly, flakes, flake-blades and cores of Levalloisian type occur in small numbers in the Middle Gravels at Swanscombe, and they may well have been part of the repertoire of Swanscombe Man.

On the evidence obtained at Lehringen, and at a later mammoth-butchering site at Tomsk in Siberia, we may conclude that many untrimmed flakes were used as tools by Palaeolithic hunters. Stopes claimed that he could recognise signs of use on some of the untrimmed flakes found in the Swanscombe gravels. This is usually very difficult when the flakes are in river gravel. The commonest uses of flakes would have been as knives and scrapers, but Stopes found one flake-blade in the Barnfield gravels which appeared to have been deliberately serrated for use as a saw.

The division of the earlier Palaeolithic industries into those of core-tool tradition and those of flake-tool tradition is becoming blurred through the progress of our knowledge; but there remains, nevertheless, an element of truth in this distinction. Bifacial hand-axes are essentially core-tools. A number of those found in the Barnfield Middle Gravels have been fashioned from flakes instead of from nodules, but in this case the traditional idea has still been preserved, for a flake which is trimmed bifacially into the form of a hand-axe is being treated as a core.

The hand-axes associated with the Swanscombe skull can be closely matched in the Somme valley assemblages classed by the Abbé Breuil as Acheul III. However, it is doubtful if the seven stages of Acheulian recognised in the Somme are precisely applicable to the sequences found in other parts of north-west Europe, so for the present it is perhaps wiser to describe the industry of Swanscombe Man as Middle Acheulian.

Our knowledge of the culture of Swanscombe Man may be supplemented by considering evidence from other sites of comparable age within the Thames valley. The gravels of Furze Platt, near Maidenhead, forming the Lower Boyn Hill Terrace, appear to be precisely equivalent to the Swanscombe Middle Gravels. Thanks to Mr. Llewellyn Treacher and Mr. A. D. Lacaille, we have an extensive knowledge of the artifacts of the gravels of the Lower Boyn Hill Terrace, which include the great hand-axe that is one of the treasures of our British Museum (Natural History) collections. After examining this specimen, one finds it difficult to regard Acheulian Man as merely an animal getting a living. Surely we see him here as an artist enjoying the exercise of his skill as a worker in flint. Many of the Swanscombe hand-axes of normal size are superbly flaked and finished with a perfection which appears to exceed the requirements of bare necessity.

In regard to the general aspects of the culture of Swanscombe Man, one has no reason to doubt that he was typical of the period to which he belonged. In Lower Palaeolithic times all men lived by hunting animals and gathering wild foods, worms, grubs, roots and berries—just as men beyond the margins of civilisation do today in Australia and South Africa. It has been suggested that hand-axes were used for digging up roots and grubs. Some of the plano-convex pick-like forms may have been so used, but Henry Stopes, who examined thousands of hand-axes from the Swanscombe gravels, noticed how many of them had fine undamaged points, and concluded that these were certainly never used for, or intended for, digging.

The term hand-axe is unfortunate because, with the possible exception of the straight-topped variety known as the cleaver, they were probably not used as axes in the usual sense. The typical hand-axe (the term is the English equivalent of the more expressive French name, *coup-de-poing*) was evidently a general purpose tool, used mainly for cutting and scraping. Mr. A. J. Arkell has shown by practical demonstration that some types of hand-axe serve excellently for skinning game, and that, no doubt, together with dismembering the animal, was one of their chief uses.

Dr. L. S. B. Leakey found that, at certain levels in the lake beds exposed in the Olduvai Gorge, Tanganyika, there were concentrations of hand-axes very suggestive of butchering-sites at the fluctuating lake-margins. In the midst of one of these concentrations, which included a fair quantity of waste flakes and lumps of raw material, excavation revealed the dismembered skeleton of a hippopotamus. It is perhaps, not too far

fetched to see in these remains the relics of a communal feast such as occurs from time to time in Africa today. If a hippopotamus is killed and
brought to shore, scores of natives collect in the course of a few hours
and spend the next day or two cutting up and consuming the carcase. Each
man brings his own iron knife and, owing to the toughness of the animal's
skin, these are constantly re-sharpened. Instead of re-sharpening their
hand-axes, Acheulian hunters may frequently have discarded them, as
they became blunted, and made new ones.

It may well be that the majority of the flint implements in the Swanscombe gravels were chipped in similar circumstances. Anyone who has
seen M. Leon Coutier fashioning a flint hand-axe will realise that a skilled
worker requires less than five minutes to complete one. With ample supplies of flint nodules close at hand in the river-cliffs, there would have
been no need for the early natives to take great care of their implements;
new hand-axes were probably made whenever there was an important
kill. Thus, in spite of the profusion of hand-axes in the gravels here and
at other localities in this valley, we need not suppose that the Acheulian
people were ever very numerous. At certain points by the river, where
animals came to water, or at boggy places into which they could be driven,
kills would have been more frequent than elsewhere. We have only to suppose that, on an average, ten tool-making individuals frequented the river-
banks at Swanscombe during a week and that each made and discarded
there two or three hand-axes, and we would have accounted for more than
one million of these tools being possibly incorporated in the river-bed at
that locality within thirty generations.

Judging by the habits of primitive peoples living today on a comparable level of subsistence (such as the Australian aborigines and the African
Bushmen), we may presume that among the Acheulians the *family-
group* would have been the foraging unit, but that a number of these,
forming a *band,* would have co-operated in some activities, as in the hunting of large game. In Australia a band varies in size from 30 to 100 individuals, but, according to Professor Julian Steward the average number is
35. A single band usually operates within a fairly well-defined territory to
the exclusion of others. The size of this territory varies from about 150 to
500 sq. mi. or more, depending on the mobility and hunting skill of the
band, and on the abundance of game and other foods. In the case of a
riverine band the length of the territory considerably exceeds its breadth.
In 1833, Charles Sturt encountered only about fifty aborigines (probably
a single band) along the whole of the Upper Murrumbidgee River, which
is nearly as long as the Thames and situated in an area of dependable
rainfall. Within the territory of a band, one might expect to find a marked
uniformity of tool-types, and it is possible that, by plotting the areal distribution of hand-axes with local or idiosyncratic traits at a particular
horizon in the 100-ft. Terrace of the Thames, we may eventually be able

to form a rough estimate of the number of territories into which the valley was divided during, say, Middle Acheulian times.

A provisional distribution map of Acheulian hand-axes in Britain and north-east France suggests that their makers lived mainly in open country, and that their movement was largely confined to shore-lines and river-valleys. At that time, of course, Britain was joined to the Continent, forming a large peninsula.

The population of the British peninsula during Pleistocene times no doubt fluctuated widely with climatic changes and with the consequent variation in the abundance of game and in the character of the available wild foods. On the basis of the range of population-density in Arctic America, Professor Grahame Clark has estimated that the population of Britain in Upper Palaeolithic times (under a sub-glacial climate) would have been between 250 and 2000, probably nearer 250 in winter months. During interglacial times the situation was different, but it is unlikely that the Lower Palaeolithic population of Britain ever comprised more than about a dozen bands. So long as there was the possibility of free movement between France and Britain, this population would probably not have been genetically isolated.

The hand-axe people were evidently skilled hunters of large and fast-moving game, to judge by the quantities and character of the meat-bones found, for example on the Acheulian camping-sites at Olorgesailie in Kenya and at Torralba in Spain. We can only guess at some of the methods they employed; but fall-traps, snares and slings are probable. The flint artifacts in the Acheulian gravels at Swanscombe include polygonal lumps which were considered by Stopes to be possibly missiles. The finding at Olorgesailie of deliberately-shaped stone balls, sometimes in groups of three, was regarded by Dr. Leakey as evidence that the African Acheulian hunters used the bolas, but this is still regarded as questionable.

All-wood spears were probably the principal weapons of Lower Palaeolithic hunters in Europe. The point of one made in yew-wood was found by Mr. Hazzledine Warren in the water-logged peaty deposit with type Clactonian industry at Clacton-on-Sea. At Lehringen, near Bremen in Germany, a complete yew-wood spear nearly 8 ft. long and with fire-hardened tip was recently found within a skeleton of *Elephas antiquus* in a lake-bed of Third Interglacial age [Movius, 1950]. Scattered among the elephant bones were about two dozen untrimmed flint flakes which had evidently been used by the hunters in skinning the animal. The Lehringen culture is regarded as probably a Levalloisian facies of Late Acheulian. . . .

Henry Stopes made one observation in regard to the culture of Swanscombe Man which as far as I know has not been contradicted by later workers. He said that he had never seen any evidence in the Swanscombe gravels that the hand-axe people used fire. In his Stopes Memorial Lecture, published in the last volume of our *Proceedings,* Mr. Hazzledine Warren made the same observation in regard to the culture of Clactonian man at Clacton. Dr. Leakey found no evidence that fire had been used by the Acheulian people at Olorgesailie. Thus it seems probable that some Lower Palaeolithic groups ate their meat raw, or perhaps dried like *biltong.* On the other hand, evidence of the use of fire has been found at the Early Acheulian camping site in Torralba in Spain (over 3600 ft. above sea-level), and at numerous Late Acheulian, Late Clactonian and Mousterian sites in Europe and Asia [Oakley, *1956*].

As regards the perishable aspects of Acheulian culture, it is worth while recalling that, in his description of the Acheulo-Clactonian floor in the Middle Terrace sands at Stoke Newington, Worthington Smith recorded the discovery of two artificially-pointed birch stakes, 4 ft. long, associated with charred wood, branches of *Clematis* and matted fronds of *Osmunda regalis.* He believed that these remains, which were mingled with the flint flakings, represented a Palaeolithic dwelling: a wind-break such as the Tasmanians used.

It was fortunate that the Swanscombe skull was found in deposits which yielded abundant faunal remains, because these enable us to determine its relative age with fair precision, and, at the same time, to deduce the character of the biotope.

The larger Mammalia in the Middle Gravels at Swanscombe have been studied by Mr. M. A. C. Hinton and the late Miss D. M. A. Bate. They include (according to the latest revision): *Elephas antiquus, Elephas* cf. *primigenius, Rhinoceros mercki* (*megarhinus*), *Cervus elephus* (large), *Dama clactoniana, Megaceros, Bison* and *Equus,* which indicate that the Thames was bordered by woodlands interspersed by grassland. This fauna is very similar to that of the preceding Lower Gravel Stage, although horse and bison appear to have become commoner, suggesting an increase in the proportion of grassland. . . .

Thus, although the fallow deer (*Dama*) and most of the other large mammals in the Swanscombe Middle Gravels indicate beyond doubt that interglacial conditions prevailed in the Thames Valley during their deposition, it must be admitted as a possibility that in highlands, particularly in higher latitudes, glaciers were already beginning to re-advance. This may well have caused a shift in the distribution of cold-tolerant forms such as the lemmings, with the result that they spread into regions where, hitherto, they had been unknown under fully interglacial conditions. . . .

When one considers the distribution of Acheulian industries in Africa and recalls the fact that they occur not only in interglacial river-gravels, but also in the Older Loess of France, it begins to appear very probable that the hand-axe people, like the Australian aborigines, were mainly adapted to life in open grassland, rather than to wooded country. Perhaps the Clactonian industry represents the facies of Lower Palaeolithic culture which was more related to forest life.

4

RECONSTRUCTION OF HOUSES

¶ The purpose of archaeology is, in its broadest sense, to achieve an understanding of the life and culture of peoples long vanished from the earth. Such understanding must, of course, be based primarily on the material remnants, often very scanty, of the activities of the former inhabitants of the archaeological site. Since man has lived in artificial structures for a considerable time and in many parts of the globe, the remains of buildings which formed the center of his activities are crucial to reconstruction of past cultures. Houses, however, are often built of the most perishable materials: wood, grass, straw, and so on. Only rarely is the archaeologist fortunate enough to find ancient structures of stone, brick, or earth, and even then the details of framing or of roof construction may be lost through decay. The most painstaking technique and cautious inference are necessary to recover an accurate picture of ancient buildings. A summary of Paleolithic house remains in Russia, published by Boriskovski (1956), is a good example of such technique.

¶ Usually, only the barest traces of former construction remain in a site. Most frequent are postholes, which may be distinguished often only by faint differences in the soil and in floor surfaces packed by the feet of the inhabitants, and by hearths. All of these are features easily lost in hasty or careless excavation and, once gone, can never be recovered. On the basis of these slight variations in the very matrix of the site, the archaeologist must reconstruct the possibilities of original building construction, attempting to fulfill all the conditions given in the excavation data, but remaining within the limits of allowable inference. The following extracts from several reports have been selected to show not only the care required in excavation, but also the ingenuity necessary to reconstruct the form of the original buildings.

Reconstruction of an Arizona Pithouse

McGregor's article on Winona Village in Arizona[1] is an account of actual excavation and is valuable for its detailed consideration of technique and of the type of information on which reconstruction was based. One will note that the author's remarks concern themselves at first only with the details of excavation and material reconstruction, where possible; only subsequently does McGregor turn to the question of the use of the building, drawing on information from the reconstruction and from material objects found, finally concluding that the structure might have been a ceremonial one. In this connection, a discussion by Watson Smith on the problem of identifying a kiva is well worth reading (Smith, 1952:154–165).

The deep pit structure, N. A. 2134A, was the second object of interest investigated at Winona Village. Originally it consisted of a large circular depression of extraordinary depth, which was filled with quantities of red cinders, irregular volcanic bombs, and other pyroclastic material. Some question was felt at first as to whether it might not be a fumarole instead of a structure, but the original pit, sunk in the center of the depression, quickly settled this, by bringing to light quantities of sherds, and small amounts of charcoal.

The method of opening this site was similar to that employed in digging other pit sites in this area. A test was first sunk in the center of the depression, and at a depth of slightly over a meter burned roof material was found. When this was reached the test in the form of a trench, was extended east and west until the side walls were encountered. These were followed, and the overlying material cleared to expose the fallen roof. The walls were found to be a rough masonry of basalt boulders, held together by clay, and near their bases sufficiently well preserved to make tracing them easy.

The fill of this site consisted of an astonishing number of rocks, mostly large volcanic fragments, thus making work very difficult. Clay, sherds, and charcoal were solidly massed between the rocks, thus suggesting the site had been deliberately filled with rocks and clay after it burned.

After the removal of the overlying material the floor was cleared progressively north from the south wall. This work was of course all accomplished by hand, each beam and artifact being located accurately on a plan as it was uncovered, and before it was removed. The clay floor was found to be well preserved along the east and north walls, the rest being most easily traced by the presence of a layer of charcoal and ashes. Only one floor was found, and tests below it failed to show any indication of disturbance of the coarse red cinders into which it had been dug. Where

[1] J. C. McGregor, *Winona Village: A XIIth Century Settlement with a Ball Court near Flagstaff, Arizona,* Museum of Northern Arizona, Flagstaff, 1937, Bulletin 12, pp. 19–23. By permission of the Museum of Northern Arizona.

the floor reached the sides it curved gently to the plaster on the walls, which was rather well preserved, particularly on the north wall.

Two main postholes were found on the center line of the structure (see

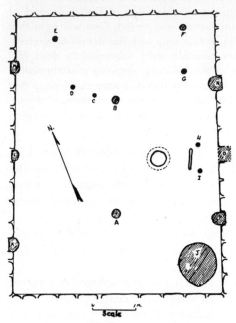

Fig. 4.1. Floor plan of pithouse. A, B, main post supports; C-G, additional postholes; H, I, ladder posts; J, cache; K-M, P, breaks in wall and floor; O, ventilator.

Fig. 4.1). Posthole A contained a somewhat rotted juniper post which was over a meter long and still in place, but burned to the floor level at the top. Post B was also of juniper, but slightly smaller in diameter. It is of interest that the two main supporting posts, which were set into the ground, were of juniper, while almost all of the rest of the supporting poles, and posts, were of pine. This might possibly indicate a knowledge that juniper would be more resistant to rot than pine when partially buried.

The other smaller postholes, C, D, E, F, and G, all contained fragments of rotted posts, none of which were useable in dating. Their odd arrangement does not give any clue as to their possible purpose, but the finding of what appears to be a fragment of a "batten" stick, near E, suggests that they might have somehow served as supports for looms. Shallow postholes F and I almost certainly represent the bases of a double pole and rung ladder, which protruded through the smokehole above the firepit.

The firepit was definitely formed of baked clay, with a low (about 2 cm.) raised rim, and contained some ashes. Between the firepit and the ventilator opening, O, was a flat sandstone slab, set on edge, which served as a deflector. This was badly broken by heat during the fire, and could only partly be reconstructed. The ventilator opening was originally capped by a flat rock lintel, also broken by the heat of the fire. This ventilator was not traced out completely to the surface, to determine, if possible, the method of roofing, and other construction features.

In the southeast corner a large pit, J, evidently a cache, was found. Although the rim was poorly preserved the shape had apparently originally not been truly circular. It was only a ragged hole through the floor, and into the cinders below, and was not clay lined. At the time of the fire, this pit was undoubtedly not covered, for it contained several sherds, some burned roof material, and quantities of small charcoal fragments, suggesting that other materials, possibly pots, were removed from it by the inhabitants after the fire.

One of the most interesting features of the entire site was the presence of five ragged holes through the floor at K, L, M, N, and P. These extended slightly back into the wall, and in every case contained charcoal fragments of relatively small poles. Above these holes faint traces of grooves were found in the walls, as though poles had been incorporated in the walls and plastered over at these points. The only explanation thus far suggested is that they served as a form of roof support.

The walls proper were only interesting in that they were constructed of a very crude masonry, and that large blocks of rock had been set in to form the first course. This is a characteristic feature of pithouse masonry in this area. Plaster was preserved at the base of the north wall, and in spots on the south wall. It had been applied in a thick coat, and then lightened in color by the additional application of a whitewash. When in use the room must have been very well finished.

Some idea of the roofing system may be had from the position of the two main support posts. This would suggest that a main beam, or gable, had been laid across them, lengthwise of the site. However, no remains of this beam were found preserved as charcoal. Smaller posts, about two and a half, or three inches, in diameter then crossed this beam from east to west. Apparently there were four such poles in each end of the site. Across these, again at right angles, were placed thin splints, or "shakes," which were split, and averaged only a quarter inch thick, and two inches wide. This was covered in turn by a layer of cedar bark, and finally above this was a relatively thin layer of roofing clay, apparently only about two inches thick. The upper surface of the clay was carefully smoothed and finished, the under surface showing the impression of bark, splints and occasionally poles. The maximum height of the walls in the corners was two and a quarter meters, or about seven feet. Judging from the general level about the original depression it must have had walls at least a foot higher than the present height, thus making the site at least eight feet deep, an extraordinary depth for any structure found in this area. The size of the site, other than depth, is extraordinary as well, for it is almost fifteen by twenty feet, approximately twice as large as the average pithouse found in this vicinity.

Twenty-five separate specimens of charcoal beams were found resting on the floor of the room, although these probably represented only about eight individuals. As has been stated before, these unfortunately proved to be of such short sequences, or so complacent, that only four of them could be successfully dated [by dendrochronology].

The question is of course almost immediately raised as to whether this structure represents a pithouse, or a kiva [underground ceremonial chamber]. Considering first the possibility of its having been used as a dwelling the following factors are in its favor. 1. It is a rectangular pit structure, in general not greatly different from other masonry lined pithouses found in this area, particularly from slightly earlier periods. 2. It contains the characteristic ventilator, firepit arrangement, of such houses, and 3. was entered through a hole in the roof above the firepit. Here however, the similarities end.

The following features would favor its designation as a kiva. 1. The unusually large size, and depth, is probably the most outstanding feature. A rectangular pit structure, slightly smaller, but almost as deep, and masonry lined, was found by Dr. Cummings at Turkey Hill Pueblo, which because of its nature, and location, must certainly have been a kiva. It also contained a firepit and ventilator arrangement, but did not show a deflector, at least at the time the writer visited the site. 2. The firepit, slab deflector and ventilator arrangement is definitely reminiscent of kiva construction, although it has occasionally been found in pithouses in this area. 3. The presence of what appears to have been a charred weaving stick, lying on the floor, near the north end of the room, indicates that weaving was practiced here, but weaving, at least as practiced by the Hopis today, may be found either in kivas, or dwellings. 4. Probably one of the most striking evidences for a kiva is the fact that no complete vessels of decorated pottery came from this site, although several large undecorated jars were found here. 5. Also many fragments of red, pink, and yellow pigments, and stones for grinding them, were found in this room, thus indicating an unusual use of paints. 6. What appears to have been a stone bird was found on the floor, the only present explanation of its presence being that it was used ceremonially. 7. Last, the gabled roof support is so unusual for this area that it may be considered at least different from that of the common house type, which is characteristically quadrilateral.

It is of course not possible to definitely determine to what use this one structure was put until several more have been excavated in this immediate area. If all of the other pithouses are found to be smaller, and to conform to the usual pattern for houses of this general region, then only may it definitely be termed ceremonial and a kiva, otherwise it must be considered a house.

House at the Snaketown Site

The section following is an extract from E. B. Sayles' discussion of Snaketown houses.[2] With the generally good conditions of preservation in the American

[2] E. B. Sayles, "Houses," in H. S. Gladwin, E. W. Haury, E. B. Sayles, and N. Gladwin, *Excavations at Snaketown: Material Culture*, Medallion Papers, Gila Pueblo, Arizona, 1937, no. 25, pp. 79–84. By permission of H. S. Gladwin and E. W. Haury.

Southwest and the possibility of dating individual features by pottery types so that the house remains could be chronologically arranged in terms of another dating system, it was possible here to trace the development of the general house type as well as the evolution of the several components of the dwellings. While the section is not a point-by-point account of excavation technique, Sayles' description gives many clues to the techniques involved and the inferences on which the conclusions were based. In this respect, note his comments on post holes dug into rubbish, the use of plaster for floors, and the like.

Beginning with the earliest houses of the Vahki Phase an evolution of house types through the various periods can be readily traced. No modifications have been recognized which point to outside influences. Only in the Sacaton Phase, as represented by a single instance of a square pithouse, is there found a variation which might be considered as intrusive. Otherwise every house uncovered conformed to a generalized plan which may be summed up as:

Single unit house built in a shallow excavation;

Covered entrance passage, near the middle of one side;

Basin-shaped firepit near the entrance;

Walls and roof supported and framed with timber; covered with smaller timbers and earth.

Variations within this plan distinguish the types in the different periods. The development from early to late is clearly seen, the trend being from the large square houses of the Vahki Phase, becoming progressively smaller, but still square, or rectangular, in the Estrella, Sweetwater and Snaketown Phases: changing to rounded corners or ends in the Santa Cruz Phase: and elliptical in the Sacaton Phase; an evolution which leads up to the prototype of the Pima round house.

The details in many of the houses were found to be similar in different phases. For the sake of brevity, a description of these has not been included with each phase, and is now included in this discussion.

WALL TIMBERS

With the change in the floor plan, the position of the roof supports was changed so as best to serve their purpose. No fixed plan was followed other than that, in oblong houses, the major roof supports were along the main axes and toward the ends. When the shape later became equalized in width and depth, as in the Pima round house, the supports were placed toward the center, as in the early square types.

Like the major roof supports, the position of the secondary roof supports was not fixed but certain trends in their use can be followed. In the earlier houses, post holes in which the secondary supports may have rested were not as close together nor as large, as a rule, as those in later houses. It may be that as houses decreased in size it was found that some of the weight of the roof could be carried by the wall supports. This would also relieve the interior space of the heavy posts which were used to support the roof in early houses, making it possible to use smaller major roof supports in the later houses.

ROOF CONSTRUCTION

As far as we can determine, the roof was built in the same general fashion throughout the series, as indicated in Fig. 4.2. The positions of the major roof supports were shown by the larger post holes within the floor space and at each side of the entrance-way. Secondary supports were also used around the periphery of the floor. Rafters rested on these upright posts and across these were smaller timbers supporting a matting of

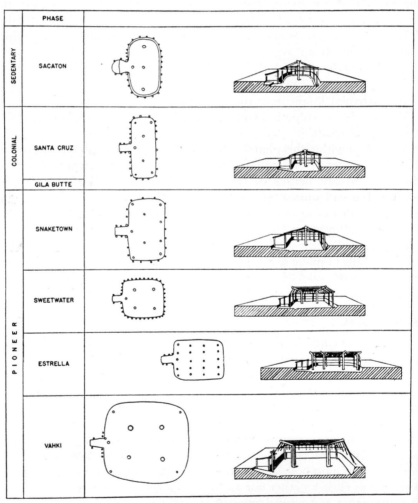

Fig. 4.2. Floor plans and postulated reconstruction of house types found at the Snaketown site, Arizona.

twigs, reeds, and grass, which was covered with earth. In many of the houses, it appears that the builders may have had trouble with sagging roofs. This was remedied by putting in additional supports as occasion arose as is indicated by the large number of post holes found in those floors built over trash.

The timbers supporting the roof and composing the main wall material were usually cottonwood or mesquite, rarely juniper; cottonwood and mesquite were also used for the rafters and lighter covering of the roof. This was thatched with arrow-weed, grass, and similar materials, the heavier kinds also serving to fill in the spaces between the wall posts.

There is nothing to indicate the height of the walls or whether there were smoke holes in the roof.

FLOORS

The character of the floor material was the same in all houses. Some of the earlier houses were built directly on hardpan, and this seemed to be the kind of footing which was preferred. Toward the end of the occupation, when much rubbish had accumulated, the Hohokam were evidently satisfied if only a part of the floor had a firm base. When the floor rested on rubbish or soft fill, caliche was brought in and plastered over the soft area. Since many of the houses, even in the Pioneer Period, rested partly on soft material, the floors were easily defined by the coating of plaster. As a rule, in all burned houses, the floor was well defined whether it was covered with plaster or not. In houses not burned, the floor sometimes appeared as a packed surface and was difficult to distinguish from the original hardpan.

A packed surface was evidently the sort of floor used by the Pima in their round houses. They did not, however, make any excavation for their dwellings.

POST HOLES

It was possible to determine the original size of post holes only when these had been dug into firm soil or imbedded in floors which were well preserved. From a large number of charred stubs found in place it was learned that the major roof supports ranged in size from 15 cm. to 30 cm., and the secondary posts from 5 cm. to 15 cm.

FIREPITS

The trend in the development of firepits was from a flattened basin with steep sides to a hemispherical one, the later type being smaller than the earlier.

BURNED HOUSES

Many of the floors uncovered showed that the houses had been burned. There was nothing to indicate whether they had been burned intentionally, as was the practice of the Pima when the occupant of a house died, or whether the burning was accidental. So seldom was any paraphernalia found on the floor of a house, suggestive of accidental burning while the house was occupied, that it is inferred that many of them were burned intentionally after personal property had been removed. This burning may have been a part of the funeral rites.

OUTSIDE AREAS

It may be that the failure to find household property on the floors of burned houses was largely due to the fact that household duties were carried on outside of the houses. This is suggested particularly in early times by the finding of outside pits and ovens identified with the Pioneer Period.

DWELLINGS

No shelter or structure was identified other than the type that served as a dwelling. However, houses may have been used at times for other purposes as is suggested by the square pit-house. This is more definitely established in House 8:6G, in which the firepit had been covered with earth. Since this house was filled with vessels, which had evidently been placed on the floor or on shelving of some sort, it was obviously in use as a storage house. It may be that the larger houses identified with the earlier phases were community houses although they possessed only a single firepit. The smaller houses, too, may have sheltered more than a single family.

There was nothing in any of the houses that was suggestive of ceremonial use.

ORIENTATION AND DEFENSE

None of the houses was oriented as if to conform to a plan such as the Pima round houses which Russell (1908) reported as facing to the east. There was nothing in the arrangement of the houses or the choice of location which would indicate any provision for defense.

CONTINUOUS OCCUPATION

The line of development of house types as defined at Snaketown suggests continuous occupation through all phases from early to late. This is further implied by the accumulation of rubbish which, without exception, showed no sterile deposits which might indicate an abandonment of the site at any time after it was first occupied.

From time to time shifts are obvious in the density of house clusters belonging to different phases, a trend also indicated by the position of the trash mounds. It would appear that, as these shifts were made and new houses built, many of the floors belonging to the older houses already in ruins were destroyed. Since the Sacaton Phase represents the last of the prehistoric occupation of the site, more floors belonging to this phase were found than in any earlier phase.

Not only was the Sacaton Phase the last of the prehistoric occupation at Snaketown but, from the evidence presented by the house remains, it would appear that it represented the densest occupation of the site during its entire history.

No evidence of occupation during the Classic Period was found within the boundary of the Snaketown site. There were, however, two other sites nearby which have been identified by their cremations and pottery as belonging to the Soho Phase of the Classic Period. None of the dwellings at either of these sites were uncovered, but the arrangement of walls at one of them suggested that there may have been a building composed of one-story adjoining rooms.

As noted previously, the last of the continuous prehistoric occupation at Snaketown is represented by the Sacaton Phase of the Sedentary Period. No evidence of the following Santan Phase, of this period, as represented at Casa Grande to the east of Snaketown, was found at the site.

No data are available at present to account for the time which elapsed between the Classic Period and the time when the Pima occupied the area formerly held by the Hohokam. Indications point strongly to the Pima as being the cultural descendants of the Hohokam. The analogy between the Pima type of single unit dwelling and that of the Hohokam is close. It is outstanding when compared with the intrusive pueblo type of dwelling found in the Civano Phase. As shown by Gladwin, Haury, and others, the community dwelling or pueblo which has been identified with the Salado Branch, and the single unit house of the Hohokam, existed side by side.

The use of an earth pit in house building is widely distributed, being common both to the Old and New Worlds. Certain features in construction, such as the support of a flat roof on centralized posts, walls and roof of timbers covered with earth, a side entrance, and a simple firepit in the floor, are found in northeastern Asia, across the Bering Strait, throughout many parts of North America west of the Mississippi River, and into South America.

Houses can be said to constitute a type when they consistently show a combination of specialized features such as those which are to be found among the Hohokam. Analogies between house types in contiguous areas, known to be contemporaneous, point either to actual contacts, or to common derivation from a well established ancestral form.

Since dwellings are the least mobile of all traits, a wide distribution of common features of construction probably indicates a considerable age for their origin. To what extent the Hohokam culture affected, and was affected by, contemporaneous cultures, what may have been its origin and its influence upon later developments, can only be determined after considering all available data.

Reconstruction of a Southeastern House

This short selection from a paper by Webb and DeJarnette[3] deals with a restricted though crucial problem of house reconstruction. Postholes are almost always the primary data of building reconstruction except in structures where stone, brick, or rammed earth was used. Here the authors attempt a reconstruction based almost entirely on the pattern of the postholes and the location of a firepit, fulfilling all the necessary conditions dictated by the material remains while admitting the possibility of other reconstructions which might also take into account these conditions. The work is admittedly a *tour de force*, but one designed to show what can be done.

The site described by Webb and DeJarnette, Seven Mile Island, dug in the course of a three-years excavation under the Tennessee Valley Authority, contributes much to our understanding of Southeastern prehistory.

Feature No. 2 is a post-mold pattern of a very interesting structure on "floor B." In the construction of this building, the small posts of the wall were not set in trenches, as was often done, but they appear to have been driven in from above. This, and their possible settling, due to the weight of the structure, compressed the earth layers under them, as may be observed in Fig. 4.3, which shows a close-up of a longitudinal section of several individual molds. In the floor plan of the post-mold pattern, it will be observed that in each corner of the structure, inside of the line of small post molds, is a large pit. This pit is elliptical in form at the floor surface; the major axis of the ellipse, 3 feet long, lies along the diagonal of the structure. The pit tapers toward the bottom, nonsymmetrically, to terminate in a circular post mold of 1-foot diameter at a depth of 3 feet. Fig. 4.4 shows a vertical section of such a corner post mold. Fig. 4.5 shows a view from above of one of these molds, carefully excavated. All four molds were very similar in size and form. The figure shows how a post 1 foot in diameter could have been inserted in this pit and made to stand erect against a solid vertical wall by having the pit filled on the inside only, and the clay well tamped in position. From the position of these four large post molds it seems certain that these four corner posts, braced from the inside, carried much, if not all, of the weight of the superstructure. It is believed that the smaller vertical posts, which evidently leaned inward toward the structure, were attached to horizontal logs overhead, supported by the four corner posts. This structure pattern, approximately 20 by 23 feet, presents very definite evidence of the manner of its construction. Fig. 4.6 shows how the larger corner posts were set inside the line of small posts. On the floor, just inside the line of small

[3] W. S. Webb and D. L. DeJarnette, *An Archaeological Survey of Pickwick Basin in the Adjacent Portions of the States of Alabama, Mississippi, and Tennessee,* Smithsonian Institution, Bureau of American Ethnology, Washington, D.C., 1942, Bulletin 129, pp. 46–48. By permission of the Smithsonian Institution.

posts, there was a small banquette of puddled clay. This banquette, before it was cut away by excavation, extended entirely around the structure wall, except at the doorway on the north side. On the outside of the line of small posts, there was a channel pressed into the sloping clay floor, which extended beyond the walls of the structure. This channel seemed to form a gutter and probably assisted in the drainage. This gutter also extended on all sides of the building, except at the doorway. The doorway is in the eastern end of the north wall and faces the river. This doorway was marked by two posts about 4 inches in diameter, set nearly in the gutter, with an elevated section of clay between them. The manner of setting these smaller posts was the same as that used for the corner posts. Holes were dug—large at top, small at bottom—one wall of the hole being kept vertical. The post was thus set vertically, but nonsymmetrically, and held in place by earth tamped behind it.

Fig. 4.3 (Top). Longitudinal section of post molds, Feature No. 2, Seven-Mile Island site. Note deformation of loading layers under posts. Fig. 4.4. Longitudinal section of post mold, Seven-Mile Island site. Fig. 4.5. Vertical view of corner post mold, Seven-Mile Island site. Fig. 4.6. Feature No. 2, showing vertical section of west and south walls and central fire basin.

Slightly to the east of the center of this floor, a fire basin had been constructed by digging a cylindrical hole somewhat larger than 1.8 feet in diameter and 1 foot deep. This hole was carefully plastered with puddled clay which was worked into a smooth rim to unite with the clay floor about its edge. When burned, this clay-lined fire pit was brick hard.

When uncovered, it was found filled with ashes containing much burned bone.

Based on the facts which are presented by this floor and post-mold pattern, the artist has prepared a drawing reconstruction of this building. Fig. 4.7A shows the building from the outside and Fig. 4.7B shows the inside construction. This reconstruction is an attempt to show how a building might have been built using the following observed specification:

Fig. 4.7A (Above). Exterior view of reconstruction of house, Feature No. 2, Seven-Mile Island site. Fig. 4.7B (Below). Reconstruction of same structure, interior view.

1. Four large corner post molds.
2. Outside lines of small post molds.
3. Outside clay gutter.
4. Inside banquette of clay.
5. Door in east end of north side.
6. Nonsymmetrically placed fire basin.

The fire basin may have been off center because of the diagonal logs overhead. This type of bracing would have been very effective engineering for posts set in holes dug nonsymmetrically as was the case here. The artist in this restoration used cane thatching, since there was no evidence of earth covering and no evidence of wattle walls at this floor level.

While in all such reconstruction it must be admitted that there must be of necessity a high degree of uncertainty as to some details, yet it is believed that it is worthwhile to attempt to demonstrate how a structure could have been erected at this site to meet all conditions known to exist. The artist seems to have accomplished this objective.

Reconstructing a Plains Indian Earth Lodge

Before the Great Plains were invaded by buffalo-hunting horse-riding peoples in the historic period (after 1700 A.D.), the fertile bottomlands of the major streams such as the Missouri River were occupied by sedentary corn-growing tribes who lived in earth-lodge villages. Many of these village sites have been excavated, among them the Talking Crow site in South Dakota which was investigated by Carlyle Smith of the University of Kansas. A burned earth lodge assignable to occupation of the site by the Arikara tribe in the period 1700–1725 was reconstructed on a small scale and then burned in order to gain some idea of features encountered in the remains of the original structure. The following account[4] gives the details of this interesting and successful experiment.

In addition to the several excerpts offered in this chapter, the reader may wish to consult the account of a full-scale reconstruction of a prehistoric Japanese pit-dwelling (Fujishima, 1957) and the proposed reconstructions of the Neolithic structures in the Köln-Lindenthal site in the Rhineland by Buttler and Haberey (1936).

Most of the earth lodges excavated at the Talking Crow site had burned to the ground. In all probability this occurred after the abandonment of the site and was caused by prairie fires sweeping unchecked through the area. In 1950 the log cabin of a Sioux Indian, not more than 200 yards from the old village site, met a similar fate. Had the houses burned while the village was occupied we would have found evidence in the form of pottery vessels still in place by the fire and collections of other artifacts stored in various places for ready use. Actually the houses contained only fragments of incomplete pots, large broken tools and small tools which had been lost or mislaid by the occupants.

The fact that the houses had burned helps us in working out the details of construction because many of the beams were preserved in the form of charcoal. We have accounts of early explorers and descriptions by ethnologists of the earth lodges that were in use during the period of recorded history. However, the houses at the Talking Crow site differ in a few details from those previously described and we had to supplement our observations by experimentation.

A copy of one of the houses found at the site was constructed on a scale of one-twelfth natural size (see Fig. 4.8B). This resulted in a structure measuring 35 inches in diameter instead of 35 feet. The model was based on the excavation of House 8, a round earth lodge with four center posts and a covered entrance passage oriented to the southwest. Opposite the

---

[4] Carlyle S. Smith, "Digging Up the Plains Indian's Past," *University of Kansas Alumni Magazine*, vol. 52, no. 4 (December, 1953), pp. 4–5. By permission of the author.

doorway was a bison skull such as those frequently associated with religious shrines among the Arikara and Pawnee. A basin shaped fireplace
marked the center of the house.

To build the model, a circle 35 inches in diameter was drawn on the
ground and the area was then excavated to a depth of one inch to represent the full scale excavation of one foot in depth. In the house we were copying it was found that posts at irregular intervals in the outer wall were larger and penetrated deeper into the soil. It was assumed that these represented the main outer wall posts. Similar holes were dug around the edge in the model. The holes for the four center posts then were dug. Wood cut to the proper lengths for the upright posts was inserted in the holes. Cross pieces were placed across the four center posts to form a square. Similarly pieces of wood were placed from one outer post to the next as shown in the photograph (see Fig. 4.8A).

Fig. 4.8A. First step in reconstructing an earth lodge in small scale.

Fig. 4.8B. Dirt is heaped over the framework to form walls and roof.

Fig. 4.8C. Completed model burned and studied to determine if charred remains approximate the original excavated earth lodge.

The burned remains of the excavated house indicated the former presence of beams radiating out from the fire place. Similar pieces were placed on the model leaving an opening at the center for a smokehole over the fire place. Short posts were set around the outer edge of the house leaning against the encircling lintels. The entrance passage was enclosed in a similar manner.

In the excavated house the charred remains of willow

rods and bundles of grass were found on the floor. From historical sources we know that a layer of willow boughs was placed at right angles across the rafters. Then the willows were covered with bundles of grass oriented with the rafters. Over these two layers was spread about six inches of earth. In the model we could not reproduce the willows to scale so they were omitted and grass alone was used. Damp earth was spread over the grass and compacted by patting with the hand. Earth was banked against the outer walls. Fine dry dust was sprinkled over the completed house and as a final touch the entire surface was soaked with water from a pressure sprayer to simulate the effects of rain. Pieces of wood were leaned against the outside and connected at the tops with horizontal pieces to simulate the method used historically to help retain the earth on the roof. To provide a scale in the photograph a clay model of an Indian about five inches tall was placed in the doorway.

Later we burned the model house in order to determine whether or not the charred remains would approximate the appearance of the excavated house (see Fig. 4.8C). Because of the limited air space in the model it was necessary to place dry grass soaked in gasoline on the floor. In less than an hour the roof collapsed. Combustion continued around the edge of the house for some time. The smothering effect of the mantle of earth caused most of the wood to turn into charcoal rather than ashes. When the burning had ceased the collapsed house was sprayed with water to simulate the effect of weathering.

The ruin was in the form of a raised ring of earth with a depression at the center, closely resembling the remains of old earth lodges to be seen on archaeological sites. The earth was removed from the model and the floor swept clean. The roof timbers were found to radiate out from the center exactly as in the full size house. The pattern left by the burned-off posts duplicated that found in the large house.

5

PREHISTORIC ECOLOGY

The study of prehistoric ecology has progressed with remarkable speed in the past few years. This study, essentially the human geography of prehistoric times, derives its data from a variety of sources, chiefly from the floral and faunal remains found in archaeological sites. These data are often analyzed and interpreted by specialists outside the field of anthropology, and for this reason the prosecution of such studies is frequently expensive both in time and money. The returns, however, are potentially great enough to place it among the most productive of archaeological endeavors.

W. W. Taylor in his comprehensive criticism of archaeology characterized that discipline as one which operates on four separate levels or steps: "*first*, the definition of problem in terms of a conceptual scheme; *second*, a gathering, analysis, and criticism of empirical data; *third*, the ordering of these data in chronological sequence; and *fourth*, the search for and, to the extent that it is possible, the establishment of reciprocal relationships within this series" (Taylor, *1948:32;* see also Kluckhohn, *1940*).

The data of prehistoric ecology fit into this framework at all levels. In the first and second stages they are scarcely to be distinguished from any other kind of archaeological information; they should be considered and gathered the same as any other evidence of man's past activity. On the third level these data are significant in the same way as geochronological data, since they are based on considerations external to archaeology proper and are therefore not subject to the same error. If a site is given a certain date because its faunal remains are thought to belong to a certain period, this dating may be either right or wrong. But it will not be wrong because of errors or inconsistencies in archaeological theory and will therefore not compound such errors. In other words, successions of biota can provide tests of cultural chronologies.

Finally, the data of prehistoric ecology provide important information concerning the evolution of culture. The Iversen article which follows i perhaps the most striking example of this, giving, as it does, a remarkably precise picture of the relationship between the natural environment and agriculture. The most extensive work on this aspect of prehistoric ecology has been done in Europe. A brilliant summary of that work is provided by Clark's *Prehistoric Europe (1952:* chaps. I–VI).

Man's Influence on Vegetation in Denmark's Stone Age

Iversen's paper,[1] quoted below, is an outstanding example of the use of ecological data. In it pollen profiles from various parts of Denmark are examined and inferences are drawn from them that have proved to be of great importance to both local and general archaeology.

Pollen analysis is potentially one of the most important tools in the investigation of prehistoric ecology. Plants are the primary indicators of ecological change and these same plants produce large quantities of pollen which, under favorable humid circumstances, are preserved. The amount of surviving pollen is so great that sampling problems are obviated and the results of analysis are therefore relatively conclusive. The difficulty presented by pollen analysis is that its prosecution requires specialized knowledge. Besides being a valuable aid in cultural reconstruction pollen analysis has also been used successfully for chronological purposes, especially in Europe (Zeuner, 1952).

In the present selection Iversen does not discuss in detail the process of forest clearance and the techniques of cultivation. He has published an article on these subjects which gives a most interesting account of modern experiments in the use of Neolithic stone axes for tree-falling (Iversen, 1956). Other experiments to test the efficiency of stone axes are described by Clark (1952:94), Leechman (1950), Woodbury (1954:40–42), Nietsch (1939:70), and Morris (1939:137).

For general summaries of the influence of man on the earth's surface, see Thomas (1956) and Heizer (1955).

Following upon the final glacial period the vegetation in Denmark at first developed according to the same laws as those governing events in the inter-glacial periods; all changes were merely an expression of alterations in climate and other natural factors. The primitive cultures of the Early Stone Age could have but little effect on the forest growth. The hunters had their paths as the animals their tracks; and just as the vegetation around bird colonies receives its character from the manure supplied to it, that in the immediate vicinity of Mesolithic settlements was characterized by midden plants. Man's influence on the vegetation did not extend far; the virgin forest closed in a few paces outside the settlement, and there nature alone determined what was to grow.

All this went through a radical change with the introduction of farmer

---

[1] Johannes Iversen, *Land Occupation in Denmark's Stone Age,* Danmarks Geologiske Undersøgelse, Copenhagen, 1941, II Raekke, no. 66, pp. 20–26. By permission of the author.

culture to the country. Then, and not before, the forest picture began to be altered by man, and there can be no doubt that the changes thus brought about were just as profound and just as interesting as those which earlier were associated with climatic and other purely natural causes. It would therefore be anticipated a priori that they would be clearly identi-fiable in the pollen diagrams.

In pollen diagrams the Danish Late Stone Age begins at a place close to zone border VII–VIII, after Jessen's zonal divisions of the diagrams. This must mean that farmer culture started at about this time and it would be a very attractive task to find its traces in the pollen-floristic development of these strata. With this in view I have made a careful analysis of material from particularly suitable localities in various parts of the country. In order to bring new elements to light I have also made systematic counts of less common types of pollen (pollen of cereals, weeds, *Hedera, Viscum*, etc.), which provide information just as valua-ble as the pollen of the trees. This has entailed the counting of much greater quantities of pollen than otherwise, a time-consuming labour but one that has also been to the benefit of the other pollen curves, the statistical uncertainty having thus been reduced to a minimum.

On the basis of some selected pollen diagrams from Zealand, Funen, East and Middle Jutland I shall now examine one by one the various phases in the aforesaid critical stage of the vegetation development round about zone border VII–VIII and at the same time endeavour to grasp their nature. . . .

It is in the middle of the Oak Period. For about two thousand years *Quercus, Ulmus* and *Tilia* together have formed the high forest; there was a little *Pinus* in poor soil; *Alnus* grew especially in wet places with a little *Betula. Viscum album* was a common parasite on those trees that make suitable hosts, and flowering *Hedera helix* climbed wherever it could obtain a hold and was of a luxuriance seen nowadays only in south-ern and western Europe.

Then occurred some rather inconspicuous but important changes in the forest picture. *Fraxinus excelsior,* which formerly had played only an un-important role, increased in frequency at the expense of *Ulmus,* whose curve fell rapidly. The curve for *Hedera* describes exactly the same course as the *Ulmus* curve; it falls abruptly, and above this level *Hedera* even in *per mille* diagrams, no longer forms a continuous curve. In most cases the *Quercus* curve displays a slight rise. These small pollen-floristic changes can scarcely be connected with human interference; for even if one might at a pinch explain the decline of *Ulmus* as the result of the at tentions of domestic animals, the simultaneous decline of *Hedera* can no more be explained in this fashion that the increase of *Fraxinus.* As the same course of development can be shown to have taken place all ove the country, in parts both fertile and unfertile, it is reasonable to assum a climatic cause. One factor alone, the marked decline of flowering *Hedera*, gives an indication as to the direction in which the climate must have changed. *Hedera* is distinctly an Atlantic plant, partial to warm summers and mild winters, that is to say a climate which from early times has been connected with the "Atlantic Period" of the post-glacial age. As that very period must, according to the theory, have extended over the time during which *Hedera* was so common in Denmark, followed by the more continental "sub-Boreal Period," whose cold winters must have been inimical to *Hedera's* growth, it seems the obvious thing to do to connect the fall in the *Hedera* curve with the change from "Atlantic" to "sub-Boreal" climate. Consequently, in our pollen diagrams I have laid the border between these two climatic periods where the *Ulmus* curve falls, this being simultaneous with the decline of *Hedera*. If then we place the zone border VII–VIII at this point, we find that Zone VII corresponds to the Atlantic period and Zone VIII to the sub-Boreal, thus obtaining perfect concordance between the classical scheme of climatic periods after the Ice Age (Blytt, Sernander, Hartz) and the pollen-floristic division according to Jessen. In Norwegian diagrams (from Jaeren) the border between the Atlantic and sub-Boreal climatic periods was similarly drawn recently by Faegri (*1940*); and although a comparison between Norwegian and Danish diagrams is rendered difficult by the natural differences between these two regions, Faegri's border seems to be in full conformity with the one described above. . . .

Just above the zone border VII–VIII as plotted here, i.e. in the beginning of the sub-Boreal Period, the curves in most Danish pollen diagrams describe a very peculiar course which bears witness of a remarkably sudden change in the composition and state of the forests. The elements of the high forest, *Quercus, Tilia, Fraxinus* and *Ulmus* undergo a distinct but contemporary decline, while *Betula* reveals a transitory, *Alnus* a more lasting increase in pollen frequency, and at the same time the *Corylus* curve reaches a very pronounced maximum. What is the significance of this conspicuous minimum in the curve for the "Oak Mixed Forest" (*Quercus + Tilia + Fraxinus*)? Can it be the expression of a temporary lowering of the temperature?

There are various arguments against that interpretation. It must be realized that this climatic decline must have been of a sudden and actually a catastrophic character to depress the curves of the Oak Forest so abruptly and violently, and this would be incompatible with the rapid advance of the hazel. Nor is there any apparent decline in *Viscum*, though its thermal requirements are greater than those of *Quercus* and *Tilia*. It would also need some explaining why it was *Betula* and *Alnus*, but not the *Pinus*, that profited from the altered conditions. On the contrary, the pollen of *Pinus* as a whole declines in frequency in this zone. The hypothesis fails entirely when we have to explain the important fact that the phase is initiated with a sudden increase in the pollen of herbaceous plants.

In order to circumvent these difficulties, one might postulate a climatic change of another character than a general decline. A lowering of the ground-water level as a consequence of a very dry period would cause birch and alder to move out over marshy areas previously occupied solely by fern plants. This would explain the increase of *Betula* and *Alnus* pollen and the relative decrease in that of the other trees. Here again, however, the increase in the pollen frequency of the herbs forms an obstacle, and the explanation must be dropped.

There remains the influence of man. It seems reasonable to place the minimum in the curve of the Oak Mixed Forest in connection with forest clearance. Originally my idea was this: the clearance chiefly affected the Oak Forest of the high ground, whereas the marsh forests with their alder and birch escaped. Accordingly, the latter trees must display a relative increase in the diagrams. Doubtless this phenomenon did assert itself, but it cannot be the whole explanation. In the diagrams from salty fjord deposits this form of curve is handsomely developed, though there are no marsh forests at the borders of salt fjords.

On the other hand, we arrive at a natural and satisfactory explanation of the courses of the various pollen curves if we assume that the pollen-floristic changes express the vegetation developments in a region where land-tilling people have occupied the land and cleared this dense primeval forest with axe and fire. Now as this explanation requires that fire was largely made use of, it would be natural to expect that traces of it could be found. I recollected a suspicious, sharply delimited stratum of charcoal in Ordrup Mose just under the problematic zone, and subsequently embarked upon a precise and complete analysis of the sample series that had been collected. The result seemed to affirm my supposition that there was some connection between this charred layer and the minimum in the curve of the Oak Mixed Forest, and I shall now go through the diagram from that aspect.

During the Litorina transgression Ordrup Mose was a fjord in the Øresund; the charred layer was near the upper edge of a thick deposit of saltwater gyttja (gyttja = organic mud). On the extreme left of Fig. 5. is a silhouette representing the frequency of charcoal fragments in slides from the deposit just under the charcoal layer, from that layer itself and from the deposits overlying it. It will be seen that the substratum to the fire-deposit also contains some charcoal; this is only natural, as the section lies in the immediate vicinity of the well-known large Mesolithic Bloksbjerg Settlement, whose primitive inhabitants still seem to have been in occupation when the new farming people took the area into possession and forced them out. On the left of the pollen diagram there are also silhouettes to indicate the changes in the pollen numbers of various tree

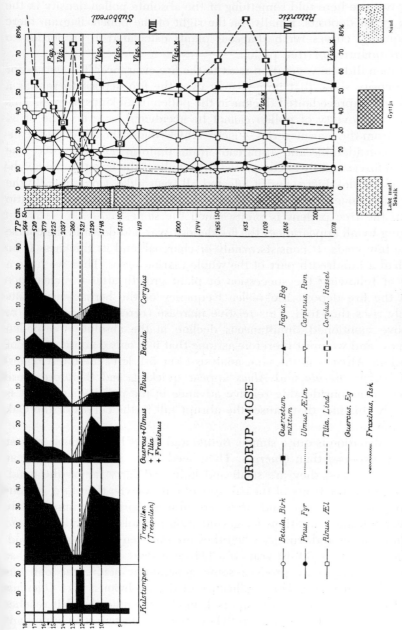

Fig. 5.1. Pollen diagrams at Ordrup Mose, Denmark. *Left:* proportion of pollen per square centimeter of preparation. *Right:* relative percentage of pollens in stratigraphic order (TP, tree pollen; depths in centimeters).

per square centimetre of slide; in contrast to what is the case with the pollen diagram, which exhibits only the relative changes in pollen frequency, we are here told something of the absolute pollen density in the various gyttja deposits. Finally, on the right of the pollen diagram there are frequency curves for herbaceous plants calculated in proportion to the total quantity of tree pollen.

How then did the vegetation react to the fire clearance? The curves for pollen density show that immediately over the fire deposit there was a sudden and unprecedented decline in the pollen of all kinds of trees. This conspicuous poverty of pollen cannot be accidental, as every one of 34 samples from the marine series, 4 metres thick, under the fire deposit contained a considerable and apparently quite uniform pollen density. The clearance fire evidently encompassed the whole of the forest in the neighbourhood of Bloksbjerg, and it affected all trees alike. Consequently the pollen diagram exhibits no great change: the relative frequency ratio between the tree pollens is pretty much the same.

Judging by all appearances the fire deposit was laid down in the course of some few years. It consists mainly of charcoal, and its thickness is no more than a hundredth part of the whole marine series. Thus we have a chance of following the succession of plant growth after the clearance fire. In the fire deposit the pollen frequency of the herbaceous plants suddenly rises threefold. This relative increase corresponds very well to the above mentioned simultaneous decline in the absolute tree-pollen frequency, and we must therefore assume that it is only a consequence of this decline. Already in the same analysis (Fig. 5.1, left) the forest regeneration begins. *Betula* and *Alnus* appear quickest, and therefore these trees record a considerable relative advance in the pollen diagram; it is principally this fact that causes the abrupt fall in the curves of the Oak Mixed Forest.

The explanation is quite simple. *Betula* and *Alnus* have a much greater power of dispersal than *Quercus*. Their seeds form regularly every year in large quantities, they are small and light and carry far on the wind, whereas the heavy fruits of the oak spread only slowly; therefore, in contrast to *Quercus*, *Betula* and *Alnus* are able to spring up immediately wherever suitable conditions for germination prevail. In addition, *Betula* and *Alnus* flower and fructify when they are only ten or twelve years old whereas *Quercus* is 30–40 years old before it does so. This means that *Betula* and *Alnus* may produce some generations before the oak has even reached maturity. The significance of this is obvious. Like *Quercus Corylus* has a poor power of dispersal, but on the other hand it reaches maturity before *Betula* and *Alnus*. These two circumstances may perhaps explain the curious features of its curve.

The tree that profited most from the clearance fire was *Betula;* shortly after the land occupation it reached a higher frequency than ever since the Birch-Fir Period. This is very interesting, for nowadays too it is mainly *Betula* that makes its appearance after a forest fire. The great dispersal and early maturity of this tree is not the sole explanation, however; after ordinary forest clearances in fertile regions *Betula* does not usually appear. The fact is that its seed germinates only when the soil conditions are favourable. On ashy soil, however, these conditions are exceptionally favourable.

The uppermost analysis in the diagram reveals a decline in the *Betula* curve. This is not accidental; all diagrams with a marked minimum on the curve of the Oak Mixed Forest show that *Betula* flourishes only for a short time. The birch is the tree requiring most light, it cannot tolerate shade, and it only gets a chance when the forest is cleared of other trees. The birch is the pioneer among our trees, and the brief *Betula* maximum above the charcoal deposit is therefore very significant.

Throughout the foregoing the expression "clearance fire" has been employed. But the question arises of whether the vegetal development evidenced by the pollen flora might not just as well have occurred as the result of a natural forest conflagration.

In the first place one might answer that natural forest fires occur almost exclusively in conifer forests; indeed, it requires a good deal of effort to make a foliferous forest burn. This is a negative argument only, but fortunately we have much positive evidence to show that agriculture was brought to the region just at the time when the fire occurred.

As we have seen, the pollen frequency of herbaceous plants rises immediately after the fire. A "non-tree pollen diagram" plotted on the pollen of herbaceous plants and heather, shows that in the main it is chiefly the same plants as those that were growing there earlier, first and foremost *Chenopodiaceae* and *Gramineae*. But next we find for the first time some pollen of plantain (*Plantago*), not, be it noted, of the salt-marsh plant *Plantago maritima*, but of the weeds *Pl. major* and *Pl. lanceolata*. The pollen of these two plants is to be found in all our diagrams as soon as we come to the "land occupation phase"; this is its first appearance, but thereafter it has a continuous curve up to the present day. Apparently *Plantago* came to Denmark together with the first farmers in the same manner as it has since followed the European all over the world, wherever he has settled. *Plantago* has been called "the white man's trail" by the American Indians; the trail of the Neolithic conquerors is the *Plantago* pollen in our diagrams. In Ordrup Mose the course of the *Plantago* curve is typical; it starts where the Oak Mixed Forest begins to fall, and reaches its maximum where the other is at the minimum. Side by side with *Plantago* a common weed was *Artemisia cf. vulgaris;* its pollen was found in large quantities, and in historic times too it was a greatly detested field weed, one that became of minor importance only with the era of modern deep ploughing.

It is a familiar fact that in the Late Stone Age a good deal of cereal cultivation took place, and therefore it was to be expected that cereal pollen would also be demonstrable in the fire deposit. Firbas showed that the pollen of cultivated cereals is larger than that of "the wild grasses," *Elymus arenarius* alone having pollen as large. If nevertheless one finds hardly any cereal pollen in Stone and Bronze Age deposits, where *Plantago* pollen often occurs in large quantities, the reason must in part be that barley and wheat, the cereals that were cultivated in those ages, are self-fertilizing and give off scarcely any pollen. Notwithstanding this unfavourable circumstance there was some cereal pollen in the strata directly overlying the fire horizon—not much, it is true, but sufficient to prove that cereals were cultivated.

Further evidence of the arrival of farmer people is provided by the finding of a bone which Dr. M. Degerbøl identified as the tibia of a domestic cow. With the aid of a little gyttja picked out of the hollows in the bone it was possible to date it with fair accuracy. It belongs to the lower part of the lake marl, i.e. just in the Oak Mixed Forest minimum. This closes the chain of evidence.

Avifauna of a California Shellmound

The discussion below[2] is an example of the kind of inferences regarding cultural behavior that can be drawn from biological data. The site from which the bird bones were collected was a large prehistoric shellmound on the eastern shore of San Francisco Bay, California, a site first excavated in 1902 by Dr. Max Uhle, the famous Peruvianist (Uhle, 1907). In 1924, salvage excavations were performed by Schenck (1926) and the bone material from these excavations was analyzed by Dr. Howard.

The important question of how the archaeologist can determine whether a site was occupied only seasonally or the year round has received too little attention. Clark (1952:25–28) summarizes a body of European data which bear on this problem, and Thomson (1939) has written a useful casehistory of an Australian group, the Wik Monkan, in which the nature of evidence of seasonal activities is examined.

A study of the materials used by a people is often the chief means of obtaining knowledge regarding the habits of that people. Anthropologists have investigated to the utmost every source of information regarding the Emeryville shellmound, with the exception of the skeletal remains of vertebrate animals found therein. Until now these remains have been studied only as they have been worked by the Indians as artifacts, or have been hastily identified as a means of obtaining an idea of the animal

[2] Hildegarde Howard, *The Avifauna of Emeryville Shellmound*, University California Publications in Zoology, Berkeley, 1929, vol. 32, pp. 378–383. By permission of University of California Press.

eaten by the Indians. Several other aspects regarding the habits of the "Emeryville Indians" have been revealed in the present study of bird remains.

Earlier in this paper we noted the fact that the long bones of the larger birds are broken, most of them transversely through the middle, others with the shaft intact, but the ends missing. In examining the artifacts made from bird bones, we find a great number of whistles. These are made of long bones which are broken, or cut off at each end, and a hole cut in the middle of one side. Schenck (1926:222–223) remarks upon the presence of tubes which he considers to be artifacts in the process of manufacture. Many of the broken bones in the collection here studied may come under the heading of tubes. The whistles of bird bone, examined by the writer, are broken in two in much the same manner as observed in all of the larger long bones of the collection. Schenck (op. cit.: 224, 276) speaks of the "killing" of artifacts—the breaking of the artifact before placing it with the dead. These broken whistles may, then, have been "killed." Considering the fragility of bird bone, however, may they not have been weakened or fractured in the process of cutting the hole in the shaft? Similarly, may not some of the other bones, not classified as artifacts, have been broken at the first application of the knife? This idea is, of course, merely a suggestion, and could hardly be applied to all of the broken bones. There is still another aspect to be considered. Some of the pieces of bone are charred at the broken end. This may indicate that in some cases the breaking was a part of the preparation of the bird for eating. Mr. Gifford has suggested to the writer that since netting and snaring were apparently the chief means of capturing birds, the wing bones might have been broken at the time of capture, to prevent the escape of the bird before it could be killed.

The avifauna of the Emeryville mound is such as to indicate a hunting range restricted to the vicinity of the Bay shore. The predominating species are water birds; and the land birds which are present could all have been found close to the Bay. Birds that are distinctive of hill-country, such as the Golden Eagle and the California Road-runner, are absent. The Valley Quail is the only chaparral species represented and it undoubtedly would have been found near the Bay in the brush bordering Temescal Creek.

A particularly notable feature of the shellmound avian collection is the presence of over two hundred specimens of nestling cormorants. These specimens were taken from various depths and localities in the mound. Both Farallon and Brandt cormorants appear to be represented, though in the immature state the distinguishing characters of the bones of these two species are weakly marked. That these birds had not left the breeding grounds is attested by the fact that practically all the main skeletal elements are present in an immature state; these include pelvis, shoulder girdle, and wing bones, as well as the leg bones, which latter being composed of more than one ossification center, would be expected to lag behind the rest of the skeleton in reaching maturity.

Evidently, then, the "Emeryville Indians," over a long period, were in the habit of robbing cormorant rookeries. In view of the fact that the raft-like tule balsa is the only type of craft known to have been used by the Indians of this part of the state, it is highly improbable that this rookery was outside the Bay. Within the Bay, Alcatraz, Angel, and Goat Islands would all have been possible nesting sites, Angel and Goat islands being, perhaps, most accessible. Though the proximity of these latter islands to the mainland and its predatory animals might have proved a deterring factor in the establishment of a rookery, we cannot say that such was the case, since today cormorants are known to nest even on the mainland. Dr. Loye Miller reports the presence of a Brandt Cormorant colony near Scripps Institution, La Jolla, and Willett reports a Baird Cormorant colony on cliffs along the shore near San Luis Obispo. Willett also reports Brandts nesting on rocky islands such as are accessible from the mainland at low tide.

It has been suggested that there may have been a colony of tree-nesting cormorants in this region. Such a colony would have been possible for the Farallon Cormorant, but the Brandt is known to nest only on rock surfaces. However, wherever tree rookeries of Farallon have been reported, they have been situated inland. Certainly, trees suitable for nesting were present on the Bay shore; but would the birds have chosen such a site with the islands so near at hand? Considering the improbability of this choice, as well as of the fact that a tree-nesting colony would not explain the presence of Brandt young, it seems more logical to believe that the rookery visited by the Indians was located on one of the islands in the Bay, possibly Alcatraz Island, upon which, according to travelers' accounts written before 1850, a colony of sea-birds was nesting.

Since the San Francisco Bay shellmounds first became known to anthropologists, the question of duration of residence on a particular site has been raised. In calculating the ages of mounds upon the basis of rate of accumulation of material, the results have often been influenced by the possibility of a non-continuous residence of the Indians on the site.

A study of the bird bones included in the Emeryville mound has thrown some light on this question. We have seen that the preponderance of species in the mound is of ducks and geese; these are represented by adult bones only. With but four exceptions, all the ducks to be expected around the Bay are primarily winter visitants, though a few of them have been known to hold over in small numbers through the summer. The genus *Mergus*, of whose presence in the mound the writer is assured, since its skeletal characters are sufficiently characteristic to permit of identification, has been recorded by present-day observers only from

January 1 to April 11. All the geese are strictly winter visitants, the extreme recorded dates of inhabitance running from October 1 (Common White-fronted Goose) to the last week in April (Black Sea Brandt). On this evidence, then, we can say with certainty that the shellmound was occupied during the winter months.

Next in abundance to the Anatidae are the Phalacrocoracidae—the cormorants. The cormorants are resident species, but we find that nearly one-half of the 525 specimens of cormorant are of young, nestling birds, probably of Farallon and Brandt.

If we may judge the rate of growth of Farallon and Brandt cormorants by their near relative, the Double-crested, we will expect eight weeks to elapse after hatching before the young are able to fly, though they are able to swim as soon as the body is fully feathered, or about six weeks after hatching. The young are naked when hatched but down begins to grow in about ten days, and within three weeks the bodies are covered with thick, short black down; the wings and tail then begin to grow, before the body plumage is fairly started. As soon as the wings and tail are developed the chicks begin wandering away from the nest, though not attempting to swim. At this time they are of almost adult bulk. From the condition of the immature bones of the Emeryville collection, it appears that it was at this stage in development that the Indians made their raids on the cormorant rookeries. The bones are practically as large as those of the adult bird, but they are in an early stage of ossification, when undoubtedly the birds were unable to do more than unsteadily wobble about on land.

The following accounts are cited as indicative of the time of year when the rookeries were probably visited by the Indians. The egg-laying season extends from the middle of May to the last of July, with that of the Farallon slightly in advance of that of the Brandt.

Ray reports visiting a Farallon cormorant rookery on the Farallon Islands on May 29, 1904, at which time he found nests containing well incubated eggs, and others with naked young. Within a week he revisited the rookery and found the babies with the black down coming in. On May 30 and June 3, Ray visited a Brandt colony where he found the birds still building nests, or beginning to lay their eggs.

Bent quotes from Loomis' account of visiting Brandt Cormorant rookeries at Seal Rocks and Point Carmel, Monterey County, in 1895. On June 25 he visited Point Carmel and found all but eleven nests with eggs apparently well incubated. Ten of the eleven nests contained young which had just hatched; in the other the young were larger. On July 2, on Seal Rocks, he found nearly all the nests with young, varying in size from newly hatched chicks to those large enough to leave the nests when approached.

Other records, from regions farther removed from San Francisco Bay, will not be quoted, though they are in general agreement with the dates given for the coast of central California.

To summarize the above evidence: May 29 marks the approximate time of hatching of Farallon Cormorants on the Farallon Islands. Three weeks from that time the young would be covered with down, and within a week or two more they would reach the stage of development shown by the bones in the mound. The date of such development, then, would be around the twenty-eighth of June. The Brandts on the Farallons were found to begin laying about the first of June. This date is in agreement with the record for Point Carmel of June 25, when incubation was approaching completion or the eggs had just hatched. About four weeks from this time, or about July 23, the young would reach the stage when they could leave the nest. The record of July 2 for Seal Rocks is somewhat earlier than this, but the period is, of course, influenced by individual nesting dates. The optimum time of obtaining young of Farallon and Brandt cormorants of the size found in the mound, is therefore from the middle of June to the last of July. The Emeryville shellmound must, then, have been occupied by the Indians during the summer.

The presence of a tarsometatarsus of a young Great Blue Heron pushes the summer occupancy of the mound back into May. Early in May the young herons are able to move about in the nests, though as yet unable to fly. At this time there is much squabbling as the young endeavor to push one another from the nest. The bone here referred to is possibly that of a young one which was pushed out, and failing to catch himself upon a lower limb of the tree, fell to the ground.

Undoubtedly the Emeryville site was occupied both winter and summer. Since there are no species of birds whose inhabitance of the Bay region is restricted to the intervening spring and fall months, we cannot prove from this line of evidence that the residence of the Indians was altogether continuous. Certainly, however, food was plentiful during those months and there is no reason to suppose that they should have gone elsewhere.

Paleolithic Housing

The paper by Hrdlička,[3] quoted below, is concerned with the relationship between occupation sites and the then contemporary climate. Containing no original data, it is simply an astute observation drawn from previously collected material. It may be that the conclusions would not hold up too well under the later refinements of the European Paleolithic sequence but this does not detract from the originality of the idea or the imaginative use of the data.

[3] A. Hrdlička, *The Skeletal Remains of Early Man*, Smithsonian Miscellaneous Collections, Washington, D.C., 1930, vol. 83, pp. 331–333. By permission of the Smithsonian Institution.

Later analysis of the utilization of caves for occupation in Upper Paleolithic times has shown that these sites were used chiefly in winter (Clark, 1947:160). K. P. Oakley (1956:104) has treated the problem of the period when Paleolithic man began to live in caves and has concluded that "the most likely explanation is that few, if any, of the earlier hand-axe people were equipped with fire and that until men had fire at their disposal regular occupation of caves and deep rock-shelters was too hazardous. In such situations small groups of human beings would have been extremely vulnerable to attack by predatory beasts unless they had fire as a protection."

There is a prevalent idea that Neanderthal man was essentially a cave-dweller, and this idea seems generally to carry with it a sense of inferiority. The records now available throw a different light on this matter. Analysis of 360 better-known paleolithic sites in Europe and the neighboring regions (from records compiled principally by MacCurdy, [1924]) gives the following interesting information:

TABLE 1. Dwellings in the Open and in Caves During Paleolithic Times

Period	Sites in the Open		Rock-Shelter or Cave	
	Number Recorded	Percent	Number Recorded	Percent
Pre-Chellean	11	100	—	—
Chellean	32	94	2	6
Acheulean	36	78	10	22
Mousterian	45	34	88	66
Aurignacian	24	18	112	82
Solutrean	10	14	62	86
Magdalenian	17	10	148	90
Azilian and Tardenoisian	4	9.5	38	90.5
Accompanying Neolithic	22	22.5	76	77.5

The figures (see Table 1) and chart (see Fig. 5.2) show some curious and important facts. Man begins as a dweller in the open, but already since the warm Chellean period he commences also to utilize rock-shelters and caverns, and then, as the climate cools, he gradually takes more and more to the caves. In these phenomena the Mousterian period shows nothing striking, nothing individual. It falls harmoniously into the curve of the progress of cave-dwelling, to be followed equally harmoniously by the Aurignacian and the succeeding periods. Mousterian man occasions no perceptible disturbance in the human housing conditions of the time, and what is even more remarkable, no disturbance or change whatsoever is found to be occasioned by the advent of the Aurignacian. Aurignacian man follows in the footsteps of his predecessor without a marked interruption. Like the Neanderthaler, he builds, in the open, huts of perishable materials that leave no trace, and he utilizes the caves exactly as much as, and eventually even more than, the Neanderthal man. He continues, in fact, on many of the same sites and in most of the same caves that the latter has used, without introducing any detectable innovation. He, also, like the Neanderthal man, leaves here and there a whole series of occupational strata which testify to much the same habits of life. Yet Aurignacian man is often represented as a new-comer,

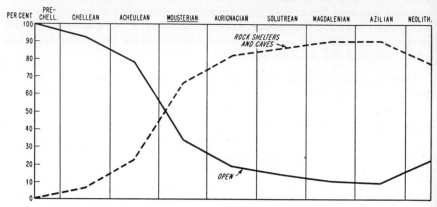

Fig. 5.2.   Frequency of open and rock-shelter or cave sites used during the Paleolithic Period.

of a different species from that of the Neanderthaler, and mentally vastly superior.

The Fauna of Belt Cave, Iran

This report[4] deals with material excavated by Carleton Coon under the auspices of the University of Pennsylvania at Belt Cave in Iran. The site is important since it covers parts of both the Mesolithic and Neolithic of that region, radiocarbon dates ranging from 10,560 ± 1200 to 8004 ± 900 years old. Coon's reconstruction of the habitation of the site is based on the analysis of the faunal remains. His results demonstrate the great utility of paleofaunal information. Belt Cave is near the southeastern shore of the Caspian Sea. Tamtama and Bisitun caves lie to the west and were excavated during the 1949 season.

I have broken up the material from Belt Cave into two sections (see tables, pages 149, 151). With 1170 identified specimens, this gives us much more to work with than did the other caves. Here we can expect a different picture. The cave is situated between forest and grassland, and fronted by swamps leading to the sea. The altitude is at about sea level, the winters mild, thus eliminating the need of seasonal shifts, the summers damp and warm. How this climate varied during the period represented by the occupation of the cave remains to be seen.

[4] Carleton S. Coon, *Cave Explorations in Iran, 1949*, Museum Monographs, University Museum, University of Pennsylvania, Philadelphia, 1951, pp. 42–52. By permission of F. G. Rainey, Director, University Museum, University of Pennsylvania

Belt Cave, Mammalian Fauna, Raw Data

	Ga.	Cp.	Ov.	Bo.	Ce.	Cd.	E.A.	S.	Cn.	Fl.	Vl.	Ph.	Vv.	R.	Total
B		3	2					1							6
1		3	1	1				2		1					8
2	2		5	2	4			1	9		1				24
3			2	1	6			1							10
4		4	1	1				2	1						9
5		5	3	1				1	1		2				13
6	1		10	2											13
7	1		7	3											11
8			4	1											5
9	1		5	1		1						1		1	10
10		5	10	6									1	2	24
11	67	4	4	20	1							1			97
12	106	3	8	37	4	1					1				160
13	236	1	5	22	1	1				1	1				268
14	123	1	3	31					3		2	3			166
15	169	3	4	5	1						1	2			185
16	28		1	18											47
17	16	1		1	1							1			20
18	14			2	1			1	1			5			24
19	9			1								1			11
20	3													1	4
21	6			1							1	2			10
22	2			2								2			6
23	1			1											2
24	3			1		1			6			11			22
25												7			7
26				1								1			2
27	2			1	1		2								6
Total	790	66	52	162	10	5	2	9	21	2	7	37	3	4	1170

Ga. — Gazella
Cp. — Capra
Ov. — Ovis
Bo. — Bos
Ce. — Cervus
Cd. — Cervid
E.A. — Equus Asinus
S. — Sus
Cn. — Canis
Fl. — Felis
Vl. — Vulpes
Ph. — Phoca
Vv. — Viverridae
R. — Rodentia

In contrast to what we have seen before, this is a bovid cave. The bovids are by far the most numerous among the ungulates, which are by far the most numerous of all classes. Ninety-four per cent of identified bones are ungulate, and of these, ninety-eight per cent are bovid. In a sense, these percentages resemble the very beginning and the post-

Pleistocene in Bisitun. The cervids appear in two loci: the very bottom, the earliest occupation; and the Upper Mesolithic occupation from [levels] 18 to 11. There are none in the Neolithic although deer must have existed in the Elburz forests, then as now.

The Upper Mesolithic is the period of the gazelle (*gazella subgutturosa Güldenstädt*) par excellence, and secondarily of the ox (*Bos primigenius*). Sheep and goats both begin at this time, far inferior in numbers to the gazelle. During the early Neolithic the ox is absent (except for its occurrence in Level 10) until Level 5, when it was probably domestic. The pig comes in similarly in Level 5. Not included in this table are some additional bones of the pig, which were identified by Dr. Frazer from some previously unidentifiable scrap. They are: an ulna from Level 13, and three astraguli, from Levels 2, 12, and 15. They are all mature. This brings the total for *sus* to thirteen. Horse is notable for its absence.

Twenty-one specimens of canids were identified. In Level 24 the specimens are two mandibles and three large teeth. These are undoubtedly *canis familiaris*, the domestic dog, and not wolf. The breed was very large and heavy-boned. Levels 4 and 2 also yield unquestionable dog. Other canids, possibly jackal, come from 24, 18, and 14. Level 15 yielded a left maxilla of *canis familiaris* with its three incisor teeth *in situ*.

As for felis, there are actually three specimens, one each in Levels 12 and 13, and a third which cannot be counted since its number came off and its layer is hence unknown. I am certain by the condition of the bone that it belongs near or with the other two. This is a small feline the size of a large housecat, from which it cannot otherwise be distinguished.

The seals, although found throughout, are most typical of the earliest levels, in which they actually constitute 20 out of 27, or 74 per cent, of identifiable specimens. These were very small animals, fully adult in most instances. They may turn out to form a new species. The two specimens from Level 5, Neolithic, were teeth used as jewelry. The viverridae are: Level 10, one of the *mustelidae;* Levels 11 and 17, *putorius* (pole-cat). The rodents: Level 1, *castor fiber* (beaver); Level 10, one each of *hystrix* (porcupine) and *muridae* (mouse); Level 20, *citellus* (spermophile).

So abundant are the specimens from Belt Cave that we can do more than merely identify them, and tell what parts of the animal the hunters brought home. All sorts of other problems can be investigated, among which is that of domestication. With this in mind, we may divide the collection on several axes: mature and immature animals; those used for meat and skins alone, as contrasted to those providing other products and services; and those which have at some time and place been domesticated, as contrasted to those which have always been wild everywhere. Of these three, the key distinction is that based on degree of maturity. To it the other two lend added controls.

The table on page 152 gives the raw data for maturity and immaturity

Belt Cave, Mammalian Fauna, Refined

	UNGULATA Bovidae								Total Bovidae	Ungulata %	Others			Total Ungulata	Ungulata %	OTHERS				
	Gazella	%	Capra	%	Ovis	%	Bos	%	Total Bovidae	Ungulata %	Cervid	Equid	Suid	Total Ungulata	Ungulata %	Phocidae	%	Others	%	Totals
Ceramic Neolithic B, 1–7	4	5.6	39	54.9	15	21.1	13	18.3	71	89.9			8	79	84.0	2	2.1	13	13.8	94
Early Neolithic 8–10	1	3.0	14	42.4	12	36.4	6	18.2	33	97.0		1		34	87.2	1	2.6	4	9.2	39
Late Mesolithic 11–17	745	81.2	13	14.2	25	2.7	134	14.6	917	98.9	10			927	98.5	4	.4	10	1.1	941
Mixed Mesolithic 18–21	32	88.9					4	11.1	36	94.7	1		1	38	76.0	8	16.0	4	8.0	50
Early Mesolithic 22–27	8	61.5					5	38.5	13	72.2	4	1		18	41.9	19	44.2	6	14.0	43
Totals	790		66		52		162		1070		15	2	9	1096		34		37		1167

Belt Cave, Maturity of Specimens, Raw Data

	Phoca		Gazella				Capra				Ovis				Toes. c/o		Sus	
	I	T	I	M	H	T	I	M	H	T	I	M	H	T	I	M	I	T
B							1	2		3	1	1		2				1
1								3		3	1			1				
2				2		2	3	2		5		2		2		1	1	2
3								2		2	1			1				1
4							2	2		4	1			1	1			1
5	1	2					3	2		5	1	2		3	1	1	1	2
6			1			1	4	6		10	2			2	3			1
7				1		1	6	1		7	3			3				
8							1	3		4		1		1				
9		1			1	1	1	1	3	5		1		1				
10							1	4		5	1	5	4	10	1	4		
11				6	61	67	1	2	1	4		4		4				
12				13	92	106		1	2	3			8	8				
13				25	211	236	1			1			5	5				
14	1	3	1	22	100	123		1		1	2	1		3				
15		2		13	156	169			3	3			4	4				
16			2	7	19	28							1	1				
17				7	9	16	1			1						1		
18	1	5		9	5	14												1
19		1		8	1	9										1		
20				3		3												
21		2	1	3	2	6												
22		2		1	1	2												
23				1		1												
24	2	11	1*		3	3*												
25	1	7																
26		1																
27					2	2												
Totals	6	37	6*	121	663*	790	27	30	9	66	11	18	23	52	6	8	2	9

* One horn immature.

I — Immature   H — Horn
M — Mature   T — Total

of specimens, in the species in which immature individuals occurred. Two exceptions must be noted. One of the gazelle horns in Level 24 was immature, which changes the totals of the "immature" and "horn" columns. One ox vertebra, from Level B, was immature. This did not seem to deserve statistical treatment.

Aside from the one calf, six species had more than one immature speciman: *phoca, gazella, sus, capra,* and *ovis,* which I shall now call seal, gazelle, pig, goat, and sheep. The sheep and goat series is represented not only by bones identified as such, but also by a group of 14 toe bones identified as sheep or goat.

Animals used for food and skins alone, or speaking more generally, for products which can be obtained only by killing the animal, are the wild animals and one potentially domestic species, the pig. Animals which furnish secondary products which can be obtained without killing are the sheep, goat, and ox. These products include milk in all three cases, hair in the case of the goat, and wool in that of the sheep. The ox also is of value as a draft animal and a beast of burden.

The table on page 152 shows two distinct breaks in the stratigraphic series: one comes between Levels 7 and 8, in that the vast majority of immature specimens occur between 7 and the top; and at 10, which is the dividing line above which gazelle specimens are extremely scarce. Now we know that 10 is the bottom of the Neolithic spill level, while 7 is the level at which pottery begins. Hence these two divisions follow a pattern already established.

In the table on page 154 we have combined our data into mature and immature by species within these three stratigraphic divisions. In the case of seal, of 37 specimens, 6 or 16.2 per cent are immature. The specimens in the two upper divisions are statistically too few for reliability, except that they show that the practice of killing immature animals existed in all levels at which seals were taken. This probably means that the inhabitants of the cave clubbed seals at their breeding places, obtaining cubs as well as mature animals. This seems to be a perfectly normal situation.

Again with gazelle, the vast majority fall below Level 10, but all show a minor tendency to kill young animals. One out of 4 were immature in the two upper levels, or 25 per cent; if we count bones only in the lower levels, 4 out of 122, or 3 per cent, were immature. Gazelles are hard for hunters on foot to catch, even with dogs. The mature animals must have found some way to shelter their young from attack.

The one specimen of pig found in the lower level was without much doubt as wild as the gazelles, but the specimens in the upper levels may well have been domesticated. One must remember that in a country where there is plenty of mast for pigs to eat, it is more profitable to let them grow and develop meat and fat than to kill them shortly after birth. Most of our specimens are teeth, and while they are permanent teeth they are unworn. The "mature" category in this case means simply old enough to have cut permanent teeth, which in a pig is not very old. The question of domestication, in the case of this animal, is open. On the

Belt Cave, Maturity of Specimens, Refined
ANIMALS WITHOUT SECONDARY PRODUCTS

	Phoca				Gazella				Sus			
	I	M	T	%I	I	M	T	%I	I	M	T	%I
B, 1–7	1	1	2	(50.0)	1	3	4	(25.0)	2	6	8	(25.0)
8–10	0	1	1	(0)		1	1	(0)				
11–27 With horns	5	29	34	14.7	5	780	785	.6		1	1	(0)
Without horns					4	118	122	3,3				
Totals With horns	6	31	37	16.2	6	784	790	.7	2	7	9	22.2
Without horns					5	121	126	3.9				

ANIMALS WITH SECONDARY PRODUCTS

	Capra				Ovis				Capra & Ovis			
	I	M	T	%I	I	M	T	%I	I	M	T	%I
B, 1–7	21	18	39	53.8	10	5	15	66.7	36	25	61	59.0
8–10	3	11	14	21.4	1	11	12	8.2	5	26	31	16.1
	3	8	11	27.3	1	7	8	12.5	5	19	24	20.8
11–27 With horns	3	10	13	23.1	0	25	25	0	3	37	40	7.5
Without horns	3	4	7	(42.8)	0	6	6	(0)	3	15	18	16.7
Totals With horns	27	39	66		11	41	52		44	88	132	
Without horns	27	30	57		11	18	29		44	59	103	

I — Immature
M — Mature
T — Total

basis of all the evidence from this site and elsewhere, I am inclined to favor the opinion that the pig was domesticated in late Neolithic times.

The real problem comes with the goats and sheep. In the upper levels, from Level 7 upward, immature specimens outnumber mature ones. To my mind this means only one thing: the occupants of the cave were slaughtering half their kids and goats. In order to do this, the animals must be domesticated, and furthermore there must be some basis of selection. The only feasible basis is sex, which means that the mature female animals were milked. In the earliest Neolithic, represented by Levels 8 to 10, the cave dwellers slaughtered only a fourth to a fifth of kids and an eighth of lambs, if we follow the count of bones alone, or even fewer if we include the evidence of horns. Including the goat/sheep toe bones, one sixth to one fifth is the ratio. Now there is a great difference between killing four or five adult animals to every lamb or kid, and butchering six lambs or kids to every four goats or sheep. To my mind this means that the people who deposited Levels 8 to 10 kept domestic goats and sheep, but on a different basis from their successors. If they had not yet taken up agriculture, or if they had done so only in an incipient way, they would be much more dependent on their flocks for food than were their successors. They would also have more time/energy per individual for herding, and hence could keep larger flocks; they would also have more land near their dwellings for pasture. If at the same time they had not begun milking their animals, there would be less incentive for killing off the male young. Since meat and skins would be the chief purpose of keeping animals, it would be worth while to let them grow to mature size before slaughtering them. Hence one can postulate an Early Neolithic period of little or no agriculture, with sheep and goats kept largely for meat and skins. Young goats were killed more frequently than young sheep. This may mean that they had already begun to use wool.

Let us now turn to the Mesolithic period, as shown by Levels 11 to 27. In the first place, gazelle bones far outnumber sheep and goat, as do those of ox. If these people had begun herding, it must have been only as a sideline. In the case of sheep, there is no evidence of the slaughter of lambs at all. In that of goats, the ratio of kid butchering is the same as later, leading us to suspect that goat herding began in the Mesolithic.

Turning to the evidence of the ox, we find only one vertebra in the entire collection which would indicate the butchering of veal. The numerous ox bones in the late Mesolithic cannot be shown to have been anything but wild. In fact, the bones indicate an extremely large animal. The gap between the last occurrence of ox in the Mesolithic and its tardy return in the later Neolithic suggests a change in use. The oversized bones of the Mesolithic are not found among the Neolithic specimens. Further, the fact that the Neolithic oxen were butchered when mature may only mean that the males were used for draft and packing, the females for milking also. It seems more likely, since Dr. Frazer has identified the Mesolithic ox as *Bos primigenius*, and the Neolithic ox as the ordinary *Bos*, these animals were domesticated in the agricultural Neolithic, but this cannot be proved by any means at my disposal.

The following hypotheses arise as a result of the foregoing evidence:

(1) During late Mesolithic times the people who inhabited Belt Cave were hunters, going to both the forest and the plain for their game. Their

principal prey were gazelle and ox. They also hunted wild sheep and wild goat. During this period they began to domesticate the goat, purely as a meat and skin animal.

(2) In early Neolithic times, before the inhabitants of Belt Cave adopted cereal culture, pottery making, weaving, and the use of stone axes, they kept both sheep and goats as animals for slaughter.

(3) After having adopted cereal culture, pottery making, weaving, and the use of stone axes, they began milking their sheep and goats and shearing their sheep. They also domesticated the ox and the pig at this time, or a little later.

These hypotheses are based on very scanty material, and require much more excavation and more professional techniques of analysis before they can be either substantiated or replaced by more firmly founded hypotheses. In the meanwhile, I offer them tentatively only, as a basis for future work.

It is notable that the problem of immaturity in animal bones is purely a post-glacial problem. In neither the Bisitun nor the Tamtama Pleistocene deposits was a single recognizably immature specimen found. In the upper levels of Bisitun, however, 7 immature specimens appeared, as follows: Level A *sus,* 3 out of 5 specimens; *cervinae,* 2 out of 75; *equus,* 1 out of 13. Level B: *capra,* 1 of 2. This data, such as it is, accords fully with the Belt Cave material.

The [species] identification of the bird remains from the three caves (Bisitun, Tamtama, and Belt) has not yet been made. Dr. Alexander Wetmore of the Smithsonian Institution has agreed to do this, for a later report. In the meanwhile, we can, however, make a few observations, particularly of a quantitative nature (see table on page 157). Bird bones, both scrap and otherwise, are easy for an amateur like myself to separate from mammal bones, with a fair ratio of success. They are hard, brittle, hollow, and shiny. The head of the femur and the distal end of the tibia are usually distinctive. The ulna in particular would be hard to mistake, since it possesses a row of pin-like protrusions for pinion attachments.

In Bisitun, birds cannot have formed a large part of the local diet at any time represented in the deposit. However, birds were five times as frequently eaten in the pit and rockfall periods as in the Brown Earth cultural optimum. Thus they go with bovids rather than with the horse-elk diet. When we have the identification of these birds, no doubt some climatic significance will be revealed by the list of genera and species. In Tamtama Cave the ratio, one half of one per cent, is the same as for the pit and rockfall periods at Bisitun, which Tamtama resembles in many other respects. It may be noted in passing that 181 pieces of tortoise carapace, plastron, and bone were recovered from Tamtama, representing at least a dozen of these reptiles. This points up the conclusion reached elsewhere that the Tamtama folk were relatively more

Bird Bones

BISITUN

	Bird Bones	Total Bones	% Bird
A	1	1542	.0
B	3	452	.7
C	1	239	.4
D	5	1148	.4
E	1	1912	.0
F	3	6894	.0
G	2	355	.6
Total	16	12,542	.1

TAMTAMA

Bird Bones	Total Bones	% Bird
13	2766	.5

BELT

Layer	Bird	Total Bones	% Bird
1		256	0
2	1	817	.1
3	1	295	.3
4	2	292	.6
5	2	344	.6
6	2	818	.2
7	2	470	.4
8	9	352	2.6
9	3	255	1.2
10	3	699	.6
11	11	1008	1.0
12		1286	0
13	2	1643	.1
14	15	1261	1.2
15	50	1154	4.3
16	4	580	.7
17	6	543	1.1
18	3	458	.7
19	3	346	.9
20		277	0
21	2	122	1.6
22	1	158	.6
23	1	107	.9
24		293	0
25	3	113	2.6
26	3	39	7.7
27	3	15	20.0
Total	140*	14,001	1.0

* Total of 140 includes the 138 listed by layers plus eight from which the layer numbers were rubbed off in handling, owing to the extreme hardness and shininess of the surface. Judging by color, texture, etc., these 8 were Mesolithic.

concerned with collecting slow game and gathering than with hunting, as compared to the classic hunters of Bisitun.

In Belt Cave, the situation is different. The marshes along the Caspian shore provide a splendid bivouac for migratory aquatic birds, where they are netted and shot in great numbers today. The long column for the Belt Cave shows that bird hunting was also in vogue in three prehistoric periods: the Early Mesolithic, where the bird vies with the seal as a source of food; the Late Mesolithic of Levels 14 and 15, notable also for ox; and the pre-ceramic Neolithic from Levels 8 through 10, with many of the bones no doubt trodden into Level 11. After the beginning of cereal cultivation, there seems to have been less time for fowling. At the risk of later disproof, I may say that many of the bones of the birds eaten at Belt Cave were large, and that the aquatic tribe was probably well represented.

Fauna and Climate in Pleistocene Palestine

The Mount Carmel caves in the northern part of Israel were excavated in the early 1930's under the direction of Professor Garrod. Their importance is shown by the fact that they form the basis of the Upper Paleolithic-Mesolithic sequence of the Near East. Moreover, it was in the smallest of the three caves, Mugharet es-Skhūl, that an important series of Neanderthaloid burials were discovered by Theodore McCown.

The report below,[5] written by Bate, concerns the faunal collections from these expeditions. Bate interprets the collections as supporting the conclusions of changing climatic conditions and concludes that the preponderance of the steppe-form *Gazella*, over the woodland-form fallow deer *Dama* indicates a relatively dry climate. Her conclusion has been challenged by Haas (Stekelis and Haas, 1952), who maintains that this preponderance may be due simply to hunters' preference. Furthermore, Miss Bate did not try to determine the number of individual animals represented (the technique for this type of analysis is clearly outlined by Leroi-Gourhan, 1952), and therefore one cannot be certain whether numerical preponderance of bones of one species does in fact mean that more individuals of the species were killed and eaten.

The ultimate correctness of Bate's view, however, does not in any way detract from the usefulness of the method. Zeuner, in a recent edition of his book *Dating the Past* (1952:229–231), accepts without modification the sequence of pluvial phases proposed by Garrod and Bate on the basis of their interpretation of the gazelle and deer remains.

The collection of animal remains which forms the subject of the present work was obtained during the excavation of the Wady el-Mughara Caves undertaken by a joint expedition of the British School of Archaeology in Jerusalem and the American School of Prehistoric Research, with Miss Garrod as Field Director. A full account of the caves and their excavation, with descriptions of their deposits and archaeological contents, has already been given by Miss Garrod in the first part of this volume.

[5] D. A. E. Garrod and D. M. A. Bate, *The Stone Age of Mount Carmel*, Oxford, 1937, vol. 1, pp. 139–142, 145, 147, 148, 149, 151, 153. By permission of the authors and The Clarendon Press.

An endeavour has been made to use this great collection of animal remains as a basis for a detailed history of the unfoldment of the faunal assemblages which succeeded each other during a not inconsiderable portion of the Pleistocene period in Palestine. This history of the fauna is inextricably interwoven with that of the changing climatic and environmental conditions, a fact which makes it possible to picture in broad outline some of the varying aspects of the country during this time.

Much further work in this direction is needed, with results from detailed geological and soil investigations. A recent paper by Dr. Zeuner (1936) clearly demonstrates how many lines of research may be necessary for a correct understanding to be reached regarding the climate of any past geological period.

But for two factors of primary importance it would have been impossible to make full use of the Wady el-Mughara Collection. First is the nature of the truly remarkable succession of deposits found in two neighbouring caves which were accumulated as a result of what appears to have been uninterrupted human occupation from a period in which a Tayacian industry occurs, up to Natufian (Mesolithic) times. The great depth of these deposits is only indicated in Miss Garrod's diagrammatic section which, with her archaeological chronology, I have used with her permission for my chart on the time distribution of the species (see Fig. 5.3). To this I have added a column giving notes on the climatic indications based on the study of the fauna.

The second of the two important factors is the good collecting and general labelling of the animal remains, to which I cannot pay too high a tribute, and for which I cannot be too grateful. Without it some interesting species would certainly have come to light, but even a partial interpretation of the succession of the faunal assemblages and their climatic implications would have been impossible.

Owing to their state of preservation and the almost invariable presence of adherent matrix, specimens could only be labelled in bulk in the field, and this proved sufficient, since it was accompanied by scrupulously careful packing. Subsequently, as a preliminary to the study of a species, individual specimens were marked in Indian ink with the name of the cave and of the Level from which they came. Exception was made only in the case of the smallest specimens, which were separately labelled in glass-topped boxes. This led to a table being made for each species recording the number of identified specimens found in the different Levels, even when these amounted to several thousands, as in the case of the Gazelles and *Dama mesopotamica*. The time distribution chart [Fig. 5.3] is based on these tables; it has not been found practicable to indicate the varying quantities of each species, but a reference to this will be found in the text.

The very large collection consists almost entirely of remains of mam-

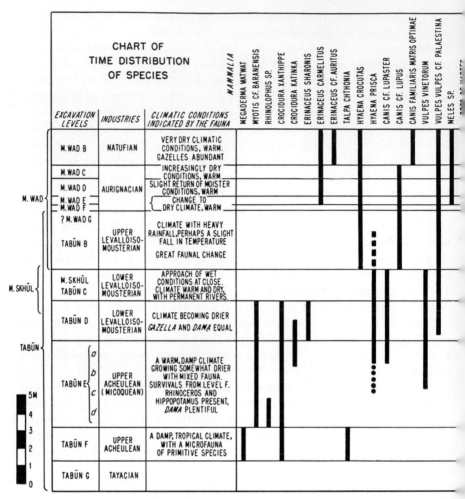

Fig. 5.3. Chart of time distribution of faunal species in Palestinian caves.

mals, of which fifty-two species have been determined. The specimens
are generally in a fragmentary state of preservation, due to the animals
being used for human food. Due also, no doubt, to the fact that the
animals, with few exceptions, were introduced by man, is the rarity of
remains of the larger carnivora, *Elephas* and other very large species.

Numerous fragmentary Tortoise and Lizard remains come from the
Aurignacian Layers of M. Wad, but they have not yet been studied. It is
remarkable that, in spite of the proximity of the sea, fish remains are
negligible in quantity. A certain number of bird remains are preserved,
and a few already identified have proved to be of interest.

It is evident that some knowledge of the physiography of the country
is essential to an understanding of its fauna. Briefly stated Palestine, as

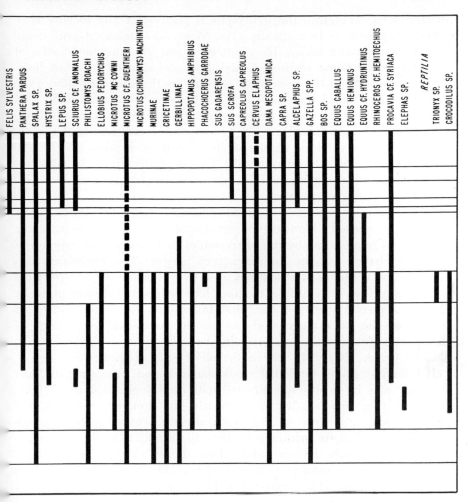

politically defined to-day, may be described as a narrow strip of country based on Gaza on the south, and extending northwards over slightly more than three degrees of latitude. This area is roughly divided longitudinally into three sections. To the west lies the coastal plain bordering the Mediterranean; eastwards, and practically parallel, is the great central mountain ridge which rises over 2,000 feet above the Mediterranean Sea. The eastern border of the land is occupied by the Jordan Rift Valley which ranges from Mediterranean level at Lake Huleh in the north to more than 1,200 feet below this in the Dead Sea area, which is a region subject to great heat.

These varied topographical features necessarily result in a great range of temperature, and differences of flora, etc., within a comparatively re-

stricted area. Therefore the geographical position of any locality is of
special significance faunistically. The Wady el-Mughara Caves could
hardly have a more favourable position for providing a general view of
the Pleistocene fauna of the country. They are situated in a low limestone escarpment at the mouth of the wady on the landward side of the
coastal plain, which here is only between three and four miles wide. This
escarpment lies at the south-western edge of Mount Carmel, and is therefore almost midway between Gaza to the south and Beirut to the north.
Furthermore, it is close to the single important western gap in the
mountain ridge which separates the Jordan Valley from the Mediterranean, and which seems to have played an important part in faunal
migrations from east to west.

This environment of greatly varied influences is reflected in the fauna,
which is composed of an astonishing mixture of types throughout the
long period represented by the succession of cave Levels. The component
elements change but the mosaic pattern persists. The attainment of a
clear understanding was at first obscured by this composite nature of the
fossil record. Two special lines of attack have helped to solve the problem.
One is a special study of the micro-fauna, and the other a detailed
survey of the persistence and comparative numerical occurrence of
the species. Some of the most important results are shown in the *Dama-
Gazella* graph (Fig. 5.4) and in the chart (Fig. 5.3).

It is easy to understand that small mammals may evolve rapidly, and
that they may be so closely connected with conditions of soil and vegetation that they are usually more sensitive to climatic conditions and
changes than are many of the larger animals. This is evident in the
present collection, in which a number of primitive small species are
found in the early Levels, while they appear to be completely replaced by forms of modern type in the Levels of later age than Tabūn B
(Upper Levalloiso-Mousterian). On the other hand some of the larger
species such as *Dama mesopotamica* and *Cervus elaphus* seem to survive
almost throughout.

Among the larger species it is found that remains of *Dama mesopotamica Gazella* (probably several species) are present in greater quantity
than those of any other species throughout the Levels above the middle
of Level E of Tabūn. These two forms represent animals of typically
different habits; Deer are ordinarily woodland animals, preferring a
moist climate, while Gazelles are characteristic of dry or desert country.
In this connexion it is important to remember that these environmental
preferences are reflected in the anatomy of these animals. Deer have
low-crowned petaloid cheek teeth suitable for browsing on deciduous
leaves and other soft herbage, and hooves adapted for soft ground. The
cheek teeth of gazelles are, on the other hand, narrower, higher crowned
and more goatlike, fit to cope with coarse herbage and scrubby growth,

while their slender cannon bones and small and close, hard feet are fitted for rapid progress on hard ground.

The census taken of the remains of *Dama* and *Gazella*, both the actual and comparative number of specimens, is set forth in the accompanying graph (Fig. 5.4). Since they are probably of similar age the specimens

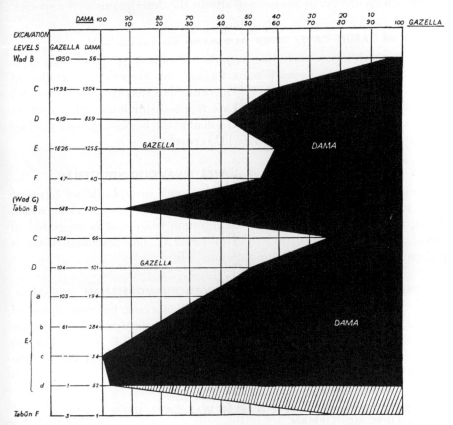

Fig. 5.4. Graph showing the comparative frequency of *Dama* and *Gazella* during the period of human occupation of Tabūn and M. Wad. This is suggested as an indication of varying moist (*Dama*) and dry (*Gazella*) climatic conditions. The actual numbers of specimens are given in the left-hand column. The earliest part of the deposit is shown shaded owing to the very small number of specimens obtained.

from Wad G and Tabūn B have been grouped together, but only a small portion are from the former Level; i.e. *Gazella* 58 and *Dama* 104 specimens. In Level F of Tabūn *Gazella* is represented by only three and *Dama* by a single bone, therefore no definite climatic condition has been indicated in the graph. Fortunately, remains of other species obtained from this Level provide convincing evidence of damp tropical conditions (see section on faunal assemblage of Level F of Tabūn). I am much indebted to Dr. F. Zeuner for his kind assistance in arranging these results, which form the chief key to the climatic fluctuations which took place during the period covered by the Levels of the Wady el-Mughara Caves. That this is a substantially correct picture is supported in many instances by evidence provided by other species. This evidence is set forth in a general way in the accounts of the faunal assemblages of the several Levels which are given below, and also in the descriptions of the species.

LEVEL E AT TABŪN CAVE; UPPER ACHEULEAN OR MICOQUEAN

This is a rich fauna, including a number of extinct species of early type. Some survivors from Level F occur throughout. Midway immigration of Asiatic forms increases, together with continuous decrease of *Dama*, until equality with Gazella and Level D are reached simultaneously. A warm, damp climate is indicated, perhaps tropical at the beginning, with gradual approach to drier conditions as Level D is reached.

LEVELS D AND C AT TABŪN CAVE; LOWER LEVALLOISO-MOUSTERIAN

These levels have provided a rich fauna with several distinct forms of early type. Some species known in Level F survive into Level D, which intergrades with Level E. Fresh immigration from Asia is suggested in Level D. The climate grows drier in Level C, but perennial water is present for the needs of Hippopotamus, etc.

THE DEPOSIT OF SKHŪL CAVE; LOWER LEVALLOISO-MOUSTERIAN

The fauna includes *Hippopotamus* and *Rhinoceros*, but commonest of all is a very large *Bos*. Chiefly owing to this it is suggested that a heavier rainfall had started prior to the wet period of Tabūn B [Cave]. For the present the Skhūl [Cave] deposit may be correlated with that of the end of Level C.

LEVEL B OF TABŪN AND LEVEL G OF M. WAD CAVE; UPPER LEVALLOISO-MOUSTERIAN

The chief feature of the faunal assemblage of these Levels is the evidence it provides of a great faunal break. From this Level onwards the fauna is of modern type. Remains of *Dama mesopotamica* constitute the principal part of the collection; this indicates a considerably increased rainfall.

LEVELS F-C OF M. WAD CAVE; LOWER TO UPPER AURIGNACIAN

The faunal assemblage of these Levels is of modern type, and includes new arrivals such as Wolf, Badger, Marten, Hare, etc. The fauna suggests a much drier climate than during Tabūn B, and desiccation increased until Wad B, with the exception of a damper phase during Wad D.

LEVEL B OF M. WAD CAVE; NATUFIAN

This fauna is of modern type, but still shows important differences from that of the present day. Gazelle remains are very plentiful, those of Fallow Deer now rare. This suggests a condition of aridity. That domestication of animals had now begun is shown by the remains of a large Dog.

6
POPULATION

Population size is an important factor in cultural reconstruction since many cultural factors are substantially affected by the size of the community. A group of 5000 living in a given area is a very different thing from a group of 500 living in the same area. They have entirely different problems of subsistence, social control, health, and the like. It is, therefore, essential that we have some idea of the size of the population if we are to achieve even a general impression of the character of the culture we are dealing with. Once we know even roughly the size of the community, it begins to "come alive" to us. We begin to see our pile of dirt in terms of a group of people and their products and interactions.

The following three studies are concerned with this problem. It is interesting to compare them because the approaches and the use of the results are quite different. For the Cosgroves (1932), the estimate of population size is a necessary step towards estimating the length of occupancy of the site. Their estimate is based on the number of rooms found and their probable correlation with family units. They combine this with the number of burials found and an ingenious estimate of the death rate, based on comparisons with known death rates, to achieve their estimate of the duration of the site. Hack (1942), on the other hand, is interested in the relative size of the population and its increase and decrease over a period of time. His estimate is based on the assignment of arbitrary units to factors of site size, houses, and sherd areas. There is no way to know how many people each unit represents, but it is possible, by this method, to determine whether the population was increasing or decreasing at a given point of time. This can then be correlated with ecological and historical factors, as Hack does, to tell us something about the overall population history of the area and what influenced it. A similar study has been made for the region just to the west by Schwartz (1956).

Duration of occupation of a site can be determined with some exactness if the refuse deposits, together with the village cemetery where the occupants were buried, are excavated so the number of households and graves can be determined. If we apply what is already known concerning mortality rates in man and family size among recent peoples of similar cultural level, the period of occupancy can be calculated. The Swarts Ruin example (Cosgrove, 1932) is one such attempt, and Hooton's analysis of the Madisonville, Ohio, graves is another (Hooton, 1920). Snow's summary computation of the duration of occupancy of Indian Knoll, Kentucky (Snow, 1948:387), Hooton's reconstruction of the growth and decline of the prehistoric population of Pecos Pueblo, New Mexico (Hooton, 1930: chap. 11), the Ricketsons' estimate of the population of the Maya city of Uaxactun (Ricketson and Ricketson, 1937:15–24), and Cook's article on vital statistics among aboriginal groups (Cook, 1947), provide information on this much neglected subject. Steward's and Birdsell's surveys of environmental factors as limiting the population of hunting-gathering groups are other contributions to this field of investigation (Steward, 1955: Pt. III; Birdsell, 1953).

Length of Occupancy and Size of Population of the Swarts Village[1]

Attempt was made to estimate the time during which the village was occupied. A primary requisite for such a calculation is knowledge of the size of the population throughout the life of the community, from which, if we know the death rate, and if we find the bodies of all the dead, we can arrive at reasonably accurate results. But the size of the population of Swarts proved difficult to determine. We tried to segregate the dwellings of different families so that by approximating the size of family groups, we might estimate the number of people in the pueblo at different times. The scattered arrangement of the Early houses and the entire lack of system in the grouping of later rooms made this a baffling task. We finally arrived, nevertheless, at an estimate of 5 people to a family, which is considered conservative and probably an underestimate, when the high death rate of infants and children is noted. An allowance of 1 room to a family in the 44 more primitive and scattered houses of the Early and Middle Period occupations would give an average population of 22 families, or 110 people; an allowance of 2 rooms would reduce it to 11 families, or 55 people. The 120 rooms of the Late Period, with an

[1] H. S. and C. B. Cosgrove, *The Swarts Ruin; Report of the Mimbres Valley Expedition, Seasons of 1924–1927*. Papers of the Peabody Museum, Harvard University, Cambridge, 1932, vol. 15, no. 1, pp. 100–103. By permission of J. O. Brew, Director of the Peabody Museum, Harvard University.

allowance of 3½ rooms to a family, would result in the accommodation of 35 families, or 175 people, living there during that time.

In all, 1009 burials were found in the thorough clearing of the ruin and it is not likely that many were overlooked. There were 75 definitely associated with the Early occupation and the remaining 934 belonged, as far as could be seen, to the Late Period.

The following discussion by Mr. W. W. Howells, who is furnishing a report on the skeletal remains from this ruin, clearly shows how the death rate for the Swarts village was obtained:

To determine the length of time over which a given site was occupied, we must know the total number of deaths, the death rate, and the size of the population.

TOTAL NUMBER OF BURIALS

This is the sole factor of which we are in possession. It is tabulated below according to age; moreover it is divided into two sections, the "Early Period" including burials from the Early and Middle Periods lumped together. The age percentages are calculated from the totals of the sub-groups. The expedition excavated the site very thoroughly, and Mr. Cosgrove believes that very few burials were missed and that the total number would not be brought much above 1009.

	0-10 years	Age at Death 10-20 years	20-X years	Total
Early period burials				
Number	39	0	36	75
Per cent	52.00	0.00	48.00	—
Late period burials				
Number	423	29	482	934
Per cent	45.29	3.10	51.66	—
Total				1009

DEATH RATE

Dr. Hooton arrived at an approximate death rate for the population of the cemetery at Madisonville, Ohio, in the following ingenious manner. He unearthed the mortality rates for nine European countries, together with the proportions of age at death, over a certain period more than fifty years ago. He assumed that, should the percentages of the age divisions agree closely with those of one of the above countries, the death rate of that country might be accepted as suitable for the Madisonville site. Switzerland fulfilled the conditions, but her death rate of 2.38 per hundred per annum was raised to 3, to allow, in this case, for burials which had escaped the spade, and for warriors dying abroad.

European Death Rates

Country	Year	Age 0-10	Age 10-20	Age 20-X	Year	Death rate per hundred
Italy	1872–77	52.37	4.22	43.41	1865–78	2.99
France	1866–77	32.28	4.25	63.47	1865–77	2.46
England	1860–70	44.23	4.56	51.21	1865–78	2.20
Prussia	1875–77	52.43	3.51	44.06	1865–78	2.72
Bavaria	1871–77	52.61	2.22	45.17	1865–78	3.09
Austria	1865–77	52.38	4.05	43.57	1865–78	3.18
Spain	1865–70	51.86	4.37	43.77	1865–70	3.12
Russia	1870–74	62.33	4.13	33.54	1865–75	3.67
Switzerland	1873–77	36.94	3.72	59.33	1870–78	2.38

In the present case, the same figures were used, and Bavaria and England measure off with the two periods respectively. However, the figures for England are not altogether reliable, as the mortality rate and age proportions deal with different groups of the population. Moreover, further machinations will relieve us of the assumption that close correspondence in age proportions with any country entails as close a correspondence in the death rate, as of course a particular country may deviate somewhat from the postulated pattern.

Dr. Hooton observes that there is a close correlation between infant and child deaths and the height of the rate of mortality. This is shown to be the case by dividing the death rate into the proportion of deaths under 10 years, and listing these ratios.

Country	Ratio
France	13.12
Switzerland	15.52
Austria	16.47
Spain	16.62
Russia	16.98
Bavaria	17.03
Italy	17.52
Prussia	19.64
England	20.10
	————
Average	17.00

Considering the fact that the majority of these ratios hover within half a point of the average, 17.00, it seems legitimate to obtain death rates for the Mimbres population by reversing the process used above and dividing the ratio 17.00 into the percentage of child and infant deaths of both groups. This gives:

Early Period   3.1 deaths per hundred per annum.
Late Period   2.7   "   "   "   "   "

The advisability of raising either of these figures is doubtful, in view of the probable peacefulness of the people and the lack of epidemics.

Since it was probable that numbers of houses fell into disuse and were left unoccupied during the time necessary to build settlements of the Early and Middle Periods which contained 172 living quarters, large communal rooms, and inclosed plazas, an allowance of either 1 or 2 rooms for the

Early Periods and an average of not over 3½ rooms to a family in the Late Period seemed logical as it gave a population commensurate with the size of the settlement.

Based on a death rate of 3.1 for the Early and Middle Periods and 2.7 for the Late, a single and 3½ room assignment respectively for these periods would require 22 years to create a cemetery of 75 for the Early Periods, and 198 years to build up a cemetery of 934 in the Late times, a total occupation of 220 years. With 2 rooms to a family in the Early Periods and 3½ rooms during the Late, the number of the first inhabitants would be decreased by one-half, which would be in better proportion for the small settlements of those times. In this way the results would show an occupation of 242 years as another estimate for the occupancy of Swarts.

We present the above calculations for what they are worth, fully realizing how many unknown quantities are involved.

Population Changes in the Jeddito Valley Region, Arizona[2]

A reconnaissance of sites in the Jeddito Valley and the Antelope Mesa region was carried out in 1939, by Mr. William H. Claflin, III. This work gives us some idea, although a very rough one, of the course of the rise and fall of the Pueblo population in the region. Notes were taken on the size of the sites found, and sherd collections were made which were later classified by Dr. J. O. Brew. The field notes give only a rough estimate of the size of the ruins for many of the sites are partially destroyed, or partially covered. Generally the length of the site is recorded, or is noted as a large or small sherd area, or a large or small group of houses. The writer in attempting to gain some idea of population changes adopted an arbitrary system of valuing such notations as follows:

Length of site:	
10 yards	2 units
20 yards	5 units
30 yards	10 units
40 yards	20 units
50 yards	30 units
100 yards	70 units
Sherd area	2 units
House	2 units
Large sherd area	20 units
Large group of houses	20 units

[2] J. T. Hack, *The Changing Physical Environment of the Hopi Indians of Arizona,* Papers of the Peabody Museum, Harvard University, Cambridge, 1942, vol. 35, no. 1, pp. 78–80. By permission of J. O. Brew, Director of the Peabody Museum, Harvard University.

Some of the sites were occupied through several divisions of the Pueblo chronology, so that they had to be counted more than once. For instance a site called Pueblo II–III, 20 yards long, is given a value of 5 units in Pueblo II and also 5 units in Pueblo III. This evaluation probably exaggerates somewhat the relative size of the Pueblo II population, for in general the villages or house groups which were occupied during Pueblo II and III times were larger in Pueblo III than in Pueblo II. The large ruins, Awatovi, Kawaika-a, Chakpahu, and Kokopnyama, are so much larger than any of the others that they were treated in a different way. It is known that they were considerably larger in Pueblo IV time than in Pueblo III time; accordingly each one is given a value of 300 units in Pueblo IV and 100 units in Pueblo III.

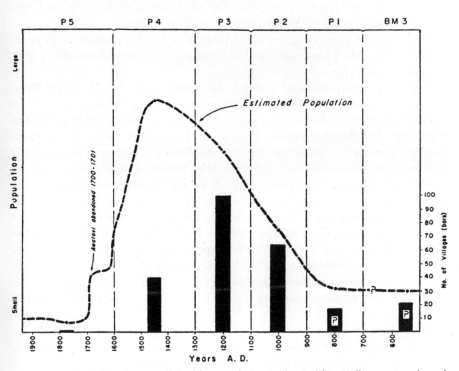

Fig. 6.1. Probable changes of Pueblo population in the Jeddito Valley region, based on a reconnaissance survey by W. H. Claflin, III. The bars represent the number of ruins belonging to each period. Vertical columns refer to cultural periods from Basketmaker 3 (III) through Pueblo 5 (V).

This method obviously yields results which are relative and of no quantitative value, but it does enable one to construct a curve showing population trends, as shown in Fig. 6.1. The number of villages occupied during each period from Basketmaker III to the present are shown as bars at the base of the diagram. The data for Pueblo I, and Basketmaker

III are at the present stage of the study less certain and the relative population at these times may be in error, but there is no doubt that population was greater in Pueblo II times than in Pueblo I. There is also no doubt that population was still greater in Pueblo III as not only did the number of villages increase but also their average size. In Pueblo IV time, however, the number of villages declined very markedly but the larger villages were so much larger than any earlier ones as to leave no doubt that the population increased.

It is probable that when the Spaniards came to the Hopi country, Awatovi was the only large village occupied, although there may have been some people at Kawaika-a. Thus a very abrupt decrease in population occurred at the end of Pueblo IV time which may have been unconnected with the Spanish conquest. The destruction of Awatovi in 1700–1701 brought another abrupt decline in population.

The curve of Fig. 6.1 gives a fair picture of the fluctuations in population since Pueblo I time, although the values and slopes of the curve may be greatly in error.

If a curve were worked out for the First, Second, and Third Mesa regions, it would probably be similar, except that there would be no decline, or in any case [only] a slight decline after Pueblo IV time, for the region is still thickly settled. Why should the other parts of the Hopi country remain settled while the Jeddito Valley region was abandoned? This may be answered by comparing the history of the stream systems of the two regions. The Jeddito Wash in Pueblo III time flowed at the level of the valley floor, as did the Oraibi, Polacca and Wepo Washes. Around 1300 A.D. they were probably all incised, making flood-water farming equally poor in all the regions. In Pueblo IV time, however, the Polacca, Wepo and Oraibi Washes apparently again spread out over the valley floors, whereas the Jeddito remained in a channel, at least in the Antelope Mesa region. This may possibly explain the abandonment of the region, however, and this explanation may thus be sufficient but not necessary.

But why did the Jeddito Valley region increase in population at the end of Pueblo III time when conditions for farming began to become poor? This may be explained by the assumption that the increase in population occurred because of migrations from the still less favorable areas to the north. If a population curve were made for the upper part of Black Mesa, and Kayenta, San Juan or Chaco regions, it would probably show an increase in population from Basketmaker time to Pueblo III time and an abrupt decline with complete abandonment at the end of Pueblo III time. It is obvious that most parts of these regions are of a different character from the Hopi country. The Tsegi Canyon furnishes a striking example. This region contains hundreds of Basketmaker and Pueblo ruins, all Pueblo III in age or older. The inhabitants must have farmed on the canyon floor. In 1884, it was farmed by Navahos, and was a rich verdant region. It is now almost deserted due to the disastrous effects of the recent epicycle of erosion. It has been shown that this canyon floor was dissected at the end of, or shortly after Pueblo III time, and it would have been just as impossible to farm in it then, as it is now. The same events occurred and the same line of reasoning applies to many stream valleys of the Plateau region, such as Chaco Canyon, Navaho Canyon, and the canyons of the upper Tusayan Washes on Black Mesa, where because of the narrowness of the alluvial floor, an epicycle of erosion quickly destroys every available farming space.

In the Hopi country, however, dissection of the valley floor is not so complete or so disastrous. Even when the main streams are incised, the tributaries still supply akchin [arroyo mouth] fields with water, and may continue to do for a long time interval. Furthermore, the unusual quantities of dune sand in the Hopi country enables the inhabitants to practice sand dune agriculture, not possible in other areas where eolian deposits are not so abundant. Thus a substitute for the destroyed flood-water fields is available.

Furthermore the abundant sand of the Hopi country provides a better intake area for springs, which alleviates the effect of drought which presumably accompanies and is the prime cause of an epicycle of erosion.

Thus the Hopi country, like the Rio Grande region to the east, may have become a haven of refuge for migrating peoples forced to leave their settlements in less favored areas. Its population increased during the period of stress and privation, while that of other areas to the north declined.

Population Estimates of Mesolithic and Neolithic Communities

The following account[3] deals with the possible demographic situation in three culture groups. First is Star Carr, a Mesolithic site in Britain, second is Jarmo, an early Neolithic site of Iraq, and third is Bronze Age Sumer. These three instances represent different levels of economic and social development and therefore provide a comparative view, however limited, of the intimate relation which exists between subsistence means and nature and size of social groups. The perspective in the present article is, therefore, rather wider than in the two preceding selections in this chapter.

For additional material on this subject the reader is referred to the works of Birdsell (1950; 1953), Howell (1952), and Steward (1936).

[3] R. J. Braidwood and C. A. Reed, "The Achievement and Early Consequences of Food-Production: a Consideration of the Archeological and Natural-Historical Evidence," *Population Studies: Animal Ecology and Demography*, Cold Spring Harbor Symposia on Quantitative Biology, Cold Spring Harbor, New York, 1957. pp. 23–29. By permission of the Long Island Biological Association.

STAR CARR

The following attempts (Star Carr, Jarmo, and Sumer) to establish population figures for prehistoric and early historic peoples illustrate nicely to what curious lengths we must go, what questionable analogies we must make, in any effort to produce population estimates for human cultures for which we do not have good written records.

Star Carr (Clark, 1954) represents an early post-glacial, late pre-boreal, lake-side, temporary occupation site in Yorkshire, east-central England. The culture, represented archeologically by chipped flint and worked bone, antler, and wood, is probably best called Proto-Maglemosian; in the larger view it was basal "mesolithic," and has been dated by C^{14} [radiocarbon] to 7538 ± 350 years B.C. At that time ice still occupied much of the Scandinavian highlands, and England was broadly continuous with continental Europe across a dry-land North "Sea."

Due to the good preservation and recovery of a wide range of animal and plant remains (the latter identified not only from pollen but from numerous woody remnants), the climate and more detailed ecological conditions can be reconstructed with fair accuracy. The fauna,[4] mostly aquatic birds and forest or meadow mammals, consisted of species found in the area today (or that would be there, if not eliminated within historical times). The vegetation was somewhat peculiar to the times, and perhaps could not be duplicated today. There was a dominant birch forest (chiefly Betula pubescens), but a substantial amount also of Scots pine (Pinus sylvestris). Although this period of time is within the "preboreal," it must be noted that its latitude and the general oceanicity of the British climate ensure that conditions were not particularly severe, and this is indicated by the fauna (particularly the presence of wild pig and roe deer) and by many of the plants. While the Scots pine is today naturally limited to areas north of England (with some rare relict exceptions), every other species identified at Star Carr can be found in Yorkshire now, although one, the marsh plant Eleocharis uniglumis, seems to be unknown north of Yorkshire and some others (Carex strigosa, Chenopodium rubrum, Solanum nigrum) are local and rare as one passes north into Scotland. Lastly, the presence at Star Carr of the sedge, Cladium mariscus, almost certainly means that there cannot have been very severe frost.

---

[4] Here, as in archeological sites in general, only the bones of animals used as human food are represented. The total fauna, or the population proportions of the different species identified, may actually have been quite different than would be inferred from analysis of the food-animals alone. The practice of regarding the result of such human "culture filters" as representative of total faunas can lead to quite erroneous conclusions inasmuch as technological or other cultural changes could alone alter the archeological faunal results when no actual changes occurred.

One visualizes, then, a climate not unlike that of Yorkshire today, in spite of the persistence of massive ice in Scandinavia; the predominance of birch, which was to be succeeded by pine and subsequently by a mixed-oak forest and by alder, must therefore be viewed as a part of a changing situation in a general post-glacial series of forest successions and is not necessarily indicative of a particularly cold local climate at Star Carr.

The lake-side settlement, barely large enough for four or five family groups, was occupied only during the winter and early spring, approximately October into April, as evidenced by the different growth and shedding cycles of the antlers of the cervids represented. The main food during this period, when plant sources would have been at a minimum, was cervid meat (red deer, *Cervus elaphus;* roe deer, *C. capreolus;* and moose or European elk, *A. alces*); of these the red deer was the most important. A wide variety of other mammals are more sparingly represented, as are a number of aquatic birds. As with hunting and gathering people in general, the Star Carr people probably ate everything edible they could find; much of this leaves no archeological record, although many of the plants represented have actually been used for food into present times.

The site was abandoned during the late spring, summer, and early autumn; later Maglemosian people spent most of this time fishing, away from their winter quarters. The site may have been occupied for some 20 winter seasons, or probably longer; during this time there was at least one period of several years of non-occupancy. Possibly four, probably not more than five, family groups lived at Star Carr at any one time; considering the known high infant mortality and short life expectancy of primitive peoples, each family would usually have consisted of two parents and three children, with a minimum number of elders. The total group then was probably not in excess of 25, of whom some five were adult men who could hunt large game.

A rough estimate of population density, considering the above circumstances, could be gained by comparison with the known density of more recent peoples living under identical conditions. Unfortunately, such identical ecologic and cultural circumstances cannot be duplicated, but somewhat similar conditions were found, prior to European invasions, in the region of southern Minnesota, Wisconsin, and Michigan. Here were deciduous forests, multiple water-side situations, large populations of aquatic and forest birds, many species of small mammals, a great variety of edible plants, and two large cervids and a smaller one (wapiti, *Cervus canadensis;* moose, *Alces americana;* and a smaller deer, *Odocoileus virginianus*). The winters in this part of North America are colder than they presumably were at Star Carr, but the native Indians were at a higher technological level than were the Proto-Maglemosians, and thus should have had a greater population density.

Kroeber (1939: particularly Map 18 and Table 7) is the best source for pre-European populations of the United States and Canada. In general, forest-living peoples away from the sea had low populations, even when they practiced a crude type of agriculture. Where a special food plant such as wild rice, which could be gathered annually and stored in large quantities, was available, a locally higher density would be present, but an overall examination of the evidence leads to the conclusion that a general figure of five persons per 100 sq. km. (= 13 per 100 sq. mi.) is probably an overestimate of the population density of a primitive hunting-collecting people who must depend on a forest environment for survival throughout the winter.

If at Star Carr there were approximately 25 persons, they would then have occupied about 200 sq. mi., a territory of 14.5 x 14.5 miles, which seems not unreasonable. There would have been, thus, only 7,538 people in an area the size of England and Wales.

It is interesting to note that 25 persons living on 200 sq. mi. of mixed forest and open land in no way approach the theoretical maximum that could be supported by such an area, which, by analogy with the somewhat similar situation in pre-Columbian Wisconsin, should have been able to maintain 7,600 people (Deevey, 1956), even if only animal food is considered and nothing is derived directly from plants! Actually, the Star Carr people could have lived easily on red deer alone without effect on the deer population, since their 200 sq. mi. should have supported 3,400 Cervus elaphus (at one animal per 50 acres; Darling, 1937). To be cautious, let us calculate one red deer for each 100 acres, or 1,700 per 200 sq. mi. Half of these are females who should, again being conservative, produce 500 young annually. At 420 pounds of dressed meat per adult red deer (Clark, 1954:15), which is probably an underestimate, 25 people (15 of them children) could theoretically have survived on 50 deer a year (daily requirement of 25 people = 60.5 pounds lean meat, on the basis of a need of 11,400 calories per day per family; Clark, 1954:16). Actually, of course, the Star Carr people did not have to live on any one food; they utilized a variety of animals, including probably fish in the summer, and doubtless much plant food also.

The main point here is that, as Deevey (1956) has already shown, the population of the primary hunting and collecting culture is not limited by the potential amount of food, but by man's ability to get it during the leanest season. Proto-Maglemosian man was probably often hungry, even starving, in country which should have indefinitely maintained a population at least 100 times (10,000%) as high (or 38 people to the square mile). That no hunting and gathering culture ever approached this population optimum (the nearest seems to have been accomplished by some of the acorn-gathering groups of California, at approximately 2.0 per sq. mi.; Kroeber, 1939:Map 19) is an indication of the human technological level of the hunting-collecting level.

JARMO

The origins of agriculture, accompanied by the beginnings of animal domestication, mark a milestone in human cultural evolution, well-known to prehistorians and anthropologists under Childe's catch-phrase of "The Neolithic Revolution." Unfortunately, the classic term "neolithic" as invented for and applied to European late prehistoric cultures cannot be applied with any clarity of meaning to southwestern Asia, where the agricultural revolution actually occurred. Whatever the terms used, the importance of the "revolution" cannot be over-emphasized.

Jarmo, in the hill-country of east-central Iraq, is the best-known of early archeological sites which had cereal agriculture and animal domestication. Flint sickles are found in earlier (Natufian culture) sites in Palestine, but these presumably were used only for the reaping of wild grasses. The lower strata at Jericho, a town beside a great gushing spring in the desert of the Jordan Valley, have been claimed to represent remains of more ancient farmers than those of Jarmo, but only preliminary reports (Kenyon, 1956; Zeuner, 1956) have been published, and little is known as yet of the agriculture of these early levels of Jericho.

Jarmo was an unwalled village atop a low hill, at an elevation of approximately 2600 feet, in the foothills of the Zagros Mountains of east-central Iraq. The region today has almost 20 inches of rain annually, limited to winter and spring; at the time of occupation of the village, some 6700 years ago, the area may have been slightly drier, an opinion reached independently by both Wright (1952) and Bobek (1954), although Butzer (1957) thinks that by 5000 B.C. this slight aridity was already shifting toward a more humid phase. The forest of that time, probably of scattered oaks and other deciduous trees, has long since been cut; today, with rare exceptions, the land is treeless except on the higher ridges, and the incessant overgrazing by the sheep and goats leads to rapid soil erosion. One millennium's progress may be another millennium's destruction.

Permanent water undoubtedly was available from a stream that flowed around the base of the hill, although now, after 7000 years of deforestation and soil erosion, the stream dries except for a few pools which remain throughout summer and autumn. The temperature in winter may drop to freezing; during the late spring and summer hot, dry winds from the continental inland sweep the country, and it is a rare day the temperature does not reach 100°F. In this climate, grain is planted with the first rains of early winter and matures fast in the spring heat; harvest for wheat and barley is in May. Then the rainless land bakes until October.

Excavations at Jarmo in 1948 and 1950–51 (Braidwood, 1952) showed that the village was continuously occupied for perhaps a quarter millennium, after which it was abandoned, never to be re-occupied.

We do not know the agricultural techniques of these early villagers; in the absence of archeological records other than their preserved grain and flint-bladed sickles we can only speculate. They had no plow, for they had no draft animals. They had diploid and tetraploid wheats, *Triticum monococcoides* and *T. Dicoccoides*, and a primitive two-row barley. The goat was, we think, the only domesticated food animal, and presumably the major source of protein, although it cannot be known if they had yet learned to milk the animals. Hunting, however, was not uncommon, but whether or not a necessary part of life we do not know; we find bones of wild pigs, gazelles, sheep, goats, cattle, red deer, roe deer, onagers (?), wolves, and foxes mixed with those of the domestic goat, although the latter predominate. Collecting of snails for food was common; we find millions of shells of *Helix (Naegelea) salomonica* throughout the excavations. A few fish and fresh-water crabs added to the protein variety. Presumably collecting of native vegetables and fruits would have been common, although again we do not know how necessary for the dietary pattern; a few such plants (acorns, pistachio nuts, lentils, and peas) have been tentatively identified amongst the archeological materials (Helbaek, 1953). In general, it would seem that the diet of the people of Jarmo was varied, adequate, and well-balanced—probably more so than that of the villagers of the same area today.

It is not impossible that a more detailed notion of the subsistence pattern can be arrived at, as the excavation areas are enlarged, and more food traces are reclaimed, quantitively recorded, and studied for their dietary implications. This study will be carried forward, we hope, in connection with observations on the actual dietary routine of the villages of the present-day workmen. This latter will be comparatively useful, with certain cultural qualifications taken into account (e.g., both chickens and turkeys and their eggs, now utilized, are later additions, while in Moslem Kurdistan, the eating of pork or of snails would of course no longer be considered).

The first two season's excavations at Jarmo revealed some details of house construction, house size, and house distribution (Braidwood, 1952). Extrapolating this information over the whole of the mound would have resulted in an estimate of approximately 30 houses, each presumably representing a family unit. Further excavation in 1955, sampling the whole of the mound, illustrated one of the basic types of statistical difficulties with archeological sampling; fully a third of the mound either was trash-pile or had never had houses. Thus we are reduced to some 20 houses, but at the same time some portion has been lost to erosion of the stream around the base of the hill, so perhaps 25 houses is our best informed guess as to the size of Jarmo at any one time.

How many people to a house? The best we can say is that each house certainly appears to be a separate family unit, comparable in size to a Kurdish village house of the same area today. The Jarmo houses had perhaps a few smaller and more numerous rooms, but the detailed inner arrangements of a Kurdish home, we must confess, are only vaguely known to us. Actually the house size, the mode of house construction, and the pattern of house distribution are so remarkably similar to those of the adjacent Kurdish villages of today that we feel we can compare them directly with a high degree of validity.

Today, in these nearby agricultural villages, there is one family per house. Barth (1953:19) gives a census for one such small village; ten house-holds had 51 people, or five per family. The higher figure of seven per house-hold was given us by excavation workmen from another village. If we take the median figure of six per family-household, 25 houses would indicate a Jarmo population of 150 people.

Although an estimate, we think it one within the bounds of close probability, for the nearest occupied villages today, Chalgah and Kani Sard, have respectively 18 and 13 houses, as counted on air-photos and Barth also lists 13 house-holds for Kani Sard. At six occupants per house we would thus have 108 and 78 inhabitants for these two villages; unfortunately we have no direct count to verify these figures. These are relatively small villages for the area today; some others in the same general region number over 200, so our estimate of 150 for Jarmo seems eminently reasonable.

A somewhat cursory survey of the area around Jarmo reveals two other village-sites, as yet unexcavated, which archeologically would be classified as the same age. Considering this trio of ancient villages, two are close together and the other is somewhat farther away (3.0 miles), but the average distance between them is 2.3 miles. Taking a detailed map of the same area today, we find that the distances between a dozen pairs of adjacent contemporary villages range from 1.4 to 3.0 miles, but the average is 2.38 miles. (This last statement is true only for continuous farmlands; much of the country is too hilly for farming.) The idea emerges that possibly the density of villages has remained approximately the same for 7000 years, an idea that needs to be tested by further archeological exploration.

There must, for each topographic and environmental region, be an optimum relationship between size of village and area of farmland. This relationship, as yet unstudied, would vary between plains, foothills, and mountains, but for the Jarmo foothills, the limiting factor is obviously not (as we had assumed it would be) the distance a man could walk to the farthest fields, do a long day's work, and return to the village at night. This distance would seem here not to be more than one and a half miles, straightline. In the higher mountains to the north and east, where arable land is sparse, a farmer may daily go twice this far or more to his fields as a matter of course.

Inspection of the report of the 1947 census for Iraq confirms our above discussion as to probable village size for the area here being considered. Villages in this census are not listed separately, but in the Nahiya of Chemchemal Center (the smallest political division for the area in which Jarmo lies) 64 villages are present, of which only 21 had a population over 200.[5] The total population of these 64 is 10,125, or an average of 158 persons per village. The remarkable closeness of this figure to the 150 persons we had already estimated for Jarmo is so striking that we must hasten to add that we were as surprised as anyone; we did not, as some might suspect, work from both directions toward a similar figure.

If we consider that these present-day Kurdish villages of the Nahiya of Chemchemal Center are generally 2.38 miles apart and have a mean population of 158 per village, we can easily calculate that each village would have 5.66 square miles, or 27.7 people per square mile. Putting the matter another way, each villager (man, woman, or child) is supported by 22.8 acres. Actually, due to soil-stripping and gullying, only a small part of the 22.8 acres is farmed in some parts of the Nahiya; conditions were undoubtedly better in these respects at the time of Jarmo.

Pursuing the matter somewhat further, we find the adjacent nahiyas of Agchalar and Sangao to have mean village sizes of 144 and 118, respectively; all three nahiyas, with a total village population of 25,842 in 185 villages (42 or 22.7% of them with more than 200 persons each), average 140 persons per village, which is again close to the 150 we had originally estimated for Jarmo. Since the three nahiyas have a total area of 943.7 square miles, the population density of village-farmers is 27.37 per square mile (2,737 per 100 square miles); each villager of these three nahiyas is supported by 23.38 acres (compare with the figure of 22.8 acres per person in the paragraph above, calculated on the basis of distances between villages picked at random).

If our data are even roughly valid, the somewhat tentative conclusion which we cautiously offer is that, for the Zagros foothills with which we are dealing, there has been no great population change during the last 7000 years. Once established and having reached a certain degree of efficiency, village-farming life would seem to have gone on with little basic change through all the turmoils of military and religious upheavals.

[5] We are aware of the possible or even probable errors in any Near Eastern village census (Crary, 1955), but the figures here quoted for the Chemchemal region seem reasonable to us in the light of our own experiences in the area.

The assumed beneficial results of technological improvements such as the use of the plow and steel sickle and the addition of sheep, cattle, and fowls to the domestic animals, have seemingly been offset by other factors. May these not be deforestation, soil deterioration, and soil erosion?

SUMER

Our third attempt at an evaluation of relations between environment and human populations brings us out of the dark of prehistory and into the barely lighter shadows of early written history (with no gain thereby on population data), to the middle of the third millennium B.C., some 4500 years ago.

Southern Mesopotamia, that was Sumer, otherwise the Land of the Two Rivers, is an alluvial geosyncline, between the lower reaches of the Tigris and Euphrates. It is a brutal desert land that is part marsh, a land with a miniscule of rain but heavy floods, a place of searing summer heat but chill winter mists.

It is a land that man must water to live, since the rainfall is scant and erratic, averaging but some four inches annually. Some years there may be no rain, but another time (as in December of 1954) the whole country-side is drowned by rain. In the spring the rivers flood and may overflow, to destroy all the crops as well as the irrigation system. Both rivers have made major changes in course within historic times; without the dykes that man has built they would by nature follow now one course, now many, changing often. It was actually this circumstance that allowed man to begin farming there, as he scattered his villages along the many inter-twining branches that were in a way natural canals.

The problem of the original settlement of southern Mesopotamia, which took place during the level of the village-farming community, ca. 4250 B.C., is not at issue here. Suffice it to say that the Sumerian city states began to appear ca. 3500 B.C. and are not only archeologically but historically well expressed by 2500 B.C.

The Sumerian city state of ca. 2500 B.C. may be pictured as a walled town, with its houses and walls built of sun-dried mud brick. Some meaner houses may simply have been of reed matting. The temple of the major city god stood near the center of the town, and most towns also had smaller temples for other gods as well.

There appears in some cases at least to have been open land and gardens within the walls; the market undoubtedly lay along the canal banks. The canals, which were quite local and not integrated as yet into any major system, were not only used for irrigation and navigation, but were also sources of fish and potable water. Outside the walls were the fields, probably reaching at most no more than a day's walk. It is doubt-ful if outlying villages (other than temporary reed shelters for harvesters, etc.) were a feature of the city state complex.

The archeologists concerned with Sumerian Mesopotamia have not thought generally to save primary evidence of the food eaten. For this knowledge we must turn to illustrations of grain and of the domestic animals (sheep, goats, and cattle) as pictured in representational art. Domestic pigs, although not so popular as an art form (Van Buren, 1939), were important as food-animals; at least pig bones were the most numerous in the one Sumerian site where the osteological remains have been salvaged and studied (Hilzheimer, 1941). The cuneiform writings are another source of information on daily life, including diet.

From these various sources we can determine that barley was the main food, with wheat the only other cereal of any importance. Grain was ground by hand into a bran or coarse flour, which perhaps was generally eaten as a mush and not baked into bread, although bread was also known. Beer was a standard item, the breweries being associated with the temples is part of their economic activity. Meat from cattle, sheep, and goats was unimportant in the daily diet of the people; sheep were kept for wool and milk was an important item of food, so probably wool and milk-producing animals were killed for food only when nonproductive otherwise. Pigs, as mentioned above, must have been eaten in considerable numbers; fish were probably the most important single protein food. Oil was derived from sesame seed. Garlic, onions, and other vegetables are mentioned, and for fruit they had dates, we know, and from these a wine was sometimes made. In spite of this diversity, the average farmer's family probably had a rather drab daily diet, with a high dependence on barley and a relatively low (although probably adequate) fat and protein intake. Actually, a stratified society was coming into being, and, as we know from the temple records, some classes got more rations than others.

The temples controlled the economic life, and thus the daily activity of the people, in considerable detail. Through their temples, the gods owned land and flocks, and collected taxes, a part of each crop. The master of the temple, in the name of the god, conscripted labor for maintenance of dykes, canals, and ditches; stored the grain for each year's food and for next year's planting; assigned land to be tilled or left fallow; specified the crop to be grown; and supervised the labor. Associated with the temple were a large number of special workmen of both sexes (including some slaves), who no longer tilled the land but were millers, weavers, brewers, scribes, metal-workers, carpenters, leather-workers, stone-cutters, etc., and overseers of various sorts.[6]

[6] If we seem to have dwelt overlong on general description of the Sumerian city states of *ca.* 2500 B.C., we could not do less in justice to the ecology of these people, which we reconstruct here from the evidences of archeology and the earliest cuneiform writings. The ecology of man is not a simple thing of his physical and biological environment, of the food available to him, of figures on rainfall and humidity. Human ecology embraces all of these plus the full range of human behavior and culture,

The intellectual and cultural achievements of the Sumerian city states of the mid-third millennium B.C. are rightly emphasized, but this importance does not necessarily imply a tremendous population, any more than the similar importance of Athens in the fourth century B.C. implies a tremendous population. Still, for ancient Sumer, the time is so long ago (romantic mists and all that), there is a blurring in many minds with later mighty empires of the same region (Babylonian, Assyrian, Sassanian, even Abbasid). There is a mental picture of vast temples, vast palaces, vast irrigation works, of a whole land industriously cultivated, of many great and splendid cities—the population must have been tremendous, a teeming of many millions!

The common estimates of 30 million for the population of southern Iraq during the "golden" period of the Abbasid Caliphate (750–1258 A.D.) are probably exaggerated, but such exaggerations are then easily pushed back into Sumerian times of more than 3000 years earlier, primarily because of the supposed similarity in extent and complexity of irrigation. Such an extent and complexity did not exist in Sumer, since no overall integrated irrigation system had been constructed at the time we are considering. Direct comparisons are not, therefore, valid in any way. Actually the population situation in Sumer was quite different, as we think the whole of southern Mesopotamia at that time supported no more than approximately half a million people.

It is not enough to realize that the city states were small (a town in a few-score square miles of farming-land), or that most of the cities themselves, as shown by archeological excavations, were no larger than many country towns of today. We need somewhat more exact data, and find them in the present-day walled town of Erbil in northern Iraq.

Erbil is the only really ancient city still occupying its original mounded site, still living atop all the layers of its urban ancestors. A Jarmo-like village may well lie at the base, with each successive stratum of history buried in turn until we find the modern thriving town atop them all. It is a very active living fossil, a very rare surviving type of the ancient walled mound-town.

The population that lives on the mound of Erbil is approximately 6000. From this figure, and knowing the area we have calculated that there are 213 people to the acre. This population density for Erbil may be taken as an upper limit in computing densities for the ancient towns of Sumer, in as much as there is no longer market, open land, or gardens on the Erbil mound. However, the market was not necessarily on the mound in the

including such non-biological (or are they?) factors as tools, cities, commerce, agriculture, government, religion, art, communications, and science. All of human ecology, as here considered, enters into consideration of population studies of any culture, but the relationships become more involved (as witness today's population studies) as the cultures become more complex.

ancient cities either, although considerable economic (and thus space-consuming) activities did center around the temple. Too, the mosque of present-day Erbil is probably relatively smaller than the typical temple of a mid-third millennium Sumerian city. We will, therefore, decrease our maximal estimate to 200 persons per acre, and regard it as indicative of population density for the inhabited portion of any Near Eastern walled town, whether for Erbil or ancient Sumer. If this figure is too high, then our final estimate of Sumerian population will also be too high.

Having done this, above, we found that Frankfort (*1950*) had attacked the same problem in a different way. From the excavations in three Sumerian cities he knew, he measured house-sizes, estimated the number of people per house, and counted the houses per acre. If he calculated six persons per house, the result is 120 persons per acre, but if he estimated ten per house, it is 200, the latter our figure exactly. (Ten persons per house is, of course, a higher house-hold number than we had previously considered true for an agricultural village, but Frankfort emphasized that he measured "moderately sized houses" in which one would expect to find servants and possibly relatives.) Frankfort then considered modern Aleppo and Damascus, where, from census figures, he calculated 160 persons per acre. (He also figured and discussed the mound of Erbil, as we do, and for the same reasons, but he did not know its population.) It is our opinion that Aleppo and Damascus, not being walled towns today, are not as densely packed as were the ancient towns and as is Erbil, and so it is our inclination to retain our figure of 200 per acre. However—and here lies the difficulty of population studies based on most archeological work—no Sumerian town has been excavated completely; instead they have rather been nibbled at. Thus, and primarily due to lack of finances, the sampling has been inadequate; we do not know for any Sumerian town the ratio of dwelling area to non-dwelling area.

Frankfort gave population estimates on four Sumerian cities which had been partially excavated; we checked him in detail on two of these. For Khafaje we agreed with Frankfort's figure (12,000 people) almost exactly, but for Tello, or Lagash, our figure was more than three times that of Frankfort's (19,000). We were confused until Delougaz told us, as he had also told Frankfort, that no more than one-third of the area within the walls was occupied by dwellings at any one time. We concluded at this instant that population studies of ancient Sumer were to be based more on knowledge gained from personal experience than on that gleaned from published reports.

To make this long story somewhat shorter, we conceded that Frankfort knew the local situations for the four cities he was considering; at 200 persons per occupied acre, these four would average approximately 17,000. We honestly confess that we do not know whether or not such a figure has any real meaning, but, considering that there were probably never more than twenty city states in Sumer at any one time (T. Jacobsen, *personal communication*) we would arrive at a figure of somewhere around 350,-000. Certainly no such figure should ever be quoted, as, after all our calculations, we can have no real faith in its validity, since our statistics are admittedly mystical. We have, indeed, in arriving at such a figure, not considered some of the larger cities such as Kish and Uruk (Warka), which might swell the total, nor have we considered that a number of small and possibly unknown towns have not been included.

Our advisers on things Sumerian (Jacobsen and Adams) "feel" happier with a population figure of approximately half a million for mid-third millennium Sumer. We do not know of any reason to disagree with them. We asked an archeologist from Georgia who knew nothing of all this, but many years ago had had one season's excavation in southern Iraq, what he thought the population of ancient Sumer was. Without hesitation he answered, "About half a million." If we had only asked him in the first place, we could have saved ourselves several days of work and worry.

We measure the total area of mid-third millenium Sumer at 10,235 square miles (26,625 sq. km.), using a map of ancient sites published by the Government of Iraq, Directorate-General of Antiquities. Not all of this land was farmed, of course; much of it was marsh and desert, but until we know from future research something of the actual extent of each city state, we cannot compute area farmed, or calculate the number of acres necessary to support an individual. However, on the basis of the above estimates (using 500,000 population), the population density of all of Sumer would have been 49.83 people per square mile (4983 per 100 square miles), or 12.9 acres of farm- and waste-land per person.

7

SURVEY AND SITE RECOGNITION

At this point the focus shifts from what archaeologists find out by excavation to the way in which they start collecting field data. This chapter concerns techniques of discovering archaeological sites.

The techniques of site survey employed in different terrain or settlement areas may be infinitely varied, while the objectives of the survey may be limited to several broad categories. At the simplest level, the mere desire to ascertain whether a given region, a blank spot on the archaeological map, contains evidence of prehistoric occupation often leads to the formulation of specific problems. Such problems may be connected, for example, with migrational or settlement patterns, with cultural relationships between prehistoric groups, or even with economic or ecological aspects of one group. The problems may have obtruded or suggested themselves earlier, and the archaeological resources of an area are then examined with an eye toward collecting data to test a previously considered theory.

The survey may be expected to disclose information primarily on the basis of surface evidence, pottery or broken tool fragments, for example, or on surface evidence plus that taken from exploratory or test pits. On the other hand, it may be the necessary preliminary to the solution of problems which must involve intensive excavation at a future date.

In any problem the following factors are important:

1. A thorough knowledge of all the previous archaeological or ethnographical data published or otherwise available for the area under consideration. The historical background of a now vanished group may be gained either from earlier ethnographic or historical studies or from contact with local inhabitants, perhaps ancestors of the aborigines, or early

186

settlers from other regions. Even if the local residents, of whatever an-
cestry, have only vague memories of the early historic conditions, they
may know something about occupation sites as landmarks or as aspects
of antiquarian tradition.

2. Knowledge of both the present and prehistoric physiographic or
geographic conditions of the area surveyed. Such knowledge is often of
immeasurable value in interpreting cultural manifestations even in areas
which have not previously been studied with specific cultural problems in
mind.

3. The ability of the archaeologist to recognize and identify prehistoric
sites when no informants are available and when there are no previous
studies to be used as general guides.

In the surveys described in the following selections one or another of
these factors is always present. The details of the field techniques vary.
Thus Willey employs aerial photographs to spot the sites before actual
physical investigation in the field; Phillips, Ford, and Griffin use an auto-
mobile, Meggers and Evans a dugout canoe. Beals, Brainerd, and Smith
proceed on foot from a base camp. Each of the modes of transportation
used was thought to be the one best adapted to obtain information on
the location and nature of prehistoric settlements.

Mounds in the Plain of Antioch

R. J. Braidwood, while conducting a survey for the Oriental Institute of the
University of Chicago, evidently had little trouble in identifying the large number of mounds in the Plain of Antioch, in the Near East, as archaeological sites.
Nevertheless, as will be seen in the following description,[1] great care was exercised in learning details about each location and in collecting the surface
artifacts so that a meaningful chronology might be derived from their analysis.

Since a survey of the type represented in this volume has not often been
done in the Near East, a word may be added to put on record the
methodology employed. The field map was made from the "État Major"
maps and the cadastral maps. . . . Fortunately most of the larger
mounds could be accurately located on the field map from the cadastral
sheets, and concrete bench marks which the Travaux du Cadastre had
set on the located mounds could then be used in the field as known points
from which to make observations with the compass. The position of any
mound which did not appear on the maps was fixed by taking compass
bearings on it from two or three known points and plotting these on the

[1] R. J. Braidwood, *Mounds in the Plain of Antioch: An Archaeological Survey*,
Oriental Institute Publications, University of Chicago, Chicago, 1937, vol. 48, pp. 3–4.
By permission of the Director of the Oriental Institute.

field map with the aid of a protractor. The compass used was of the Brunton type, with a light tripod.

It was not deemed necessary to measure the size of individual mounds. They are described as "large" if they approach the size of Catal Huyuk, which is approximately the largest in the plain, being about 400 meters long, 250 meters wide and 30 meters high, or "small" if they are no larger than Tell Dhahab, which is a little round mound no more than about 25 meters in diameter. Anyone who is interested in excavation and wishes more exact measurements will, we assume, visit the plain himself to inspect the mounds.

The field party was composed of the writer, our head foreman Abdullah, two of the more intelligent workmen, who knew the plain well and spoke Turkish and Kurdish as well as Arabic, and several boys, who assisted in picking up sherds. Natives who lived near a given mound were questioned as to the name or names of the mound, their ideas of what the names meant, whether any other names were once in use, and whether the antiquities were known to have come from the site. The natives would usually assist in picking up potsherds.

The collection of sherds from the surface is best done during the winter or late fall, when the grass has dried up and blown away and the rains have washed out a new crop of sherds. However, many of the mounds in the plain are inaccessible at that time on account of floods and bad roads. Because of this and the force of other circumstances, it was necessary to make the survey in the late spring. Each collector was given a sack and told to collect all the sherds he could find, regardless of the size or type of fragment. This is necessary, as there is a natural tendency to pick up only painted wares and rim sherds, and a number of meaningful cooking wares and burnished wares may easily be missed. The slopes and the talus of a mound usually gave the greatest yield, but in many cases there were open cuts and gullies which were rich in sherds. Such cuts are valuable, though they tend to make the particular periods represented in them appear over-important in comparison with the periods represented by sherds from other parts of the mounds. When the party returned to the expedition house, the sherds were washed and then sorted, and notes were made as to the periods represented in terms of the ceramic chronology of Tell al-Judaidah.

It was also necessary to note in the field the approximate size and form of each mound, its apparent water supply, whether it is now occupied by a native village, and whether there is an extrusion of fortification walls or other architectural features. Masonry extrusions were found only on mounds near the foothills, where there is a natural supply of stone at hand; out in the plain, however, the mounds have been denuded of stone by the natives.

Site Survey in Arizona

In northeastern Arizona, identification of sites is not as easy as the recognition and plotting of mounds on the Antioch plain, though often ruins of architectural features do serve to place sites. Beals, Brainerd, and Smith, engaging in archaeological survey and excavation with the Rainbow Bridge-Monument Valley Expedition during the years 1933–38, were interested in sites of whatever description, even modest ones which might be identified by the presence of only a few potsherds and soil darkened by charcoal. Their basic aim, like Braidwood's, was to collect ceramic material systematically in order to use it as the foundation of a regional chronology.[2]

Although the membership and direction of the site survey differed in the various years, the general method was uniform. Most of this work was carried on from the Tsegi Canyon camps. Each morning one or more small parties would leave camp on foot to survey a definitely defined area. The group was always led by an experienced archaeologist and might consist of from two to six men. The ideal was to cover every square yard of ground so thoroughly that no prehistoric remains could possibly be overlooked. The group leader usually assigned to each man a particular portion of the area, himself remaining in a position within call of the others. Each man carried a number of blank "site cards," printed forms on which pertinent data relative to each site discovered could be entered. He also carried a set of small cloth sacks and paper bags, for the purpose of collecting and carrying sherds, and perhaps a camera and a compass.

Because of the nature of the terrain it was usually expedient for one man to cover the valley floor, another the sand dunes against the sandstone cliffs, a third the relatively level bench which usually exists along the uppermost stratum of the Wingate sandstone, and a fourth the talus at the foot of the higher Navajo sandstone. This position enabled each man to remain about on one level with a minimum of scrambling up and down, and also permitted the entire group to progress forward in a fairly uniform front. Of course local conditions frequently required alterations in this formation.

Whenever any member of the surveying party came upon a prehistoric site, as evidenced by the presence of potsherds, flint chips, masonry remains, or charcoal concentrations, he immediately made a collection of sherds and worked flint from the surface and painted a site number on a rock as nearly the center of the site as feasible. Usually the group leader went to each site located and entered descriptive field notes on a standard

[2] Ralph L. Beals, George W. Brainerd, and Watson Smith, *Archaeological Studies in Northeast Arizona*, University of California Publications in American Archaeology and Ethnology, Berkeley and Los Angeles, 1945, vol. 44, no. 1, pp. 7–9. By permission of University of California Press.

site card. Less frequently this was done by the man finding the site. Usually a sketch plan and often a photograph were also made, especially if there were notable architectural features.

At the end of the day the site cards and sherd collections were taken back to camp. Either at the local camp, or later at the Marsh Pass base camp, all site cards were copied in duplicate on a typewriter. All sherds were washed in plain water to remove all mud and earth, next in a dilute muriatic acid to remove lime deposits, and finally in a baking-soda solution to neutralize the acid. After the sherds had thoroughly dried, the appropriate site number was either written on each sherd with India ink or stamped with a rubber stamp. The collection was then resacked or boxed in sealed cartons and stored, pending its final shipment to the Expedition's permanent laboratory. In addition to the washing and cataloguing, a preliminary attempt was made to reconstruct broken vessels from sherds, whenever this appeared possible. As has been said, the cartographers worked in collaboration with the archaeologists, and each site was spotted on the map as soon as possible after its discovery.

Site Survey on the North Pacific Coast

In the preceding surveys, as may be seen, the concern was not so much with the sites as with the surface collections. Information given by local inhabitants was of course valuable, but not absolutely necessary. The chief factors involved were scrupulous care and systematic recording, with a well-defined problem, chronology largely based on sherd collections, immediately at hand.

In some areas, where surface collection is not feasible, for example, where materials such as potsherds are not present or easily perceived on the surface of the site, the natives of the country must be pressed into service in order to begin the survey. Thus Drucker, on the American Northwest Coast, outlines his goal and proceeds to attack the problem by sample excavation.[3]

The aim of the survey was to apply the direct historical approach to the regional archaeology, testing sites which on historic or other evidence were known to have been inhabited during historic times, to define if possible the historic and protohistoric horizons, and to set the stage for linking them with, or distinguishing them from, the prehistoric cultures of the area. It was found that the coast sites lend themselves exceptionally well to this method, for because of their considerable size many of them reveal a series of levels underlying the historic ones (identifiable through the occurrence of contact goods of various sorts) which by reason of their depth must have been laid down in prehistoric times. Conditions are thus

[3] Philip Drucker, *Archeological Survey on the Northern Northwest Coast*, Smithsonian Institution, Bureau of American Ethnology, Washington, D.C., 1943, Bulletin 133, pp. 24, 25, 62. By permission of the Smithsonian Institution.

extremely favorable for checking possibilities of culture stratigraphy or change. . . .

An attempt to apply the direct historical approach to a new archaeological field ordinarily must be based on the records of the period of early European contacts, utilizing them to determine tribal distributions and to identify sites. For the Northwest Coast, however, historic records are less essential, though of unquestionable value as a check and guide, because of the fact that the native cultures there persisted little modified much longer than in many other parts of the New World. The nature and effects of European contacts on the Northwest Coast differed markedly from those in other areas. The chief difference lies in the fact that there have been no major populational movements, voluntary or enforced, since earliest historic times. Despite the steady numerical decrease of population and the tendency for survivors of decimated groups to assemble in central or stronger villages, the sites of early historic times (and many of them go well back into the prehistoric period) are not only still known and occasionally utilized, but are also considered the property of the rightful heirs of the past occupants. Most of these sites in British Columbia have been set aside by the Canadian Government as Indian Reserves. Consequently the identification of historic horizons with ethnically known groups does not constitute anywhere near as difficult a problem as in the Plains or the Southeast. Any tolerably well-informed modern native can tell to what ethnic group, and what division within the group, a given site belongs; indeed, he can ordinarily point out a number of the older people who were born there . . .

In the following pages, archaeologic sites located during the survey of Coast Tsimshian and Kwakiutl territory in 1938 are described. The methods used in the reconnaissance were as follows: Each site found was located on a chart of the district, and a site-card was made out for it, recording the following information: site designation, chart reference, location, water supply, type of deposit, length, width, height, house remains visible, burials, plant cover, owned by, mapped, photo, remarks, date.

Sites to be tested were trenched, laying out the test pits to cut across the edge of an historic house, where traces of these could be seen. Artifacts recovered from the tests were located as to vertical position, and in the case of cuts made partly in the sloping face of the midden (for drainage) the horizontal distance from a fixed datum was also recorded. During the latter part of the survey it was found very helpful to note also the matrix in which the artifact lay, as a check on depth measurements, which are sometimes difficult to make accurately in deep pits and ones put down from sloping or uneven surfaces. This makes it possible to locate every artifact precisely on the trench profiles. All these data were recorded by means of artifact slips of the type used by the University of California archaeologic surveys. Most of the digging was done with shovels, scraping the bottom of the trench, then shoveling out the dirt thus piled up. It was thus possible to uncover most of the artifacts without disturbing them. Want of time and somewhat low artifact yield prevented use of trowels as the chief tools. Faunal remains recovered were kept in foot level bags. After completion of each cut, profiles were drawn, vertical measurements from top to bottom being taken at 3- or 4-foot intervals. The dip of various layers was read off with a Brunton compass. Samples were taken of the various layers. The point at which each sample was taken was noted on the profile, as a check. A sketch map was then made of the site with a Brunton [surveyor's compass] and tape.

Site Survey in the Tropical Forest

The Amazonian jungle is obviously a different sort of area to search for archaeological sites than arid Arizona or the coast of British Columbia. A clear statement of site survey techniques in the tropical jungle comes from the recent report by Meggers and Evans,[4] a husband-and-wife research team. The reader may wish to compare this account with that of Drucker and Contreras (1953) who surveyed in the Tabasco and Veracruz jungle of southeastern Mexico.

PROBLEMS AND COMPROMISES IN FIELD TECHNIQUE

Archeology in the tropical forest of South America presents, in addition to the usual problems, many difficulties that are not encountered in the more arid or more accessible parts of the New World. Manuals of field procedure and precision methods of excavation technique frequently cannot be followed, and the field situation must be met with an understanding of what is pertinent and what is unprofitable in order to gain the maximum of information in the shortest possible time. Otherwise, one could easily spend a full year in the field and have very little to show for it. This we learned, however, only by experience. For the benefit of those who may follow us, we will outline briefly some of the major problems and compromises.

Evans, who had recently returned from 9 months of fieldwork on the coast of Peru, superintended the assembling of the field equipment. We included all those items that had been essential or helpful in the work and some of these proved to be even more important in the tropical environment, particularly specimen bags of unbleached muslin, and duplicate sets of field notes. In the hope that aerial photographs might reveal the location of the Marajoara mounds as they do ruins on the coast of Peru, we secured permission to examine those taken of Marajó Island by the United States Air Force, going to some difficulty since they were still classified as

[4] B. J. Meggers and C. Evans, *Archeological Investigations at the Mouth of the Amazon*, Smithsonian Institution, Bureau of American Ethnology, 1957, Bulletin 167, pp. 6–11. By permission of the Smithsonian Institution.

"confidential." The results were highly disappointing because the forest growth obliterated all but the most abrupt and extreme alterations in the terrain. Later, after experience on the ground and in low elevation flights over the savanna and jungle, we became fully convinced that aerial photography has nothing to offer as a means of locating archeological sites in the Amazon area. However, we derived one important benefit from the aerial survey of the Amazon. As a result of this work, the Aeronautical Chart Service of the United States Army Air Force has been able to revise and correct its World Aeronautical Charts to such a degree of accuracy that when on the ground we could follow each bend and curve of all but the smallest streams. From the standpoint of a more useful scale for groundwork, the Aeronautical Chart Service made available the Preliminary Work Sheets, Scale 1:500,000, from which the final copies of the World Aeronautical Charts, Scale 1:1,000,000, are made. Not only did these maps save us considerable time and trouble, but they gave a degree of accuracy to the site locations and the geographical features of the area that otherwise could not have been attained.

In addition to these excellent maps, we took along surveying equipment, such as a plane table and tripod, alidade, and stadia rod, on the assumption these materials would be useful in the mapping of each archeological site. Two weeks in the field demonstrated that not only was it impossible to carry this equipment, but also it was completely nonfunctional for several reasons: (1) Generally, the sites were not large enough or with enough surface features to warrant the use of the alidade and plane table; (2) to sight a line through vegetation required a cutting operation that was not economically feasible or practical; (3) a sufficiently accurate map could be obtained with greater ease and in less time with grid paper, a compass, a tape, and a hand level. In other words, we made a compromise in technique here because if we had not done so we would have had to sacrifice results in terms of the number of sites we could examine and we are convinced that a site map so derived would show no more pertinent information than is now available on our various plans.

Field technique must be adaptable to the situation so that the most scientific data can be obtained under the peculiar local circumstances. To demonstrate the point, it is pertinent to mention why we used the system of sinking several small strata cuts, generally 1.5 by 1.5 meters, into various sections of the site instead of digging a long trench or a larger, single strata cut. Again, the site situation is the determining factor. In all the sites of the Tropical Forest level of culture the accumulation of refuse is too shallow to make it essential to dig a large cut to provide sufficient space to throw out the dirt as the cut increases in depth. The nature of the refuse makes it more functional to place several small cuts in various parts of a site in order to test more of the occupation zone. Trenches are not feasible because of the quantity of trees and their root systems that cover most sites. A series of small cuts can be finished in a limited time going from the surface to sterile [base], whereas a larger excavation might not reach completion in the time available at certain sites. The question has been raised as to why we did not trench the large Marajoara mounds in two directions. Our answer is threefold: (1) Property owners were extremely hesitant to allow any digging in their mounds because they offer the only high ground for their cattle during the wet season and also because they do not want their "treasure" disturbed. Permission to dig even small test holes was difficult to obtain and permission to trench the mounds would never have been granted. (2) Sufficient labor for extensive trenching activities was not available at any cost. (3) Scientifically speaking, it was far more important to test several sites than restrict ourselves by extensive excavation on one site. This approach has permitted us to evaluate and interpret more extensive digging conducted earlier by Farabee and others.

For those who have not had the fortune or misfortune, depending on one's viewpoint, to work in Amazon archeology, the tremendous problem created by roots cannot be overemphasized. Although the cuts were laid out originally with square sides, the first layer of digging always produced roots that often caused a slight modification of shape; however, the area covered in each cut was always well controlled. Not only was it impossible to polish the walls of strata cuts, but if they had been polished they would have shown no details. The intense rainfall, high humidity, and easily leached soil take out any materials that would make a clear-cut line of strata distinguishable on the walls of cuts. In the artificial mounds of the Marajoara Phase, soil conditions did vary and here it was possible to smooth the walls of the cut sufficiently to plot the various features. In all the other sites the excavation technique was careful and well controlled, but not carried to the point of diminishing returns by trying to follow out preconceived ideas that no strata cut is properly executed unless the ritual of polishing and smoothing is faithfully carried out. In other words, the entire excavation technique in Amazon archeology can be summarized in a few words: not once was technique abandoned because of lack of interest, nor was it modified to the extent that the data obtained would be unreliable; but it was necessary at all times to be realistic about technique and to apply the method to the peculiar local situation that would bring results, rather than blindly become a slave to technique irrespective of the total results.

Rain and humidity create problems that can only be appreciated if one has tried to work in a tropical forest situation in part of the rainy season. Granted, we stayed in Belém classifying our materials at the height of the rainy season, but some of the fieldwork had to be conducted during this part of the year. Tarpaulins were used to cover the excavations to keep them from filling with water during a downpour, but even then we were digging in mud. Survey trips in dugouts up streams and rivers, going from intense sun one hour to a heavy shower the next, made it difficult to keep notes and photographic equipment dry. Cameras and film had to be kept in air-tight cans dehydrated with silica gel. The intense rainfall in the Amazon not only creates physical hazards that restrict the work and actually makes it impossible to undertake archeological fieldwork during February, March, and April, but it reduces the archeological evidence to objects of stone or pottery. Postholes, matting, thatching, and other details of house construction are so quickly destroyed by decay that unless the posts burned (apparently an extremely rare situation) there is absolutely no evidence of such features. Proof of this factor is easily obtained by digging on the site of a former *caboclo* house where the exact position is known. If over 5 years have passed, the area has passed into secondary growth, posts and postholes have disappeared, all decayed vegetable matter has been leached out or washed away and except for areas darkened with charcoal or ashes there is no sign of the occupation other than occasional broken artifacts. Bone materials destroy rapidly even in secondary urn burials. Except in those urns in which the water supply was constant (in other words the jar broke and was filled by rain or by seepage and remained moist throughout the dry season) or where the urn and its lid had kept the contents constantly dry, bone has turned to dust, usually distinguishable only as fine white flecks in light gray to black soil. The few bone scraps we were able to salvage were in extremely poor condition and had to be treated with a dehydrating agent mixed with a stabilizing cement, such as acetone and duco or acetone and ambroid.

None of the problems and compromises mentioned so far have been dictated by another situation inherent in the Amazon area, one that has a decided effect on the method of carrying out the fieldwork—the lack of modern transportation facilities and the sparse population. In spite of all the modern mechanical aids to mankind, one is reduced to the necessity of utilizing the primitive, local means of transportation. More than once after a slow and difficult dugout trip we wished for an outboard motor, but there were many other situations in which paddling in a dugout was 100 percent more practical than traveling by outboard motor. To use motors it is necessary to haul all the gasoline from a main base and establish caches of fuel. To do this would involve organization and planning of supplies that would be more time consuming and frustrating in the long run than the use of local transportation. By taking advantage of the larger sailboats, sailboats with auxiliary motors, or launches to traverse some of the longer distances, traveling light when going by dugout, and depositing our collections and main equipment at various bases, we were able to reach all areas fairly easily. Those who have never traveled in the interior of the Amazon, along the smaller streams where only a hunter, wood cutter, or rubber cutter might live, sometimes find it difficult to understand the importance of the dugout as a means of transporation. Not only is it a sturdy craft, capable of taking a lot of punishment from submerged debris, but it is quite stable, easy to propel, and will hold a fairly large load. Nevertheless, in archeology more than once we had to keep in mind the fact that, although we went "empty handed" to a site except for a few digging tools, specimen bags, and photographic equipment, we always returned laden down with sherds. This is not to say that we *now* feel that our final results have suffered as a result of the limitation of transportation (after completion of the study, we have only one site that we feel could be better interpreted with another day's work), but several times we had to take into consideration the fact that another bag of surface material or another test excavation would be out of the question because of the lack of hands to carry the resulting sherds back to the dugout, or because the waterline of the dugout would be lowered below the margin of safety. Archeology in the Amazon is not like that of areas of the world where one can drive to the site, load the car down, and then drive back again if necessary.

Fortunately, the cultures are simple, the sites are small, and a maximum of data can be secured with a minimum of digging. The problem of labor in the Amazon is much more severe than in many other parts of the New World. Most of the people live by working on cattle ranches, cutting wood, gathering rubber, or by hunting. Miles and miles of rivers and streams can be traveled without seeing any human habitation. Local labor is consequently not available in quantity. If one had the financial resources to buy a boat large enough to house a crew of men and to transport food for this crew, then labor could be brought from Belém to the interior. However, this is not practical for many reasons. The expense of such a project would be prohibitive on the budget of most New World archeological expeditions; the laborers would not be familiar with the local situation and it would still be necessary to hire local guides; permission from landowners to trespass with such a large crew would not be easy to obtain; transportation of such a large crew to more remote sites would overtax the available facilities. As a result of this acute labor shortage and the necessity of constantly changing guides as we moved from one area to another, we found ourselves doing a larger part of the actual excavation work than would normally be expected. Only during the first month on Marajó did we have the same workmen long enough for us to train them to work in a strata cut. Otherwise the guide went hunting or dug in another part of the site for sherds to increase the sample from the site. In the long run, however, such a system means that one does not have to question the data when analysis might suggest inadequate or careless excavation technique that can so often be blamed on an inexperienced crew.

Looking back on the Amazon situation and having the benefit of a second tropical forest expedition behind us before writing this introduction, we believe we have found the equipment best suited for South American tropical forest archeology, as well as developed the ability to travel light with a minimum of unessential equipment but with a maximum of protection for such things as cameras, exposed film, notes, etc. In spite of this we still have no general solution for the problems of transportation. Regardless of how much planning is done before hand or how much money one has available, there is no way to avoid traveling by foot, by horse, by bullock, by dugout, and by sailboat, even though occasionally the airplane, jeep, truck, car, outboard motor or launch may be thrown in for the sake of variety. In other words, the local situation frequently cannot be predicted. One might carry an outboard motor and gasoline for weeks and then discover that the local conditions of a particular stream make use of the motor impossible, and paddling a dugout the only resort.

There is one universal fact, however, and that is the contribution of the local guide to the success of South American tropical forest archeology. This guide is essential and invaluable not only because of his knowledge of the location of sites along a specific stream and in the adjoining area, because of his hospitality, his ability to obtain extra fish and game to supplement the food supply, and the use of his thatched shelter as a base, but also from the standpoint of his intimate knowledge of the local customs, the local problems, the local geographic features, and most of all for his ability to arrange for an extra helper, a dugout, an extra set of paddles or whatever else might be needed. A good guide can anticipate the archeologist's requirements and make archeology in the Amazon more than just hard work.

Survey in the Lower Mississippi Valley

In regions where roads allow surveying with automobiles as the chief mode of transportation, large areas may be covered with relative ease. In the Lower Mississippi Valley, Phillips, Ford, and Griffin were faced with the problem of covering a huge area where mobility was a most important factor. The skillful way in which this survey was conceived and executed is given considerable space here because it demonstrates how closely the survey is involved with a definite goal, that is, how every action aims toward the solution of the previously determined problem.[5]

There is a general agreement among students of Southeastern archaeology that the climax of the late prehistoric cultures is the archaeological

[5] P. Phillips, J. A. Ford, and J. B. Griffin, *Archaeological Survey in the Lower Mississippi Alluvial Valley, 1940–1947*, Papers of the Peabody Museum, Harvard University, Cambridge, 1951, vol. 25, pp. 39–43. By permission of J. O. Brew, Director of the Peabody Museum, Harvard University.

facies long recognized under the designation "Middle Mississippi." At a comparatively late date—A.D. 1400–1500 is probably not too late for its peak of development—this culture type was firmly established over an immense area. The large prehistoric settlements represented by the remains at Cahokia, Moundville, Etowah, and Macon, not to mention some of the less-known but equally impressive sites described in the present work, are thought to have been occupied about this time, or even later. By 1939, when the present Survey was first discussed, an immense amount of data on Middle Mississippi had accumulated, but the problem of its origins and development appeared to be as far from resolution as ever. There was a general impression, shared by many students of Southeastern culture, that this was because the "central" Mississippi Valley, the assumed center of distribution of the culture, had not been sufficiently investigated. It was primarily to make good this lack that the present Survey was undertaken.

The existing status of archaeological studies in what we have defined elsewhere as the Survey Area was such as to make it a very attractive field for research. Except for the University of Chicago's work at Kincaid and other sites in southern Illinois, the investigations sponsored by the St. Louis Academy of Science in southeastern Missouri, and excavations by the University of Tennessee at the Shelby Site, in the vicinity of Memphis, Tennessee, none of which had been published, the area had been largely untouched by modern methods of investigation.

To understand this apparent neglect, it is necessary to review briefly some of the earlier work in the area. From the earliest beginnings of what used to be called "Mound Archaeology" it received its full share of attention. Private collectors were busy as early as the seventies and the Peabody Museums of Harvard and Yale, the Davenport Academy of Sciences, and the Bureau of American Ethnology of the Smithsonian Institution soon followed. The long series of investigations of the latter culminated in the publication of Thomas' monumental report of 1894 (Thomas, 1894) and Holmes' monograph on the pottery in 1903 (Holmes, 1903) both of which gave a great deal of space to the archaeology of the area. Thomas' problem may be summed up in the question: "Were the Mound-builders Indians?" Consequently, the Bureau's investigators, under his direction, gave particular emphasis to mounds, enclosures, and other features of a constructional nature. Their reports provide invaluable data on such features, many of which have since disappeared, and all of which have been altered almost beyond recognition, but in questions involving the analysis of culture materials, particularly pottery, they contributed very little. Holmes' great treatise went far to make up the deficiency, and it is to this remarkable pioneer effort that we owe the term, "Middle Mississippi." It is important to remember that as used by Holmes, it was a broad typological concept applied to pottery alone. So far as our particular area is concerned, it has remained just that. The large-scale excavations and comparative studies necessary to convert that concept into a culture context have not been started. The latter investigations of Peabody, Moore, Brown, Lemley, Dickinson and Dellinger, had, except for the last three named, been concerned almost entirely with burials and their associated artifacts. A mass of material, chiefly ceramic, was saved from the commercial pothunter, whose activities in this area have been unremitting, and is now moldering on museum shelves. Not unnaturally, the misconception arose that the field has been fully exploited through all this effort, professional and otherwise. Nothing could be farther from the truth. It so happens that in the Lower Mississippi Valley profusion of burial offerings is a late development characteristic of the Mississippian cultures, but not of the earlier cultures that preceded them. In planning the Survey, we had to accept the melancholy conclusion that accumulated materials were mostly late and therefore of little use in solving the questions we were interested in, but we could take heart from the circumstances that few of the earlier sites in the area had been disturbed. Pothunters had shied away from them in disgust, and professional archaeologists often followed their example. The problem, therefore, was not primarily that of securing with better methods more material of the sort already obtained, but of securing material that had not been obtained at all. We have been accused of coming in as outsiders and "skimming the cream" of the archaeology of the region. The metaphor is imprecise. The cream, in the sense of the topmost layer, had long ago been skimmed and safely removed to the collector's shelves. It was the less attractive but far more important material that lay underneath that we were after.

This brings us again to what we may call the main Survey problem. We have spoken of the desirability of investigating Middle Mississippi on what was assumed to be its home ground in the hope that some light might be thrown upon its antecedents. These, it could be assumed, lay in a period dominated elsewhere by cultures of Hopewell-Marksville affinity. Originally recognized as a specialized development in the Ohio Valley, by 1939 the fundamental nature and wide distribution of this earlier culture type was beginning to be appreciated. Its known limits had been so widened as to include almost the entire Southeast, using the term in its broadest sense, and as a result, the Survey area appeared as central rather than peripheral to the distribution. Marksville-type pottery had been reported by Lemley and Dickinson in 1937 from sites on Bayou Macon in southwestern Arkansas and by Ford in 1936 from sites in the lower part of the Yazoo Basin. In the northern part of the Survey Area, however, north of the Arkansas River, no signs of this culture had as yet been found. We had every reason to expect them, and may anticipate here by stating that they appeared on the first sites investigated in the spring of 1940. Thus, on the first day in the field, the Survey problem shifted from the general one of putting a floor under Middle Mississippi to the more specific one of the relationship between Middle Mississippi and an earlier Hopewellian culture, to which we gave the provisional name of Baytown, and it has remained there ever since.

With a slight foreknowledge of the abundance of sites in the Mississippi Alluvial Valley, the writers approached the project in the winter of 1939–40 with a long-range point of view, which needless to say did not take into account the imminence of a second world war. The plan, insofar as it was formulated, envisaged three stages of work: (1) preliminary site survey and analysis of surface collections; (2) stratigraphic tests on a large number of sites; (3) small-scale excavations on key sites, selected on the basis of the results of (1) and (2). . . . In terms of the Mississippi River Commission grid, we have so far covered with unequal thoroughness 49 out of 171 quadrangles included within the area we have somewhat brashly designated as the Survey Area. In so doing we have catalogued 385 sites, the majority of which have not been heretofore referred to in print. Twenty stratigraphic tests have been carried out on 11 sites, 18 of which were sufficiently successful to warrant description in this report. Stage 3, that of site excavation, remains in the status of hopeful planning for a non-foreseeable future.

SURVEY METHODS

It should be thoroughly understood that a complete archaeological survey, of the sort now in progress in many states, was never contemplated. Our catalogue of sites makes no pretense of completeness. The object was merely an adequate sampling of sites, sufficient to provide a safe coverage of the area and to insure against the omission of any significant cultural manifestation. This looks well on paper but is actually difficult to carry into practice. Deliberate avoidance of sites, particularly large and fruitful ones, requires a scientific rigor which the writers cannot claim to possess. It is inevitable, therefore, that our sample is weighted somewhat on the side of larger and more conspicuous sites. It must also be pointed out that this crude sampling method of reconnaissance, combined with certain conditions of the archaeology itself, notably the paucity of stone "workshop" sites and shell heaps, is unfavorable to the finding of early pre-ceramic manifestations, though we know from stratigraphic excavations that such existed in the area.

The general procedure in the first season (spring, 1940) was to establish headquarters in a town affording reasonable accommodation and work out from there within practicable limits, using both cars for reconnaissance, with the idea of getting a large sampling of sites and as much surface pottery as possible for purposes of preliminary classification. Temptations to get busy with shovels were ruthlessly suppressed. In subsequent trips, where two vehicles were available, as in the spring of 1941 and 1946, one was fitted up for excavation while the other carried on the Survey. It was, however, at all times a strictly motorized reconnaissance. Only rarely were attempts made to run down reported sites that could not be reached by car, or at least by jeep, and these were almost invariably unsuccessful. We made an effort to traverse all public roads and as many private roads as were passable, and thus managed to view from a reasonable distance practically all the cultivated land, which, in the flood-plain sections is practically equivalent to all the land that would have been suitable for Indian occupation and a great deal more besides. The term "reasonable distance" perhaps requires some explanation. In the cultivated portions of the flood plain a site with mounds or midden accumulations, however small, is generally visible from a considerable distance. This is the way the great majority of sites were located. A large number, of course, were found on information picked up along the roadside at the cost of innumerable coca-colas and some indigestion. If there are mounds in the neighborhood, everybody knows about them; in fact, almost everybody has dug into them. The presence of pottery and stone fragments, even where no mounds are present, is likewise a matter of common observation in this stoneless land. Other sites, and this applies to fairly large mound groups, were found by studying contours on the excellent Mississippi River Commission maps, and a few sites are actually designated as "Indian Mounds" on these maps. Our indebtedness to interested local students of archaeology has already been gratefully acknowledged. Information from published sources was used whenever possible but was often found to be insufficiently specific as to location.

The basis of cataloguing is the grid system used by the Mississippi River Commission in mapping the area. Their quadrangle sheets, comparable to those of the U.S. Coast and Geodetic Survey, cover 15 minutes of latitude and longitude (about 14 by 17 miles) at the scale of 1:62,500. They are numbered in tiers from north to south, and lettered in ranges from west to east. Each quadrangle is accordingly designated by a number and a letter. Site 12-N-3, for example, is the third site which was encountered in quadrangle 12-N. Finds have been catalogued in the same way with an additional term designating the particular location on the site from which the collection was taken. Fortunately, the entire area contemplated in the Survey has been mapped by the Commission, so it will be possible to follow this system throughout.

In the field each car was equipped with a bound volume of quadrangle sheets which was constantly in use. The route of the car was followed on the map in colored pencil and points at which information was sought or obtained were likewise indicated. This enabled us to judge the significance of negative evidence. Information obtained was noted on the map margins for future verification. Sites, when found, were laid down directly on the sheets, which can be done with considerable accuracy. At the same time a printed site index card was filled out, giving, along with other pertinent information, the site location in terms of quarter section, section, and township. As a further check, a descriptive location was given with reference to local landmarks. Mapping of sites was held to a minimum. For most sites a sketch map with estimated distances was deemed sufficient. This was drawn on the back of the site card which was furnished with a grid for that purpose. Large sites, particularly mound groups, where assemblage becomes an important factor, were mapped with plane table, and alidade. . . .

In the initial stage of the Survey—and for all practical purposes we are still in that stage—it was our view that the sole object of surface collecting was to get adequate samples of associated material. The emphasis was therefore on the collection rather than on the site. The difficult question as to what exactly constitutes a site was deliberately avoided. We followed convenience rather than principle. In general, any area showing more or less continuous indications of occupation was regarded as a site, regardless of the extent or number of mounds involved. This is at variance with the approved methods used in some current State Surveys, in which village site and mounds, however closely related, are catalogued as separate units. In our case, this would have resulted in many times the number of sites and great increase of paper work without any corresponding return. The looser, more economical method was, in our opinion, entirely consistent with the purposes of the Survey. However, with an increase of emphasis on the problem of correlating archaeology with abandoned river-channel position, the site as such takes on a greater importance, and we shall undoubtedly be obliged in the future to modify our care-free methods in the direction of closer definition of site and local topographical relationships.

In respect to actual collections, we have been somewhat more particular. Separate collections were made on different areas of a site wherever there was the slightest indication that they might differ in content. If, at the time of sorting, they were found to be the same, within the normal limits of variability, they were thrown together again to make a larger count for the site. No ideal canon for surface-collecting methods was formulated, much less followed. The system of picking up every sherd within a specified area is a counsel of perfection. On many sites it would be a physical impossibility. Generally speaking, our only concern was to get as large a sample as possible and a reasonably honest one. The last is not as easy as it sounds. On sites where sherds are thick enough to be shoveled into sacks, it is difficult not to favor decorated and rim sherds. The only sure way to eliminate this difficulty is to hire local people to pick sherds up at so much per sack. You sometimes get brickbats and other extraneous material, but the sample is an honest one.

Aerial Photographic Maps as Survey Aids in Virú Valley

In the Virú Valley in Peru so many sites had to be mapped that some short cut was necessary to ensure full recording for the survey. In using aerial photographic maps for this one purpose, Willey also found that the value of a surface survey was enhanced by the information gained from a study of the aerial maps. The technique outlined below[6] is avowedly specialized: it can be used to best advantage as Willey says, in "large areas without vegetation cover."

The procedures in field and laboratory for the Virú Valley program have been described previously (Willey, 1946; Ford and Willey, 1949: 18–19). The present section will paraphrase these earlier accounts but will also consider certain problems, methods, and techniques that have a specific bearing upon the settlement-pattern study.

The basic data for analysis and synthesis of prehistoric Virú settlements are the descriptive observations on archaeological sites or other prehistoric works in the Valley. These data were compiled as notes, maps, and photographs during the course of a 4-month survey of the Valley. In this period 300 sites were recorded. They were visited by Ford, who was conducting the ceramic survey (Ford, 1949:34–35), myself [Willey] and two workmen. At each site notes and photographs were made, and at many of them a detailed map was prepared.

The mapping techniques were based upon aerial photography, and to describe the processes it is necessary to refer back to initial preparations which were made before entering the field. In embarking upon an investigation of settlements or site layouts it was obvious that maps would be crucial and would represent the greatest expenditure of time and effort in the field. If a large number of sites were surveyed, adequate instrument maps could not be prepared in the field time allowed. The problem, then, was to find a way of making a relatively accurate site map in a short time. I am indebted to Ford for a solution to this problem through the use of aerial photos and for his help in setting up the mapping laboratory at our Trujillo headquarters.

Before leaving Lima we had purchased air photographs of the Virú Valley. These had been prepared three to four years previously by the Peruvian Air Force and were assembled at the National Air Force Laboratories at Las Palmas near Lima. The prints were coordinated quadrangle mosaics, each of which encompassed 2 minutes of latitude and 3 minutes of longitude at a scale of 1:10,000. Twenty-two of these quadrangles, each

---

[6] Gordon R. Willey, *Prehistoric Settlement Patterns in the Virú Valley, Perú,* Smithsonian Institution, Bureau of American Ethnology, Washington, D.C., 1953, Bulletin 153, pp. 2–6. By permission of the Smithsonian Institution.

measuring 23 by 16 inches, were needed to give adequate coverage of the cultivated valley bottoms and margins of Virú.

Study of the air photos showed numerous archaeological sites in the Virú Valley, most of which were unreported; and this preliminary review proved to be most helpful in the field survey. Walls of dwelling sites, mounds, ancient roads, and canals were sharply defined; and, in many cases, features could be appreciated in the air photographs that would have been missed if we had passed over them without previous knowledge in a ground survey. It was this clarity of definition in the photos that suggested the particular mapping technique employed. Such a technique is feasible in country like the Peruvian coast where there are large areas without vegetation cover and where there are abundant structural remains visible on the surface.

Preparatory to going into the field, a site map was made from an air photograph with the aid of an epidiascopic projector. This was done by placing one of the 1:10,000-scale air photographs in the epidiascope and projecting the image, in a dark room, onto a screen equipped with drawing paper. The section of the air photo so projected was a small rectangle about 3 by 2 inches. This was arranged to include the site, or sites, in question and the surrounding country. The enlarged projection was then traced in pencil, and this tracing formed the outline map which was then carried into the field to the site under consideration for detailed checking. The projection enlargement was a little over 15 diameters of the original on the air photograph. This particular ratio was accidental, being arrived at by adjusting for a convenient distance between epidiascope and screen. As the air photos were on the 1:10,000 scale, the projected tracings were at a scale of approximately 1:700. This scale was standardized and used throughout our Virú mapping work. All of the site maps illustrated in this report were made in accordance with it.

Field checking included chain measurements made on the ground. In many cases, there would be features which did not show to advantage on the air photos. These were then measured and plotted. Wall thickness, wall heights, doorways, subfloor cists, room banquettes, masonry and adobe types, and a multitude of other details not revealed in the air photographs were measured or recorded during our visits to the site. In addition the relationship of one site to another, of sites to canals or cultivation plots, of sites and refuse heaps, and similar observations were noted during the ground survey, sometimes with reference to the air photos.

The sites, as surveyed, were numbered in a consecutive system with the prefix "V" (for Virú), hence the designations V-1, V-2, etc. As the survey progressed these sites were marked on a duplicate set of the large aerial photo quads which were carried with us in the "jeep." Later, they were copied onto the second, and cleaner, set of quads which were kept in the laboratory and from which the projections were made. The sites were also entered on a master site map of the Valley. This map was prepared by the geographer, F. W. McBryde, who worked from an aerial photograph taken at a 1:25,000 scale.

There are a number of comments to be set down concerning the site maps made with the help of the epidiascopic projections. It should be emphasized that they are not as accurate as a plane table or instrument map, but are more accurate than sketch maps or maps made only with compass and chain. There are a number of reasons for their lack of accuracy. We have mentioned the indistinctiveness of site features in the air photos. Besides this, there is the element of distortion in the photograph. I am not technically competent in aerial photography and cannot discuss the error factor with precision, but, in comparing ground and air-photo projection measurements, I found this margin of error to be small for practical purposes. For example, if a wall measured 50 meters, by scale, on the projection map, there would be an error of less than 1 meter in the measurement of this same wall on the ground. Thus the projection maps seemed effective and accurate enough for the settlement-pattern study.

There were, of course, sites which did not show to advantage on the photographs and for which any but the most gross projections were impossible. Steep terrace dwelling sites, because of the slope, could not be satisfactorily projected. The maps which I made of many of these are little more than sketches supplemented with chain measurements and occasional compass readings. At other times, heavy *monte* growth covered a site so that it was impossible to use the air photographs for anything more than general location data. These sites, which were usually on flat ground, were more successfully mapped than the hillside sites, as the chain measurements were more simply and accurately taken. For most site maps the direction arrow indicates the true north, as this was obtained from the aerial quads. There are some exceptions to this, however, where, because of a lack of a projection, a direction reading was taken by compass. In these instances, the map has been reproduced with a magnetic north designation.

Throughout, heights of mounds, buildings, and walls have either been estimated by eye or checked with a hand level. Contour elevation, as it is used on some maps, was taken in another way. The Servicio Aerootografico provided us, in addition to the air-photo quads, a partial series of contour maps at the same scale. These contour maps, with intervals of 10 meters (and 2-meter subdivisions in some cases), had been made from the air photos, not from ground surveys. They did not offer a complete valley coverage; but, where available, we used them for epidiascopic projections in the same manner as the air photographs. After completing a site tracing from an air-photo projection, the matching contour map was inserted into the epidiascope at the same place and orientation as the air photo. This was done by means of north-south coordinate lines drawn through both. When the contour map was properly adjusted in the machine, the contours were traced onto the map projection, over the site outline, and the meter elevation figures recorded. These superimposed contour projections were only moderately successful. Many of them are inaccurate. For example, the reader will note that canals will occasionally cross from a lower to a higher contour when actually the canal is running down grade. In these cases it is certain that the air-photo projection is the correct one; the contour projection wrong. In spite of this, I decided to use the contour lines, when available, to indicate general slope and elevation of terrain. A 10-meter interval is a large one, and is useful only for steep slopes; but there are many of these in Virú, and the fact of a site being on a precipitous hillside or relatively flat ground was worthy of indication. Within the contour lines there were often lesser elevations that were significant, and these have been indicated by a hatched symbol.

Site mapping was carried out on those locations or features where, in effect, there was something worthy of mapping. Of our 315 Virú sites, at least half showed no noteworthy surface features. These were "mapped" in the sense that they were located on the air quads and, eventually, the master-site map, but individual drawings were not made. Such sites were midden piles without rock or adobe walls, earth and refuse mounds of the Lower Valley which appeared only as low hillocks, and many of the smaller dwelling-construction of pyramidal mounds about which no surface data seemed particularly significant except gross size and general location. Because of the differential in the construction of sites in the Valley, those in the middle and upper portions having rock foundations while those in the lower sections being of adobe, more middle and upper region sites were mapped in detail. There are numerous exceptions to this, however, as there are many adobe-walled Lower Valley buildings whose surface outlines are reasonably clear.

A series of symbols have been used in the site maps. These indicate stone masonry walls, adobe walls, superimposed terraces, and all the other necessary features of the map. In some cases these are supplemented with names, such as "road," or "canal," "massive wall," etc. Proportion and scale have been sacrificed slightly to the symbols. For example, in the scale we used it was impossible to indicate a stone wall in proper symbol that would be rendered less than 1-meter wide on the map. Actually, most rock-walled dwellings had thinner walls than this; however, features of this sort are described in the text where dimensions are given.

Theoretically, the survey sites were selected at random. Actually, a number of factors tended to skew our sample, and these should be pointed out. As indicated in the previous paragraph, sites of the upper drainage offered better possibilities for mapping; hence, we included in our sample more upper- than lower-region sites. Also, as any archaeologist knows the big impressive sites command one's attention before the minor midden heap; and it is only fair to say that we have, proportionately, given a better coverage to big sites than to small ones. In retrospect, we see the Virú-settlement job as a much larger one than we had anticipated. Our total of 315 is no more than one-quarter of the total prehistoric sites in the Valley. This estimate is made from observations in the Valley and from inspection of the air photographs. In the interests of a fair sample, we did, however, inspect all regions of the Valley, going inland to a point 10 kilometers above the Huacapongo-Upper Virú confluence. Furthermore, we attempted to include a representative sample of sites of all different functional classes, i.e., burial places, dwellings, temples, fortifications, etc.

Plant Growth as Indicators of Buried Features

The techniques used in identifying sites or site features from plant cover may be quoted from numbers of survey reports. Of the following examples, two are from the Near East and one from the United States. The United States record, which in this case is from Florida, could be duplicated in many other areas—in California, for instance. The reason for peculiar plant growth patterns is not as immediately apparent in the shellmounds as it is in the buried walls of the buildings examined by Frankfort, Jacobsen, and Preusser, in the graves found at Carchemish (N. Syria) by Woolley, or in the sand-covered irrigation canals of the Ptolemys. Note that the same conditions or explanation of the lack of growth where walls lie below the surface is given by Nelson in the American Southwest and by Frankfort and his collaborators in the Near East. Gladwin (1957:257) describes recognizing a buried adobe wall at Casa Grande, Arizona, from a straight line of grass which appeared on the desert floor after a wet winter.

IDENTIFICATION OF BURIED WALLS[7]

Toward the end of the season a third field of inquiry offered itself and was, provisionally at least, explored. The thin grass which appeared after the rains and covered some of the hills of our site did not grow evenly over the surface. Where there were remains of walls just underneath the surface, it scarcely grew at all, whereas it flourished on the looser soil between the walls. Where there was no grass, we could derive information from the color of the soil, which was lighter where the rain water had been absorbed by the loose filling of ancient rooms than it was above ancient walls, where the upper layers remained water-logged and dark. By means of the grass we could follow the walls of a large building which extended immediately south of the one we were excavating.

[7] Henri Frankfort, Thorkild Jacobsen, and Conrad Preusser, *Tell Asmar and Khafaje: The First Season's Work in Eshunna, 1930–31*, Oriental Institute Communications, Oriental Institute, University of Chicago, Chicago, 1932, no. 13, p. 11. By permission of the Director of the Oriental Institute.

LOCATION OF GRAVE PITS[8]

The river bank was of hard gravel, the made soil overlying it very shallow, and only disturbed to the depth of about three inches by the feeble Arab plough; the field, being fallow, was covered with sparse growth, for the most part shallow-rooted, but with a mixture of sturdier weeds of a sort whose roots go deeply down; if one looked carefully it became manifest that these weeds were sometimes single, but often in clumps of four or five plants, but a clump never measured more than six feet across; at some time or another the gravel subsoil had been broken up, so that the plant roots could penetrate it, and it had been broken up in patches which would be just the right size for graves; the broken pottery on the surface represented either shallow burials or, more probably, offerings placed above the graves at ground level, and every deep-growing weed or group of weeds meant a grave-shaft. The deduction proved correct.

SHELL HEAPS AND FLORAL ASSOCIATIONS[9]

Apart from the purely archaeological value involved, the shell heaps of Florida are interesting from other points of view, one of which is that of the floral associations. John K. Small repeatedly stressed the unique plant habitat formed by the shell heaps. Concerning the shell heaps of the Daytona region, Small says: "The presence of a kitchen-midden is indicated by the plant growth. These dunes are naturally covered with a scrubby growth of shrubs and small trees, but wherever there is a shell-midden, we find dense hammock, usually so dense that herbaceous and shrubby growth is sparse. The most interesting phenomena connected with the vegetation are the tropical elements there represented."

At another point he says:

"These Florida shell-middens are extremely interesting from several standpoints. Their floristics should be made a systematic study by some one, for they support a more or less specialized vegetation. They are artificial objects or habitats and are fast disappearing, their flora being destroyed along with their disintegration. . . . The great shell-heaps between Daytona and New Smyrna are fast being leveled, and with the process the rare wild-pepper plant (*Peperomia cumulicola*) is disappearing."

Some of the plants to which Small referred are listed below, this list being of plants which seem to reach the northern limit of their distribution on the shell heaps of the Halifax River region. The heliotrope vine (*Tourne*

[8] Leonard Woolley, *Digging Up the Past*, Penguin Books, Harmondsworth Middlesex, 1949, p. 31.

[9] John W. Griffin, "Green Mound—A Chronological Yardstick," *The Florida Naturalist*, vol. 22, no. 1, p. 3. By permission of *The Florida Naturalist*.

fortia poliochros) was discovered by Small on Green Mound in 1922, and was the first noted occurrence of this plant on the North American main-land.

Peperomia cumulicola, wild pepper
Psychotria undata, wild coffee
Epidendrum tampense, tree orchid
Eugenia simpsoni, spice tree
Ardisia escallonioides, marlberry
Zanthoxylum fagara, wild lime
Tournefortia poliochros, heliotrope vine
Chiococca alba, snowberry
Epidendrum conopseum, tree orchid
Capsicum baccatum, red pepper
Rapanea guianensis, myrsine
Scheopfia chrysophylloides, whitewood.

TRACING THE PTOLEMAIC IRRIGATION SYSTEM IN THE FAYUM BASIN[10]

During the first season (1924–5) a group of small mounds with Graeco-Roman sherds, and a long line of low eroded embankment south of the L. Basin were noticed. A cutting into the mound exposed the wall of a mud-brick house. As the site was clearly a small settlement of classical age, and our programme was already overloaded with prehistoric questions, inves-tigations were not pursued, nor was the purpose of the embankment ascer-tained. Not until the 1927–8 season did we involuntarily return to the prob-lem.

Exceptionally heavy rains in November, 1927, promoted an unusual growth of desert plants in the low-lying basins; on December 7th, happen-ing to cross the embankment, my attention was drawn to what seemed for a moment an optical illusion—a faintly green path on the face of the desert. Closer scrutiny showed the colour to be due to myriad sprouting seedlings in the act of breaking the desert surface. Lying prone on the ground this effect, studied in perspective, confirmed the first impression of a parallel-sided path of plant growth following the base of the embank-ment. This path could be traced westwards to what appeared to be its end on the southern slopes of the X. Basin. Four days later, the track, now clearly defined by increased growth, was trenched, and thirty-five cross-sections at intervals, showed a narrow unlined channel, attaining in places a depth of 6 ft. This and other channels were traced intermittently to a point about half a mile north of Kom Aushim (Karanis).

It became evident that we had found an irrigation system, of which the sand-filled channels were so completely merged in the desert surface that

[10] G. Caton-Thompson and E. W. Gardner, *The Desert Fayum,* Royal Anthropo-logical Institute of Great Britain and Ireland, Gloucester, 1934, pp. 140–141. By per-mission of the Honorary Secretary of the Royal Anthropological Institute.

only the cooperation of plant ecology, with its sensitive register of differential moisture in disturbed ground, had revealed their existence.[11] The plants, which reached their maximum growth in January and had withered away by early March, belonged mainly to the genus *Mysembrianthemum*.

Time Differences Reflected by Flora Covers on Sites

In addition to aiding in identifying sites, peculiarities of plant cover often serve as bases for formulations of other conclusions. Thus Nelson, working in the Southwest, Drucker and Bank (1953) on the American Northwest Coast, and Mathiassen in the Arctic have all been concerned with plant cover and have speculated on vegetational anomalies as time indicators. These examples serve to emphasize the proposition that site survey is not always merely a matter of finding sites or artifacts, or even of solving immediate problems. It also affords opportunity to put together factual details in such a way that new, perhaps unsuspected, aspects of the original problem may be brought to light.

Even in virtually treeless Greenland, vegetation has been of aid to Mathiassen in identifying prehistoric sites. Throughout his monograph on Disko Bay archaeology and in a similar work on the archaeology of the Julianehaab District (Mathiassen, 1936:21, 28, 38, 43) references are made to a type of terrain or soil at or near the sites of ancient villages or homesteads.

In certain cases where the vegetation was of no particular help in disclosing the site location, it served as a hint concerning the ages of certain sites. Such use as a time marker is only secondary and rough, however; the artifacts and their associations must remain here the primary instruments for determining relative chronology.

THE SOUTHWEST[12]

The flora of the Tano habitat, while moderately important, cannot be adequately treated at the present time for lack of data. The region specifically considered in this paper is itself relatively poor, but it is hardly to be doubted that the inhabitants of the Galisteo drew upon the products of their entire tribal range, and until that range has been more thoroughly examined the subject may rest. Speaking generally, the Galisteo basin is open and barren except for a thin sprinkling of forage grasses and weeds. A certain species of prickly-pear cactus (*Opuntia*) is common in places along the high margin of the basin and further constitutes an annoying element to the archaeologist in that it flourishes to an unusual degree on the debris of the ruined pueblos.

The general appearance of the [Pueblo Blanco] ruins calls for a word of

[11] For a second case of an ancient canal marked by vegetation see the airphoto of the region near Ur in *Desert Markings near Ur* (Anonymous, 1929).

[12] N. C. Nelson, *Pueblo Ruins of the Galisteo Basin, New Mexico*, Anthropological Papers, American Museum of Natural History, New York, 1914, vol. 15, pt. 1, pp. 39, 86, 104, 106. By permission of the American Museum of Natural History.

comment. In the case of all the preceding pueblos [discussed in this report] there have been some building ruins which appeared young and others which were either dismantled or in a relatively advanced stage of decay and obliteration due to weathering. If we except buildings II–IV, which may possibly have been slightly dismantled, the majority of the ruins at Blanco are about equally weathered, and this weathering appears to have reached a relatively advanced stage. That is to say, while the buildings of this pueblo, like those of the preceding, were constructed largely of stone, and must, when first collapsed, have presented rough and uneven surfaces, full of holes and crevices, the tops of the ruins are today approaching a smooth condition and the debris is firmly packed. The holes and crevices have all been closed as the result of time and the workings of natural agencies. This has made it difficult for cactus seeds to find lodgment and thus obtain a start; and, if appearances are not entirely deceptive, the old crop is on the point of dying out. The prediction seems therefore not unwarrantable that in a few decades the visiting archaeologist will find the ruin as free from this pest as the valley floor itself. But can this weathering process and the consequent condition of the cactus growths after all furnish a sure key to the relative ages of the various ruins? Perhaps not. An element of uncertainty is introduced into the problem by the fact that the pueblos in question were not built of precisely the same materials. The better the nature of the building stone at hand the less adobe was employed in the masonry construction and, vice versa, when the building stone was scarce or of poor quality much adobe was used. This fact alone would alter the resisting power of any given ruin very considerably. Nevertheless, if care is exercised with respect to the above variations in constructive material, there can be no doubt that the examination of the superficial conditions of a pueblo ruin is of some value in the effort to determine its age.

Prior to the Museum's excavations [at Pueblo Galisteo] the presence of pueblo ruins would hardly have been noticed by anyone coming near, unless he had passed directly over the spot. This is because the ruined edifices were constructed almost exclusively of adobe and are in many cases so washed out and weathered away as to be well-nigh indistinguishable. Careful inspection, however, reveals a number of low ridges relatively free from vegetation and sometimes marked by a few small, angular boulders lying scattered over the surface. There are no cacti here, as in the case of the other pueblos and there probably never were any. A certain species of weed, sometimes called "snake-weed" by the local inhabitants, thrives to the exclusion of everything else all over the valley floor and its absence generally marks the location of a ruin.

Buildings VII–XIV are also easily apparent to the trained eye, but the remaining structures are very faint, at least so far as surface contour is concerned. Yet shortly after a heavy rain, owing to the difference in texture of the adobe walls and the debris filling the rooms, the former stand out quite plainly as dark lines on the smoothly washed surface.

THE NORTHWEST COAST[13]

The cover of the sites is unusual. The eastern half of midden 1 [at Roscoe Inlet] and most of the face (the slope to the beach) supports a growth of long tough grass of a distinctive light green color. Occasional nettles grow among the grass. The rest is wooded. Midden 1A is, in fact, covered with such a heavy stand that it was not recognized as a midden from the fore-shore. The timber consists entirely of young hemlocks (*Tsuga heterophylla* Raf. Sargent) except for a small clump of alders which follow the course of the creek cutting through midden 1. The hemlocks grow in most cases on decaying logs, house posts, and fallen beams, extending their roots along the grain of the timber—a type of growth noted by Sudworth as character-istic of the species. This habit probably has enabled them to become es-tablished where other conifers could not. In a number of instances sizable hemlocks were seen growing in a row on a very slight ridge—seedlings had become established on a fallen beam and had continued to grow after the beam had almost completely decomposed. . . .

Another time indicator . . . is the type of cover on the sites. It will be recalled that at all but one place (Roscoe Inlet) the sites were devoid of the normal forest cover, supporting instead deciduous bushes, grasses, and the like. The apparent reason is that conifers require a slightly acid soil, whereas the shell content of the middens makes the deposit basic. The hemlock cover at Roscoe Inlet is less a contradiction than it appears, for there the trees grew chiefly on the fallen house timbers. Both Harlan Smith and Reagan, however, report sites covered with normal forest. Seemingly, the only way to account for such sites is that sufficient time has elapsed since their abandonment to allow precipitation to leach out the calcium carbonates of the upper levels. Whether this leaching process proceeds at a rate near enough constant to make it possible to calculate the time represented by such strata is a matter for a soils expert or chemist, but other things being equal, a site which supports a stand of mixed coni-fers can safely be assumed to be considerably older—at least, last occupied at a much earlier date—than sites with distinctive deciduous cover. Al-though the 1938 survey found no such wooded middens, it cannot be as-sumed they do not occur in the regions surveyed. Obviously, such places would be difficult to find except by very careful combing of each district. Our party was looking for late sites with historic levels. The possibility that ancient hidden sites may occur should not be overlooked when the time comes to do intensive work in the area.

[13] Philip Drucker, *Archeological Survey on the Northern Northwest Coast*, An-thropological Papers, Smithsonian Institution, Bureau of American Ethnology, Wash-ington, D.C., 1943, Bulletin 133, pp. 82, 114. By permission of the Smithsonian Institution.

THE ARCTIC[14]

The ground is stony moraine gravel; in several places, however, there are outcrops of rock in the form of low knolls and on the north side of the settlement the rock forms steep bluffs down to the sea. South of the stream a low rocky point runs far out; the south coast at its west end is formed of rock, more to the east a low cliff of moraine gravel. Apart from the rocky knolls, some of which are naked, others overgrown with willow, heather and lichen, the terrain where the houses lie is marshy and covered with a thick layer of moss and having a vegetation of *Vaccinium uliginusom, Empetrum nigrum, Betula nana*, species of *Carex* and *Luzula*, etc. Round about and growing over ruins I–II and V is a quantity of *Alopecurus*, but it has not the luxuriant, sappy-green character that one sees on more recent settlements; the houses more to the north, VI–X, have no vegetation to distinguish them from the surrounding tundra.

The most northerly group of ruins, VI–X, lies rather isolated from the others and all fairly close together. Their appearance, state of preservation and situation, all argue that they are contemporaneous, that they have been inhabited at the same time. Before excavation their appearance indicated that they were the earliest houses at Igdlutalik. No thick growth of grass announced the presence of any ruins; in the vegetation there was nothing to distinguish them from the surrounding boggy plain with its crowberry and bilberry bush. The ruins themselves were not at all prominent in the terrain: shallow depressions, sometimes surrounded by a very low mound of earth, from which another depression, the passage, runs westwards towards the sea; in some cases we were not even sure that they were ruins until our excavation proved it; only very occasionally was there a stone projecting from the boggy peat. Nor had the middens any covering of grass; everything argued that the organic rubbish which feeds the plants had long been decomposed.

[14] Therkel Mathiassen, *Contributions to the Archaeology of Disko Bay*, Meddelelser om Grønland, Copenhagen, 1934, vol. 92, no. 2, pp. 39, 42. By permission of Meddelelser om Grønland.

8

STRATIGRAPHY AND STRATIFICATION

Stratigraphy, the sequential layering of deposits (whether due to natural or cultural agencies) which have accumulated over the course of time, is the chief means of determining the relative ages of those layers and their contents. Geologists employ the principle of stratification (sometimes called the "Law of Superposition") to work out the history of the growth of the rock strata composing the earth's crust.

Archaeologists also employ this principle of interpreting a series of layers, for the lowermost stratum of an archaeological deposit will normally be the oldest and the uppermost layer will be the most recent. There are rare instances of the reversal of the normal order of strata due to human or natural agencies. In archaeology, no principle has more general significance and application than stratigraphy.

According to Daniel (1950:77–78), the Danish archaeologist Worsaae (1849:23–24) was the first to demonstrate the validity of the three-age system (Stone, Bronze, Iron) proposed by Christian J. Thomsen (1836) who was curator of the Danish National Museum from 1816 to 1836. Before Worsaae's three-age system of prehistory could be conceived of and proved with reference to the circumstantial facts of the occurrence of artifacts in the ground, it was necessary, first, that prehistoric implements be demonstrated as man-made and not the product of natural forces, and second, that there be admitted a time span for human history which was of sufficient duration to provide a means of dating the finds which were made. Not until the middle of the seventeenth century was the first effective recognition made that chipped flint implements were man-made, and not until 1723 did a Frenchman, Antoine Jussieu, explain satisfactorily for the first time the artificial nature of archaeological European flint implements by comparing them to American Indian flint tools and reach the conclusion that ancient European peoples made and used these implements (see Shorr, 1935; Kendrick, 1950: 121 ff.). Shorr's survey of the beginnings of research into prehistory also provides the information that not until 1744 do we have the first discovery, by a person aware of the significance of the implications it had for the history of man, of the archaeological association of bones of man himself, of man-made implements, and of the bones of extinct animals. This discovery was made by J. A. Esper, a German Protestant minister, in a Bavarian cave.

For extended treatments of the development of the disciplines of archaeology and paleoanthropology, see Boule and Vallois (1946: chap. 1), Breuil (1942–45), Crawford (1932), Daniel (1950: chaps. 1, 2), MacCurdy (1924:9–24), and Piggott (1937). E. Lartet (1861:213) says that the French investigator Tournal in 1828 made the first claim and presented adequate evidence in print for the coexistence of man and extinct animals, and not until 1800 was the first notice published (by John Frere) of ancient flint implements found under conditions suggesting high antiquity. It will thus be seen that the appreciation of the facts that flint implements were made by man and that they were geologically old is a relatively recent intellectual achievement of man.

We present here one of the accounts referred to above—John Frere's paper published in 1800, in which he describes the finding of Acheulean hand axes in Suffolk, England (see also West, 1956).

Precisely who should be given credit for being the first American archaeologist to conduct stratigraphic excavations, or to recognize stratification in an archaeological site, is far from clear. Thomas Jefferson may qualify for this honor, as judged from his account of 1784 excavations printed below. Jefferson's interest in American Indians was very great (Chamberlain, 1907). He collected Indian vocabularies and his curiosity was aroused by the local Virginia mounds containing graves (Lehmann-Hartleben, 1943).

Frederick W. Putman in 1877 published an account of explorations in a Tennessee burial mound, and it is clear that he recognized that the deeper graves were older than those nearest the surface, but he seems not to have appreciated the fact that he was demonstrating a cultural sequence.

W. L. Gabb, a geologist, observed between 1869 and 1871 an archaeological sequence of preceramic-ceramic culture levels in a cave on Samana Bay, Dominica, B.W.I. The following quotation is taken from his report:

In the cave where I slept there is an extensive and interesting kitchen-midden divisible into two eras; the older marked only by shells and a few turtle and fish bones, resting on the rocky floor, and through which I excavated to a depth of nine feet. Over this is a thinner layer of ashes with bones of birds, agouti, fish and turtles, and an abundance of pottery evidently of the immediately pre-Columbian era. Over this, liberally intermixed with bat guano, is a modern deposit of broken earthen and iron kettles and beef and pig bones, indicative of a higher, or at least, more modern civilization, though justice requires us to admit that the pottery is inferior in workmanship, in elaborateness and in beauty of design to the preceding era.[1]

W. M. F. Petrie, in 1890, excavated by artificial levels in the slope of the mound of Lachish, in Palestine, with the result that he was able to establish a firm ceramic sequence.

Of the following accounts dealing with stratigraphy, some are chiefly of historical interest (e.g., those of Frere, Jefferson, and Peabody). N. C. Nelson's summary of his Tano excavations marks the beginning of a new era in American archaeology, since it called attention effectively to the results which stratigraphic excavation could produce. Refuse deposit stratigraphy at Tano is not basically different from that encountered by Haury in his sectioning of the fill layers of Snaketown Canal, and the same may be said for the layered deposit in Sandia Cave. The lengthy extract from the Monagrillo shellmound report by Willey and McGimsey is of especial interest in providing a comparison of results achieved by two methods of stratigraphic excavation. Tobler's successful attempt to arrange the Tepe Gawra tombs in their proper sequence is archaeology at its best, for not only does such excavation have to be done with utmost attention to detail, but also the analysis of records requires a superior sense of judgment. The Hiwassee Island mound dissection was carried out with great thoroughness, and the presentation by Lewis and Kneberg is a model of clear description. The suggestions by Kidder, Jennings, and Shook for excavating a Middle American mound or pyramid are nearly unique, since archaeologists who have dug these large structures have rarely described the methods employed. Wheeler's advice on recording internal strata in such fashion that the diagram will be intelligible and meaningful is worth careful reading.

An Eighteenth Century Discovery of Paleolithic Tools

John Frere's account,[2] published over 150 years ago, is the first notice and illustration of Paleolithic tools which were recognized as dating from what we now know as the Pleistocene Epoch, a period which to him was of such antiquity that he ascribed the tools to a time "beyond that of the present world." Slightly

[1] W. H. Gabb, "On the Topography and Geology of Santo Domingo," *Transactions of the American Philosophical Society*, Philadelphia, 1881, n.s., vol. 15, pp. 146–147.

[2] John Frere, "Account of Flint Weapons Discovered at Hoxne in Suffolk," *Archaeologia*, 1800, vol. 13, pp. 204–205.

earlier (in 1770) John Leland published a bifacial handaxe found in 1715 in association with "elephant" bones, but the implement was ascribed by him to a Briton of the Roman period.

LETTER TO THE REV. JOHN BRAND, SECRETARY, READ JUNE 22, 1797

Sir,

I take the liberty to request you to lay before the Society some flints found in the parish of Hoxne, in the county of Suffolk, which, if not particularly objects of curiosity in themselves, must, I think, be considered in that light, from the situation in which they were found. [See Figs. 8.1A and 8.1B]

They are, I think, evidently weapons of war, fabricated and used by a

Fig. 8.1A (Left). Acheulean flint hand ax from Hoxne, Suffolk. Fig. 8.1B (Right). Acheulean hand ax found by John Frere at Hoxne, Suffolk.

people who had not the use of metals. They lay in great numbers at the depth of about twelve feet, in a stratified soil, which was dug into for the purpose of raising clay for bricks.

The strata are as follows:

1. Vegetable earth 1½ feet.
2. Argill 7½ feet.
3. Sand mixed with shells and other marine substances 1 foot.
4. A gravelly soil, in which the flints are found, generally at the rate of five or six in a square yard, 2 feet.

In the same stratum are frequently found small fragments of wood, very perfect when first dug up, but which soon decompose on being exposed to the air; and in the stratum of sand (No. 3), were found some extraordinary bones, particularly a jaw-bone of enormous size, of some unknown animal, with the teeth remaining in it. I was very eager to obtain a sight of this; and finding it had been carried to a neighbouring gentleman, I inquired of him, but learned that he had presented it, together with a huge thigh-bone, found in the same place, to Sir Ashton Lever, and it therefore is probably now in Parkinson's Museum.

The situation in which these weapons were found may tempt us to refer them to a very remote period indeed; even beyond that of the present world; but, whatever our conjectures on that head may be, it will be difficult to account for the stratum in which they lie being covered with another stratum, which, on that supposition, may be conjectured to have been once the bottom, or at least the shore, of the sea. The manner in which they lie would lead to the persuasion that it was a place of their manufacture and not of their accidental deposit; and the numbers of them were so great that the man who carried on the brick-work told me that, before he was aware of their being objects of curiosity, he had emptied baskets full of them into the ruts of the adjoining road. It may be conjectured that the different strata were formed by inundations happening at distant periods, and bringing down in succession the different materials of which they consist; to which I can only say that the ground in question does not lie at the foot of any higher ground, but does itself overhang a tract of boggy earth, which extends under the fourth stratum; so that it should rather seem that torrents had washed away the incumbent strata and left the bog-earth bare, than that the bog-earth was covered by them, especially as the strata appear to be disposed horizontally, and present their edges to the abrupt termination of the high ground.

If you think the above worthy the notice of the Society, you will please to lay it before them.

I am, Sir,

with great respect,

Your faithful humble Servant,

John Frere

Excavation of a Virginia Burial Mound in 1784

Although Thomas Jefferson excavated a century and three-quarters ago, his account[3] has a modern ring in that he dug to solve a problem, and recorded his findings in detail and with accuracy. Going beyond mere reporting, Jefferson extracts a number of valid inferences from his data.

[3] Thomas Jefferson, *Notes on the State of Virginia*, ed. W. Peden, Chapel Hill, 1955, pp. 97–100. By permission of the Director of the University of North Carolina Press.

I know of no such thing existing as an Indian monument: for I would not honour with that name arrow points, stone hatchets, stone pipes, and half-shapen images. Of labour on the large scale, I think there is no remain as respectable as would be a common ditch for the draining of lands: unless indeed it be the Barrows, of which many are to be found all over this country. These are of different sizes, some of them constructed of earth, and some of loose stones. That they were repositories of the dead, has been obvious to all: but on what particular occasion constructed, was matter of doubt. Some have thought they covered the bones of those who have fallen in battles fought on the spot of interment. Some ascribed them to the custom, said to prevail among the Indians, of collecting, at certain periods, the bones of all their dead, wheresoever deposited at the time of death. Others again supposed them the general sepulchres for towns, conjectured to have been on or near these grounds; and this opinion was supported by the quality of the lands in which they are found, (those constructed of earth being generally in the softest and most fertile meadow grounds on river sides) and by a tradition, said to be handed down from the Aboriginal Indians, that, when they settled in a town, the first person who died was placed erect, and earth put about him, so as to cover and support him; that, when another died, a narrow passage was dug to the first, the second reclined against him, and the cover of earth replaced, and so on. There being one of these in my neighbourhood, I wished to satisfy myself whether any, and which of these opinions were just. For this purpose I determined to open and examine it thoroughly. It was situated on the low grounds of the Rivanna, about two miles above its principal fork, and opposite to some hills, on which had been an Indian town. It was of a spheroidical form, of about 40 feet diameter at the base, and had been of about twelve feet altitude, though now reduced by the plough to seven and a half, having been under cultivation about a dozen years. Before this it was covered with trees of twelve inches diameter, and round the base was an excavation of five feet depth and width, from whence the earth had been taken of which the hillock was formed. I first dug superficially in several parts of it, and came to collections of human bones, at different depths, from six inches to three feet below the surface. These were lying in the utmost confusion, some vertical, some oblique, some horizontal, and directed to every point of the compass, entangled, and held together in clusters by the earth. Bones of the most distant parts were found together, as, for instance, the small bones of the foot in the hollow of a scull, many sculls would sometimes be in contact, lying on the face, on the side, on the back, top or bottom, so as, on the whole, to give the idea of bones emptied promiscuously from a bag or basket, and covered over with earth, without any attention to their order. The bones of which the greatest numbers remained, were sculls, jaw-bones, teeth, the bones of the arms, thighs, legs, feet, and hands. A few ribs remained, some vertebrae of the neck and spine, without their processes, and one instance only of the bone which serves as a base to the vertebral column. The sculls were so tender, that they generally fell to pieces on being touched. The other bones were stronger. There were some teeth which were judged to be smaller than those of an adult; a scull, which, on a slight view, appeared to be that of an infant, but it fell to pieces on being taken out, so as to prevent satisfactory examination; a rib, and a fragment of the under-jaw of a person about half grown; another rib of an infant; and part of the jaw of a child, which had not yet cut its teeth. This last furnishing the most decisive proof of the burial of children here, I was particular in my attention to it. It was part of the right-half of the under-jaw. The processes, by which it was articulated to the temporal bones, were entire; and the bone itself firm to where it had been broken off, which, as nearly as I could judge, was about the place of the eye-tooth. Its upper edge, wherein would have been the sockets of the teeth, was perfectly smooth. Measuring it with that of an adult, by placing their hinder processes together, its broken end extended to the penultimate grinder of the adult. This bone was white, all the others of a sand colour. The bones of infants being soft, they probably decay sooner, which might be the cause so few were found here. I proceeded then to make a perpendicular cut through the body of the barrow, that I might examine its internal structure. This passed about three feet from its center, was opened to the former surface of the earth, and was wide enough for a man to walk through and examine its sides. At the bottom, that is, on the level of the circumjacent plain, I found bones; above these a few stones, brought from a cliff a quarter of a mile off, and from the river one-eighth of a mile off; then a large interval of earth, then a stratum of bones, and so on. At one end of the section were four strata of bones plainly distinguishable; at the other, three; the strata in one part not ranging with those in another. The bones nearest the surface were least decayed. No holes were discovered in any of them as if made with bullets, arrows, or other weapons. I conjectured that in this barrow might have been a thousand skeletons. Every one will readily seize the circumstances above related, which militate against the opinion, that it covered the bones only of persons fallen in battle; and against the tradition also, which would make it the common sepulchre of a town, in which the bodies were placed upright, and touching each other. Appearances certainly indicate that it has derived both origin and growth from the accustomary collection of bones, and deposition of them together; that the first collection had been deposited on the common surface of the earth, a few stones put over it, and then a covering of earth, that the second had been laid on this, had covered more or less of it in proportion to the number of bones, and was then also covered with earth; and so on. The following are the particular circumstances which give it this aspect. 1. The number of bones. 2. Their confused position. 3. Their being in different strata. 4. The strata in one part have no correspondence with those in another. 5. The difference in the time of inhumation. 6. The existence of infant bones among them.

A Stratified Mound in Mississippi

Although Willey and Phillips (1955:743) have called the work of Hawkes and Linton (1916, 1917) "one of the earliest systematic stratigraphic excavations in North America," earlier recognition of cultural-historical implications of archaeological stratigraphy is a matter of record. Thus Charles Peabody, in a report published in 1904, describes work carried out in a Mississippi mound in 1901–1902. Here, in the Edwards Mound, clear stratification of the mound, which had been erected and used at two different periods, was noted. The pertinent sections of Peabody's report is printed below.[4]

The Edwards Mound may be considered as a typical Indian mound of the later period placed within a typical village site. The characteristic features are, first, the division of the mound into an upper and lower part, separated by strata A and B and second, the variety and richness of the articles found at or near the surface of the surrounding field.

Below the "Critical level" [i.e., below the A-B strata (see Fig. 8.2)]

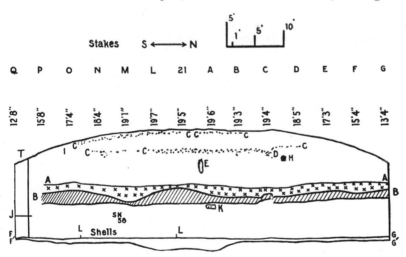

Fig. 8.2.   Cross section of the Edwards Mound, Mississippi.

were the greater number of full length burials; above it the greater number of bundle burials. Below the "Critical level" were found but five of the sixty-eight [pottery] vases, and very few manufactured articles of any kind, while above it they were frequent. These facts, coupled with the

[4] C. Peabody, *Exploration of Mounds, Coahoma County, Mississippi*, Papers of the Peabody Museum, Harvard University, Cambridge, 1904, vol. 3, no. 2, pp. 51–52. By permission of J. O. Brew, Director of the Peabody Museum, Harvard University.

amount of ashes in stratum B and with the rude ring of [post] holes . . . induce to the opinion, that the mound has been built in two periods: that the lower portion was gradually built and used as a burial place, that a stockade of posts was set up about the centre to the east of a later apex; that, after a period of occupancy, this stockade was burnt down, and another population continued to build the mound to a conical apex some ten feet higher. Further we conclude that the latter people buried their dead from time to time, generally intrusively in the bundle fashion and deposited pottery, and necklaces of stone, shell and glass beads with the bones; further that the latter people were undoubtedly Post Columbian and were well skilled in working stone, and had some acquaintance with white people and other tribes, at least by trade. More than this can hardly be asserted.

Ceramic Sequence at Tano, New Mexico

Between 1912 and 1916, N. C. Nelson, then a young curator in the American Museum of Natural History, conducted excavations and site reconnaissance in New Mexico. In 1914 he excavated a stratified refuse heap at Tano ruin, and in 1916 published his now famous paper, "Chronology of the Tano Ruins, New Mexico,"[5] which is considered the first modern, detailed demonstration of archaeological stratigraphy in North America (for comment see Spier, 1931; see also Nelson, 1917).

In the course of archaeological investigations pursued in New Mexico under the auspices of the American Museum during the past four years some chronological data have come to light which it seems proper to bring to the attention of students without further delay. The data consist mainly of observations on the stratigraphic relationship of several widely distributed types of pottery. Other facts of importance, such as architectural variation, exist, but these are less convincing and besides seldom immediately useful in determining the relative age of a ruin. This preliminary treatment is therefore deliberately confined to a presentation of the stratigraphy, together with a brief outline of the distinguishable ceramic features and the application of the results thus obtained to the ruins in the limited area under investigation.

GENERAL CONSIDERATIONS

As is well known, there are in the Southwest several more or less localized types of prehistoric pottery, such as ornamentally indented coiled ware, several distinct varieties of painted wares, and likewise, a somewhat varied group of glazed ware. Dr. J. W. Fewkes (1914) has only recently

[5] N. C. Nelson, "Chronology of the Tano Ruins, New Mexico," *American Anthropologist*, vol. 18 (1916) pp. 159–180. By permission of Walter Goldschmidt, Editor.

made us acquainted with another hitherto little-known ceramic type of a unique character which was most intensively developed in the Mimbres valley but which occurs also in the adjacent Rio Grande country and probably beyond, towards the Pecos river. This fine, relatively ancient ware is of the painted order and seems to mark the southeastern limits of Pueblo culture in the United States.

To the north of the Mimbres center, extending up the Rio Grande drainage basin almost to the Colorado boundary, is another ceramic area characterized primarily by glazed pottery. The eastern limit of this area is somewhat uncertain, but it appears not to extend beyond the longitude of the lower Pecos and Red rivers, while in the west it remains within the Rio Grande basin except for a slender arm extended by way of Laguna and Acoma to the Zuni valley where it again expands, taking in the country drained by several tributaries of the Little Colorado, close to the Arizona–New Mexico boundary. Leaving out of account probably sporadic occurrences in the Hopi country in the northwest, at Ysleta del Sur to the south, and also at reported minor sites along the Canadian river and elsewhere on the eastern plain, glazed pottery is distributed over an area approximating 20,000 square miles in extent, a stretch of territory which may be said to constitute the northeastern border section of Pueblo culture.

The greater portion of the country in question seems unfit for almost any sort of aboriginal existence, being either mountainous or desert-like plateau, lacking water. But the flood-plain of the Rio Grande and some of its tributaries, likewise the lower levels of the high relief with its springs and small patches of tillable soil offered inducements to a sedentary agricultural people. There is hardly a suitable spot that does not show some trace of former Indian life. To be sure, many of the settlements were small and perhaps temporary. But, disregarding those sites, there are on record for the region about three hundred ruins, some of them very large. Judging from results obtained in the Tano district alone, it is safe to say that a thorough-going examination of the entire glazed pottery area would reveal probably twice the listed number of abandoned pueblos. The situation thus developed, area and environment being taken into consideration, becomes analogous to that observed in parts of California and in the Mound Builder area. That is, the implied population mounts to figures out of proportion on the one hand, to the productivity of the country and on the other, to the historically known facts. We may, therefore, reasonably suspect a lengthy occupation by either a shifting or a changing population; in other words, that the ruins in question are not of the same age.

Hitherto no archaeological work of consequence has been done within the limits of the glazed pottery area, except in the northwestern part of it, i.e., in the Pajarito Plateau district, where Dr. E. L. Hewett and his associates of the Archaeological Institute of America have been engaged for some years. However, the conditions here do not seem thus far to have yielded precise chronological information. At the same time it is only fair to state that it has been more or less apparent to every student since Bandelier made his first observations that the Rio Grande Pueblos underwent certain cultural transformations in prehistoric times. In the region under investigation by the American Museum, a district which lies southeast of the Pajarito plateau and somewhat central in the glazed pottery area, this fact was evident from the beginning. Thus, traces of "small-house" ruins marked by sherds of painted pottery of the black-on-white variety, as well as by coiled ware, were found in several places during the reconnaissance and it was easy to see that these sites antedated the large Tano ruins, say of the Galisteo basin, which were characterized chiefly by glazed pottery. At the end of the first season's work one of these glazed types of pottery had been eliminated as of historic date, having been found constantly associated with bones of the horse and other domestic animals and in fact only in particular sections of such pueblos as San Cristobal, San Lazaro, San Marcos, Galisteo, and San Pedro Viejo, all but the last of which were known as Mission centers down to about 1680. But there were still apparently at least two distinguishable types—with several variants—of glazed pottery, the relative ages of which could only be surmised because both occurred in association with the strictly historic ware, though not with the same frequency. As no actual excavation was undertaken during 1913, nothing further was accomplished until 1914, when the importance of the subject had fairly impressed itself. By the opening of the season it was reasonably certain, both from internal evidence and from various general considerations, what was the chronological order of the four apparent pottery types, but tangible proof was still wanting.

This desideratum, as it happened, was obtained at the first site excavated, viz., San Pedro Viejo or Paako, a pueblo ruin lying on the southwestern edge of the Tano territory, near the head of the valley separating the San Pedro and Sandia mountains. Later, these findings were verified and supplemented by data obtained from a refuse deposit at Pueblo San Cristobal on the east-central border of the Tano country, i.e., at the west base of the Trans-Pecos highlands, about seven miles south of Lamy. Again in 1915, verifications were made at the abandoned pueblos known as San Marcos, Cieneguilla, and Arroyo Hondo or Kuakaa, these last sites being all well toward the northern and northeastern limits of the Tano range and not far from Santa Fe. The result of these observations is the identification and chronological order of four, or practically five, successive styles of pottery corresponding to as many periods or stages in the history of the people occupying the late Tano and adjacent Pueblo territory. What follows is intended merely as a brief outline of the facts in the case.

STATISTICAL DATA

The data required to establish a chronology were of course to be looked for only in those places that bore evidence of long settlement. Actually superposed successions of ruins or large stratified refuse deposits are not as common, however, as might be expected, and where they do occur, there is often no appreciable differentiation in the remains. Nevertheless, at San Pedro Viejo two superpositions were discovered, one showing contact of the historic type of glazed pottery with another earlier type of glazed ware, and the other showing contact of the older of the two preceding glazed types with the black-on-white ware. These were, however, merely clean-cut superpositions showing nothing but time relations. Towards the end of the 1915 season another case of contact similar to the last of the two mentioned above was found at Pueblo Kuakaa. But, as before, these sections, being incomplete in that they showed no trace of the fourth type of glazed ware, could not be taken at face value. That is to say, while the positions of the two extreme members of the pottery type series were fixed, the chronological order of the two middle members was not proved, though strongly suggested. However, at Pueblo San Marcos and also at Pueblo Cieneguilla, both in the ruins proper and in the refuse heaps, the ancient type of glazed ware twice noticed in contact with the black-on-white ware was found actually mixed with it, the one gradually replacing the other. This latter was the evidence wanted, because it accounted for the otherwise unknown time interval that separated the merely superposed occurrences of types and from the point of view of the merely physical relationship of contiguity, connected them. The remaining fourth type of pottery could now take only one position in the series, namely, that of third, counting from the bottom. But all these various superpositional and transitional sections are incomplete and fragmentary, each showing merely the time relations of two successive pottery types at some place or other in the total series of four or five types. Hitherto no complete section has been found, and probably does not exist unless possibly it be at Pueblo Pecos. This site, according to Bandelier, shows evidence of settlement in the days of black-on-white pottery and, as is well known, was inhabited down to about 1838. The Tano section that comes nearest to filling the requirements was found at Pueblo San Cristobal. Here are to be seen the dwindling remains of a large refuse heap, still measuring about ten feet in depth on the vertical exposure in the bank of the creek which has undercut and carried away the missing part. Human burials were visible at different levels of this debris when first seen in 1912, and in order to obtain some skeletal material a five-foot bench was excavated from one side of the artificial deposit to the other, along the edge of the creek. At that time it was noticed in a general way that different types of pottery fragments prevailed at different levels but no effort was made, until too late, to keep them separate. This happened partly because I was not continually present during excavation, having decided beforehand that chronological data were to be obtained in the ruins only and not in burial mounds where grave diggers in overturning the debris again and again had surely destroyed the planes of stratification. But as all data from the ruins remained inconclusive after practically three seasons' work I returned to San Cristobal in 1914 to make a test. A visibly stratified section of the refuse exposure showing no evidence of disturbance was selected and a block of this measuring 3 by 6 feet on the horizontal and nearly 10 feet deep was excavated. I performed this work with my own hands, devoting fully three days to the task. The potsherds from each separate foot of debris were kept apart and the finally classified numerical results appear in the following table.

This test is not perhaps all that could be desired; but inasmuch as its results in their general bearings agree absolutely with the partial data obtained before and since at other sites, no effort has been made to strengthen the inevitable conclusions. Had a greater volume of debris been handled, the figures of the table might possibly have lined up a little better and possibly not, because a larger block of debris would doubtless have included areas disturbed by burials, etc. Even with the conditions as given, viz., a visibly stratified and undisturbed block of deposit, accidents are entirely probable and no stress should be laid on individual figures, which at best are more or less arbitrary. The table as a whole is, however, consistent and intelligible.

Examining the table as it stands, we see at once that column 1 has no chronological significance, corrugated cooking pottery of essentially the same style having been in use throughout the time period represented by the ten-foot accumulation of debris. Column 2, likewise, is relatively useless for chronological purposes because the so-called "biscuit ware" indicated by it runs a rather unsteady course from beginning to end. The rest of the table is as satisfactory as could well be expected, whether we study the columns as individual or related units. Column 3, representing black-on-white painted ware—called Type I—has its maximum expansion at the bottom and becomes negligible about halfway towards the top. The few fragments found in the upper four feet indicate probably heirloom vessels held over from early days or else specimens dug out of the ruins and not at all that this type of ware continued to be manufactured. Whatever historical significance attaches to the fact that the ware was at its maximum development when the refuse began to accumulate we must leave for later consideration. The 4th, 5th, and 6th columns, representing contemporary variants of early glazed ware—called Type II—show very nearly normal frequency curves. That is, the style of pottery indicated came slowly into vogue, attained a maximum and began a gradual decline. At the point where the maximum is reached the preceding style will be noticed to have come to practical extinction. Column 7, standing for a ware combining painted and glazed ornamentation—called Type III—barely gets a showing; but it appears to make the proper start for another normal frequency curve, such as would be expected. This curve might doubtless have been completed by excavation in other refuse heaps of later date than the one here tried. As no such supplementary test was made the succeeding style

TABLE 2. Stratigraphic Occurrence of Pottery at the Tano Ruin

Thickness of Section	Type I: Two- & Three-Color Painted Ware			Type II: Two-Color Glazed Ware			Type III: Three-Color Glazed Ware
	Corrugated Ware (1)	Biscuit Ware (2)	Black-on-White Painted Ware (3)	Red Ware Black or Brown Glaze (4)	Yellow Ware Black or Brown Glaze (5)	Gray Ware Black or Brown Glaze (6)	Gray, Yellow, Pink and Reddish Wares, Combination Glaze-and-Paint Design (7)
1st ft.	57	10	2	24	23	34	5
2nd "	116	17	2	64	90	76	6
3rd "	27	2	10	68	18	48	3
4th "	28	4	6	52	20	21	
5th "	60	15	2	128	55	85	
6th "	75	21	8	192	53	52	1 ?
7th "	53	10	40	91	20	15	
8th "	56	2	118	45	1	5	
9th "	93	1 ?	69				
−8 in.	(126)		(103)				

The figures 69 and (103) in the 10th foot of Column 3 may need explanation. This 10th foot of debris in actuality measured only 8 inches in thickness and contained 69 potsherds. Had the debris measured a full 12 inches it should have contained about 103 potsherds. This will also explain the lower figures in Column 1.

of glazed pottery called Type IV, and referred to already as of historic date, cannot appear at all in this statistical way. Its position in the chronological type series is, however, fixed by an abundance of sound evidence. Finally, there may be mentioned, as Type V, a painted style of ware which is clearly the forerunner of modern Pueblo pottery, though it takes its start prior to 1680. This particular ware does not seem to occur at San Cristobal or in any but the westernmost of the supposed Tano ruins and is therefore perhaps of Keresan origin. With these few remarks we may leave the statistical aspect of the table to speak for itself and turn our attention to its pottery classification.

DESCRIPTION AND CLASSIFICATION OF POTTERY

As will readily be perceived, the validity of the numerical data set forth in the preceding table depends upon the classification of the pottery. In attempting this the same difficulty arose that confronts the student in dealing with any other series of related phenomena: there were overlappings and minor variations that for the sake of simplicity had to be ignored. Consequently, the separation of the Tano pottery into nine stylistic groups—seven of which appear in the table—is only an approximation to the actual facts. Future study of the ceramics is sure to compel further subdivision. But the basic characters here seized upon, are sufficiently distinct to warrant the classification as far as it goes; to have noticed minor variations would not have affected one way or the other the chronology to be established. The leading superficial characters of most of the ceramic styles are indicated at the head of each column of the table. Those styles or contemporary varieties of styles that mark successive time periods have been named "Types." In part this terminology is no doubt arbitrary, but will serve present purposes. Finally it must be stated that in attempting the following comprehensive description of the pottery it was found necessary to consult the material dug out of the ruins as well as that obtained from the refuse heaps.

Corrugated or Coiled Ware (Column 1 of Table 2)

This ware is almost invariably covered with soot and was evidently made exclusively for cooking purposes. Hence it naturally shows no such finesse of technique as is found to characterize the coiled ware outside the glazed pottery area. The ware ranges evenly from top to bottom of the refuse heap and occurs at all Tano ruins from the earliest to the latest; but as it undergoes no appreciable modifications in form, finish, or composition it must be left out of account for the present as chronological data. The leading characters of the ware are as follows:

1. Form, Size, etc.   Normally a jar (olla), spherical body, short neck, flaring rim; occasional shoe or bird-shaped pots with knobs suggesting

wings and tails; bowls uncertain. Sizes range from miniature to medium, approaching large.

2. Surface Finish. Plain coil of primary and sometimes apparently secondary origin; indented coil (finger, fingernail or sharp implement being used) with occasional effort at ornamental effect. Coiling and indenting often obscured either by wear or by "wiping" during process of manufacture. Some specimens of later times show evidence of a micaceous wash.

3. Paste Composition. Gray colored clay, more or less tempered with coarse sand or crushed rock of crystalline nature. In early times some crushed pumice stone may have been added, while in later times micaceous substance was occasionally mixed in. Vessel walls are thin and brittle, the latter fact being due probably to constant use over the fire.

Biscuit Ware (Column 2 of Table 2)

This peculiar kind of pottery, which can be detected even by the touch, may or may not be a lineal descendant of the local black-on-white painted ware that precedes it (see Column 3 of Table 2). At any rate, it is the only style of painted pottery to maintain its vogue side by side with glazed ceramics from the beginning to the end of the latter's existence. There seem to be two kinds of biscuit ware, the most common being of a dull white or light gray color, the other of a dull yellowish tone. This latter has its probable forerunner in a more or less distinguishable variety of the black-on-white ware, but the prototype of the former has not been found thus far. Judging from both the time and space distribution of the typical biscuit ware, it seems probable that this was not manufactured by the Tano themselves, but was secured by trade either from the Keres or the Tewa in whose old territory it is very abundant. The most common ware exhibits the following characters:

1. Form. Bowls, often asymmetrical, hemispherical body with slight constriction near the top and a more or less flaring rim; with or without a flattened edge. Vessel walls unusually thick. Sizes range from small through medium towards large.

2. Surface Finish. More or less smoothly polished, with and without an exceedingly thin wash of the paste material, in colors ranging from dull white to gray, depending on length and nature of use.

3. Ornamentation. Geometric design on one or both sides, more or less crudely executed, in dull black paint. Rim edge sometimes dotted. Awanyu symbol common.

4. Paste Composition. Homogeneous, finely granulated, light in weight, soft and porous, lacking cohesive strength. Tempering material practically absent, though occasional quartz-like crystals occur. The composition suggests nothing so much as ground-up pumice stone or volcanic tufa, a substance which is so very abundant in the Pajarito region where biscuit ware is most plentiful.

We come now to the type series of the pottery which establishes the chronological relations of the Tano ruins.

Type I: Two- and Three-Color Painted Ware (Column 3 of Table 2)

The pottery actually figuring in the table is a local variety of the black-on-white ceramics commonly identified with the generalized substratum of Southwestern Pueblo culture. Bandelier generally associated the ware with "small houses," i.e., with what might be called a pre-pueblo stage of sedentary life; but the data now at hand enable us to state that the large quadrangular form of village typical of the Rio Grande valley in later times was fully developed before the black-on-white pottery went out of style. The ware as a whole is perhaps not quite so fine as that of the Mesa Verde and Chaco regions on the one hand or of the Upper Gila and Mimbres regions on the other. It is particularly lacking in variety of form. In decorative symbolism it approaches the abandoned northwestern Pueblo area rather more than the southwestern and is little, if at all, inferior to it. The characterization of the ware follows:

1. Form, Size, etc.   Bowls predominate; ladles, i.e., bowls, with handles, occur; jars very rare. Body form of bowls hemispherical. Rim section almost invariably plain, with top edge flat, rounded or pointed; occasional flaring lip. Bowls come in small and medium sizes, vessel walls uniformly rather thin. Jars are miniature and medium.

2. Surface Finish.   Some bowls show trace of coiling or of basket mould on the outside. Surface rubbed more or less smooth on one or both sides. Slip or wash on one or both sides (often crackled) in colors—like the paste —ranging from dull white to blue-gray, depending on length and nature of use.

3. Ornamentation.   Applied inside of vessel (very seldom outside), rather skillfully, in black paint. Design geometric, rectilineal and curvilineal; hachure work and bands of thin parallel lines common; occasional pieces with paint dots on edge of rim as in Mesa Verde ware.

4. Paste Composition.   Variable on close examination. Matrix always of a grayish color, sometimes almost white with a bluish tinge (color of wood ashes), fine grained, closely knit, hard, and firm. Tempering material varies. Sand or crushed rock of a crystalline nature occurs in some pieces, but crushed basalt is more common. Sometimes the two are mixed and both may be nearly absent, as in the apparent prototype of biscuit ware.

Attention must be called at this time to the fact that an exceedingly small percentage of a black-on-red painted ware is generally mixed with the black-on-white, as is the case in the Chaco, Mesa Verde, and other districts. Thus far only bowl fragments have been found. These show a gray colored paste, red slip on both sides, geometric design in black on the inside, and sometimes a design in white on the outside. The ware is of a decidedly pleasing appearance and is probably a forerunner of the most prominent variant of the next type of ceramics to be considered.

Type II: Two-Color Glazed Ware (Columns 4, 5, 6 of Table 2)

As indicated in the table this ware comes in three distinct varieties of color—red, yellow, and gray—with ornamentation done in black or brown glaze. There are, however, several reasons besides brevity of treatment for grouping the three kinds of pottery under one and the same heading. Thus the variants to be described all bear some resemblance to the preceding type, they have in addition a number of common characters, and they are practically contemporary. Individually considered, the red ware seems to have arrived first—in fact it was probably the transition form, while yellow and gray wares held out the longest and gave rise no doubt to the succeeding type. At first sight the shift of types seems rather violent. For ages black-on-white and black-on-red wares had been in vogue and now we find the black-on-white replaced by black-on-gray and black-on-yellow wares, the black-on-red only having held over. More striking still is the fact that ornamentation is now applied with glaze instead of paint. Nevertheless, there are indications enough to suggest that the transition from Type I to Type II was not very sudden in any sense of the word; but as yet details on this point await investigation. The outstanding characters of the ware are as follows:

1. Form, Size, etc. Bowls predominate but jars occur, the former in sizes varying from small through medium towards large, the latter from miniature towards large. (A) Bowl bodies are hemispherical as in Type I. Rim sections mostly plain, but a few are swelled or show inward or outward curve. (B) Jars have more or less vertically compressed bodies; round bottoms, wide mouth, with or without neck, with or without flaring lip. The miniature forms have short bottle necks and have two loop-handles set on the body near the neck.

2. Surface Finish. Smoothened by rubbing on one or both sides. Slip applied on one or both sides (extra thick on ornamented side), in red, yellow, and gray color, the same color covering the entire vessel.

3. Ornamentation. Applied on upper half of jars and on inside of bowls (seldom outside) in the form of glaze of a color ranging from greenish-brown to black, depending to some extent on its thickness and also on color of slip beneath. Glaze sometimes crackled. In some cases the ornamental substance is of a consistency halfway between glaze and paint, in others it is a genuinely vitrified coating, resisting a knife point, and every bit equal to the glaze on modern crockery. Design is geometric, executed with an effort at precision but somewhat simplified in comparison with Type I, the component parts being generally done in much heavier lines than in the painted ware, because the glaze had a tendency to run and thus to spoil all

attempts at a fine-line pattern. Symbolism partly the same as in Type I, partly different. Some conventionalized bird figures occur on later developments of the ware.

4. Paste Composition. Resembles Type I sometimes but in general is less hard and firm, also lighter in weight. The tempering material has less of basalt and more of sand. Color of matrix varies greatly, depending evidently not on nature of clay used but on color of slip applied to vessel. Often it is gray in the center as in Type I, e.g., and red near the exteriors; but in other cases it is red clear through as if coloring matter had been mixed into the paste. There is of course, also, the occasional possibility of the red color being due to oxides in the clay.

Type III: Three-Color Glazed Ware (Column 7 of Table 2)

The distinguishing feature of this type of pottery is that its design element, or part of it, is outlined in glaze and filled in usually with red paint, the combination design being placed on a ground color or slip of a different order such as yellow, pink, gray, and even some shade of red. This ware, while not well represented in the Table for the San Cristobal refuse heap, is diffused apparently over the entire glazed pottery area and is especially abundant in the large Tano ruins. It was in use for some time after the Spaniards came to New Mexico but is nevertheless essentially of prehistoric date. The ware is doubtless a descendant or a development with modifications, good and bad, from the preceding type, though the detailed proof of this statement remains to be worked out. But while the new type of ceramics has gained in diversity of form and general adaptability, it has lost not a little in decorative elegance. Its main characters may be summed up as follows:

1. Form, Size, etc. Bowls and jars are about equally abundant and both occur in sizes ranging from small through medium towards large. There are also a few vessels of the jug type with combination spout-handle, resembling the common Peruvian specimens of that order. Vessel walls are a little thicker than formerly but show some range. (A) Bowl bodies hemispherical. Rim sections decidedly varied in thickness and curve. (B) Jar bodies more or less vertically compressed, often slightly asymmetrical, bottoms round (jars from the Keresan territory have flat or punched up bottoms), mouths wide, necks vertical or contracting, lips absent or flaring.

2. Surface Finish. Rubbed smooth on one or both sides, except on inside of jugs where coiling is often left undisturbed. Two different-colored slips were generally applied to different parts of the vessel. Thus in the case of a bowl the outside bottom—the part invisible when placed right-side up—was usually painted red while the rest of the surface, inside and out, received a slip of some light shade of yellow, gray, pink or even red, which served as background for the ornamental design. In the case of a jar the lower half of the body and the inside visible portion of the neck

was generally (not always) painted red while the outside of the neck and the upper half of the body received a slip in one of the several colors enumerated above, and which here also served as background for decoration.

3. Ornamentation. Applied as already indicated on the outside of the neck and upper part of the body of jars and on the inside as well as on the upper outside portion of the bowls, partly with glaze and partly with paint, the latter usually red. Exceptions occur where no ornament has been added on the outside of bowls or on the neck of jars. The characterizing feature of this pottery type, viz., the ornamental figures outlined with glaze and filled in with red paint, are generally confined to the neck portion of the jars and to the outside of the bowls; but sometimes the combination design does occur also on the body portion of a jar as well as on the inside of a bowl, in which case the outside of the bowl is usually left blank or is merely marked by a few dashes of plain glaze. Designs mostly geometric as before, more or less crudely executed, and in part spoiled by the glaze running beyond its intended limits; quite a number of conventionalized bird figures; some more or less realistic bird figures, mammal figures, etc.

4. Paste Compositions. Not so uniform as to be a leading character by which to identify the ware. Some of the paste is like that most common in preceding types; but in general it is more porous and brittle than formerly. The colors range through various shades of brown, red, and gray; sometimes red with a gray core, resembling the gray of previous types. The tempering material varies much in nature and quantity, fine sand, coarse sand, or crushed rock, varicolored granules of uncertain nature—perhaps crushed potsherds, etc., being used. Accompanying the mass of type ware are a few specimens probably of contemporary date which except for general crudeness of finish might be regarded as two-color ware of the preceding type. These are mostly miniature and small vessels of the "prayer bowl" variety, rectangular in outline, flattened bottom, more or less vertical sides, usually painted red, decorated with a few dashes of glaze and in one instance with a semi-realistic bird figure.

Type IV: Historic Two-Color Glazed Ware

This style of pottery, though very short-lived, has been singled out as a chronologic type because it is strictly characteristic of those ruined Tano pueblos that were inhabited between 1540 and 1680. It has been found also in ruins whose historic occupancy is not a matter of record, e.g., at Pueblo Tunque; but here as elsewhere, the ware occurred in association with bones of domestic animals, fragments of copper, iron, porcelain, etc., and never under any other condition. The characterizing peculiarities of this pottery are its diversity of forms and its simplified but execrable decoration. In other words, the ware, while somewhat specialized and perhaps more adaptable to use, is far less artistic than formerly for the reason principally that it is not genuine Indian art but a poor European imitation. It represents the breakdown of Pueblo culture under the first century of stringent Spanish regime. The detail features of the ware may be summed as follows:

1. Form, Size, etc. Bowls, jars, platters of various odd outlines, cups or mugs with loop-handles, melon-shaped vessels, rectangular vessels, etc. Sizes range from miniature towards large. Thickness of vessel walls have considerable range. (A) Jars have more or less vertically compressed body, often somewhat angular in outline, round or flattened bottom, wide mouth, no neck as a rule, with or without flaring lip. (B) Bowls show hemispherical body, convex bottom. Rim exceedingly varied in thickness and disposition, being either vertical, incurving or outcurving; lip absent or outflaring.

2. Surface Finish. Decidedly varied, some red ware being polished to a high degree like modern Santa Clara black pottery, some rubbed to an average degree of smoothness as formerly, and some merely scraped but not smoothed at all. A slip appears on most (not all) of the ware, usually in a gray color, sometimes yellow or cream color and occasionally red.

3. Ornamentation. Applied as before on one or both sides of a bowl and on the upper portion of the body of a jar, in the form of glaze. The color and general appearance of this glaze is a very characteristic dark brown when thickly applied and of a greenish hue when the coating is thin. Generally the iridescent glaze substance is of such striking and excellent quality as to incline one to the opinion that it was compounded after a Spanish formula. The fact that the artist could not control it at all seems suggestive of the same idea. The designs attempted, though of the very simplest geometric nature, were almost invariably ruined by the running of the glaze.

4. Paste Composition. Varies but slightly from preceding type, but there are exceptions of closely knit, hard and firm matrix. Normally the paste is porous and brittle. Tempering material either coarse or fine crystalline. Colors are brick red, reddish, brownish, and gray.

Type V: Modern Painted Pottery

Whether the Tano potter actually revolted against the degenerative tendency of his art during the first three-fourths of the seventeenth century, or whether his more advanced and at the same time more conservative Keresan neighbor came to his assistance is uncertain. But the fact remains that some time prior to the Rebellion of 1680, painted pottery of a decidedly modern stamp began to replace the glazed ware at the village of San Marcos, and to a slight extent elsewhere. At Cienega and Cieneguilla the painted pottery occurs in such profusion, and with no admixture of glazed ware, as to lead one to conclude that these settlements were of post-Rebellion times, though history is silent on the subject. Now it happens that ware of this sort is found in considerable abundance at the ruins of Pueblo Kotyiti (excavated 1912) and also at the nearby ruins of Pueblo Kuapa of earlier date in the Keres country to the west of the Rio Grande. In the Tano ruins of pre-Rebellion times it is scarce, however, and may not occur in quantity except at San Marcos. For this reason we may dismiss it for the present with a few delineatory remarks.

The material at hand for the Tano ruins consists of but a few fragments and it will therefore be impossible to go into any details. Bowls and jars both occur, possibly also other forms. Seemingly there are no more vertical jar rims, but the bowl rims show at least several of the former variations. Vessel surfaces are more or less well rubbed. The undecorated portions of the ware—bottoms, etc.—are generally painted red, the other portions ordinarily a light pink. The ornamentation, placed on this pinkish ground-color, is done with black paint. Sometimes the figures are merely outlined with black paint and filled in with red paint, as in Type III. The decorative lines are generally thin, straight or curved and done with only a fair amount of precision. All designs are geometric, with some few of a semi-floral nature. The vessel walls are rather thicker than formerly. The paste is of light weight, porous, and brittle, containing a good deal of sand. Its color ranges between red and dull yellow, the latter resembling at times the color of unburned adobe.

SUMMARY

The present paper is, of course, not a study of Tano ceramics but merely an attempt to establish the basis for a chronology. To that end the principal styles of pottery have been described in more or less tedious detail chiefly to convince the student that the differences, particularly of the so-called successive types, are real and not imaginary. Only the grand divisions, peculiar not to the Tano district but in a measure to the whole glazed pottery area, have been considered and merely from a concrete or objective point of view. Subdivisions of styles, such as "Frijolitan" and "Standard Pajaritan" suggested by Dr. Kidder probably exist also in Tano ceramics. At any rate transition material is present. But these are matters for future discussion.

The principal difficulty in making the classification has been to devise a terminology that shall be readily intelligible and also simple enough to be permanently useful. Both archaeology and geology suffer confusion by the use of geographic words that are meaningless without an appended definition. For that reason I have avoided repeating Dr. Kidder's terms such as "Schoolhouse," "Frijolitan," "Pajaritan," etc., though the latter two are both convenient and expressive and may for all I know be desirable labels for local modifications of a particular type of glazed pottery. On the other hand, a terminology that is self-explanatory is necessarily clumsy. Still, for the present, I see no scheme more convenient in the prosecution of my own work than the preceding classification which may here be summarized.

Type I. Two- and Three-Color Painted Wares.   1. Black-on-white.
2. Black-on-red. 3. Black-and-white-on-red.

Type II. Two-Color Glazed Wares.   1. Black-(or brown)-on-red.
2. Black-(or brown)-on-yellow. 3. Black-(or brown)-on-gray.

Type III.   Three-Color Glazed and Painted Wares.   1. Black-glaze-and-red-paint-on-gray. 2. Black-glaze-and-red-paint-on-yellow. 3. Black-glaze-and-red-paint-on-pink. 4. Black-glaze-and-red-paint-on-red.

Type IV.   Historic Two-Color Glazed Wares.   1. Brown-(or green)-on-gray. 2. Brown-(or green)-on-red. 3. Brown-(or green)-on-yellow.

Type V. Modern Painted Wares.   1. Black-on-pink. 2. Black-and-red-on-pink.

The above types of pottery succeed each other in the order given; but accompanying them from beginning to end, without undergoing any marked changes are two additional types, viz.: 1. Corrugated or coiled wire. 2. Biscuit ware (i.e., a surviving variety of black-on-white ware).

APPLICATION OF CHRONOLOGICAL DATA TO THE TANO RUINS

Accepting the foregoing chronological deduction as essentially correct, we may properly conclude this study by trying out our scheme on some of the ruins in the territory to which it applies. A limited amount of data in the way of potsherds, etc., is available for several subdivisions of the glazed pottery area and judging from these it seems probable that the entire region underwent about the same stylistic changes. But for the present purposes it will be enough to illustrate the possibilities of chronological determination by applying the facts at hand to the Tano district from which alone our data are nearly complete. Substituting for the five successive pottery types a corresponding number of time periods we get the following results, set forth in tabular form (see Table 3).

The table must for the present be left to speak for itself. It is not complete in some respects and it may even be incorrect on two or three points; but the final report on the alignment of the Tano ruins will not differ very much from the indications above presented. Of particular interest is the steadily decreasing number of ruins marking the successive Pueblo periods, but until the capacities of the various ruined villages have been estimated it is useless to put definite constructions upon the figures. The off-hand impression is, however, that the housing facilities during the first three periods of Pueblo history in the Tano district remained very nearly uniform because as the villages decreased in number they increased in size. This might mean among other things that the population remained fairly stable.

In conclusion it may be well to repeat that the foregoing attempt to establish a chronology is based on purely concrete and numerical data. It is a study largely of small fragments of pottery, their number, nature, and physical contact relations. But the case for chronology can be strengthened by the investigation of architectural modifications, although these at best

TABLE 3. Assignment of Tano Ruins to Culture Period

No.	Name of Locality	Pre-Pueblo Period	I	II	III	IV (1540-1680)	V (1680 on)	No. of Rooms Excavated
1	White Rock Cañon, No. 1		X	X				
2	" " " " 2		X	X				
3	Boom Camp		X	X				
4	Los Aguajes			X	X			33+
5	Santa Fé		X					
6	Agua Fria, No. 1		X					
7	" " " 2		X	X				
8	Cieneguilla		X	X	X		X	132
9	Cienega, No. 1						X	
10	" " 2			X				
11	" " 3		X					45
12	" " 4	X						Trenched
13	La Bajada " 1		X					
14	" " " 2			X	X			84+
15	Canyoncito, " 1			?	X			9+
16	" " 2				X			
17	" " 3		X					
18	" " 4	X						
19	Arroyo Hondo, " 1		X					12
20	" " " 2		X	X				108+
21	Peñas Negras		X					
22	Chamisalocita Cañon		X					44+
23	Alamo Cañon		X					27+
24	Mansanaria, " 1		X					Trenched
25	" " 2		X					5+
26	Lamy " 1		X					
27	" " 2		X					2
28	" " 3		X					17
29	San Marcos		X	X	X	X	X	172+
30	Cañon Casita		X					
31	San Cristobal		X	X	X	X	?	239+
32	Largo			X	X			13+
33	Colorado			X	X			47+
34	Shé		X	X	X			28+
35	Blanco		X	X	X			47+
36	San Lazaro		X	X	X	X	?	60+
37	Galisteo		X	X	X	X	?	25+
38	Gipuy (Old Domingo)			X	X			
39	Ojito Juan Pedro			X				
40	Pinavetitas Cañon				X			
41	San Pedro Viejo (2)	(X)	X	X	X	X	?	174+
42	Uña de Gato, No. 1		X					
43	" " " 2			?	X			
44	Tunque			X	X	X		239+
45	Algodones	X						
	Totals	4	29	21	19	6	3	1562

cannot serve as a sound classificatory basis. Furthermore, when the very considerable quantities of crushed pottery vessels obtained during three seasons of excavation have been assembled and put in shape for comparative study it would be possible to observe either a series of sharp breaks in the symbolism on the pottery, or else a gradual development of motifs. Such a study it now seems probable will show that the successive styles of ceramics arose the one from the other and that therefore, by inference, we may assume a relatively steady and uneventful career for the people inhabiting the Tano territory.

Stratigraphy of Lovelock Cave, Nevada

In the fall of 1911 the dry archaeological deposit of Lovelock Cave, Nevada, was reported by commercial guano miners to the University of California. L. L. Loud, a preparator in the Museum of Anthropology, worked at the cave between April and August, 1912. He made a large collection of artifacts, most of which were basketry materials in a state of perfect preservation due to the completely dry conditions of the deposit. Loud, in describing his excavation method says: "Owing to the character of the deposit and the lack of assistance it was necessary to excavate the material in irregular masses, often bounded by large boulders fallen from the roof. These irregular masses have been called lots . . ."[6]

In 1924 M. R. Harrington, then attached to the Museum of the American Indian, Heye Foundation (New York), was sent to Nevada to continue excavations in Lovelock Cave, mainly in the west end of the cave where Loud had been unable to work. Loud accompanied Harrington, partly to enable the latter to synchronize the excavations with those of twelve years earlier. Loud and Harrington published their report in 1929.[7] Loud's sections report the 1912 excavations, those of Harrington the 1924 work and a reconstruction of the history of the cave's occupation. Although Loud worked alone, and was thus hindered in any large-scale effort, and worked mainly in the east end of the cave where the refuse deposits were thinner, it is quite apparent that he did not conduct stratigraphic excavations, and indeed it is probable that he was not in 1912 even aware of the principle that relative depth of artifacts could be translated into relative differences in time of their deposition. He presents his data without reference to time distinctions—his report is purely descriptive.

In 1924 Harrington was aware of the principle of superposition in yielding archaeological sequence; this was undoubtedly because of his knowledge of the stratigraphic work of Nelson at the Tano Ruins in New Mexico, as well as through his own work in 1922 and 1923 in the Ozark shelters (Harrington, 1924), where he succeeded in demonstrating by stratigraphy an earlier "Bluff-Dweller" and later "Top-layer" culture.

---

[6] L. L. Loud and M. R. Harrington, *Lovelock Cave*, University of California Publications in American Archaeology and Ethnology, Berkeley, 1929, vol. 25, no. 1, p. 29. By permission of University of California Press.
[7] *Ibid.*, p. 9–13, 18–28.

Harrington writes of Lovelock Cave:

When the deposit was especially deep, the "lot" had to be dug in levels; the upper 4 feet first, then the next, then the next. Lot 15, at the southwest end, was dug in 6 levels for stratigraphic purposes, in the only part of the cave where such procedure might give some hope of yielding results.

The structure of the deposits was noted. Storage pits and grave pits were measured and recorded. The depth of each specimen of consequence and its position with respect to the median line of the cave, established for measurement purposes by Mr. Loud during his former stay, were recorded. The measurements of depth have only relative value, because the original surface of the cave floor had been removed by the guano-diggers to varying depths, except for a narrow strip along the inner edge of the rockfalls blocking the cave mouth. But even if the surface had remained unbroken, the bottom was so irregular, and the deposit consequently so much deeper in some places than in others, that an object found at a depth of only 2 feet near the middle of the chamber might belong to an older horizon than one found 8 feet deep at the southwest end.[8]

STORAGE PITS

Many artifacts were found during the course of the general digging in the deposits of refuse of the cave proper, but most of our best specimens came from the storage pits and from the graves.

The pits, called by some investigators cists, cache pits, or caches, were simply holes dug by the Indians in the cave floor of their day for the purpose of storing seeds, pine nuts, dried fish or other food, or for the storage of such valuables as fur robes, ceremonial plumes, decoys, and rabbit nets.

Usually these pits had been opened and the contents removed, presumably by the owners. Some showed evidence of having been used a number of times, but in a few cases the owner had never returned to recover his buried store, and the pit remained unrifled until our time.

In all, we opened 40 such pits in the Lovelock cave, exclusive of graves, of which there were 8. These pits varied in form from a shallow bowl-shape to a deep pot-shape, or in figures from 2 feet to nearly 5 feet in depth, with diameters ranging from 1 foot 10 inches to 4 feet. Some were oval and one of these had diameters of 5 feet 8 inches and 4 feet. The depths were not calculated from the surface of the ground, but from the level of origin when that could be distinguished, that is, the level which was the floor of the cave at the time the pit was dug. This is shown in the section (Fig. 8.3). The lower pit must be considerably older than the upper one; in fact, it is evident that it was dug during the earliest occupation of the cave, when its floor consisted only of a thin layer of guano resting upon the lacustrine deposits left by the waters of Lake Lahontan. The upper pit to the left, on the other hand, was dug after the Indian deposits had accumulated to some depth. The same thing is revealed in Fig. 8.4 even more clearly, for

[8] *Ibid.*, p. 5.

pit 10 was dug from one distinct floor level, while pit 9, although almost equally deep when found, originated in another higher floor level, and is consequently not so old as pit 10. From such instances it appears that storage pits did not belong exclusively to one particular period of the cave's occupancy, but had been dug from time to time since it was first occupied.

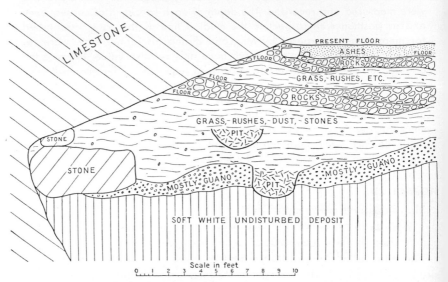

Fig. 8.3.　Stratigraphic section in southwest end of Lovelock Cave.

To prevent the food or other things stored in each pit from becoming mixed with the dusty refuse in which it was dug a lining was provided, sometimes for the bottom only, sometimes covering the sides as well. Grass was the most frequent lining material, rushes next; then scraps of old baskets, pieces of rush mats, water plants from the lake, shredded bark, and a sort of felt made from the down of the cat-tail rush. In two instances sage twigs were employed. Sometimes two or more materials lined a single pit.

Some pits were used over and over again, being cleaned and relined to receive the new crop of seeds, pine nuts, or dried fish. Occasionally the cleaning was omitted, and the new lining laid upon several inches of dust and debris that had accumulated in the pit since last used. In the case of pit 12, a false bottom concealed the real treasure the pit was intended to house.

A description of all pits would entail repetition, so typical ones have been selected. Pit 4 lay in lot 7, near the northeast end of one of the great masses of fallen rock blocking the mouth of the cave. Its greatest depth from the present surface was 3 feet 10 inches, but when first made it was only 2 feet deep, for 1 foot 10 inches of refuse had been deposited subsequently upon its "level of origin." It formed a deep oval bowl, with diam eters 2 feet and 2 feet 3 inches. In the bottom lay some downy feathers and the beak of a duck, possibly relics of storage of decoys or decoy parts. Then came a rectangular piece of rush matting forming a bottom and fragments of baskets forming the sides, all representing a later use of the pit. After this use the pit had evidently stood empty for some time, for several

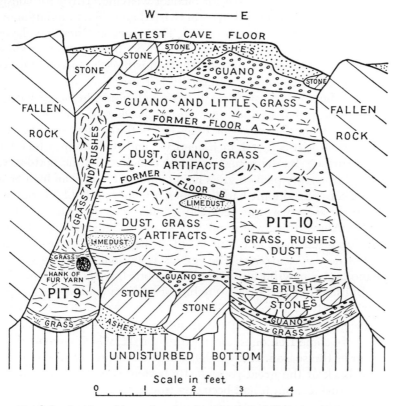

Fig. 8.4. Stratigraphic section showing pits 9 and 10 in Lovelock Cave.

inches of loose trash had gathered. The next user simply laid a new bottom over the accumulated rubbish. This bottom consisted of a conical twined pack basket smashed flat, an old, worn-out, coiled, bowl-shaped basket, several fragments of twined baskets, and a small breechcloth or apron made of fiber, apparently shredded bark. Upon this lay 198 bunches of small feathers, each carefully tied together with strings. These represented the leavings of the latest recognizable contents of the pit. It appears that they were used in decoy making. The pit belongs to the later period.

Pit 9 was one of the deepest found in the front part of the cave, its bottom lying 6 feet below the present surface; yet it belongs to the later period, being dug from a level only 14 inches below the present surface, which makes the original depth of the pit 4 feet 8 inches. It is a good ex-

ample of the pot-shaped type of pit, the diameter at the top being 2 feet
8 inches, while at the bottom it is 3 feet 4 inches. One side of the pit is seen
in Fig. 8.4. At the very bottom was a tightly packed 6-inch lining of grass,
rush mat fragments, and pieces of baskets. This lining was possibly the
first used after the pit was dug. Then came 14 or 15 inches of dusty rubbish, containing a hank of yarn for blanket weaving. This yarn consisted
of strips of fur and of downy bird skin twisted around a foundation of native strings and shreds of worn-out nets. Then came another grass layer, in
which were 126 small dried fish, overlooked doubtless in the darkness of
the cave by the last user of the pit. Above this the pit contained only the
rubbish that had accumulated since its last use.

Pit 10, not far to the east of pit 9, was much older; in fact belonged to
either the transitional or the older period as may be seen in Fig. 8.4.,
for it was dug from a level about 3 feet below the present surface. As the
pit at that time was 3 feet 1 inch deep we find its bottom 6 feet 1 inch
below the surface. Its diameter was 2 feet 6 inches. On the bottom was a
3-inch layer of tightly packed grass lining, upon which lay an inch or so of
bat-guano, showing the pit had lain open a while, probably during a period when the cave was not occupied by man and the bats had it all to
themselves. Above this lay a number of stones weighing 10 to 20 pounds,
possibly deposited there to get them out of the way when the old tenants
returned or new ones arrived. The next user, without removing the stones
and guano laid a new bottom lining of sagebrush twigs and stems. In the
dusty rubbish above this layer were bits of basketry and matting, plus the
usual strings, etc.

There were many pits with yield as poor as pit 10, or poorer. In contrast
to these were some rich ones, among them pit 12, which gave us the best
single find of the season. It lay in lot 7 near the center of the front of the
cave, just back of the great rockfall. Its bottom was 5 feet 1 inch below
the present surface, but it had been dug from a level 2 feet 8 inches below
the present surface; so its original depth was only 2 feet 5 inches. It was
oval in outline, measuring 2 feet 8 inches by 2 feet 4 inches, the long axis
lying east and west. At 3 feet 6 inches below the present surface, or 10
inches below the pit's "level of origin" lay a bag made of rush matting,
flattened out, resting on two layers of mat fragments of similar material.
Beneath this were three large pieces of twined pack basket and a large
coiled basket bowl somewhat distorted. Underneath this were more pack-
basket pieces; while similar fragments were laid around the walls, giving
the whole thing the appearance of a well lined pit intended for seeds or
other fine material. It was so cleverly arranged that looking in from above
no one would guess that anything could be concealed beneath such a lining. On this bottom lay several large stones such as were frequently thrown
into discarded pits, apparently to get them out of the way. When the layer
of mats and basketry was removed it was seen to be a false bottom (see

Fig. 8.5), for beneath it lay a bulky package wrapped in rush matting; a rush bag full of feathers; feathers wrapped in a piece of mat; a bunch of feathers tied with string; and two bundles of snares made of string and twigs, all in excellent condition. Some water-fowl hunter had hid his decoys here against another season. He may have filled the pit with refuse as

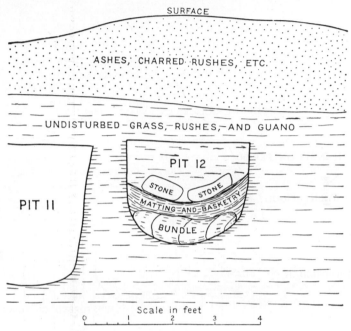

Fig. 8.5. Section of pit 12 showing position of decoy bundle, Lovelock Cave.

an added precaution, but if not, anyone who looked into it saw only the stones and the lining of an apparently empty storage cache. The age of this pit is transitional or later.

STRATIGRAPHIC SECTION

Our stratigraphic section, lot 15, did not yield results equal to expectations, but did shed a little light on the culture sequences of the cave. The lot was laid off on the southwest end of the cave floor where lay the only area large enough and apparently undisturbed. It was 6 feet wide from southeast to northwest and 8 feet long from northeast to southwest, where it touched the overhanging ledge. This was on the surface, but as the deposit was taken off level by level, the length increased, for the layers extended back under the ledge, until at the bottom lot 15 was nearly 16 feet long (See Fig. 8.6).

First level—surface to 18 inches deep. Level 1 consisted mostly of ashes and of rocks from the roof, with very few artifacts, except near the surface where relic hunters had thrown some rich "back dirt." On account of this back dirt, the origin of which was unknown and the limits of which were hard to trace, this cut was made only 18 inches deep, with the idea of ignoring its contents altogether, and starting afresh at 18 inches, in deposits we knew to be undisturbed. Only two articles in its contents, however,

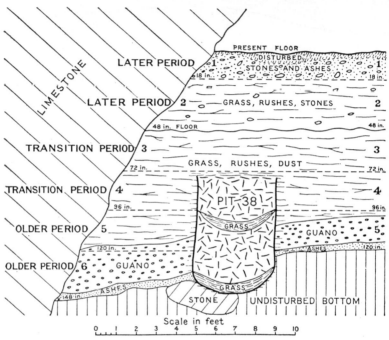

Fig. 8.6. Diagrammatic section of stratigraphic area (lot 15), showing cultural levels, Lovelock Cave.

were obviously out of place. These were two large feathers attached to short lengths of rush rope, a type of artifact we had hitherto found in the lower levels. The other objects from this level were a stick bent into loop form to make a paddle for stirring mush, such as is still used by the Northern Paiute and Washo; a bunch of vegetal fiber; 5 "quids" or "chews" of rush fiber; a piece of tanned skin, possibly buckskin; a strip of twisted dog skin, once forming part of a woven blanket; a strip of downy bird skin from a similar blanket; 4 pieces of baskets, including a coiled one of rather coarse weave, made on a 3- to 4-rod foundation; another specimen of similar structure but much finer; and two pieces of stiff twined basketry, rod and splint, one piece a little finer than the other; 2 pieces of common twined rush matting; 1 piece of extra fine matting with fiber-cord, twined warp; 1 piece of a twined rush sandal; some twisted rush rope; some braided rush rope; a twisted rush ring; two pointed arrow foreshafts of greasewood; the sharp point of a digging stick; and a wooden fire-drill hearth.

Second level—18 inches to 48 inches deep. The second level extended from 18 inches to about 48 inches, where there was a distinct hardpacked floor, which formed with the bottom of the cut. The depth was a little less than 48 inches on the northeast side, and a little more on southwest side. This level contained many stones, large and small, fallen from the roof, and was not very rich in artifacts. The deposit showed no trace of distrubance.

The artifacts found included 14 fragments of cane arrows, 6 of which showed traces of feathering and 8 of which were still provided with their pointed foreshafts of greasewood; 12 such points or foreshafts without the cane shafts; and 11 basket fragments, including a coarse coiled weave such as was reported from the first level, another of finer but similar weave in staff rod-and-splint twining, and some examples of rod-and-splint wicker weave. There were also the usual rush ropes twisted, and braided; the common rush matting held together with rows of rush twining; the quids or chews; and the bunches of fiber. Among the more unusual objects were: a bone awl; a bunch of feathers tied together; a pointed stick with a cord attached; a fragment of an object of soft stone with a groove near the point; two arrow foreshafts for flaming arrows, one wrapped with inflammable rush, the other having bound to it a piece of charred punky wood which had doubtless been burning when it was shot into the cave; several fragments of decoy birds made of rushes; a section of the dried windpipe of some animal; and some felted vegetal down.

Lastly, there was a complete rectangular bag or case woven of rushes and wrapped in a piece of rush mat, which lay on the floor of the level (about 48 inches deep) in the west corner of the "lot" at the base of a large fallen rock. This contained a skin bag of red paint, tied with a strip of old net; a small coiled basket; the horn of a mountain sheep; a wooden fire-drill hearth; a bundle of shredded sagebrush bark tinder; a number of greasewood sticks for making arrow foreshafts; several completed foreshafts; a small bag made of animal intestine; three green paint-stones and one white paint-stone.

Third level—48 inches to 72 inches deep. The third level was made only 2 feet deep—that is, from 48 to 72 inches, not because we encountered a natural dividing layer as at the bottom of the second level, but because we encountered material of a somewhat different character. The material composing this level was mostly dust, grass, and rushes, with comparatively few stones, and with many more artifacts in proportion to the total bulk than in the second level.

The contents comprised a 3-feathered cane arrow with a wooden foreshaft, with decorations in green. Some of the fine transverse striping near the notch suggests the work of northern California tribes. Unlike most arrow foreshafts found here, this one was slotted for a point, but the point was missing. It had probably been a stone one. Two obsidian arrow points were found in this level, and one of these may belong to the arrow. Then there were 4 other pieces of cane arrows, one of them with a wooden fore-shaft in place, and seven separate, pointed foreshafts of greasewood.

Most interesting and suggestive was the finding in this level of two wooden foreshafts for atlatl darts.

Among the 25 basket fragments were multiple-rod coiled and pitched specimens, single-rod coiled specimens, and wicker rod-and-splint weaves, all similar to those in the preceding level; the only new thing in basketry being the openwork twined technique. In rush matting there were the common types, as in the rush cordage; but in addition there was fiber cord-age, much of it of Indian hemp, and in one instance a heavy cord made by twisting together scraps of old nets. There were also fragments of netting, a strip of twisted downy bird skin from a blanket, and five bits of cord, wound with fur, from fur-cloth blankets. Some of this fur looks to be from the fox and some from a small rodent of rat type, but not muskrat. A piece of a bag woven of rushes; a bundle of straight plant stems, apparently of wild blue flax (*Linum lewisii*); a bundle of bark fiber; some pieces of sticks and cane burned at one end; some feathers; a piece of white paint; a bit of tanned skin; a deer hoof from a rattle or ornament; and a chip of crystal also appeared. Of slightly greater interest were two broken snares; a string from a feather-cloth blanket made by twisting downy feathers about a cord, the only example of this found in the cave; some disk beads of shell strung on a braided string; two wads of rushes used as stuffing for a decoy; a stuffed duck head, part of a decoy; a crudely chipped "fish knife" of slate such as were picked up by the dozen at aboriginal sites around Humboldt lake; a piece of the rib bone of some animal, serrated on the edges; and finally 3 bone awls made of animal shoulder blades, L-shaped, with a projection at the proximal end of the awl at right angles to the shaft forming a sort of handle.

Fourth level—72 inches to 96 inches deep. The fourth level had no nat-ural bottom, no dividing layer, to show us where to stop, so the 2-foot cut was made arbitrarily. The composition of the deposit was about the same as in the preceding level.

Two pits, numbers 38 and 39, originated in this fourth level and pene-trated the white substratum forming the bottom of the cave. The exact point of origin of pit 39 could not be determined, but pit 38 was clearly dug from a point near the upper surface of the level. Measuring 4 feet 6 inches from north to south and 4 feet 2 inches from east to west, it reached a depth of nearly 6 feet below its level of origin, or 12 feet from the surface. In the bottom was a typical grass lining, and about 3 feet above, another, showing that the pit had been used at least twice. It contained some large pieces of pine wood, brought from the distant high ranges, some shell beads, some fine strings, and a bundle of snares.

Pit 39, which lay just to the east, reached a depth of 10 feet 11 inches from the surface and originated in the fourth level, so it might have been anywhere from 2 feet 11 inches, to 4 feet 11 inches deep when first dug. Its diameter was 3 feet 4 inches. The grass lining had been disturbed and mixed in the lower part of the pit, possibly when the owner removed the contents of which he overlooked a number of little dried fish.

The arrow fragments and foreshafts typical of the upper levels were not found in this one, but instead a single pointed foreshaft so large that it probably belonged to an atlatl dart rather than to an arrow, and also part of a typical atlatl dart foreshaft.

In basketry there appears for the first time, a fine twined, flexible weave, of the same type but different material as that made by the Klamath, Modoc, and Pit River Indians today. In addition there was the rather coarse coiled basketry, made on a 3- or 4-rod foundation, the openwork twined basketry, and the rod-and-splint wicker basketry noted in the third level. A slight variation is seen in the introduction of occasional rows of twining in the wicker basketry. The matting, the rush cordage, the fiber cordage, and the pieces of rush bags were about the same as in level 3, but some of the netting was dyed.

For the first time in place were numerous feathers of eagles and other large birds, tied to pieces of rush rope. Among miscellaneous articles were bundles of grass and basket splints; strips from bird-skin and fur-cloth blankets; quids or chews of rush fiber; scraps of buckskin; Olivella-shell beads, some strung on a buckskin thong; a shell disk bead; some deer hair; a piece of animal bone with incised decoration; a flat oblong object of slate with a hole in the middle, suggesting the so-called "gorgets" found farther east; a well made stone ball, perhaps an inch in diameter; a broken stone knife or dart point; and a ball covered with interwoven leather strips.

Fifth level—96 inches to 120 inches deep. After digging a little way into this level the grassy refuse gave place to guano with a slight admixture of grass and rushes. This continued throughout except on the very bottom, where lay a stratum of ashes of varying thickness, resting on the white lacustrine deposit forming the bottom of the cave. This bottom was found at about 120 inches deep, in some places a little more, in others a little less, over the northeast end of the "lot." Toward the southwest the whole deposit grew gradually deeper, until at the far western corner, it measured 148 inches in depth. Everything below 120 inches belonged to our sixth level.

Our fifth level contained few artifacts, except toward the southwest end, where it struck the upper part of a deposit of basketry and other articles, most of which lay in the level below. From the fifth level, there were neither arrows nor atlatl darts, but in basketry there were the finely woven flexible twined weave first noted in the preceding level, the rather coarse 3-rod coil found in all the preceding cuts, and two new things. One of them was a coiled basket, possibly a woman's hat, made on a flexible single-rod foundation which looks to be split rush. This had a braided rim and had once been covered on the outside with small dark downy feathers and quills, which had been woven into the basket as it was made. The other new find was a soft, flexible, twined bag with rounded bottom, somewhat torn, but still 10¾ inches wide and 13½ inches deep. The material has disintegrated to fiber, but looks as if it might be split rush.

The common rush matting was found, as was also twisted rush rope, fiber cordage, and net fragments, with the usual Olivella-shell beads; and various large feathers attached to rush rope such as appeared in level 4. There were also a piece of a stick for stretching nets, a bundle of very small canes, and a block of wood cut in cubical form which may have been used as a ball.

Sixth level—120 inches to about 148 inches deep. The disadvantage of running arbitrary levels is well exemplified by the fact that the bottom of the 120-inch cut runs directly through a deposit of basketry, in the south-west end of the "lot," leaving part of the deposit in the fifth level and part in the sixth. The thickness of the sixth level, which lay directly upon the original bottom of the cave varied from nothing at the northeast end of the "lot" to 2 feet 4 inches at the southwest end. The composition was mostly guano with some admixture of stones, grass, rushes, and on the very bottom, ashes.

Of weapons we found only a large, heavy, pointed foreshaft of greasewood, larger than those commonly used for arrows, which may have been part of an atlatl dart. In basketry there were the same type of coarse coiled basketry on a 3- or 4-rod foundation, some finely woven flexible twined basketry with patterns in black, and pieces of another twined bag, showing patterns in black. There were also some pieces of the common rush matting, some bits of netting (in part dyed red or brown), and a long stick for stretching nets, with some of the net still fastened to it.

There were other worked sticks in the deposit, some undoubtedly digging sticks, and one curved specimen with a piece of braided hair rope attached; a piece of worked pine bark; and six badly disintegrated "sickles" of mountain sheep horn. The usual Olivella-shell beads were present, some strung on cord; also a piece of shell; a broken L-shaped bone awl; and two wooden objects suggesting pendants, one perforated, the other grooved for suspension. The best objects were a complete, though small, woven rabbit-skin blanket or cape, carefully rolled up and laid away, and a unique headband composed of many tufts of rather short black hair wrapped and strung together with native twine, beneath which was tucked, in one place a tiny bi-pointed bone implement.

The best of these things, as well as the best of those found in the fifth level, were found in connection with two deposits of skulls and loose human bones.

Deeper than any of these things, at 154 and 158 inches in a near-by "lot," were some pieces of flexible basketry with decoration in porcupine quills. These have been described by Orchard (1925).

INTERPRETATION OF STRATIGRAPHIC SECTION

At first glance the contents of the different levels offer little in the way of culture sequence, for certain things like rush matting and cordage are found with little if any change in all levels. But certain other classes of objects yield some suggestive results and warrant dividing the occupation of the cave into three periods: Early, Transitional, and Late. Two levels may be assigned to each period.

For instance, in the case of weapons we have:

1. Arrows (2 fragments)[9]	Surface
No atlatls or darts	18 inches
2. Arrows (26 fragments)	48 inches
No atlatls or darts Floor	
3. Arrows (1 complete, 13 fragments)	72 inches
2 darts for atlatl	
4. No arrows	
1 large point-foreshaft, probably for dart for atlatl	96 inches
5. No arrows	120 inches
6. No arrows	148 inches
1 large point-foreshaft probably for dart	

The table suggests that the bow and arrow was the standard weapon after the floor at 48 inches was laid down, but that earlier the bow and arrow and the atlatl and dart were synchronous. From the presence of typical arrows no deeper than 72 inches we may guess that still earlier the atlatl and dart alone prevailed, but the evidence of our stratigraphic section is too slender to be satisfactory. Fortunately objects found in the adjoining "lots" at depths corresponding to the third, fourth, and fifth levels strengthen the evidence. These were unmistakable pieces of atlatls, foreshafts of atlatl darts, and curious crooked clubs often found with atlatls in the ancient Basket-Maker region farther east. As no arrows were found in the lower levels of the nearby lots either, it is clear that the atlatl with its darts was the typical weapon of the Lovelock cave people until the period

[9] The distinction between the arrows and the atlatl darts found in the Lovelock caves lies mainly in their diameters, the darts being distinctly thicker and heavier than the arrows. This is best brought out by the foreshafts, arrow foreshafts ranging from $\frac{3}{16}$ to $\frac{5}{16}$ inch in diameter (only one specimen measured over $\frac{4}{16}$), while dart foreshafts run from $\frac{6}{16}$ to $\frac{7}{16}$ inch in diameter.

represented by the third level, when the bow and arrow supplanted it.[10]
Adding these additional data to our diagram, we have:

1. Arrows (2 fragments)   Surface
   No atlatls or darts   18 inches
2. Arrows (26 fragments)   48 inches
   No atlatls or darts   Floor
3. Arrows (1 complete, 13 fragments)
   Atlatl (1)
   Darts (2)   72 inches
4. No arrows
   Large point-foreshaft, probably for dart
   Darts   96 inches
5. No arrows
   Atlatl (1)
   Darts
   Crooked clubs of Basket-Maker style (4)   120 inches
6. No arrows
   Large point-foreshaft, probably for dart   148 inches

A somewhat similar change is shown in basketry, as will be seen in the
following diagram:

1. Coarse coiled basketry, 3- or 4-rod foundation   Surface
   Fine coiled basketry
   Coarse twined basketry (rod and splint)
   Slightly finer twined basketry
   No flexible basketry
   No woven bags   18 inches
2. Coarse coiled basketry, 3- or 4-rod foundation
   Fine coiled basketry, 3- or 4-rod foundation
   Coiled basketry, single-rod foundation, coated with pitch
   Coarse and fine twined basketry (rod and splint)
   Wicker basketry (rod and splint)
   No flexible basketry or twined bags   48 inches
3. Coarse coiled basketry, 3- or 4-rod foundation
   Coiled basketry, single-rod foundation, coated with pitch
   Openwork twined basketry
   Wicker basketry (rod and splint)
   No flexible basketry or twined bags   72 inches
4. Coarse coiled basketry, 3- or 4-rod foundation
   Openwork twined basketry
   Wicker basketry (rod and splint)

---

[10] Cane arrow shafts measured from $\frac{4}{16}$ to $\frac{6}{16}$ in diameter, while a typical dart
shaft (the only one available for measurement at this writing) was $\frac{9}{16}$ inch in
diameter. It may be of interest to note here that typical Basket-Maker dart foreshafts
from Grand Gulch, Utah, now in the Museum of the American Indian, Heye Founda-
tion, range from $\frac{6}{16}$ to $\frac{7}{16}$ inch in diameter, and the dart shafts, which in this case
are of wood and not cane, run from $\frac{7}{16}$ to $\frac{8}{16}$ inch.

Same with occasional twined rows
Fine weave twined basketry, flexible   96 inches
5. Coarse soiled basketry, 3- or 4-rod foundation, sometimes
   feathered
   Finer coiled basket on single flexible rod foundation, probably
   a hat, braided rim, outside once covered with dark downy
   feathers
   Fine woven flexible twined bag, brown   120 inches
6. Coarse coiled basketry, 3- or 4-rod foundation, sometimes
   feathered
   Fine twined basketry, flexible, patterns in black
   Fine flexible twined bag, brown with black patterns   148 inches

The rather coarse coiled basketry alone continues from start to finish. Differing from the weapon diagram, the transition period for basketry seems to be represented by the fourth level, for at that time the soft woven bags and flexible baskets hitherto used were given up, and stiff wicker and twined baskets came in—most of them pack baskets—and these lasted until the end; in fact they are still used by the Northern Paiute. This gives us two transition levels, the third for weapons, and the fourth for basketry.

The presence of a feathered coiled basket in the fifth level is interesting, and so is the single-rod pitched coiled basketry in the second and third levels; but their application, if any, to our problem is not clear.

A study of other specimens from different levels casts light on the relative ages of other characteristic products of the cave—the decoys, for instance. In the stratigraphic section they first appear in the transitional third level and seem to have lasted until the end. This is backed by finds elsewhere in the cave, where it was possible to determine the horizon of the decoys. In general they are associated with the upper third, or at most the upper half of the deposits. Pits containing them originated well above the central level. Moreover, the stuffed type of decoy—one of the two types found—is still used by the Northern Paiute.

Another characteristic thing, the rush sandal, appears only in the top level of the stratigraphic section. This is not enough to establish its relative age, however, especially as we are not sure that all of the material in this uppermost cut really belongs where we found it. But throughout the cave, and outside in the rockshelter near the southwest entrance, rush sandals were found in the upper portion of the deposit, and we have no examples of them from the lower levels or from the deeper pits.

On the other hand, the feathers of eagles and other large birds, attached to rush ropes, appear in the fourth and fifth levels of our stratigraphic section and when found in situ elsewhere in the cave were always in the lower half of the deposit.

The stone balls, of which one is recorded from the fourth level, seem also to be associated with the older half of the deposits, as are the ovoid and bi-pointed stones which, although not found in the stratigraphic section, are reported nearby at depths of 130 and 139 inches.

Another characteristic product, and one of the most unique, the L-shaped bone awl, occurs in our transitional third level, and also in the sixth level, and in the older pits in other parts of the cave.

It seems certain that fur-cloth blankets were used during all the occupation of the cave. But there is a type of feather cloth, made by twisting strips of downy bird skin around a long cord or rope which was then woven into a blanket, that appears mostly in the upper levels of the deposit, although we have one piece as deep as the fourth level. The only piece of typical feather cloth, found in the whole cave, such as is associated with early Pueblo culture in the Southwest and was made by weaving together cords wound with downy feathers, not bird skin, was found in the third or upper transitional level of the stratigraphic section.

Still another early type is the sickle-shaped implement of mountain sheep horn, of which a number were found in the sixth level of the section, and a perfect example nearby at 72 inches deep.

Of the objects found throughout the deposit, plain matting was the most abundant. It had warp and weft both of rushes and the rows of twining two or three inches apart. In the top level a much finer weave of matting also appeared, the twining in this being fiber cord instead of rush. In the third level was a coarse type of matting woven entirely of rush, as usual, but with the rows of twining much closer together than in the ordinary type.

Netting was found in all levels except the upper one of this section, but it was found near the surface elsewhere in the cave, so doubtless it belongs to the upper level too. Little difference can be noted in the netting found at different levels, except that very fine netting occurs mostly in the older deposits, and here also there are more examples of nets dyed red or brown, than may be found elsewhere.

Rush ropes were abundant in most of the levels and no essential difference could be found between the older and the later ones. Olivella-shell beads and pointed digging sticks occurred from start to finish.

Sectioning the Snaketown Canal

The excavation of the Snaketown site in southern Arizona by a team of workers attached to the now disbanded research center called Gila Pueblo produced one of the most comprehensive published reports on a single site in the Southwest.[11] The ancient Hohokam canals at Snaketown were sectioned by E. W.

---

[11] E. W. Haury, "The Snaketown Canal," in H. S. Gladwin, E. W. Haury, E. B. Sayles, and N. Gladwin, *Excavations at Snaketown: Material Culture,* Medallion Papers, Gila Pueblo, Arizona, 1937, no. 25, pp. 50–58. By permission of H. S. Gladwin and E. W. Haury.

Haury, and his report is an excellent example of the rich results which come from careful excavation and thoughtful analysis of the data. For further information on culture phases at Snaketown see Chapter 10.

No single accomplishment of the Hohokam commands as much respect as their canal systems, designed to irrigate otherwise unproductive land. This achievement forms the very foundation of their complex culture and on it all of their accomplishments were more or less directly dependent. Further, it was their reliance on agriculture which almost completely eliminated hunting as a factor in Hohokam economy, as shown by the scarcity of animal bones and hunting implements. The extent, and some of the details, of the Hohokam canal systems of the Gila and Salt River Valleys have been well described in the literature of the past 30 years but many questions still remain.

The task of clarifying the canal problem at Snaketown was undertaken not to define the extent of the system but rather to ascertain details of the canal, and, most important of all, to determine, if possible, the age, or the phases, during which the system was in use. On this point, practically all descriptions and discussion of the past have failed to contribute any definite evidence, owing chiefly to the facts that the Hohokam chronology was so imperfectly known and that little digging in the canals themselves had been attempted. Due to favorable circumstances at Snaketown, very satisfactory evidence bearing on the problem of age was gathered.

Only one ancient canal was traceable in the immediate vicinity of Snaketown. Motz' survey followed this for somewhat over a mile to the east and about the same distance to the west of the site making a total of about three miles. Several short sections were obliterated by erosion, which is not surprising since the canal's path is at right angles to the present natural drainage channels. It clings closely to the edge of the upper terrace of the valley which, in this region, supports the arid desert growth. Topographic and man-made changes have made it impossible to determine at precisely what point the canal joined the river. At first it was thought that the intake must have been located at Gila Butte where the Gila is cutting into the southern slope of the hill; a map of the Pima canals in this section shows short stubs of old canals at this point. Levelling with the surveyor's instrument, however, made it clear that the intake must have been somewhat higher up-stream. Search to the east of Gila Butte revealed a short section of prehistoric canal which apparently had its intake about five miles to the east. While the full extent of this canal could not be traced, if projected westward, it would have passed north of Gila Butte to connect with the eastern end of the Snaketown canal. The contours of the land show that such a route would have been feasible. If this reconstructed course of the Snaketown canal is correct, its total length was over ten miles, a short distance as compared with some of the others in the Gila and Salt River Valleys, such as that which supplied water to Casa Grande which was over 16 miles in length (Cummings, *1927*:10).

About half a mile west of Snaketown the canal divides, the south fork continuing to run for a short distance along the brink of the terrace while the north fork swings away from the terrace edge into the flat desert land where it finally disappears. This branch apparently served a series of Classic Period settlements located west of Snaketown. From the sherds in the excavated sections of the Snaketown canal, it is believed that, although Snaketown was abandoned prior to the Classic Period, the canal continued to be used after the abandonment.

The Snaketown canal is recognizable today in the best preserved sections as a shallow channel, flanked by inconspicuous ridges. These measure, on an average, about 10 m. from crest to crest above the fork in the canal, and slightly less below this point. The direction of the canal was governed more or less by the topography, but there were no great obstacles, such as hills or arroyos, to turn it sharply from one side to the other. Recent erosion has cut the canal at several places but apparently little difficulty was experienced with gulleys in older times. The drop in the grade of the canal, as determined from the present surface conditions over a stretch of three miles, was less than 8 m. or an average of about 2.5 m. per mile. Curiously the north fork has a greater fall than the south fork, although running farther from the river.

In the southwestern section of Snaketown the canal was obliterated. [There is] a slightly higher elevation here in the form of a ridge which runs along the edge of the terrace. A part of this has been caused by the canal itself, due to the continued washing in of silt and consequent repeated cleaning of the ditch. Where the canal is not visible, wind-blown material and the debris of modern occupation account for the fill. A series of houses now occupies this elevated, and hence better drained, area, overlooking the present fields of the Pimas.

The fact that the Snaketown canal ran along the edge of the terrace, when it might have been placed without difficulty much farther back in the desert, is in itself a suggestive point as regards the location of the land which was cultivated. It will be recalled that Snaketown was situated on the highest of the Gila River terraces and that immediately below lay another terrace, very flat and bearing a dense cover of mesquite. Its width varies from three-quarters to one mile whence it drops off to the flood plain in which the river now runs in a shallow channel. A walk over this terrace shows fields in full cultivation, others abandoned and partially over-grown with mesquite, and still others covered with large mesquite, the old canals and low earth ridges of the borders being the only testimony of cultivation by the Pima within historic times. Fig. 16 [not reproduced here] shows the extent of the Pima canals on this terrace and it is significant that none occur on the upper terrace. The largest Pima canal, now abandoned, follows the base of the upper terrace paralleling the ancient ditch on the higher level. With this evidence it is clear that, then as now, the main fields of the Hohokam were on the rich alluvial plain of the lower terrace in the vicinity of Snaketown, while auxiliary fields west of Snaketown undoubtedly were cultivated on the upper terrace where the canal ran at some distance from the edge of the terrace.

TEST 1

The canal tests tell a highly interesting story of silting up by nature and re-excavation by man to preserve the systems. The task of maintenance must have been almost as great as the herculean efforts expended in the original digging of the canals, a fact which has not been fully realized.

Test 1 exposed three superimposed canals. The first or oldest, was the largest, the second the smallest, and the third and most recent was of intermediate size (see Fig. 8.7).

First Canal

Excavated into native soil; the channel being somewhat irregular. Apparently the water never ran much over 1 m. in depth and not long enough, without changes in the channel, to develop the mineral crust seen in the two upper canals.

Sherds were the only criteria for ascertaining the age of the first canal. At the time it was dug, the surface must have been littered with sherds now found in the embankments of earth thrown up along the edges of the ditch. These sherds were predominantly of the Santa Cruz Phase, and none were later than this phase. This may be taken as an indication that occupation at Snaketown had already entered the Santa Cruz Phase when the first canal was dug, about 800 A.D. It is possible, of course, that in digging this canal, all traces of a former one may have been obliterated, but, lacking such evidence, the date given must stand as an approximation for the oldest canal in this series of three.

Through extended use, this canal became partly filled, followed by a slight pause in the filling when a new bottom was formed, lying approximately 1 m. above the original bottom. Silting then continued until the original surface level must have been nearly restored, the canal thus being almost completely silted up. The pottery in the upper part of this accumulation belonged to the Sacaton Phase, indicating a span of not less than a century between the original digging and the last stage in the filling process.

Second Canal

Dug into the sediments filling the first canal (see Fig. 8.7); channel considerably smaller than first canal and crusted with a lime deposit.

The sherds in the bottom of this canal and in the silts which formed date from the Sacaton Phase, about 900–1100 A.D. During this same phase, the

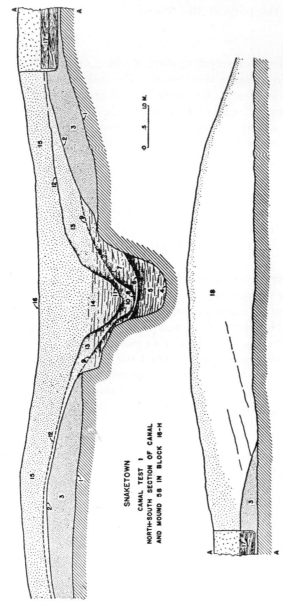

SNAKETOWN
CANAL TEST 1
NORTH-SOUTH SECTION OF CANAL
AND MOUND 58 IN BLOCK 16-H

0 .5 1.0 M.

Fig. 8.7. Section through the Snaketown Canal and Mound 58 showing the superposition of three canals and the relationship of the rubbish mound to the canals. 1, old surfac-e; 2, surface after first canal was dug; 3, material removed during digging of the first canal, contained sherds not later than Santa Cruz Phase; 4, bed of first canal; 5, sediments; 6, channel floor where water ran for a time after partial sedimentation; 7, sediments; 8, lime crusted bed of second canal; 9, probable surface when second canal was in use; 10, stratified sediments, much Sacaton Phase pottery; 11, lime crusted channel of third canal; 12, surface when third canal was in use; 13, sediments and sandy material into which third canal was excavated; 14, stratified sediments; 15, sandy material deposited by wind and water since last canal was used; 16, present surface; 17, Pima cache, a wooden box with various iron tools; 18, rubbish mound (58) dating from Sacaton Phase overlapping deposit 3 with Santa Cruz Phase sherds.

rubbish mound (No. 58) on the north bank of the canal began to accumulate, the rubbish overlapping the soil containing Santa Cruz Phase sherds thrown out during the excavation of the first canal. Sediments finally filled this canal as was the case with the first in the series.

Third Canal

Channel excavated into silt of second canal; sides and bottom of canal crusted with lime, there being two layers in the bottom about 10 cm. apart, the upper sealing in the lower.

Numerous Sacaton Phase sherds were found between the two layers of crust in the bottom, but none appeared in the final sediments. Thus, the most that can be said as to age is that this canal was used during the Sacaton Phase or later. It was thought, however, that its use might have extended into the Classic Period, in which case the canal would have been in operation after Snaketown itself was abandoned. That this was the case was proven by the conditions encountered in the second test.

Before leaving this test, it will be well to say that, although the last two canals in this series were not originally excavated to as great depths respectively, as the first, all three were lower than the present lowest contours of the site, showing that water could not have been taken from the canal and led by means of laterals to the actual village as was done at Los Muertos, a large site of the Classic Period (Haury, 1945) located about ten miles north of Snaketown.

After abandonment, wind and water have laid 2 m. of silt above the top of the last canal.

TEST 2

A second test was made about one-half mile west of Snaketown where the canal divided. If the supposition be correct that the uppermost canal of the series in Test 1 was maintained by the Hohokam during Classic Period times, evidence to this effect should be found near their houses. Fig. 8.8 reveals the conditions as encountered in the trench dug at this point.

Valuable evidence was found in waterworn sherds of Casa Grande Red-on-buff of the Classic Period in the beds of the canals, affording proof that the canals were in use when this type of pottery was being made. Absence of underlying canals in Test 2 suggests further that the canal did not reach its greatest length until late in Hohokam times. The two lowest canals at Snaketown were estimated to have been in use from 800 to 1100 A.D., and we have good evidence to show that the upper canal in Test 1 and the extension of the same in Test 2 was used at 1300 and possibly somewhat later. As a conservative estimate, this gives us a life of about 500 years for the Snaketown canal.

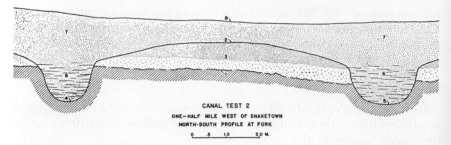

Fig. 8.8. Section through Snaketown Canal at fork. *1,* caliche-clay line with overlying soil deposit; *2,* surface at time canals were in use; *3,* earth removed from excavation of canals; *4,* bed of south fork; *5,* bed of north fork; *6,* stratified sediments containing Classic Period sherds; *7,* sandy material deposited by wind and water since canals were used; *8,* present surface.

DISCUSSION

Following are a few facts of general interest regarding the Snaketown canal.

Although a width of 10 m. from crest to crest showed that we were dealing with a large canal, the actual water channel was comparatively small. Thus, assumptions based on surface indications that all canals are large, may need revision. This is not said with the intention of belittling Hohokam accomplishment in the development of irrigation systems, but rather to show that surface conditions may be misleading. A few canals do stand out because of their apparent size, as for example, those in the Park of Four Waters east of Phoenix, but it should be borne in mind that excavation here has never revealed the exact size of the channel which carried the water.

The small secondary ditch in the bottom of the main canal found by Cushing (Haury, *1945*) did not occur in the Snaketown canal. In a test trench dug across a canal in the Gila Valley by Dr. Byron Cummings in 1926, a similar inner canal was encountered. It may be that this feature is to be found only in the larger canals which apparently have broad flat bottoms in contrast to the deep and narrow Snaketown canal. These secondary channels would serve to confine the water during times of scarcity.

In view of the flat grade of the canal—a drop of about 2.5 m. to the mile —it was surprising to find sherds as much as 5 cm. across which had been carried far enough to round off the corners. Coarse sand and fine gravel also occurred, especially in the deeper parts of the channels. It is probable that this material represents detritus carried into the canal by small freshets which broke in somewhere along its course. As a rule, however, the water apparently ran quietly with practically no load, as shown by the formation of a mineral crust in the canal bed.

There is evidence that the volume of water carried in the canal fluctuated, as it does in the canals of today; but some water must have remained in the ditch most of the time, as shown by the presence of fresh-water snail shells (*Helisoma trivolvis* Say and *Succinea avara* Say).

When the Hohokam first developed canal irrigation is a question which cannot yet be settled. For the first time, however, estimates with sound foundation can be made. Taking the evidence of the Snaketown canal at its face value—the allocation of the oldest canal of the series in Test 1 to the Santa Cruz Phase—we can say that the beginning of canal irrigation was not later than about the middle of that phase, or about 800 A.D. But because none of the later canals in Test 1 showed any improvement or marked difference from the earliest, it may be inferred that the Santa Cruz Phase canal does not represent the first attempt at canal-building by the Hohokam. In the belief that irrigation must have started before culture reached its peak in the Colonial Period—in fact, irrigation would have been mainly responsible for that rise—one is tempted to place the beginning of the trait as not later than the closing phases of the Pioneer Period, or sometime before 500 A.D. As support for this idea, we find that, prior to the Santa Cruz Phase, there were eight or more centuries of intensive occupation at Snaketown for which we cannot say definitely that canal-irrigation was employed, although from the nature of the grinding tools as far back as the Vahki Phase we believe that agriculture was practiced. It would not be possible for a sizable community to subsist in this arid region on agriculture without some form of irrigation, assuming that there has been no appreciable climatic change in the last 2000 years. We may ask, then, by what form of irrigation were the crops raised? There are several possibilities. The first is that of irrigation by canal. But no tangible evidence can be advanced in support of the idea that canals were in use as early as the Vahki Phase. Holding to the belief that irrigation by canal, once acquired, would accelerate culture advancement without much of a lag, a logical assumption would be that this form of water supply was not acquired until the final phases of the Pioneer Period, a few phases before the peak of development was reached. A second possibility is that of flood water irrigation. As has been pointed out by Bryan (*1929:* 445), the areas utilized in flood water farming vary, the choice depending upon the local topographic conditions. One of these is supplied by the environment of Snaketown, as the village lay adjacent to the broad valley of the Gila River, the floor of which was subject to the inundation of sheet floods. Knowing the valley, the Hohokam could have selected such spots where, in times of flood, the water was not swift enough to wash out the crops and did not carry enough silt to cover them. There would be no evidence today of such a method, as the Hohokam would have been wholly dependent upon the flooding of their fields by natural forces, but the practice is one which, without much stretch of the imagination, could have been the forerunner to canal irrigation. A third possibility takes a climatic change into consideration. Both Brooks (*1926:*393) and Huntington (1933:324) have advanced the idea that a wet period culminated a few hundred years before the time of Christ. This period might conceivably have fallen within the range of occupation at Snaketown. Under such conditions, dry-land farming would have been possible. With progressive desiccation setting in, farming on such a plane would have become increasingly precarious unless new means were developed to meet the contingency. The logical solution was, of course, the development of canals. Whether this attainment was purely of local origin or whether it was brought in from some source where it had been previously established, will doubtless be a subject for perpetual discussion; but the fact remains, that in the environment of the Hohokam along the Gila River, the fingering out of flood water in small channels on the flood plain, the sheet-like spread of water on the desert during heavy rains, and the effects of this on adjacent vegetation, could not have gone unnoticed by the Hohokam. Although natural conditions thus favored a local and independent development of irrigation systems, we may never know whether or not the Hohokam profited by the example thus set by nature.

It is a fact that the establishment of many of the late Hohokam settlements, from the Sedentary Period on, was made possible by the canals which brought the water needed for domestic purposes to the village. Hence, a survey of all Hohokam sites with emphasis on their relation to streams, might prove a useful method in ascertaining when canal irrigation came into being. For example, the discovery of early Colonial and Pioneer Period villages far from streams would be a decided lead.

The maximum size of the canals, both as to width and depth, and the greatest scope of the systems, was pretty definitely not reached until the Classic Period, about 1200–1400 A.D. The systems then dwindled, ending in the small but nevertheless efficient systems of the Pima of the eighteenth and nineteenth centuries. Both Font and Garces, writing in the eighteenth century, tell of well developed irrigation among the Pima (Russell, 1908:29, footnote; 87, footnote d). Recent reclamation projects have again brought large and intricate canal networks to this area, some of which now lead water to land never before cultivated by the Indian.

Stratigraphic Deposits of Sandia Cave

A classic example of cave stratification is presented in the deposits of Sandia Cave, New Mexico, excavated by F. C. Hibben of the University of New Mexico.[12] The particular importance of this site is in the lower materials, referred to as the Sandia culture, which are probably the oldest certain evidence of man in the

[12] F. C. Hibben, *Evidences of Early Occupation in Sandia Cave, New Mexico, and Other Sites in the Sandia-Manzano Region*, Smithsonian Institution, Miscellaneous Collections, vol. 99, no. 23, pp. 11–15, 16–18. By permission of the Smithsonian Institution.

New World found to date. The radiocarbon dates of the Sandia materials and their significance have been discussed by Hibben (1955) and Crane (1955). For a general review of the evidences of early man in the New World see Wormington (1957).

The well-defined stratigraphy of Sandia Cave is one of its outstanding features. Fig. 8.9 illustrates the precise nature of this stratigraphy and shows that it extends, with slight variations, throughout the cave. Stratigraphic sequences of this sort are of the utmost importance in determining relative chronology.

The deposits of Sandia Cave have no physical connection with any exterior deposits. For this reason, correlations with glacial phenomena and Pleistocene chronology known from open sites are somewhat difficult. Groupings of the strata within the cave necessarily are referable mainly to periods represented only by phenomena occurring within the cave. However, the problem of exterior factors such as stream erosion or accidental wash into or through the cave is practically eliminated. All objects and matter in the cave appear to have been deposited there originally. There was no deposition from the outside nor were original internal deposits redistributed by such factors as stream wash, solifluction, faulting, or other natural agencies of disturbance. These deposits, then, may be regarded as primary and may be judged in their relative positions. Such items as fire areas with undispersed lenses of charcoal reaffirm the undisturbed nature of the deposits. Naturally, a problem of this sort involves considerations different from those of a river-terrace or river-sediment site.

The uppermost stratum, labeled "recent deposit" in Fig. 8.9, is for the most part wind-blown dust, bat guano, and pack-rat dung. The guano deposits occur in the greatest concentrations in the front portion of the cave, thinning toward the back, and disappearing altogether at about meter 70. Beyond this, only a very light covering of dust represents the uppermost stratum. The make-up of this layer is varied in places by the addition of small rocks and large slabs that dropped from the roof in recent times (see Fig. 8.10) and, at the very mouth of the cave, by a considerable quantity of wind-blown and pack-rat-deposited leaves and vegetable material. This top layer is entirely dry. Owing to this circumstance, and also to the fact that mammal forms found in it are for the most part living species, it has been labeled "recent."

In several places this recent accumulation extended to the roof. This completely blocked the passage and possibly accounts for the fact that here is almost no wind-blown material in the rear portions of the cave. At several places, in the first meters, where the accumulation reached the roof it even extended up into fissures where bats formerly roosted. From some lenticular stratification in this recent layer, it appears that there were intervals when the bats did not use the cave, possibly when it was completely blocked and they could find no entrance.

Beneath this recent accumulation is the second definite stratum, a layer

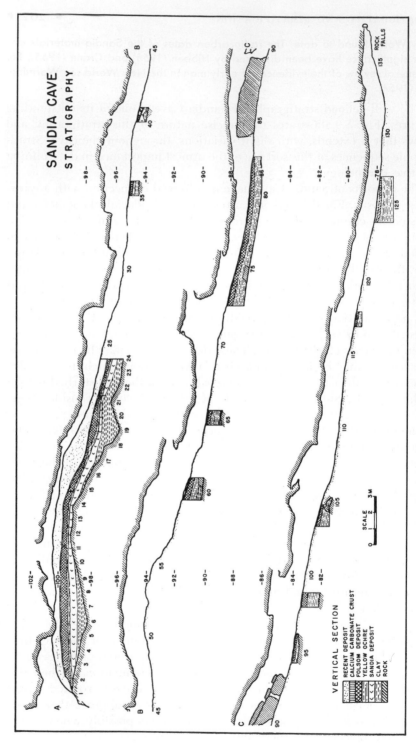

Fig. 8.9. Sandia Cave, vertical section showing stratigraphy.

of calcium carbonate that extends in a continuous crust from the mouth to the extreme rear of the cave. This crust varies from a laminated lime formation a few centimeters thick to a crystalline cave-travertine layer as much as 30 centimeters thick. In some places sheets of stalagmitic mate-

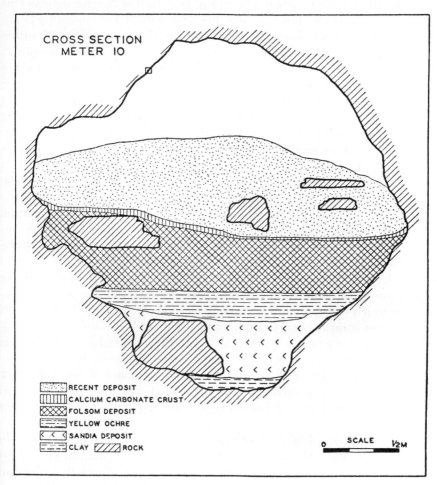

CROSS SECTION
METER 10

RECENT DEPOSIT
CALCIUM CARBONATE CRUST
FOLSOM DEPOSIT
YELLOW OCHRE
SANDIA DEPOSIT
CLAY   ROCK

SCALE
0   ½M

Fig. 8.10. Cross section of Sandia Cave at meter 10.

rial formed on the wall, and an occasional stalagmite protrudes upward from the calcium carbonate crust into the recent layer mentioned previously. Throughout the cave the crust was durable and practically impenetrable. In the front of the cave, near our meter 7, the Boy Scouts had dug through the crust to a limited extent in a search for treasure. The hardness of the lower layers, however, soon discouraged them. Near the rear of the cave, in two places at meter 75 and at meter 90, large sections of the roof had dropped subsequent to the formation of the calcium carbonate. These large pieces of rock broke completely through the crust and partially buried themselves in the debris below. At several places rocks of varying size from an earlier fall are incorporated in the crust. Most of them are completely encased in a layer of calcium carbonate.

Below the calcium carbonate capping is a stratum of cave debris. This has been termed the Folsom layer because typical Folsom artifacts are included in it. This Folsom stratum is composed of mixed material with a preponderance of stone and bone fragments. In addition, there are pieces of yellow ochre, crinoid stems, charcoal fragments, flint chips, and other cultural material. Originally, the Folsom layer apparently was a cave floor strewn with accumulated debris. Many of the fragments of animal bones also indicate the lairing of animals, either carnivores or cave-dwelling mammals in this same cavern. That the material was originally unconsolidated and loose seems evident from the size of the individual particles as well as from the fact that much of the material has drifted down the slant of the passageway toward the back of the cave, possibly as a result of the continual passing of animals, or men, or both.

The Folsom layer is now, however, consolidated into a cave breccia. Much of the material has a hardness comparable to somewhat friable concrete. Many of the fragments of stone, artifacts, and even some of the bone pieces are covered with crystalline calcite. Waters highly charged with calcium carbonate from the stalagmitic crust above the Folsom layer have consolidated most of the material into a solid mass. That moisture destroyed much of the bone material seems evident. Most of the fragments were almost completely disintegrated as far as the bony structure was concerned, their presence being indicated only by cavities left in the breccia or by the arrangement of the calcite crystals. Evidently because of the porous nature of the Folsom deposit and the amount of moisture once present there, only a small number of bone pieces were fossilized, and then usually with the addition of a heavy calcium crust deposited on their surfaces.

Although charcoal in very small fragments was relatively abundant in some parts of the Folsom stratum, it was nowhere concentrated in what might be construed as a fire area or hearth. It is significant that charcoal fragments extended to the very surface of the layer. A few pieces are embedded in the lower portion of the stalagmitic crust.

The Folsom stratum extends considerably farther back in the cave than would be expected. Even at meter 100 it is thick enough to be readily distinguishable. Artifacts and signs of occupation are, however, limited to the front portion. Only one large blade referable to the Folsom complex was found in the excavated section from meters 72 to 83. The whole Folsom layer naturally thins toward the back of the cave (see Fig. 8.9).

Beneath the Folsom stratum and in unconformable contact with it, is a layer of sterile yellow ochre, finely laminated and evidently waterlaid

The laminations consist of differentiated streaks of light and dark ochre of a vivid yellow hue. Here and there lenses of the material were consolidated almost to the consistency of rock, apparently by a binding of calcite. All the ochre, in spite of its seemingly pure nature, is pervaded with calcium carbonate. Its mode of deposition, a purely geologic problem, is discussed by Professor Bryan in the appendix to this paper [not reprinted here].

The top surface of the yellow ochre layer obviously suffered some erosion, apparently physical. In some sections a path or passageway, worn by the movement of men or mammals back and forth through the cave, may be noted on the top of the layer. Folsom debris lies immediately above this unconformity, and the destruction of the topmost layers of the yellow ochre is indubitably referable to Folsom times.

The yellow ochre represents another wet period and is absolutely sterile as far as bones, cultural material, or even rock fragments are concerned. This sterility indicates a totally different set of conditions from those surrounding the deposition of the layers both above and below it.

The yellow ochre stratum, with the possible exception of the calcium carbonate crust, is the most constant in the cave. The layer increases in thickness toward the back of the cave (see Fig. 8.9), where, in certain test pits, it achieves considerable depth. In some places in the rear of the cave the yellow ochre extends to and rests on bedrock, to the exclusion of other strata.

Beneath the yellow ochre is another layer of cave debris. This represents the lowermost or earliest occupation of Sandia Cave. The material of this layer is more finely divided and less consolidated than that of the artifacts, charcoal, crinoid stems, and brownish colored dirt, evidently wind-blown and mixed with vegetable and animal material. This stratum, because of the cultural items included, and its lower and distinct position in this cave, has been termed the Sandia level.

The top surface of this Sandia layer is not heavily consolidated and the yellow ochre rests directly upon it with no unconformity noted. Apparently, the yellow ochre was deposited directly on top of the other cave debris, represented by the Sandia layer, with no disturbance other than the infiltration of the moisture carrying the ochre. There was, however, not sufficient calcium carbonate in the yellow ochre to consolidate completely the Sandia layer. Only in some isolated portions, usually near the top, has any consolidation taken place. Even this has not formed a breccia, as in the Folsom stratum, but a friable and noncrystalline mass. The yellow ochre has, however, heavily impregnated the Sandia level with the typical yellow, finely divided dust.

That the Sandia stratum as a whole was moistened by the superincumbent yellow ochre layer seems evident. Bones are poorly preserved, and most of the identifications were made from teeth. Cultural evidence seems to indicate occupation of the cave to the very surface or topmost portion of the Sandia layer, where the yellow ochre lies upon it. Presumably, the Sandia layer represents a dry period in the cave's history, interrupted and made untenable by the succeeding wet period of the yellow ochre.

Portions of this Sandia layer were less disturbed or "scuffed" than the Folsom layer above. Two hearths, to be discussed subsequently, were found in position. Occasionally, bones, partially articulated, and cultural remains were discovered in situations where apparently they had been covered over with little or no disturbance.

The Sandia layer does not extend as far back into the cave as the Folsom. As Fig. 8.9 indicates, the Sandia stratum has almost feathered out at meter 40. As a matter of fact, as in the case of the Folsom occupation, it is remarkable that evidence is found so far back. No cultural indication in the Sandia layer occurred beyond meter 23.

Beneath the Sandia stratum, in some places, is another layer. This is the so-called clay layer, an accumulation of disintegrated limestone, almost white in color. Except for the inclusion of large numbers of crinoid stem segments, the material is sterile. The clay is homogeneous and compact in nature. It is laminated, evidently water-deposited, and contains a considerable amount of calcium carbonate. The top surface is pitted sporadically with small hollows apparently of human origin. In many places, the clay stratum completely fills a stream course or channel associated with the original formation of Sandia Cave.

The clay layer also feathers out toward the rear of the cave, and apparently does not extend beyond meter 70. However, it may occur sporadically farther back then this.

SIGNIFICANCE OF THE STRATIGRAPHY

Stratigraphic sequences involving the Folsom complex have long been sought. Data on post-Folsom sequences were expected when the cave investigations were started, and they would have added to our knowledge of the cultural growth of the Paleo-Indian. But instead of another hunting culture to help fill the gap between Folsom man and the earliest Basket Maker remains in the Southwest, we have in Sandia Cave a complex earlier than the Folsom (see Fig. 8.11).

The priority of the lowermost, or Sandia, cave occupation is clear. How much time lapse occurred between the Sandia and Folsom levels is a matter of conjecture. Although there are cultural affinities between the two, over and above the fact that both represent a hunting economy, the interval between them was undoubtedly considerable. This seems indicated both by the evidence for an intervening wet period and by the thickness of the yellow ochre itself.

Since the initial use of the cave by man there has been a succession of

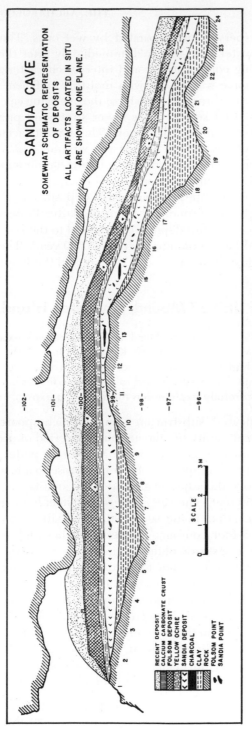

Fig. 8.11. Sandia Cave, vertical section, meters 1–24, showing location of artifacts and fire areas.

dry periods interspersed and separated by wet ones. The yellow ochre layer, obviously water-laid, followed immediately after the Sandia occupation. The ensuing comparatively arid interval characterized by Folsom cultural material gave way to one with moisture sufficient to consolidate the deposit into a cave breccia and to form the overlying calcium carbonate of travertine crust that sealed in the lower strata and prevented the intrusion of later objects into earlier levels. The deposits accumulating during the subsequent dry period formed the stratum which is designated "recent." This succession of dry and wet periods has an important bearing on the chronological significance of the entire sequence in that it provides the basis for a geologic interpretation of the deposits and their correlation with Wisconsin glacial chronology. From the latter Professor Bryan concludes that the sterile ochre deposits correspond to the last ice advance of the Wisconsin and have a nominal date of 25,000 years. The Sandia group lived in the cave just before this nominal date and the Folsom just after it.

Excavation of Unit 37 Mound, Hiwassee Island, Tennessee

The extensive site of Hiwassee Island in Tennessee was excavated and reported on by T. M. N. Lewis and M. Kneberg. One of the main platform mounds (Unit 37) had been added to several times and structures had been erected on its summit. The methods used to determine the history of the building of this mound are carefully explained in the following extract from the report.[13]

This large, truncated, substructure mound which apparently had been the the focus of community life throughout the period of occupancy of the extensive village area by peoples of the Mississippi pattern, was the key to the sequence of the components. Its summit rose to a height of approximately 22 feet above the adjacent ground level, and its longer basal diameter was about 150 feet. The sides rose rather steeply to the summit, the dimensions of the latter being 60 by 90 feet. Plate 11 [not reproduced here] shows the 2-foot contours, the test trenches and an embankment and a terrace on the east side of the summit. Apparently this summit alteration had taken place subsequent to historic occupation. Its purpose is unknown, but it undoubtedly represented the work of early white settlers, since it cut through the top humus and a portion of a former occupational level. The mound had never been cultivated and was covered by a good growth of large timber on the sides and summit; this had been an effective preventative against ordinary erosion, but a portion of the northwestern side had been cut away during high water stages of the river. This erosion had not affected any of the major evidence contained within the mound,

[13] T. M. N. Lewis and M. Kneberg, *Hiwassee Island, An Archaeological Account of Four Tennessee Indian Peoples,* University of Tennessee Press, Knoxville, 1946, pp. 28–33. By permission of the University of Tennessee Press.

but had destroyed some of the underlying village deposit. It is probable that at one time a considerable area of the village may have been present on this side of the mound. During normal stages of the river the shore line was some 200 feet from this side of the mound. Natural soil profiles between the eroded side of the mound and the lower river terrace showed deep village deposits. It can be assumed, therefore, that the mound had originally occupied a more central location with respect to the village than at the time of investigation.

In order to clarify the excavation technique employed in connection with this large and complex earthwork we shall use for illustrative purposes an hypothetical example of a simpler substructure mound than the

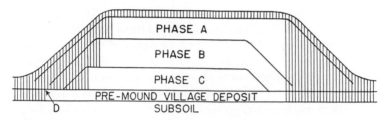

Fig. 8.12. Diagram of substructure mound excavation technique.

one under consideration. It has been customary for us to stake off a grid system of 10-foot squares upon the surface of this type of mound and carry four test trenches 5 feet in width into the mound along the coordinate axes from points beyond the periphery. The schematic diagram in Fig. 8.12 represents a soil profile through the center of an hypothetical example. A trench is begun at the left of the mound, as indicated by the hachured lines, and dug to the depth of subsoil. It is carried forward into the mound by vertical cutting. In order to avoid the destruction of postmolds contained in the floor patterns of community buildings present upon the surface of the premound village deposit the trench is stepped up at point D to the top of this deposit. It is usually not difficult to distinguish between the darker premound deposit and the overlying lighter colored mound-fill. The trench is then carried forward upon the surface of this deposit until the summit of Phase C becomes apparent on the side and end profiles, whereupon the trench is stepped up to the level of that summit and carried forward until the summits of Phases A and B are reached. Then a test trench is begun at the opposite end of this central axis, as shown at the right of the figure by hachured lines. In this hypothetical example we have shown the summit of the uppermost phase, A, as extending to the right beyond the summits of the two lower phases, hence it is to be expected that the summit of Phase A would appear on the side and end profiles of the test trench before those of the two lower phases. At this point the trench is stepped up from subsoil to the Phase A summit where it is carried forward to meet the trench from the opposite direction. The same excavating procedure is followed in the case of the test trenches which are carried into the mound along the other coordinate axis. When the completed coordinate trenches intersect on the summit of Phase A, the resulting four quadrants of humic mantle are then removed. Subsequent to the recording of architectural and other evidence present upon the summit, the test trenches are then carried down through the fill of Phase A to the summit of Phase B. The profiles of both the north-south and east-west coordinate trenches are recorded phase by phase until the excavation of the mound has been completed. These profiles serve as a control for the horizontal stripping of the fill from the summits and for the removal of the fill of the side slopes.

This was the technique followed in the case of the Hiwassee Island substructure mound, and this combination of vertical and horizontal excavation made it possible to obtain a complete series of vertical profiles along the north-south and east-west axes, and to expose an entire building level at one time. As the levels were exposed from time to time the features associated with them were plotted and photographed. The removal of the side slope fill of each constructional phase was carried out concurrently with the removal of the fill which overlay each building level, thereby revealing the form of the substructure during the successive periods.

In order to present an intelligible explanation of the various constructional phases of which this mound was composed, and its stratigraphic relationship to the village deposits, the discussion will begin with the manifestations present upon the earliest level beneath the mound and will consider the evidence as it occurred in time, rather than in order of excavation.

The same original humus zone which lay upon the subsoil beneath the village deposit was found to extend beneath the mound. This dark soil averaged 0.9 of a foot in thickness and contained a proportionately large amount of pottery of Hamilton Focus types. Also included in this layer was material from the succeeding component, which, because of its association with the old land surface, probably represents the culture of the Hiwassee Island Component at the time of its initial occupation and shortly after the abandonment of the site by the people of the Hamilton Component. Overlying the old land surface and merging into it was a village midden deposit ranging in thickness from 0.4 to 1.5 feet. This will be referred to in the subsequent discussions as the pre-mound village deposit. Fig. 8.13, illustrating the east-west and north-south profiles of the mound, shows both of these underlying layers and the successive constructional phases.

Each of the seven major phases of mound construction served as a foundation for large community buildings. From the beginning of occupation by people of the Mississippi pattern this immediate area had apparently

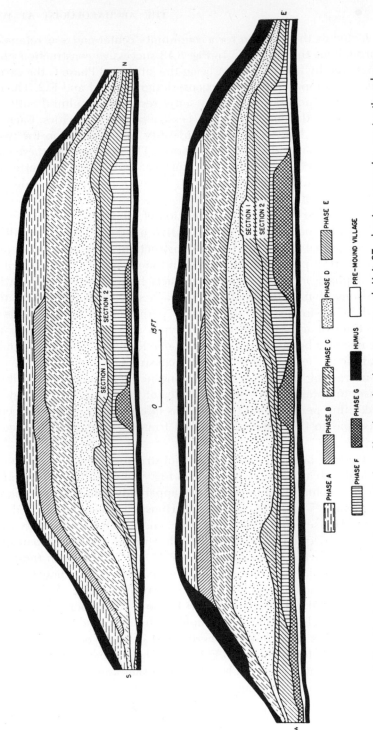

Fig. 8.13. North-south and east-west central profiles through substructure mound, Unit 37, showing successive construction phases.

PHASE A   PHASE B   PHASE C   PHASE D   PHASE E

PHASE F   PHASE G   PRE-MOUND VILLAGE   HUMUS

SECTION 1
SECTION 2

0   15 FT

been selected as the location for a community center and was retained as such throughout their history. In Fig. 8.13 successive construction phases are designated by letter, Phase A being the latest and Phase G the earliest. Phase E was composed of two sections, designated E 1 and E 2. The total mass of the mound does not in any sense represent a cultural entity, except, perhaps, as the end result of successive building activities. Each constructional phase had its individual identity as a foundation for two or more buildings in use at a particular period. The first group of these buildings was constructed upon the land surface, and it was only after considerable time and much rebuilding that the location assumed the form of an elevated foundation.

The rather clearly defined superposition of phases furnished an important means of separating culture-indicative materials into temporally sequent series, since the fill used in the construction of each successive phase contained refuse previously discarded in the village. Thus, the fill of any particular phase included types of artifacts from all earlier occupations. Comparisons of inclusive materials in each successive phase with those included in its immediate predecessor permitted us to determine the relative time of appearance for new types of artifacts, since any type which came into being during the use of one level was generally found for the first time in the fill of the succeeding constructional phase. By the process of subtracting older types and adding newer ones it was possible in most cases to obtain a fairly adequate idea of the cultural technology during succeeding periods, and to relate this information to the architectural sequence and to the materials obtained from the unstratified village deposits.

The deposits beneath the primary substructure phase contained the archaeological features which appear in Fig. 8.14. Building 70, the earliest example of a community building, was apparently contemporaneous with dwelling houses 73 and 74. The floor of House 71 was superimposed upon the floor of House 74 after its destruction, and the large community Building 69 was subsequent to Building 70. The ground plan shows part of another structure which was subsequent to House 74. Although these were the only traceable wall patterns, the entire area surrounding them was filled with postmolds which originated upon the surface of this deposit. This situation did not apply, however, to the southern portion of the area which was entirely lacking in postmolds, refuse pits and midden. A great many refuse pits occurred elsewhere, most of them being precedent to the structure patterns shown in Fig. 8.14. The contents usually consisted of a few fragments of animal bones, mussel shells and an occasional potsherd, and the accompanying soil was very dark from the decayed organic inclusions. These pits appeared to have been dug during the earliest occupational period of the Hiwassee Island Component. The presence of two buildings of the community type and the existence of an unoccupied area

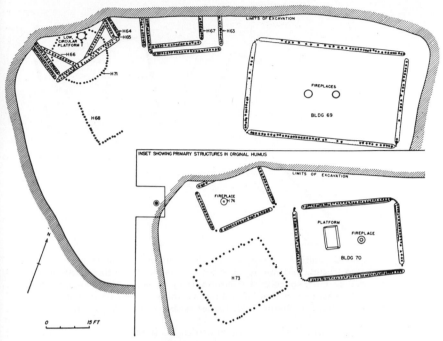

Fig. 8.14. Pre-mound primary and secondary construction levels, Unit 37. Inset showing the earliest structures matches the plan of the secondary structures at "limits of excavation" in upper left hand corner. Target symbol is a matching point for all subsequent levels. Dwelling houses are distinguished from community buildings by the letter H.

to the south strongly implies that there was a planned layout for the village when it was first settled.

The next period of the community center is shown in Fig. 8.15. It is designated as Level G. This level represented the first phase of elevation of the substructure, although it can scarcely be called a single unit of construction. Building 58 had been erected directly above Building 69 but was somewhat smaller. There was no evidence of any fill between the floors of the two structures, but the sequence was clearly shown by the embankments which had been thrown up against the northern and western walls of Building 58. These were 2.5 feet high and approximately 5 feet wide at the base, and they covered a portion of the wall pattern of Building 69. The truncated pyramidal elevation in front of Building 58 was 3.5 feet high and had basal dimensions of 23 by 27 feet. A similar pyramid several feet to the west was associated with Buildings 57 and 62. Building 57 had been constructed upon an earthen foundation about one foot in height, and this was connected with the last mentioned pyramid by a narrow ramp.

A stockade which surrounded Building 62 was, apparently, an integral part of the community plan which, at the time of Level G, included three

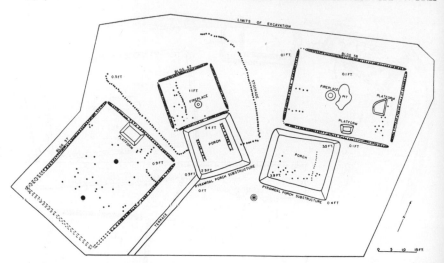

Fig. 8.15. Level G, Unit 37, community center structures. The south portion of Building 57 could not be traced, and the hypothetical completion of the floor pattern is based upon the positions of the two central roof-supporting columns. All elevations indicated are relative to the lowest datum reading of Level G which was the base of the pyramidal porch substructure in front of Building 62. Target symbol is matching point for all levels.

buildings and two small pyramids. Seemingly, it enclosed a courtyard at the rear of the building. It was not possible to trace it completely for the reason that a section of the postmold alignment had been obliterated by subsequent building activities at the northwest end. It seems likely that the stockade was not in use during the entire occupation of Level G, since archaeological evidence indicated that the several successive dwelling houses which had obliterated a portion of its northwest side had been built during the Level G period. Houses 66 and 67 were erected after the removal of the stockade; House 63 lay above House 67; House 65 succeeded House 66, and finally, House 64 followed House 65. To the west and northwest of Building 62 were several postmold alignments which were precedent to the stockade, but their significance could not be determined. Since there was a difference of approximately one foot between the floors of the structures upon this level and those beneath, it is possible that intervening structures may have existed and that all evidence of them had been obliterated by the buildings associated with Level G.

The next time period is represented by the erection of a single uniform foundation, designated Phase F (see Fig. 8.16). The fill of this new constructional phase was composed largely of subsoil clay with some admixture of village debris. It covered the underlying manifestations to a height of 3.5 feet above the floors of the Level G community buildings, and its summit was just slightly higher than the summits of the pyramids of Level G. The primary shape of this substructure was nearly quadrilateral, and its front side faced the southeast. Two successive additions were made

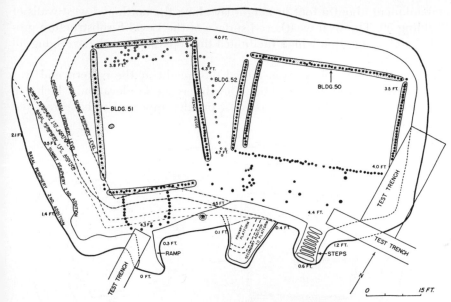

Fig. 8.16. Level F, Unit 37, substructure and associated buildings. All elevations indicated are relative to the lowest datum reading of Level F which was the base of the ramp. Target symbol is matching point for all levels.

along the front and side of the western portion, adding 5 feet to the summit area on both occasions, and increasing the final overall dimensions to 55 by 105 feet. The basal dimensions exceeded those of the summit by about 10 feet. Three projections extended from the front side of the substructure. Two of these, one a ramp and the other a stairway, provided access to the summit of this level; the intermediate tongue-shaped projection had a level top, and its function is problematical. It was evident that all three of these features were in use during the occupancy of Level F.

The patterns of the two buildings upon Level F were well defined. Building 50 at the eastern end had been constructed at the time when the main part of the foundation was built, that is, before the two additions at the western end. Building 51 was not erected until these additions had been made. The incomplete pattern shown on the ground plan of this level and designated Building 52 may have been a structure which was found to be of inadequate size, which decision occasioned the two additions to the substructure. In all probability only a portion of the building was erected before the plans were altered, since the side slope of the primary substructure had not been affected by weathering between the time of its completion and the time when the first addition was built against it. The same condition was observed on the side slope of the first addition which also was apparently inadequate. It was quite evident that the two additions were made almost immediately. The partial remains of a heavy embankment about a foot in height lay along the north and west walls of Building 50. The well weathered surface of the Level F substructure provided a cleavage line which facilitated the separation of the overlying fill of Phase E 2.

When this new phase was added the height at the eastern end was greater than at the western end. This difference in elevation, which can be seen in Fig. 8.13 on the east-west profile, appeared to have resulted

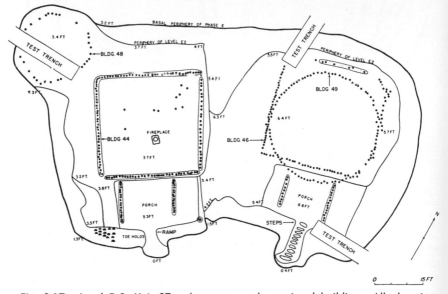

Fig. 8.17. Level E 2, Unit 37, substructure and associated buildings. All elevations are relative to lowest datum reading of Level E 2 which was the base of the ramp. Target symbol is matching point for all levels.

from an effort on the part of the builders to cover the embankments surrounding Building 50 of Level F. The general plan of this new substructure phase corresponded very closely to the pattern established by Phase F, as can be seen by comparing Figs. 8.16 and 8.17. The main difference consisted in an addition at the north-west corner to accommodate the small structure, No. 48. In front of the community buildings the substructure had been increased in height approximately 3 feet, forming small pyramidal eminences. This had necessitated the rebuilding of the ramp and stairway used with the previous level. Building 44 was almost at the same level as Building 51 of Level F, the additional fill at the eastern end raising the foundation only slightly over one foot. The circular structure, Building 49, had been erected prior to the small pyramid, since part of its wall pattern lay beneath it. Building 46 was contemporaneous with the pyramid.

The composite form of Phase E 2 was not only duplicated in the succeeding phase, but its special features were stressed, as is apparent in

Fig. 8.18. In erecting Phase E 1 the shape of the substructure at its base was little modified, but the reconstruction of the summit portion gave sharper definition to the areas supporting the structures and emphasized the differential elevation. This did not entail the addition of much fill but seemed to have been largely a process of renovation. This building level represented the period during which contact occurred between the peo-

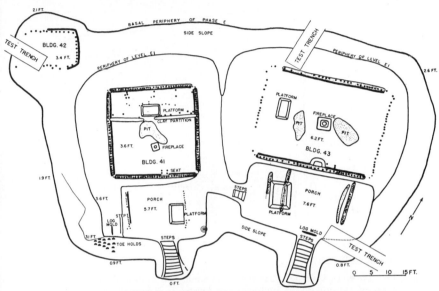

Fig. 8.18. Level E 1, Unit 37, substructure and associated buildings. All elevations indicated are relative to the lowest datum point of Level E 2 which was the base of the steps in front of Building 41. Target symbol is matching point for all levels.

ple of the Hiwassee Island Component and those of the Dallas Component. The fill above it contained the first cultural materials identified as being of the Dallas type. Although there was no evidence that the community buildings on this level had ever been replaced, the weathered surface of the substructure did suggest that this phase and the two associated buildings had been in use for a considerable period. A large number of special architectural details suggest that this period represented an era of prosperity among the people of the Hiwassee Island Component. Probably the community had attained a position of influence in the region; and the center of its public life, as represented by the buildings upon the substructure, was the scene of important political and religious activities. Such a community might be expected to attract new elements of population from other areas and to assume gradually a cosmopolitan aspect. The cultural elements which appeared during this period seem to point to assimilation of new people, rather than to the borrowing of ideas.

In spite of the fact that the next building phase, D, exhibited a marked change in the plan of the substructure, there was an obvious continuity shown in the arrangement of the buildings and their architectural features (see Fig. 8.19). This new addition involved a fill which varied from 2 to 7 feet in thickness and extended the substructure over a much greater horizontal area. The summit was approximately 11 feet above the level of the surrounding village and its dimensions were 60 by 80 feet. The basal dimensions were about 90 to 125 feet. In contrast to the earlier re-

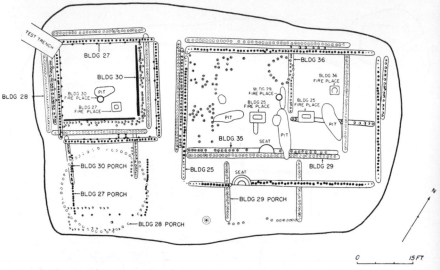

Fig. 8.19. Level D, Unit 37, substructure summit and associated buildings. Postmolds in each series of superimposed buildings are keyed to differentiate the individual wall patterns. Target symbol is matching point for all levels.

construction of the foundations which seemed to have been primarily for renewal, this new constructional phase appeared to have been prompted mainly by a desire to increase the size, especially the height. After its completion, Level D had apparently been used for a long period, if the large number of buildings erected upon it, as shown in Fig. 8.19, may be given that interpretation. Upon the eastern end of this summit four buildings had been erected successively. Building 36 was the first. This was followed in turn by Building 35, 29 and 25. Apparently only Building 28 was contemporaneous with the porch-like pattern in front. At the western end, Building 30 was the earliest, Building 28 next and 27 last. Each of these had contemporaneous accessory structures in front of them. The arrangement of dual buildings and accessory structures was similar to that of the preceding levels.

It has been mentioned previously that cultural materials included in the Phase D fill indicated the presence of the Dallas culture. Further evidence in support of this may be adduced from the fact that a burial which belonged to the Dallas Component was made at the northwestern edge of the substructure, either during the last part of the occupation of Level E 1, or while Level D was in use. It was covered by the fill of the next constructional phase, C. The occurrence of this burial in relation to the mound phases is particularly important in view of the complete absence of any burials which could be associated with the Hiwassee Island Component. None of those occurring in the village area was earlier than any of the archaeological features belonging to the Dallas Component, and there was none in association with the earlier levels of the mound. This burial, then, has important implications for interpreting the changes in artifacts, architecture and substructure characteristics, because it implies the presence of people of the Dallas culture, rather than a diffusion of Dallas ideas to the Hiwassee Island type of community.

Phase C, shown in Fig. 8.20, was another massive addition to the mound. In its simplicity of form it was similar to Phase D, the summit being ap-

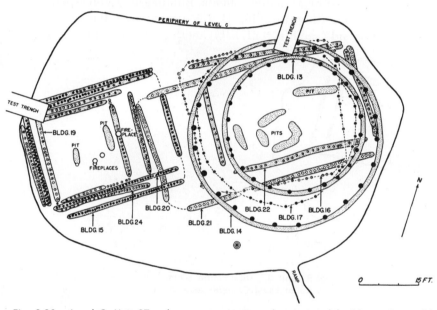

Fig. 8.20. Level C, Unit 37, substructure summit and associated buildings. Postmolds in each series of superimposed buildings are keyed to differentiate the individual wall patterns. Target symbol is matching point for all levels.

proximately the same shape. Two series of buildings had been constructed upon this level. The earliest structure at the eastern end was Building 22 and, apparently, it had been contemporaneous with Building 24 at the western end. Building 21, which succeeded 22, was quite large, and its associated building at the western end, Building 19, was contrastingly small. The next pair of structures were Buildings 17 and 20, and these were in turn followed by Buildings 16 and 18. Building 18 was indicated only by a fire-hardened floor and fireplace, the postmolds having been eradicated by subsequent building activities. The continuous rebuilding operations which took place upon this level had resulted in an accumulation of about a foot and a half of fill above the original Phase C summit. Before the erection of any more structures at the eastern end, a half foot of sandy fill was placed upon the floor of Building 16, and upon this was built the large rotunda, Building 14. Building 15 at the western end was contemporaneous with the rotunda, but no fill had been added beneath it. However, following the abandonment of Building 15, an addition of two feet of fill was made to the western end of the summit. At the time of our investigations this addition was designated as Phase B, but it did not actually comprise a constructional phase in the sense of rebuilding the substructure; rather, it represented a chronological unit which was later used in the analysis of the materials contained within it. This additional elevation covered a portion of Building 14, following which the latter was replaced by a smaller rotunda, Building 13. Contemporaneously with the latter building, Building 11 was erected upon the new elevation at the western end (see Fig. 8.21, left); another structure, Building 10, was

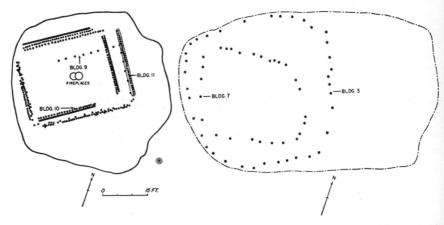

Fig. 8.21. *Left:* Level B, Unit 37, substructure summit and associated buildings. Building 11 overlays Building 15 of Level C. *Right:* Level A, Unit 37, substructure summit and associated buildings.

built sometime later, and Building 13 served as a companion structure for both successive buildings at the western end. The last building, No. 9, was a typical Dallas structure.

The last addition to the mound was Phase A (see Fig. 8.21, right). Its summit was level and embraced an area about 50 feet wide by 85 feet long. Approximately one foot of fill was added at the western end and 3 feet at the eastern. A large portion of the summit had been reddened by fire, probably from burning buildings. Three fireplaces and numerous post-molds attested to the former presence of buildings of the Dallas type. Buildings 3 and 7 were the only distinguishable structure patterns. Some of the postmolds were 1.5 to 2 feet in depth, while others were quite shallow and, therefore, had originated at a higher level. These appeared to be molds from the basal ends of posts belonging to structures which had been erected upon the summit of the mound after a period sufficiently long to allow a layer of humus to accumulate. Pits dug by curio hunters, and root disturbances made it difficult to trace out any structure patterns upon this level. Added to this were the disturbances resulting from the erection of buildings upon the summit by the Cherokee or other historic peoples. The top soil at the eastern end seemed to have been used in recent times to form an embankment across the summit. This borrowing of soil had resulted in the eradication of most of the postmolds which had existed in that area. The few shallow ones which remained indicated that structures had been erected upon that portion of the summit.

A rather heavy humus layer covered the western portion of Level A. It was not attributable entirely to decayed vegetation. Much of it probably represented decayed organic matter discarded during historic Indian occupation. The layer contained a number of European trade articles, and similar articles were found with burials which were intrusive to the top and side slopes. Twenty-three burials occurred in the mound. Four were in pits originating upon Level A and were typical Dallas Focus burials. All others, with the exception of the one previously discussed in connection with Phase D, were intrusive to the mound. Six bundle reburials, which included the partial remains of thirteen individuals, appeared to have been made after some of the recent humus mantle had begun to accumulate. Two of these were accompanied by historic trade articles, from which we have inferred that the other reburials also belonged to the historic period. Four other burials which were found near the base of the mound at the southwestern side, appeared to have been Dallas Component burials, but their stratigraphic association was somewhat difficult to determine due to the redeposition of side slope fill at this point. In method of interment and in the nature of accompanying articles they resembled other burials of the Dallas Component; hence, we have assumed that they were contemporaneous with the four burials interred in Level A. Taking all evidence into consideration, we have concluded that Level A represents the final period of construction by people of the prehistoric Mississippi community.

Stratigraphy in the Monagrillo Site, Panama

The Monagrillo shellmound on the Pacific coast of western Panama was excavated in 1948 and 1952. The report on these excavations by Gordon R. Willey and Charles R. McGimsey[14] has particular interest in the present con-

[14] G. R. Willey and C. R. McGimsey, *The Monagrillo Culture of Panama*, Papers of the Peabody Museum, Harvard University, Cambridge, 1954, vol. 49, no. 2, pp. 12, 15–16, 39–43, 43–50. By permission of J. O. Brew, Director of the Peabody Museum, Harvard University.

nection because of the authors' technique of excavation in arbitrary levels of 10 to 50 cm. thick, the analysis of the artifactual remains (chiefly pottery), the determination of the physical layering (called by the authors "geologic strata"), and the correlation of the cultural stratigraphy based on level-digging with the geologic stratigraphy. This excavation constitutes an example of the American method of digging by mechanical levels in homogeneous midden or trash accumulations, followed by a comparison of the cultural stratigraphy demonstrable from the analysis of the level digging with that which would result from reliance upon collecting from the actual geologic strata which make up the shellmound.

This selection is also of interest in view of Wheeler's criticism of arbitrary-level technique of excavation as an "outworn method" (Wheeler, 1954:53). The defense of the American method of "metrical stratigraphy" has been made by Thompson (1955). No archaeologist would argue that arbitrary-level excavation is preferable to the method of excavating deposits which have visible stratification by "peeling" off the layers separately and keeping materials from each layer as a single lot. But most American archaeologists who have had experience with unstratified refuse deposits, which can only be excavated by arbitrary levels, would scarcely agree with Wheeler's stricture that the method is "outworn."

EXCAVATION PROCEDURES

As stratigraphic control was an objective in virtually all of the excavations, the individual tests were quite limited as to horizontal dimensions. Test pits were almost always laid out as 3 × 3 or 3 × 2 m. cuts. In the four long trenches which we excavated, one in 1948 and three in 1952, the actual digging proceeded by section units which were connected to make the trenches. All sherds and other artifacts were segregated by these sections. Vertical control in most cuts was by arbitrary levels. These levels ranged in thickness from 10 to 50 cm., usually maintained at a standard measure within a single excavation unit. In some cases, where, through error in digging, pit floors were carried down below specified depths, levels varied from 5 to 15 or 20 cm. There are also excavations where, for special reasons, collections were segregated by natural strata, or by certain features, rather than by the relatively thin, arbitrary levels. In general, however, the uniform consistency of the mound and the absence, or near-absence, of structural or burial features made practicable the system of small horizontal and vertical control units.

The objectives of the 1952 excavations were three-fold. First, it was our purpose to search the site carefully for possible stratified deposits which would enable us to place, in a relative chronology, the Monagrillo ceramic style and its associated remains. Second, data on the physical history of the mound were important desiderata. Finally, our third purpose was simply that of obtaining a larger sample of Monagrillo artifacts. In pursuing these objectives it was clear that our methods and attack were to be, essentially, one. The story of the physical growth of the Monagrillo tumulus could best be studied, it was reasoned, by cross-sectioning trenches. These same trenches could be excavated by sections and levels as means of control in our stratigraphic check. In addition, the augmentation of the Monagrillo artifact sample could be made from such cross-sectional trenches or from such additional pits as was deemed necessary.

In consequence, we initiated the East, Central, and West Trenches. In the East Trench, Sections 5 and 15 were put down first. These measured, as did all but one section of this trench, 3×2 m., and the long axes of these sections were oriented on a north-south line. The East Trench progressed by cutting sections, sequentially, north of Section 15 and both north and south of Section 5. Each 3×2 m. section block, excavated in 10 cm. levels, was carried into sterile soil before an adjoining block was commenced. The Central Trench progressed in the same fashion, working southward from the initial cut, Section 1. As is evident on the map (see Fig. 8.22), the Central Trench was not extended all the way across the body of the mound but bisected only the south ridge. Sections 1, 2, 5, and 6 of the Central Trench measured 3×2 m. Section 3 was excavated as a 3.50×2 m. block (by error); and, to compensate for this, adjoining Section 4 was laid out as 2.50×2.00 m. West Trench excavations were begun as 3×2 m. blocks. Section 16, the first excavated, lay near the crest of the south ridge midden, directly in alignment with the older cuts of the South Trench and separated by only 50 cm. from Section 1 of the South Trench. Section 7 of the West Trench was placed on the north ridge. The remaining sections of this long trench, for the most part 3×2 m. cuts, were excavated, sequentially, in both directions from the Section 16 and Section 7 starting points. Operations in the Central Trench were completed by mid-February. Digging was not complete in the East Trench until early in March, and the final section was removed in the West Trench on March 6.

Coincident with these three major north-south trenches, a number of smaller excavations, numbered as "pits," were made elsewhere. As a check in the alvina flat on the north side of the mound, Pit XI, a 3×1 m. cut, was put down on the line of the west face of the West Trench about 18 m. north of its northern terminus. For a similar outlying exploratory purpose, Pit XII, another 3×1 m. pit with its long axis lying north-south, was excavated off the west edge of the shell midden in the low-lying neck of the peninsula. Pit XIII, a 2×2 m. pit, was located near the western edge of the mound some 20 m. east of Pit XII and still within the limits of the refuse deposits. Pit XIV, 3×2 m., lay still another 20 m. eastward of Pitt XIII. It was near the western end of the trough and lay on a north-south line with Pit X (1948 season). Pit XIV was excavated to check the depth and nature of the deposits at the western end of the site. Pits XXIV, XXV, and XXVIII lay on an east-west line. All were 3×2 m. They were excavated to observe the strata in the western end

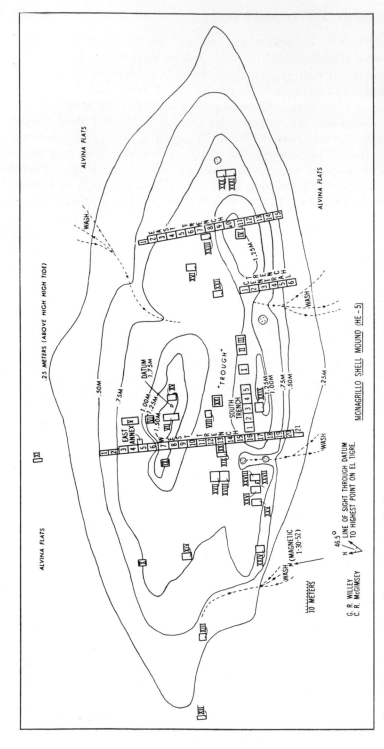

Fig. 8.22. Map of the Monagrillo site (He-5), with excavation units indicated. Arabic numerals refer to sections with trenches; Roman numerals refer to pits. Contour interval 2.5 m.

of the south midden ridge, and, in effect, they serve as a continuation of the 1948 explorations of the South Trench. Pit XXIX, a 3 × 3 m. cut, was located just 50 cm. south of Section 3 or the South Trench. This was near the very crown of the south midden ridge, and this carefully excavated pit was made as a check on the 1948 stratigraphic studies of the South Trench sections. Similarly, Pit XV, a 3 × 2 m. cut, was carried down in the knoll of the north ridge, but a few meters west of the 1948 excavation, Pit VII. Pit XV was, in this case, made as an additional check into the deepest part of the north ridge deposits. At the far eastern end of the site, two contiguous pits, XXV and XXXI, each 3 × 2 m., form the beginnings of a cross-trench at this easternmost terminus of the mound. These pits serve a similar purpose as those at the western periphery of the midden accumulation, that of determining the dip and disappearance of its outermost limits. The pits, XVII, XVIII, XIX, XX, XXI, XXII, and XXIII, were excavated in the last two weeks of our stay at Monagrillo during the early part of March. They were made to follow up hints of stratigraphy that had been disclosed in Section 13 of the West Trench. All of these pits lay within the trough area of the site and were of importance in disclosing the somewhat complex nature of the trough fill deposits. Pit XXVII, a 1.50 × 1.00 m. column, was excavated on the west side of Pit XXVIII. This was a control cut in which all materials were screened and from which complete shell and other samples were removed for careful study. Pit XVI, lying a little to the west of the East Trench, was opened to study the ash and fire pits so common to this particular locality of the mound. This pit was one of the very few not carried down to sterile deposits.

CULTURAL CORRELATIONS

The archaeological site presents two primary factors to the archaeologists: (1) the cultural and depositional forms; and (2) the quantity and distribution of these forms. From these all else must be inferred or deduced.

The geological section of this report discussed the form and distribution of the deposits in general. Later chapters describe in detail the form and resultant categories of the specific cultural content. The preceding general discussion of the distribution and quantity of the elements comprising the deposits was sufficiently detailed for those elements which were laid down by natural agencies since they relate primarily to the problems of delimiting and correlating the various strata and establishing a temporal sequence of the strata and their included material. However, in order to reconstruct the cultural situation as completely as possible, a more detailed analysis of the distribution and quantity of the cultural forms or cultural content is required.

In making this analysis several things are assumed. The geologic strata delineated in the preceding section, or appropriate combinations of them, are utilized without question. Proof of the sequence or contemporaneity of these strata rested entirely on an interpretation of the geologic factors involved. If at any future time a different interpretation is justified, the following section must be reviewed and adjusted accordingly. The major cultural category employed in this analysis is the pottery type. These pottery types also are assumed in a sense, since they were originally categorized on the basis of observable descriptive cohesiveness of form. In another sense, these geologic correlations are an actual test of the types as they are set up, for unless they prove to be logical, meaningful entities when viewed in the light of their stratigraphic associations, they are without chronologic utility and for many problems must be redefined.

The categories of material culture available for analysis are few indeed. Pottery and stone objects are necessarily of greatest concern while fire pits are of interest in connection with one stratum. These three, along with the shell and bone directly resulting from the occupants' dietary requirements, make up approximately 99 per cent of the cultural residue remaining to the archaeologist. Somewhat surprisingly, no discernible tools of shell and few of bone were encountered. The single human skeletal remnant encountered might be considered to constitute the final one per cent of material evidencing former occupation.

CORRELATION OF GEOLOGIC STRATA AND CULTURAL CONTENT

The most cursory glance at a cross section drawing of the He-5 mound [not reproduced here] is sufficient to show that absolute depths and distances are meaningless for cultural interpretation. Only after the cultural content of the mound has been correlated with the natural depositional strata is it possible to draw any conclusions concerning the pottery, stone artifacts, and other man-made phenomena.

It will be recalled that, with the exception of Pit XIX, all the material from He-5 was excavated in arbitrary levels generally ranging from 10 to 50 cm. in thickness. These levels were excavated without regard to the natural geologic strata. In fact, the nature of the deposits was such that in the majority of instances it was impossible to determine the precise boundaries of the geologic strata during actual excavation. They were discernible only after careful study of the completed pit or trench profiles. The pottery, as well as the other artifacts, was counted and tabulated in relation to the arbitrary levels. Therefore, it was necessary to correlate these arbitrary levels and their tabulated contents with the geologic strata defined in the preceding section before further stratigraphic analysis could proceed.

The profile drawings and field notes of each pit were reviewed, level by level, and on the basis of this review each level was assigned to one of the geologic strata. The stratum number was then entered opposite that level on pottery tabulation sheets. In some cases, of course, a simple designation was not possible for a single 10 cm. level would transect several depositional strata. This was particularly true in those locations where the natural strata have a pronounced dip. In these instances all soil strata involved were listed unless the field notes specifically stated that all of the pottery from the arbitrary level had been found solely in association with one or another of the strata. When these comparisons and tabulations had been completed for all excavation units, the results were compiled and summarized on the Geologic Correlation Sheet (Table 4). This chart lists separately every geologic stratum, and every combination of strata necessitated by the above analysis, with the amount of pottery (by type) included in each.

A similar analysis was also undertaken for all the nonceramic elements within the deposit which were presumed to have resulted directly from human activity.

THE DELINEATION OF CULTURAL STRATIGRAPHY

Once the material was correlated with the natural strata it became pertinent to determine whether we were dealing with an individual cultural unit, a single, cohesive, "phase" ("A cultural complex possessing traits sufficiently characteristic to distinguish it, for purposes of preliminary archaeological classification, from earlier and later manifestations of the cultural development of which it formed a part, and from other contemporaneous complexes."), or a number of separate cultural entities; and, if the latter were the case, how these phases correlated with the natural strata.

The mixed levels of the Geologic Correlation Sheet made it somewhat unsatisfactory as a check on positive associations between pottery types and natural strata. Therefore a subsidiary chart, the Stratigraphic Correlation Sheet (Table 5), which consisted solely of the material from the unmixed levels, was abstracted from it. The mixed or combined levels of the Geologic Correlation Sheet were temporarily ignored since consideration of many of them necessitated decisions as to its proper allocation before any basis for such allocation had been established.

From this Stratigraphic Correlation Sheet there emerged a definite pattern which indicated that most of our previously established pottery types had stratigraphic or distributional significance. While some Monagrillo sherds occurred in all sections of the deposit they were predominant only in the first eight strata. The two Alvina types were found almost exclusively in Stratum 9. El Tigre Plain pottery was associated primarily with Stratum 10, although a few scattered sherds occurred in earlier strata.

The almost completely independent stratigraphic associations of the three major pottery divisions (see totals in Table 5) suggested that they represented disparate cultural entities rather than segments of a cultural continuum (a suggestion strengthened by an inspection of the pottery itself). Before this conclusion could be accepted entirely, the occasional

TABLE 4. Geologic Correlation Sheet

Stratum	Monagrillo Plain	Monagrillo Thin Yellow Ware	Monagrillo Variant	Monagrillo Red	Monagrillo Incised	El Tigre Plain	Alvina Plain	Alvina Red	Unclassified	Totals
1a	12	34	—	2	—	—	—	—	—	48
1	267	—	—	9	—	—	—	—	—	276
1, 2	33	1	—	—	—	—	—	—	—	34
1, 5	28	1	—	—	—	—	—	—	—	29
2	17	2	—	3	—	—	—	—	—	22
2, 6	24	1	—	4	—	—	—	—	—	29
3	245	20	—	7	2	4	—	—	—	278
3, 7	95	2	—	5	—	2	—	—	—	104
3, 4	40	—	—	—	—	—	—	—	—	40
3, 5	250	41	—	6	1	—	—	—	—	298
4	209	10	—	5	9	9	—	—	—	242
4, 7	364	6	21	7	—	10	—	—	—	408
5	126	19	—	3	—	—	—	—	—	148
5, 8	75	6	—	—	—	—	—	—	—	81
6, 8a	67	2	—	—	—	—	—	—	—	69
5a	307	2	—	8	—	—	—	—	—	317
5, 5a	51	1	—	—	—	—	—	—	—	52
5a, 8	615	7	—	19	—	1	—	—	—	642
7	1939	5	66	28	7	23	—	1	—	2069
8	11,951	51	10	268	40	36	6	—	3	12,365
7a	40	—	1	—	—	—	—	—	—	41
8a	266	5	—	4	—	10	—	—	—	285
7, 7a	77	5	—	7	—	—	—	—	—	89
7a, 9	6	—	—	—	2	—	—	—	—	8
7, 10	367	2	—	6	2	801	—	—	3	1181
7, 11c	6	5	—	—	—	—	—	—	—	11
8, 9	17	—	—	—	—	—	—	—	—	17
8a, 9	381	10	8	—	—	—	228	25	—	652
8, 10	1370	10	—	36	—	1698	2	—	—	3116
8, 11b	16	—	—	—	—	—	—	—	—	16
9	74	—	—	3	1	—	176	28	—	282
10	22	—	—	—	—	5003	3	—	1	5032
9, 11c	9	—	—	1	—	—	3	1	—	14
11a	158	11	—	2	2	2	1	—	—	176
11b	687	18	—	14	—	8	—	2	—	729
11c	80	3	—	2	—	172	—	—	2	259
10, 11c	4	—	—	—	—	163	—	—	—	167
9, 10	—	—	—	—	—	4	—	—	—	4
Surface	6	—	—	—	—	207	—	—	—	213

TABLE 5. Stratigraphic Correlation Sheet

Stratum	Monagrillo Plain	Monagrillo Thin Yellow Ware	Monagrillo Red	Monagrillo Incised	Monagrillo Variant	El Tigre Plain	Alvina Plain	Alvina Red	Other	Totals	El Tigre Total	Alvina Total	Monagrillo Total
1a	12	34	2	—	—	—	—	—	—	48	—	—	48
1	267	—	9	—	—	—	—	—	—	276	—	—	276
2	17	2	3	—	—	—	—	—	—	22	—	—	22
3	245	20	7	2	—	4	—	—	—	278	4	—	274
5	250	41	6	1	—	—	—	—	—	298	—	—	298
6	126	19	3	—	—	—	—	—	—	148	—	—	148
4	209	10	5	9	—	9	—	—	—	242	9	—	233
5a	307	2	8	—	—	—	—	—	—	317	—	—	317
7	1939	5	28	7	66	23	—	1	—	2069	23	1	2045
8	11,951	51	268	40	10	36	6	—	3	12,365	36	6	12,320
7a	40	—	—	—	1	—	—	—	—	41	—	—	41
8a	266	5	7	2	1	—	—	1	3	285	—	1	281
9	74	—	3	—	—	—	176	28	1	282	—	204	77
10	22	—	1	1	1	5003	3	—	1	5032	5003	3	25
11a & 11b	845	29	16	2	—	10	—	1	2	905	10	1	892
11c	80	3	2	1	1	172	—	—	—	259	172	—	87
Total	16,650	221	368	65	80	5257	185	31	10	22,867	5257	216	17,384

intermingling of pottery types, such as the El Tigre sherds deep in the Monagrillo strata or Monagrillo sherds in apparent association with the El Tigre Stratum, needed to be investigated.

Strata la, 1, 2, 5, 5a, and 6 contained only Monagrillo sherds, but in the East Trench in Strata 3 and 4 there were a few El Tigre sherds as well. In each case the overlying Stratum 7 was very thin and disturbed by a heavy concentration of El Tigre material which extended down to, or almost down to, the lower strata. The four sherds from Stratum 3 were about 50 cm. below the nearest El Tigre deposit, but the chance of accidental intrusion from above is high since the soil of Stratum 3 is very loose.

Strata 7 and 8 also contained material other than that classified as Monagrillo. The mixture here appears to be similar to the situation in Stratum 10 where Monagrillo and rare Alvina sherds occurred in an otherwise El Tigre context. In both instances the mixture probably resulted from the method of analysis. If a 10 cm. level consisted overwhelmingly of fire pit areas it was classified as Stratum 10, and, since the fire pits had been excavated into the Monagrillo strata, it was inevitable that in the entire level some Monagrillo sherds would occur. Conversely, where no fire pits were evident in the profile or mentioned in the field notes Stratum 10 was not designated on the Correlation Sheet; and El Tigre sherds which had spread from nearby fire pits were thereby included in otherwise pure Monagrillo levels. Pit XVI was excavated for the express purpose of determining the relationship between the fire pits of Stratum 10 and El Tigre pottery, and careful observations pertaining to the same problem were made in connection with several other pits and trench sections. In every case a clear cut association was evident between the fire pits and El Tigre pottery as opposed to the surrounding deposits where Monagrillo pottery was predominant. The areas immediately adjacent to the fire pits showed some mixture.

Ninety-seven per cent of the Alvina material was associated with Stratum 9. A few sherds of that type also occurred on or near the surface of the north or south ridges in apparent association with Strata 7, 8, and 10. These few sherds undoubtedly represent material which had been left on the surface of the ridges at the time of the deposition of Stratum 9. The Monagrillo sherds in Stratum 9 probably reached the trough through erosion of the north and south ridges.

Stratum 11, which consisted of eroded material, showed a mixed pottery content. It is, however, significant that in the lower levels—11a and 11b— El Tigre sherds were rare whereas they were the predominant pottery of the upper and later section—11c.

It, thus, is clear that a difinite stratigraphic division exists between the Monagrillo, the Alvina, and the El Tigre pottery complexes.

No stone or bone was found in direct or inferential association with the fire pits of Stratum 10. Although a few shells occurred mixed with the ash they were of the same species as those in the surrounding stratum and probably represented accidental inclusions. Some bone and shell was found throughout Stratum 9 but it was concentrated most heavily in the same areas as the Monagrillo sherds and therefore probably stems from the same source. That is, it represents material washed into the trough from the bordering north and south ridges. It is possible that some of this shell was associated with the Alvina sherds but none such could be positively identified. Stratum 9 contained few stone artifacts, but the two that were present—a small polished celt, and a projectile point—were totally unlike anything found in association with any of the Monagrillo strata. Therefore, while the stratigraphic evidence is no more definitive than for some of the shell and bone, it is considered probable that the two stone implements represent material associated with the similarly divergent Alvina sherds and the deposition of Stratum 9 itself.

From this it is evident that the three major changes in the cultural material and content of the mound were invariably associated with stratigraphic divisions.

There is considerable internal consistency within the Monagrillo Phase so there can be little doubt that it forms a cohesive cultural unit. Insufficient evidence is available for the others—Alvina and El Tigre—to determine the possible existence of internal divisions.

The Monagrillo Phase is associated with the first eight natural strata and presumably covers a considerable span of time, correlating with the abandonment of the old shore and the creation and subsequent filling of the lagoon. The filling of the trough continued after the practical disappearance of the lagoon and the Monagrillo Phase abandonment of the site. Since the Alvina material occurs in all levels of the trough fill, the Alvina occupation must have begun not very long after the Monagrillo occupation ended and have continued intermittently for some time. The El Tigre occupation followed but how much time separated it from the two preceding periods is impossible to determine on the basis of present evidence.

FURTHER QUANTITATIVE AND DISTRIBUTIONAL ANALYSIS OF THE MONAGRILLO PHASE

The purpose of this section is to determine what other inferences can be drawn concerning the human occupation of the site on the basis of a more intensive analysis of the quantity and distribution of discrete elements or artifact categories within the deposit.

Two kinds of problems present themselves. The first is concerned with the nature of the artifact inventory: the material present, the predominance of particular types, variations between stratigraphic units within a cultural phase, artifact differences between cultural units, etc. The second has to do with the nature of the occupation itself: the intensity of the occupation (how frequently, how much), changes in the nature of the occupation within a cultural phase, differences between cultural groups in the type of occupation, etc.

The small area occupied by the Alvina and El Tigre complexes and the limited amount and little variation of the material did not permit extensive analysis of these complexes along such lines. Therefore, the following discussion deals primarily with the Monagrillo Phase.

Methodology

No one technique of analysis can provide a satisfactory set of answers to all of the above questions. Problems relating to the nature of, and changes in, the artifact inventory are generally discussed by the use of trait lists and horizontal percentage analysis. A technique, herein called the *concentration index*, also is useful in this regard as well as being the primary method of analyzing the nature of the occupation itself.

Percentage Analysis

The technique of analysis, whereby the numerical relationships existing between any or all of the various object categories of a stratigraphic level or other specific unit are expressed by percentages, is called *percentage analysis*. It also includes the use of these percentages for comparison between specific units.

These percentages (e.g., 92 per cent of the pottery in Stratum A is type 1) yield information on the internal content and proportions of the material culture of the unit under consideration. Analysis of internal content and proportion often permits subdivision of a cultural unit and facilitates differentiation between cultural units. It also makes possible interpretations concerning the relative popularity of the unit's constituent elements. As a number of recent studies have shown (Phillips, Ford, and Griffin, *1951;* Brainerd, *1951;* Robinson, *1951*), an elaboration of this technique permits seriation of otherwise unstratified material.

Percentage analysis of constituent elements of a specific provenience unit largely ignores the nature of the unit itself. An interpretation of the percentage relationships internal to a specific unit (25 per cent of the pottery in Stratum A is type 1 but type 2 makes up only 5 per cent) does not necessitate assumptions concerning the unit except that grouping the material into the unit was legitimate and pertinent to the problem. Similarly when the internal percentage relationships of two or more specific units are compared (type 1 makes up 25 per cent of the pottery in Stratum A but only 20 per cent of the pottery in Stratum B) no assumptions about or commitments of the specific units are made except that comparisons between them are valid for the problem being investigated. In other words, neither the nature nor the areal and temporal extent of the units considered need be known before the percentages can be calculated and compared. This freedom accounts in no small measure for the versatility of the technique but it also acts as a limitation, particularly when the nature of a unit itself is the object of the inquiry.

The Concentration Index

In an undisturbed stratum two factors determine the amount of cultural debris per cubic unit; the rate of natural deposition, and the rate of cultural deposition. If the rate of natural deposition is constant or its effect can be estimated, then further variations in the amount of cultural material per cubic unit reflect changes in the rate or the nature of the deposition of that cultural material. For example, if deposition is occurring at a site through the action of natural agencies, occupation by a small group over a period of time would result in much less material residue than would an occupation by a similar but larger group over the same period. Similarly intermittent occupation would tend to cause heavier concentrations of cultural material interspersed through areas of little material while constant occupation would tend to result in a fairly constant amount of deposition throughout.

If this is granted it becomes pertinent to determine methods whereby the rate and nature of cultural deposition or changes therein can be expressed and interpreted.

At least initially, percentage analysis is not applicable, for the size and nature of the unit as well as the included material is now of primary importance. Nor are the absolute amounts of cultural material contained in the units of much value for this problem unless the size of the units and the rates of natural deposition are taken into account. Five hundred sherds from a 10 cm. level might signify one thing; the same number from a 50 cm. level would, under otherwise similar circumstances, mean something else. Similarly, 500 sherds in a level subjected to rapid natural deposition would denote an entirely different situation from one where the same amount of cultural material was present but the rate of natural deposition was extremely slow. A technique is required which suggests the relative rate of cultural deposition, and which, combined with other factors will permit an interpretation of the causes affecting this result. The concentration index fills this need.

The concentration index is nothing more than the number of items of a particular category of material in an area, expressed in relation to the volume of that area. For example, the designated unit of volume in this report is a 50 cm. cube (that is a cube 50 cm. on a side); thus if 100 sherds were found in one cubic meter of a certain stratigraphic level the concentration index would be 100/8 or 12.5. Expressed verbally this means that there was an average of 12 or 13 sherds for every 50 cm. cube of the cubic meter under consideration.

It can readily be seen that the size of the concentration index will be determined by both natural and cultural depositional factors. Variations in the rate of natural deposition between strata will cause changes in the index despite the fact that the character of the human deposition has remained constant throughout. This factor of natural deposition is at once a hindrance to and an essential element of any interpretative analysis concerned with the varying nature of the cultural deposition. Interpretation of index variations as cultural in origin is directly dependent upon the assurance with which the affect of natural accumulation can be predicted. On the other hand if natural deposition is absent or negligible, distinction between the major factors of cultural deposition is impossible. Differentiation between them is dependent upon concurrent operation of natural agencies of deposition, for continuing natural deposition separates non-continuous cultural deposits. In short, it insinuates the element of time. The following discussion, then, is based on the assumptions that natural deposition is continuing apace and that it is either constant or the general trend of its affect is predictable.

There are three major factors of cultural deposition which affect the concentration index. The first is the nature and frequency of occupation. More frequent or longer periods of occupation will result over a period of time in a higher rate (amount of cultural deposition relative to total deposition) of cultural deposition. A change in this deposition will be revealed by a change in the concentration index. The second factor is population. The rate of deposition of cultural debris is to a certain extent directly proportional to the number of humans concerned. Therefore fluctuations in population should result in variations in the concentration index. The third factor is the per capita popularity of the particular material categories under consideration. Changes in the index of a category of objects (e.g., pottery) can be brought about by the simple fact that the objects became more or less popular and were therefore being used— and discarded—at a different rate.

One final general point should be brought out in regard to the concentration index: in any one situation the index would appear to have what might be called a saturation point. After a certain concentration of material has been reached, no further increase in popularity, population, or frequency of occupation could conceivably cause more material to be deposited within any given area. Below this point the index serves as a valuable indicator or change.

Careful investigation of all available data, including the concentration index, should give strong indication as to which of the four factors (one natural, three cultural) has played a decisive role in any particular instance. The first step in such an investigation is to determine whether vagaries of cultural or natural deposition are at the root of the index variations. Only a close analysis of the pertinent geologic factors can provide a satisfactory answer to this. In archaeological sites it is rarely possible to determine the rate of natural deposition with mathematical precision; however, it is possible in many cases to decide whether natural deposition has been approximately constant or what the trend and relative proportion of its influence has been. Generally, that is sufficient to allow a decision as to whether the differences in the concentration index result primarily from variations in natural deposition, although in some instances the verdict must remain in doubt.

If the action of natural agencies satisfactorily accounts for any variations in the index then the analysis need go no further; but if it is felt to be insufficient cause or seems contrary to the index, then further investigation is required. There is a simple and fairly reliable method for sorting out one of the factors of human deposition. Index fluctuations resulting from variations in the popularity of individual categories of material culture can generally be distinguished from those caused by the remaining two factors—population and frequency of occupation. This method requires either a number of disparate object categories (e.g., pottery, stone tools, bone implements, etc.) from each stratigraphic unit or, alternatively, the existence of a category whose per capita popularity is unlikely to change, such as the shell residue of a basic shellfish economy. If used with reasonable caution shell, where shellfish is the staple food, or alternatively, shell and bone, is perhaps the most reliable category, for while artifacts can be expected to vary in popularity through time, the per capita consumption of protein is less likely to differ. Of course the possibility of variation resulting from changes in the availability or nature of the supply must be considered. However, if shell, stone tools, and bone artifacts tend to maintain proportionately parallel indices, level by level, while the pottery index increases proportionately it would seem a safe assumption that the use of pottery among the group concerned was increasing. On the other hand, if they all showed approximately proportional changes, it would be reasonable to suspect that all were reacting equally to population changes or changes in intensity of occupation. It is conceivable that no pattern at all would be discernible among the major categories of material culture, but, if so, that fact alone would have interpretive significance. It is possible, of course, to conduct a similar analysis of individual types within any category of material culture.

It is more difficult to make a satisfactory decision between the final two cultural alternatives. The solution to the problem no longer lies entirely in the study of index differences between stratigraphic divisions. Larger populations and increased frequency or length of occupation amount, in the long run, to the same thing—greater deposition over a shorter period of time—and thus could result in identical index variations between stratigraphic divisions. The only indications come from a study of the structure and composition of the individual deposit and by computing the concentration index for successive small levels (e.g., 10 cm.)

within the stratigraphic divisions under consideration. If the material has been excavated in uniform units and so recorded this study involves nothing more than the inspection of the artifact frequencies themselves for they are already related to a standard cubic unit—the one used in excavation.

Inspection of the composition of the stratigraphic divisions will reveal one of three situations or some combination of them in regard to the cultural content. When the comparison is between units with only scattered material, little information can be gained as to whether differences are the results of varying length of occupation or of changes in population size. Presumably, the occupation was intermittent and probably brief unless there is reason to believe that the preservable material inventory of the occupying groups was exceedingly limited.

Lensing also indicates intermittent occupation of the site. If there was a change in the frequency of the occupation but no change in population size, the lenses should appear at greater or lesser distances apart while the concentration index for the individual lenses would remain approximately constant. If a population size change had occurred the index should vary slightly, and the relative areal extent of the lenses should change. In fact, in a case involving fairly small lenses the areal extent of the lens is probably a more reliable indicator.

If the cultural material appears to be distributed fairly heavily and consistently throughout the stratigraphic division, probabilities favor steady occupation. This may be only a specialized case of lensing if the stratigraphic division has been so defined that one lens makes up the division. A review of the concentration indices of successive units within the division should reveal oscillating fluctuations if the occupation was intermittent because of the inevitable depositional lensing. The internal concentration indices normally would not oscillate greatly (though of course some variation is bound to occur) if the site had been permanently occupied by a relatively stable group. This oscillation might develop if there were a small permanent occupation with occasional, perhaps seasonal, large population influxes or, alternatively, if a small group shifted its concentrated occupation to various points over the site.

If the internal concentration indices of a heavily occupied stratum increase or decrease more or less consistently (even if they are oscillating they may show some such trend) the variation probably reflects changes in population size.

Problems of Sampling

Questions concerning the validity of interpretations based on numerical samples of otherwise unknown populations or universes fall into two major categories; (1) the validity of the individual samples, and (2) the significance of differences existing between the samples. There is also the question of the relation of the sampling results to the information originally required. This last, while not a problem of sampling as such, does bear on the sampling problem in that the required results affect the type of sampling to be done.

The problem of determining the validity of the samples (how accurately do they represent the universes from which they were drawn?) has two interrelated facets. Is the sample random? Is it adequate? A small sample properly gathered is all that is required from a randomly distributed universe with little internal variation. As distribution within the universe becomes less random and the variation increases, the number and size of samples required to adequately represent it likewise increases.

Random distribution can never be assumed in an archaeological situation, but material within a single stratum of refuse is more likely to approach this condition than is that from a series of contemporaneous architectural units. The amount of internal variation often is not known until laboratory analysis has begun—a fact which argues powerfully for as much field analysis as possible. At He-5—primarily a refuse deposit—there were areas of slight concentration of cultural debris within a stratum, but no stratum taken as a whole exhibited great internal variation. There was also a limited artifact inventory throughout and little internal artifact variation so that an excessive size or number of samples was not necessitated. The absolute area of our sample, that is, the total volume of each stratum excavated, ranged from approximately 10 cubic meters of Stratum 2 to approximately 200 cubic meters of Stratum 8. Numerically, the absolute sample size of pottery, on which most interpretations were based, ranged from 44 sherds in Stratum 2 to more than 12,000 sherds in Stratum 8. These samples represent varying proportions of the total stratum (the universe) of which they are a part. Relating these partial samples to the universes from which they were drawn, only one per cent of the estimated total of Stratum 2 was excavated while approximately 15 per cent of the estimated total of Stratum 1 was dug, with about 5 per cent being the average.

In view of the relatively random distribution and limited variation within the mound it was felt that in every stratum except Stratum 2, and perhaps, Stratum 6, the sample was of adequate proportional and absolute size and the pit locations were sufficiently distributed to give reasonable assurance that the samples were representative of their respective strata. In Strata 2 and 6 doubt is thrown on the results not only by the small areal size of the sample but by the small numerical size. Even if it could be assumed that the total sherds recovered were proportionate to the total number in the stratum, the number of sherds representing each type was so small that an accidental clustering of a few sherds of a type could completely skew the results of a percentage analysis.

The second question is concerned with the significance of differences existing between the samples. This problem can also be subdivided; statistical significance and cultural significance. The separateness of these two is occasionally overlooked. Statistical significance does not prove any interpretation by eliminating error due to factors of chance in the sampling process. In other words, if statistical significance is indicated, the sample differences probably represent actual differences which exist between the entire universes from which samples were taken. It is another question entirely whether such differences between the total universes had any cultural or interpretive significance. These questions will be discussed in connection with the consideration of the specific strata.

The question of sample size and the significance of sample differences is often not so much one of statistical validity as one of archaeological validity. A great deal of archaeological interpretation is necessarily based, at least in part, on the assumption that the amount and proportion of material of a particular category found archaeologically reflects approximately the situation as it existed at the time that material was in use. How finely interpretations may follow similarities and differences so represented is an interesting question which, while given frequent consideration, perhaps has not yet been sufficiently analyzed. No blanket rules could be established, but perhaps certain indications as to minimal requirements could be suggested.

Summary

The two problem areas outlined (the nature of the artifact inventory, and the nature of the occupation) are not mutually exclusive. However, the different information required frequently necessitates varied techniques of analysis which manipulate the basic data in a number of different ways.

Careful analysis of the geologic situation and the concentration index can reveal insights into the nature and cause of differences in the occupations of the various stratigraphic and cultural units within a site, suggesting whether observable differences are primarily the result of: (1) changes in the popularity of individual items of material culture; (2) the number of people occupying the site; (3) the frequency and/or length of their visits; or (4) whether they are the result of nothing more than differences in the rate of natural deposition. Frequently interpretations suggested by a varied or changing artifact inventory or the percentage relationships of a unit's constituent elements also bear on the question of the nature of the occupation.

Percentage analysis is used primarily in discussing the popularity variations which occur in the artifact inventory. The results of this are often applicable to other problems such as seriation. The concentration indices of the components of an object category within any one stratum are proportional to the percentages of those components, but percentages can be used for such popularity analysis with much greater facility.

By its very nature detailed analysis such as this cannot be definitive. The results are built on a series of assumptions and considered probabilities which pyramid. In many instances the samples are small causing additional difficulties as well as doubts. Nevertheless, while the resulting conclusions are not proven facts, they are carefully considered and reasoned inferences; and as such they have a certain value not only as suggestions as to what might have occurred but as indicators of potentially fruitful areas of investigation.

SHELL

Shell and pottery were by far the predominant cultural elements present at He-5, and it is upon these two that most of the cultural interpretations depend. By and large, the other categories of cultural material merely supplement or substantiate the conclusions drawn from the analysis of the shell and the pottery.

Information concerning the nature and amount of the shell present at the site stems from three sources: (1) general observations made in the field notes and on the pit profiles; (2) a series of spot samples of material from Stratum 1 and Stratum 8 (taken from the West Trench, Section 17), from Stratum 3 (the *Tivela* shell lens in the upper portion of the stratum), Stratum 4 and Stratum 7 (all taken from the West Trench, Section 7); and (3) the analysis of the total shell sample recovered from Pit XXVII. The detailed identification and analysis of these shell samples is contained in Appendix I of this report [not reprinted here].

Relative Popularity of Shell Species

The following is based primarily upon the complete analysis of the shell sample from Pit XXVII, and only the major trends are discussed here . . . The percentages are based upon proportional weights.

The most obvious and important trend is that noted in the discussion of the geological history of the mound. Throughout Stratum 1 *Ostrea chilensis* constitutes approximately 70 per cent of the shell present. This species decreases rapidly after the deposition of Stratum 1, reaches a low point toward the beginning of Stratum 8 but enjoys a resurgence of popularity toward the end of Stratum 8. *Ostrea mexicana* follows this same general pattern but fluctuates more and is only a minor component of Stratum 8. *Tivela gracilor*, in almost exact contradistinction to the *Ostrea* trend, composes less than 10 per cent of Stratum 1, increases steadily to a maximum of approximately 70 per cent toward the middle of Stratum 8 and then decreases slightly. *Natica unifasciata* also follows this pattern.

A few species such as *Pecten circularis* and *Anadara grandis* were associated primarily with Stratum 1. *Pteria sterna* becomes significant in Stratum 5, rises to 20 per cent in the lowest section of Stratum 8, then again fades out. Some species were found only in association with Stratum 8, but these formed only a minor portion of the shell present there. In general, Stratum 8 exhibits a more diversified shell content than do any of the other strata.

Two other patterns of occurrence are evident. Nine or ten species, such as *Scapharca tuberculosa, Donax punctostriatus, Protothaca grata,* and perhaps *Tellina eburnea* follow a pattern somewhat as follows: they are absent or unimportant in Stratum 1, reach a peak during Stratum 5, fall off during the early part of Stratum 8 (at the very time *Tivela* reaches a peak) and then tend to increase toward the top of Stratum 8. In the case of *Donax punctostriatus* and *Protothaca grata,* the second peak far outstrips the first, and they form a significant portion of the final deposits of Stratum 8.

Unfortunately, little information is available on the precise environmental requirements of these various species; however, in the light of the geologic history of the immediate area and what information is available some interpretations are suggested.

Oysters (*Ostrea*) prefer a rocky or mud bar area while *Tivela* favors soft sand. It is possible, of course, for these two conditions to occur in relative proximity to each other but the popularity trends of the two species, when compared to the geologic history of the mound, suggest that before the formation of the lagoon oysters were the predominant species in the immediate vicinity of the site and were most utilized for food. When the lagoon formed *Tivela* became numerous and the dietary emphasis shifted to them. The resurgence of *Ostrea* and, perhaps, that of *Donax punctostriatus* and *Protothaca grata* toward the end of the Monagrillo occupation suggests that as the lagoon filled and dried, *Tivela* became scarcer and the inhabitants were again forced to rely increasingly upon oysters, which were now gathered further afield, probably to seaward of the offshore bar (the new coastline).

The diversified shell content of Stratum 8 reflects the increased amount of shell fishing. Many of the shells may represent species accidentally gathered and later discarded at the site.

The Nature of the Monagrillo Occupation

The five samples from which the concentration indices for shell were computed consisted of material gathered from the pit profiles. The volume estimate was not made in the field so a slight error may have been introduced by a change in the density of the sample but the inter-strata index differences are so great that this factor could never have seriously affected the results. The weight rather than the number of shells was used in the computation.

As a result of the heavy sorting and loss of material in Stratum 1, little information is available on the nature of the occupation and the concentration is unreliable. However, the very nature of the site at this time, subjected as it was to periodic wave action, is sufficient to suggest that occupation must have been sporadic. The site probably served as little more than a temporary base for shell-fishing expeditions.

No shell concentrations are present in Stratum 2 or in most of Stratum 3. Some oyster shell lenses occur in the upper half of Stratum 3 and sporadically in the contemporary Stratum 5. The distribution of the shell lenses during this period indicates that, while no area of the site was completely avoided, the west-central section of the south ridge was preferred, probably because it was slightly farther from the areas of greatest wave action. At any rate shell lenses occur most frequently in the general area of the Central Trench and the southern section of the West Trench. These lenses are never more than 20 cm. thick. Their areal extent never exceeded 3.00 m. in a north-south direction; and, while the east-west dimensions are not known so exactly, a lens could never be traced from one trench to another or from one pit to another. This suggests that while occupation of the site was heavier than it had been, the groups were small and the visits not only intermittent but for short periods of time.

The first lenses of predominantly *Tivela* shell are thicker and more extensive. These occur more frequently on the peripheries of the mound in Stratum 3 and the eastern end of Stratum 5. The lagoon was now well formed so wave action was no longer a deterring factor. The lenses occasionally are as much as 50 cm. thick and in one instance extend over 7.00 to 8.00 m. The groups were apparently increasing in size and were staying for longer periods of time. Still, the concentration index shows that even during the deposition of a fairly large shell lens the occupation was by no means as intense as it became later.

During the deposition of Stratum 4 and Substratum 5a there are the first indications that the occupation may have been permanent. The shell of 5a is scattered fairly thickly throughout and tends to be more finely crushed. The shell lenses of Stratum 4 are very thin, only a few centimeters, and almost never extend for more than a meter. However, they occur with great frequency. A possible explanation for the depositional difference between these two more or less contemporaneous strata will be suggested in connection with the discussion of Strata 7 and 8. The low concentration index obtained in Stratum 4 is the result of the extremely thin shell lenses. The sample from Stratum 3 was taken entirely from within a shell lens, but this was impossible in Stratum 4 and much of the material represents the naturally deposited brown sand which separated the lenses. Taken as a whole there appears to be a heavier concentration of shell in Stratum 4 than in Stratum 3.

The appearance of Strata 7 and 8 suggests heavy, continuous occupation and the large concentration index supports this view. Appearance alone suggested that a great deal more shell was contained in Stratum 8, and it was thought that this was the main occupation area. The concentration index shows that the amount of shell present in the two strata was almost the same. The difference lay in the degree and amount of fragmentation. In Stratum 8 the impression given is one of whole shell; although, of course, close examination reveals numerous fragments. On the other hand, Stratum 7 appears to contain primarily shell fragments with only occasional whole shells present.

The differences in quality between the contemporaneous strata, 7 and 8, may, possibly, be explained by the hypothesis that the north ridge (Stratum 7) was used primarily as a living area while the south ridge (Stratum 8) was a depository for refuse. This suggests a neatness not always associated with the occupants of shell mounds, and if the ancient inhabitants were bent on throwing part of their trash somewhere other than where they were living, it is difficult to understand why they didn't utilize the trough. It is, however, inescapable that the crushed condition of the shell on the north ridge indicates that that area was subjected to heavy traffic. It seems improbable that the south ridge material could have maintained its unfragmented condition had similarly heavy occupation occurred. Since there is a large amount of ash mixed with the north ridge deposit—thin ash lenses even occur—as well as a number of lenses of black organic stain, none of which occur in the south ridge, the hypothesis may have some basis in fact. A number of other factors having to do with the relative deposition of pottery, bone, and stone also offer some substantiation.

This separateness of refuse and living areas may account also for the disparity between the shell lenses of Substratum 5a and Stratum 4 although in this case the living area seems to have been on the south ridge. The small shell lenses scattered so thickly throughout Stratum 4 would, then, represent more or less individual refuse deposits.

The depth of both Stratum 7 and Stratum 8 varies over the site but suggests that the longest, heaviest occupation occurred in the general area of the West Trench.

Tomb Sequence at Tepe Gawra

The report by Arthur Tobler[15] on the excavation of Tepe Gawra, a large Mesopotamian *tell*, contains a masterful demonstration of the sequencing of a large series of tombs. Tobler (1950:67) summarized his method of analysis as follows:

[15] Arthur J. Tobler, *Excavations at Tepe Gawra*, Museum Monographs, University Museum, University of Pennsylvania, Philadelphia, 1950, pp. 51–65. By permission of the Museum of the University of Pennsylvania.

The means employed to determine these strata of origin have included the establishment of a *terminus ad quem* by ascertaining in the case of each tomb whether it was crossed by the walls of any stratum lying over it. Most tombs, happily enough, were so crossed by later building walls, and the upper limit of their stratigraphic source was thus fixed. In other cases, factors such as the elevation of the floor and walls of a tomb in relation to the elevations of the floors of overlying strata; the association of tombs with temples; and the location of tombs in open areas of the various settlements proved decisive in attributing a tomb to a particular stratum.

In addition to the more numerous graves . . . described in Chapter III, eighty tombs were discovered. These tombs have been distinguished and separated from the simpler graves for the following reasons. First, they represent an elaborate and different type of burial, in which an enclosure was constructed either of *libn* (sun-dried mud-brick), or of stone, or of a combination of both materials. This enclosure, or tomb, was moreover often roofed with mud-bricks, matting, stone slabs, or wood. Second, unlike the simple graves, which were found in almost all levels of the mound, as well as in Area A at its foot, these tombs were discovered only in Strata IX through XIII, and are thus a type of burial characteristic of only a limited period in the history of Tepe Gawra. Third, a number of the mud-brick tombs contained rich collections of objects; these burial furnishings have few parallels with the objects discovered in occupational debris. Fourth, and largely as a result of the factor just mentioned, the stratum or strata in which the builders of these tombs lived have, up to the present time, remained unidentified, and the tombs thus represent one of the major stratigraphic problems encountered at Gawra.

The present chapter has been organized into four main sections, dealing respectively with: (A) the stratigraphic origin of these tombs; (B) details of their construction; (C) a description of the skeletal remains contained by the tombs, together with notes on the burial customs they illustrate; and finally, (D) a description of the funerary furnishings. [The present excerpt comprises most of Section A; omits B-D.] Following this outline we may proceed to a discussion of the most difficult aspect of the tombs, viz., the problem of identifying their builders and relating them to definite strata.

A. THE STRATIGRAPHIC PROBLEM

Late Tombs

It has been suggested by the actual excavator of most of the tombs that they contained the dead of a people inhabiting some locality near Gawra, at a time (between Strata IX and VIII-C) when Gawra was unoccupied.[16] Certain objections may be made to this view. In the first place, there is no site within a radius of a few miles of Gawra that was large enough in the period represented by the tombs to have accounted for their presence, and it is difficult to believe that any large site still more distant (as for example, Nineveh), can be held responsible. If, on the other hand, nomads are accounted as the people who constructed these tombs, they must have had a rich material culture, far exceeding that of the inhabitants of Gawra and other North Mesopotamian sites in this period. Furthermore, such a culture is not usually associated with nomadic peoples. Lastly, there is no evidence of any considerable period of time having elapsed between the abandonment of Stratum IX and the construction of Stratum VIII; on the contrary, the evidence points to an unusually brief interval.[17] In view of these objections it seems more reasonable, if indeed not actually necessary, to assume that the builders of the tombs had been inhabitants of Gawra at some period. If so, it would then follow that they must be connected with some level or levels of the mound.

The problem of connecting these tombs with known occupational levels is extremely difficult because only a few parallels may be drawn between objects from the tombs and those found in the debris of overlying strata. It is this fact which constitutes the greatest attraction of the theory discussed in the preceding paragraph; namely, that the tombs and their furnishings are the products of a people foreign to Gawra. To be sure, some relationships may be established between objects from the tombs and those from occupational debris of Gawra building levels and graves. While these analogies furnish additional arguments to the effect that the tombs were the products of Gawrans, they are, unfortunately, not numerous or specific enough to provide positive evidence as to particular stratigraphic sources. For the most part, the tombs have yielded objects which are either unduplicated by those recovered from occupational debris (e.g., gold rosettes, pendants, and studs; ivory combs; ivory pins; etc.), or other types of objects having no value in narrow relative dating, such as beads. Pottery vessels and seals—the most valuable comparative media—are, on the other hand, uncommon as tomb furnishings. As a result, the evidence obtained from a study of the funerary equipment of the tombs may only be used to check the possible stratigraphic sources suggested by other methods, but is in itself inconclusive.

Let us examine still further the theory that the tombs contain the physical and material remains of a people who lived near Gawra, and who, presumably because of the sanctity of our site, chose to bury their dead

---

[16] Charles Bache, "Prehistoric Burials of Tepe Gawra," *Scientific American,* vol. 153, no. 6 (December, 1935), pp. 310–313. The deepest, and hence the earliest tombs, however, namely those in Strata XI-A, XII, and XIII, had not yet been discovered.

[17] Cf. E. A. Speiser (*1935:27*): ". . . Stratum VIII is primarily the continuation of an established civilization after a brief break following the destruction of Stratum IX."

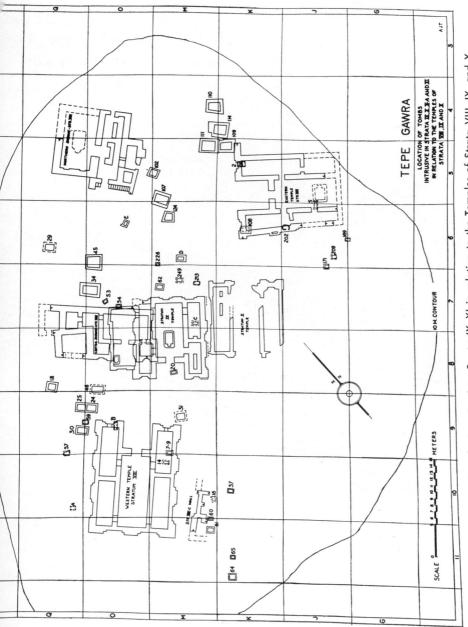

Fig. 8.23. Location of tombs intrusive into Strata IX–XI in relation to the Temples of Strata VIII, IX, and X.

on the mound of Gawra at a time when it was crowned only by the deserted and ruined buildings of Stratum IX. A necessary consequence of this theory would be that the floor levels of the tombs would occur, within reasonable limits, at approximately the same depth, since the tombs are assumed to have originated at about the same height above the plain. The

TABLE 6. Possible Stratigraphic Sources of the Tombs Appearing on Fig. 8.23

	Tomb No.	Elevation of Tomb Floor	In Stratum	Crossed by Walls of Stratum	Possible Strata of Origin
Group I	61	11.13	X	VIII-A	VIII-B, C, or IX
	60	11.39	X	VIII-A	VIII-B, C, or IX
	16	10.72	X	VIII-A	VIII-B or C
	37	10.83	X	VIII-A	VIII-B, C, or IX
	64	10.74	X	—	?
	65	10.68	X	—	?
Group II	14	11.27	X	VIII-A	VIII-B, C, or IX
	7-9	10.70	X-A —	IX	X
	31	10.78	X	VIII-B	VIII-C or IX
	B	—	X	VIII-C	IX
	A	—	X	VIII-B	VIII-C or IX
Group III	57 (cist)	10.61	X	VIII-B	VIII-C or IX
	30	11.96	IX	VIII-A	VIII-B or C
	59 (cist)	—	X	VIII-A	VIII-B, C, or IX
	25	—	IX	VIII-B	VIII-C
	24	—	IX	VIII-B	VIII-C
	46	—	X	VIII-A	VIII-B, C, or IX
	18	11.87	IX	—	?
	20	12.13	IX	VIII-A	VIII-B or C
	C	—	X	VIII-B	VIII-C or IX
Group IV	29	11.74	IX	VIII-A	VIII-B or C
	34	10.25	XI	VIII-C	IX, X, or X-A
	45	10.25	XI	VIII-A	VIII-B, C, IX, or X
	53	11.51	X	VIII-C	IX
	54	11.80	X	IX	IX ?
	E	11.33	X	VIII-C	IX
Group V	62	11.60	X	VIII-C	IX
	226	—	XI	X	X-A
	249	9.59	XI	X	X-A
	D	11.93	X	VIII-C	IX
	213 (cist)	10.86	X-A	VIII-C	IX or X
Group VI	124	9.62	XI —	—	?
	107	9.33	XI —	—	?
	102	9.30	XI —	VI	?
Group VII	111	10.02	XI	VIII-C	IX, X, or X-A
	109	ca. 9.42?	XI —	VIII-C	IX, X, or X-A
	114	9.42	XI —	VIII-C	IX, X, or X-A
	110	9.43	XI —	VIII-A	VIII-B, C, IX, X, or X-A
Group VIII	2 (cist)	11.75	X	VIII-C	IX
	108	10.47	XI	VIII-C	IX, X, or X-A
	202 (cist)	10.82	X-A	VIII-C	IX or X
	5	11.67	X	VIII-C	IX
Group IX	171	—	XI	—	?
	209	11.14	X-A	VI	?
	169	9.49	XI	—	?

third column of Table 6 lists the elevations of the floors of all tombs appearing on Fig. 8.23, but does not include the deepest tombs discovered in Strata XII and XIII, for which no elevations are extant. It may be seen, however, from a glance at that table that the elevations of the tomb floors range from 9.30 m. above the zero point to 12.13 m.; a difference of close to three metres. This difference would be considerably widened if the exact elevations of the tombs intrusive in Strata XI-A, XII and XIII could be included; however, a rough calculation may illustrate our point. The elevation of the floor of Stratum XIII is approximately 6.50 m.; as three tombs (G36-150, G36-151, and G36-155) had been sunk into Stratum XIII, their floors were therefore about this elevation. The highest tomb discovered (No. 20) had a floor elevation of 12.13 m., hence the extreme range in elevation of the tomb floors is about 5.63 m., which is an impossible figure for burials from a single stratum. It is obvious on the basis of this evidence alone that not all of the tombs are to be attributed to a single stratum, or to a single interstratigraphic interval. A two- or three-metre difference in elevation could be explained if it is supposed that the buildings of Stratum IX had collapsed and formed small hummocks above the comparatively flat floor of that level. But we are not even prepared to accept this explanation, for Stratum IX was not extensively occupied; in fact, the buildings of that level covered only a little more than half of the available area of the mound. It would surely have been the flat, open area to the rear of the Stratum IX Temple which would have been selected for the location of the tombs, if they are all to be attributed to this stratum, or to an interval between Strata IX and VIII-C. Moreover, if this area had been selected, the floors of the tombs would occur at elevations which likewise would be fairly constant; certainly, a vertical range of over five metres would then be inexplicable.

The horizontal distribution of the tombs proves the contention that Stratum IX, or a period following the occupation and desertion of that stratum, cannot have been the only time when these tombs were constructed. On Fig. 8.23 the locations of forty-five of the total of fifty-three mud-brick and stone tombs intrusive in Strata IX, X, X-A, and XI have been plotted. The tombs discovered in still lower strata appear on Plate XXIII [not reproduced here], and will be discussed later. It will readily be seen from a glance at Fig. 8.23 that the tombs occur in a broad, crescent-shaped belt extending from the eastern, through the northern and western sections of the mound, leaving only the southern area unoccupied. It has just been observed that, if the tombs are to be attributed only to Stratum IX, it might logically be expected that they would occur in the northeastern and eastern half of the mound, as this part of Gawra (to the rear of the IX Temple) was unoccupied at that time. The fact that many of the tombs ignore the locations of the buildings of Stratum IX may thus be taken as the final and conclusive piece of evidence contradicting that theory. But what does the location and distribution of the tombs then suggest?

If the first of our plans showing the distribution of the tombs (Fig. 8.23) is again referred to, it will be seen that the belt of tombs is not formed of an unbroken series of related units; on the contrary, the tombs occur in groups with at least five main gaps breaking their continuity. In four of these gaps, the outlines of the three temples of Stratum VIII and the single temple each of Strata IX and X have been placed in their actual locations, the Central Shrine of VIII and the Stratum IX Temple overlapping in part. A few tombs, to be sure, encroach on the limits of the temples, or are found within those buildings; a circumstance that will find an explanation later. For the most part, however, the interruptions in the series of tomb locations are filled in by the temples themselves. The significance of this fact is at once apparent. It suggests that the tombs were deliberately concentrated near certain religious buildings of Gawra, and also that the tombs are associated with the temples of at least three main strata, namely, VIII, IX, and X, and consequently must have originated in those strata. The wide range in elevation of the tomb floors, implying a multiple rather than a single stratigraphic source for the tombs, is thus confirmed by the horizontal distribution of the tombs and their association with the religious edifices of no less than three main strata.

A broad basis for the stratigraphic attribution of the whole body of tombs has now been established, but only the fact that the tombs were constructed by, and contained the remains of Gawrans of Strata VIII, IX, and X has emerged. The specific attribution of individual tombs is a task that still remains, for at the present stage of this inquiry it cannot be stated with any degree of assurance whether Tomb 46,[18] to take a single obvious example, may on the basis of its location alone be attributed to Stratum VIII or to Stratum IX, since it lies equidistant from the Western and Central Shrines of VIII and the Temple of IX. It must be remembered, furthermore, that the Western Shrine of Stratum VIII was in use only in the C, or earliest phase of Stratum VIII,[19] while the Central Shrine

---

[18] "Locus" numbers were assigned to the tombs, as well as to the graves and, in fact, to any specific point in any level of Gawra which was of interest, whether a burial, a cache of objects, an architectural detail, or any other feature worth noting. In the present chapter, however, the numbers have been retained, while the word "Tomb" has been substituted for "locus" in order to distinguish still further the tombs from simple graves. It will be noted that the tombs do not all bear the same kind of designation. In the third, fourth, and fifth seasons, the loci were given a simple numerical designation such as 5, 102, 249, etc. In the sixth season, a new numerical series was begun, prefaced by the unit "G36-," indicating the year of excavation, while in the seventh season they bore the prefix "7-." The five tombs identified only by capital letters were not numbered in the field during the third season, and I have arbitrarily assigned these designations to them to facilitate reference.

[19] Speiser, op. cit., pp. 26–27, 30–31.

continued in use throughout all three phases. Consequently, is Tomb 46 to be considered as contemporaneous with Stratum VIII-A, VIII-B, VIII-C, or IX, since merely by association it could be related to the Western Shrine (VIII-C), the Central Shrine (VIII-A, B, or C), or the Stratum IX Temple? And with which temples and strata are all other tombs to be related?

It has been found possible, by superimposing the plans of all strata containing and overlying the tombs, to determine the level or levels in which most tombs could possibly have originated. It is obvious that if walls of any stratum overlying a specific tomb cross over its location, that tomb must have been constructed before the walls had been built. Similarly, if the walls of any stratum are found to have been cut and broken directly over the location of a tomb, it follows that the shaft of that tomb is almost certainly responsible, and the tomb must therefore have originated in a still higher stratum. By employing these two principles it has been found possible in most cases to establish the limits of the stratigraphic sources of the tombs, for if a tomb should have been discovered in Stratum X, and its location is crossed by walls of Stratum VIII-B, for example, that tomb in all likelihood originated in Strata VIII-C or IX; the only intervening levels. Certain exceptions to and qualifications of this method will be pointed out later, but for the present let us examine the results arrived at by its application.

Table 6 lists all tombs appearing on Fig. 8.23, together with pertinent data. The extreme right-hand column lists all possible stratigraphic sources for each tomb. These sources, as has been explained, are determined by listing the strata lying between the stratum into which the tomb intruded (fourth column), and the stratum whose walls first cross over the tomb location (fifth column). As the tombs were found in groups, they have been so listed in order of their occurrence, and these groups have, for convenience in reference, been numbered. There are, however, a few tombs which are more or less isolated, and these have been inserted between the grouped tombs, again in the order of their occurrence on the plan. Our inquiry is directed at present only to the tombs discovered in Strata IX–XI; the earlier tombs, intruding into Strata XI-A–XIII will be discussed later in this chapter.

We have now determined all possible stratigraphic sources of the forty-five tombs appearing on Fig. 8.23. The results listed in the last column of the table are not conclusive and decisive in each instance, for some tombs still command possible sources in two or three strata, while Tomb 110, one of the important members of Group VII, may possibly have originated in any one of five different strata. Still others, such as Tombs 64, 65, 18, 226, 124, 107, 171, and 169, are not crossed by the walls of any overlying stratum; as a consequence, there is absolutely no indication as to their sources. Nevertheless certain tombs may be singled out to furnish indisputable proof as to the origin of the whole body of tombs appearing on Fig. 8.23 in Strata VIII-B, VIII-C, IX, X, and, in two instances, in X-A.

The first of these key tombs is No. 7–9. This tomb, uncovered in Stratum X-A (Squares 9–10 M), belongs to the second group of Fig. 8.23 and Table 6. It is crossed by the fragment of a wall in Stratum IX, east of Room 917. The only possible stratigraphic source of this tomb is, therefore, in X.

Next are Nos. 24 and 25 of Group III, which form one of the two double-tombs discovered. These had been constructed at the bottom of a shaft leading into Stratum IX (Squares 9 Q-O), although the elevation of their floors is unfortunately not specified in the field records. No walls of Stratum VIII-C cross over this double tomb, but in the next, or B-phase of Stratum VIII, walls of the small room northeast of Room 881 and immediately adjoining it cross over both ends of the tomb. This double tomb is therefore of VIII-C origin, since that is the only stratum lying between VIII-B and IX.

Group IV provides us with two tombs having definite strata of origin. These are Nos. 34 and 53, in Square 7–0. No. 53 was intrusive in Stratum X; although the floor of No. 34 rested in Stratum XI, and is therefore listed as intrusive into that stratum in Table 6, the tops of the walls of this tomb reached into Stratum X, so that it must have originated in a stratum above X. As both tombs are crossed by the walls of Room 883 in Stratum VIII-C, the only stratum to which they may be assigned is, consequently, Stratum IX. In that stratum they were located near the temple, being situated north of the northern corner of Room 904, which forms an addition to the original temple building. The substantial difference in elevation between the floors of these tombs (1.26 m.) may be regarded as militating against the attribution of both of them to the stratum. However, the roof of Tomb 34 was only 68 cm. lower than the roof of No. 53, the former having much higher walls. Furthermore, Tomb 34 contained an adult burial and, although it had been robbed in ancient times, enough of its furnishings had been overlooked or scorned to hint at the original wealth it must have contained. Tomb 53, on the other hand, contained only the bones of an infant, undisturbed since the day of burial. The difference in elevation between these two tombs arises, therefore, because one (No. 34) was a rich burial of a presumably important personage, while the other did not require the protection that added depth would have afforded, as it contained only an infant and was completely devoid of furnishings.

Tomb E, an isolated tomb in Square 6–0, is intrusive into Stratum X. Since it is crossed by Stratum VIII-C walls, the only possible source of this tomb is in Stratum IX.

Group V in Squares 6–7 M, and just south of Tomb E discussed above, provided our next certain examples: Tombs 62, D, 226, 213, and 249. The first two of these had been constructed at the bottom of shafts terminating in Stratum X. Both are crossed by walls of VIII-C (Room 884), so that the only possible level from which their shafts could have been dug is Stratum IX. Like Tombs 34 and 53, these burials associate themselves closely with the Temple of Stratum IX, being located directly to the rear (northeast) of that building.

Tomb 249 of the same group has a floor level from 2.00 to 2.34 m. below those of Nos. 62 and D. For this reason alone a source in a stratum lower than that attributed to Nos. 62 and D would seem apparent, which is confirmed by walls of Stratum X crossing over the location of this tomb. As it was discovered in Stratum XI, the only remaining stratum from which it could have been dug is X-A.

Also to be assigned a Stratum X-A source is Tomb 226 which, like No. 249, was found in Stratum XI and is crossed by walls of Stratum X. Tomb 226 thus originated in Room 20 of Stratum X-A, while the shaft of No. 249 was begun in Room 21, immediately adjoining. We have no clue why these rooms should have been selected for the site of tomb shafts, when open areas of the X-A settlement were so readily available. Even the fact that these tombs had their source in X-A is surprising when it is recalled that no temple existed in Stratum X-A to attract burials of any type. Nevertheless, whatever the answer to this riddle may be, there can be no doubt that both 249 and 226 did indeed originate in Stratum X-A.

Ten tombs have now been found to be related to specific strata. It will be noted that four other tombs listed in Table 6 (Nos. B, 54, 2, and 5) also have but a single stratum in which they could have originated. All four tombs, however, are crossed by walls of the Western and Eastern Temples of Stratum VIII, or by walls of the Stratum IX Temple. There is the possibility, therefore, that these tombs were deliberately placed underneath the foundations of their respective temple buildings as a propitiatory or ritual gesture, and that they may even contain sacrificial victims. This surmise is strengthened by the fact that all contained the bones of infants, and is confirmed by a far larger number of child burials discovered near the Western and Eastern Temples when Stratum VIII-C was excavated,[20] and by numerous graves, usually of infants or children, associated with the temples of almost all levels, which will be described in Chapter III. If the explanation is accepted that these four tombs, Nos. B, 54, 2, and 5, are related to the strata possessing the temple buildings rather than to underlying strata, why should not all tombs located within temple buildings, or crossed by the structures themselves, be similarly attributed to the strata possessing those buildings?

Altogether ten tombs are crossed by the walls of temples or are situated within their confines; they are Nos. 7–9, 14, B, 54, C, 108, 202, 5, 2, and

[20] *Ibid.*, pp. 141–142, Plate XII (inset).

109. We have already discussed Tomb 7–9, and found it had its source in Stratum X. The reason for attributing it to that stratum was a wall fragment in Stratum IX which crossed over the site of the tomb. Consequently, it cannot be related to the Stratum VIII-C Temple lying above it, and the association of this tomb with the Western Temple must be regarded as accidental. Tomb 108 may be questioned as a sacrificial burial on different grounds. Although it is similarly located under a corner of the Eastern Temple of VIII-C as Tomb 2, which we are prepared to accept as a burial of the sacrificial type, Tomb 108 has a floor elevation of 10.47 m., as contrasted with the 11.75 m. elevation of the floor of Tomb 2, 11.24 m. for Tomb 202, and 11.67 m. for Tomb 5; all of which occur within the limits of the same temples. Tomb 108 thus occurs from 0.77 to 1.28 metres deeper than the others, and lies no less than 2.50 metres below the foundations of the Eastern Shrine in Stratum VIII-C. As No. 108 contained only an infant equipped with two beads, there would have been no reason for excavating such a deep shaft, and certainly no apparent reason for sinking the shaft of this tomb 1.28 m. deeper than Tomb 2, which at least contained more beads. Tomb 108, like Tomb 7–9, is therefore only fortuitously associated with a Stratum VIII Temple. Instead, a Stratum X source is suggested by its location, since it would in that stratum be situated within the angle formed by the junction of the outside walls of Rooms 1080 and 1085, southwest of the area designated as 1086 on the Stratum X plan, and just off the street leading to the Stratum X Temple. In this corner of the X settlement the tomb shaft was excavated and orientated with two sides of the tomb parallel to the walls of the two buildings, and only a few centimetres away from them.

The floor elevation of Tomb 109 (ca. 9.42 m.), in Square 5-K, is among the lowest of the tombs appearing on Fig. 8.23. In addition, most of the area of this tomb lies outside the limits of the Eastern Temple, with only part of the southeastern wall of the tomb being crossed by a wall projecting from the Temple. These circumstances suggest that Tomb 109 is not to be connected with Stratum VIII, and is not a tomb of the sacrificial type; this tomb will be discussed later with other members of the important Group VII.

Of the ten tombs which may be interpreted as containing sacrificial victims, we have now eliminated three (Nos. 7–9, 108, and 109) as having no connection with the overlying religious structures of Strata VIII and IX. The remaining seven tombs, however (Nos. 14, B, C, 54, 2, 202, and 5), may be regarded as definitely related to temple buildings, and hence in all likelihood contain sacrificial victims. These are to be grouped as follows. Belonging to the Western Temple of Stratum VIII-C are Tombs 14 and B; to the Eastern Shrine, also of Stratum VIII-C, are Tombs 2, 202, and 5. Each of these temples thus had a tomb containing an infant placed underneath the foundations of the front of the building, and at least one more within the building itself. Tombs C and 54, on the other hand, belong to the Stratum IX Temple. Here again, one interment was made beneath the walls of the structure (although in this case under the rear wall of the later extension, Room 904), while another was within the confines of the temple proper, and below its pavement, where it occupied a position similar to that of Tomb 14, in the Western Temple of Stratum VIII-C. The position of Tomb 5 is unique, since it was apparently associated with the podium of the Eastern Temple. The Central Temple of Stratum VIII, the Northern Shrine of the same stratum, and the Stratum X Temple have no tombs lying beneath their floors or walls (cf., however, footnote 26). Just why these temples should have been ignored is not clear, but in the case of the Stratum VIII Northern Shrine, at least, it is obvious that this structure possessed no attraction whatever for tombs. Those few tombs lying near it (Nos. E, 107, and 102) originated in earlier strata, so that their apparent association with that structure is completely fortuitous.

None of the five tombs attributed to Stratum VIII Temples is crossed by walls of any stratum below VIII-C, and neither Tomb C nor Tomb 54, which have been attributed to the Stratum IX Temple, is crossed by the walls of any stratum underlying IX (cf. Table 6). Consequently, no objections on these grounds may be made to their attribution to Strata VIII and IX. Additional tombs of a sacrificial type, this time related to the Stratum XI Temple, will be discussed in the section of this chapter dealing with the earlier tombs of Gawra. Why this practice is not represented in Stratum X by tombs beneath the temple of that level is a question for which we have no answer at present.

Several additional tombs present clues which relate them to definite strata. The first of these is No. 31, one of the richest tombs discovered. This burial lies in Square 9-M in a location that would place it only forty centimetres east of the Western Temple of Stratum VIII-C, or almost five metres from the *liwan* of the Stratum IX Temple. In view of its location, therefore, this tomb may be related to either of these buildings, and consequently to either stratum. Nor do superimposed plans of the strata provide any additional information; from Table 6 we learn that this tomb was discovered in Stratum X; that the elevation of its floor was 10.78 m.; and that it is crossed by walls of Stratum VIII-B, which again leaves a choice of either VIII-C or IX for its stratigraphic source. One positive indication is available to us, however. The walls of this tomb rose to a height of 77 cm., making the maximum elevation of the tomb 11.55 m. If the tomb had been sunk from Stratum IX, therefore, the roof would have reached, or protruded above the floor of that stratum—a manifest impossibility. Accordingly, we should assign this tomb to Stratum VIII-C, where it would have had a protective cover of earth about 65 to 85 cm. or more in thickness. It was, therefore, associated with the Western Temple of VIII-C, and occupied a position opposite to the double tomb, Nos. 24 and 25, at the front of the Temple and at its eastern corner.

Next is Tomb 60 of Group I in Squares 10–11 M. Table 6 shows that this tomb was intrusive in Stratum X, and that it is crossed by walls of Stratum VIII-A, possibly having its source in any one of the three intermediate levels of VIII-B, VIII-C, or IX. That this tomb does not belong to Stratum IX is indicated by the elevation of 11.45 m. for the tops of its walls. The roof of this tomb thus lay at the level of the Stratum IX pavement, if not actually above it, and the burial must therefore have originated either in Stratum VIII-C or VIII-B. Other tombs in this group provide similar proof of their source in Stratum VIII. Tomb 61, and possibly No. 64 as well, would also have protruded above the floor of Stratum IX. In addition, Tomb 64 would have been situated within thirty centimetres of the edge of the mound, and finally, none of this group would be located near a religious or any other kind of building in Stratum IX. The problem is further simplified by the fact that Tomb 60 touches the wall lying immediately southeast of the Western Temple of Stratum VIII-C, and together with Nos. 16, 61, 37, 64, and 65—the remaining members of this group—seems to have been separated from the temple by this wall. The probability is, therefore, that this wall was standing when the shafts of these tombs were excavated, for otherwise (in Stratum VIII-B, for example, when the wall in question was covered by debris), the tombs could have been placed closer to the temple, as were Tombs 30, 59, and 24–25, on the other side of the same edifice. To be sure, the position of Tomb 60, which lies so close to the wall outside the temple, permits the interpretation that it cut through this wall, and the tomb should, therefore, be related to Stratum VIII-B. But it remains to be explained why Tombs 60, 61, and 16 form a line parallel to the wall; what, in Stratum VIII-B, was there to determine the alignment of their locations? The evidence is not entirely unequivocal, but its most logical interpretation is that Tomb 60 and, for that matter, all other tombs belonging to this group, are to be related to Stratum VIII-C, where they were separated from the temple by a wall that was extant only in that stratum. Confirmation of the attribution of these tombs to VIII-C rather than VIII-B would seem to lie in the fact that the Western Temple was actually in use only in Stratum VIII-C. In VIII-B the entrance to this edifice was blocked off and a definite effort was made to deface the building.[21] Surely tombs of Stratum VIII-B would not have been located near a desecrated shrine; they would have been placed near religious buildings still held in veneration, and the Western Temple was used as a religious edifice only in Stratum VIII-C.

This argument does not preclude the possibility that tombs of other groups may have originated in Stratum VIII-B, but it does maintain that

[21] *Ibid.*. pp. 30–31.

if tombs are attributed to that stratum they must be situated near the three temples which were then in use, namely, the Central and Northern Shrines, and the Eastern Temple. Tomb 45 of Group IV, in Squares 6 and 7–0, for example, is probably of Stratum VIII-B origin. Table 6 shows that it may have had a source in Strata VIII-B, VIII-C, IX, or X, but a more positive indication is available. The walls of Room 883 in Stratum VIII-C are missing directly over the location of this tomb; as a matter of fact, the width of the break in the walls of this room is exactly matched by the width of the tomb, and there is no way to account for this gap except by holding the shaft of Tomb 45 responsible. If we have correctly attributed its source, the tomb in question would then have been located nearly in the center of the open area separating the Northern Shrine from Rooms 837, 831, and 833.

The broken walls of Stratum VIII-C exactly above this tomb prove that its shaft must have been sunk from Stratum VIII-B. Even if this fact is ignored, however, the elevation of the top of the tomb walls (11.51 m.), would have allowed a cover of earth only 20 or 30 cm. thick between the roof of the tomb and the floor of Stratum IX. This manifestly would not have been sufficient protection; either the walls of the tomb would not have been constructed so high within the shaft, or the shaft would have been excavated still deeper. The criticism may be made that Tomb 34, which lies about two metres from the tomb under discussion, has an identical floor elevation of 10.25 m., yet it has been shown that No. 34 had its origin in Stratum IX, while it is now argued that No. 45 had a Stratum VIII-B source. The proximity of these two tombs, no less than their identical floor elevations, are factors that might beguile us into ascribing both to the same stratum. But the shaft of No. 45 definitely cut through Stratum VIII-C walls; on the other hand, the location of No. 34 is crossed by VIII-C walls, so that the attribution of both tombs to a single stratum is an impossibility.

Similarly, Tomb 29 of Group IV may also have had its source in Stratum VIII-B, although the floor elevation of this tomb is 11.74 m., compared with the 10.25 m. elevation of the floor of Tomb 45. The explanation of this difference again lies in the height of the walls of the tombs, which in the case of No. 29 rose to a mere 20 cm., so that a deeper shaft was unnecessary. This tomb, also a member of Group IV, lying in Square 6-Q, is shown in Table 6 to have two possible stratigraphic sources: VIII-B and VIII-C. In Stratum VIII-C it would be situated in the small open space northeast of Room 888; in Stratum VIII-B it would occur, like Tomb 45, in the broad, open area southwest of the Northern Shrine. The latter location seems the more probable, although the possibility that this tomb could have originated in Stratum VIII-C must be admitted.[22]

[22] Also belonging to this group of tombs are Nos. G36–40 and G36–44, both located in Square 7-Q (in the d and a quarters of that square), and both intruding into debris

Tomb 213, a stone cist in Square 7-M, and a member of Group V, is to be attributed to Stratum IX, as were Nos. 62 and D of the same group. It was intrusive into Stratum X-A, and is crossed by walls of VIII-C (Room 887), so that Strata IX or X are possible sources. This tomb, however, seems to have cut the wall projecting southeast of Room 1007 in Stratum X, and hence must have originated in Stratum IX.

Tomb 124 brings us to a consideration of the important tombs of Group VI, hitherto ignored in our discussion. The three tombs forming this group (Nos. 124, 107, and 102) are located for the most part in Squares 5-M and 6-M, and have floor elevations that are remarkably uniform, all occurring within a range of 32 cm. All three tombs were discovered just below the floor of Stratum XI, their walls extending well into that stratum. Tombs 124 and 107 are not crossed by the walls of any overlying stratum (see, however, footnote 23 below); and Tomb 102 is crossed only by Stratum VI walls. Obviously, therefore, we have now to deal with the most difficult part of our stratigraphic problem, for Table 6 gives little clue to the stratigraphic source of these tombs. By superimposing the location of Tomb 124 on the plans of overlying strata, however, it was discovered that walls of Strata X and X-A were broken and missing at the location of this tomb. The conclusion is then inescapable that the shaft of No. 124 cut through these strata, and the shaft must have begun in a higher stratum. Consequently, the source of this tomb is now limited to any one of the three phases of Stratum VIII, or to Stratum IX; an origin in any stratum later than VIII-A would imply an impossibly deep shaft.

The association of this tomb with religious buildings of Strata VIII and IX unfortunately gives us no clue as to its source; its position could be interpreted as related to the Northern Shrine of VIII or to the IX Temple, but its depth suggests that it was a product of Stratum IX. The elevation of the floor of this tomb is 9.62 m., while the walls rose to an elevation of 10.12 m. If the tomb shaft had been begun in Stratum VIII-C, to take the lowest phase of that stratum, it would have been excavated to a total depth of well over two and one-half metres, and there would have been an earth-fill upon the roof of the tomb exceeding two metres in depth. Even though the roof of No. 124 possessed a cover of stone slabs, it may be questioned whether its builders would have tested their strength to

---

below the Stratum XI floor level. These tombs, like Nos. G36–14, G36–26, G36–27, G36–30, 536–34, and G36–36 which are discussed in footnotes 26 and 27 of this chapter, are not shown on Fig. 8.23, as their exact locations cannot now be determined. As a consequence, no positive stratigraphic source may be assigned to them, but in the case of the present two tombs, which occur somewhat deeper than the other members of Group VI discussed above, a source in Stratum IX seems the most probable. In that stratum they would have been situated near the northern corner of the Temple, whereas in Both Strata X and VIII-C a complex of small rooms in this location would have effectively prevented the excavation of tombs shafts. Each tomb contained the remains of a child.

that degree. If sunk from Stratum IX, however, the roof of this tomb would have been between 1.60 and 1.70 m. below the pavement of that level; this figure is still considerable, but more reasonable. Such evidence as there is, therefore, indicates a source for Tomb 124 in Stratum IX, where it was situated to the rear of the temple.

The remaining members of Group VI, viz., Tombs 107 and 102, present us with our most interesting problem. To begin with, these two tombs were unquestionably contemporaneous, for, although separated from each other by approximately a metre and a half, they were oriented on exactly the same north-northwest to southeast axis that is not duplicated by any other tomb discovered at Gawra. The reason for this peculiar orientation will later become clear, but at present the fact that it is characteristic of both tombs is suggestive of their contemporaneity. Conversely, this orientation demonstrates that Tomb 124, just discussed, was not constructed at the same time, for that tomb possesses a more orthodox alignment, its longitudinal axis pointing northwest-southeast.

It has been pointed out in the discussion of Tomb 124 that, so far as overlying walls are concerned, we have little indication of the stratigraphic sources of the Group VI tombs, since neither 124 nor 107 are crossed by any walls of higher strata, and since No. 102 is crossed only by walls of Stratum VI. In the case of Tomb 124, we have discovered that it cut through Stratum X walls, and consequently must have originated in a later stratum, but with Tombs 107 and 102 we have no such clue, and their source in Stratum X is a possibility that must be examined. If Tomb 107 originated in Stratum X it would be exactly enclosed by the walls of the building bearing the number 1003 on the Stratum X plan, neatly fitting into that structure, whose walls would then be exactly parallel with the tomb walls. Such a coincidence is too great to have been the result of an accident, and at once suggests a relationship between Tomb 107 and the building mentioned. To be sure, the northwest wall of the tomb would lie only thirty centimetres from the northwest wall of Room 1003, compared with the 1.35 m. distance separating their respective southeastern walls, but an absolutely precise centering of the tomb within Room 1003 is not vital to our thesis. If Tomb 107 is to be related, therefore, to Stratum X, it must be associated with Room 1003 of that stratum, and that structure would then be one of a very few, other than temples, to have enclosed a tomb within its limits.

In describing the architecture of Stratum X (in Chapter I), the public, and possibly religious, character of this building was pointed out, the architectural evidence consisting of the regular plan of this edifice, the possibility that it possessed buttresses, and the fact of its niched walls. There was, in addition, one feature of this structure that was most unusual; namely, the paving of the whole interior with mud-bricks laid in regular courses to a depth of nearly one metre. As all other buildings in this stratum had only the usual earth floors, the paved floor of Room 1003 would, by itself, merely emphasize its public character. However, with the knowledge that Tomb 107 is located beneath that building, the fundamental reason for the extraordinarily thick floor is now apparent; it was intended to emphasize the sacred character of the soil beneath, and to prevent its desecration. Room 1003 must consequently be interpreted as a shrine, built to fix and protect the location of the tomb lying underneath its floor; as such, it is unique among the buildings of Gawra.

If we accept this explanation of the nature of Room 1003, do the contents of Tomb 107 which lies beneath it tend to confirm such an interpretation? It must be conceded that richer furnishings might have been expected in the burial of some personage important enough to have had a shrine erected over the location of his tomb, for Tomb 107 contained no objects of great intrinsic value, the adult burial which it enclosed being supplied merely with six stone spheres. On the other hand, the tomb of a priest need not be expected to yield a rich collection of objects, and the stone spheres may even have had some cult use not now suspected. At any rate, it is important that Tomb 102 lying outside the shrine, also contained stone spheres, for this coincidence furnishes another link in the relationship between Tombs 107 and 102.

The reason for the unusual orientation of Tomb 107 is now clear, for it was placed with a similarly oriented building. However, this orientation is also unusual for temple buildings in all strata from XIII through VIII, which always have their corners set to the cardinal points, so that the real reason for such a peculiar alignment still eludes us. But we can now explain the identical orientation of Tomb 102, for that tomb is located outside the shrine, lying only 35 cm. away from its northern corner, with the northwest wall of the tomb exactly parallel to the southeast wall of the building.

The final piece of evidence suggesting a Stratum X origin for Tomb 107 is based on the size of the mud-bricks used in the construction of that tomb. These measured 50×25 and 51×26 cm., and are thus larger than the bricks generally used in either Stratum IX or VIII. They are, however, identical in size with some of the bricks used in Stratum X buildings, and compare with the 50×23 and 50×22 cm. measurements of the bricks used in the construction of the shrine itself. The close identity in size between the bricks used in the construction of the shrine and those in Tomb 107 further serves to establish their relationship.

It was remarked in discussing Tomb 124 that all three tombs comprising Group VI had floor elevations occurring within a very narrow range of only 32 cm. The elevations of the roofs of these tombs are even more uniform, since for No. 124 we have a figure of 10.12 m.; for No. 107, 10.09 m.; and for No. 102, 10.14 m. The range in elevation of their roofs is therefore a mere five centimetres, which may be construed as evidence of their source in a common stratum. Such an argument is, however, completely fallacious, for the shaft of Tomb 124 cut into the southwest wall of the shrine, and must have originated in a stratum later than X. Tomb 107, on the other hand, cannot have a source in a stratum later than X, because its location was covered from the Stratum X floor level to a depth of one metre below floor level with an undisturbed pavement of mud-brick, which can only have been laid after the tomb had been constructed. The floor of the shrine had an elevation of 11.46 m. at its northwestern corner, and 11.24 m. at its southeastern corner. The roof of Tomb 107 consequently lay from 1.15 to 1.37 m. below the upper surface of the floor, with almost one metre of this distance being filled with the lower course of the mud-brick flooring. The floor, consequently, must have extended to within 20 to 50 cm. of the tomb roof, forming a remarkable, as well as unique, cover to the tomb.

It has already been proved that Stratum IX cannot have been the source of Tomb 107 because of the mud-brick flooring lying intact above the location of that tomb. To consider other alternatives, however, Stratum VIII-C or any other phase of the VIIIth stratum cannot have been the source of No. 107 for the same reason. In the case of No. 102, a Stratum VIII source is improbable, for it would imply an extremely deep shaft of about 2.30 m. or more. Then again, as these tombs were discovered in Stratum XI, they may even be considered of Stratum X-A origin. If Nos. 107 and 102 are to be attributed to Stratum X-A their roofs would have been about 60 to 70 cm. below the floor of that stratum. Such a comparatively shallow shaft would not have been an impossibility, although in view of the wealth contained by Tomb 102, a thicker earth cover might be expected. Another objection to ascribing a Stratum X-A source to these tombs arises from the fact that two walls east of the area numbered 16 on the plan of Stratum X-A have apparently been cut into by the shaft of Tomb 102, if we may presume that the shaft of this tomb had extended slightly southeast of the actual tomb limits. Consequently, Tomb 102, since it appears to have cut into X-A walls, and also its contemporary, Tomb 107,[23] must have originated in some higher stratum. That stratum, to repeat, can only be Stratum X, and the attribution of these two tombs to Stratum X is confirmed by a cumulative weight of evidence permitting no other interpretation.

[23] Tomb 107 is apparently crossed by two walls of Area 16 in Stratum X-A, but these walls encroach on the limits of the tomb by a matter of a very few centimetres. On the other hand, part of the southern wall enclosing this area is missing, and has possibly been cut into by the southeastern corner of the tomb. Or this circumstance may be explained if we presume the excavators of the shafts of Tomb 107 widened the bottom of the shaft slightly at its floor, so that undercutting produced the effect of X-A walls crossing over the tomb. While these walls do not decisively cross over the location of the tomb, in my opinion they definitely prohibit the attribution of this tomb to Stratum X-A.

The four tombs forming Group VII (Nos. 111, 109, 114, and 110), lying in Squares 4 and 5, M and K, include three very richly furnished tombs, and one containing a triple burial. All had been constructed at the bottom of shafts terminating just below the Stratum XI floor, and all are first crossed by walls of Stratum VIII-C, with the exception of Tomb 110, which is crossed only by VIII-A walls. We are thus confronted with three possible stratigraphic sources for these tombs, and it would be difficult to assign a specific stratum of origin to any of them were it not for the fortunate circumstances that Tomb 110 is the only one discovered at Gawra where it was possible to trace the shaft of the tomb back to its starting point.[24] The floor of Tomb 110 lay below Stratum XI, at an elevation of 9.43 m.; above this, the shaft was traced back to an elevation of 11.33 m., or to a point just below the Stratum X floor, in which stratum this tomb must have originated. At the maximum elevation of 11.33 m., the shaft extended to a height of 1.90 m. above the tomb floor; possibly another ten centimetres of hard-packed earth lay at the top of the shaft, and had once again become the floor of the stratum, so that the original shaft probably attained a total depth of two metres. A source in Stratum X for this tomb, as well as the others in this group, is logical, for they would have been located at the end of the street leading to the Stratum X Temple, and as close to that building as it was possible to be in the northeastern section of the mound. On the other hand, the present Group VII tombs may have been associated with the shrine erected over the location of Tomb 107. That building lies nearly ten metres northwest of the area occupied by the tombs under discussion; however, it is difficult to explain why Tombs 111, 109, 114, and 110, if they were intended to associate with the shrine of No. 107, were not then located north or northwest of that building where there were open areas, and where they could have been situated much closer to its holy ground. It is thus questionable whether we may consider the present four tombs as associated with the shrine of Tomb 107; however, one relationship between them is clear. This is the discovery in Tomb 110 of stone spheres similar to those produced by Tombs 107 and 102. As a matter of fact, both 107 and 110 contained an identical number of these spheres—six each—and to make the parallel even more striking, Tomb 114 also contained six stones; this time, however, natural pebbles of red jasper.

The objection may be raised that although Tomb 110 is to be connected with Stratum X, a similar attribution for Nos. 111, 109, and 114 does not follow merely because these three are grouped with No. 110. However, the elevation of the floors of Tombs 109 and 114 (9.42 m.) is only a single centimetre below that of Tomb 110, so that their source in a common stratum may at least be suspected. Tomb 111, to be sure, has a

[24] This tomb lay next to an unexcavated fringe of the mound, through which the shaft of the tomb could be followed back to its starting point in Stratum X.

floor considerably higher than the others (10.02 m.); but it joins with No. 109 to form a double tomb. This double tomb does not have a common wall, as did Nos. 25 and 24, but the southeast wall of No. 111 is built against the northwest wall of No. 109, so that it is impossible to dissociate them. Furthermore, Tomb 114 closely adjoins and almost touches No. 109 and, to a slightly lesser degree, No. 111. Finally, the orientation of all four tombs in this group is identical. All members of this group are thus interrelated, and the group may be considered a unit, so far as its stratigraphic source is concerned at least.[25] This source was proved to be Stratum X in the case of Tomb 110, and an identical attribution for Tombs 111, 109, and 114 must therefore be conceded.

Up to this point we have considered thirty-five of the total of forty-five tombs appearing on Fig. 8.23. All of these have been found to originate in five consecutive strata, viz., VIII-B, VIII-C, IX, X, and X-A. Most of the remaining ten tombs have no indications as to their specific stratigraphic sources, but it may be possible to assign a stratum of origin to them on the basis of their association with adjoining tombs, or by other means.

Five tombs of Group III, in Squares 8 and 9, Q and O, have been omitted from earlier discussion. These are Nos. 57, 30, 59, 46, and 18, of which Nos. 59 and 57 are stone cists rather than mud-brick tombs; two of these have been considered (Nos. 25–24) and attributed to Stratum VIII-C. Consequently, an identical stratigraphic source might be expected for the five tombs now under consideration, as all members of this group closely adjoin, and all are more or less closely situated to the Western and Central Shrines of Stratum VIII-C, although Tomb 46 alone may also be associated with the Stratum IX Temple. In the case of Tombs 30, 59, 46, and 18, Table 6 lists Stratum VIII-B as a possible source, but it was remarked earlier in this chapter, when discussing the tombs of Group I, that it is extremely unlikely that any burials should have been associated with the Western Temple in the A and B phases of Stratum VIII, as in those periods the temple was defiled, and its entrance blocked. It may be asserted with some confidence, therefore, that these four tombs originated no later than Stratum VIII-C; however, Tombs 57, 59, 46, and 18 have as an alternative a possible source in Stratum IX. By tracing the location of Tombs 59 and 46 on the plan of Stratum IX; consequently they must have originated in a higher stratum, which can only be Stratum VIII-C.

---

[25] The elevations of the tops of the walls of these four tombs have regrettably been omitted from the field records, but an examination of Plate XLVIa [not reproduced here] discloses that the walls of all of these tombs except No. 110 rose to approximately the same height. The concentration of these tombs near the location of the Stratum XI Temple must be construed as fortuitous because, to judge from Plate XLVIa, the walls of these tombs possessed a minimum elevation of from 60 to 90 cm. Consequently, the roofs of these tombs would have been well above the floor level of Stratum XI and must be attributed to a later stratum.

We have, however, ignored the fact that Tombs 57, 59, and 46 were intrusive in Stratum X; Tombs 30, 18, and 25–24, on the other hand, were dug into Stratum IX so that these two groups were separated by approximately 1.25 m. of debris. This circumstance might indicate a source in Stratum IX for Nos. 57, 59, and 46, and a Stratum VIII-C source for the tombs having higher elevations, if it were not for the fact that Tombs 59 and 46 cut through Stratum IX walls and cannot have originated in the same stratum. How the difference in elevation is to be explained is problematical; perhaps because Nos. 57 and 59 were stone cists covered with stone slabs, their roofs were deemed capable of supporting a heavier burden of earth, and their shafts were consequently dug deeper. No. 18, however, was a mud-brick tomb having no trace of a roof or the material with which it might have been made, but since this tomb had been disturbed and apparently thoroughly plundered, it is possible that it, too, originally possessed a stone slab cover or wooden roofing, either removed by the tomb robbers or destroyed by them.

To sum up, Stratum VIII-C is the only stratum—if we may treat these tombs as a group instead of disconnected units—in which Nos. 57, 30, 59, 46, and 18 could have originated, since in Stratum VIII-B they would associate with a building which had lost its religious function, and because two of those tombs cut through Stratum IX walls, and must as a consequence have originated in a later stratum. An attribution of Nos. 57, 30, 59, 46, and 18 to Stratum VIII-C would also agree with the source ascribed to Tombs 25–24, and thus date the entire group to the earliest phase of the VIIIth stratum.[26]

The isolated tomb in Square 10-Q, designated by the letter "A," is similarly to be attributed to Stratum VIII-C. This tomb has two possible sources, Strata VIII-C and IX, but as it is apparently associated with the Western Temple it undoubtedly originated, like the tombs of Group III, in Stratum VIII-C.

Tomb 20 is our next example. This is another isolated tomb in Square 8-M, situated exactly at the entrance to the Stratum IX Temple, although it can have no relation to that structure, since the floor of the

[26] In addition to the seven tombs forming Group III of Fig. 8.23, four additional tombs were discovered in Squares 8-Q, and 8-O which are not shown on that plan. They are Nos. G36–14 (8-Q), G36–26 (8-O), G36–27 (8-Q), and G36–30 (8-O), of which Tombs G36–14 and G36–26 were intrusive into Stratum X-A, while the other two were discovered just below the floor level of Stratum XI. All four tombs, therefore, form a part of Group III, but it will be noted that they occur much deeper than the other members of the group, and presumably had their origin in some stratum or strata earlier than that attributed to the members of this group discussed above. Possibly Tombs G36–14 and G36–26 originated in Stratum IX or X; on the other hand, Tombs G36–27 and G36–30, since they had been sunk deeper than the others, probably belong to Stratum X or X-A. No. G36–26 was a cist, but all four tombs contained the bones of children.

tomb rested on the floor of the stratum. It had, therefore, been sunk into Stratum IX from an overlying level, and since Table 6 shows it is crossed by walls of VIII-A, the only possible sources of this tomb are Strata VIII-B or VIII-C. The floor of this tomb was determined to be 12.13 m. above the zero point, the highest elevation of any of the Gawra tombs. The height of the tomb walls is not specified, but if they were only ten or twenty centimetres high the roof of the tomb would then have occurred at about the level of the Stratum VIII-C floor; therefore the origin of this tomb in Stratum VIII-B must be presumed. Indeed, it is probable that the location of this tomb is to be explained only by attributing it to Stratum VIII-B, for had it been of VIII-C origin it would almost certainly have been situated closer to the Western Temple.

Three tombs, Nos. 171, 209, and 169, comprising Group IX and situated in Squares 6-J and 6-G, round out the discussion of the stratigraphic sources of the tombs shown on Fig. 8.23. Tomb 171 was discovered in Stratum XI, at an unknown elevation; it is not crossed by the walls of any overlying stratum. Tomb 169 also was intrusive in Stratum XI; its floor has an elevation of 9.49 m., and like No. 171 it is not crossed by walls of any higher stratum. Tomb 209, discovered in Stratum X-A, has the highest elevation (11.14 m.) of any in this group. It is first crossed by walls of Stratum VI. With such limited evidence from the strata overlying these three tombs positive stratigraphic attributions are hardly possible. However, it will be noted that two of these tombs were intrusive in Stratum XI; the other was sunk into Stratum X-A. The difference in elevation of their floors is thus over one and a half metres, and as a consequence, two different strata of origin seem to be indicated. The position of Tomb 169 shows that it cuts through Stratum X-A and X walls; in all probability, therefore, this tomb originated in Stratum IX, where it may have been associated with the large building southeast of the Temple. Tomb 171, since it was likewise intrusive into XI, is also to be attributed to Stratum IX, although a Stratum X source is not improbable. Tomb 209, which has the highest floor elevation of any tomb in this group, in all likelihood was the product of the inhabitants of Stratum VIII-C, and was associated with the Eastern Temple.[27] Although these attributions appear reasonable, it must be emphasized that no positive

---

[27] Two additional tombs, Nos. G36–34 and G36–36, in Squares 7-K and 7-J respectively, are to be considered with the three tombs of Group IX just discussed. Tomb G36–34 was intrusive into Stratum XI, as were Tombs 171 and 169 described above. Perhaps, like those tombs, it is also to be attributed to Stratum IX, but it is located in or near the Stratum X Temple, and may consequently be contemporaneous with that edifice. In the lack of any other evidence substantiating this hypothesis, however, it has seemed wiser to regard this tomb as a Stratum IX product. Tomb G36–36, on the other hand, was discovered in Stratum X and is, therefore, more probably of Stratum VIII-C origin, like No. 209 of the present group.

stratigraphic sources may be assigned to these three tombs with the evidence now at hand.

Technique of Excavating Middle American Pyramids and Tombs

A. V. Kidder provides us with a statement based on the results of his long experience in the excavation of large Mesoamerican pyramids.[28] Many of these structures have been rebuilt or added to from time to time, and the excavator's problem is to determine the nature and position of the various constructions contained within the mass of the pyramid. A briefer, though valuable, discussion of the methods of excavating Maya structures has been published by Robert E. Smith (1955;12).

We believe . . . that one should begin the exploration of any Meso-american mound by cutting a narrow trench, or running a tunnel at ground level, from well outside the mound to its center. This should enter from the side rather than the front. The front may often be identified by the presence of a bulging projection indicating the former position of a stairway. If no such evidence can be made out, and if, as is commonly the case, the mound forms part of a quadrilateral assemblage, it will usually be found to have faced on the enclosed court.

The lateral penetration trench will give a cross section of any inner construction which may exist. It will also reveal the nature and depth, and the line of junction with undisturbed architectural material, of such relatively nonsignificant surface deposits as humus and debris from fallen superstructures. These can then be removed with far less danger than if they are dug into blindly.

After the trench has been opened and its sides carefully examined (this should be done both while they are fresh and after they have dried), the buildings that have been identified should be cleared one by one, always leaving adequate control sections for back-checking upon problems not envisaged during the original excavation. This removal of one structure after another, starting always at the trench where the section shows each phase clearly, enables one to keep full record of each increment to the mound. It also simplifies photographic recording. The trench provides a take-off whence one can work from the known to the unknown, thus largely preventing the unwitting damage often caused by outside approaches. The procedure might be modified by extending the trench inward a step at a time as buildings successively examined

[28] Alfred V. Kidder, Jesse D. Jennings, and Edwin M. Shook, *Excavations at Kaminaljuyu, Guatemala*, Carnegie Institution of Washington, Washington, D.C., 1946, Publication 561, pp. 27, 28, 90, 92. By permission of the Carnegie Institution.

are cut away. This is feasible only if conditions are such that a new structure is easily and surely recognizable and the total preview afforded by the deep preliminary lateral cut will generally, we believe, be most satisfactory.

The adobe used in all these [Kaminaljuyu] structures was so much alike that it was next to impossible to detect a change when digging passed from one into another. Even seen in cross section in the sides of a penetration trench, and often when we knew within centimeters where such a trench must have passed through a junction, we could not locate the line of separation between two buildings. This forced a revision of the technique usually employed in dirt digging. We abandoned the use of the broad flat blade of a mattock, which cuts a thin shaving of earth and leaves a wide, smooth mark, and employed only the pointed end of a hand pick for all advance or exploratory work because adobe plaster when damp shows no appreciable differences from fill either in texture or in color, and offers no resistance to a broad-bladed cutting tool. However, it does not bond or fuse with fill laid upon it, and a line of cleavage nearly always exists, if the adobe finishing coat was in reasonably good condition when covered. In order to take advantage of the tendency of superior fill to cleave from such plaster, we dug with hand picks, using light blows, twisting the point so that the earth caught by it would be levered forward and out, ripped loose rather than sliced through. Each stroke removed a little material below and behind the tool's point, and when a plastered surface was reached the fill through which we were working would flake away from it and we could then follow the newly discovered surface laterally.

As the season wore on it appeared that the difficulties encountered in recognition of superpositions applied only when the sides of a penetration trench were freshly cut and damp. After the adobe had dried, junctions became relatively clear because of shrinkage and the formation of cracks. Once thorough drying had taken place, subsoil, junctions between buildings, plastered surfaces, thin floors, all outlined themselves distinctly.

A word as to the excavation of the tombs. The first ones encountered . . . we sank into from above—an undesirable method, as one never knows where the floor will be or where grave-goods may lie, and so, even if the preliminary exploratory pit be small, one risks ruining some fragile specimen by coming down upon it unaware. Another drawback to the vertical approach is that it is always difficult to recognize changes in the nature and the "lay" of fill while it is being taken out from above. In our early work we attempted to record these phenomena from the sides of a gradually enlarged exploratory pit. But in a deep tomb one is badly cramped; and the drying fill slumps and trickles down upon the section of the floor that is under examination, causing much extra work and endangering objects that are being cleaned.

In the procedure finally adopted, tombs were excavated entirely from the side and the removal of the fill and the clearing of the floor constituted two separate operations. The size of the grave was first determined, a simple matter as the dark, relatively soft fill could easily be distinguished from the clean, hard clay through which the shaft had been sunk. Then a pit as wide as the shaft and sufficiently large to give ample room for shoveling was dug just outside the tomb, if practicable on the north, that side being chosen because we had learned that mortuary furniture seldom lay close to the north wall. The pit was carried down to the level of the tomb floor, exposing the entire north face of the fill . . . A diagram recording its composition and stratification, if any, was made, after which the work was pushed southward, the floor of the excavation being kept at about 50 cm. above that of the tomb. The fill was taken out in vertical slices about 1 m. thick, each slice divided into 1-m. columns, which were removed consecutively . . . Columns rather than complete tomb-wide slices were cut because the latter would have permitted observation of only east-west faces, whereas diagrams of the two faces of each column could later be combined to form both east-west and north-south sections. This somewhat involved method was necessitated by the fact that the fill, in most cases, was not merely a simple dump of earth but contained remains of roofing, collapsed platforms, and debris of dismantled buildings which yielded important evidence for the history of the tomb.

The bulk of the fill out of the way, the 50-cm. layer left on the floor was taken out, also in blocks 1 m. square . . . This final operation was of course done entirely with trowel and brush. Work began at the north end of the tomb and was carried southward, specimens and bones being brought to light, noted, recorded on the ground plan, and taken up.

At first, we attempted to clean and keep in place all skeletons and vessels, in order to get photographs of the entire contents of a tomb. But we soon found that materials left *in situ* prevented access to others, that some of them deteriorated badly during the several days they often had to lie open to sun and air, and that they were in danger of being stepped on or damaged by falls of earth from the drying walls of the tomb. Furthermore, decayed bones and shell, rotted pyrite-incrusted plaques, and crushed pottery, particularly vessels that had coats of stucco, suffered severely from the brushing necessary to expose them for photography. Hence we noted and removed each specimen as we came to it, the more fragile ones, as soon as their nature and size were ascertained, being undercut and taken out, still encased in earth, for final treatment in the laboratory. In such cases, exposed parts of objects were covered with several layers of moistened tissue paper and the whole lump was solidified with a heavy coat of paraffin.

The Identification and Interpretation of Strata

This second methodological note is by R. E. M. Wheeler,[29] one of the leading British archaeologists, who was, for a time, head of the Archaeological Survey of India. In this note, using examples from India, he illustrates correct, i.e., meaningful, and incorrect methods of recording archaeological stratigraphy.

The correct interpretation of a section . . . is a matter of accurate observation, clear-thinking, and experience. Let us pause for a moment to consider this in practice. We will assume that the draftsman has correctly identified the changes of material, i.e., the strata, and (measuring from a carefully levelled datum-string) has accurately transcribed them to squared paper. His delineation will probably appear as in Fig. 8.24A. But this delineation, although indicating the presence of strata, does little or nothing to indicate their varying character and significance. It is a meaningless collection of lines—a procession of letters not yet divided into words. A more ambitious draftsman may attempt to indicate something of the individuality and diversity of the strata, and Fig. 8.24B illustrates

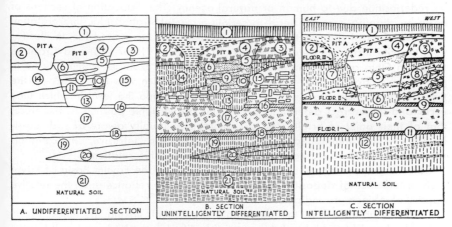

Fig. 8.24.   Recording of archaeological stratigraphy.

such an attempt. This fails in two main respects. First the general evenness of tone throughout the section produces the unmeaning monotony of a sentence spoken without inflection, and so fails largely to convey the intended impression. The draftsman has not realized the varying significance of the facts which he is recording; he has failed to see the wood for the trees. Secondly, he has not realized that his rendering is not merely

[29] R. E. M. Wheeler, "The Recording of Archaeological Strata," *Ancient India*, no. 3, pp. 148–149. By permission of P. Banerjee, Office of the Director General of Archaeology in India.

a transcription of accurately measured or even accurately emphasized lines: it is, or should be, also an accurate *picture* of what he sees. Not only should lines of demarcation be transcribed from measurement, but also the size, shape and position of brick-bats, bones, sherds or other materials which, by their character and quantity and by their "angle of rest" in the soil, combine to indicate the nature of a stratum and the method of its accumulation. An intelligently drawn section is far more than a diagram; it is a *picture*, representing not merely the skeleton but also the vital flesh and blood of its subject. Fig. 8.24C is Fig. 8.24B corrected in this sense.

However rudimentary and obvious these details may seem, I have no hesitation in emphasizing their importance. A well-drawn, i.e., intelligently recorded, section is relatively a rarity. But it is nevertheless a basic necessity of modern fieldwork.

Reversal of Trash Layers at Chetro Ketl, New Mexico

The normal position of objects in layered deposits may, at times, be changed by redeposition due to human or natural agency. The dislocation of sections of earth by slipping can also lead to serious errors of stratigraphic interpretation unless the fact of that earth movement is noted and accounted for. In illustration, we cite instances detailed by W. H. Holmes (1919:67, 80) and Crabtree (1939) in Ohio and California localities. Burials, for example, commonly lie in pits whose bottom is at a lower point than that which was the surface at the time the grave was dug—such graves are intrusive into the level in which they occur and the correct determination of their stratigraphic position is, therefore, that of their point of origin. The archaeologist is usually aware of such possibilities as those mentioned and, by use of the term "intrusive," indicates his recognition of the disturbance of normal stratigraphic relations.

Caton-Thompson and Gardner (1934:21) noted in the Fayum Basin of Egypt such disturbance of deposits that they could place no reliance upon the relative depths of objects as indicators of age. They say:

> The inhabitants had the deplorable practice of sinking fire-holes; two hundred and forty-eight of these were identified in the bedrock level; later occupants, as the level rose, burrowed theirs into the accumulating rubbish; and the extent to which in doing so they must have shifted the earlier deposit and its contents cannot be ignored. True, in places the horizontal bands of blown sand or of ashes gave a localized control of the neolithic stratigraphy; but in the main it must be regarded as suspect. The cultural homogeneity revealed throughout the deposits must be accepted then only in the light of these conditions.

In some deposits whole layers or strata may be reversed so that the "law of superposition" reads backward—the strata are, so to speak, upside down. There are a number of instances of reversed stratigraphy in the archaeological literature and the two selections presented here have been deemed sufficient to illustrate the subject. For other examples see Coon, 1952:20; Bennett, 1953:33;

Colton, *1946:297–299*. Haury (*1955:*133) gives a hypothetical example of reversed stratigraphy.

Dr. Florence Hawley has published many important papers on Southwestern archaeology and ethnology. The passage below,[30] taken from her published doctoral dissertation, is a classic example of reversed stratigraphy. She has also published a separate note on this particular subject (Hawley, *1937*).

Chetro Ketl is one of the fifteen or so large pueblo sites in Chaco Canyon, New Mexico. According to tree ring dates the buildings of Chetro Ketl were erected between 945 and 1116 A.D.

Directly east of Chetro Ketl rises the east refuse mound, one of the largest trash piles ever found in connection with southwestern pueblo sites. Located as it is in line of discharge of storm waters from one of the cañon rincons behind it, this mound has received the silt of many centuries as an accumulation covering its eastern periphery to a depth of 12 feet 8 inches, and apparently to a greater depth on the northern and western sides. There has been no deep excavation on those sides.

This dump was examined in 1922, when trenches 11 feet wide were cut from north to south and from east to west. In 1929 a pit was sunk at the center of the dump. Neither the material from this work nor that of the earlier year was ever studied in detail. This excavation left the mound badly cut before we began trenching in 1930.

The east dump is roughly oval in shape. Although at present the surface of the dump slopes upward from the west, the old surface level as followed in the excavations was found to dip toward the east. At the center the mound was approximately 20 feet deep.

Our objective was to discover what the dump might yield of pottery sequences, to learn whether its depth was accounted for by long accumulations of daily sweepings alone, and to find the relation of the dump strata to the periods of Chetro Ketl building.

Stratigraphic excavation, stratification by soil composition, charcoal dating, and the statistical treatment of potsherds taken from the excavation were the techniques employed in study of the Chetro Ketl dump.

1. Excavation. The dump is located directly east of the pueblo. It seemed logical to suppose that people coming from the pueblo at first should have emptied their baskets of trash near the outer walls. Later they would dump on both sides of the growing mound, but as material was thrown from the peak on the farther side, eastward, the dump would grow not only vertically but also from the west eastward. As the peak of the mound would move ever farther eastward, a more precipitous slope would be found on that side than on the west.

With this as a premise to be tested, it was decided to sink a trench 12

---

[30] Florence M. Hawley, *The Significance of the Dated Prehistory of Chetro Ketl*, University of New Mexico Bulletin, Monograph Series, Albuquerque, 1934, vol. 1, no. 1, pp. 31–35, 51–57, 57–61. By permission of University of New Mexico Press.

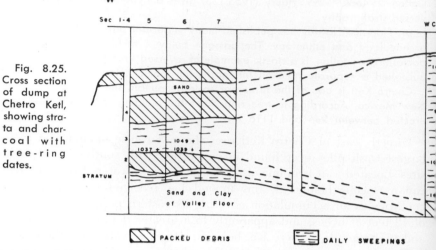

Fig. 8.25. Cross section of dump at Chetro Ketl, showing strata and charcoal with tree-ring dates.

feet long through the west side of the dump, to examine the center with a single pit, and to carry a trench down the eastern slope from the old central cut to where the eastern edge met the present ground level. The depth of each excavation was to be determined by the level of the original valley floor, wherever it might be encountered. The project was found to require so much time that further excavations were not attempted; intensive work carried out with requisite detail and care was obviously of more value than extensive work without detail. As time became an element before the planned excavations were completed, it was decided to carry the lower levels of excavation of the east trench to the bottom only in alternate sections, each section being 4 feet square. This allowed for plotting the strata of excavated sections from data; the intervening unexcavated sections could be plotted approximately through extension of the strata lines from excavated section to excavated section.

The four foot square sections above mentioned formed the horizontal unit adopted for the work. Vertically the material was to be taken out in 8 inch levels. From each level the material was screened, sacked, and labeled as it was removed. Later the sherds were washed, classified, counted, the percentages taken for each level, and the results tabulated and plotted for each section.

The western trench was started where a wash had eaten into the edge of the mound. For the first 16 feet east of that cut excavation was carried no lower than the stratum of sand which appears to have blown over the dump shortly after its abandonment and before the debris from the center of the mound washed down over it in a 16-inch cover. The next 12 feet, sections 5, 6, and 7, were thoroughly examined to the bottom, 16 feet below the surface. The west central pit uncovered the original valley floor at a depth of 20 feet. The east trench, 18 feet deep where it

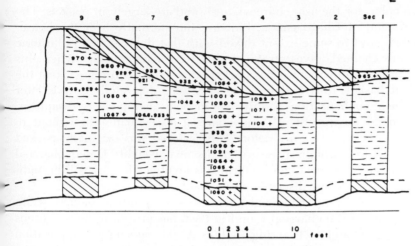

approached the center of the mound, was 13 feet deep at its eastern end, 36 feet from the center, where the dump surface meets the present ground level. Obviously the eastern side of this dump extends much farther eastward beneath the deep accumulation of sand washed over it since its abandonment.

2. Stratification by soil content and contour. The strata of different materials present in this dump could be seen on the side and back walls of trenches as excavation cut downward. The contours were outlined definitely enough so that they could be traced by an observer in the trench. The sides were in even alignment and sharply cut, ready for photography, when a cloudburst one summer afternoon filled the trenches with water. The upper walls of the trench crumbled, ruining any chances for pictures, and necessitating a delay of a week for cleaning away the debris and reestablishing the measurements of depth attained just before the disaster. Measurements and drawings necessarily became the data for the final cross section chart of the dump (see Fig. 8.25).

The strata seen differed in soil composition and color as well as in pottery content, discovered in subsequent sherd classification. Study of the structure of the strata showed two types to be present:

(1) Strata 1 and 3, as numbered on the chart, composed of daily sweepings, showing ash, charcoal, and potsherds heaped in small overlapping mounds as thrown from the baskets of the women;

(2) Strata 2 and 4, predominantly composed of old sweepings packed in lumps, gray in color, containing some stone, ash, and charcoal, but without laminations or outlines of small piles seen in the strata of daily sweepings. This material appears to have been debris removed from some abandoned section of the pueblo cleaned out for new building or from an old dump which was moved.

In sweepings piled directly onto the dump, a stratum may be variegated in color, for the ash, charcoal, and sand are largely in pockets. The light red sand of Chaco cañon, blowing intermittently over the household debris, and to some extent mixed with that debris when prehistoric floors were cleaned, gives strata of this type a light color. When this material is first thrown out it has pockets that indicate to some extent the individual baskets-full of debris as they were deposited. If it is later moved such configuration is lost; laminations and pockets disappear, and a general mixture of ash and charcoal disseminates throughout to give the whole mass a gray color. This material was originally packed down, probably through pressure of its own weight. Dated charcoal pieces and sherd percentages confirm this identification, as will be indicated in the following discussions of stratification.

3. Dating of Dump Charcoal. The dating of refuse mound strata through study of the charcoal found in them has proven to be a rigorous application of Douglass' tree ring analysis. As the value of this application has been tested under the unusual and adverse conditions found in the Chetro Ketl dump, use of this technique in clarifying sequences in other southwestern dumps is anticipated.

Our first season of work on this refuse mound consisted of the west trench excavation, from which little charcoal was saved because the possibility of using such material for dating strata was yet unrealized. Later charcoal was carefully sifted from the strata of the east trench, but before this was dated, solution of the complex problem of relative period of these strata was attempted through the techniques described above. The results of this effort led to broad hypotheses later substantiated by the charcoal dating, but until that task was accomplished no certainty in exploration of the peculiar stratification was possible. The charcoal specimens, which averaged under an inch in diameter, were pieces of branches burned in household fireplaces during the periods represented by the strata which held them. Most of them were of piñon, a wood slightly more difficult to work than pine; some were of pine and of Douglas fir and easily readable, and some were of juniper, cottonwood, and brush, and could not be used. The rings of most averaged approximately .5 mm. in width; many were microscopic. Examination was made with a 20 diameter hand glass, occasionally supplemented with a higher power lens.

As branch rings studied in modern pines are found to be somewhat more erratic than stem rings in response to weather conditions, and as most of these charcoal records were from piñon and hence more difficult than if from pine, extreme care was necessary in cross dating their charts with each other and in determining their actual dates. The master chart of this Chaco piñon was found to correspond, with but few variations, to the master chart of the yellow pine.

Of the entire dump collection, not more than 20% could be dated with confidence. The significance of even this small proportion, however, was paramount in definitely corroborating and dating the pottery sequences, in providing a key to the relationship of strata not lying in a normal chronological sequence, and in determining the relation of these strata to the Chetro Ketl building periods.

4. Potsherds in the Refuse Mound. Before examination of the dump could be attempted, it was necessary to establish a typological classification of pottery so that the groups could be recognized and treated statistically. The following classification was made in 1929 after several bases of distinction for representative types were tried. Difficulty lay in adequately distinguishing variations of the general Chaco black on white ware by some criteria that should be valid in marking the distinctive departure of type from type. Designs, paste composition, and paint were tried as classificatory data, but none were found to be adequate. General surface treatment of polish and slip were finally adopted as the most serviceable of sub-class criteria for this situation. It was supplemented to some extent by less distinct points of departure in design, paste, and paint. The classification was used for all subsequent work, but not with a preconceived idea of the series of classes necessarily representing a chronological sequence. That they arranged themselves in a manner suggestive of a developmental order was obvious, but it was not until after an examination of the pottery distribution through the 1931 excavations of the western side of the dump that the classes were admitted to be, in general, sequential. Even here contradictions appeared in the fact that some of the apparently latest strata and latest pottery appeared low in the pile, but the variation in soil make-up of the various strata and the dating made possible by collected charcoal indicated that almost one half of this dump was of material much older than the rest and out of chronological order. Briefly put, part of the dump was upside down. The evidence and discussion of this peculiar situation will be taken up in the detailed description of each stratum.

Four strata are encountered in trenching through the [east dump] refuse mound. They are numbered from the bottom upward, number 1 being the stratum first laid down and number 4 the last (see Fig. 8.25).

Stratum 1. Directly above the undisturbed sand of the original valley floor, as uncovered in the west trench, lies a thin layer rich in charcoal. The upper part of this stratum is lighter in color and more sandy than the bottom, a difference that is indicated by the line drawn through this stratum on Fig. 8.25. Small mounds and pockets of ash, sand, and charcoal identify the formation with that seen today in the accumulating dumps of the modern pueblos. Basketful by basketful the trash was thrown out, marking the pockets and lenses of charcoal and ash we find in excavation, first near the outer wall of the village and then farther eastward. The peak of the mound grew progressively eastward. As diagrammed in the chart, the highest point of the first stratum located in the west branch was at the west side of section 5; its peak probably lay somewhere between there and the western edge of the mound. The stratum remained almost horizontal through section 6 and dipped downward through section 7, showing that the valley floor evidently sloped eastward here. Stratum 1 runs out somewhere between section 7 and the west-central pit. There is no trace of it in the east trench.

That accumulations grew up around the spreading base of the mound is probable, but while we are dealing with material uncovered by a trench near the center of the dump, the problem of peripheral chronologies need not be considered.

Of the charcoal saved from stratum 1, not a piece was datable; ring sequences were too short or too erratic. As will be indicated in the discussion of stratum 3, which is dated, strata 1 and 3 are so similar in pottery distribution and soil composition as to appear of closely sequential periods. Stratum 1 was obviously the first to be laid down, at least in the section of the dump examined. Approximate dates for this stratum will be given subsequently.

As previously stated, distribution of corrugated ware throughout the different strata shows no consistent variation. The discussion of potsherd content of the strata will be based on percentages of the three types of black on white wares as described in the section on Pottery Classification.

Black on white sherds from stratum 1 occur in the following percentages (based on total sherds as 100%):

Polished black on white	33.2%
Semi-polished black on white	22.2%
Unpolished black on white	9.5%

Stratum 2. The second stratum illustrated in the cross section of the dump (Fig. 8.25), is slightly thicker than the first. It shows its peak in section 5, slopes rather precipitously downward in section 6, straightens somewhat in section 7, and appears in a thin layer as the lowest deposit almost 20 feet beneath the top of the dump in the west-central pit. Throughout the east trench its depth remains fairly constant, but the uneven surface of the ground on which it was deposited appears in the varying levels of its base line.

Stratum 2 consists of a mass of refuse that comes out as packed clods of debris. Its gray color appears to be the result of general mixing of ash and charcoal throughout. The marked difference in structure between this layer and the mounded and pocketed layer of daily sweepings beneath it led to comparison of the former with other material taken from the pueblo. In appearance the material of stratum 2 is found to be very similar to that removed in digging through the debris of the Great

Sanctuary. Except for the fact that it is filled with clods and stone, the material of stratum 2 is similar to that of Stratum 1 and 3 after that material is removed and mixed in the discard pile.

This material of stratum 2 could have been thrown onto the dump in its mixed state if it came from old refuse areas in the pueblo cleared of accumulations to permit the erection of new rooms or kivas. Old abandoned rooms and kivas are frequently filled with debris in modern pueblos. If any of these were to be cleaned out for re-use, or if old dumps were to be moved from one location to another, the mass of material after being deposited the second time would show few or no laminations. The whole would be comparatively homogeneous.

When found on a new dump, such material would be mixed with appreciable amounts of pottery in use at the time of the second deposition, for the daily household sweepings would be cast onto the growing pile week by week. These small contributions to the growing stratum would accumulate more slowly than the older twice moved material cleared from elsewhere and re-deposited as quickly as the builders could transport it in their baskets.

The black on white potsherd percentages for this stratum are:

Semi-polished black on white	26.5%
Polished black on white	14.0%
Unpolished black on white	9.5%

It is noticeable that while polished black on white ware was predominant in stratum 1, of daily sweepings, the semi-polished is predominant in stratum 2, composed mainly of old debris.

Only one charcoal specimen from stratum 2 is dated. It was cut about 1090 A.D. (1060 + ca. 30 rings estimated to have been burned off the exterior). This specimen gives the approximate date when the top of stratum 2 was being deposited; it is not the date of the material predominantly composing the stratum. Evidence for this statement comes from study of strata 3 and 4 and will be taken up subsequently.

Representative dates on the dump strata are marked on the cross section chart (Fig. 8.25), according to the levels from which they were taken.

Stratum 3. The third stratum is a thick layer of ash, charcoal, sand, and other debris. Although it makes up less than half the total thickness of deposit in the area cut by the west trench, it composes almost the entire central section of the dump, as cut by the west-central pit, and two-thirds of the eastern section. It is chiefly an accumulation of daily sweepings, into which was mixed a small amount of the old debris which largely composed strata 2 and 4. The peak of stratum 3 is seen at the present surface of the mound in the west-central pit and at the upper western edge of section 9 in the east trench.

Polished black on white ware is predominant in stratum 3 just as in stratum 1, also of daily sweepings. The proportions of black on white ware in stratum 3 run as follows:

Polished black on white	27.3%
Semi-polished black on white	16.9%
Unpolished black on white	5.5%

A large collection of charcoal was taken from stratum 3, and more specimens are dated than from any other one stratum. As usual, the difficulty of estimating the number of rings burned off the exterior of specimens is present. Two groups of dates are found, one in the late 900's, one in the 1000's and early 1100's. Let us first consider this latter group.

In Protocol 2 [not reproduced here] the underlined figures are the latest obtained for each level, that is, the dates on pieces having the fewest rings burned from the exterior. Nevertheless corrections for the missing exterior rings must be made in each case. The estimated date thus obtained is given in parenthesis.

The date found nearest the bottom of this mound is 1084 + ca. 6, or 1090. It comes from level 18, section 5, at the bottom of stratum 3 in the west trench. The date of 1067 + ca. 20 is found at level 26, west-central pit, two feet above the bottom of stratum 3, and 1060 + ca. 30 at level 27, section 5, marking the top of stratum 2 and the bottom of stratum 3 in the east trench. 1090 is taken as a fairly close approximation of the actual date which marks the top of stratum 2 and the bottom of stratum 3.

The latest date on stratum 3 is 1106 + ca. 4, or 1110 approximately. This comes from level 15, section 8. From level 17, section 4, comes the date of 1105 + ca. 5, or approximately 1110. When allowance is made for the slope of the stratum, these dates are seen to come from a horizontal plane slightly above the center of stratum 3 and roughly parallel with the top of the dump. The rate of deposition of this stratum and the computed dates of its upper levels will be discussed later.

The other group of stratum 3 dates, clustering around the middle 900's, is represented by seven scattered pieces of charcoal whose dates group with those of stratum 4. Stratum 4, as will be seen in its detailed description, is composed of a gray unmarked mass of material in general similar to that of stratum 2, containing a preponderance of semi-polished black on white ware dating in the late 900's. That some dates in the 10th century should come from small masses of the same material observed scattered through the mound-marked main contents of stratum 3 is not a matter of coincidence. Apparently a small amount of old debris was being moved during the period of deposition of this stratum. To judge by the position of the early dated specimens in relation to the depth of the stratum, this process of clearing was being started during the latter part of the period of stratum 3 and developed into a major operation at Chetro Ketl during the period of stratum 4.

Stratum 4. Stratum 4, the uppermost on the dump, is of the same unstratified packed debris as stratum 2 and shows a similar general potsherd distribution. It represents a period of clearing away the old debris originally deposited elsewhere in the pueblo.

On the west side of the dump the stratum is divided horizontally by a layer of sand. It seems evident that the top of the lower strip of this debris was the surface of the dump at the time that it was abandoned, and that for some time sand blew over it until a layer averaging 16 inches thick accumulated. The few sherds which drifted into it were probably washed down from the peak of the dump. Unless caught by bushes, sand rarely accumulates on the peak of a mound; we find none on this. The prevalence of westerly winds in the cañon would explain the presence of sand on the west slope but not on the east.

Above the sand is another layer of debris, identical in type to that below the sand. It would appear that after the sand had accumulated on these slopes, the peak began to weather and erode, washing farther and farther down the sides of the dump, until finally a layer about as thick as the sand had accumulated. If this washed material came from the peak of stratum 4 at the top of the dump, the sherd percentages in it might be expected to compare with those of the rest of that stratum, which would be the lower strip of stratum 4 debris in sections 5, 6, and 7, west trench. The relative distribution found in the potsherd count is seen to be identical in both the upper and the lower levels of the stratum.

The peak of the dump today shows no remains of stratum 4, which we presume once existed there as on the slopes where it is still found. If the material of the upper layer of stratum 4 on the west slope weathered off the peak of the dump, it is reasonable to suppose that stratum 3 might be left uncovered at the top of the mound. Eight hundred years of the brief but torrential summer rains and heavy winter snows characteristic of the Chaco might easily move between one and two feet of soft material from the peak of a mound protected by no ground cover.

The potsherd distribution of stratum 4 shows the following percentages:

Semi-polished black on white	33.5%
Polished black on white	16.2%
Unpolished black on white	9.9%

The dates on charcoal from stratum 4, with one exception, all lie in the middle 900's. An average of 10 to 20 years must be added to each to account for the rings burned from the exteriors. That these specimens are not merely centers of branches from whose exterior a large number of rings has been burned is finally proved by the fact that the present exteriors of these are as early in date as the interiors of most of the charcoal from other strata. As ring size indicates, both groups come from small burned branches, and as both groups average the same in diameter and in ring width, it is obvious that the group with exterior dates in the 900's is not one with the group giving interior dates in that period. These early dates represent the old removed debris itself. Referring to the dates of the building periods, we see that these dates of stratum 4 material come into the little known period of masonry I (945–1035). The material composing stratum 4 would appear, then, to have been deposited originally at some other spot during the period of masonry I, and the potsherd distribution of the stratum should then represent, in general that of the period of masonry I.

The material was later re-deposited on the east dump as the fourth stratum. The one date in this stratum falling after the year 1000 is 1054. From the exterior of this specimen approximately 50–70 rings are burned away. Adding an average of 60 years to this last ring present gives an approximate date of 1124 for level 9, section 5, from which the specimen was taken. It was found directly above the remains of the only interment in the mound. Its presence may have been intrusive if the burial was intrusive; otherwise, it must have been deposited in daily sweepings thrown out at the time the older material was being transported. In either case, it evidently represents the period shortly before or after the dump was abandoned and before the abandonment of the pueblo, for the burial accompanied by Chetro Ketl pottery was without doubt that of a resident of the pueblo.

That stratum 4 was laid down after stratum 3 is self-evident. Whether or not this one piece of charcoal came to its position in the stratum by accident or by deposition can not be decided with certainty. We do know, however, that if the upper levels of stratum 3 were post-1110 A.D., the material of stratum 4 must have been laid down between that time and the time of abandonment of the pueblo.

RATE OF REFUSE ACCUMULATION

Unfortunately we do not have dates from all the strata of the east dump, but if we consider all the other data that may bear on the relationship and relative dating of these strata, an approximate chronology can be constructed. Our approximation to a final date on the top of the dump can be checked against the latest dates known on Chetro Ketl and on other Chaco ruins. If we can figure the rate of accumulation of daily sweepings in stratum 3, which is best dated, and then discover the proportionate amount of similar daily sweepings mixed into the other strata which are preponderantly of old debris, we can compute approximate dates for the latter.

First let us consider the actual dates with which we may deal. The bottom of stratum 3 and the top of stratum 2 have been given the approximate date of 1090. The east trench gives the best series of dates for this stratum: from level 17, section 4 comes the date of 1105 + ca. 5, and from level 15, section 8 comes the similar date of 1106 + ca. 5, both dates being rounded off as 1110. If we consider 1090 as the date of the top of level 27, or bottom of level 26, section 5, and 1110 the date of level 16, section 5 (following the slope of the stratum between sections 4 and 8 where levels 17 and 15, respectively, date 1110), we have 10 levels representing an accumulation period of 20 years. The rate of accumulation is seen to be about 2 years per level.

That the center of a dump would grow faster than the sides is apparent; peaked mounds in themselves evidence the tendency to dump on a center. The rate of deposition of 2 years per [8 inch] level is figured for the east slope of the Chetro Ketl dump. This area is chosen both because of the maximum number of dates present and for consideration, and because stratum 4 is here still present and unmodified by the sand layer and the mass of eroded material found on the west slope. Except for figures on stratum 1, we will continue our estimates of the age of the dump through data from the east slope, but the dates on upper and lower borders of strata and the final date of beginning and end of deposition on this dump pertain to the entire cross section investigated.

Level 20, section 5, dates 1090 + ca. 10, or 1100. As this level is six levels above that dated 1090, the rate of deposition would indicate it should date about 1102. The actual date plus an estimation of burned-off rings is seen to check closely with the calculated date.

Level 15, section 8, five levels higher, gives the date of approximately 1110, as cited above. Level 11, section 4, dating 1099 + ca. 20, or 1119, is at the top of stratum 3, four levels above the date of 1110 and by rate of deposition would calculate to date 1118. The two figures again are seen to closely approximate each other and consequently to check the estimated local rate of deposition.

RELATIVE DATING OF STRATA 1, 2, AND 4

Referring to the significance tests, we see that strata 1 and 3 are essentially alike except for proportions of polished black on white ware. About 6% more polished ware was made during the period of stratum 3 than in the period of stratum 1. As stratum 3 was obviously later than stratum 1, it is to be expected that more fine ware might have been made during the later period.

The contents of stratum 2, preponderantly of old debris but partly of daily sweepings, as previously described, would contain some daily sweepings presumably approximating the composition of stratum 1, which similarly, resemble those of stratum 3. That a marked change would have taken place between the daily sweepings in each of these pairs is improbable when we consider that strata 2 and 4 were preponderantly of old debris and consequently would have been laid down during brief periods of time.

If strata 1 and 3 are both of daily sweepings and essentially alike, their rate of deposition can be thought of as essentially the same, providing the pueblo population remained of the same relative size in proportion to the surface of the dump in use. That the pueblo size did not increase unduly during the long period of stratum 3 deposition appears in the map of pueblo additions between the years 1100 and 1116. Strata 2 and 4, statistically indicated to be essentially different in content of polished black on white, although both are preponderantly composed of old debris high in semi-polished black on white ware, may owe that difference, entirely to admixtures of different proportions of the types of sweepings of strata 1 and 3 respectively.

If strata 2 and 4 are known to contain some part of the sweepings typical of stratum 1 and 3 respectively, then the rate of deposition of strata 2 and 4 should be proportional to the rate of deposition found for stratum 3 in ratio to the amount of sweepings present. This proposition is dependent of course, on the proviso that pueblo population did not greatly increase in that time and that any other possible disturbing factors, of which we have no evidence, may be considered negligible. The rate to be figured is thus seen to be only roughly accurate.

In figuring the periods covered by the deposition of each stratum, let us work from the top of the dump downward, using the columnar chart of pottery percentages found in each stratum, as data. Considering the limitations of our technique, there is no advantage in using more detailed figures than the rounded percentages which may be read from the columns.

Stratum 4. If polished black on white ware is taken as 100% in stratum 3, which is composed almost entirely of daily sweepings, semi-polished black on white figures to be 64% and unpolished black on white as 20%. We know stratum 4 to be preponderantly of old debris with some admixture of daily sweepings. Let us measure the variation between contents of stratum 3, which is of sweepings, and stratum 4, which is mixed. In the latter, polished black on white ware is represented by a 3½ cm. column. If this be taken as a unit, 100%, and if we had 64% semi-polished black on white, as in stratum 3, the column representing the semi-polished ware theoretically would rise only 2.1 cm. in height. Actually it measures 6.8 cm., which is 4.7 cm. or 223% excess. Of the unpolished ware we find, similarly, 1.35 cm. or 208% excess beyond the theoretical .65 cm. expected. This situation points to the presence of daily sweepings in stratum 4. The two figures may be averaged as about 215%.

If the average of 5 levels for stratum 4 would have required 10 years for deposition providing the material had all been sweepings, then in its actual composition of 100/315 daily sweepings, the stratum would take 100/315 × 10, or 3.2 years of accumulation. As stratum 3 was figured to have been completed about 1119, we estimate the top of stratum 4 to have been laid down about 1122. As admitted previously, we lack dates on the latest period and on the time of desertion of Chetro Ketl, but this date of 1122 may be compared with 1127, the latest on Bonito, and 1123 and 1124, the latest dates on Yellow House and Kinbiniola, respectively.

Stratum 2. If we take the amount of polished black on white ware present in stratum 1 as 100%, we find 45% semi-polished and 20% polished ware. Using these percentages as the yardstick for comparing the amounts of each in stratum 2, we find there a 3 cm. column of polished black on white representing the 100%, an excess of about 4 cm. or 290% semi-polished ware beyond the 1.35 cm. to be expected in sweepings according to the proportions of stratum 1, and an excess of 1.5 cm. or 250% beyond the .6 cm. to be expected of unpolished ware. These figures indicate between 250 and 290% (averaged as 270%) more old debris than daily sweepings in stratum 2. (The use of polished black on white ware as the standard unit for comparison in both types of strata would be entirely valid only if no polished black on white ware had been made during the early period represented by the old debris. We do not know this to have been the case. But the fact that the polished ware runs low in stratum 4, which is seen to contain lenses of daily sweepings mixed with the twice moved material, dating at the end of the 900's, indicates that but little polished black on white ware could have been made in that early period. Our figures are necessarily incorrect in proportion to whatever small amount of polished black on white ware was made at that time. Not more than a rough approximation of period is claimed for the figures obtained.)

From the data at hand, it can be seen that of the three levels of stratum 2, 100/370 will be daily sweepings. If it were all daily sweepings, the accumulation period would be 6 years; with 100/370 sweepings, only 1.6 years would be required for deposition.

If the top of stratum 2 in section 5 at the center of the east trench be dated at 1090, then the bottom would date about 1088. As nothing is found beneath stratum 2 on the east side of the dump, this would be the date when deposition was first begun here.

Stratum 1. Beneath stratum 2 in the West trench is stratum 1, two levels thick. At the daily sweeping accumulation rate of 2 years per level, this would take 4 years for accumulation, making the bottom of the layer date about 1084. This would be the date of original deposition on the west side of the dump.

SUMMARY OF EAST DUMP STRATA, COMPOSITION AND DATES

Reviewing our strata dates from top to bottom of the east dump, we find, first, stratum 4, composed almost entirely of twice-moved debris, dating from about 1122 at the top back to about 1119. The debris itself dates in the late 900's.

Stratum 3, preponderantly of daily sweepings dates from about 1119 at the top to 1090 at the bottom.

Stratum 2, preponderantly of old debris was quickly redeposited from elsewhere. It dates from about 1090 back to 1088. The contents of the strata appear to be in general so similar to that of stratum 4 that we suspect most of it belong to the late 900's.

Stratum 1, apparently entirely of daily sweepings, dates from 1088 back to 1084, when the portion of the east dump investigated was first used for deposition.

The total period of deposition on this dump in this portion investigated appears to have been approximately 38 years, from 1084–1122. This seems a very short period for the accumulation of such a large mound, but when one considers that the material of strata 2 and 4 are indicated by the charcoal to be old refuse hastily redeposited, the discrepancy between size of dump and time of accumulation is not so apparent. Working from averages and proportions, as has been necessary, the dates and periods are understood, moreover, to be approximations only.

As we have no record in the section of the dump excavated of material from the period between the end of the 900's and 1084, we must suppose that some other dump or another part of this dump was in use during that period.

Reversed Ceramic Sequence at Samaria

The ancient site of Samaria in Palestine has received much attention by Biblical archaeologists. It was first excavated by Harvard University in 1908–1910; a number of additional investigations have been carried out since that time. The history of these investigations and a summary of the results achieved is given by C. C. McCown (1943:chap. 13).

Crowfoot's 1935 excavations at Samaria provide us with an unusually clear instance of reversed stratigraphy.[31]

The round tower which was discovered in 1933 was then assigned tentatively to the Israelite period. The masonry and, in particular, the dressing of the stones was not like that of any of the Israelite walls with which we were familiar, but the build and plan of the tower were exactly like those of a round tower discovered by the Harvard Expedition at the south-west corner of the summit which was attributed by Reisner to the reign of Jeroboam II. We assigned the new tower to the same reign on this authority. But we had some qualms about it and decided to look for better evidence this year [1935].

[31] J. W. Crowfoot, *Report on the 1935 Samaria Excavation*, Palestine Exploration Fund, Quarterly Statement for 1935, London, 1935, pp. 182–194. By permission of L. G. Peithan, Secretary, Palestine Exploration Fund.

A shaft was accordingly sunk in the north-east quadrant against the inner face of the tower, and the filling was very carefully removed in layers corresponding with the tower courses. The filling in the top strata on the levels of courses XI to VII was not very instructive; near the tower it consisted entirely of white limestone chips and a little further back broken stones, dark coloured earth, and potsherds, mainly of the Israelite period, were mixed with more white chips. Gradually as we descended, the character of the filling changed. From the bottom of Course VII to Course III the dark debris reached up to the tower but it was now divided into zones on the line of each course by a thin trickle of white chips, which became thicker from Course III downwards. It was quite clear that, except perhaps in the uppermost strata, this filling had not been disturbed since the tower was built; it plainly represents the rising platform of the builders, the different zones or strata are the separate fillings added as each course was laid in position, and the white chips which divided them are the chips which fell from the stones as they were dressed in place. If the filling had been disturbed, these white lines must have been broken. Consequently the latest sherds found in these strata give the earliest possible date for the construction of the tower. The following table compiled by Dr. Ben-Dor shows how the potsherds were distributed:

Course	Israelite	Post-Israelite	Hellenistic	Total
XI	40	3	—	43
X	17	8	1	26
IX	113	28	—	141
VIII	28	3	—	31
VII	48	8	—	56
VI	151	91	5	247
V	100	97	3	200
IV	50	106	5	161
III	16	26	—	42
II-I	12	26	2	40
				987

It is obvious that the masons built their platform from the materials lying to hand; the top of the surface debris was the first to be thrown into the pit, it included a few Greek and Hellenistic sherds, a great quantity of sherds from the post-Israelite and Persian periods and some Israelite sherds; as the platform rose higher the builders shovelled in debris from lower levels and in these Israelite wares preponderated.

9

AGE-DATING BY RATE OF ACCUMULATION

The archaeologist is always faced with the problem of determining the age of the materials he is excavating. There are many methods which can be employed. (For a summary of these see Heizer, *1953* and Griffin, *1955*.)

One method, apparently rather unfashionable at the moment, involves estimation of the time required for the accumulation of soil in sites, of mineral in buried bones, and the like. That such progressive accumulations occur cannot be questioned. The calculation of the time involved, or of the rate of deposit of these accumulations, if these can be determined, may permit the archaeologist to suggest the age, however approximate, of the site or materials with which he is working.

As pointed out by Matson (*1955:169*), radiocarbon dates in deep-layered deposits may be used to estimate the rate of soil accumulation if there is reason to assume that the rate of deposition has been fairly steady for the period covered by the site. Radiocarbon dates may be used as known points in time from which to extrapolate backward or forward, a method which has already been employed by geologists (Kulp, *1951*).

A review of the principles and problems encountered in calculating rate of deposition in geological deposits has been published by Kay (*1955*), and a survey of geological time-rate deposition has been presented by Flint (*1945*).

There is no question that the rate-of-accumulation method has been at times poorly employed by archaeologists, but at the same time there have been some highly satisfactory results from its use. The reliability of results is directly proportional to the amount of evidence available and to its quality, which varies from poor to excellent. A number of archaeologists have condemned the method, among whom may be cited Clark (1947:139), Randall-MacIver (1933:17), Schenck (1926:208–212), and Woolley (1949:79). Wheeler, criticizing Petrie's conclusions on rate of alluvial deposition in Egypt, says: "Such calculations have, if any, a purely academic or abstract interest. They make no allowance for the intermittencies and vagaries which, alike in human and in geological history, defy the confines of mathematical formulae."[1]

An early discussion of the calculation of rate of soil accumulation is that of J. Luffkin, member of the Royal Society. Discussing discoveries of elephant remains at great depths near Colchester, he says:

> But 'tis easily explained, why these Bones should at this Day be found at such Depths, if we consider the alteration or rising of the Vallies, by the continual washing down of the loose Earth or soil by the Rains and Snows from the adjacent Hills, and by the annual Rottings of the Grass, Sedge, etc., for Proof whereof take the following Instance from Dr. Plott's Nat. Hist. of Staffordshire . . . speaking of a Moss, etc. wherein there was found a Lump of Coins of Edward IV of England (supposed to be lost in a Purse or Cloth now rotted away) at 18 Feet deep, which being about 200 Years since (that is, when they were found) whoever pleases to compute it will find this Moss grew about one Foot in 11 Years, or one Inch per Annum and $\frac{1}{12}$ proxime.[2]

Felix DuBois, discussing the age of the mosque at Djenne, says:

> It is possible to determine the great age of this monument . . . On the very thick front walls which are normally rather more than one metre in thickness, I have found successive layers of plaster measuring no less than 90 cm. in thickness. [On account of the torrential seasonal rains annual replastering of walls is necessary.] Now, to determine the age of old houses, native masons count 12 cm. thickness of plaster per century, which give us the end of the XVth century as the age of the Mosque, and this date tallies with that given by the Tarik [a seventeenth-century history of the Sudan].[3]

Ghirshmann (1938:88) notes, in relation to the excavation data from Sialk, that before the Sialk IV period there are 17 superimposed strata of mud brick huts, totaling 28 meters in thickness. By taking 75 years as the life of such houses, Ghirshmann calculates the age of the north mound as the second half of the fifth millenium B.C., and of the south mound as the second quarter of the fourth millenium B.C. As Daniel (1950:212–213) notes, these dates are now considered too recent.

[1] M. Wheeler, *Archaeology from the Earth*, Oxford University Press, London, 1954, p. 29.

[2] J. Luffkin, "Part of a Letter from Mr. John Luffkin to the Publisher Concerning Some Large Bones Lately Found in a Gravel Pit Near Colchester," *Proceedings of the Royal Society, Philosophical Transactions*, 1701, vol. 22, p. 246.

[3] Felix DuBois, *Tombouctou la Mystérieuse*, Paris, 1897, p. 183.

Another instance of error resulting from such computations is presented by Harrington (1933:171), who calculates the antiquity of the Gypsum Cave culture, using as his measure the age of the Basket Maker culture, or 1500 B.C. This date is now known to be too early for the Basket Maker culture, and the validity of the calculation is thereby destroyed (cf. Kroeber, 1948:671).

Wheeler, even though he is critical of the method, made at least one attempt to compute the age of a site by rate of accretion. He writes:

> . . . in 1946 the careful digging of a small area on the platform of the Harappa citadel . . . showed the undoubted continuance of the mature Harappa culture through the six successive building-phases of the site. Thus, the same excavation revealed a variant culture at a lower level, beneath the defences; but the six phases of substantial baked brick construction of the upper levels may be regarded as the produce of several centuries, perhaps four or five in number. [Footnote here reads: The salt which today rapidly disintegrates baked brick on exposure both at Harappa and Mohenjo-daro would be considerably less abundant and noxious if the soil were regularly cultivated and the surface-water, which now evaporates through the desert-sand and drags up with it the deep-lying salt, were absorbed systematically by plant-life. There is no evidence that anciently the walls of these cities suffered materially from salt. It seems reasonable therefore to assume something like seven or eight decades as the lifetime of a Harappa building well-constructed of baked bricks.] On the same calculation, the ten occupation-levels of Mohenjo-daro might, so far as excavated, represent more than seven centuries of essentially uniform ceramic.[4]

Accounts of similar attempts to compute the age of archaeological materials or deposits occur in the following works: Heizer (1953:24); Cook (1946); Hansen (1942:105); Meighan (1955:23–24); Hawley (1934:57–61); Cummings (1933:55); Dall (1877:51–52); Jochelson (1925:117–119); Hutchinson (1950:65–71); Kubler (1948); Bird (1938); Orsi (1922:138–139); Petrie (1904:10–11); Randall-MacIver and Mace (1902:50–52); Pumpelly (1908:I, 54–57); Lothrop (1928:195–197); Vaillant (1935:166–167, 257–258); Nüesch (1902:221–228); and Wedel (1941:141, 144).

The point which the editors of the present volume wish to make is that the archaeologist will often find that the only available method for estimating age is the rate-of-accumulation technique. He may elect to ignore the method in the belief that it is too unreliable, or he may apply the method and reserve judgment of its absolute accuracy. But in view of the many difficulties in the employment of the radiocarbon dating technique (sample collecting, cost of laboratory runs, wide margin of

[4] Wheeler, op. cit., p. 29.

error, and probable future abandonment of the method due to atmospheric enrichment by radioactive elements), the rate-of-accumulation method should not be completely forgotten, since it may in future be the only possible one available in particular instances. ⌣

Duration of Occupation of Ash Hollow Cave, Nebraska

The report on Ash Hollow Cave, Nebraska, by J. L. Champe[5] presents a most interesting example of dating. The cave contained many charcoal fragments which, in stratigraphic lots, were subjected to dendrochronological analysis. The ages of the levels which produced no charcoal were then estimated by extrapolation.

The excavation techniques described made possible the recovery of considerable amounts of charcoal from the floor deposits. In general, the individual bits of charcoal were small, but items as large as a walnut or larger were saved. In most instances all of the charcoal saved from one block was catalogued under a lot number, which might represent one or several specimens.

In February, 1944, all of the charcoal, 148 lots in all, was turned over to Harry E. Weakly for study. Weakly has reported a sequence developed from non-archaeological wood specimens from Lincoln County, Nebraska, which extends from the present to 1480 A.D. and with a little less reliability, to 1420 A.D. This sequence has been recognized by Wedel and has been found useful by Hill and Metcalf. These authors have accepted a date of 1706, which Weakly assigned to charcoal from Ch-1, the type site of the Dismal River Aspect.

A second sequence, not yet published, has been built up by Weakly from wood collected near Redington, Morrill County, Nebraska, which is in the North Platte Valley some two hundred miles west of Lincoln County. Ash Hollow is very nearly midway between these stations, and also in the North Platte Valley, hence especially well located for comparison with both the Redington and North Platte sequences.

When the charcoal was turned over to the tree-ring analyst, it was agreed that the dendrochronological and the stratigraphic studies would be carried on in complete independence of each until it had been determined that the tree-ring analysis would yield significant results. Each lot of charcoal, whether one of more pieces, carried the block and column designation given it in the field. These were left uncorrected by the laboratory audit previously mentioned. No further information was sup-

---

[5] J. L. Champe, *Ash Hollow Cave*, University of Nebraska Studies, Lincoln, 1946, no. 1, n.s., pp. 23–33. By permission of University of Nebraska Press.

plied by the archaeologist. The cave was known to be stratified but the actual lenses, as now identified, and their relative positions within the floor deposits, were known only to the writer.

Study of the charcoal was only possible when the analyst's regular duties permitted, which was, for the most part, during the winter months of 1944–45 and of 1945–46. A preliminary report of specimens from 46 of the 148 lots was made by letters from Weakly to the writer, dated March 22 and April 5, 1945. Careful comparison of the charts of the usable material from these lots led Weakly to postulate eleven tentative sequences separated by ten gaps of unknown duration. A specimen from the sequence made up of material nearest the surface was dated at 1676, plus a few years allowance for outer rings burned away. These data were reworked by the archaeologist, the corrected locations and lens assignments for each lot determined, and the depths were plotted against the actual section under 8NR2, used as an ideal section (see Fig. 9.1). Close correlation between lens and sequence is apparent, although in several cases, more than one sequence corresponds to a single lens. Since these data were independently derived, the correlation of the tree-ring and the stratigraphic sequences provides a strong confirmation of the accuracy of both archaeological and dendrochronological observations and inferences.

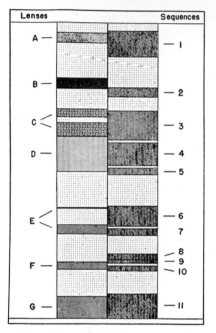

Fig. 9.1. Comparative section for lenses and sequences, Ash Hollow Cave.

The terminal date of 1676 and the total number of rings in each of the eleven "floating" sequences postulated in this first report, provided a basis for preliminary estimates of the age of the lenses. Allowances for ten gaps, on purely arbitrary grounds, made these estimates highly speculative for the lower levels. It seemed clear, however, that more work on the charcoal might be expected to do much to close these gaps and to make the dating more certain.

Work on the charcoal during the winter of 1945–46 has made possible the use of data from 93 lots, which now seems to include the greater part of the usable material from the cave. These new data, and the stratigraphic information made available to the analyst, brought about the reduction of the eleven original sequences to seven with excellent correspondence, after 1420 A.D., with the Redington sequence.

Sequence I corresponds to Lens A, and is dated from 1587 to 1684, plus an allowance of some 20 years for missing rings. A gap between Sequence I and the combined sequences II and III is bridged by the Redington material, while the two sequences together extend from 1517 to 1210 A.D. The Ash Hollow sequences then seem to extend published dates for the area to a date more than two hundred years earlier, but, for the present, no overlap with the earlier sequences is possible.

Sequences IV and V are now combined into Sequence D, associated with Lens D and now 154 years in length. Sequences VI and VII have been united as Sequence E, of 246 years; Sequences VIII, IX, and X become Sequence F, 102 years long, while Sequence XI, now 86 years, becomes Sequence G but remains relatively unchanged.

Each of these newer sequences will be presented in a chart showing the items which make up each sequence, and the implications of these data will be discussed briefly. The preliminary nature of this material can hardly be overemphasized but the importance of even a tentative dating of the lenses, and of the cultural complexes identified, may justify this first statement in connection with the present study. A full report of the dendrochronology of this material is planned for the near future, together with other tree-ring data for the western Central Plains. Changes in the detail of the present sequences are to be expected, but neither the tree-ring analyst nor the archaeologist now expects significant changes in the dating of the Ash Hollow charcoal.

SEQUENCE A

Sequence A is made up of twelve items from nine blocks. Three items come from blocks containing matrix over Lens A; eight items derive from six blocks within Lens A, and the last lot comes from a column in which Lens A is not definitely represented. Dismal River sherds lay just below nine of these items, two charcoal specimens were directly associated with Dismal River pottery and the one remaining is the doubtful occurrence already mentioned.

Consideration of the bar chart (Fig. 9.2) shows that two items, from widely separated blocks, include al-

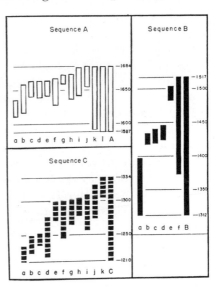

Fig. 9.2. Tree-ring sequences for lenses, A, B, and C.

most all of the lens sequence. These items are supported, in the later half of the sequence, by the other ten specimens. Except for one item, all of the terminal dates fall after 1658 and four of them come at the very end of the sequence. If a few years are allowed for missing rings on the outside of these specimens, the most probable dates of occupation would seem to be from 1675 to 1705.

This sequence stands alone so far as the Ash Hollow data is concerned, but fortunately it can be cross-matched with Weakly's Redington sequence. This matching permits the dates already given and also bridges the gap between Sequence A and Sequence B, from the lens just below.

SEQUENCE B

Sequence B (Fig. 9.2) is made up of six items from six blocks and covers 205 years. It is made possible by the very satisfactory overlap of two large items, which are supported, to some extent, by four shorter pieces. Cross-matching with the Redington sequence is satisfactory, adding some further support and extending the Redington data backward to 1312.

Direct pottery associations are not clear; a Dismal River sherd is reported from one block and a typical Upper Republican rim occurred in another.

SEQUENCE C

Sequence C (Fig. 9.2) covers the time period from 1210 to 1334 A.D. and so overlaps 22 years on Sequence B. Although this is not a long overlap, the matching is described as of a very high order and entirely convincing to the analyst.

Eleven items are included in the sequence, and these vary from 22 to 68 years in length. No single specimen spans the entire time period but there are three to six items for any particular year in the sequence, except for a few years at the beginning and end.

Direct association with Upper Republican pottery occur in five of the eight blocks represented. Two lots are from blocks just above pottery of this kind, and one association with type X ware is noted from a block laid down late in the occupation. The evidence is too meager for more than a suggestion of the occupation date, but the terminal dates show that it must have been after 1255. Since seven of the eleven specimens terminate after 1298, an estimate of 1300 A.D. for the occupation seems conservative.

SEQUENCE D

Sequence D (Fig. 9.3) covers 154 years and includes 26 items from 15 blocks. It was impossible to match any of this material with the preceding sequence although the time gap so indicated need not have been very long.

Pottery associations are noted for six of the 15 blocks, all of these are

Woodland with two exceptions. An Upper Republican sherd is reported from a block which intersects both Lens C and D, and one block contains eight sherds identified as type Y. Eleven of the blocks were within Lens D, one block included both C and D, two contained matrix below Lens D, and one lay in matrix nearly twelve inches below the bottom

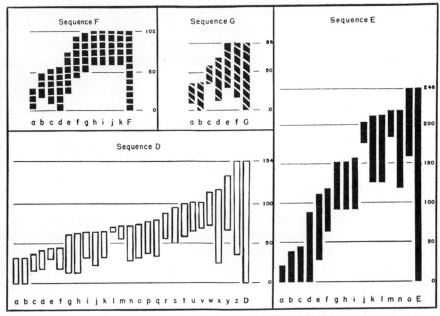

Fig. 9.3. Tree-ring sequences for lenses D, E, F, and G.

of Lens D. This last occurrence may be the result of pitting of the type shown in the west face of column 5NR3.

The analyst notes that there is evidence of drouth in the ring patterns near the close of Sequence D. This fact may explain the complete break which is apparent between Sequence D and the long sequence from 1210 to the present. It is also of some importance to theories which involve the possible relationships between the Woodland and Upper Republican manifestations in the Central Plains.

SEQUENCE E

Sequence E (Fig. 9.3) includes 15 items from ten blocks, extending 246 years. No pottery associations occur in these blocks. The individual specimens are of good length and cross-match well so that the sequence seems well supported except for a few years near the fifty-year mark covered by only two specimens.

Five of the ten blocks are from Lens E, four include matrix with Lens E and one specimen is from the matrix several inches above Lens E.

This lens, however, is some twelve inches below the bottom of Lens D over much of the cave, so this one migrant item does not seem significant.

Several very early occupations are indicated, followed by one in or just after year 225 in this sequence.

SEQUENCE F

Sequence F (Fig. 9.3) includes 1–2 years and is made up from eleven specimens from five blocks. There were no pottery associations. The sequence itself seems well supported and there are some suggestions of two occupations, one near year 60 and the other at the end of the occupation of the lens. Stratigraphically, this lens is well separated from either Lens E above or Lens G below, but there is no ready means of estimating the time intervals which correspond to the strata differences.

Five of the six blocks were within Lens F and one block included matrix above the Lens F stratum.

SEQUENCE G

This last short sequence of 86 years (Fig. 9.3) is derived from three blocks just above the tight conglomerate forming the original floor of the cave. Six items are reported with satisfactory cross-dating for the entire sequence. Two or perhaps three occupations are indicated for the lens, probably occurring after year 40.

Some comment is needed regarding the wood from which this charcoal is derived, and also of the kinds and amount of variation which might be anticipated.

Much of the charcoal actually used in the sequences is cedar or juniper with occasional items of pine. Juniper has been found unreliable for cross-dating elsewhere but Weakly finds it entirely workable on the Central Plains. He thinks this may be attributed to a different rainfall pattern resulting in a very few double rings.

The use of branches as well as stems for cross-dating has been discussed by Glock (1937) who gave this matter special attention in his study of the Ponderosa Pine.

As a matter of curiosity the rings from three sections of the best branches and those from one section of root were measured and plotted. Agreements are fairly good if the nature of the materials is considered. Agreement between root and branches goes so far that practically every crest in one graph is represented in the others. A comparison between figures 33 and 25 [not reproduced here] shows a fairly good agreement, especially so if the graphs were smoother. The major features are almost identical, and smoothing eliminates minor details which furnish the discrepancies, not only between the root and the branches but also between these and the stem.

The matter of branches touches the archaeological phases of tree-ring work in two ways. First, the presence of branches in material being dated may explain the occurrence of ring sequences partly out of harmony with the chief record. Therefore it would be well to be able to distinguish branches if possible. Branches are likely to be eccentric, that is, to show a degree of hyponastic development. Second, the more a given amount of tree-ring material contains portions of a single tree, the more localized the possible inferences. Branches or roots add little or nothing to an ecologic record if the stem is available.

The possibility that charcoal from a single lens might show very considerable variation in age has been suggested. On speculative grounds, it would not be surprising to find specimens of wood many years apart in age recorded from a single lens. Such a situation could come about, for example, if wood-gatherers should collect long dead branches from the ground and include them in the same lot of fire-wood with recently dead twigs pulled from living trees. Great variation in age might be anticipated if the supply of fallen trees considerably exceeded the demands of fire-builders, and the conditions for preservation of down timber permitted great age-differences to develop.

The situation at Ash Hollow, however, argues against such an occurrence. Timber is nowhere abundant within the Hollow and is very scanty, at the present time, within a half-mile of the Cave. It is also apparent that very few fallen branches would remain on the floor of the Hollow near the Cave. At this point, almost the entire width of the canyon floor is an old wash, with banks of sand and gravel that indicate floods of considerable extent and moderate frequency. It seems very unlikely that fallen timber would remain near the Cave for more than a few years at the most.

Perhaps the best evidence relevant to this discussion is provided by the actual records of the charcoal from the lenses themselves. No unaccountably large variations are reported, although almost all of the usable wood has been considered and placed, except for three or four unassigned specimens. It may be assumed, then, that mixing of the type suggested must have been most unusual at Ash Hollow, and that no significant error has been introduced by this means.

SUMMARY OF STRATIGRAPHY AND DENDROCHRONOLOGY

The first stratigraphic and dendrochronological studies were carried on independently so that they could be used for mutual confirmation if significant results were obtained. Seven lenses were identified by the archaeologist and lettered successively from the top down, beginning with A and ending with G. Independent work on the charcoal from the cave resulted in the identification of eleven tree-ring sequences separated by ten gaps. These sequences were numbered from top to bottom, beginning with I and ending with XI.

These sequences and the blocks from which the material was derived were carefully compared with the lenses and other stratigraphic data by the archaeologist, resulting in the excellent correlation between the two lines of evidence shown graphically in Fig. 9.1. This correspondence was taken as confirmation that both sets of inferences were acceptable, and thereafter work on the tree-ring data was carried on with benefit of the stratigraphic data.

At present, the greater part of the cave charcoal has been examined and it has been found possible to reduce the original sequences to seven. The most recent of these sequences now extends from 1210 A.D. to the present, after cross-matching with non-archaeological wood from Redington and Lincoln County, Nebraska. This sequence includes all of the usable wood in Lenses A, B, and C. A minimum suggested date for the Lens C occupation is 1300 A.D. or perhaps a few years earlier. Wood from Lens B covers the period from 1312 to 1517 but the major period of occupation would seem to be from 1450 to 1517. Lens A is datable by comparison with existing sequences, and it appears that the period of occupation is probably from 1675 to 1705 at the earliest.

Lens D is represented by Sequence D, of 154 years. Since there is no matching between Sequences C and D, the occupation of Lens D must have terminated before 1210 A.D. The terminal dates of the 26 specimens in this sequence grade evenly from the year 34 to the end of the sequence, and this may indicate a long time of occupation. An allowance of fifty years for the gap between Sequences C and D would seem to be a reasonable one. These fifty years added to the 154 years in the sequence would permit a suggested date of *circa* 1000 A.D. for the beginning of Sequence D, and it is probable that the actual occupation is nearly as long. This estimate for the Woodland occupation seems conservative, but is is interesting to find that this new estimate is almost identical with earlier placements for the Woodland occupation of the Central Plains.

A date for the lower margin of Lens D of 1000 A.D. permits a rough estimate of the age of the three lower lenses, based largely on the relative depths of deposition. Such a procedure is clearly speculative but it seems to be the best inference which can be drawn from available data. The total number of rings from the cave charcoal is 992, and the center of distribution is about the center of Lens D. This is also near the mid-point of the total floor deposit, which suggests a rough correlation between the depth of deposit and the elapsed time after the earlier part of Lens D. On this basis, the first occupation, indicated by Lens and Sequence G, could be placed not long after 1 A.D., and might be estimated as from 1–1000 A.D. The occupation indicated by Lens and Sequence F could then be assigned to the period of 300–400 A.D. and Lens and Sequence E could be placed between 600–850 A.D. Obviously, the exact dates are chosen arbitrarily but the relationship between them is consistent with present scanty data. The four floating sequences seem well established and it is to be hoped that further research in other caves and deposits will supply wood to fill in some of the existing gaps.

Age and Duration Estimates at Khafajah, Iraq

The ancient site of Khafajah, ten miles east of modern Baghdad in Iraq, is on the Diyala River just above its confluence with the Tigris. Excavation of the site was begun by the Oriental Institute in 1933–1934 and continued for six more seasons. The site consists of various large mounds, which contain the architectural remains of mud brick buildings, both private dwellings and sacred structures. The excerpt from the report given below,[6] deals with the chronology of the five temples found on Mound A, which measures 600 by 900 meters in area.

This volume records the history of a sacred temple named Sin (or Salam), which was rebuilt many times from its earliest phase in the "Proto-literate" period well into the latest part of early Dynastic times. The Proto-literate period includes a number of early Mesopotamian culture phases "in the course of which writing first appeared and developed until it reached the stage in which the phonetic principle (as in rebus writing) began to be employed. Stratigraphically these cultural phases roughly correspond to Archaic Strata VII–III at Warka, or to later Uruk and all of Jamdat Nasr periods." The Proto-literate period is subdivided into four phases: a, b, c, d. This publication deals with Proto-literate phases c (Sin Temples I–III) and d (Sin Temples IV–V), and the following Early Dynastic I (Sin Temples VI–VII), Early Dynastic II (Sin Temples VIII–IX), and Early Dynastic IIIA (Sin Temple X) phases.

DYNASTIC AND PROTO-LITERATE PERIODS

For lack of adequate historical material the absolute dating of the cultural periods to which the temples described in this volume belong and even estimates of their duration are still highly controversial matters. It is tempting, therefore, to utilize any indication provided by the ruins themselves which can be interpreted as bearing upon this problem. At least in one point in the excavations, near the entrance to Sin VII, we believe we have found such an indication. An examination of Fig. 9.4 will lead us to this point. The floor in the foreground and on both sides of the stairs is that of Sin VII 1, to which the lower three steps, covered with bitumen, and the lower parts of the walls (a) also belong. The steps of the second occupation and the corresponding walls are marked b, and the dark lines between walls a and b mark the levels of floors which had been removed. It is to be noticed that the faces of the walls of the second occupation on both sides of the stairway project slightly over the faces of the walls of the first occupation. Just as in the case of the stairway, this additional thickness was the result not of a rebuilding but of an accumulation of many layers of mud plaster on the face of the original wall. The latter can be discerned as an unbroken surface at c, where part of the later plaster had

[6] Pinhas Delougaz and Seton Lloyd, *Pre-Sargonid Temples in the Diyala Region,* Oriental Institute Publications, Chicago, 1942, vol. LVIII, pp. 125–135. By permission of the Director of the Oriental Institute.

been removed (cf. Fig. 9.5). Whereas frequent replastering of stairs was necessary in order to adjust them to the unequally rising levels of town and temple, no such necessity existed in the case of vertical walls. Indeed, it appeared during the excavations that there was no perceptible relation-

ship between the two. On the other hand, one can easily explain the replastering of the walls as part of the necessary routine for the upkeep of any adobe building; in fact, annual replastering of the roofs and exposed walls of buildings of this type at the end of each summer in preparation for the winter rains is still a very common annual routine in the Near East. A detailed view of the part marked c in Fig. 9.4 is given in Fig. 9.5. The original face of the wall appears at a, while b marks the face of the wall of the second occupation. In between we found no less than sixteen layers of mud plaster; and, if we assumed that the annual routine of plastering was regularly kept, it follows that it took at least sixteen years to add this thickness to the wall.

To determine the rise in floor level corresponding to this increase in wall thickness, we must turn once more to the outside of the temple as shown in Fig. 9.4. The dark line d marks the level of the floor of the second occupation when the plastering began, since the first layer was applied only from this line upward. The last and uppermost layer stops short of the somewhat higher line e, which marks a corresponding floor level. It follows that in sixteen years the level rose from d to e—approximately 12 cm.

Fig. 9.4 (Above). Main entrance into Sin Temple VII, showing remains of the first (a) and second (b) occupations. Fig. 9.5 (Below). Successive layers of mud plaster on the outer wall near the stairway of Sin Temple VII, accumulated during the second occupation of this building period.

Having thus determined the relationship between time and the rise of levels at one point we may attempt to utilize it as a basis for conclusions of a more general character. It should be realized, however, that no precise results can be expected, for, obviously, there can be no general answer to the problem of the rate at which debris accumulated. Indeed, even in normal circumstances—that is, when the rising of levels results only from the normal use of buildings, from their deterioration due to normal wear and tear, and from subsequent rebuildings—the rate of accumulation depends on innumerable factors, such as the locality of ruins, their age, position within the town, and orientation, function of the original building, etc. Consequently an observation concerning this problem made at one particular point cannot be indiscriminately applied to other buildings. But, even when applying such evidence to only one building where conditions did not greatly vary, no very precise results can be expected. Even if our basic assumptions are sound—that is, if the layers of plaster represent a similar number of years and if the accumulations were more or less uniform—the calculated results cannot be considered as precise, since they are affected by possible errors in measurement of the two initial quantities, namely the 16 years and the 12 cm. of debris.[7] Moreover, as we shall see, it is possible to approach the problem from various standpoints, leading to different results. With these reservations in mind we may proceed with our calculations.

The simplest application of the established relation is to use it for estimating the length of the whole building period in question, namely the duration of Sin VII. In dealing with this building period alone one may be justified in assuming that at a given spot, near the entrance, the rate of debris accumulation was fairly uniform.[8] Under this assumption, since a layer of about 75 cm. accumulated here between the lowest floors of the first and second occupations, the length of the first occupation would have been $^{16}/_{12} \times 75 = 100$ years. Adding 16 years for the duration of the second occupation, in accordance with our interpretation of the primary evidence, we obtain a total of 116 years for the whole of Sin VII. Before proceeding with further generalizations, we should recall that during the same time the rises in other parts of the temple were different, amounting to only about 35 cm. in the middle of the court and 55 cm. in the sanctuary.

Inasmuch as the spot in front of the temple near the stairway was well

---

[7] Ten per cent for the total error in either direction, though not very likely, is possible, and therefore all figures arrived at should be presented thus: number of years ±10% of same. For this degree of accuracy a unit of ten years is quite sufficient, and we shall accordingly round off the numbers derived from the calculations to the nearest ten.

[8] In reality there is some ground for assuming that the accumulation of debris was somewhat faster in the second occupation than in the first which would mean that the duration of Sin VII 1 might have been somewhat more than that calculated below.

protected and little affected by building activities, we may further assume that the rate of accumulation of debris here did not greatly vary in the different building periods and, on the basis of this assumption, estimate the duration of time covered by the five preserved rebuildings of the Early Dynastic period (Sin VI–X). The height of accumulated debris from the floor in front of Sin VI to the highest preserved floor outside Sin X was about 5.50 m.; resorting to the simple calculation, we find $^{16}\!\!/_{12} \times 550 \doteq . 730$ years.[9] In this calculation we assume not only that the floors were rising uniformly during the different occupations but also that the accumulation of debris *between* building periods went on at the same rate. It is, however, more likely that the rise of level between the last floor of one building period and the earliest floor of the next went on at a faster rate than when the building was actually in use. We therefore have to consider the result arrived at as a maximum, if the method itself is sound. An opposite alternative is to disregard completely the layers accumulated between building periods and to apply the same calculation to the total height accumulated during the occupations only. Consulting Plate 14A, [not reproduced here] we see that two noticeable gaps occur, one between the last occupation of Sin VII and the first occupation of Sin VIII and the other between the last floor of Sin IX and the first of Sin X. As far as Sin VI is concerned, it seems probable that the floors here rose gradually until they reached the level of Sin VII 1. The accumulation during occupations, then amounts to about 3.50 m. out of the total accumulation of 6 meters; consequently we may figure the time as $^{16}\!\!/_{12} \times 350 \doteq . 470$ years. Since we now have allowed no time at all for the 2 meters of accumulation between rebuildings, we must consider this number of years as a minimum for this method of calculation.

We may attempt to check the results obtained by this direct method in several ways, considering each result independently on its own merits.

First, let us take the case of the sanctuary, where the rise must have been fairly regular. Here the accumulation during the 116 years of Sin VII[10] was 55 cm. The whole accumulation from the first floor of Sin VI to the third floor of Sin X was approximately 4 meters; and the same simple calculation gives us $^{116}\!\!/_{55} \times 400 \doteq . 840$ years. Here again we as-

---

[9] The sign $\doteq$. means "is approximately equal to."

[10] In the sanctuary we were unable to distinguish between the accumulations of debris during the first and second occupations. We therefore assume that the layer between the earliest and the latest floor represents the total accumulation during this building period, while the thin layer between the floors of Sin VII 2 and VIII 1 is the result of the leveling of the ruins. In the courtyard, on the other hand, we attribute the accumulation between the floors marked VII 1 and VII 2 to the first occupation only. The reason for this is that the bitumen-plastered ablution place was found on the floor of the second occupation, and it is likely that the layer of debris between floors VII 2 and VIII 1 represents not only the debris accumulated by the leveling of the ruins but also that accumulated during the second occupation.

sumed that the whole of the accumulation was due to a natural process, although it is clear that in reality some of it was due to rebuilding activities. The time obtained is consequently exaggerated. In order to be able to judge the extent of this exaggeration we shall once more adopt the opposite procedure, basing our calculations on only the accumulated rising of floors within each of the building periods and disregarding the layers between them. This can be more easily achieved in the court, where the distinction between the floors used in each building and the layers between building periods is more readily made. By adding up the various layers accumulated during occupations and allowing the same accumulation for Sin VI as for Sin VII we obtain a total "natural" rise of about 2.15 m. Since here the accumulation corresponding to the 100 years of Sin VII 1 was 35 cm., it follows that the time involved would be $100/_{35} \times 215 \cdot = . 610$ years.

The problem permits still another approach, which likewise can be considered in various ways. We may take the duration calculated for Sin VII (116 years) as typical for all building periods and, multiplying it by 5, obtain 580 years for the duration of Sin VI–X. On the other hand, one may consider the 16 years of the second occupation of Sin VII as typical for all occupation floors and, multiplying this by 14, the total number of floors (1 in Sin VI, 2 in Sin VII, 3 in Sin VIII, 5 in Sin IX, 3 in Sin X), obtain about 220 years as a result. This number must be considered as a gross underestimate, for Sin VII 2 was but a secondary occupation which left no impression whatsoever on the level of the main area inside the temple. Obviously a much longer time must be allowed for each of the *original* occupations of the five building periods, even if we assume that the *secondary* occupations of each of them were not longer than this particular one. Taking the period of 100 years previously arrived at for the first occupation of Sin VII as typical for an original occupation and 16 years for each of the nine secondary occupations, we arrive at a still different number: $5 \times 100 + 9 \times 16$, that is, about 640 years. Now let us tabulate in order of magnitude the various results arrived at:

TABLE 7.   Duration of Sin Temples VI-X

Estimate	Years Calculated[a]	Error Allowed	Range (in Years)	Comments
a	220	±20	200–240	Grossly underestimated
b	470	±50	450–520	Apparently underestimated
c	580	±60	520–640	Possible
d	610	±60	550–670	Possible
e	640	±60	580–700	Possible
f	730	±70	660–800	Apparently overestimated
g	840	±80	760–920	Clearly overestimated

[a] It may be noted, by the way, that the arithmetical mean of the numbers in the second column is approximately 580 or, if we eliminate the two extreme numbers as not sufficiently reliable, about 610.

The range of each estimate is represented graphically in Fig. 9.6 by a horizontal linear segment the length and position of which are determined by the abscissas corresponding to the limits of the range. It is to be seen that for certain intervals these segments overlap. The distribution of these

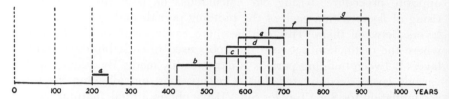

Fig. 9.6.   Diagram representing estimates of duration of Sin Temples VI–X.

segments over the time axis, which is divided by centuries, shows the number of possibilities falling within each century as follows:

Duration of Sin VI–X in Centuries	Number of Possibilities
Less than 2	0
2–3	1
3–4	0
4–5	1
5–6	4
6–7	4
7–8	2
8–9	1
9–10	1
More than 10	0

This brings out even more clearly that the range of 200–240 (a) is isolated from all the other possibilities, not coinciding even in part with any of them. This and the exaggerated estimate (g) at the other extreme may be eliminated as not sufficiently reliable.

The five remaining estimates, b–f, are again graphically represented in Fig. 9.7 on the same principle as in Fig. 9.6. The overlapping parts of the various ranges are represented by proportionate lengths of horizontal bands. Taking now ten years as a unit, we find the distribution of possibilities in various time intervals is as follows:

Time Interval (years)	Number of Possibilities
Under 420	0
420–550	1
550–580	2
580–640	3
640–660	2
660–670	3
670–700	2
700–800	1
Over 800	0

It is to be seen that, although the number of possibilities increases and decreases symmetrically between 420 and 800 years, their disposition within this range is not entirely symmetrical, indicating that the probable dura-tion is rather nearer 600 than 650 years.[11] In round figures six centuries can, therefore, be accepted as probably a close estimate of the time be-tween the building of Sin VI and the third occupation of Sin X. Taking

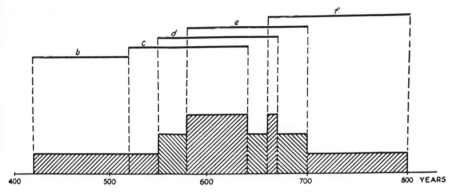

Fig. 9.7. Diagram correlating usable estimates of duration Temples VI–X.

into consideration the two later occupations of Sin X, traces of which were found at the west end of the ruins, we estimate the total duration of Sin VI–X at about 650 years. Dividing this period proportionately to the thick-ness of the debris accumulated during the different phases of the temple, we obtain: 250 years for Sin VI and VII, 220 years for Sin VIII and IX, 180 years for Sin X.

The length of time represented by the earlier ruins (Sin I–V) can be estimated on somewhat similar principles. Again two different methods can be adopted. First, we may assume that the accumulation of debris outside the earlier temples, in a position relatively similar to that where the original observations were made, was at approximately the same rate as in the later temples. Such a position is the courtyard northeast of the sanctuary near the stairways leading to the top of the artificial terrace in the last two rebuildings of this group, Sin IV and V. Here the layer of debris between the lowest floors of Sin I and Sin V in Q 42:16 is approxi-mately 3.40 m. However, it should be noted that the slope of the second and third floors of Sin IV clearly indicates that at least part of this accu-mulation is due to building activities. On account of this we may con-sider the "natural" accumulation as approximately 3 meters. Resorting to the simple formula previously used we obtain $\frac{16}{12} \times 300 \cdot = . 400$

[11] The appearance of the graph depends, of course, on the margin of error al-lowed. It may be noted that a slight increase of the latter (from 10% to 12%) would lengthen ranges c and f sufficiently to overlap at about 650, producing, at this point, a peak of four coinciding possibilities. On the other hand, even a lesser de-crease of the allowed error would shorten ranges d and f enough to eliminate the peak between 660 and 670. In both cases the range of three coinciding possibilities between 580 and 640 would hardly be affected.

years for this accumulation. On the other hand, we may assume that the accumulation of debris within the sanctuaries of the earlier five and the later five building periods was at approximately the same rate, apart from the heightening of the ground produced by the building of the artificial terraces. The total accumulation between the lowest floor of Sin I and the assumed later floor of Sin V is approximately 3.60 m., of which about 1 meter is the height of the artificial terrace of Sin IV. The remaining 2.60 m. may be regarded as of the same character as the accumulation of 4 meters between the first floor of Sin VI and the third floor of Sin X. Since our previous calculations gave approximately six centuries as the duration of the later five building periods, we have $^{260}/_{400} \times 260 = 390$ years.

The results are close enough to deserve attention, and we may accept four centuries as the approximate duration of the first five building periods: or, allowing again about 10 per cent as a possible margin of error in each direction (400 ± 40), from 360 to 440 years. The two major phases of this total length can be estimated on the basis of the relative thickness of their debris (excluding the height of the artificial terrace of Sin IV) as 225 years for Sin I–III and 175 years for Sin IV–V. We may now attempt to employ these results in estimating the lengths of the cultural periods during which the various phases of the Sin Temple existed.

Sin I was built, as we have seen, at about the middle of the Proto-literate period. On the other hand, there is archaeological evidence that Sin V survived into the earlier part of Early Dynastic I; the length of the last two phases (c and d) of the Proto-literate period, represented by Sin I–V, would then be somewhat under four centuries. The estimate of the total length of this period depends upon the estimate of its earlier two phases, to which our evidence does not extend.

The Early Dynastic period is represented by the later five rebuildings (Sin VI–X), the first of which (Sin VI) belongs to the early part of Early Dynastic I and cannot be very far removed from the beginning of this period, since there is no perceptible break in cultural tradition between this building and Sin V, which survived from the preceding period. At the other end, even the highest preserved floor of Sin X certainly does not represent the end of Early Dynastic III. This is clearly demonstrated by the comparative stratigraphy of the Sin Temple and the Temple Oval. The building of Temple Oval II and Sin X must have been very nearly contemporaneous, but while no later traces than the fifth occupation of Sin X were preserved, there existed above Temple Oval II an entire new rebuilding (III) of the same temple complex which still must be attributed to the Early Dynastic period on account of its building material (plano-convex bricks) and the character of finds associated with it.[12] Though it is

---

[12] H. Frankfort, "Progress of the Work of the Oriental Institute in Iraq, 1934/35," *Fifth Preliminary Report on the Iraq Expedition,* Oriental Institute Publications, University of Chicago, Chicago, 1936, LIII 106, Chronological Table.

likely that Temple Oval III survived beyond the Early Dynastic period, we must allow some time for its existence in the Early Dynastic period after the latest preserved occupation of the Sin Temple. The duration represented by Sin VI–X must therefore be augmented at both ends to cover the whole of the Early Dynastic period. In view of these circumstances, a total addition of about a century does not seem exaggerated. We obtain thus approximately 750 years for the total length of the Early Dynastic period.

While this is considerably longer than some other estimates, the writer can see no serious objections to it from archaeological considerations. Moreover, in his *Sumerian King List* Dr. Thorkild Jacobsen comes to the conclusion that 350 years must be allowed for Early Dynastic III alone.[13] This estimate arrived at by Jacobsen independently and on an entirely different basis, certainly also implies that the whole of the Early Dynastic period must have been considerably longer than was hitherto generally thought. Our conclusions may, to some extent, be tested by correlating them with those of Jacobsen and by examining whether the results of such a correlation are supported or contradicted by facts known from the excavations. Furthermore, by establishing such a correlation we extend considerably farther into the past the chronology derived from the King List, to cover the earlier buildings and cultural periods with which we are concerned in this discussion.

Since no royal inscriptions of the Early Dynastic age were found at Khafajah, we have no direct means of connecting any of our buildings with rulers named in the King List; but a fairly close indirect connection is provided by the Ninhursag temple at al-Ubaid, which, on the one hand, is dated by inscriptions to Aannepada, second king of the First Dynasty of Ur,[14] and, on the other hand, shows very close affinities with the Temple Oval at Khafajah.[15] However, since three phases of the Temple Oval at Khafajah are known, we have to consider to which of these the temple platform at al-Ubaid is most closely related. Architecturally, the use of kiln-baked bricks for the revetment of the platform, the close spacing of the buttresses, and the general use of flat bonding instead of bricklaying in herringbone fashion are all features characteristic of the later part of the period in which plano-convex bricks were in use[16] and do not commonly occur in the earlier stages of the Temple Oval. Stylistically, some

[13] Oriental Institute, University of Chicago, Assyriological Studies, Chicago, 1939, No. 11, Table II.

[14] Though neither the foundation tablet nor the gold bead bearing the name of this king was *in situ* (cf. Hall and Woolley, *Al-Ubaid*, pp. 79 f.), there is no conclusive evidence to disprove the accepted view that the tablet refers to the building the ruins of which were excavated.

[15] It was this view that led the writer to his search for and discovery of the oval around the temple platform at Al-Ubaid (cf. Iraq, V 2); it seems, then, to be fairly well substantiated.

[16] Cf. Oriental Institute, University of Chicago, Studies in Ancient Oriental Civilization, No. 7, p. 29.

of the objects recovered in front of the al-Ubaid platform are also more akin to similar objects of the latest stage of the Early Dynastic period than to those from its earlier phase. We may, then, relate the temple platform at al-Ubaid to Temple Oval III at Khafajah and consequently tentatively date the later occupation of Temple Oval II to the beginning of the First Dynasty of Ur. Since the stratigraphic and chronological relations between the Temple Oval and the Sin Temple are known, we thus obtain a hypothetical connection between the buildings under discussion and the King List.

The buildings are correlated graphically in Fig. 9.8 against a vertical time scale. For simplicity's sake a precise length in years is assigned to

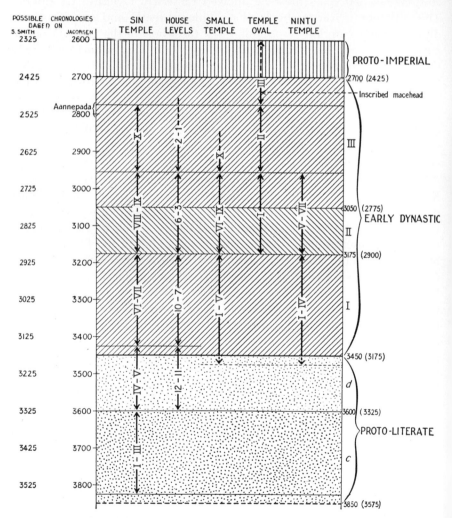

Fig. 9.8. Diagram showing tentative dates of the Proto-literate and Early Dynastic periods and of buildings at Khafajah belonging to those periods.

each group of building periods, though we must remember that each figure is affected by positive and negative margins of error, the influence of which is discussed on page [359]. In Jacobsen's proposed chronology Early Dynastic III extends from 3050 to 2700 B.C. Within this period Mesannepada and Aannepada reigned at Ur some 80 years, between 2850 and 2770 B.C. or, in the lower chronology based on Sidney Smith, between 2575 and 2495 B.C.[17] In allowing 75 years for the existence of Temple Oval III in the Early Dynastic period we must date its building to about 2775 (or 2500); that is, indeed, within Aannepada's reign. From this point backward we assign years as follows: to Sin X, 180 years; to Sin VIII–IX, 220 years; to Sin VI–VII, 250 years; to Sin IV–V, 175 years; to Sin I–III, 225 years.

Next we can try to establish the approximate lengths of Early Dynastic I and II and of the last two phases of the Proto-literate period ("Jamdat Nasr"). By definition the beginning of Early Dynastic II coincides with the building of Sin VIII, which falls, in our chart (Fig. 9.8), at 3175 B.C. (or 2900 B.C. according to the lower chronology); thus we obtain an approximate length of only 125 years for Early Dynastic II. Early Dynastic I is represented by the whole length of Sin VI and VII and an additional 25 years allowed for the survival of Sin V into the Early Dynastic period; its total length thus amounts to 275 years, and it begins at about 3450 (or 3175) B.C. Deducting the 25 years of assumed survival of Sin V into Early Dynastic I from the 175 years represented by Sin IV and V, we obtain 150 years for the latest phase of the Proto-literate period, while Proto-literate c is represented by at least the 225 years of Sin I–III. The arbitrary allowance of 25 years between the beginning of this phase and the founding of the Sin Temple would bring the beginning of Proto-literate c to about 3850 (or 3575) B.C. Since the remains below the Sin Temple suggest contemporaneity with the Warka Archaic Strata V or IV, we may perhaps allow, as a very rough estimate, three more centuries for the first two phases of the Proto-literate period, which would bring its beginning to about 4150 (or 3875) B.C.

By using the stratigraphic relations between the Sin Temple and other buildings on Mound A we can include in this chart some of the other architectural remains shown in the table at the end of the volume. In the case of the Temple Oval we allow the same length for Oval III as for Oval II. If that is correct, Oval III would have survived through the Proto-impe-

[17] The length of this period does not depend upon the absolute chronology adopted. If a lower date for Hammurabi, which seems substantiated by recent evidence, is adopted, all absolute dates given in this table have to be correspondingly lowered. This amounts only to shifting the scale of time in relation to our chart. For instance, if we accept the lowest date yet offered for Hammurabi, Sidney Smith's 1792–1750 (see his *Alalakh and Chronology* [London, 1940], p. 29), we shall have to shift the scale of time by 275 years, as in the extreme left of Fig. 9.8, and Early Dynastic III will extend from 2775 to 2425 B.C. Dr. Jacobsen informs me that he himself now inclines toward a lower chronology not signally different from those advocated by Smith and Albright.

rial period, into the first years of Sargon's reign,[18] an assumption which seems to be supported by the fact that we found Rimush inscriptions immediately above the ruins of Oval III.[19]

We may now see how the rather unexpected results concerning the comparative lengths of the subdivisions of the Proto-literate and Early Dynastic period tally with facts known from the excavations. According to Figure 9.8 the whole of Temple Oval II and the whole of Sin X fall approximately in the middle of Early Dynastic III, while Temple Oval I and Sin IX survived about 90 years into Early Dynastic III. The style of statuary found in Sin IX[20] and the inscriptions found there and in Nintu VII seem to support this view. An inscribed macehead dated by Dr. Jacobsen approximately to the time of Eannatum[21] is placed in our chart at 2740 (or 2465), about the middle of his reign. This date falls within the period indicated for Temple Oval III, where, indeed, the macehead was found.

It remains to be seen to what extent an allowance of about 10 per cent for error in each direction in each of the represented periods will affect the general results.[22] Taking Early Dynastic III as fixed and within it the date of 2500 B.C.—according to the lower chronology—as a point of departure, the error allowance would bring the building of Sin X and Temple Oval II to 2680 ± 20, that is, still well within Early Dynastic III. Similarly, the beginning of Early Dynastic II would fall at 2900 ± 40, that of Early Dynastic I at 3175 ± 70, that of Proto-literate c ("Jamdat Nasr") at 3575 ± 100, and that of Proto-literate a at 3875 ± 140. It is evident that the relative lengths of the various cultural periods would remain practically unaffected by such errors and that even the absolute dates would fluctuate between comparatively narrow limits.

To emphasize once more that our results cannot be regarded in terms of precise dates we may summarize them as follows: If we accept the end of the 25th century B.C. as the approximate date of the end of the Early Dynastic period, we may date the beginning of Early Dynastic III to the first half of the 28th century B.C.; the beginning of Early Dynastic II to between the middle of the 30th and the middle of the 29th century B.C.; the beginning of Early Dynastic I to between the middle of the 33rd and the end of the 32nd century B.C.; the beginning of the Proto-literate period to between the end of the 41st and the middle of the 38th century B.C.; and in it the beginning of the "Jamdat Nasr" phase to between the beginning of the 37th and the beginning of the 35th century B.C.

[18] Cf. Oriental Institute, University of Chicago, Assyriological Studies, Chicago, 1939, No. 11, Table II.

[19] Oriental Institute Publications, University of Chicago, LIII 106.

[20] See *ibid.*, XLIV 7.

[21] See *ibid.*, LIII 148 f.

[22] The 10% margin of error allowed in each direction (see n. 7) is, of course, to some extent arbitrary. However, if the principles of our method are fundamentally correct, such a margin is considered to be fairly adequate. If, on the contrary, the principles are erroneous, no larger margin of error will improve the results.

10

CROSS-DATING

When a foreign ("intrusive") object of known date is found in an archaeological site in association with local objects of hitherto unknown date, it is often possible to assign an approximate age to the previously undated materials. The validity of such an assignment depends heavily upon the clearness of the association of the objects involved. Thus a well-excavated site with distinct strata and features is highly desirable if the cross-dating method is to be used. And the ideal "intrusive" is one which is short-lived in time, easily distinguishable, and widely distributed in space (often through trade). Pottery types are particularly satisfactory in fulfilling these requirements (see, for example, Haury, 1940:95–96). One method of identifying foreign pottery is by comparing the total petrographic characteristics of wares (see Shepard, 1942, 1956; Felts, 1942; Gladwin, 1937).

It is desirable, of course, to know the antiquity of the intrusives in absolute numbers of years. Yet foreign types can be useful even when only their relative dates are known, that is, dates related to specific archaeological sequences elsewhere. Foreign types thus dated can show at what point in the stratigraphic record site "A" was contemporaneous to culture "Y." Relative cross-dating recently formed the basis for a large-scale attempt to correlate certain regional chronologies in the Old World (Ehrich, 1954). Cross-dating is so widely used in modern archaeology that the reader is referred here only to a few representative examples: Gadd (1932); Gifford (1949); Kidder, Jennings, and Shook (1946); Krieger (1946, 1947); Stone (1949); Di Peso (1958:144–149); Shepard (1948).

A word of caution on the point of associations may be added. The excavator should always be aware of the possibility of finding "heirloom" pieces, which date from earlier times, in association with items of later manufacture and use. Not uncommonly such heirlooms or antiques occur far from their point of original manufacture. For some examples, see **Delougaz and Lloyd (1942:4)**, **Vaillant (1931:247)**, **Kroeber and Strong (1942:116)**, **Ritchie (1954:67–68)**, **Smith (1940:246)**, **Drucker (1955:30)**, **Strong and Evans (1952:201)**, **Wheat (1955:174–184)**.

Cross-Dating at Snaketown

The selection below[1] is from the Snaketown site report, by Emil W. Haury. This site is on the Gila River in arid southern Arizona and is one of the type sites of the Hohokam culture. The study of the Snaketown site was made after certain of the pottery types of the Anasazi culture to the north and of the Mogollon culture to the east had been dated by means of tree-rings (dendrochronology). Due to the absence of beam material, the tree-ring method could not bo applied directly at Snaketown. Fortunately, however, intrusive Anasazi and Mogollon pottery types with "dendro-dates" were excavated at Snaketown in association with Hohokam types. This permitted cross-dating Hohokam phases and the assignment to them of absolute year dates.

The equation of the phases of Snaketown with the cultural stages in adjacent areas must be based largely on intrusive materials. In nine cases out of ten pottery offers the surest and most reliable means towards attaining this end. In Snaketown this was especially true. Foreign pottery, both whole and fragmentary, much of which could be assigned to its phase, was instrumental in bringing about the correlation of the Hohokan with the Anasazi and Mogollon.

The value of intrusive pottery at Snaketown would be far less if the evolution of Anasazi pottery were not so well known or so accurately dated by the Douglass tree-ring method. This has made it possible to assign reliable dates to the later phases of Snaketown and estimated dates for those phases too old to have received Anasazi trade pieces. Confirmation of the sequence of phases determined for Snaketown is given by the foreign material. Intrusive sherds, if arranged serially in accordance with the order of the deposits in which they occurred, will repeat exactly the sequence determined for them by stratigraphy and tree-ring dates in the areas where they were at home.

Intrusive pottery occurring in sections of pure rubbish in the stratitests has been considered as indicative of contemporaneity. Sherds on the floors of houses have also been so regarded. Little importance, however, has been attached to any of these instances of association unless they were repeated. The securest dating information of all came from the associations in cremations of whole or nearly whole pieces of foreign pottery with local

[1] E. W. Haury, "Pottery Types at Snaketown," in H. S. Gladwin, E. W. Haury, E. B. Sayles, and N. Gladwin, *Excavations at Snaketown: Material Culture*, Medallion Papers, Gila Pueblo, Arizona, 1937, no. 25, pp. 212–219. By permission of H. S. Gladwin and E. W. Haury.

Snaketown pottery. Under such conditions there can be no question of chance association.

The list of intrusive sherds below includes those found at Snaketown, whether on the surface or in the excavations:

Anasazi:	
Lino Black-on-grey	5
Kana-a Black-on-white	55
Black Mesa Black-on-white	42
Kana-a Grey	1
Deadmans Black-on-red	42
White Mound Black-on-white	1
Mogollon:	
San Lorenzo Red-on-brown	2
Mogollon Red-on-brown	5
Mimbres Bold Face Black-on-white	31
Mimbres Black-on-white	5
San Francisco Red	115
Alma Plain	5
Alma Neck Banded	2
Three Circle Neck Corrugated	4
Dragoon Red-on-brown	19
Forestdale Smudged	47
Sonora Red-on-brown	9
Trincheras Polychrome	2
Unidentified	16

Whole or nearly whole pieces:

Anasazi:	
Kana-a Black-on-white	1
Deadmans Black-on-red	1
Black Mesa Black-on-white	1
Kana-a Grey	1
Mogollon:	
Mogollon Red-on-brown	1
San Francisco Red	1

Of this amount of trade pottery, approximately 30 per cent was placed in phases because it was found in controlled parts of the excavation. The remaining 70 per cent represents such intrusives as were picked up on the surface or came from mixed deposits. The identified pottery is naturally of greatest significance but the remainder is not without value as will presently be shown.

In the Anasazi series, all have come from the western section, i.e., the Flagstaff area. The Mogollon series included the standard types for that culture including several which have not yet been described but which, according to all characteristics, must eventually be assigned to the same complex. To facilitate discussion, these have been named in accordance with our usual custom.

Fig. 10.1 tabulates the distribution of foreign pottery in phases, 13 of the 18 types identified having been placed. A detailed type to type discussion would be of little avail here as most of them have already been described. A few, however, demand a word of explanation.

The first of these is Dragoon Red-on-brown, the focus of which lies in southeastern Arizona in the Sulphur Springs Valley and in the mountains adjacent to the Willcox playa, particularly on the west. So far it has been found only in the form of bowls, generally outcurved but sometimes with a suggestion of a flared rim. Polishing over the decoration and the character of the designs connect it directly with Mogollon Red-on-brown.

| PERIOD | PHASE | ANASAZI | | | | MOGOLLON | | | | | | | | | TOTALS |
		LINO BLACK-ON-GREY	KANA-A BLACK-ON-WHITE	BLACK MESA BLACK-ON-WHITE	DEADMANS BLACK-ON-RED	MOGOLLON RED-ON-BROWN	DRAGOON RED-ON-BROWN	SONORA RED-ON-BROWN	MIMBRES BOLD FACE BLACK-ON-WHITE	SAN FRANCISCO RED	FORESTDALE SMUDGED	ALMA PLAIN	ALMA NECK BANDED	THREE CIRCLE NECK CORRUGATED	
SED	SACATON		7	7 (1)	11	8			9	21 (1)	5	3		3	74 (2)
COL	SANTA CRUZ		2 (1)		2 (1)	2 (1)	2			10	4	1	2	1	26 (3)
COL	GILA BUTTE	1								2	4				7
PIONEER	SNAKETOWN								1	3					4
PIONEER	SWEETWATER								1	3					4
PIONEER	ESTRELLA								1	4					5
PIONEER	VAHKI									1					1
	TOTALS	1	9 (1)	7 (1)	13 (1)	2 (1)	10	3	9	44 (1)	13	4	2	4	121 (5)

Fig. 10.1. Occurrence of intrusive pottery by phase at Snaketown site. Circled numbers indicate whole vessels.

Mimbres Bold Face Black-on-white is frequently found as a companion ware.

Another type which demands a word of explanation is Forestdale Smudged. It is a thin ware, mainly occurring as hemispherical bowls, highly polished inside and out, the interior being a lustrous black, the exterior reddish-brown to grey. This type possibly gave rise to the polished and blackened interior pottery of the Upper Gila. Technologically it is related to San Francisco Red and geographically is adjacent to it. Forestdale Smudged occurs occasionally in Basket-maker III sites and was found in abundance in the White Mound Ruin near Allantown, Arizona, a late Basket-maker III site dating prior to 800 A.D. The exact focus of the type has not yet been defined but a ruin at Forestdale gives promise of being within the area of its greatest concentration.

Returning now to Fig. 10.1 it will be seen that Lino Black-on-gray, a component of the La Plata Phase (Basket-maker III), occurred prior to all other Anasazi types. It was followed by Kana-a Black-on-white, Coconino Phase (Pueblo I), which in turn was succeeded by Deadmans Black-on-white, Canyon Diablo Phase (Pueblo II), there being an overlap in the last two. The sequence of these types at Snaketown is the same as in the Flagstaff area, a fact that greatly strengthens the correlation between the Hohokam and the Anasazi phases. Deadmans Black-on-red, of admittedly long duration, occurred most heavily in the Sacaton Phase but was already present in the final part of the Santa Cruz Phase. Because Kana-a Black-on-white occurred in both Santa Cruz and Sacaton Phase associations, it is inferred that the transition took place before the Pueblo I–Pueblo II transition of the north. An added check of the Santa Cruz–Coconino Phase and the Sacaton–Canyon Diablo Phase correlations is found in the evidence of excavations of the Museum of Northern Arizona near Flagstaff. The northern pottery types, as already stated, have been dated on the basis of tree-rings.

In Fig. 10.2, an attempt has been made to correlate the phases of the Anasazi and Hohokam in a way suggested by the evidence.

The fact that is immediately obvious in the above is the absence of Anasazi material in the early Snaketown phases and its abundance in the late phases. The recovery of a single Lino Black-on-grey sherd in a satisfactory Gila Butte Phase stratigraphic position may not be admitted as sufficient evidence to establish the contemporaneity of the two ceramic stages concerned. But there is still the fact that Pueblo I (at Flagstaff) and the Santa Cruz Phase were roughly coeval, and that in the Anasazi series there was but one general stage of pottery making prior to Santa Cruz–Pueblo I while in the Hohokam series there were five. Had the Anasazi been making pottery prior to the Gila Butte Phase, the abundance of foreign material in later phases makes it practically certain that earlier northern pottery would have found its way into the proper Snaketown phases. The positive evidence in the absence of sherds in early phases may both be given equal value.

The priority of Hohokam pottery over Anasazi was suspected even before the Snaketown excavations. Cross-finds in other ruins have, in every way, confirmed the conditions encountered at Snaketown. With such a formidable mass of evidence one is driven to the conclusion that Hohokam pottery making had already passed through its early stages before the Anasazi had even acquired pottery.

What does it all mean? We may conclude first, that Hohokam pottery was not a collateral development of the Anasazi ceramic complex; second, that, because the first Anasazi pottery cannot be related in form, finish, or method of manufacture to Hohokam pottery, the germ of Anasazi pottery did not come directly from the Hohokam; and third, that once Anasazi pottery became well started on its way, it was affected directly and indirectly by the older industry in the south. This is true particularly of

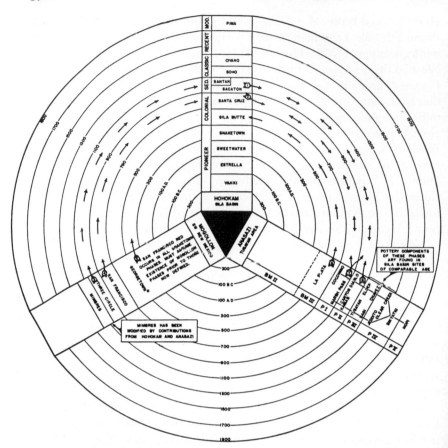

Fig. 10.2. Correlation of Hohokam, Mogollon, and Anasazi phases based mainly on intrusive pottery types in Snaketown. Dates are based on tree-ring findings in the Tusayan and Mogollon areas; the chronology from about 500 to 1400 A.D. is believed to be reasonably accurate. The chronology prior to 500 for the Snaketown phases is an estimate. Pottery types are indicated in the numbered arrows as follows: 1, Sacaton Red-on-buff; 2, Santa Cruz Red-on-buff; 3, Mimbres Bold Face Black-on-white, Three Circle Neck Corrugated; 4, Mogollon Red-on-brown, Alma Neck Banded; 5, San Francisco Red; 6, Lino Black-on-grey; 7, Kana-a Black-on-white; 8, Deadmans Black-on-white. (The exact chronological position of the Georgetown Phase is not known, except that it precedes the San Francisco Phase. On typology, it may be equated with the Estrella Phase.)

the acquisition of decorative elements, as quartering, hatching, the scroll, and life forms, all of which had been well established in the Hohokam series before they first appeared in Anasazi ceramics.

Coming now to the Mogollon series (Fig. 10.1) we find that Mogollon Red-on-brown occurred in earlier contexts at Snaketown than did Mimbres Bold Face Black-on-white, a sequence already determined by the excavations in the Mimbres area. The same holds true for Alma Neck Banded and the Three Circle Neck Corrugated. Tree-rings have given us a date of 900 A.D. for Mogollon Red-on-brown, a date considered to be near the end of the life of this type. Its association with Santa Cruz Red-on-bluff gives us our second cross-date for the Santa Cruz Phase, the other being Kana-a Black-on-white from the Flagstaff area. Similarly, Mimbres Bold Face Black-on-white, not yet dated by tree-rings but following Mogollon Red-on-brown stratigraphically, gives us an additional check as to the status of the Sacaton Phase (Fig. 10.2).

San Francisco Red is unique in that it was the most abundant of all foreign pottery and the only type to occur in every phase. Its status as an intrusive type has been well shown by Nora Gladwin's findings. From the investigations in the Mimbres it has already been established that San Francisco Red was long-lived, that its changes were so inconsequential that it could not be used as a phase or period diagnostic. But at Snaketown its cultural value supercedes its chronological value. The argument for a greater antiquity of the Mogollon over Hohokam ceramics and for the possible derivation of Vahki Red from San Francisco Red has been based on the repeated occurrence of the latter in each of the Snaketown phases.

Dragoon Red-on-brown, an off-shoot of Mogollon Red-on-brown, appeared predominantly in the earlier part of the Sacaton Phase. This position is normal since in southeastern Arizona the type frequently occurs with Mimbres Bold Face Black-on-white, also associated with Sacaton Red-on-buff in Snaketown, and in its native area is known to have Sacaton Red-on-buff from the Gila Basin as an infrequent but contemporary intrusive.

Sonora Red-on-brown is the only type of the whole lot which seems to be out of place. In Sonora it has been judged to occupy a relatively late position, whereas in Snaketown it appeared in several phases of the Pioneer Period. This must be explained on the ground that, either the pieces from Snaketown are not Sonora Red-on-brown, or, the type had a longer life than is, at present, recognized. It must be emphasized that this apparent disagreement may be due to our ignorance of what transpired in northwestern Mexico. If the Snaketown associations are valid, Sonora Red-on-brown represents the oldest intrusive painted pottery to have reached Snaketown.

Forestdale Smudged was of long duration, judging from its occurrence at Snaketown. It has already been noted as having occurred in Basketmaker III sites and hence its appearance at Snaketown in the Gila Butte Phase is not out of place. If the type was a derivative, or a collateral, of San Francisco Red, as has been suspected, the evidence at Snaketown gives us an idea as to when the branching took place.

The aggregate of foreign pottery, including such as was not placed in any phase, has a value in defining the temporal limits of the outside contacts of the Hohokam. The latest pottery was Mimbres Black-on-white (Pueblo III) which came into existence after 1000 A.D. and lasted well into the twelfth century. The sherds at hand are believed to be from vessels early in the Mimbres phase, hence probably not later than the eleventh century. The remaining types, White Mound Black-on-white, San Lorenzo Red-on-brown, and Trincheras Polychrome, may be allotted to a time prior to 1000 A.D., although the history of the latter is still imperfectly known. The character of some of the designs would tend to place the type as nearly contemporary with Santa Cruz Red-on-buff.

The failure to find Anasazi types, as St. Johns Polychrome, Tularosa Black-on-white, Tusayan Black-on-white, Four-mile Polychrome, Gila Polychrome, and Jeddito Yellow, dating from Pueblo III and IV horizons which occur in later Gila Basin sites, serves as a check in applying a final date for the Snaketown occupation. Because it was diffused as widely as any other type and its age has been so well defined, St. Johns Polychrome has become one of the best guide fossils in Southwestern archaeology. Kidder places the beginning of the type as early in the twelfth century although Roberts has evidence that would place it somewhat earlier. The absence of St. Johns Polychrome at Snaketown, then, would indicate that the village was abandoned by about 1100 A.D., or earlier if Robert's dates are accepted. An 1100 A.D. final date for Snaketown is altogether reasonable since three phases remain, the Santan, Soho, and Civano, ending somewhere about 1400 A.D. This would then leave 100 years per phase, a span of time also suggested by the presence of trade pieces whose approximate dates are known.

We may therefore conclude that by 1100 A.D. Snaketown was no longer inhabited, bringing to an end a continuous occupation which, according to our estimated dates, began before the Christian Era.

[EDITOR'S NOTE: The chronology for the earlier phases at the Snaketown site as proposed in the 1937 publication from which the above extract is taken has been questioned by H. S. Gladwin in *Excavations at Snaketown III, Revisions*, Medallion Papers, Gila Pueblo, Arizona, 1942, no. 30.]

11

SERIATION

One of the basic problems in archaeological research is to discover sequences of prehistoric cultural changes. Under ideal field conditions, sequences of cultural change may be found in clearly distinguishable layers at a stratified site, the earliest layers being those at the bottom of the deposit. Field conditions, however, are rarely ideal, and sometimes any sort of layering or stratigraphy may be impossible to detect. As a result, seriational methods have been developed to ascertain cultural changes when the stratigraphic evidence is not clear or when there is absolutely no such evidence.

Seriation makes one important assumption: the degree of similarity between items of material culture in a particular region tends to correlate with the closeness in time of the manufacture or construction of those items. Seriation involves three essential steps: first, the identification of the cultural units, e.g., pots, grave-lots, or sites; second, the determination of the relative similarity between the cultural units; and third, the arrangement of the units into a linear sequence according to their relative similarity. The linear sequence thus obtained is supposed to approximate the actual chronological sequence of cultural change. Independent evidence derived from other data is necessary to determine which end of the sequence is earlier in time.

Seriational methods in archaeology appear to have had two more or less separate developments. The earlier method, often referred to as "sequence dating," is the seriation of *excavated* materials. The originator of the sequence dating technique was Flinders Petrie (*1899*) who in the 1890's established chronological sequences of Egyptian tombs and their contents by means of pottery seriation. More recently, S. K. Lothrop (*1942*) has used an ingenious variation of this technique in analyzing ceramic grave-lots excavated in Panama as illustrated in the account appearing in this chapter.

A relatively complex statistical method of sequence dating has been introduced by Brainerd (1951) and Robinson (1951). Their method is primarily concerned with the seriation of the excavated levels of refuse deposits. The purpose is to increase the degree of precision to which cultural changes can be distinguished in such sites.

A second major development in archaeological seriation has been in the ordering of *surface* collections of artifacts, most commonly called "surface seriation." The first rigorous use of this method was probably A. L. Kroeber's work (1916a, 1916b) in the vicinity of Zuñi pueblo, New Mexico. Shortly thereafter, Leslie Spier (1917), working in the same region, made additional refinements in the method. The subsequent two decades seem to have produced surprisingly little additional development in the methodology of surface seriation. The use of this technique has been revived by James Ford (1938, 1952) and others (Ford and Willey, 1949; Phillips, Ford, and Griffin, 1951).

In any specific seriational sequence, there may be disagreements between workers about the validity of the particular assumptions involved. Accordingly, such sequences are often not widely accepted as representing the *real* chronological sequence unless they are supported by some other independent information. Thus, for example, Phillips, Ford, and Griffin (1951) checked the results of their surface ceramic seriations against sequences obtained from stratigraphic excavations.

Archaeological seriation has proved, on the whole, an imperfect, yet often extremely useful, tool. If used with caution and in conjunction with corroborating evidence, it will probably continue to be developed and refined as an aid in the reconstruction of prehistoric culture change.

Sequence Dating Egyptian Tombs

Sir Flinders Petrie was unquestionably one of the foremost pioneers in the development of Egyptian archaeology. Confronted with methodological problems for which there were few precedents, Petrie often displayed ingenuity and energy in their solution. The following excerpt,[1] from a monograph published in 1901, is a case in point. Here the great Egyptologist, in his *Diospolis Parva* report, explains his method of sequence dating (cf. Massoulard, 1949:61–69).

As it will be necessary in the account of these cemeteries to continually refer to the relative ages of the tombs, it will be better to begin with a discussion of the method by which the prehistoric age of Egypt has been subdivided and reduced to a defined order.

Hitherto it has been taken for granted that when no exact age could be stated for a particular civilization it must fall into a general limbo of "prehistoric times"; and the utmost that could be done was to name some pe-

[1] W. M. F. Petrie, *Diospolis Parva*, Egyptian Exploration Fund Memoirs, London, 1901, no. 20, pp. 4–8.

riods from the places where they were best represented—such as Chellian, Mousterian, Hallstattian, and to generally say that one such period was before another. Such a system is cumbrous, and gives no scope for exact definition.

But if we can use any definite scale of sequence, where the scale of absolute time is unknown, we can at once deal with a period as simply and clearly as if the scale of years were provided. Such a scale of sequence we have in the numbers of the burials; and if we can only succeed in writing down the graves in their original order of time, we can then be as definite in fixing their contents in a scale of graves as we would in a scale of years.

The problem then is, if we have the contents of hundreds of graves accurately recorded, how can we sort those out into their original order, and so construct a scale.

First, we need to be able to write out the record of the contents of a grave in such a way that it can be rapidly compared with every other grave. To draw figures of all the objects would be impossible, because they would need to be large enough to show small variations, and it would be impossible to compare hundreds of such together and observe their differences. It is necessary then to begin by forming a *corpus* of all the forms, numbered in order, and then to denote each form by its number.

To deal simultaneously with the records of some hundreds of graves, it is needful to state them as compactly as possible. This was done by writing out the numbers, which express the forms of pottery that were found, on a separate slip of card for each tomb. The slips were ¼ inch wide and seven inches long. All the slips were ruled in 9 columns, one for each kind of pottery. Every form of pottery found in a given tomb was then expressed by writing the number of that form in the column of that kind of pottery. Thus the whole of the pottery found in a given tomb was shown by a row of numbers which could be rapidly compared with the numbers of any other tomb record. The means were thus provided for exact definition and rapid comparison.

Having the material in suitable form we can proceed to arrange it. The general principles of arrangement I have stated in a paper in the *Journal of the Anthropological Institute* (Vol. XXIX, pp. 295 ff., 1899); here it will be more to the point to state the actual stages and details. The pottery alone is dealt with for arranging the graves, as it is very abundant and varied: and the other objects—stone vases, slate palettes, flints, etc.—when arranged according to the results of the study of the pottery serve as checks on the correctness of those results.

A brief view of the classification of the tombs and their contained pottery, to begin with, will help in explaining the processes by which such a result is reached. Here a series of seven stages is chosen to show the manner in which each period is linked to those which are before and after it.

Of course more or fewer stages might have been illustrated here; but these suffice to show how any period is linked to others, and to give a general idea of the varying styles of the periods. It would be clearly impossible to transpose any two of these groups, of the forms which are found together, without disconnecting them with those before and after. It is needful therefore to have a much finer gradation than seven stages to express the relative ages of varieties; and practically fifty stages were adopted to cover all this period. As some earlier periods may yet be found, the scale begins at 30; and running to 80, it leaves enough numbers before 100 to join up to the historic times in future. Thus the actual numbers assigned are purely arbitrary; but the order of the stages they represent is certain, and each number represents an equal quantity of burials. Now we turn to the series of steps whereby a card catalogue of grave contents was arranged in nearly the original order or sequence of the graves.

1st step. The most clear series of derived forms is that of the wavy handled vases, some of which are given as the first figures in the five lower stages of Fig. 11.1. Beginning almost globular, with pronounced ledge-handles, waved (as in stage 35 to 42) they next become more upright, then narrower with degraded handles, then the handle becomes a mere wavy line, and lastly an upright cylinder with an arched pattern or a mere cord line around it. The order of the changes is also shown by the contents; at first full of a strongly aromatic ointment, lastly filled with merely solid clay, as in the cylinder jars. The degradation of contents to a worthless substitute proves from which end of the scale the changes proceed. Here we have then a good series with which to begin a classification. To some small extent these varieties were overlapping in time, as we find cognate forms in one grave. How then are the groups which contain one type of wavy handle (W) to be subdivided? Side by side with this W pottery there is a class which since 1896 we have seen to be later than the rest, as it links on to the forms of historic age; it is lettered L. In any given group of W we can then sort out the slips, placing firstly those which contain L types that occur before, and lastly those with fresh types of L pottery. Thus the large groups are subdivided.

2nd step. Having the slips thus coarsely sorted into a few groups, by W and L, we can next sort each group by the types of Black-topped pottery (B), Polished-red pottery (P), and Rough-faced pottery (R), according as the slips contain types occurring before or not. This rough placing can be further improved by bringing together as close as may be the earliest and latest examples of any type; as it is clear that any disturbance of the original order will tend to scatter the types wider, therefore the shortest range possible for each type is the most probable truth.

3rd step. Having then all the slips which contain W sorted into approximately their original order, by the distribution of the other kinds of pottery which occur with them, we see that all the L pottery falls within the

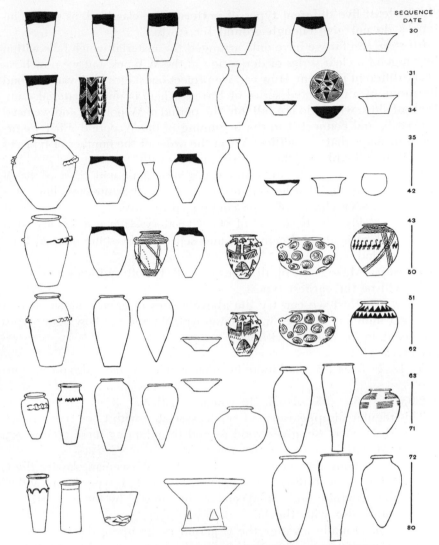

SEQUENCE
DATE
30
31
34
35
42
43
50
51
62
63
71
72
80

Fig. 11.1. Sequence date series of pre-dynastic Egyptian pottery forms.

range of W. It is practicable, therefore, to bring into the series all the slips with L, though without W. These are incorporated in the series by looking for the first and last example of every type of pottery occurring on a slip, and then placing it so that it shall be after all the first examples and before any of the last examples. If it is contradictory, as the last example of some kind of pottery was passed before the first example of some other kind is reached, then either the order previously arranged must be altered, or else we must acknowledge that the new slip contains the earliest or latest example of one of its types. In this and all the later stages only graves with at least five different types of pottery were classified, as poorer instances do not give enough ground for study.

4th step. So far we have only arranged the material which falls within the range of a clear series of derivation in the W types; but we now have a very different problem. How can we project our stages backward beyond the range of a connected series of forms? There is much material, hundreds of slips, which do not fall into the period of W pottery, and we need to classify and connect it to the beginning of the W period. First we arrange the slips that are without W, in the order of the number of types of B, P, R, found with W. Thus we have graves with

0 1 2 3 4 5 6 and more types in common with those of the W period. And we find that looking to the pottery with white cross lines (C) these successive classes of slips contain on the average

¼ ¹⁄₁₆ ¹⁄₂₅ 0 0 0 0 of the C pottery. Hence it is clear that the C pottery is at the beginning, and separated by some interval from the W period.

5th step. Make a list of all types of B, P, R pottery found with C, as these will be the earliest types.

6th step. Next we can try the above classes of graves which contain different numbers of types in common with W, and see how many types they contain in common with C.

Graves with

0 1 2 3 4 5 and more in common with W, have also on an average

2.0 1.2 .67 .25 .1 .1 in common with C.

This regular disappearance of types associated with C, as types associated with W increase, gives good ground for adopting these groups as a true classification of the period before W.

7th step. Thus clarifying the period before W, we can classify the C end of this scale according to the proportion of B, P, R types found with C which they contain; and the W end of the interval by the proportion of types found also with the W period.

8th step. Finally arrange the C period by grouping the instances of each type of C as near together as may be; and group similar types together so far as allowed by other kinds of pottery.

9th step. The decorated pottery (D) has so far received no attention; but as the graves containing it have at this stage been already roughly sorted by the statistics of the other pottery found with it, we can now use it as a means of further sorting. It is valuable material for this purpose, as the detail of the decoration is more likely to vary than the mere form which we have to judge by in other classes. Each type of D was therefore examined, and its occurrences concentrated together, as far as was possible without upsetting the W series, or spreading out the range of other kinds of pottery.

10th step. Having now about 700 slips of graves sorted into their original order by these various considerations, we now make a first division into fifty equal stages, numbered 30 to 80, termed *sequence dates* or S.D., and then make a list of all the types of pottery, stating the sequence date of every example that occurs in these graves.

11th step. So far only graves containing pottery of well-marked characters, as C, W, L, etc., have been dealt with. Now on the basis of the list made in the last step we incorporate all the other graves which contain enough pottery to define their position. So far as they may modify our views of the S.D.'s of the types, the list of S.D.'s is amended.

12th step. All of the material being now built together, and in approximate order, the further processes are for more exact arrangement in detail. All the slips containing C pottery were placed together at the beginning; but there is also a large number of slips which come before D and W, but which do not contain C pottery. Should these really be interspersed among the graves which contain D, and is it a mere accident that these do not contain C? The only test for this is the frequency of new types of other classes of pottery. If the post-C graves are really of the period of C graves we should find fewer new types beginning in post-C, as they would have already anticipated in C. Or if C and post-C graves are already in their true order, the frequency of new types should be the same throughout. Taking the new forms we find that on each slip on an average there are of new types

	B	P	F	D	R
in C period	1.3	.59	.07	.07	.14
in post-C	.26	.19	.05	.03	.28

Hence many post-C slips should go into C, as the newer types have already been largely anticipated in C. There are some other considerations, rather too complex and detailed to state fully here, from the actual number of pots of new types, the starting point of R pottery, etc. Finally, instead of 44 graves being of C and 148 of post-C, 47 were transferred to the C period, leaving 91 in C and 104 in post-C; some of these were however returned back again on studying the range of each type. The motives of arrangement have therefore come to a balance, and it is unlikely that there is any serious error of sequence.

13th step. The previous arrangement is confirmed if we ignore the C pottery entirely, and date all its slips solely by the other pottery which they contain.

14th step. After this rearrangement of the whole period before W, the sequence dates of the types of pottery were all retabulated.

15th step. Having exhausted the statistical methods of arrangement, and obtained all we can from them, we now turn to the treatment by the extent of range of each type of pottery. As already mentioned, the shortest range of any type is probably the nearest to the truth. Hence we look over the list of S.D.'s of each type, in the list of types and wherever the first or last example is far out from the rest, the slip containing it is examined to see whether it can be brought closer to the others. We may graphically imagine this sorting to be represented by an elastic thread for each type, attached to all the slips containing that type, and then the resultant position of all the slips under the tension of all the threads will be the probable truth; the weakness of each thread being in proportion to the true extent of diffusion of its type. Every instance of wide dispersion is examined, and concentrated as much as is possible without scattering another type. Thus the position of many slips has to be a compromise between bringing one type early or taking another late; and the likelihood of a type being extended is judged by the range of the other types most like it. Often several types hang together, and must all be transferred if one is moved, and then the ranges of twenty or thirty types have all to be reviewed at once. Most of these changes are however but small, not extending beyond one or two stages of the whole range of fifty.

16th step. The material thus mechanically arranged in its main outlines by various tests, is then subject to an artistic and subjective review, as to credibility of style and development, and similarity of forms in different classes of pottery; any likely alterations which do not violate the statistical probabilities are then made; but this is only a finishing matter, and is not allowed to weigh against the more solid facts.

17th step. The whole series (900 slips) is then redivided into 50 equal groups; and the list of the S.D.'s of each type is re-formed accordingly.

18th step. A list of all the graves that have been entered on slips, and of all others not yet examined, is then formed, with the sequence date of each grave stated in accordance with the ranges of its pottery types. This list serves for the subsequent dating of all the other objects found in the graves.

At the end of the period the question of whether the cylinder jars of pottery were all descended from the wavy-handled vases, or were copied from the earlier stone vases, was also tested statistically by the number of types of other pottery; but the results showed that they must be connected with the wavy-handled pottery jars. A class of the rudest shallow graves, with only black topped pots, was classed as 30, as they were clearly before the C pottery beginning at 31.

It should be observed that these various steps of arrangement cannot be taken in a different order; but that each has its proper place in relation to other steps.

The resulting sequence dates for each class of objects will be afterward discussed in dealing with the stone vases, flints, metals, etc. Here we give the sequence dates for all the varieties of pottery known, both those in the *corpus* of forms in *Naqada,* and those new forms published here. These tables are the essential basis for all further study of the prehistoric, and from them the relative age of any newly-discovered tombs containing pottery can be at once read off.

Potsherd Chronology of Sites near Zuñi Pueblo

The scope and versatility of A. L. Kroeber in diverse fields of anthropology is well illustrated by this account[2] of his archaeological investigations in the vicinity of Zuñi pueblo, New Mexico. Kroeber here gave the method of surface seriation its first rigorous use in America. Taking time out from his ethnological research at Zuñi, he collected and analyzed potsherds in such a way that he was able to distinguish five archaeological sub-periods prior to the existence of modern Zuñi. This paper has served as the foundation for subsequent developments in the technique of surface seriation, such as that of Spier (1917) in the same region.

In the course of a study of family life made at the pueblo of Zuñi during the summer of 1915, I recorded the native names of a number of ancient villages in and near Zuñi Valley. A late afternoon walk a few days afterwards brought me to where Mattsakya once stood, a mile and a half east of the town of Zuñi. The wall outlines which Mindeleff traced have mostly disappeared in thirty years, save for two rooms and where a prairie dog hole had laid bare a few feet of masonry that otherwise would have been hidden. The quantity of broken rock on the surface, the sharp rise of the knoll, and the maintained shrine, or rather two, on its summit—the last, as it proved, an almost certain evidence of former occupation of the spot—all however indicated a ruin even to the novice in archaeology. A few moments revealed a pottery fragment or two. At first the sherds were difficult to see and harder to distinguish from the numerous minute slabs of stone. A quarter of an hour, however, practised the eye; and the short time remaining before darkness sufficed to fill my pockets.

A few afternoons later, I went out in the opposite direction, toward Pinnawa, a mile or more to the west. Proceeding first to the northwestern edge of the present suburbs of the town to see the communal "scalp house," I noted another shrine or monument a few hundred feet to the north, directly in front of the government day school. This occupied the center of a slight rise, perhaps a yard above the surrounding plain and two hundred or more feet in diameter. The ground was strewn with small rounded and variously colored pebbles, such as do not occur in the fine red clay of the levels of Zuñi Valley. In a few seconds sharp-edged fragments of flint or chert appeared, and then occasional bits of pottery. A passing Zuñi named the spot Shoptluwwayala; its shrine is connected with

[2] A. L. Kroeber, *Zuñi Potsherds,* American Museum of Natural History, Anthropological Papers, New York, 1916, vol. 18, pt. 1, pp. 7–21. By permission of the American Museum of Natural History.

the yellow Sallimoppiya dance character. The pottery was not abundant; but a pocketful was secured.

I went westward, still on the north side of the broad bed of the Zuñi River, toward a knoll nearly a mile ahead, into which the stream had cut a vertical bank. The rise in the ground made me suspect an ancient site of human occupation. Again the smooth pebbles were conspicuous; and then bits of chipped rock and potsherds were seen lying here and there. Hattsinawa was the name the Zuñi gave me next morning. As at Shopt-luwwayala, there was not a single building stone visible, nor anything that might have been a fragment of one; nor did the cut bank reveal any, although pottery pieces lay on the surface to its edge. Another pocketful was the harvest.

I followed the river bed down a couple of hundred yards, and walked across the remnants of the stream—most of which was flowing through ir-rigation ditches into Zuñi fields—at Pinnawa. This site is the terminus of a long spur running from the southern hills to a low end at the river. Only a few steps from the stream there lay some broken rock of the type that litters Mattsakya but is wanting at Shoptluwwayala and Hattsinawa. Pot-tery at first was scant; but as I proceeded up the nose of the hill, the throw-out from every prairie dog hole was decorated by from one to half a dozen fragments. Toward the summit of the knoll and the inevitable shrine—only a few yards from the wagon road—both rock and potsherds lay thick, with chipped pebbles here and there. The site is also more extensive than either of the two preceding ones; and a few minutes sufficed for a larger haul.

It was immediately apparent that red, black and patterned potsherds predominated here, as they seemed to have preponderated at Mattsakya, while white fragments had been in the majority at both Shoptluwwayala and Hattsinawa. I therefore attempted to pick up all sherds visible in cer-tain spots, rather than range over the whole site and stoop only for the at-tractive ones. In this I may not have been altogether successful, for a red, a patterned, or a deep black fragment catches the eye more readily than either a "black" or a "white" one that ranges toward dull gray. But at least the endeavor was conscientious.

Next morning my finds were washed and dried—an unnecessary pro-ceeding, I soon found—then sorted and counted. A tabulation thoroughly confirmed the mental impression of the evening before. At Mattsakya and Pinnawa, black or blackish pieces predominated; red ones were fairly nu-merous, white ones less so. At Shoptluwwayala and Hattsinawa, white pre-dominated, and black and red were rare. The corrugated ware showed similarly: at Mattsakya and Pinnawa black sherds were as abundant as white, at the two other sites the black were lacking, the white frequent. The black corrugated ware usually runs to a dark or dull gray, the white is nearly always pale buff, pinkish, or light gray; but there were few doubtful pieces. There were other differences. At the "black and red" sites, a few three-colored sherds were found; at the white ones, none. The two former were extensive and heavily littered with good-sized rock fragments, as one would expect at a stone built ruin. The latter showed no rock, but a somewhat more sandy soil than prevails in most of the red clayey Zuñi plain, with some admixture of waterworn pebbles, scarcely any more than an inch in length, and of surprisingly diverse colors. The presence at Mattsakya and Pinnawa of one or two tiny bits of obsidian, which was unrepresented at Shoptluwwayala and Hattsinawa, was not altogether conclusive, on account of the small total yield of the two last named; but it seemed significant, as it does still. Finally, Mattsakya and Pinnawa had been previously mentioned to me by Zuñi informants as places inhabited in the *innote* or long ago. Shoptluwwayala and Hattsinawa were named only on designation and inquiry.

There could be no doubt that here, within a half hour's radius of the largest inhabited pueblo, were prehistoric remains of two types and two periods, as distinct as oil and water. The condition of the sites indicated the black and red ware ruins as the more recent; but certain misleading observations of the pottery in use in the Zuñi homes of today left me in doubt for a time. These observations rested upon fact, but the facts are due to the influence of American civilization, and would not have obtained a couple of generations ago. Once these circumstances were comprehended, the chronological priority of the white ware type became certain.

I recalled the surveys and excavations of many years ago, and a confused impression of a mass of sherds and similar uninspiring pieces obtained for the Hemenway Expedition under the direction of the memorable Cushing, sent in an exchange from the Peabody Museum to the University of California, and now stored there in a pile of trays. But an accumulation of dust and the familiar name Halona were all that emerged with distinctness. I searched my mind for published reports of the work that must have been done in the region—vainly: if anything was in print, it had been forgotten in fifteen years during which my reading on the American Southwest had been desultory; and I was remote from bibliographies. Victor Mindeleff's study of pueblo architecture, for which I had sent in connection with researches into the clans and town growth of Zuñi itself, I found truly admirable, and it contained valuable plots and descriptions of ruins; but they did not touch on my problem. The final clinching was given by Hodge's most useful summary of the history of Cibola and Zuñi, included in that tremendous research which will always be fundamental to all studies of the Zuñi and which is the great labor of the life of Matilda Coxe Stevenson, who died far away while I was forming my first friendships with her old friends. In Hodge's meaty compendium I found that Mattsakya and perhaps Pinnawa were inhabited Zuñi villages in 1598, and in all likelihood when Coronado stormed Haȝoiʰkɥ in 1540, and that at least Mattsakya was a place of abode until the great revolt of 1680.

The fate of Mattsakya was also that of Kyakkima, a better preserved ruin nestling against the giant cliffs of Towwayallanna, four miles southeast of Ittiwawa, "the middle," as Zuñi is for the world, in the belief of its residents. The pottery of Kyakkima should accordingly be that of Mattsakya. It proved to be so. A hundred seconds on its debris settled the identity.

Not only, then, are there the type and period of white ware and the type and period of black and of red ware, but the latter is the more recent. It belongs in part to the time of early American history; the former is wholly prehistoric. I call the historic Type A, the prehistoric Type B, since further exploration or study may reveal another prehistoric Type C.

Pinnawa was revisited, and a larger collection of fragments brought home. Their relative numbers tallied as they should with the first lot, considering the chances of accident in such small series. Sherds continue some distance to the south of the wagon road that crosses the spur just south of the little summit of the site. My companion and I continued a quarter of a mile south, or southeasterly, up the gently sloping ridge to Tetlnatluwwayala, a shrine of one of the war god twins. The shrine led me to believe in an underlie of ruin; and it was there. There was no shadow of doubt as to period: every sherd but one was white. Even the corroborating pebbles, and absence of building sandstone, did not fail. The pottery was not abundant on the surface and again the industry of the prairie dogs proved a boon.

We went on along the ridge, down a slight dip, across the deeply washed trail that the bearded gods tread as they file from the southwest into Zuñi in the evening of the first summer solstice dance, and up again to the next low summit, where I remembered seeing a piece of lava, perhaps from a thousand year old grinding slab, on an earlier walk dictated by want of exercise and before thoughts of archaeology entered my mind. The spot is perhaps an eighth of a mile from Tetlnatluwwayala. As nearly as the lieutenant governor could later follow my index from a Zuñi roof, he judged it to be Te'allatashshhanna; but he may have misjudged the direction of my finger, or meant a more distant place. I am not certain of the name. I could not find the lava; but a short distance to the west, and a little higher, was another shrine. The hillock was of loose white sand, wind deposited and in spots wind eroded, though mostly covered with vegetation. In one of the bare depressions, and over a small patch on the leeward slope, lay a handful of pottery fragments. Again all but one were white.

We rode to Kyakkima with the lieutenant governor. As we approached the trickle that issued from the spring at the foot of a recess in the cliffs, a whitish spot on the sandy soil caught my eye. I sensed a type B sherd; but the officer said Kyakkima lay ahead. We drank at the head of the spring; then crossed the streamlet and ascended the steep slope to the east. Here was Kyakkima, where some five hundred Zuñi once lived in a town of four levels. On the higher terraces the walls that Mindeleff plotted still stand; half way down is the ever present shrine with the dry rotting prayer sticks from which the plumes have blown. The site is large, the pottery abundant, and much of it attractive. I filled one pocket with an average sample, in which dull black was picked up undiscriminatingly with striking black on red and black on yellow patterns. Then we hunted pretty pieces. To keep any of the collection in the open pockets of the only coat among us on the ride home, part of it had to be jettisoned. The plain black pieces were abandoned; but unless some wandering Zuñi sheep herder or traveler has in mild surprise brushed them from the large rock by the spring, they still lie on its surface, to verify my count of them, while the reader scans this page.

But the white spot was not forgotten, and before the horses were remounted a ramble over the slope west of the rivulet produced a couple of dozen sherds—two red, all the remainder whitish. As usual, building stone was not in evidence, but pebbles and boulders occurred through the sandy soil. There is no shrine; nor does there appear to be a Zuñi name for the exact spot. I have named it Kyakkima Sunnhakwi, Kyakkima West. It is not a site that suggests itself for habitation. Possibly it is only the outer fringe of a once larger settlement of period B of which the main portion is covered by the Kyakkima of period A.

It is unnecessary to continue the narrative. Other "ruins" subsequently visited conform to the two types; such data concerning them as were noted, are included in the tabulations and in the memoranda appended. It is observable that of the type B sites, Hattsinawa and one other show a fair proportion of red ware. They therefore belong to the end of age B, or possibly to the first dawnings of that later period which was still blooming in the sixteenth and seventeenth centuries of our era.

The white slip pottery of the prehistoric time in Zuñi Valley is clearly, in general, of the familiar Cliff-Dweller type. Even the black and white checker board ornamentation so familiar from museum and private collections, is represented. A deviation from the colorless grayish white of most Cliff-Dweller specimens to a light buff or yellowish or pinkish white in many of the Zuñi pieces, may be the result of a peculiarity of the local clay.

Careful explorers in Arizona have warned against too much weight being given to color when inferences are drawn. Yellow ware in a ruin may be more indicative of the chemical constitution of the soil than of a type of civilization. I am ready to subscribe to this caution as heartily as anyone. It does not apply to this study of Zuñi antiquity because every ruin touched lies within the same valley, because all those examined are within an hour's distance of the pueblo, and because at least two pairs of ruins of differing periods are only a quarter of a mile or less apart.

Zuñi pottery of 1915, which may be found in every household, is overwhelmingly a white or creamy yellowish white slip ware, patterned either with black or with black and red; but in the latter case, the areas of black exceed those of red. The reason for this prevalence of white surface is that the pottery in use is confined principally to two types: water jars, usually large but low; and great open bowls for bread kneading. Now and then may be seen a canteen of breast shape, also with black or black and red ornamentation; a high jar, of plain polished red, used both for storage and as a drum; and a water jar, usually small, with red inside and bottom —the red being burned yellow ocher. There are some black cooking pots: I have seen a number with handles or knobs, none really corrugated. Most of them stand unused in interior storerooms; occasionally one is set on the hearth fire to parch or pop corn, more rarely to cook in. The Zuñi woman now cooks in a frying pan or in agate ware, and serves food either in this vessel or in a china dish or rectangular lava bowl. A hundred, perhaps twenty-five years ago, this was not the case; and I am confident that debris from the town streets of that time would have shown nearly the same proportion of blackish ware as occurs at Mattsakya and Kyakkima, simply because the native cook pots had not yet gone out of use before American made substitutes. A few holes dug a yard or two deep in the streets or fallen houses of Zuñi will confirm or disprove my prediction.

I now began to observe sherds around the town. In the course of an afternoon's survey on the housetops, I gathered as many pieces as I could carry without interfering with the work in hand. More than half were blackish, and at that I probably desisted sooner from trying to pry out of the hard baked clay obstinately imbedded pieces of this shade than gaily colored ones.

It seemed however that the prevalence of black on the roofs might be due to the blowing over of chimneys, which in former times were regularly, and now still often, made of cracked or broken cook pots. Stooping through the streets of the town was hardly calculated to enhance my standing in Zuñi, so I delegated the task to four children of my "family," who fell to the work with zeal, and I am confident observed as closely as they could my instructions to collect without discrimination. An afternoon netted them over a thousand fragments, large and small. A third of these I class as black; more than half were black or black and red on white, and at least some of the white sherds are from jars of this type. My youthful aids reported that in the vicinity of the great plaza, in the very heart of the town, black pieces were scarce, but that toward the northwestern edge of the pueblo proper—not of the suburbs or outlying houses—they became numerous. Both red and black on red pieces were found, though they aggregate only two or three percent of the total.

I believe this collection reasonably trustworthy. While dark sherds may have been a little slighted, they are far more numerous than I should have predicted after a month of frequenting Zuñi homes. When the changes in habits are considered that recent years have worked, it is a fair inference that a similar gathering made in a stratum a few feet below the present level of the streets would contain about one half black pieces, and correspondingly fewer of the patterned water jar type. In short, Zuñi potsherds of 1915 actually approximate those of type A, while those of 1815 may be expected to differ hardly at all, in color proportions, from those of 1615 or perhaps 1515. I suspect that a gradual diminution of the red ground ware, and perhaps of corrugated, is the chief change that has taken place (in the features considered) in the centuries since the discovery.

A few minor alterations may however be noted. The round lines of the deer and birds and scrolls on some modern Zuñi jars, are almost utterly lacking from the historic sherds. This fact substantiates the conviction gained from museum inspection of modern Pueblo ware, that these designs are not native but the result of European influence, though to the Zuñi woman of today they seem as truly Shiwwi or pure Zuñi as do the angles she paints around them, or with which she covers the whole of the next jar she makes. Patterns in type A pottery are not infrequently lustrous—perhaps not a true glaze, but with a distinct glassy shine. The art or custom of producing this has perhaps died out since the sixteenth century. Red ware with overpainted white lines is still occasionally manufactured, though I believe mostly in bric-a-brac and tourist articles; but this was infrequent also in period A. Most of the vessels in use today have their black pattern, if not a true black, at least a very dark brown. This is due to the mixing of the pigment with water containing either cedar, or ky'ahhewe, or another plant extract. The small, four-sided, step-edged bowls still used for sacred cornmeal—whose average age may be a generation more than that of household bowls and jars—mostly have their frog and tadpole patterns in walnut brown, the above dyes not having been used with the pigment. Much of the type A "black" decoration is of the same shade; especially on yellow or yellowish background. The prayer bowls also incline to a yellowish slip; so that they connect the twentieth with the sixteenth century in two ways. A distinct green, usually lustrous and sometimes bright, which is occasional on type A pieces, seems however to have no equivalent today.

The ware of type B, of type A, and of today, shows white or gray along the fractured edge. It is rarely reddish, or red like Southern California pottery. This is presumably a characteristic of the local clays. There are some ancient and modern fragments, mostly thick and coarse, burned red through; but the majority of red pieces are covered with a highly polished slip of that color.

History tells us that the people of period A were Zuñi, speaking and essentially living as now. The men and women who inhabited the sites of period B belonged to the unidentified prehistoric past. We cannot say that they were or were not Zuñi; but there is no known fact which prevents them from having been of this nation. That their ruins are low and soil-covered can be explained by reason of their age; that they are small in extent, in the open country, and located with reference to water supply or farm land or unknown considerations rather than for defensive protection, indicates a somewhat different life in the prehistoric period. I have not turned a spadeful of earth in the Zuñi country. But the outlines of a thousand years' civilizational changes which the surface reveals are so clear, that there is no question of the wealth of knowledge that the ground holds for the critical but not over timid excavator.

Table 8 is a summarization on the basis of the three fundamental colors,

TABLE 8. Percentages of Pottery Types in Zuñi Region

	Period A								
	Matt-sakya	Pin-nawa	Kyak-kima	Kol-liwa	Site W	Tow-wayal-lanna	Wim-may-awa	Shunn-tek-kya	All Sites Combined
Wholly black	63	52	61	51	72	(40)	56	49	53
White or black on white	27	22	20	26	24	23	22	36	25
Containing any red	10	26	19	23	4	37	22	15	22
Total	100	100	100	100	100	100	100	100	100

	Period B								
	Shop-tluw-way-ala	Hatt-si-nawa	Tetl-natluw-way-ala	Te-'allat-ashsh-hanna	Kyak-kima West	He'i-'tli'an-nanna	Site Y	Site X	"Haw-wikku B"	All Sites Combined
Wholly black	7	19	—	5	—	3	—	1	9	5
White or black on white	90	71	98	95	92	97	100	96	79	92
Containing any red	3	10	2	—	8	—	—	3	12	3
Total	100	100	100	100	100	100	100	100	100	100

black, white, and red. Of sherds colored differently on their two sides, or having a pattern in two or three colors, all containing any red have been counted as "red"; of the remainder, all are included under "white" which bear any white. This arrangement gives red somewhat the advantage and black the disadvantage among the three colors; but any other method of summarizing would have been subject to an equal degree of arbitrariness. At any rate, Table 8 reveals clearly, even to those who may not care to absorb the more numerous figures of the preceding lists, the distinctness of the two periods. In the historic time, "A," black preponderates, and red about equals white ware. In the prehistoric period, "B," white is overwhelmingly in excess and both black and red occur only scatteringly.

As my study progressed, I frequently found it difficult to divide the corrugated pottery into "black" and "white," and the difference between periods A and B as regards this ware became apparent as one of total frequency rather than of differences of tint, though it is true that period B corrugated samples are almost throughout distinctly whitish. I also recalled that real corrugated ware is said by the Zuñi not to be made today, and is very scarce among the street debris, while most of the period A ruins show an appreciable percentage, though small compared with the type B sites. Further, the only really large proportion of corrugated pieces from any period A locality was at site W, which in its lack of building stone and general appearance resembles a type B site; next to it comes Pinnawa, which is more decayed as a ruin than even Mattsakya, and far more than all the others. It therefore seemed as if a progressive decrease of the proportion of corrugated ware of any color were a characteristic of the lapse of time in Zuñi Valley irrespective of "period"; and I arranged the sites in order accordingly. Two of the minor sites of period B did not fit into the series; but both of these also showed other special characteristics, in their slip ware. On the other hand, Hattsinawa, which I had before classed as late B on account of its high proportion of red sherds, as well as because it is located on a more distinct knoll than any of the other B sites, comes nearer to the A ruins, in its frequency of corrugated ware, than any B sites except Kyakkima West, and from this latter the sample was of the smallest.

A subdivision of the two periods was thus indicated. I tested the obtained sequence of sites with several color characteristics. The results, which are given in detail in Table 9, are surprisingly corroborative and allow of a tentative discrimination of five sub-periods, or six if modern Zuñi be included. Briefly, corrugated ware preponderated in the very earliest epoch, and diminished through all periods until it has died out in the present. On the other hand, three-colored pottery—black and red patterns on a white or yellow ground—is wanting in B, appears sporadically in early A, becomes more numerous in late A, and reaches its climax today. Black on red ware, on the other hand, is most abundant about the middle time. It has not been found in early B, while late A and the present reveal a decline from middle and late B and early A. For red and for black pottery in general, the relative figures for period A are not worth anything; but in both classes the period B sites show an increasing approximation

TABLE 9. Subdivisions of A and B Periods by Percent of Pottery Types

Period	Site	Corru-gated	Three Colors	Black on Red	Any Red	"Black" Ware
Present	Zuñi	0ª	0	1		
Late A	Towwayallanna	1	8	3⎫		
	Kolliwa	—	7	2		
	Shunntekkya	2	7	2		
	Wimmayawa	2	4	1	22ᵇ	53ᵇ
	Mattsakya	3	4	3⎬		
	Kyakkima	4	3	2		
Early A	Pinnawa	10	1	8		
	Site W	24	—	1⎭		
Late B	Hattsinawa	27	—	5	10	19
·	Kyakkima West	12ᶜ	—	4	8	—ᶜ
Middle B	Shoptlawwayala	40	—	2	3	7
	"Hawwikku B"	49	—	6	12	9
Early B	Te'allatashshhanna	66	—	—	—	5
	Site X	71	—	-	3	1
	Tetlnatluwwayala	72	—	—	2	—
?—B	He'i'tli'annanna	—	—	—	—	3
	Site Y	—	—	—	—	—

ª Present, but less than half of one percent.
ᵇ The variation between sites here lumped seems due more to accident or selection in collecting than to differences typical of period.
ᶜ Unfortunately only 25 pieces are available from this site.

to period A proportions in the order of their age as suggested by the corrugated ware. I believe it may be concluded, while type B and type A sites can normally be distinguished without the least uncertainty, and the separateness of the two is fundamental, that nevertheless they do not represent two different migrations, nationalities, or waves of culture, but rather a steady and continuous development on the soil.

I am aware of the thinness of my foundation in rearing a structure of half a dozen eras on nothing more than three or four color and texture features of a few thousand sherds gathered on the surface of some fifteen closely grouped spots. I was tempted to buttress my chronological classification by further collecting, especially at sites from which my representation was little more than vanishing. But my stay in Zuñi is short; the time that gathering, sorting, and tabulating would require, is scarcely available; and even twice or three times the number of surface fragments would not suffice to convert my tentative conclusions into positive ones. The final proof is in the spade; and that involves money, a gang of men, months of time, and an examination, if possible, of all ruins within a given radius. The real confirmation of my chronology I must thus of necessity leave to the future. But I am confident that however the present classification be altered in detail or supplemented by wider considerations, in essentials it will stand—because the essentials are obvious on the ground.

The problems of prehistoric Zuñi and of the earliest Southwest will be solved only by determined limitation of attention. There has been treasure hunting in this fascinating region for fifty years, some with the accompaniment of most painstaking recording, measuring, and photographing; but these dozens or hundreds of efforts, some of them costly, have produced scarcely a rudiment of true history. It is fatal for the investigator to exhume pottery in the morning, note architectural construction at noon, plot rooms in the afternoon, and by evening become excited over a find of turquoise or amulets. Such procedure may allow areas and even sites of most distinctively different type to be discriminated, but the finer transitions, on which ultimately everything depends, will be lost sight of under the wealth of considerations. One feature at a time, then another, then correlation, is the method that will convert Southwestern archaeology from a delight for antiquarians into a historian's task. The fine bowls, precious jewelry, and beautiful axes that already cumber our museums, will find their use; but that time is at the end of study, when they can be placed and used with meaning, not at the beginning, when they confuse and weary. At present five thousand sherds can tell us more than a hundred whole vessels, and the bare knowledge of the average size of a room in a dozen contiguous ruins may be more indicative than the most laborious survey of two or three extensive sites.

Particularly does the necessity of concentration apply geographically. A promising site here and another a hundred miles away may show striking differences in innumerable respects. But in the present chaos of knowledge who can say which of these differences are due to age and which to locality and environment? With the chronology of Zuñi, of the Hopi country, of the Rio Grande, of the San Juan, and of the Gila worked out independently, comparison may yield momentous conclusions; but comparison at present, however suggestive, will bear no certain fruit. If the investigator who enters this greatest of American archaeological fields allows himself to be appalled by the length and variety of the labors of those who have preceded him, his outlook will be dreary; if he recalls that but for a few scattered scratches the field is virgin as regards real history, and if he wisely limits himself, and proceeds by the common sense plan of one thing at a time and that hammered at until it yields, he surely has before him one of the most promisingly productive of scientific problems.

Tomb Seriation at Naga-'d-Dêr, Egypt

George A. Reisner's excavations in Egypt have made his name one of the most famous in this field. At Naga-'d-Dêr, near Abydos in Upper Egypt, Reisner conducted extensive excavations for Mrs. Phoebe A. Hearst. The collections from this site are at the University of California.

Although not all of Reisner's assertions on the course of Egyptian cultural development are supported by presently available data, his method, which he carefully explains, of determining the sequence of time in the great cemetery remains a model and his report deserves careful reading.[3] His sympathetic reconstruction of life in the provincial community whose dead were buried at Naga-'d-Dêr is culture history at its best.

Reisner's technique of tomb seriation was developed slowly, and the reader may wish to consult his report on the dynastic cemeteries at Naga-'d-Dêr for an account of an earlier attempt to establish the developmental trend of tomb structures (Reisner, 1908).

The Cemetery N 500–900 on the east bank of Naga-'d-Dêr (see Fig. 11.2) was begun some time in the latter part of Dyn. II, probably in the reign of King Khasekhemuwy. The capital of Egypt was still at Thinis, and Khasekhemuwy himself was buried in the old royal Thinite cemetery at Abydos, which is about ten miles farther south on the opposite side of the valley. The series of archaeological groups which took their source in the neolithic culture of the early predynastic period may be conveniently distinguished as follows:

(a) Early predynastic or neolithic group.

(b) Middle predynastic or early copper group.

(c) Late predynastic group; practical use of metal.

(d) Dyn. 0 to the reign of King Zer; practical use of metals; writing; first period of intensive manufacture of stone vessels; beginning of sculpture (statuettes, figures, and small reliefs); united monarchy.

(e) King Zer to accession of Khasekhemuwy; culmination of the early dynastic period; second period of stone vessels; continued development of all arts and crafts.

(f) King Khasekhemuwy to accession of Sneferuw; third period of stone vessels (period of degeneration); beginning of wheel-made pottery; first period of stone architecture; temples of Zoser at Step Pyramid.

(g) Dyn. IV; second period of stone architecture (large limestone blocks and granite); the building of the royal pyramids at Medûm (?), Dashûr, Giza, and Abu Roash; culmination of statuary and relief.

(h) Dyn. V–VI; impoverished royal family; third period of architecture (spread of technical knowledge of quarrying and construction in stone); spread of sculpture in all its forms; introduction of new corpus of stone vessels and new pottery forms; end of the first union of Upper and Lower Egypt and the first period of cultural development, followed immediately by a complete breakdown of the administration and the arts and crafts.

From the discovery of the practical use of metals to the reign of King

[3] G. A. Reisner, *A Provincial Cemetery of the Pyramid Age, Naga-ed-Der*, Pt. III, University of California Publications, Egyptian Archaeology, Oxford, 1932, vol. 6, pp. 185–192. By permission of University of California Press.

Fig. 11.2 (*Facing*).   Plan of Cemetery N 500–900, Naga-'d-Dêr.

Khasekhemuwy, a thousand years or more had elapsed. When Cemetery N 500–900 was begun, the intensive manufacture of stone vessels was entering on its third phase with the new forms and materials introduced by Khasekhemuwy. The Egyptians at court were in the full use of tools and weapons of hardened copper, writing, and sculpture, although the latter had not reached its climax, and were on the point of translating the old crude-brick architecture into limestone. About this time, a certain small community, certainly an agricultural village, near Naga-'d-Dêr, began burying their dead on the "western" end of the "northern" bank of the South Wady. The Cemeteries N 1500 and N 3000 were probably older cemeteries of the same community and contained the graves of more important families. These older cemeteries were still growing by the addition of large corbel-vaulted graves and small graves of different types including the stone-roofed well-graves (type iv a) which was the first type to be made in Cemetery N 500–900.

The centre of growth of Cemetery N 500–900 consisted of several nucleus graves each of which formed the beginning of a small burying-ground. The cemetery thus founded continued to grow from these nuclei and by the addition of later nucleus graves during Dyn. III. Almost contemporaneous with the first graves of the early "western" cemetery, a very small family group, perhaps a unit of the same community, began another burying-ground. This isolated small cemetery (called group j) consisted of only about twenty-eight graves [shown as filled circles in northeastern part of site map] made during the whole period to about the end of Dyn. III, and ran its course independently of the main cemetery. The family was not only small but also very poor.

Early in Dyn. III, about the time that Zoser was building the Step Pyramid and its temples, the more important members of the community transferred their burying-place from N 1500 to N 500–900. There was then no site empty in N 1500 on which a tomb like the stairway corbels of N 1500 or the stairway mastabas such as N 585 or N 593 could be built. The king at Memphis was building stone walls with dressed surfaces, but at Thinis, the previous capital, even the nobles were still using crude brick. The great men who built the enormous crude-brick mastabas at Bêt Khallâf just across the river from Naga-'d-Dêr had developed or adopted the stairway mastaba for their tombs. Two of these, K I of the reign of Zoser and K 2 of the reign of Sa-nekht (the King Neferka, or Raneferka of the unfinished pyramid of Zawiat-el-Aryan), are among the largest mastabas of Egypt, and may well have been the first of the true stairway mastabas (type IV A) to be made in Upper Egypt. Following the model of K I, but on a much smaller scale, the first of the larger tombs built in N 500–900 in succession to the stairway corbels of N 1500 were rather poorly made stairway tombs of type IV B. The first was probably N 585 set on a level site free of previous constructions and well away to the "east" from the small tombs of types iv a, b, and d which had already been made in the early "western" cemetery. Soon after, N 593 was built on the free space left between N 585 and the small graves. Both these formed the nuclei of small groups of stairway tombs of lesser size: (II) following N 585, N 586 (= a 38) (type IV B), N 530 (type iv e), and N 546 + 604 (type v d (I)); (III) following N 593, N a 29 (type IV V), Line II was carried on into Dyn. IV. But Line III and three other outlying small stairways, N 518, N a 115, were confined to Dyn. III.

The two nucleus tombs, N 586 (= a 38) and N 593, were undoubtedly of the reign of Zoser. The next tomb to be built (N 573 + 587) was the first of the main line of six mastabas, the largest tombs in the cemetery. This was placed on a primary site a few metres "east" of N 585 and was built on the model of K 2 at Bêt Khallâf dated to the reign of King Sanekht, the successor of Zoser, and the builder of the unfinished pyramid at Zawiat-el-Aryan. The stairway tombs of husband and wife are included in one mastaba, a type which was not used again at Naga-'d-Dêr but came into common use at Giza in the reign of Cheops, in the shaft mastabas of stone. N 573 + 587 was undoubtedly the tomb of the headman of the community of that time, visibly a man of considerable means, equal to the greatest persons buried in Cemetery N 1500. Sixteen very fine stone vessels were found in N 587 and four in N 573 although otherwise both burial chambers had been completely plundered.

In the main line of lesser size and perhaps subsidiary to it come the two stairway mastabas of type IV A, N 574 and N 599. These appear to me to belong to important members of the headman's family and are later than N 573 + 587 but earlier than N 689. Unfortunately, the skeletons were not sufficiently preserved to warrant definite conclusions as to the sex, but that of N 599 was probably a female. I surmise that the owner of N 599 was the wife of N 574 and that N 574 was a headman, of a shorter term, who came between him of N 573 + 587 and him of N 689. After N 574 and N 599, the next large mastaba in the line is N 689, clearly the tomb of the chief personage of *his* time, quite equal in resources to the first-mentioned headman of N 573 + 587 and certainly not over a generation or two later. I take it that the badly destroyed mastaba N 688 (type IV A) was the tomb of his wife. That would give us three generations of headmen of the community from the time of King Sanekht (Neferka) to the end of Dyn. III:

(1) N 573 + 587, the headman and his wife in one mastaba.

(2) N 574 and N 599, headman and his wife in separate mastabas.

(3) N 689 and N 688, headman and his wife in separate mastabas.

Three generations would cover between 60 to 80 years, and Cem. N 500–900 would thus show between 80 and 100 years for Dyn. III. This corresponds roughly to the usual estimates made for the length of the dynasty. But it is possible that N 574 does not represent a separate generation, in which case the time indicated would be shortened to 70–90 years. If any trace were to be found in this small provincial cemetery of the great advance in architecture and sculpture taking place during this time at Memphis, it would be in these large mastabas of the main line; but both here and at Bêt Khallâf, all the material shows that the men of this time in Upper Egypt still held fast to the traditional arts and crafts of the early dynastic period.

Down to the end of Dyn. III, the cemetery of the headmen (that is, the spaces between the large mastabas from N 573 + 587 to N 688) had been kept free of small tombs. If, as I assume, these tombs represent a direct line of descent, the influence of the headmen would have been sufficient to prevent any intrusion. In the meantime the minor members of the community were being buried in the continuation of the "western" cemetery of small graves. In spite of the slow growth "eastward" of the cemetery of small graves, the tombs of the headmen were getting farther and farther away; and minor members and adherents of the chief family, especially the funerary priests, must have long since wished to occupy with their small graves the vacant spaces between the large mastabas. By this time, the end of Dyn. III, the grave types iv a and iv b with stone-roofed wells had degenerated into the simple pit type iv c which is so difficult to distinguish from the similar pit grave, type v f of the middle of Dyn. IV. Certainly after the burial of the headman of N 689 and perhaps later than that of his wife in N 688, small graves of type iv c (or v f) began to be intruded in the space between N 573 + 587 and N 689.

Soon after the beginning of the intrusion between N 573 + 587 and N 689, after the burial of the owner of N 688, and early in Dyn. IV, a more important family group was founded between N 689 and N 688 with the medium-sized shaft mastaba N 629 (type v d (I)). This group grew by the addition of two medium-sized shaft mastabas, N 579 (type v d (I)) and N 577 (type v c), followed by the small tombs N 579 (type v b) and N 578 (type v b), both attached to N 577, and then N 614 (type v f) and N 580 (corbel type v a). This group extended well into Dyn. IV and was begun about the same time as the large mastaba N 561 b.

While these two intrusive groups were being founded and in the early stages of their growth, the fourth and next large mastaba, N 561 b (type IV C), was built about 8 metres "east" of N 688 and with its "southern" face on a line with the "northern" face of N 688. In between a small knoll was left empty. The fifth large mastaba, N 739 (type V A), was built on a contiguous site immediately "east" of N 561 b and very close to it in time. It seems to me that these two belong to the same generation although N 561 b was made first, perhaps as much as ten or fifteen years before N 739. I believe this pair again represents man and wife, and that the man was buried in N 739, being the fourth headman in the series. In his burial chamber was a diorite bowl on which the Horus-name of Sneferuw was scratched, proving that the man lived in that reign although he may have died as late as the early part of the reign of Chephren.

After the construction of N 561 b and the burial of its owner, the knoll which had been left empty between N 688 b and N 561 b was taken by a medium-sized mastaba, N 645 (corbel type v a), N a 351 (type v f), and N a 352 (corbel type v a). Burials in the older "western" cemetery had nearly ceased, and the ground "north" of the mastabas N 689 and N 688 began to be occupied by graves of types v d (I), v f, v a, and v b.

After the construction of N 739, the chief locus of growth in the cemetery was north of N 739 and N 561 b in a large complex of small c.b. [crude-brick] mastabas very many of which were entirely intact. The two nucleus graves were first N 786 (type v c) and N 788 + 789 (types v c and v a). There were 12 mastabas in this complex, 8 of type v a (corbel), 2 of type v c (built chamber and shaft), and 2 of v b (arched vault). Two other graves of type v f were one earlier and one later than the complex. The old cemetery continued growing by the interspersion of small graves of type iv c or v f.

At some point during the formation of the complex "north" of N 561 b, the sixth and last of the large mastabas (N 610) was built on a long knoll which ran roughly "E-W." N 610 was 17 metres long, considerably larger than N 739. The subsoil "east" of N 739 was soft and the surface although level enough for about 10 metres dropped beyond that to a water-channel and farther "east" the ground was broken by ridges and slopes. It is clear that the builders of N 610 selected the best possible site available at the time. They were forced to adjust their mastaba to the form and trend of the knoll so that the mastaba itself was of irregular rhomboidal form ("E" end, 13.4 m.; "W," 8.8 m.), orientated "E-W" instead of "N-S," and had an internal offering chapel on the "western" end of the "S" face instead of the "southern" end of the "W" face. The position of the offering room is that of a mastaba built on the "west" bank of the Nile, although this mastaba faces "south" instead of "E." Normally the "west" bank mastabas face "E." The orientation of the mastabas of the first six dynasties conformed to the direction of the valley and the offering rooms were on the side facing the approach from the valley (the land of the living). Thus the orientation of the mastaba (and the grave) was based on functional considerations (convenience in bringing offering to the dead) and was not laid down by ritualistic rules. The internal offering chapel in N 610 is the earliest found at Naga-'d-Dêr. This type of chapel was introduced at Giza in the reconstructions of the mastabas built for the sons and daughters of Cheops. As originally constructed all the mastabas of the unified plan in the Cheops royal cemetery had been designed for external chapels and some of them were so constructed; but the cores of many of them had been cut out behind the "southern" niche and internal chapels inserted. N 610 is of different form with the chief niche enlarged by a complicated variation of the brickwork into a cruciform room. This form of niche-room is well known from c.b. mastabas at Medûm, Giza, and Saqqarah. The Saqqarah mastabas prove its use in Dyn. III, but many of the other examples are from the first two reigns of Dyn. IV. Just across the valley from Naga-'d-Dêr, at Reqaqna, Prof. Garstang found two tombs with this niche-room, R 62 and R 64, both of about the same date as N 739. R 64 was the tomb of the king's scribe, Shepses, and contained a diorite bowl inscribed with the name of Sneferuw. N 610 is manifestly a generation later than N 739 and was, I take it, the tomb of the fifth headman of the community, the last to be buried in Cemetery N 500–900, probably some time in the reign of Chephren. In addition, N 764, added to the "eastern" end of N 610, contained, I believe, the grave of the wife of this headman. There was certainly no further site left on the wady bank suitable for a large mastaba. With the spread of knowledge of quarrying, it was now possible for the well-to-do men of Upper Egypt to cut chambers and shafts in the limestone which is here of a very good quality although with two intervening strata of *tufl* (geological clay). Just "north" of N 500–900 stands a limestone hill which separates our cemetery from the sloping plain the "western" edge of which was taken by Cemetery N 3000 (Dyn. II). On this plain "east" of Cemetery N 3000 stands a small group of crude-brick mastabas of medium size each of which has a shaft grave with shaft and chamber cut in the limestone. These are of Dyn. V. Above, the rock slopes up to a cliff and above the first cliff rises a second slope terminated by a second cliff. In the upper cliff have been excavated the earliest of the rock-cut chapels also with rock-cut burial shafts. It is probably in these mastabas with rock-cut shafts and in these early cliff tombs that the continuation of the cemetery of headmen is to be found.

At this point, about the end of Dyn. IV, the change in burial custom took place, probably an advance in the process of mummification, which produced the more extended burial on the left side with the knees bent, and with it brought in the long wooden coffin with the long shaft and the long burial chamber. The rest of the Cemetery N 500–900 is filled with the graves of this new type (Dyn. V–VI). These graves of type vi a-d lie in rows after the manner of family groups. It was therefore of the same character as the old "western" cemetery, growing in family groups, each founded by a nucleus grave. Judging by position and by contents, the latest appear to be in the "NE" quarter, and the cemetery probably tended to grow "westwards," "eastwards," and "northwards." Toward the "west," twenty-six graves were intruded in the outskirts of the cemetery of headmen as far as N 689. Traces were found of crude-brick mastabas over several of these graves and the spacing indicates that all of them had been surmounted by mastabas of some sort. In Cemetery N 3500 there were a number of pit graves with small oval mounds of mud-plastered rubble as mastabas, and it may be that part of the type vi graves under discussion were covered by similar mounds. In Cemetery N 100, some of the rock-cut tombs which entered the steep slope of the hill-side were crowned with crude-brick mastabas built on the slope just above, and possibly some similar type was used in Cem. N 500–900 for the graves cut in the steep slope of the gravel. With these graves of type vi, we have reached Dyn. V; but, in spite of the rock-cut tombs of this period, all the graves in Cem. N 500–900 have been cut in gravel. This fact is a clear indication of the poverty of the community, but the contents of the graves do not indicate any greater poverty than is indicated by the contents of the small graves of Dyn. III and IV in this same cemetery. There are no more large tombs like the tombs of the headmen; but the mass of the community appears to have held to the old traditional burial-place down to the end of Dyn. VI. There are a few graves later than this but they are intrusive and may not belong to the same community. It is improbable that the community came to an end of Dyn. VI although it may have shifted its dwelling-place to another site. Archaeologically the graves in the cliffs of the intermediate period present the continuation of the graves of type vi in Cemetery N 500–900, and probably the later graves of our community are in the rock-cut tombs of the slopes of Cemetery 100 under the large cliff tombs of the chief men.

It is now possible to reconstruct in imagination the appearance of Cemetery N 500–900 at the various stages of its history. The cemetery was in use for four or five centuries, and as it grew from "SW" to "NE," the older graves were neglected and fell into decay. Thus the appearance was constantly changing always with a new and well-kept portion from which the tombs gradually changed with different degrees of neglect to a part which lay in utter ruin, battered down by wind, sun, and an occasional rainstorm. Let us imagine the cemetery as it was at the end of Dyn. III when the main part was in its best condition. The wady bank was covered with a dense maze of crude-brick mastabas whitened with plaster (sulphate of lime), in places built one against the other (family groups). Each tomb had a small offering-place around its southern niche; and narrow paths between the tombs led to each of these offering-places. Farther east, a group of white stairway mastabas presented larger blocks rising slightly above the skyline of the small "western" mastabas; and beyond these the large mastabas N 573 + 587, N 599, N 689, and N 688 lifted their whitened masses to a height of 1 or 2 metres above the ground. Imagine an irregular conglomeration of rectangular white blocks rising higher and higher up the wady bank—a village of the dead which in the early dawn on the great festivals of the dead was thronged with living offerers. Already the white was broken by black spots in the early "western" part where here and there a neglected mastaba had fallen into decay.

A century or so later, the white cemetery of Dyn. III–IV had reached its extreme limit at Mastaba N 610 + 764. The area covered was greater.

The spaces between the great tombs of the headmen had been filled with smaller mastabas and the fresh group "north" of N 561 b was complete. All the "western" end of the cemetery was shining white including probably the great stairway mastabas, and N 585 with its subsidiary group. The newer small mastabas of type iv c and v f were also well kept. But the old "western" cemetery was mostly in ruins, and no doubt the older large mastabas showed signs of decay.

Another century or two and the cemetery of small mastabas of type vi had covered the higher part of the wady bank above N 739 and N 610 + 764 with its dull irregular mounds, all of which were plastered with mud though some were whitened. It may be assumed that the early "western" cemetery was in utter ruin, and all but the latest of the large mastabas in much the same state. The offering services of N 561 b, N 739, and N 610 may have been maintained for twenty-five to fifty years after the burial of their owners and the mastabas kept more or less in repair. But by the end of Dyn. VI all the mastabas, large and small, of Dyn. II–IV had without doubt been abandoned to the weather.

The decay of this white cemetery is not without interest to the archaeologist. The first marked result of weathering was the disappearance of the white plaster, which shaled off and fell on the ground around the mastabas. Then the upper part of the crude-brick walls began to crumble and filled the spaces between and round the mastabas with black earth (Nile mud). As these retaining walls decayed the gravel or other filling of the mastaba began to leak out on top of the black earth around the mastaba. When the accumulation of the debris around the mastaba reached the height of the crude-brick walls now partially decayed, these walls were protected against further rapid decay. At this point, the surface of the cemetery consisted of mounds (the filling of the mastabas held by the walls as preserved) and small hollows (the former spaces between the mastabas). The mounds were high or low according to the original height and size of the mastabas, still contained in their debris. The next step was a slow equalization of the inequalities of the surface by weathering and in particular by heavy rainfall which occurs periodically (I think about every ten years) at Naga-'d-Dêr. This not only washes down the tops of the mounds and fills in the hollows but it also cleans the surface and tends to conceal the walls buried in the debris. When sufficiently heavy to produce streams of water, these cut down the whole surface and in some cases the decayed tops of the buried walls. In fact, I know of cases where rain water has actually denuded a cemetery below the original surface and removed every trace of the superstructures, and in one case cut down a whole plain by a metre or more below the old surface. The "eastern" part of Cemetery 500–900 was in the stage of weathering described above with the ruined mastabas buried in the debris and the burial chambers intact. The area of group j had been denuded below the old level and all remains of super-

structures swept away; but the weathering of the surface had also removed all evidence of the presence of graves and a majority of the graves
of group j had escaped plundering.

The next stage in the decay of the cemetery was the first plundering
directed to the recovery of the precious metals (above all gold) from the
tombs. When a tomb is known certainly to contain gold, the first plundering takes place almost immediately in the same or the next generation. It
is to be noted that the intact tombs (in particular the large mastabas N 561
b and N 739) contained no gold in their intact chambers. The large stairway mastabas were all completely plundered by thieves who manifestly
worked undisturbed, I think a century or more after the placing of the
burials. Probably at this same time, a search was made of the smaller
graves also. Many of them have been entirely cleared out. The search for
gold was probably repeated in a desultory way from time to time through
the centuries. All these surreptitious excavations resulted in a certain
amount of earth thrown out of the burial pits and shafts to lie on the surface and weather slowly away. Then some time about the fifth century
A.D. or a little later, a Christian community began burying its dead in long
narrow pits which ran "E-W." Similar Coptic graves were found all over
the "southern" part of the Naga-'d-Dêr field. At the present there is a
Coptic monastery on the "southern" edge of the village of Naga-'d-Dêr
and beside it a large cemetery used by the Coptic community of Girga.
These old Coptic burials in Cemetery N 500–900 were the cause of considerable damage to ancient structures and deposits and above all they
broke up the hard old surface and hastened the denudation of the "western" part of the cemetery. In recent times, 1880 to 1900, the *fellahîn* of
Naga-'d-Dêr had regularly excavated *sebakh* for fertilizing material in
the middle and "western" parts of the cemetery. During this work, they
came on a number of stone vessels which found a ready market with a
merchant of Girga who engaged in the traffic in antiquities as a side line;
and a desultory search for antiquities was in progress in Cemetery N 500–
900 and elsewhere when we arrived and stopped it for the time being.

During the long period Dyn. II–VI, covered by the graves of Cemetery
N 500–900, Egypt passed through the culmination of its greatest cultural
period and produced an enormous number of wonderful monuments,
many of which are still preserved to us. The great royal cemeteries near
Memphis extending from Medûm on the south to Abu Roash on the north
contain the pyramids and temples of Zoser (the step pyramid of Saqqarah), the step pyramid at Medûm, the two great stone pyramids at
Dashûr one of which is the tomb of Sneferuw, the unfinished tomb of
Sa-nekht at Zawiat-el-Aryan with the finished pyramid of a contemporary
king beside it, the pyramids of Cheops, Chephren, and Mycerinus at
Giza, and the pyramid of Radedef at Abu Roash. Around each of these
great pyramids stand the tombs of the royal princes and the great nobles,

many of which are famous in the modern world for the beauty of their reliefs and paintings. Furthermore the majority of the finest sculptures in the museums were found in the tombs and the chapels of this period—the Chephren statue, the Nycerinus statues, the "Sheikh-el-Beled," the statues of Prince Rahotep and his wife, and literally hundreds of statues and statuettes of other persons. Memphis appears as one of the most brilliant of the courts of history, the product of the greatest of the ancient civilizations of the world. Of all this glory practically nothing was reflected in the daily life of our obscure agricultural community at Naga-'d-Dêr. Men heard tales no doubt told by casual passers-by and perhaps some had been carried off to Memphis to work on the heavy jobs of pulling and hauling. But the products of the great arts and crafts were not for the people of our village. They found the crude brick of their ancestors sufficient for their needs and held to the old materialism that placed in the burial chamber the objects used in life together with actual food and drink. Their periodic offerings to the dead were made in real food and drink as it still is among the *fellahîn;* and offering formulas learned by heart were of course recited. At Giza and Saqqarah the contemporary tombs have elaborately sculptured and painted walls which provide the scenes of daily life, pictures of offerings and lists of food and drink. At Cemetery N 500–900 it is not until Dyn. V–VI that any writing appears attached to the superstructure of the tomb, and then only a few pitiful flakes of limestone with the name and title rudely scratched on the surface. Yet this little community was not standing still. In the commoner objects of daily use it almost kept pace with the centres of Egyptian culture, probably because many things were manufactured at the great centres and distributed to rich and poor alike in payment for grain, cattle, hides, and similar standard necessities produced by the soil. The development of the types of large tombs from the corbel-vault with stairway through the true stairway mastaba to the shaft mastaba was the same, perhaps slightly delayed, as the development of large tombs in the great cities. The development of the small tombs is almost the most rapid and the richest in its variations which is to be met in the Nile Valley. It presents a great contrast to the provincial cemeteries of the Middle and New Kingdoms when for centuries no change in the form of the tomb can be distinguished. The community of our cemetery was an ordinary provincial community, poor enough, but with plenty to eat and drink after the taxes were paid, and probably enough to buy such goods as the merchants of the local market town imported from the great centres of manufacture. I conceive them as living much as such a community of *fellahîn* live to-day, travelling once a week to the local market, paying their ferry-fares with loaves of bread, and haggling the day through with some merchant, exchanging grain or other produce in small quantities for cloth, pots and pans, leather sandals, baskets, or whatever else was beyond the skill of the village craftsmen. They were in no hurry and the bargaining might go on for weeks over the same object. And many a man went, not because he had any business, but to amuse himself with the activity of the crowd. I daresay that every market provided other less healthful amusements for those with the means to pay. The excavation of Cemetery N 500–900 was an unimportant piece of work as far as beautiful finds are concerned, but nevertheless it gives us the under side of the brilliant picture presented by the royal monuments of Giza and Saqqarah.

Seriation Analysis of Pottery Collections

A research team, made up of Philip Phillips, James A. Ford, and James B. Griffin, made an archaeological survey of the lower Mississippi River valley in the 1940's. Ford, who had earlier evinced an interest in surface seriation as an archaeological technique (1938), was the principal author of the following selection from their report.[4] This account is noteworthy both for its clear exposition of the assumptions involved in the method as well as for its use of stratigraphic evidence to validate the results of the surface seriation.

Now the 346,099 sherds from 383 sites, collected by the Lower Mississippi Survey and duly classified as described in Section III, could be stored away in cabinets and forgotten for the time being. The data were safely on paper and time would heal our wounded consciences and dim our suspicions that at several points our classification was less than perfect. During the winter of 1947 Phillips turned to the problems of physiography, and the identification of historic sites; Griffin began the description of pottery types; and Ford started work on analysis assisted and checked at every point by his somewhat fearful colleagues.

The basic assumptions which served as a foundation for the analytical procedure need to be stated in some detail. They will help to explain the procedure followed and it is hoped will prevent the reader from accepting the conclusions in an any more "positive" sense than the writers intend. We consider these assumptions as a set of probabilities which lead to conclusions that are our best guesses. Not that we intend to apologize for this admission. This we think is the real method of science. We are trying to expose our limitations and are not setting out to prove anything beyond all doubt.

A. In the portion of the Mississippi Valley which was surveyed and for the greater part of the span of history which is being studied, the aboriginal people were presumably agriculturists. The population was rather

---

[4] P. Phillips, J. A. Ford, and J. B. Griffin, *Archaeological Survey in the Lower Mississippi Alluvial Valley, 1940–1947*, Papers of the Peabody Museum, Harvard University, Cambridge, 1951, vol. 25, pp. 219–233. By permission of J. O. Brew, Director of the Peabody Museum, Harvard University.

numerous, as will be shown later, and was collected in small villages. For these reasons it seems reasonable to think that there was comparative stability of peoples. These Indians did not wander as did the historic Indians of the Plains, and from the archaeological evidence, there seems to have been little or none of the frantic shifting of tribes that marks the post-contact history of the Eastern Indians. We are assuming then until the evidence indicates the contrary that the people who carried the cultural traits we are studying were probably relatively stable geographically and that for the most part population changes were slow gradual ones.

B. While the prehistoric populations were comparatively stable in the larger geographic sense, this does not appear to have been true of the great majority of village sites. Some sites were inhabited throughout the time span which is being studied. Most, however, were occupied for a short time in proportion to the entire chronology. This assumption was based on archaeological experience in other parts of the Southeast and on a preliminary glance over the collections gathered in this survey. The condition seems to be due to the limitations of the agricultural methods and equipment of the Indians. After a field had been cleared and used for crops for a few years, the grass and weeds probably moved in and took over. With the inefficient tools which the Southeastern Indians had, control of this vegetation very likely became so difficult after a few years that it was easier to ring and burn trees for a new field than it was to continue planting in the old one. In the course of a few decades, when all the desirable agricultural land in the vicinity of a village had been opened up to weeds in this fashion, the village would have to be moved to a new location. This was the practice of the Southeastern tribes in the early Historic Period before they acquired plows, and such names as "Chickasaw Old Fields" and "Tuckabachee Old Fields" undoubtedly refer to such weed-grown abandoned land.

The securing of short time-span collections is essential if the method of seriating of surface collections is to be successfully applied. For this reason, careful attention was paid to the combinations of sherd material which were gathered from various parts of each village site. In the course of field work, where it was evident that one portion of a site yielded a different complex from that found on another part, two or more separate collections were made. These were labeled "A," "B," etc., and were treated all through the course of analysis as though they came from different sites. A cross section of the ceramic styles in vogue at these different sites at one instant in time would have been the ideal material for seriation purposes, but that, of course, is an unattainable goal.

C. The third assumption has already been stated in the foregoing section on ceramic classification. Until the evidence suggests differently, we are assuming that in any large area cultural continuity in both time and space is to be expected as the normal state of affairs. A gradual change of feature with the passage of time and across the area, when it is viewed on any one time horizon, was our very idealized concept of the cultural history with which we are dealing. This does not mean that we did not anticipate the possibility of finding evidence of (1) the replacement of one population bearing a certain variety of culture by another population having entirely different customs; (2) the replacement of cultural features through acculturation from sources outside the region in which we are working; or (3) the specializing of cultural complexes in certain regions due to their being protected from the prevailing patterns of the area as a whole by such factors as geographical isolation, peculiarities of population distribution, linguistic barriers, or political groupings. These conditions were some of the things of which we expected to get hints from our study.

So we did not begin our analysis with any assumption that changes in ceramics, such as the shift from clay- to shell-tempering, necessarily indicate any abrupt cultural or population replacement. If the refuse deposits of the two time periods really should have a layer of clean white sand separating them after the classic model of stratigraphy, we wanted to be shown by the evidence.

D. Our fourth basic assumption has also been stated in the discussion of ceramic typology. We are assuming that each of our pottery types is a more or less sensitive instrument for measuring cultural change with the passage of time and distribution over space. We are a little complacent about this assumption and feel that we are on fairly certain grounds because we went to great pains to set up and adapt each type for exactly those purposes. Rearranging, merging, and splitting of type groups were guided by preliminary analysis and the resultant information about chronological relations.

However, as has been made clear in the type descriptions, all of the types are not equally well adapted for this purpose. Because of the practical difficulties of making distinctions, some of the types, especially the undecorated ones, include material that represents long spans of time and large amounts of area. In other examples we are aware that the original concepts have changed during the classifying so that the resultant categories are somewhat broader than would have been desired. Mazique Incised is an example of this latter kind of type weakness. Despite this, we feel that we are fairly aware of this factor and thus have it under reasonable control.

E. The next point to be considered is not a basic assumption but rather a logical derivative of the preceding discussions. It has to do with the relative popularity of types through time. If our pottery types are successful measuring units for a continuous stream of changing cultural ideas, it follows that when the relative popularity of these types is graphed through time, a more or less long, single-peak curve will usually result. Put in another way, a type will first appear in very small percentages, will gradually increase to its maximum popularity, and then, as it is replaced by its succeeding type, will gradually decrease and disappear.

This interesting phenomena can be illustrated by endless examples taken from any span of culture history. Consider the popularity curve of the "Charleston" dance fad in the United States. A specific political concept, a particular word, or any other carefully defined cultural type will show the same popularity curve that Spier found in the history of Zuñi pottery.

This is an interesting phenomenon but do not let us be misled. We have not discovered a natural law operating independently of our own humble efforts. This peculiar characteristic of type popularity distribution through time is something we have helped to bring about through our own conceptualization of the pottery types that manifest said behavior. How the curves come out is partly controlled by how the types are defined.

F. The sixth assumption is also a derivative of the foregoing discussions. If a complex of cultural materials representing a space-time continuum of culture history is classified in a consistent manner, the popularity curves of the various constituent types will form a pattern. Each portion of this pattern will be peculiar to a particular time and area. This concept may best be illustrated from contemporary culture. Lacking accurate data, as this sort of information is usually ignored by historians, let us manufacture some for purposes of illustration. Let us say that in the State of Ohio in the year 1920, the following were the relative popularities of the indicated types of travel for distances over 5 miles:

	Per Cent
Walking	5
Steamboats	5
Riding horses	5
Automobiles	20
Horse and buggy	15
Airplanes	2
Gasoline-powered boats	5
Railways	43

Here is a ratio of popularity of transportation types which will never be exactly repeated in Ohio or anywhere else.

Now let us take a look at a supposed history of the relative popularity of transportation types in Ohio for a period extending sometime before and after 1920 (see Fig. 11.3). Not only is the pattern different for each ten-year interval, but the quantitative picture of this stretch of culture history is a unique thing. The pattern of the popularity peaks of the different transportation types have never been repeated. A similar graph for Texas would doubtless show larger popularity of horse-riding. There wouldn't have been any steamboat travel at all in Utah. Indiana would

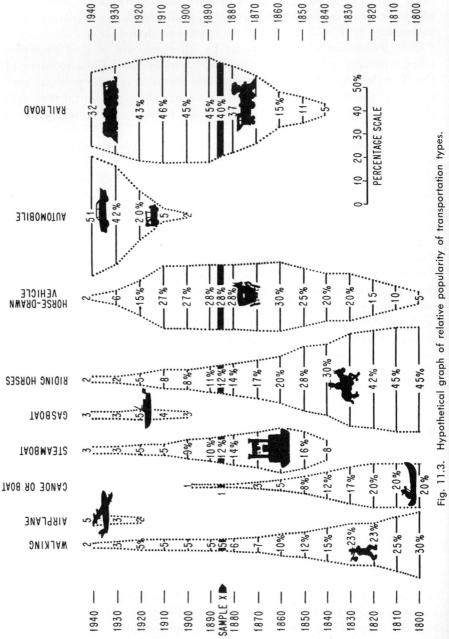

Fig. 11.3. Hypothetical graph of relative popularity of transportation types.

show the same type as Ohio but in differing quantities and temporal relations.

So long as we maintain our classifications strictly as they are, we may review any number of representative samples of Ohio transportation history, and the same frequency pattern will result. The only way in which the pattern might be changed would be to change the classification. This can be done in a number of different ways. Let us show a few:

1. Travel without vehicles
   Vehicles that travel on land
   Vehicles that travel on water
   Vehicles that travel in air
2. Man-powered travel
   Animal-powered travel
   Steam-powered travel
   Gasoline-powered travel
   Electric-powered travel
3. Travel 0–5 miles an hour
   Travel 5–10 miles an hour
   etc.

Note that in each case where the classification is rearranged, the quantitative-historical picture would be completely different. This is not to say that it would be any more true or false than the scheme which we illustrated in Fig. 11.3. All of these classifications will measure time change in a cultural feature. The point of interest to the classifier is that the first scheme with the finer type divisions will do the job a little more accurately than the others. Still finer divisions which will do even better jobs will occur to the reader.

While this fanciful illustration is set up, let us go a little farther and show how the dating and seriation techniques that will be discussed later will work. Suppose that we have a sample of the transportation habits of the Ohioans for an unknown date which showed the following percentages of popularity:

	Per Cent
Walking	5
Riding horses	12
Horse and buggy	28
Paddling and rowing boats	1
Steamboats	12
Automobiles	0
Airplanes	0
Railway	40

When this information is graphed after the fashion used in Fig. 11.3, and the graph is placed on this chronology, it will be seen that the type frequencies of this sample, which we may as well call "X," will fit the chronology at only one point. As our figure shows, it dates about 1885.

Let us suppose again that we are faced with a situation in which we are merely provided with frequency data on the transportation customs of Ohio for a number of years. We do not know the dates of these samples and have no idea as to their chronological sequence. We can't get a complete history out of this data but we can do something. By rearranging our samples, we can find the type frequency pattern and the relative order of the samples. We will not know the calendrical dates of the samples, the relative lengths of time occupied by the various sections of the chronology, or even which end of the chronology is the most recent in time, but we can develop the quantitative-historical pattern. This, in effect, is the seriation technique we have used.

This rather far-fetched bit of imaginary analysis is only worth-while if it brings out the point that systematic classification of cultural data representing a particular range of time creates in each case a characteristic quantitative pattern. We had this in mind as our sherds from the Mississippi Valley area were classified, and the analytical procedure that will be described were the steps which were taken in search of these patterns.

G. Two more assumptions which we have made may be grouped together. We have assumed that our sampling of sites in each part of our Survey Area has been sufficiently thorough. We think that we have secured a sample of the pottery which was made during each stage of the chronologies which we will present so that no large time gaps remain unrepresented.

We are also guessing that a random sample of over fifty sherds is sufficient to indicate the proportionate type frequencies existing in the refuse from which the material was collected. A total of fifty is considered to be usable, but not particularly reliable. One hundred is much better and every sherd above one hundred is all to the good. It will be noted that some of our collections are quite large.

The foregoing assumptions which we made at the start of the analytical work, and which we intended to act upon until the evidence indicated that they were wrong, may be summarized as follows:

A. The distribution of prehistoric populations of the Survey Area was relatively stable.

B. The majority of the village sites were probably inhabited for a short time as compared to the entire time with which we are dealing.

C. The culture of the area in the main probably changed gradually rather than by means of mass migration from other areas.

D. If propositions A and C were true, the pottery types which we had defined would each show a single-peak popularity curve when measured through time, but the duration of such peaks, and the resulting curves, would vary from one type to another.

E. If D is true, then all the pottery-type frequency curves would be different in each part of the area on each time horizon, and a distinct pattern will appear when each part of the area is viewed through time.

F. Our sampling technique has been successful in getting samples representing continuous segments of time in all parts of the area and also in securing enough material from the sites which we will treat to give a more or less reliable picture of the material available on the surface.

ANALYTICAL PROCEDURE

The first step in our ceramic analysis was a simple and tedious one. On the sheets which recorded the classification of the material from each collection, the totals of these collections were run up on an adding machine, and the percentages of each type calculated by slide rule. The "Unclassified" sherds were included in these totals. This was done for all surface collections which contained more than fifty sherds, as well as for each level in the stratigraphic excavations.

Then a roll of graph paper marked with a centimeter-millimeter grid was secured. On a piece of this paper a "key" was prepared very carefully. This key indicated the position of the axis of each type from which bars showing the relative frequency of the types were to be drawn. The best spacing of the types along the key was something that had to be developed in the course of the analysis to prevent overlapping of the frequency bars.

After the first key was worked out, the type frequency data for each collection was placed on a 5-centimeter-wide strip graph. This second step was also a routine mechanical matter and took some time to accomplish, particularly as this work several times pointed out defects in the positions of the types on the key. When the key was changed, all strip graphs made with the old key had to be discarded. Finally, however, all of the classification data was in this graphic form.

While this work was underway, the classification data was being analyzed in another way by several student assistants at the American Museum. This was a distributional study of type frequencies. For each type a sheet of tracing cloth was placed over a map showing all site locations. Then, the percentage frequency of the type at each site, say Mulberry Creek Cord-marked for example, was recorded in its proper geographical position on the traced map. Now, if the above-discussed assumptions are correct, that the average village site was inhabited for a relatively short period (see assumption B, above), and that our Survey work has gathered a sample of the material from sites representing each time period in all parts of the area (F, above), then in each part of the Survey Area there should be sites which show Mulberry Creek Cord-marked near or at its popularity peak. Other sites, which cover time ranges before or after the maximum popularity of the type, will, of course, show their occurrence in smaller percentages. With all of this in mind, the completed distribution maps of Mulberry Creek Cord-marked were inspected with particular attention to maximum occurrences. It was seen that it would be possible to draw lines which would enclose maximums in descending order, after the fashion of contour lines. If we wished to coin a new word and help our science to become more profound, we might call these "Iso-ceramic Lines"—but let's not.

These distributional studies made plain something which we knew already from classifying the material: there would be both quantitative and qualitative variation at all time periods in the different parts of the Survey Area. They also showed something else which we had suspected would be true. Regional specialization tended to increase with the passage of time so that late complexes from the northern and southern ends of our Survey were more unlike than were the early. This is a common phenomenon for cultures at this stage of development and seems to be owing to factors such as decreased population mobility due to an increased dependence on agriculture; the establishment of more stable centers, such as ceremonial mound groups and towns; and an increase in the cohesion of political groupings made possible and necessitated by the improved food supply and consequent population increase; to which was added the increased availability of cultural ideas which could be combined to form "new" varieties.

With this data in hand, it was decided that the practical way in which to treat the chronology of the Survey Area would be to divide it up into sub-areas based on the differences that could be observed in the material of the latest time horizons. A chronological column could then be worked out for each sub-area and comparisons between the areas could be made at the different time levels. We realized that the procedure which we were adopting was fully as arbitrary, and indeed was of the same kind of high-handed ruthlessness as were our decisions in regard to ceramic classification. We are again preparing to set up artificial boundaries, which this time are geographically defined, and draw the borderline cases back toward the selected concepts.

From the beginning, the Lower St. Francis River area in Arkansas looked like a "natural" for a "Focal Grouping." Here are a number of highly similar sites, already known in archaeological literature (Parkin, Rose Mound, etc.), that seemed to stand off by themselves. This happy condition was improved by the fact that Survey work was not extended very far up the St. Francis River above these sites, so we were ignorant of any gradual transition toward any different-appearing complex in that direction. All the arbitrary decisions which would trouble us lay to the south and east. Ignorance and a classical tradition; it couldn't be better. We immediately set up a Lower St. Francis area and accepted the sites in quadrangles 11-N and 12-N as appropriate for starting chronological analysis.

The second area also looked good. Its literary background is provided by Calvin Brown's description of the material from the Walls Site near Memphis. The material from this and a number of closely related sites differed in a number of respects from the typical St. Francis area complex. That this distinction proved to be partly due to difference in time does not lessen the initial lure of the situation. A *Memphis area* was defined and the sites included in quadrangles 13-O, 13-P, 14-O and 14-P were taken as nuclear for starting the analysis.

We had a little more difficulty about the other three areas which were eventually set up. The literary background did not focus our attention so effectively, and we knew a little too much about "transitional" sites and material. After several false starts the following areas and beginning quadrangles were selected (see Fig. 11.4):

St. Francis Basin   11-N, 12-N
Memphis area   13-O, 13-P, 14-O, 14-P
Sunflower area   16-N, 16-O, 17-N, 17-O
Lower Yazoo Basin area   19-M, 19-N, 20-M, 20-N
Lower Arkansas River area 16-K, 16-L, 17-K, 17-L

It must be emphasized again that these areas have been set up solely for purposes of seriation and are therefore not to be confused with "foci" in the Midwestern taxonomic sense, or any other sort of cultural grouping.

It will be seen that the starting quadrangles for each area are geographically separated from the starting quadrangles of the other areas. This was intentional and was for the purpose of emphasizing the differences. The borderline cases were dealt with later as will be described.

By the time the study had reached this stage, we already had at hand considerable information as to the outlines of the ceramic chronologies in the region. One source of information was the sequences which had been worked out in the adjoining regions by Webb and his associates in northern Alabama; Jennings along the Natchez Trace Parkway in north-central Mississippi; Ford and his co-workers around the mouth of the Red River in Louisiana. A second very essential source of information were the stratigraphic excavations made by Phillips and Griffin, described in detail in a later section of this report. These revealed portions of the ceramic histories which could be used as partial backbone for the chronologies. Our third source of information was the preliminary seriation analyses which we had made while classifying the site collections. So we had a rather good idea as to the relative time positions and distributions of many of the ceramic types. Despite this, the analytical procedures described here were followed out in detail, so far as possible, as though we had been completely innocent of such fore-knowledge.

Five sheets of heavy paper about 48 inches long and 20 inches wide were laid out on a large table side by side. The 20-inch width of these sheets corresponded to the length of the strip graphs which recorded the

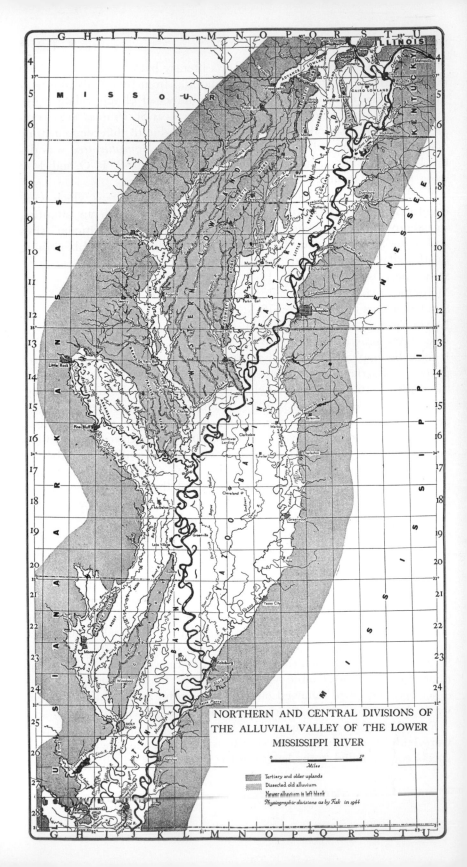

NORTHERN AND CENTRAL DIVISIONS OF
THE ALLUVIAL VALLEY OF THE LOWER
MISSISSIPPI RIVER

Miles
0   50

Tertiary and older uplands
Dissected old alluvium
Newer alluvium is left blank
Physiographic divisions as by Fisk in 1944

type frequencies of each collection. Each of these sheets was headed with the name of one of the seriation areas, and they were placed on the table in the geographical relation of the areas from north to south. Then all of the strip graphs that represented collections from sites included in the quadrangles that served as the nucleus, or starting point, were separated out and placed on the appropriate sheet. The strips were laid horizontally across the sheets and were held in place at the edges by paper clips. As they were arranged and rearranged, particular care was taken to see that the type axes coincided.

We were now ready to begin the search for the quantitative patterning of pottery types, which for reasons that have been discussed in the foregoing, should exist in the area chronologies. This work was started with site collections of the Lower Yazoo Basin area. These were relatively easy to seriate as two stratigraphic excavations were available to serve as guides for part of the history. The deepest of these excavations, Jaketown (20–0–1) Cut A, had fourteen levels and seemed to cover the greatest range of time. Accordingly, the strip graphs representing these levels were arranged on the sheet in the order in which they had come from the ground and immediately showed the frequency patterning for the time covered by the cut. The strips representing the second strata excavation, Shell Bluff (19–0–2) Cut A, were next put in place. The graph of the top level of this cut was slid along the sheet of paper until a point was found at which all its type frequencies best fitted the corresponding frequencies of the Jaketown cut. It was clear that the second level at Shell Bluff was older than the top level, but we could not know how much older it was in relation to the picture given by the Jaketown cut. Consequently, the second-level graph was placed below the first and slid downward until the best fit was secured.

Vertical arrangement of the material in the ground gave some control over the collections from the stratigraphic pits, and we knew that the collections from the lower levels had to be older than those from the upper. However, for the surface collections we had no such guide. All we had was our assumption that the majority of these surface collections represented relatively short spans of time (see B, above) and the logic which led us to think that a quantitative patterning must be there.

The surface-collection graphs were taken one at a time and compared with the beginning that had been made with the stratigraphic material. If they fitted somewhere along the time represented by the excavations, the graph was fastened down to the backing sheet with paper clips. If percentages of such late types as Neeley's Ferry Plain and Bell Plain were too large, and proportions of such older types as Baytown Plain, Larto Red Filmed, and Mulberry Creek Cord-marked were too small, the

Fig. 11.4 (*Facing*). Areas of the Lower Mississippi River Valley for chronological analysis by seriation.

collection was obviously later and the graph was placed above the excavations. These surface-collection graphs were shifted about in vertical relation to one another until patterning was developed as is shown in the upper part of Fig. 17 [not reproduced here].

The data from the starting quadrangles of the other four seriation areas were dealt with in a similar fashion, Figs. 17–21 [not reproduced here]. Where stratigraphic information was available, it was used as a guide. Where there was none, the surface-collection graphs were shifted about to develop the best patterning that could be secured. In this way the five chronological columns were developed side by side.

The next phase of the analysis was to assign the sites in the intervening quadrangles to one or another of the five areas which had been set up. All of the site-collection graphs for each of these remaining quadrangles were seriated and then compared to the five area graphs. For example, the chronological patterning of quadrangle 18-M looked more like the chronology begun for the Lower Yazoo area than any of the other sub-areas, so the collections from this quadrangle were fed into the Yazoo graph at the points where they fitted best.

Now, the area chronological graphs were virtually complete and good patterning of types could be seen. Apparently, our assumption that most of the surface collections represented relatively short lengths of time was correct. But while the majority did, some obviously did not. In a number of collections, early and late types were associated together in a fashion that showed either that the sites had been occupied for a long time, or there had been reoccupation. In order to clear up the patterning, the strips representing these collections were taken out. The numbers of these long time-span collections as compared to the shorter-lived sites that are used in the final graph are as follows:

Area	Number of Short Time-Span Surface Colls. Used in Finished Graph	Number of Long Time-Span Colls. Taken Out to Clarify Graph
Lower Yazoo Basin	48	1
Lower Arkansas River	19	1
Sunflower	81	9
Memphis	66	7
St. Francis	37	0
Colls. used in graphs	251	Discarded 18

Although eighteen surface collections with respectable sherd totals have been eliminated from the graphs because of the special requirements of this kind of analysis, this does not mean that the effort devoted to these sites has been lost. It may be expected that these are places where rather long spans of history may be examined in stratigraphic relation, if there is any depth to the deposits. So far, tests have been made in one of these sites, 20-0-1 (Jaketown). It was quite evident why surface collections from this site were useless for seriation purposes; the occupation covered practically the full range of ceramic history in the area.

HANDLING OF THE DATA FROM STRATIGRAPHIC EXCAVATIONS

The incorporation of the data from the stratigraphic excavations into this analysis was done in a purely arbitrary fashion. Each level was treated as though it were a separate surface collection from a distinct site, except for the fact that care was taken to keep the levels in proper vertical order. The relation of stratigraphic levels to the soil profiles revealed by the walls of the excavations, which is discussed in detail in the next section of this report, was not worked out at the time this analysis was made, but had it been available would not have received consideration in this phase of the work. The seriation of the data in these five subareas was an attempt to discover the chronological patterning of the pottery types in each region and to reveal the consistency with which the types followed that pattern. In this handling of the data it was expected that such anomalies as the reoccupation of sites after they had been abandoned for any considerable length of time would be revealed by comparison with the evidence given by neighboring sites as to the chronological pattern of each sub-area.

There are some discrepancies between the interpretation given to the stratigraphic data in this section, written mainly by Ford, and the section on Stratigraphy, written by Phillips. These disagreements are not basic differences as to the gross outlines of the chronology; there are no differences as to this. They have to do principally with the problem of whether the evidence indicates that there was a break in the deposition between the Baytown refuse characterized by clay-tempered pottery and the shell-tempered Mississippian deposits. In most cases this involves a question as to whether late Baytown (period D-C) or the early Mississippian Phase (period C-B) is missing in the stratigraphic sequence. With the evidence which we have at present it does not seem possible to resolve these discrepancies to everyone's satisfaction, so we will allow them to stand. However, they can be explained by the fact that Phillips' judgments have been based on detailed examination of the internal evidence supplied by each strata cut while the guesses of Ford have attempted to reconcile the evidence given by both surface and excavated collections.

CO-ORDINATING THE AREA CHRONOLOGIES

We are now in possession of five quantitative graphs representing the ceramic history of the five selected areas. However, these are relative histories. There is no absolute chronological scale by which the appropriate amounts of vertical spacing, which represents time that should be given to the early, middle, or late portions of each can be measured. The best that can be done is to try to correlate them one with another. This was done in the following fashion. Six strings, spaced and running parallel, were stretched from end to end of the table on which the graphs lay. Then portions of the graphs were adjusted up or down until the same types showed comparable relative quantities under the appropriate string. Thus, the third string down from the top, which has become line C on the time scale used in the finished drawings [not reproduced here], was made to mark the point in each graph where Baytown Plain and Neeley's Ferry Plain were about equal, Mulberry Creek Cord-marked had practically disappeared, Bell Plain was just getting a start, and Larto Red Filmed was almost gone. In each case this procedure was a compromise. If the upper portion of the Lower Arkansas graph had been slid downward until all the percentages of Bell Plain were equal to those in the Sunflower and Memphis areas along the C horizon line, then the Baytown-Neeley's Ferry relationship would have been all out of adjustment. All the type patterns were considered in this correlating process and the A to G time-scale arrangement given in the five final graphs is the end result of many compromises. So this scale is presented as a time framework for the chronologies. Time F in the Yazoo area, for example, is supposed to be the same as F in the Lower St. Francis.

The necessity for compromises of this kind was not unexpected. As a matter of fact, they are an inherent part of this kind of cultural analysis. The groups of ideas to whose products have been tagged such names as Mazique Incised did not spring up simultaneously all over the area. They moved from one part to another, and that took time. For example, the ideas of red slipping on clay-tempered vessels (Larto Red Filmed) apparently was moving from south to north through the region, while cord-marking on clay-tempered pots (Mulberry Creek Cord-marked) was moving from northeast to south. Naturally the former is earlier to the south and the latter to the north.

The student who is particularly interested in the history of this area, or of the procedure by which this balancing was done, may check it—if he has the time and patience—by placing the five area graphs [not reproduced here] side by side and following across the relative time position of each type. This process has been a subjective weighing of the evidence provided by each type position and of course is always open to question. As a matter of fact, there has been considerable question as to certain aspects of this arrangement which should receive attention at this point. Griffin and Phillips are of the opinion that the late materials in the Arkansas area actually date somewhat later than they are represented in the graph of that area. They think that the pottery type Wallace Incised probably extends up to the time when the Quapaw were discovered by the French. This opinion is somewhat reinforced by the fact that the type is practically confined to the region in which the Quapaw were described and occurred in appreciable amount in the top levels of two cuts in the Menard Site (17-K-1), and on the surface of the near-by Wallace Site (17-K-3) which there is reason to believe may have been the site of the Quapaw village of Osotouy (Uzutiuhi), first visited by the French in 1686. As additional evidence, Clarence B. Moore excavated burials in the fields near the Menard Site that were accompanied by European material. Admitting that the cemetery excavated by Moore almost certainly is of Quapaw origin, Ford has hesitated to raise the upper part of the Arkansas graph for several reasons. First, to do so would also bring the types which accompany Wallace Incised up to a later date where their proportions would not be consistent with those of the same types in the neighboring areas. Second, Moore's illustrated material does not show any examples of the types Wallace Incised. However, this does not mean that he may not have found such vessels. The third and most convincing point (to Ford) is the fact that Moore does illustrate three vessels of the type Fatherland Incised, the pottery which the Natchez tribe farther down the Mississippi were making about A.D. 1700. In addition, he found "teapot vessels," another trait shared with the Natchez. Neither Fatherland Incised nor any of the late "Caddo" types with which it is normally associated appeared in the Survey collections from the Menard and near-by sites. While far from denying that this vicinity is the likely site of a historic Quapaw village from which Moore sampled the burials, it does not appear likely to Ford that the site collections and uppermost strata levels in our Arkansas area graph represent this historic occupation.

Comparison of the area graphs will show that the late collections in the Memphis area have been allowed to come up to the most recent times. This was practically forced by the large percentage of Bell Plain found on the surfaces of the late sites in that area. In contrast the other areas show much smaller percentages of this type as a very late feature. It is possible, as discussed in the next section, that a part of this Bell Plain is pothunter refuse or is burial ware which has been ripped from graves by cultivation. However, the trends in accompanying types: decrease of Barton Incised, increase of Parkin Punctated, and the appearance of Rhodes Incised and Vernon Paul Applique, suggests that there is a certain consistency to this situation that makes the increase of Bell a significant marker of the passage of time in this area—whatever may be the factors involved.

It is thought that probably none of these columns extend to the beginning of reliable historic documentation about A.D. 1700. This is consistent with the fact that the French explorers of that period indicate that the population of the Mississippi flood-plain area between the mouth of the Yazoo River, where villages of Yazoo and Tunica were found, and the northern limits to which our Survey has extended was very scanty indeed. About the mouth of the Arkansas River were found the Quapaw or Arkansea, and those are the only people who can be placed with any certainty. In the upper drainage of the Yazoo were the Tiou, Chak-chiuma, and Ibitoupa. Swanton estimates that the total of this Upper Yazoo population was less than 1000 people.

This is far from enough people to account for the number of sites which we have dated as occupied during the later Mississippian period, and, in fact, is markedly in contrast to the population picture given by the De Soto narratives for the year 1542 as will be shown in a later section.

Clarence B. Moore found burials accompanied by glass beads and other European material at several sites through the area we have surveyed. The pottery which he illustrates from the Rhodes and Bradley Places is clearly of late Memphis area types, but as Moore's report does not associate the illustrated materials with the burials that are described, it is impossible to state definitely that the European material was found with this complex. Even if it is associated with it, it should be noted that the possibilities for the aborigines acquiring glass beads probably go back somewhat before 1700 in this area, if not back to the period of De Soto's exploration in 1542.

There is some reason to expect that the ceramic complex which prevailed at least as far north as the Sunflower area in 1700 had a small percentage of incised pottery resembling in both decoration and shape the historic Natchez-type Fatherland Incised. It has already been pointed out that Moore found a small proportion of this type associated with European material near the Menard Site. Charles Peabody's excavations in the Oliver Site in our Sunflower area produced at least one vessel of this type. Again, the association with the European material which was found in some quantity cannot be determined from the report. However, the type did not appear in any of our late collections. Clearly, further search needs to be made for rare contact sites in the Survey Area with a view to determining the exact forms of the late ceramic complexes in the different parts of the region. Until this is done, it cannot be stated with certainty exactly when these columns end.

The finished area graphs are given as Fig. 17–21 [not reproduced here]. The collections are listed by site designations, 12-N-7, etc., down the left side of each graph. Collections which were made from restricted areas in certain sites are indicated as A, B, etc. (12-N-3A). The stratigraphic cuts made in certain sites are shown by staffs on the left side of the diagrams, and each level of such excavations is indicated with depth in centimeters. Each staff is shaded to aid in relating it to the corresponding type frequency bars given in the body of the charts.

The pottery types are represented by vertical "axes" which are labeled at both top and bottom of the diagrams. Equally spaced on either side of the appropriate axes are horizontial bars the length of which represents type percentages according to the scale given in the lower right-hand corner of the graph. It will be noted that only one-half of the full length of the frequency bars for the relatively abundant types Neeley's Ferry Plain and Mulberry Creek Cord-marked has been shown. These types are arranged at the left, and right hand sides of the graphs, respectively, and this device has enabled us to decrease the over-all width of the illustrations.

On the right hand side of each graph are listed the collection totals. These will indicate the amount of reliance that may be placed upon the samples. The time scale, A, B, C, etc., which relate the graphs to one another in the manner which has been described above, is on the right hand side of each. These are the smallest time divisions which we have felt justified in making in the chronologies. The more comprehensive names which we are using, Tchula, Baytown, and Mississippian are also given with the time range of each period indicated.

Explanations of complicated diagrams are tedious reading and frequently serve mainly to hide the essential simplicity of the scheme. The reader who is still confused at this point may be less so after comparing the following tabulation of types at Site 19-L-6 (Refuge) with the collection as graphed at the very top of the Lower Yazoo Basin area diagram.

19-L-6 (Refuge)

Type Name	No. Sherds	Percentage
Neeley's Ferry Plain	304	.463[a]
Baytown Plain	31	.047
Bell Plain	263	.400
Parkin Punctated	21	.032
Leland Incised	28	.043
Unclassified	9	.014[b]

[a] Half of percentage shown in graph.
[b] Not graphed.

DISCUSSION OF THE SERIATION TECHNIQUE

Such, then, was the analytical procedure followed in developing the area graphs, and some of the reasons why it was done so. The seriation of surface collections might have carried the full weight of the evidence for developing the chronological type patterning, but as some stratigraphic excavations were available in each area it did not have to. There is a tendency among some archaeologists to affect an attitude of suspicion and doubt in regard to the seriation technique, and it has often been asserted that the results of such "juggling" cannot be accepted unless supported by vertical stratigraphy. It seems likely that such an attitude may arise from one or both of two sources; either a misconception of the phenomena of cultural change and the part that typology plays in measuring that change, or a lack of understanding of the seriation technique. As a matter of fact, both seriation and the vertical stratigraphic technique have certain advantages and defects under different conditions and must be applied to chronological problems with a careful regard for their limitations.

The chief limitation of seriation is the fact that it must work with degrees of probability which are often quite difficult to measure or even estimate. Usually, the measure has to be the pragmatic one of the results obtained. In our area, for example, any one or all of the probabilities stated at the beginning of this section may not have been true. The population may not have been relatively stable. There might have been sudden and frequent movements of populations so that the cultural change in any one locality would have had little semblance of order. Had this been true, we might expect either that the development of a sequence by this means would have been impossible, or that cultural periods would have been developed which were clearly delimited, one from the other.

It is also possible that a majority of the villages might have been inhabited for very long periods of time. If this had been true, it would have been impossible to separate early and late pottery features by surface collecting and seriation techniques. There is, of course, a degree of this kind of error in all of the samples which we have handled, and this is probably the principal defect of the technique. None of the collections are the instant cross section of the ceramic content of the culture at each site which would be the ideal situation. The fact that each of the surface collections does represent a time span of a certain length must, in theory, result in a certain "fogging" of the quantitative history. For example, if we assume that we have done a perfect job of sampling and classifying and have placed one of our strip graphs so that its vertical position correctly represents the mean date of the site occupation, then it is plain that this graph will represent the early types which were fading or perhaps disappeared soon after the site was first occupied, too high in the chronological scale. Conversely, the late types which belong to the latter part of the occupation are also pulled back to the mean position and show as too early.

Again, the occasional reoccupation of sites after a lapse of time might be a disruptive factor. It is even possible that there might have been at some periods the general custom of utilizing older sites. This also would result in our securing a mixture of old and new cultural materials and would invalidate our assumption for continuous occupation. Had this happened in a majority of cases, the odds are very much against there having been any consistent pattern to the selection of the earlier sites which would be utilized. Only in the event that a region had been cleared of a previous population by conquest, and the conquerors had moved in and begun to utilize the settlements and fields of the people whom they replaced, could there be any probability of a consistent sequence of types. In such a case the seriation technique would reveal the cultural chronology, but interpretations as to cultural and population continuity might be led astray. It is very probable, however, that there would be "pure" deposits of the late phase of the earlier occupation, and the early phase of the later, which would illustrate the break in cultural continuity.

We can also be certain that none of the collections show type frequencies to the exact percentage that would be found if every sherd at a site had been gathered and classified. For these reasons, we would like to say again that success in this type of work demands numerous collections, and the imperfections of the technique are such that the majority of the indications must be taken as evidence. Two or three sherds of a type that seems to be quite late in a surface collection from a site that by all other indications is rather early do not worry the seriator at all. There are too many ways in which such a chance mixture could have occurred. He is more concerned by the fact that the overwhelming majority of the sherds of this type take a late position, and that the preponderance of the material from the site fits into the early ceramic pattern. Add to all this the uncertainties of classification which we have outlined in a foregoing section, and it is easy to see why we would like to stress the fact that success in this type of work demands a number of fairly sizable collections, and that only indications given by the majority of the situations must be accepted as evidence.

THE USE OF STRATIGRAPHIC DATA IN SERIATION

The analysis of stratigraphic data as such will be discussed at length elsewhere. Here we are concerned principally with the use of stratigraphic along with surface collections in the seriation technique and their limitations from this point of view. Phillips and Griffin in the 1941, 1946, and 1947 field seasons made a total of seventeen stratigraphic excavations at nine different sites. All of these gave the anticipated results and showed evidence of change in type frequencies with the passage of time. Of these, fourteen were clear-cut enough to be incorporated in the area graphs and three could not be used for reasons that are explained below. This high degree of success in the effort to obtain this type of evidence was directly due to a careful selection of sites to excavate. Before beginning, each excavator had a fairly clear notion as to at least a part of the chronological patterning which the site would reveal.

The principal defect, from the point of view of seriation, in the information provided by stratigraphic excavations is a result of what might be termed migration, particularly upward migration of material in midden deposits. This is most pronounced in middens in which refuse and soil were accumulated very slowly. Apparently, the activities of the Indians who lived on such sites, the digging of postholes and pits, and overturning the soil in other ways, has tended to bring old pottery and other refuse to higher levels in the growing deposit. This is particularly true of the later Mississippian horizons. Analysis of stratigraphic studies in such deposits make the older type appear to have lasted much longer than really was the case. This factor is doubtless always present in the analysis of all midden deposits. Usually, however, the distortion of the graphs is so small that it falls well within the limits of the variations that have to be allowed in this kind of analysis.

The control which we have over this accidental upward weighting of midden-deposit evidence is the comparison of such unusually slow-growing cuts with the results of other excavations in the same area. A still better check is the comparison of these cuts with seriated short time-span surface collections.

The most pronounced example of upward migration which we have encountered in this study are the two strata cuts that were made at Lake Cormorant (13-P-8). The site is located in the Memphis area and the excavations revealed about 120 cm. of refuse deposit, the material from which, when analyzed, proved to represent the entire ceramic chronology for the area from time G to A. All of the types found in the area are well represented, for the collections from each level were substantial. The popularity peaks of the types form a pattern which is in perfect agreement with the seriation graph of the Memphis area as a whole as can be seen by comparing the stratigraphic and seriation graphs (Figs. 11.5 and 11.6) with Fig. 20 [too large to be reproduced here]. However, if we were to accept the evidence offered by the Lake Cormorant Site we would have to believe that the types Withers Fabric-impressed and Baytown Plain

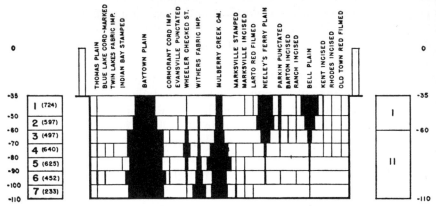

Fig. 11.5.   Stratigraphic diagram, Cut A, Lake Cormorant site.

were still being made in time B to A. All the other sites collected from the Memphis area by both the surface and stratigraphic techniques show that this was not so. We conclude then that these older types in the Lake Cormorant Site have been brought up to the surface of the midden by overturning of the soil. For this reason, it has not been possible to incorporate the Lake Cormorant data in the Memphis area graph.

The second phenomenon found in strata-cut tests is that at times they misrepresent the history of the site being studied by completely skipping or being deficient in the material that represents certain spans of time.

The reason for this is not difficult to find. While a village was occupied, the midden material accumulated at any one spot only so long as it was being actively deposited at that place. In the Southwest, where intentional dumps were utilized or in Peru where substantial buildings of stone and adobe were occupied uninterruptedly, there was little reason to change the locales of garbage disposal. However, in the eastern United States the

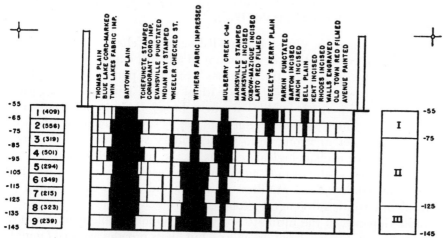

Fig. 11.6. Stratigraphic diagram, Cut B, Lake Cormorant site.

houses were impermanent structures of wood, and from the excavation of numerous sites it is clear that considerable shifting of house locations was done in rebuilding. Thus, it may happen that one of our strata pits was put down at a spot where a house stood for the first third of the time the village lasted; was rather far from any dwellings during the second third; and was again near a house during the last third. A graph of the type frequencies will—if it is clear enough—show a definite shift in percentage frequencies at the level where deposition paused. The same thing will result if the pit chanced to pass through a house floor or a courtyard which was intentionally kept clean of debris.

Ceramic Styles and Sequence at Sitio Conte, Panama

Samuel K. Lothrop's outstanding archaeological report on the site of Coclé in Panama is the source of the following excerpt.[5] Lothrop here attempts not only to arrange the excavated tombs in their chronological sequence, but also

[5] S. K. Lothrop, "Pottery of the Sitio Conte and Other Archaeological Sites," in *Coclé: an Archaeological Study of Central Panama*, Memoirs of Peabody Museum, Harvard University, Cambridge, 1942, vol. 8, pp. 183–197, 199. By permission of J. O. Brew, Director of the Peabody Museum, Harvard University.

to determine the actual span of years covered by the graves. His method involves the identification of the products of individual potters and the assignment of arbitrary life-spans to them. This technique is somewhat reminiscent of Reisner's estimation of life-spans of prehistoric generations and the attempted identification of individual families in reconstructing the history of an Egyptian cemetery (Reisner, 1932:187–188). Lothrop checks his own results by comparing them with other evidence based on cross-dating and calculation of age by rate of accumulation. A recent stratigraphic analysis of ceramic types at Sitio Conte has been published by Ladd (1957).

Style is defined by Webster as a "distinctive or characteristic mode of presentation, construction, or execution in any art, employment, or product, especially in any of the fine arts." Style in pottery may apply to both large and small groups or to individual vessels. Thus there is a distinctive Coclé style which enables us on a broad basis to segregate at a glance the products of that region from, let us say, Veraguas or Chiriqui. To make smaller divisions, Sitio Conte pottery stands out in the mind's eye from other archaeological remains in the immediate vicinity; Early and Late types at the Sitio Conte differ from each other and, as we shall show, the handiwork of families or even of individuals can at times be picked out from the general group.

Style depends in the ultimate analysis on imponderable qualities incapable of exact measurement or analysis but, in its broader aspects, tangible and impersonal factors play a part. In the case of Sitio Conte pottery, the shapes, cross-sections, basic colors and the grosser aspects of design are distinguishing features which may be expressed with exactitude. More elusive characteristics, however, such as fading of colors, the quality of line and brush technique, the minor variations of design, et cetera, likewise tell a distinct story of importance.

As one works away from the more obvious aspects of style, it is clear that the observer must become more and more of an expert in order to make distinctions of value. This introduces a personal factor because it becomes necessary to deal with intangible qualities. The student of pottery or any art can have no greater asset than an instinct or feeling which will lead him to correct interpretations arrived at intuitively before facts can be established on an impersonal basis. In a published report, however, it is best to be objective whenever possible. In the following discussion of style, therefore, we have limited ourselves almost entirely to qualities so obvious that they are capable of reproduction in our illustrations. We may point out, however, that the conclusions we reach are also supported by more elusive qualities which cannot be demonstrated pictorially except in color, although no less important in forming our opinions.

From our knowledge of native tribes existing today, we know that pottery making is an art handed down from one generation to another: a mother will teach her daughter how to shape vessels and how to apply traditional designs to them; the grandmother may assist in this instruction. Thus a family style is often created, from which it may or may not be possible to segregate the handiwork of an individual. When the daughter marries she introduces her peculiar fashion of pottery making into her husband's family. Under new surroundings, her workmanship may be influenced by her mother-in-law and sisters-in-law or vice versa. In this way, a potter may add designs to her repertoire or may acquire new techniques such as a new method for blocking out the field to be decorated. It is also conceivable that two potters may cooperate in painting a single vessel, each decorating certain portions of it.

In all probability each potter has more than one style. For instance, in Sitio Conte Polychrome ware an individual might decorate plates, bowls, cups and carafes each with a distinctive set of patterns which could be correlated only by study of pigments, fading and quality of line. In addition to Polychrome ware, the same potter might also fashion Red ware, Smoked ware and other distinctive types. It is therefore improbable that an archaeologist can segregate *in toto* the products of a given individual.

Large graves at the Sitio Conte contained over two hundred vessels, which evidently were the product of several potters. The first problem in the identification of these individuals is to determine their styles and also the normal range in the variation of repeatedly painted designs. The safest approach lies in the study of ceramic pairs, of the same size and shape, which carry the same basic decoration, for in such cases we can be practically certain that only one individual is involved.

As an example, Fig. 11.7 shows two Early Polychrome plates from the same grave, both adorned with tongue scrolls separated by rectangular panels containing footprints.[6] Filling patterns are of an unusual type with a small circle in the mouths of the YC elements. [The YC design is a scroll in the form of a Y whose tail is curled into a spiral or scroll.] At first glance, these plates seem very much alike, but, on closer inspection, it is obvious that there is variation in size, color and arrangement of practically every unit. Yet not only association in the ground but style links these vessels very definitely and one is forced to believe that one potter made them both. Figs. 142, *b*, and 143 [not reproduced here] illustrate another example of pairs found in the same grave.

A third similar case is illustrated in Fig. 11.8. Here is another pair of vessels from the same grave, practically identical in size, both adorned with a black line on the upper side of the lip, parallel panels with slight entasis and similar crab motives on the upper surface. On the other hand,

---

[6] Only a limited number of Lothrop's figures and plates are reproduced in this extract. Those which appear here give some idea of the stylistic variations in the painted pottery at Sitio Conte. Numbers for figures and plates not reproduced remain as in the original text. The figures reproduced here have been renumbered to accord with the sequence in this book.

Fig. 11.7 (*Above*). Pair of Early Polychrome plates with tongue scrolls from Grave 1. Scale about 1/4. Fig. 11.8 (*Below*). Pair of Early Polychrome plates decorated on both surfaces from Grave 1. Scale 1/4.

the alternate panels on the upper surfaces carry completely distinct designs and the bases, apart from a central element, are totally unlike in treatment. Variation in presenting the same subject may be noted in the crab patterns [on the upper surface and the base of the plate on the right] and in the three types of footprints [on the upper surface and the base of the plate on the left]. Again, however, it seems certain that only one potter is involved.

When we compare the designs in Fig. 11.8 with Fig. 11.9 we find that

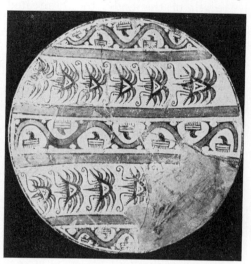

Fig. 11.9.   Polychrome vessel from Grave 32.

they resemble each other very closely and that the patterns in Fig. 11.9 fall well within the range of variation [in the two plates in Fig. 11.8]. Not only are the decorative elements basically alike, but the color, spacing and details of the brushwork are strikingly similar. Again it seems reasonable to believe that only one potter is involved, but in this case the specimens in Fig. 11.8 came from grave 1, while that in Fig. 11.9 belongs to one of the two earlier interments in grave 32. The two burials therefore are linked chronologically because the same potter is represented in both of them.

How long was the working life of a potter in Coclé? This is a question to which there can be no absolute answer, both because it might vary in the case of different individuals and because we have no knowledge of general customs. In the case of our Pueblo Indians, the women seem to make pottery as long as they are capable of turning out a reasonably good product. On the contrary, among the Lenca of Guatajiagua today the actual fabrication is done by unmarried girls only, although older women collect clay, clean it and polish the finished vessels. As a result, any given person actually makes pottery only for a few years. In the accompanying table and the ensuing discussion we have arbitrarily fixed the average working life of a Coclé potter at forty years. We believe this to be a maximum figure and it is quite possible that the chronology which emerges might be reduced by perhaps as much as fifty per cent. At any rate, we thus produce a definite set of figures and a chronological frame which are subject to discussion and correction.

It is obvious that if one potter contributed to two different burials they may be separated in time by many years. If, on the other hand, several potters produced the furnishings of the same two graves, then the chances of wide separation in time are much reduced. This is the case as regards grave 1 and the first of the three interments in grave 32. Additional links appear in Figs. 376 and 377 which show two flaring bowls similar in rim treatment, the method laying out the design, the black line running the length of the body, the bifurcated tails and the elongated crests attached to the bodies. It also seems probable that the designs in Figs. 82, c, and 88 were produced by one potter on account of the elongated claws and because the head in Fig. 88 is treated in the same fashion as that in Fig. 376. The in-sloping bowls with fringed serpents shown in Pl. I, e, and Fig. 106, d, also connect graves 1 and 32. As a result of these multiple parallels in style it seems highly probable that the two burials date within a very short period of each other and, for our present and doubtless imperfect chronological calibration, we may assume that they are contemporaneous.

PERIOD	APPROX. DATE	STRATIFIED SERIES OF GRAVES			ISOLATED GRAVES
DECLINE	1520	10, 11, 12		27, 28	58
	1510				56
	1500				
	1490				55
LATE	1480	8	26	23	43	45
	1470	9		22		
	1460	5B 5A	25		54	
	1450			21		
	1440		24		20	
	1430			19	6	
EARLY	1420	?	18			44
	1410		16			
	1400		15			
	1390	7	14			
	1380		17			
	1370	3	13	32C	29	31	48
	1360	4		32B		
	1350	2				
	1340					
	1330	1		32A		

Granted the validity of the principles and procedure we have laid down in the preceding paragraphs, the question arises as to what direction our analysis should take. Obviously the fact that particular graves in different stratigraphic series can be cross-dated is of archaeological importance. If, furthermore, the products of an individual may be detected in two or more superimposed graves, then it is clear that the burials were all introduced in the ground within the working lifetime of one potter. These two viewpoints seem to the writer to be fundamental. At the same time, the identification of the products of individual potters is so intriguing that at one time this appeared to be an end in itself. Somewhat reluctantly, however, we have confined our discussion, for the present, largely to chronological phases.

EARLY PERIOD

Styles of the Early Period

As a start we may list the following six polychrome stylistic groups of the Early period which we believe to be the products either of individual potters or of a family complex:

A. *Firm and thin-line style of grave 1 with two red pigments,* is marked by thin, firm outlines which usually have faded from black to brown, completely or in part. "Parallel" lines blocking off the field of decoration into panels show entasis or drawing together in the middle of the panel. Both red pigments used as filling colors were applied before the black outlines, but purple, which also appears occasionally, was put on after the black outline. This group probably represents at least two potters. It is illustrated as follows: grave 1, Pl. I, *h;* Figs. 21, *a,* 25, 73, 89, 90, 116, *c,* 378; grave 2, Fig. 57, *b;* grave 3, Fig. 43, *a;* grave 32, Fig. 16 [these figures not reproduced here] and Figs. 11.8 and 11.9.

B. *Firm and broad-line style of grave 1 with two red pigments.* This group may be the product of the style A potters and we believe it represents at least two individuals. Examples are illustrated as follows: grave 1, Figs. 37, 71, 74, 86, *b,* 97, *e,* 98, 379; grave 32, Fig. 30, *a* [not reproduced here].

C. *Coarse-line style of grave 1 with two red pigments,* marked by thicker, less certain outlines than in style A. Division of the field may be by parallel lines or by lines radiating from a central circular panel. The latter type of layout never occurs in style A. The two styles are in part contemporaneous because both appear in the most ancient graves but style C lingers after A. The presumption is that C represents two potters. Examples appear as follows: grave 1, Figs. 49, 56; grave 2, Fig. 380; grave 7, Fig. 48, *a;* grave 14, Fig. 47; grave 16, Fig. 48, *b* [not reproduced here].

D. *Black-line style of grave 4.* This group is distinguished by the fact that the major patterns are not entirely color-filled but are built up around a basic broad black line. Most scroll motives might be included in this category but, with a single exception, we have not felt competent to ally them with this style, which evidently includes more than one potter. Examples are illustrated as follows: grave 1, Fig. 71, 82, *a;* grave 13, Fig. 381; grave 32, Figs. 32, 46 [not reproduced here].

E. *Fringed-outline style of grave 32.* As we have frequently remarked, grave 32 was opened three times to receive successive interments, resulting in ususual confusion among the objects placed with the dead. One pottery style evidently occurred with all three burials. It is characterized by extreme flamboyancy because the major patterns are outlined by a deep fringe and usually all open spaces in the background are eliminated by inserting snail shell scrolls. The fringed style occurs not only in grave 32 but in graves 1 and 17. According to the estimate of time in the table on page 430 this indicates that it flourished for as long as forty or fifty years. It is possible therefore that all vessels with this type of adornment were made by one potter but we believe that two or more individuals produced it, not only on account of the lapse of time but on account of variation in style and quality of line. We may note that one of the few recorded instances of a fired green pigment known in the New World is applied in this style (Pl. I, *f*). More typical specimens are illustrated as follows: grave 1, Pl. I, *e;* grave 17, Fig. 70; grave 32, Pl. I, *k;* Figs. 1, 53, *a,* 58, *a,* 63, *b,* 94, *d,* 95, 106, *d,* and 115 [not reproduced here].

F. *Scroll-filled style of grave 32.* Analogous to the style just described is a second group from grave 32 which has all backgrounds blocked out by snail shell scrolls, but lacks the fringed outline of style D. It is possible that both should be considered as one unit, especially as style E probably was the product of more than one potter. On the other hand, in style F there is a more massive quality of line which may be an indication of individuality. Examples illustrated, which all come from grave 32, include Figs. 33, 63, *a,* 106, *a, c, f,* 382, *a* [not reproduced here].

The styles we have enumerated are characteristic of the Early period at the Sitio Conte and, we believe, were manufactured locally. In addition, there are several other apparently local polychrome styles, discernible to anyone who has familiarized himself with the Sitio Conte specimens, which do not form such clear-cut groups, at least as judged by our illustrations. We may call attention, however, to the following outstanding styles: Figs. 22, 23, 77, 79, *a,* and 80; also Figs. 31 and 54; also Figs. 83, 84, 91, 97, *c;* also Fig. 72; also Pl. I, *j* and Pl. I, *k.* Furthermore, there are styles which either are non-typical of the Sitio Conte or occur at various other localities in such quantity that at present they have no definite home. These we have tentatively classified as foreign importations. One of these, the polychrome style of grave 31 (Fig. 226) is characteristic only of the middle part of the Early period and is an important diagnostic of age in other sites. Another, the fine-line style of grave 5 (Figs. 149, 193), occurs only in the Late period at the Sitio Conte but is found at other sites.

Grave Sequence of the Early Period

Let us now turn to chronological details and consider the Sitio Conte graves in the northern sector of trench I (Figs. 11.10 and 11.11). The most ancient burial is grave 1, discovered intact, which at the outset of this discussion we have shown to be contemporaneous with the first interment in grave 32. Above grave 1 in the ground was grave 2, then grave 5, then grave 4. Grave 5 dates from a much later stylistic period and, in digging it, graves 2, 3 (of which the latter is not stratified in relation to 1) and 4 were partly robbed and destroyed. It is a curious fact that a large number of pottery fragments from the more ancient graves 2, 3 and 4 were discovered far above grave 5 in its shaft. The writer suspects that one other Early grave was completely destroyed by the introduction of grave 5 and that the contents were dispersed in its shaft.

What is the chronological relationship of graves 1–4? We believe it is explained by the Polychrome plates in Pl. I, *i,* and Fig. 385, which, although found in graves 1, 3 and 4, are apparently the work of one potter. Unifying characteristics include the pigments employed, the division of the field of decoration and treatment of the bird heads, crests, beaks, vi-

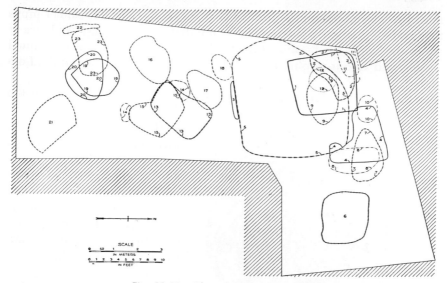

Fig. 11.10.   Plan of Trench 1, Coclé.

sors, body panels, legs and tails. These fall well within the limits of variation we have previously seen on vessels manufactured in pairs. We may therefore place a maximum span of forty years on these stratified burials, as seen in the table on page 430. This is a most important assumption for, if it is valid, other graves at higher stratigraphic levels may also be brought within the range of a time limit. As is usually the case, evidence not capable of illustration supports our conclusion.

Grave 3 is approximately on the same level as grave 4 (Fig. 11.11) but they are not in stratigraphic relationship. Hence their relative age

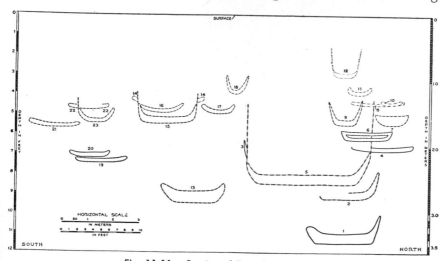

Fig. 11.11.   Section of Trench 1, Coclé.

must be determined on the ground of style. We believe but cannot prove that grave 4 is slightly older. These two burials, as well as grave 31, are of about the same age because they mark the earliest appearance of fluted vessels, and an out-sloping bowl style which became common in the Late period.

In the central sector of trench I another series of stratified graves of the

Fig. 11.12.   Polychrome plates from Grave 17.

Early period was found (Figs. 11.10 and 11.11). The oldest was grave 13. Above this in the ground was grave 15, also intact, which, however, had cut through the more ancient grave 14 (Fig. 11.11). In the case of grave 17, our notes record that the legs of the single skeleton it contained could not be found but that they would have run under grave 14 had they been in an extended position. Perhaps part of grave 17 had been looted in aboriginal times.

Our sequence from the bottom up thus runs: graves 13, 17, 14, 15. Again it seems that all can be dated within the lifetime of an individual on the basis of the Polychrome plates illustrated in Fig. 11.12. This again is inference, but the similarities are even more positive when the original specimens are seen than is evident in the illustrations.

The next problem is the correlation of the two stratified series of graves here evaluated. We believe that graves 4 and 13 are approximately contemporaneous. This statement is made partly on general correspondence in polychrome styles. It is also noteworthy that these burials both contain the most ancient examples of a purple and red polychrome style which became very common in the Late period (Fig. 390). A comparable specimen from grave 13, non-typical in shape, is illustrated in Fig. 387. In addition, graves 4 and 14 both contained fragmentary in-sloping and out-sloping bowls with banded interiors recalling the typical Late Polychrome vessel in Fig. 161, *b*. The chronological relationship between graves 4 and 13 is further emphasized by the following complete but limited distributions:

1. Red ware out-sloping bowls: graves 4, 7, 13, 32
2. Ditto, with flange: graves 4, 13, 15, 32
3. Red ware in-sloping bowls: graves 4, 13, 32
4. Smoked-ware bevelled bowls: graves 4, 13, 15, 32
5. Tubular-incised bowls: graves 1, 4, 13, 32

Of the Early period non-stratified graves, grave 32 was a compound and complex burial in which bodies were inserted on three separate occasions. What intervals separated these interments? The first, we have shown, was approximately contemporaneous with grave 1. The second burial took place long enough after the first for the bodies to have become completely disarticulated but the third burial resulted in only partial disarticulation of the second set of bodies. On the basis of the data in the previous paragraph and also of correspondence in polychrome styles (Fig. 58) we believe that the last burial in grave 32 may have been more recent than grave 13 but contemporaneous with grave 17.

In addition, we have a link between graves 15 and 32 because practically identical Smoked-ware effigy bowls of the type seen in Fig. 322 were found in each burial. There is no additional evidence to indicate a close connection and in the table on page 430 we therefore have separated them by our maximum limit for an individual potter. The correctness of this procedure is made probable by the fact that graves 14 and 17 are stratified between 13 and 15.

Grave 31, like grave 32, is another isolated and non-typical burial which can be dated only through style. It contained two fluted vessels, a form which first appeared in graves 3 and 4. It also contained examples of a foreign polychrome style (Figs. 226, 227) one specimen of which also came from grave 4. We therefore believe graves 4 and 31 were approximately contemporaneous.

Grave 29 again is non-typical and is not stratified. It obviously belongs in the Early period, however, and, on the basis of fragments of the polychrome style just mentioned, is approximately of the same age as grave 31.

Returning to stratified burials, grave 7 lay above grave 4 (Fig. 11.11) and, while definitely of the Early period, is of later date than grave 4. We believe that another burial once existed here in this series, destroyed by the natives in digging grave 5. Our reason for this is that many sherds from the shaft of grave 5, which we have shown contained material of earlier date, cannot be associated stylistically with what remained *in situ* in the graves partly destroyed in the digging of grave 5.

The chronological edifice we have built up from grave 1 to grave 15, as shown in the table on page 430, appears fairly sound both because it is based on stratigraphy and because the stylistic links are many more than we can illustrate or describe verbally. Our next step, which takes us from grave 15 to grave 16 (Figs. 11.10 and 11.11), is less positive. Graves 15 and 16 were in marginal contact with each other and the funeral furnishings in both reached the same level on the grave walls, although the floor of grave 15 was the deeper. When we excavated them we thought, according to our field notes, that grave 16 might overlap grave 15 but we could not be sure. We therefore cannot now be factually certain of their chronological relationship, although stylistically grave 15 is the older.

Grave 16 may be linked, however, with graves 6 and 24 of the Late period on the basis of the vessels illustrated in Fig. 388, which apparently are the product of one potter, and the bowls in Figs. 151, b, and 389 add grave 19 to the picture. Grave 6, 19 and 24 mark the opening of what we have called the Late period. While each of these burials contained a few survivals of Early forms, the bulk of their pottery is in Late styles, so fully developed that there is no mistaking them.

Among the few hold-overs of Early period styles encountered in graves of the Late period we can list the following:

Grave 6.   a. Drooping lip Polychrome plate with zigzag bands (cf. Fig. 134). b. Flaring Polychrome bowl with a coiled serpent pattern (cf. Fig. 95). c. Panelled Red ware carafe of Early size (small) and shape (sharp angle where neck joins body).

Grave 19.   a. Flaring Polychrome bowl with crab pattern. b. Black-and-White-on-Red ware out-sloping bowl with crab pattern. c. Black-and-White-on-Red ware out-sloping bowl with footprint pattern (Fig. 282, a).

These specimens, ten in number, are so close in style to vessels found in the sequence of graves 13–15 that a long separation in time seems unlikely. We have therefore allowed a span of only thirty years from graves 16 to 6, 19 and 24 in the table on page 430. The vessels listed mark a definite end to the Early period styles for there are no comparable pieces in graves of later date.

LATE PERIOD

Late Polychrome ware embraces about as many distinct styles of painting as Polychrome of the Early period. In general it may be said that the black outlines of patterns are more massive than in the Early period and that there is a greater tendency to render a design in part or completely in black-line alone. Color, however, is the essence of polychrome pottery and it is often lavishly employed. For the most part, red and purple are the filling colors, usually applied in equal quantities so that they contrast with each other, whereas in more ancient times purple usually is either subordinate to red or is employed to the exclusion of red. Brown rarely is seen as a filling color except in a broad-line style confined to grave 5 and cache 5. Among the larger and more important stylistic groups of the Late period we may note the following.

Late Period Styles

A. *Red-white-and-purple banded style.* This group is characterized by red and purple bands interspaced with white bands showing the slip, usually all of equal width. It occurs in graves 5, 6, 24, 26 and 43 (Pl. II, *d,* Figs. 133, 134, 175, 176, 177, *a, b, d,* 178 and 185) and therefore spans the Late period. It obviously is the product of several potters.

Although the style here considered is characteristic only of the Late period, it had been evolved at an earlier date. Our most ancient specimen probably is a fragmentary one found above grave 4, from which it seems to have been removed when grave 4 was cut by the shaft of grave 5. It consists of an in-sloping bowl (cf. Fig. 174) with vertical bands on the walls. Another specimen came from grave 13 (Fig. 387) and is approximately contemporaneous. An out-sloping bowl with concentric circles on the floor and bands on the inner rim was found in grave 14.

We estimate (table on page 430) that graves 4 and 13 may antedate the Late period by as much as seventy years. Why the banded style persisted in small quantities through this interval and then became popular we cannot state with assurance. It is possible that the specimens of the Early period reached the Sitio Conte by trade. The large number dating from the Late period may indicate that a foreign style suddenly became fashionable and was manufactured locally. It is also possible that the potters from other villages came to the Sitio Conte as the result of a successfully waged war and that they introduced new styles. Finally we may entertain the possibility that the Sitio Conte was abandoned for a time, as is indicated by sterile bands in the refuse, and that the inhabitants, settling among new neighbors, acquired new ceramic styles which persisted when they returned to their former home.

B. *Purple-and-red out-sloping bowl style.* This style is closely allied to style A of the Late period and perhaps the two should be grouped together. It was found in graves 13 (Early period) and 5, 6, 21, 23, 24, 26 and 45 (Late period—Pl. II, *c, c';* Figs. 104, 139, 140, 141, 154, 159–170 and 390). Probably these vessels are the product of several potters. With very few exceptions they are out-sloping bowls. Characteristics of this style include a massive quality of line and contrasting areas of purple and red. Designs are both geometric and zoomorphic. Like style A, style B first appears in grave 13 in the Early period.

C. *Curvilinear style.* The chief characteristics of this style are broad and forcefully curved lines with delicately tapered ends and the rather sparing use of color (Figs. 136, 146, 147, *b,* 148, 150, 153, 173, 190, 192, 199, *a,* 197 [except *c*], 218, *a,* and 391). All examples came from grave

26 with the exception of a few specimens from graves 5 and 23. This fact suggests that the entire group may have been produced by a single potter. If so, the potter possessed a remarkably large repertoire of designs. We think it more probable that two individuals were involved. In some cases a single red pigment was employed but often two shades of red were used.

D. *Heavy-line style of grave 5.* We have already pointed out that grave 5 and cache 5 contained a number of vessels painted in a peculiar fine-line style, which we classified as Foreign Polychrome style A, because it occurs in several other localities but is typical of no single site. In addition, grave 5 and cache 5 yielded a second specialized style illustrated in Pl. II, *h, i,* and Figs. 151, *a,* 152, 177, *c, f,* 184, 189, 208, 218, *b,* 219, 221 and 392. This at present is recorded only from the Sitio Conte, where it was found in such quantity that it seems to have been made in the locality. The black lines of patterns associated with this style, like those of style C, are broad and heavy but they terminate in sharp points. The chief filling color is a rich dark red; brown and purple also are used. Patterns are geometric, consisting of clawed frets, clawed scrolls, a bird wing motive and nesting circles.

With a single exception, all specimens came from grave 5, which contained two burials. The interval between them was so short that bodies in the first burial were still partly articulated when they were moved to make room for the second lot. Pottery of style D accompanied both interments but can be partly divided into two groups as a result of the position of individual pieces in the grave and their association with individual skeletons. These show certain divergences in style. The earlier material is more angled, both bowls and jars, as can be seen in Figs. 177, *f,* 184 and 392. The later pieces are more rounded. They include jars with a flat rim, found under the capstone topping the final interment (Fig. 189), a tripart vessel (Fig. 218, *b*) and various turtle effigy jars (Fig. 208). No changes take place in the nature of the designs. It seems improbable that all specimens were made by one person, but rounded and angled patterns evidently were painted by the same individual for both occur on the same vessel.

E. *Effigy style of grave 6.* Grave 6 contained ten effigy carafes which resemble each other so closely that they probably were made by the same potter (Figs. 211, *b,* 212 and 220). No examples have been found except in grave 6, so that at present this style is valueless for cross dating.

Late Period Grave Sequence

To return to the Late period grave sequence, we have shown that the most ancient graves of this epoch are 6, 19 and 24. Of these, grave 6 is an isolated burial but the other two are at the bottom of important stratigraphical series. Evidence that all three are approximately of equal age includes the vessels probably made by one potter in Figs. 388, *b, c,* and 389; also the fact that these three graves and no others are typical of the Late period but contain a few ceramic hold-overs from the Early period. In addition we reiterate the fact that graves 6 and 24 yielded some transitional forms such as the vessels in Figs. 174, *b,* and 175, *a,* which have typically Early shapes combined with typically Late decoration.

Grave 6 was located close to but was not integrated with the long stratified series of graves in the north end of trench I (Figs. 11.10 and 11.11). We date it before grave 5 because the latter contained no definitely Early period traits as did grave 6. Grave 5, we may add, can be closely equated chronologically with grave 26 which is stratified over grave 24 (approximately of the same age as grave 6) and is therefore the more recent of the two. Grave 25, placed above grave 24, can be dated as the later of the two because it was almost completely destroyed by the shaft of grave 26. The table on page 430 shows the relative age of these burials.

The largest and most lavishly furnished burials of the Late period were graves 5 and 26. When the latter was dug, the shaft was carried down to grave 24 and many objects were removed (see Fig. 11.13). Afterwards

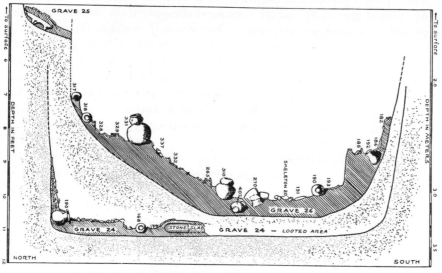

Fig. 11.13. North-south cross section of graves 24, 25, 26.

the floor of 26 was built a short distance above grave 24. We believe that individual potters working in Late Polychrome styles A and B, which we have just described, contributed to both graves. It is possible, however, that pottery was transferred from one grave to the other.

Grave 5 is linked stylistically in many ways with both graves 24 and 26 so we have placed it chronologically between them in the table on page 430. Carafe styles in grave 5 (the large type, illustrated in Pl. I, *e*, found only in the Late period) point towards grave 24 but Panelled Red and Polychrome effigy vessels (Figs. 208, 301) and gold disks adorned with figures of the Crocodile god (Part I, Fig. 91) indicate connection with 26. Features found only in graves 5 and 26 include fossil shark teeth and gold bat pendants.

To attack another problem, graves 19, 21, 22 and 23 form a stratified series in the order listed from bottom to top (Figs. 11.10 and 11.11). We have shown that grave 19 is of about the same age as grave 24. Grave 23 at the top of the series may be correlated with grave 26 in several ways. For instance, the Polychrome spouted jars in Fig. 197, *b*, *d*, *f*, are very closely related stylistically and may have been made by one potter. Both burials contained examples of a probably imported Black-line style (Fig. 241) and also of loop-leg vessels in the style of Veraguas (Fig. 336, *a*). In each case, only one potter seems to be involved.

Grave 5 also is associated with grave 23 by the presence in both of Polychrome turtle effigy vessels painted in a rather uncertain quality of line (Fig. 210). Fig. 394 shows almost identical spouted jars from both graves which presumably were fashioned by the same potter.

The isolated graves and caches at the Sitio Conte, with the exception of Early period graves 31 and 32, contained comparatively little pottery, but at times they can be assigned a chronological position on account of stylistic links. This we have attempted to do in the table on page 430. In no case is the material sufficiently abundant or are connections so direct that the date of individual isolated graves may be fixed with confidence. As a large part of the material on which this arrangement is based has not been illustrated, we shall not discuss it. Future excavations in Coclé, however, may elucidate the chronological setting of these burials. . . .

DURATION OF OCCUPATION

Turning to the broader aspects of chronology, we may remark that the length of the period of occupation shown in the table on page 430 depends on stylistic analyses, which are not open to exact demonstration, and also on the assumption that the average working life of a potter was approximately forty years, which surely is a maximum figure. The total period of about two centuries shown in the table might therefore be reduced. On the other hand, two thin sterile bans in the refuse may represent occasions when the site was temporarily abandoned, which would increase the length of occupation.

The maximum depth of refuse was about 3.1 meters (10 feet), with the exception of small inverted cones which extended farther into the ground. According to our table this represents a maximum accumulation in the center of the site of the rate of 30.5 centimeters (1 foot) in twenty years. This figure, because it includes a large amount of silt deposited by the river, is comparable to other sites where it has been possible to measure the rate of accumulation. At the Sitio Conte itself we have a check on our figures owing to the peculiar construction of grave 5. All burials had floors, established by the presence of skeletons, mortuary offerings and, in some cases, stone slabs. Grave 5 alone, however, had a definite top, indicated by a horizontal stone slab which presumably once lay flush with the surface. If the rate of accumulation which results from our stylistic analysis is correct, the top of grave 5 should have been exactly 91.4 centimeters (3 feet) below the top of the refuse. Our records show that it actually lay only 5 centimeters (2 inches) deeper than this figure.

The sterile bands in the refuse constitute a problem we cannot solve. Owing to the digging of graves in aboriginal times, these bands had been destroyed in many places and we could not correlate them with the graves. They may represent periods of flooding due either to a shift in the bed of the Rio Grande de Coclé or to unusual rainy seasons.

In final comment on the chronological framework here evolved, we have another check owing to the fact that Coclé metal ornaments reached the Mayan area in trade. In dredging the Cenote of Sacrifice at Chichen Itzá in Yucatan, over a score of metal pendants of Coclé style were recovered. The Cenote cult at Chichen Itzá is definitely associated with the period of Mexican influence in Yucatan, which dates from 1191 to 1450 [see Chapter 13 of this book]. Although none of the Yucatecan specimens from Coclé can be directly associated with the Sitio Conte, their connection with Mayan and Mexican chronology is not inconsistent with our system of dating and, from a broad point of view they indicate that we cannot be far wrong in our reckoning.

Reduction of Potsherds to Whole-Vessel Counts

When the archaeologist encounters pottery fragments in large numbers on the surface of sites or as he excavates, he saves these and, after classifying them by type, tabulates the occurrences, thus deriving conclusions as to the probable time sequence of the pottery types. Several selections in this volume provide examples of this method.

Alex Krieger has gone beyond this type of analysis and has sought more significant conclusions from the many fragments by matching sherds in order to determine how many original vessels these fragments represent. Although his estimates of whole vessels are approximate, his figures do certainly permit a more meaningful analysis of the pottery from a single archaeological site. This can be illustrated here by presenting a description of Krieger's method and the results obtained for the Davis site in eastern Texas.[7]

J. A. Ford (1951:93–94) gives his reasons for not following Krieger's sherd-matching method at the Greenhouse site in Louisiana. Here Ford dug narrow

[7] H. Perry Newell and Alex D. Krieger, "The George C. Davis Site, Cherokee County, Texas," Memoirs of the Society for American Archaeology, no. 5, pp. 75–77 [American Antiquity, vol. 14, no. 4 (1949)]. By permission of American Antiquity.

trenches. He believes that each such cutting produces only a few sherds of one broken vessel. Furthermore, the simplicity of the designs on the Greenhouse pottery would have made sherd-matching extremely difficult. Obviously, it is only when large areas, or an entire site, are excavated that such matching is feasible, as, for example, in the Davis site and Humboldt Cave, Nevada, discussed in the next excerpt.

Newell's field catalogs record over 96,000 potsherds and 1,000 other objects, not all of which are artifacts. In order to comprehend the present analysis and tabulations, it should be realized that only one tiny undecorated oval bowl was found virtually complete in the field. In addition, the sherds of some two dozen vessels were found *in situ* together and later glued, but in only six or seven cases was the vessel then virtually complete; the others were only one-quarter to one-half complete.

Despite this insignificant start, the accompanying study is based on a total of 5,031 "vessels" reached by matching and reducing the sherds within each type and group to an estimated number of actual vessels rather than individual sherds. Several hundred other "vessels" were also used, but lacked the necessary pieces for judging form, decoration distribution, etc. The determination of "vessels" was reached through a laborious process of building up batches of sherds that belonged to the same vessel by hunting for them back and forth through the huge collection.

I [Krieger] cannot recount the steps by which this was accomplished, and it was done a few days at a time over a period of years. Stated briefly, it was a matter of starting with something distinctive, such as sherds with a rather special cast to the design, a particular shade of color, paste of a certain consistency or temper, size and distribution of design elements, etc., then trying to find other pieces like them. Previously, a selection of 6,000 rim sherds had been worked over several times by Newell and myself into potential type groups and several good starts toward individual vessels were found. It also sometimes happened that pieces from two different "type" groups belonged to the same vessel with very different rim and body decoration. I suspect that there remain some such combinations still unrecognized, but the sheer mechanical task of sorting such a mass of pottery into vessels perfectly is probably impossible; moreover, it is not necessary to the basic value of the statistics reached so far and would probably not change them significantly.

Of course it was not possible to reduce all the pottery to "vessels," but two sorts of groupings were performed. First, the "vessel batches" consist of shreds belonging to a single vessel which can only partially be glued together, but enough pieces are present to judge the appearance of the complete vessel accurately. Such "batches" consist of anywhere from three or four large sherds to 225 small ones. They provide the basis for Mr. Storey's sketches of complete vessels. Second, when the sherds of a certain type had been culled for pieces belonging to the batches, the remainder was matched carefully to see whether any more combinations could be made; often more batches appeared in this way, but if not it was at least possible to determine approximately how many vessels were represented. The larger the mass of pottery, the less accurate the count would be, but as a rough scale it appears to me that if 100 rim sherds were reduced to say about 60 vessels, this would be accurate to within four or five actual vessels; if 750 sherds were reduced to some 340 vessels, the actual number would surely lie between 300 and 400 and probably considerably closer to the estimate. Approaching 2,000 sherds the reduction might come within the nearest 100 actual vessels. There is no way to check this estimate, and individuals would vary in their results.

There may be a serious question about whether this labor is justified. Certainly when the pottery collection becomes extremely large there is not much to be gained because the vagaries and accidents of preservation and recovery are largely overcome by sheer numbers. Nevertheless, the writer has long been interested in the discrepancies between the traditional sherd counts that appear in publication, and the numbers of vessels actually made by the cultural group being studied. Particularly, it is convenient to know the real relative importance of the "types" at the time they were made and used. In a previous analysis of this kind with a smaller collection of about 2,200 sherds and 62 restored vessels, it was surprising how great the differences were in percentages calculated from sherds only, and from the actual vessels found by sherd matching. Krieger (1946:185–191) refers to pottery from the Sanders site near the south side of Red River in Lamar County, Texas. This is the type site for the Sanders Focus, related in some ways to the Alto Focus, for which Davis is the type site. I know of no other reports employing this method for the total ceramic remains, although large groups of sherds from the same vessels are often noted.

In all of this matching it must be emphasized that the primary dependence was on rim sherds, for it was soon apparent that if the vessel was decorated at all, this was done from near the lip downward; how far down depended primarily on the vessel form. A carinated bowl, for example, was never decorated below the rim (the basin-shaped body sloping away from the eye and being practically invisible). The jars, their whole surfaces visible, have a variety of rim decorations but only three body treatments: plain, incised lines, and pinches or punctates made with fingernails. The barrel-shaped and cylindrical vessels, lacking a delineation between rim and body, but with the whole outer surface visible, have decorations ranging from a narrow zone just under the lip to the entire body. The simple bowls also lack a distinguishing point between rim and body, but the body curves away from the eye as it becomes the bottom, and the decoration is generally confined to the upper half or quarter of the vessel.

Globular bowls are all, apparently, decorated over the whole bulging side, only the vasal area invisible to the eye being plain. Bottles, when decorated, bear the design either over the entire body (except the base), or in a narrow zone around the shoulder area surrounding the spout; there seem to be no compromises. All engraved bottles (few have any other kind of decoration) have from four to six fine lines encircling the top of the spout just below the mouth; this seems to be true whether the body has only the shoulder lines or full-body decoration alone, the spouts being ignored; in this case alone it is the upper rather than lower part of the vessel which is unusable for analytical treatment.

The reduction of sherds to vessels is of great importance in determining the actual amount of wholly undecorated pottery. The Davis site analysis shows that only about 2.5 per cent of the total vessels were left wholly plain. Only two examples were found of a vessel decorated on the body but not on the rim, hence this factor may be ignored here; i.e., it is safe to assume for statistical purposes that rim sherds provide an accurate basis for distinguishing types against one another, and against completely plain vessels.

In this connection I should like to point out what appears to be a deep fallacy in the statistical analysis of lower Mississippi Valley pottery, to name only an area of immediate concern here. We learn from one recent report, into which went a great amount of work and thought, that the plain "types" of several Tchefuncte sites constitute up to 72.9 per cent of the pottery. The plain "types" consistently outnumber all others in almost staggering amounts, hence the cultural implication that Tchefuncte people decorated only a little of their pottery. For example, Tchefuncte Midden A yielded 22,882 sherds of Tchefuncte Plain, 7,531 Mandeville Plain, 4,759 Tchefuncte Stamped, 2,112 Tchefuncte Incised, and much smaller amounts of 13 other types, most represented by only 3 to 61 sherds apiece. Lafayette Mound 1 yielded 20,520 Tchefuncte Plain, 220 Tchefuncte Stamped, 117 Tchefuncte Incised, and smaller amounts of seven other types. In the frequency and percentage tables of the same study, we may take Tchefuncte Midden A as an example again, and in levels A to E the percentage of Tchefuncte Plain runs 51.2, 63.1, 63.3, 64.5, and 57.3. The most common decorated type, Tchefuncte Stamped, runs 8.6, 8.8, 14.6, 16.0, and 12.5 per cent of the total sherds in the same five levels, respectively. The several tables show additional cases of the plain sherds far outnumbering all the decorated types put together in each Tchefuncte period component.

A very similar situation has been published for Marksville period pottery in the Crooks site, central Louisiana. Here we learn, for example, that a total of 11,620 sherds of Marksville Plain came from the Marksville period levels, against 817 Marksville Stamped, 271 Marksville Incised, 84 "Marksville period rim," 62 LaSalle Punctated, and a remainder of 14, 8, and 5 sherds of minor types. The various sections of the site yielded percentages of Marksville Plain of 85.3, 88.0, 81.7, 82.8, 68.9, 83.4, 98.3, and 77.4; in other words, from a minimum of over two-thirds to a maximum of practically all the sherds from each section or level.

In these and similar cases which might be cited from many areas, it would be extremely instructive to know what proportion of the actual vessels was undecorated. Although it is nowhere stated that the "plain types" consist of all plain sherds from the sites, this is implicit in the tabulations. That is, the "plain types" include all sherds from plain vessels, plus sherds from the undecorated parts of all other vessels, and therefore throw the percentages completely out of gear with the cultural habits of the pottery makers. If, in such studies, the pottery had been reduced to actual vessels and allowance made for undecorated portions of vessels what would be the numerical result? The true percentage of plain pottery would undoubtedly show a significant drop. Consequently, the percentages of type representation among the decorated vessels would greatly increase. If (using only a speculative situation) the wholly plain vessels constituted but 10 per cent instead of 80 per cent of the total, the types with some part of the vessel decorated would have to be calculated as proportions of the remaining 90 per cent instead of 20 per cent. Such a re-evaluation of the "frequencies and percentages" of types would completely alter the picture of relative popularity of ceramic styles in any given village.

There is no way of knowing whether any given situation in Louisiana archaeology would be as radically changed as the example just given, but this is not improbable, and at any rate a re-alignment of ceramic tabulations on this basis would seem well worth the trial. It is no more difficult than the alternative method, and need not involve the reduction of sherds to actual vessel-counts if this is infeasible. What is needed, primarily, is to leave plain body sherds out of the statistics. This brings us to the point that archaeologists in general feel it a matter of duty to classify and count every single specimen in a collection. The theory is that such studies must be complete down to the last object in order to be accurate.

Calculation of the Number of Baskets from Fragments

A second account of Krieger's method[8] deals with the basketry fragments recovered from Humboldt Cave in western Nevada as compared to those recovered from Lovelock Cave.

From this and the preceding excerpt, the reader may appreciate some of the deadly routine work which devours time and tries the patience of the archaeologist at work.

[8] Robert F. Heizer and Alex D. Krieger, *The Archaeology of Humboldt Cave, Churchill County, Nevada,* University of California Publications in American Archaeology and Ethnology, Berkeley and Los Angeles, 1956, vol. 47, no. 1, pp. 34–37. By permission of University of California Press.

TABLE 10. Occurrence of Basket Types at Humboldt Cave and Lovelock Cave

Type	Humboldt Cave						Lovelock Cave	
	Pieces Recovered ("Straight Count")		Number of Baskets				Pieces Recovered	
	Number	Per-centage	Calculation by Match-ing Process	Per-centage	Estimated True Number	Per-centage	Number	Per-centage
Wickerware								
Burden basket	1,545	75.0	—	—	—	—	—	—
Burden basket with twine variation	21	1.0	—	—	—	—	—	—
Total	1,566	76.0	240	57.7	200	55.7	1,115	73.0
Coiled								
Circular roasting trays	392	19.0	136	32.7	125	35.0	286	18.7
Fine bowls (including feathered)	28	1.3	8	1.9	8	2.2	9	0.6
Bowls, single-rod foundation	12	0.6	6	1.4	5	1.4	2	0.1
Coarse bowls	4	0.2	2	0.5	2	0.5	12[a]	0.8
Rings or stands	2	0.1	2	0.5	2	0.5	—	—
Total	438	21.2	154	37.0	142	39.6	309	20.2
Twined								
Openwork (burden basket?)	39	1.9	12	2.9	8	2.2	38[b]	2.5
Closework, flexible, overlay	11	0.5	6	1.4	5	1.4	17[b]	1.1
Closework, flexible, plain	4	0.2	4	1.0	4	1.1	19[b]	1.2
Others	—	—	—	—	—	—	30[b]	2.0
Total	54	2.6	22	5.3	17	4.7	104	6.8
Grand Total	2,058	99.9	416	100.0	359	99.9	1,528	100.0

[a] Includes bowls and bottles; no bottles were found at Humboldt Cave.
[b] Classification uncertain from description; "others" probably includes some twine variations of wicker. See text.

In determining the relative frequency of occurrence of different basketry techniques, Krieger worked out a system of matching fragments found in the cave in order to calculate the number of actual baskets representing each technique. The usual method is simply to count the number of pieces recovered and to present this "straight count" as a record of the relative frequency of occurrence of specimen types. However, as is pointed out below, the system of matching basketry fragments to determine fairly accurately the number of complete specimens gives results differing markedly from those of a straight count. The simple straight count is likely to suggest relative frequencies rather far removed from the true ones because of differences in the size of the various baskets, which may break or tear into a number of pieces. Table 10 compares the results of the matching process in the present study with those of the straight count. The straight count of specimens from Humboldt Cave is given first, with the percentage of the total that these fragments represent. Then the figures for the number of actual baskets are presented, first as calculated by the matching process and then a revised estimate. Finally, we give the totals already published for Lovelock [Cave] where no matching of fragments was attempted. Table 11 recapitulates the totals from Table 10.

To illustrate the difference in the results of the two methods, a compari-

TABLE 11. Summary of Basket Types at Humboldt Cave and Lovelock Cave

| Type | Humboldt Cave | | | | | | Lovelock Cave | |
| | Pieces Recovered ("Straight Count") | | Number of Baskets | | | | Pieces Recovered | |
	Number	Per-centage	Calcula-tion by Matching Process	Per-centage	Estimated True Number	Per-centage	Number	Per-centage
Wicker burden baskets	1,566	76.0	240	57.7	200	55.7	1,115	73.0
Coiled (all forms)	438	21.3	154	37.0	142	39.5	309	20.2
Twined (all forms)	54	2.6	22	5.3	17	4.7	104	6.8
Total	2,058	99.9	416	100.0	359	99.9	1,528	100.0

son of the relative frequencies of wickerware and coiling in Humboldt and in Lovelock shows the straight count for the two caves in remarkable agreement: in each there were nearly four times as many wicker fragments as coiled. The matching process, however, indicates that the true proportion of wicker to coiling is actually much closer to 4:3 than 4:1. This can be readily explained by the fact that the wickerware consisted entirely of very large conical burden baskets, whereas the coiled specimens were either trays or small bowls. The large burden baskets had been broken and torn into small fragments, whereas most of the coiled pieces had worn through at the bottom and had then been discarded. Actually, the ratio may have been even closer to 1:1 than the table indicates, for the coiled specimens are on the whole more distinctive than the wicker and may thus be more accurately matched by means of texture and stitching. The revised estimate of the number of wicker burden baskets, 200, therefore may be too high; the total for the coiled, 142, is probably more nearly accurate.

The matching process serves one other use. Pieces from the same basket may come from different parts of the deposit; caches as far apart as ten feet horizontally and three feet vertically yielded fragments that matched. This circumstance lends support to our belief that the cultural material from the cache levels of the cave (that is, from the deposit below 20 in.) has an essential unity. It is interesting that Humboldt Cave, though but a fraction of the size of Lovelock Cave, yielded about one and one-quarter times as much basketry as the scientifically excavated parts of Lovelock.

12

LITHIC AND METALLIC SOURCES

An important source of culture-historical information, at times overlooked by archaeologists, is to be found in the identification of rocks, minerals, and metals from which archaeological specimens are made and the location of the sources of these materials.

A search of the ethnographic literature dealing with American Indians will soon reveal the extensive trading and traveling done to obtain locally unavailable but culturally desirable minerals and metals. While the methods of procurement cannot be easily determined by the mere occurrence of foreign mineral specimens in an archaeological context, some idea of culture contact, including intensity of contact and the cultural values placed by the ancient peoples upon particular kinds of rocks or minerals, can be determined.

Studies of this sort necessarily involve a detailed knowledge of mineralogy and an intimate acquaintance with the local geology. Sometimes, when the macroscopic study of specimens cannot determine the differences between closely allied rocks, a detailed microscopic examination of thin sections is necessary. Also, when similar materials may be procured from several different sources, a spectroscopic analysis may reveal impurities or trace elements. It is theoretically possible that two specimens might be so similar as to defy analysis by known means or that the variations occurring in materials from each of several such sources might be great enough to make exact identification of the source impossible.

In general, archaeologists cannot be expected to have the necessary knowledge or facilities to make these identifications; consequently they must request the coöperation of the specialist. The archaeologist's duty, then, lies in procuring the necessary specimens from their archaeological context and enlisting the help of the specialist in making the detailed analysis. Three recent papers (Herz and Pritchett, 1953; Pritchett, 1953: 235–236; Weiss, 1954) deal with the "fabric" analysis of Greek marbles. This joint attack by archaeologists and petrologists on the problem of whether two or more fragments of sculptured marble derive from the same, or different, originally complete stele or sculpture promises to settle such questions definitively.

While the substance of which artifacts are made is most important in studies of this kind, the importance of reject, waste, and raw material must not be overlooked. The amount and size of the discard may give an idea of the value or availability of the material in question.

The following articles deal with the problem of lithic or metallic sources in two different ways. In England, a certain artifact type was found to have a wide, spatial distribution and to be made from a variety of materials. An attempt was made to identify the material of which each item was constructed, and to plot both the distribution of artifacts fashioned of the same material and the location, if known, of its source. Even preliminary studies, like those in the following selections, show a surprisingly wide distribution of particular materials and suggest wide travel, some of it primarily by sea.

For additional references see Ball (1941), Cole (1951:131–134), Bell (1953), Bryan (1950), Heizer and Treganza (1944), and Howell (1940).

Material Sources of British Stone Axes

Stone axes of various sizes and shapes have been found in Neolithic and Bronze Age sites widely scattered over the British Isles. It was apparent that some of these axes were made of the same or similar rock and that others were quite different. Many appeared to be made of rock that was not known locally. Questions were thus raised concerning the location of the quarries from which the raw material for the axes was obtained; if the axes were not made from local rocks, where did they come from and how did they get to the place where they were found? Answers to these questions would throw light on trade and culture contact in ancient Britain and perhaps could be of aid in dating archaeological sites, but in order to obtain the answers the axes first had to be carefully analyzed and the materials mineralogically identified. The South-Western Group of Museums and Art Galleries appointed a sub-committee to undertake the investigation. The sub-committee's first report appeared in 1941, and a second one in 1947 (Stone and Wallis, 1947). The following excerpts are from the first report.[1]

[1] Alexander Keiller, Stuart Piggott, and F. S. Wallis, "First Report of the Sub-Committee of the South-Western Group of Museums and Art Galleries on the Petrological Identification of Stone Axes," *Proceedings of the Prehistoric Society*, Cambridge, 1941, vol. VII, n.s., pp. 50–72. Reprinted by permission of J. G. D. Clark, Editor.

For many years past on both formal and informal occasions, archaeologists and others . . . have been stressing the importance of a scientific examination of the numerous stone axes in public and private collections. It has been urged that an exact determination of the rock material and its original provenance, together with a knowledge of the locality at which the tool was found, would lead to far wider and more exact information in Neolithic and Early Bronze Age times.

A major hindrance to the realisation of these anticipations lay with owners who required the petrologist to identify the rocks by macroscopical characters alone. It was of little use for the geologist to point out that grinding, polishing and patination had often obliterated the few surface features available and that even if fracturing of the specimen were allowed, no real progress could be made until a thin section of the axe was obtained. Pressed for an identification even on the above unsatisfactory grounds, geologists have at times given answers which are really little better than reasoned guesses, and the archaeologists have based some equally speculative deductions upon them.

At the outset of the present enquiry it was recognized that an examination of stone implements by their macroscopic characters alone would not suffice for their precise identification. Even if a freshly fractured surface is available it is doubtful whether a correct identification can be made, except perhaps with such distinctive rocks as are found in the Presely Mountains and at Bwlch Mawr. It cannot be too strongly stressed that modern microscopical methods, applied to thin sections, form the only satisfactory criterion in the identification of implements.

On this account permission was sought by the sub-committee, and readily granted by the respective owners, to cut the implements and so obtain thin sections. It was quickly realized that a slice taken from the corner of an implement, to some degree masked the original shape, even if great care were exercised. A technique was therefore evolved of cutting a small wedge- and later, a slab-shaped piece from the stone and then grinding this small wedge or slab to the required thickness. The method also has the advantage that the void can be filled in with plaster and coloured. From the museum standpoint the appearance and shape of the axe is now exactly as it was before slicing.

In the course of these investigations over two hundred stone implements have been dealt with up to the present. Realising the difficulties of immediately determining the provenance of the rock, as each stone implement was examined, it was decided to establish a number of arbitrary groups, each with definite characteristics. The identification of the group and the determination of the locality of the rock can then be carried out as opportunity serves.

[Nine groups were reported on in this article. The description of only two of these is included here.]

Group I. Macroscopically the stone implements in this group are characterised by consisting of medium grain, dark green or greenish-grey, igneous rocks which generally weather to a rough surface.

Microscopically, it is observed that the rock is unralitised gabbro, epidiorite or greenstone in which augite, sometimes ophitic, occurs in colourless to pale brown plates which show no crystal outlines and exhibit a variable amount of alteration to green fibrous hornblende along the cleavage cracks and the outside edges of the grains. In some cases the alteration to hornblende is complete. The presence of this secondary amphibole accounts for the tough nature of these axes. The felspars, presumably albite, are much altered and are more or less riddled with small needles of actinolite. The chief accessory mineral is ilmenite which is often altered to leucoxene.

An examination of several hundred sections of greenstone from various igneous areas in the British Isles led the sub-committee to the conclusion that the peculiar characters of this group could be best matched by the greenstones of Devon and Cornwall. Collecting and examination of the rocks in these greenstone areas has been carried out, but unfortunately an exact identification still eludes the sub-committee.

Although the exact provenance of the rock from which these implements were manufactured is still unknown it is considered important to be able to state that the above twenty-eight axes are identical with each other and must have originated from one small site. Petrologists who have experienced the variability of greenstone, even within the confines of a quarry will realise how extremely small an area the working site, when found, will probably prove to be.

Further it is an impressive fact that the number of axes now placed in Group I represents about 12 per cent of the total number examined.

Group VII. Since the pioneer work of Mr. Hazzledine Warren, the igneous rock from the crags of Graig Lwyd on the northern slopes of Penmaenmawr, overlooking the sea, has been known to archaeologists as a source of material for the manufacture of implements. The rock is an augite-granophyre and forms an intrusion which gives rise to extensive screes. In hand specimens it is seen to be a fine-textured, pale bluish-grey rock, extremely tough and difficult to work when fresh, which flakes well giving good bulbs of percussion and fairly smooth conchoidal fractures. The rock weathers rapidly becoming pale grey in colour. In thin section Dr. H. H. Thomas describes the rock as consisting of "sparsely distributed small phenocrysts of turbid plagioclase felspar, small rounded crystals and crystal-groups of augite and still smaller decomposed crystals of rhombic pyrozene in a micro-crystalline matrix of quartz and felspar with rods and isolated crystals of magnetite."

Mr. T. A. Glenn published a paper on the distribution of the axes made in the Graig Lwyd factory. He gave a complete list of all "finds" known up to that date and plotted these on a map. It should be noted that the majority of these records is made from macroscopic characters only.

Dr. H. Godwin records the microscopic identification of an axe from Swaffham Engine Drain, near Upware as being of the Graig Lwyd rock.

The present investigation has added another four localities to those already known.

CONCLUSIONS

In presenting their first report the sub-committee would summarise the work as follows:

Over two hundred axes have been sliced and examined; approximately seventy-five of these may be arbitrarily classified into nine well-defined groups.

Group I. A most satisfactory group of twenty-eight identical axes

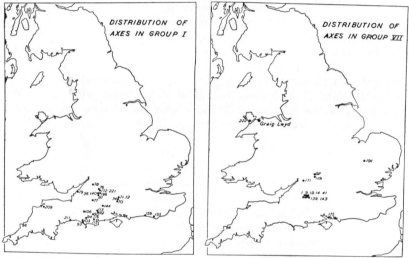

Fig. 12.1 (Left). Distribution of Axes in Group I. Fig. 12.2 (Right). Distribution of Axes of Graig Lwyd rock in Group VII.

[distribution shown on Fig. 12.1]. Although the exact original provenance of this greenstone has not been discovered the determination of such a homogeneous group is considered to be important.

Group II. One axe has been identified with a greenstone from between Lay Point and St. Ives, Cornwall.

Group III. Four axes have been matched with greenstones from a small area to the south-east of Marazion, Cornwall.

Group IV. A series of five axes consisting of a sheared tremolite rock.

Group V. Two axes of altered killas have been compared with rocks of this nature which occur adjacent to the greenstone to the east of St. Ives, Cornwall.

Group VI. A homogeneous group of fourteen axes which have been identified as emanating from the Stake Pass factory in the Lake District.

Group VII. Four additional localities have been determined for the well-known Graig Lwyd rock [distribution shown on Fig. 12.2].

Group VIII. A small group of three axes all from Windmill Hill, Avebury, consisting of siliceous rock.

Group IX. A series of three axes made of porcellanite have been definitely matched with the rock that occurs at Tievebulliagh Hill, Co. Antrim.

Of all the axes that have been submitted to us it is interesting to note that approximately 18 per cent may be placed in either Group I or VI.

The Secretary, Mr. Stuart Piggott, F.S.A., contributes the following notes on the archaeological implications of the sub-committee's work:

The archaeological results must of necessity be more tentative than those of a geological nature. It is apparent however that while the most important area supplying the raw material for the stone axes of Wessex was Cornwall, axe-factories in North Wales and Cumberland exported their products as far south as Wiltshire at least. In the first of these latter regions, the famous Graig Lwyd axe-factory holds a key position. The late Dr. H. H. Thomas and Mr. H. F. Poole suggested North Wales as a general source for the majority of the axes from North Wiltshire and from the Isle of Wight examined macroscopically, and for many of the Windmill Hill series which were more satisfactorily determined from thin sections. The routes by which axes were traded are still obscure, but the new identifications of Graig Lwyd axes from the Stow-on-the-Wold neighbourhood and from Nailsworth suggest traffic across the Cotswolds, and give added point to the Cotswold affinities of the Capel Garmon long cairn in the Conway valley. The identification of a Graig Lwyd axe from the Fenland indicates the widespread distribution of the factory's products, and it will be seen below how important this find is in establishing a chronological horizon for the trade. Apart from the axes however, archaeological evidence of contact between North Wales and Wessex in the Neolithic is practically absent.

Correlations even further west than Wales are however now substantiated by the identification from three widely scattered English sites of axes from the factory on Tievebulliagh Hill near Cushendall in Co. Antrim. These axes, from Kent, Dorset and the Cotswolds, reveal hitherto unsuspected trade contacts between Ireland and southern England in Neolithic times. The fact that the makers of the northern Irish long horned cairns used axes from the same factory is suggestive when the Cotswold specimen, from another famous long cairn region, is considered.

Perhaps the most interesting discovery made is the recognition of over a dozen exports from a very small and hitherto almost unknown axe-factory in the Lake District, above Borrowdale. Axes vaguely described as of "Borrowdale ash" have frequently been reported in the past from northern English localities on both sides of the Pennines, but now we have actually tied down a group of axes to the parent factory on Stake Pass. It is noteworthy that, apart from a Dorset specimen, all come from the Upper Thames and North Wiltshire region. The connection between this area and Cumberland comes as an archaeological surprise, and now the axes have pointed the way we may discover further evidence for trade contacts between the two regions.

Connection between Ulster and Cumberland in Neolithic times is suggested by pottery types, and it may be through the Lake District that the Tievebulliagh axes were traded into England.

With regard to the Cornish sources, the axes in some degree confirm the evidence from other lines of argument. The Neolithic A culture of Dorset as exemplified for example at Maiden Castle has close connections with that of Devon and Cornwall. This is shown by distinctive pottery types common to the regions and a west-to-east trading, if not colonising, movement had already been surmised—the connection between the two areas persisting into the Middle and even the late Bronze Age. The axes from Hembury Fort in Devon were of rocks derived from twenty miles westwards, in Dartmoor, and at Maiden Castle axes were found, again apparently of Dartmoor or Cornish origin. Two individual identifications had previously been made of Cornish rocks in South Wiltshire—a derived axe in a Late Bronze Age context on Boscombe Down near Salisbury and the battle-axe found with a beaker burial near Woodhenge. The wide distribution of axes in Group I, of probably Cornish origin, is remarkable, extending as it does to Gloucestershire, Hampshire and even Sussex, as well as the more accessible Dorset.

A typological study of the axes in the various petrological groups yields practically no results. There seems no consistency in the type represented, and at present we know of no features really significant of culture or period and must wait for the results of Mr. Bruce-Mitford's promised attempt to "wrest a coherent story from the typological confusion." The flattening of the sides of e.g. our nos. 2 and 92 is not necessarily, as the Windmill Hill evidence for flint axes shows, a late feature, though theoretically the expanded cutting edge of nos. 77 and 78 should echo a metal original and be proportionately late in the series. The Graig Lwyd specimens include part of a perforated mace-head from Windmill Hill which appears to be of the cushion type described by Eliot Curwen and assigned to the Early Bronze Age, and its stratigraphical position implies a similar dating. Other Graig Lwyd specimens show the characteristic flaking technique by which they were roughed out.

Archaeological evidence for dating by stratigraphy or associations is confined in Wessex to the specimens from Windmill Hill, where the foreign stone axes all belonged to the later periods of the site's re-occupation, and to the habitation site on the West Kennet Avenue, where two Graig Lwyd axes were found in a late Neolithic context. An axe from the Neolithic habitation site at Abingdon, Berks. has been found to be a product of the Stake Pass factory. This site must date from the late Neolithic, for not only does its characteristic pottery appear at Windmill Hill as an import at an advanced stage of the site's history, but among the Abingdon flints were a late Neolithic single-piece sickle and an Early Bronze Age dagger. The presence of the Stake Pass axe in this context and the fragments from the upper levels at Windmill Hill confirm the chronological equation afforded by other evidence. Foreign stone axes appear to have been primary at Maiden Castle, but generally speaking the exploitation of igneous rocks for axe manufacture does not appear to start in Wessex during the period of the Neolithic A culture, but to be associated with the Neolithic B folk and to continue into Early Bronze Age times.

The use of the Tievebulliagh axe-factory during the period of the building of the Irish long horned cairns is attested by the finds at Doey's Cairn, Dunloy, where two axes almost certainly from this factory were found as votive deposits in the "sealing" of the portal. The most important chronological landmark for the manufacture and distribution of the igneous stone axes is that afforded by the discovery of the Upware axe, of Graig Lwyd rock, *in situ* in a Fenland peat bed. Thanks to the work of the Fenland Research Committee and in particular to that of Dr. Godwin, the sequence of the Fenland peats and the forest history represented by the pollen grains contained in them has been worked out and correlated with the archaeology and post-glacial geology of south-eastern England and of Northern Europe generally, and a zoning of the peats over a period of time from about 8000 B.C. to the present has been possible. The Upware axe was found high up in the Lower Peat, just over the junction of Godwin's Zones VII and VIIc, and in a position which equated with a horizon immediately below the Fen Clay deposit. In terms of climatic periods, this implies a very early position in the Sub-Boreal stage, and archaeologically, a horizon later than the East English Neolithic A. The Fen Clay was laid down immediately before the arrival in the region of the A beaker folk and the equation of its position with the land subsidence which submerged the late Neolithic occupation sites on the Essex coast securely places the Upware axe in a similarly late Neolithic context—in terms of absolute chronology, somewhere about 1900–2000 B.C. The exact coincidence of this geological dating with the archaeological stratigraphy at Avebury and Windmill Hill is eminently satisfactory and of considerable importance, and this correlation between two so widely separated regions has been made possible solely by means of the petrological determination of the rock of axes exported from a single factory whose effective period of production cannot have been of very great length. It is clear that many more important discoveries await this combination of petrological and archaeological method.

Use of Smelted Iron by Precolumbian Eskimo

Helge Larsen and Froelich Rainey have worked on the prehistory of the Arctic for many years. Larsen has conducted extensive excavations in Greenland and Rainey has worked in the central and western Alaskan area. Both felt that the answer to many of the unsolved problems in the prehistory of the area lay in the area near Bering Sea. At the time of the expedition mentioned below Larsen was curator in the Danish National Museum, and Rainey was Professor of Anthropology at the University of Alaska.

Following a clue given them by Knud Rasmussen, they headed for Point Hope, Alaska, and began excavations at the recent Eskimo site of Tigara. While there, they discovered the Ipiutak site, where their work revealed an old manifestation of an early stage in Eskimo prehistory, a culture showing many resemblances to its presumed parents in Siberia. One of the discoveries which proved useful both for dating the site and in showing its relationship with the peoples of ancient and adjacent Asia, was that the people of Ipiutak used iron. It was shown that this iron was not meteoric, like that of Greenland, but terrestrial in origin. They note that iron was first used in Siberia in the middle of the first millennium B.C. and they believe that the first Paleo-Eskimo migrations to North America took place at this time. The site at Ipiutak was first occupied shortly after this period, sometime in the first half of the first millennium A.D.

Larsen and Rainey's observations on the use of iron and its significance in the Ipiutak site and L. W. Strock's spectroscopic analysis which proved the terrestrial origin of the iron follow.[2]

It is generally accepted that the composite knife was used to work antler and ivory. For the fine surface decoration found on many antler and ivory artifacts, the Ipiutak people probably used engraving tools which consisted of a slender ivory or antler shaft with a sharpened incisor of a ground squirrel or an iron point set into a slot in the end. The ground squirrel incisors, of which three were found in place, were all sharpened to a point. Enamel, of course, is an excellent tool for engraving the softer ivory and antler. It has undoubtedly been the tool of an artist. With few exceptions, these engraving tools are decorated, some of them very elaborately. The decoration is usually limited to the middle section. It is possible that the decoration had a utilitarian purpose and served to prevent the instrument from slipping in the hand of the artist, as, for instance, in the specimen with the two knobs. This implement was possibly also used as a drill, for instance, to make the dots and small sockets for inlays which occur frequently in Ipiutak decoration. This assumption is based on the shape of the butt. Almost all the engraving tools have a conical butt which shows signs of wear caused by rotation. One butt is a truncated cone with a short tip in the center. The natural explanation for this form would be that the butt has rotated in a drill rest or drill mouthpiece. No drill rests or drill mouthpieces were found, but that, of course, could be accidental. It follows then that we must find a suggestion as to how the tool was manipulated. The decoration is placed exactly where the bow-string should run, which argues against the use of a bow. The only explanation seems to be that it was turned by being rotated between the fingers or palms.

One specimen has had an iron bit. Only a small portion of the bit remained in the socket but, although highly oxidized, it was enough for an analysis. Dr. Frederick H. Pough of this museum reported after a microchemical analysis:

The engraving tool with the oxidized iron point was tested by microchemical methods to determine the presence of nickel, which would have been found

[2] Helge Larsen and Froelich Rainey, *Ipiutak and the Arctic Whale-Hunting Culture,* American Museum of Natural History, Anthropological Papers, New York, 1948, vol. 42, pp. 82–84; Appendix 3 (by L. W. Strock), p. 254. By permission of the American Museum of Natural History.

had the iron been of meteoric origin. A small fragment proved to be magnetic, indicating that sufficient residual unoxidized iron was still present in the limonite to give a positive nickel test if nickel was present. A negative reaction indicated that no nickel is present and that consequently the iron is of terrestrial origin since all meteoric iron contains at least a small proportion of nickel. A comparative test was made with a piece of equally oxidized Ovifak iron and a strong nickel test obtained, confirming the conclusion that the [Ipiutak] iron probably was refined from terrestrial ores.

On Pough's suggestion, the iron was also subjected to a spectroscopic test, which confirmed its terrestrial origin. The presence of iron in the Ipiutak find is obviously of paramount significance. In the first place, it supports our belief that the composite knife handles and other knife handles with a very narrow blade slit were intended to hold an iron blade. Second, it means that we must revise our present opinion regarding the use of iron in the Eskimo culture; and, finally, it provides excellent evidence as to the origin and age of the Ipiutak culture. Prior to the Ipiutak excavations, the general belief was that iron was introduced into Eskimo culture in the Punuk phase, an assumption that was based upon Collins' find of iron-pointed engraving tools and knife handles, with sockets designed for a metal blade, belonging to that culture phase. As the source of the metal Collins (1937:304–305) suggested Asia, where iron objects were used in China, as well as in the central part, at least about the middle of the first millennium B.C. Collins thinks that "iron in small quantities might possibly have reached Bering Strait and St. Lawrence Island more than a thousand years ago." Leaving the question as to precise date open, we now have good reason to believe that iron was known to the Eskimo of the Arctic Whale Hunting culture during an earlier phase than Punuk. The Ipiutak culture definitely antedates Punuk and is probably also earlier than Old Bering Sea, but seems to be contemporaneous with Okvik, the earliest phase of the Arctic Whale Hunting culture. Furthermore, Okvik and Ipiutak have many common traits which indicate definite contact; it is almost certain that the Okvik people had a knowledge of iron and probably also used it as did the Ipiutak people. No iron has been found in association with Okvik artifacts, but, as Rainey has already pointed out, the narrow blade slits in the true composite knife handles, as well as in its prototype (Okvik Types 1 and 2), suggest the use of metal blades. As already mentioned in our opinion the composite knife handle was originally designed to hold a small metal blade by a people who had access to only small quantities of the precious metal. Iron-bladed knives were undoubtedly also used by the Old Bering Sea people. Fifty-six composite knife handles were found at Miyowagh, St. Lawrence Island, a site in which the Old Bering Sea as well as the Punuk phase is represented. Thirty-one of these, and one from the earlier Hillside site, had such small sockets "that they must have been designed for metal blades." With our present knowledge we can thus be quite sure that iron was used by the Eskimo in the earliest known phases of their culture. As we believe that the Ipiutak culture is not only contemporaneous with but also precedes the Okvik phase, the Ipiutak engraving tool is the earliest evidence of the use of refined iron in the Western Hemisphere. The iron was, of course, of Asiatic origin.

Engraving tools similar to these are known from Okvik and Ekseavik on the Kobuk River, both with decoration around the middle. Several specimens are known from St. Lawrence Island. One, from Early Punuk, is decorated like the above, while the others are much shorter and of a different shape. It is undoubtedly accidental that no engravers have been found in the Old Bering Sea phase. In northwestern Alaska the type persisted until fairly recent times. A wooden engraving tool from Cape Smythe, which is probably contemporaneous with Old Tigara, has four sharp serrated ridges on its lower part near the middle. Engraving tools with decoration in relief have recently been reported from the Aleutians and were in use on Kodiak Island until recent time.

SPECTROGRAPHIC ANALYSIS OF IRON

A small fragment of the iron engraving tool from the Ipiutak excavations was furnished me [Strock] for spectrographic analysis in order to determine whether the material is of terrestrial or meteoric origin.

The specimen was badly corroded and cemented with other material—presumably oxidization products. A similar fragment of iron from the Shara Murun Basin, Inner Mongolia, stated to be several hundred years old, was furnished for reference, together with fragments of the Cape York, Greenland, iron meteorite.

Since qualitative spectra alone suffice to distinguish readily between terrestrial and meteoric iron, ultraviolet spectra of the specimens were recorded in juxtaposition on a photographic plate for convenient comparison. The entire samples were placed in craters of carbon electrodes and burned to completion in a direct current arc. A spectrum of pure iron to be used as a wave length reference was photographed on the same plate.

Visual inspection of the spectra revealed the striking difference in composition between the Alaskan and Mongolian irons and the Greenland meteorite. The characteristically high nickel and cobalt contents of all meteoric iron is revealed by the large number of spectral lines of these elements in the Cape York meteorite, whereas none of them are visible in spectra of the two irons. As documentary proof of this result, an enlarged positive copy of the spectrogram for the wave length region 3116 Å to 3015 Å accompanies this report. Lines due to iron are easily identified by reference to the iron reference spectrum placed on the same chart.

In addition to the iron lines in the Cape York meteorite, the following other lines have been identified in this small region of its spectrum and labeled on the chart:

Cobalt	Nickel
3044.005[a]	3037.935
3048.888	*3050.819*[a]
3061.819	3054.316
3072.344	3064.623
3082.618	3080.755
3086.777	3097.118
3089.595	3099.115
	3101.544[a]
	3101.879
	3105.468
	3114.124

[a] Strongest lines are italicized.

The average composition of 318 meteoric irons tabulated by O. C. Farrington is 90.85 per cent iron, 0.59 per cent cobalt, and 8.52 per cent nickel, which differs only slightly from published analyses of the Cape York meteorite (7.50 per cent nickel and 0.49 per cent cobalt) according to data given by V. M. Goldschmidt. Spectra of both the Mongolian and Point Hope, Alaska, irons show no trace of a resemblance to this meteoric iron composition. Further evidence of the same nature is the presence of a weak line in the Cape York meteorite spectrum due to the rare element germanium (Ge 3039.064) which geochemical investigations have shown to be a constant and characteristic constituent of meteoric iron. It is not visible in the Alaskan or Mongolian irons.

All evidence secured in this study shows the Point Hope, Alaska, engraving tool fragment submitted to be terrestrial iron readily distinguishable from meteoric iron by qualitative spectrographic examination.

Copper Bells from the Snaketown Site

The archaeological site of Snaketown, first discovered in 1927, is near the Gila River in south-central Arizona, in the heart of the area formerly inhabited by the Hohokam peoples. Excavations by the Gila Pueblo staff began in 1934 and were continued intermittently for several seasons.

The occurrence of copper bells in Snaketown and the American Southwest in general, where little additional evidence of local metallurgy has been noted, raises many questions. Were they manufactured locally or were they imported? If they were manufactured locally, were local ores or imported ores used? If the finished bells were imported, where did they come from? Central Mexico and east-central United States (south of Lake Superior) made extensive use of copper, the latter using native copper and the former smelting local ores, and thus were the most likely sources for the copper and the finished bells.

Detailed spectrographic analysis of the Snaketown bells seems to eliminate

Central Mexico and east-central United States as sources of the ore or metal and thus the area of origin of both metal and finished product was narrowed to include only the American Southwest and northern Mexico. Haury (1947) has more recently reversed his opinion of 1937 and now believes that all Southwestern cast copper objects are of Mexican origin. E. Haury's account and W. C. Root's metallurgical analysis of the Snaketown bells follow.[3]

The only metal objects found at Snaketown were made of copper. These consisted of 28 copper bells, all found on the floor of 6 G House, 8 where they had fallen from some higher point in the house on its destruction by fire. Shell beads were found with the bells with which they had been strung. The bells are remarkably uniform in size and shape, suggesting the workmanship of a single individual, and they are small as Southwestern bells go. The resonator is pear-shaped, slit at the bottom, and slightly flattened on top where the eyelet joins the bell. Small stone pebbles and copper pellets were used as clappers.

A spectrographic analysis of one of the Snaketown bells, made through the courtesy of Dr. A. M. Tozzer, Harvard University, indicated a high grade copper with less than 1 per cent of silver and traces of lead and arsenic. A similar analysis of many bells, both Southwestern and Mexican by Dr. W. C. Root, and of copper objects from the Lake Superior region, has shown that the copper in the Snaketown bell conforms, roughly, with that found in other Southwestern bells, and is distinguishable from the copper in bells from Central Mexico and copper objects from the Lake Superior area. With the last two regions eliminated, we may believe that the source for Southwestern bells was local and that the bells were made somewhere in the region.

There is no doubt that the bells were cast by the *cire perdue* method. But, as is shown by the results of a study of the structure in copper bells [Appendix III, not reproduced here] by Mr. B. H. McLeod, International Smelter, Inspiration Copper Company, Inspiration, Arizona, there are some aspects of this method of casting heretofore not fully appreciated. Mr. McLeod believes, for example, that the bells were probably not made by pouring molten metal into the molds because of the physical difficulties of so casting copper into thin objects; and further, that such a method is denied by the absence of oxygen in the copper of the bells analyzed, compelling him to think that they were made in a covered mold with the unmolten copper placed in a crucible attached to the mold and the whole laid in the fire, thus shutting out all oxygen.

Fortunately the Snaketown bells were found under such circumstances that their phase assignment was beyond question. The house in which

[3] E. W. Haury, "Minerals and Metals," in H. S. Gladwin, E. W. Haury, E. B. Sayles, and N. Gladwin, *Excavations at Snaketown: Material Culture*, Medallion Papers, Gila Pueblo, Arizona, 1937, no. 25, pp. 163–167; Appendix II, "The Metallurgy of Arizona and New Mexico" (by W. C. Root), pp. 276–277. By permission of H. S. Gladwin and E. Haury.

they occurred contained about 60 vessels of pottery, all dating from the Sacaton Phase. This limits the occurrence of the bells to between 900–1100, probably one of the earliest instances of the trait in the Southwest. Other bells from an horizon that was approximately comparable are those reported from the Cameron Creek Village (Bradfield, 1931:124), Pueblo Bonito (Pepper, 1920:269, 324–325), and Aztec (Morris, 1919:100). None of these can date much later than 1125.

Although a comprehensive study of Southwestern bells has not been undertaken, it begins to appear that the oldest bells were smaller and more consistently globular or pear-shaped than the bells from later (Pueblo IV) ruins which were not only larger, as a rule, but displayed special features, as the "wire" technique and, in one case, an effigy type (Fewkes, 1904:50). On the present evidence it may also be stated that copper bells were most numerous from about 1300 to 1400.

Before Dr. Root's statements regarding the source of copper were available, it was always assumed that copper bells signified trade from Mexico. But we now know that, if this was the case, the trade was not from Central Mexico, where the constituents of the metal in bells are different. Some of them may, however, have come from northern Mexico where the bells have practically the same impurities in amount and kind as the bells from Gila Pueblo. In Pueblo IV times the greatest concentration of bells was to be seen in the ruins of Chihuahua and in the Salado ruins of southern Arizona, the former area apparently being the better supplied. It is impossible to say as yet whether the Southwestern bells came from a single source or whether they were made in various ruins by a restricted group or guild which had knowledge of the process. Owing to the difficulty of the technique, it is not probable that the process was a matter of common knowledge.

METALLURGICAL ANALYSIS

Twenty-three objects from Arizona and New Mexico and four objects from Chihuahua were analyzed. They were found to consist of copper with a trace of silver. Except for one bell with a slight trace of tin, they contained no tin, lead, arsenic, antimony, or bismuth.

Two analyses of native copper from Lake Superior show the presence of about .01 per cent of arsenic in the copper. Objects from Central Mexico usually, though not always, contain traces of one or more of the following elements as impurities—tin, lead, iron, arsenic, antimony, bismuth.

Two pieces of copper ore were among the objects analyzed. The largest is from a ruin on the upper San Francisco River, southwest New Mexico. It consists of metallic copper mixed with cuprite . . . and (is) unlike native copper from the Lake Superior region, which seldom contains cuprite. . . .

It has generally been supposed that metal objects found in the Southwest were derived from either the Lake Superior region to the northeast, or Mexico to the south. But the absence of impurities frequently found in copper from those regions, and the presence of objects made from ores frequently found in the Southwest, of similar composition to the copper objects themselves, leads one to the conclusion that the metal was prepared and made into bells, etc., by the natives of Arizona, New Mexico, and Chihuahua from ore found close at hand. . . .

So few objects have been analyzed from northern Mexico that it is difficult to define the boundary between the metallurgy of the Southwest and that of Central Mexico. It may be as far south as Michoacan. It is equally difficult to locate the precise origin of the metal objects found in Arizona and New Mexico. While the mineralogical conditions are just those that would be expected to produce the metals found there, the lack of mines, furnaces, molds, etc., and the comparative scarcity of metal objects so far discovered would point to some other place of origin. This may possibly have been Chihuahua or a region even further south. But they certainly did not come from the Valley of Mexico. . . .

To be added to the above are 65 more analyses of objects in the Gila Pueblo collections, making a total of 88 from the region. Of 24 objects from Arizona and New Mexico all are pure copper except for traces of iron and silver, except one which contains a slight trace of antimony. Of the 31 objects from Chihuahua two contain slight traces of lead, one a slight trace of arsenic, and six contain traces of antimony.

The objects from Arizona and New Mexico appear to have been made from a copper ore free of most impurities. Those from Chihuahua seem to be from ore sometimes as pure as in New Mexico, sometimes containing slight traces of lead, arsenic, antimony in addition to silver and iron. Similar slight variations in the composition of copper ores from the same region is not uncommon.

There is nothing in these analyses to change my previous conclusions that the copper of which these objects were made came from the Southwest rather than from the Lake Superior region or Central or Southern Mexico.

The facts on which I base my opinion that the objects found in the Southwest had their origin there are these. Beads of cuprite have been found in Chihuahua and New Mexico. Cuprite is a very common Southwestern ore and is easily reduced to metallic copper. The cuprite in the beads shows no trace of arsenic, antimony, bismuth, tin or lead. Neither do most of the objects. On the other hand, copper objects from the Valley of Mexico usually contain more or less of these elements as an impurity.

Against this view are the negative facts that no metal workings have been found in the Southwest, and not very many metal objects.

Examination of these objects strengthens the view . . . that they were made by a process of casting, probably by the *cire perdue* process, as two were of wirework technique. There are no indications of plating, gilding, soldering, or the other more complex processes that were in use in the Valley of Mexico and elsewhere.

13

ART

This chapter includes five rather miscellaneous selections. The first, by D. H. Lawrence, is a brief extract from his charmingly written account of a visit to the Etruscan tombs of Tarquinia. The second selection is a description of part of a newly discovered mural of the Classic Maya, dating from some 1500 years later than the Etruscan tomb paintings. The reader then encounters a post-Paleolithic cave painting from the Spanish Levant which portrays a ritual dance—it is older than the previous two by perhaps eight to ten thousand years. From a still earlier time is the small stone pebble which was engraved by Late Paleolithic hunters. The final excerpt is from Lothrop's careful description of the battle scenes embossed upon gold disks dredged from the great natural well (cenote) at the Classic Maya site of Chichen Itza in Yucatan.

Thus, through the subject matter of art we are enabled to glimpse some features of ancient sport and relaxation, ceremony and ritual, and battle, where both victors and vanquished are represented.

Murals in Etruscan Tombs at Tarquinia

The paintings from the Etruscan tombs at Tarquinia, Orvieto, Chiusi, Véies, and Vulci have been much studied (see Bartoccini, n.d.; Poulsen, 1922; Mühlstein, 1929; Weege, 1931; Romanelli, 1951; and Leisinger, 1953). According to Leisinger (1953:24, 50), the Tomb of the Leopards and the Tomb of the Feast which are described here[1] date respectively from the fifth and second centuries B.C.

The Tomb of the Leopards is a charming, cosy little room, and the paintings on the walls have not been so very much damaged. All the tombs are ruined to some degree by weather and vulgar vandalism, having

[1] D. H. Lawrence, *Etruscan Places*, Compass Edition, New York, 1932, pp. 66–78. Reprinted by permission of The Viking Press, Inc.

been left and neglected like common holes, when they had been broken open again and rifled to the last gasp.

But still the paintings are fresh and alive: the ochre-reds and blacks and blues and blue-greens are curiously alive and harmonious on the creamy yellow walls. Most of the tomb walls have had a thin coat of stucco, but it is of the same paste as the living rock, which is fine and yellow, and weathers to a lovely creamy gold, a beautiful colour for a background.

The walls of this little tomb are a dance of real delight. The room seems inhabited still by Etruscans of the sixth century before Christ, a vivid, life-accepting people, who must have lived with real fullness. On come the dancers and the music-players, moving in a broad frieze towards the front wall of the tomb, the wall facing us as we enter from the dark stairs, and where the banquet is going on in all its glory. Above the banquet, in the gable angle, are the two spotted leopards, heraldically facing each other across a little tree. And the ceiling of rock has chequered slopes of red and black and yellow and blue squares, with a roof-beam painted with coloured circles, dark red and blue and yellow. So that all is colour, and we do not seem to be underground at all, but in some gay chamber of the past.

The dancers on the right wall move with a strange, powerful alertness onwards. They are men dressed only in a loose coloured scarf, or in the gay handsome chlamys draped as a mantle. The *subulo* plays the double flute the Etruscans loved so much, touching the stops with big, exaggerated hands, the man behind him touches the seven-stringed lyre, the man in front turns round and signals with his left hand, holding a big wine-bowl in his right. And so they move on, on their long, sandalled feet, past the little berried olive-trees, swiftly going with their limbs full of life, full of life to the tips.

This sense of vigorous, strong-bodied liveliness is characteristic of the Etruscans, and is somehow beyond art. You cannot think of art, but only of life itself, as if this were the very life of the Etruscans, dancing in their coloured wraps with massive yet exuberant naked limbs, ruddy from the air and the sea-light, dancing and fluting along through the little olive-trees, out in the fresh day.

The end wall has a splendid banqueting scene (see Fig. 13.1). The feasters recline upon a checked or tartan couch-cover, on the banqueting couch, and in the open air, for they have little trees behind them. The six feasters are bold and full of life like the dancers, but they are strong, they keep their life so beautifully and richly inside themselves, they are not loose, they can't lose themselves even in their wild moments. They lie in pairs, man and woman, reclining equally on the couch, curiously friendly. The two end women are called *hetaerae*, courtesans; chiefly because they have yellow hair, which seems to have been a favourite feature in a woman of pleasure. The men are dark and ruddy, and naked to the waist. The women, sketched in on the creamy rock, are fair, and wear thin gowns, with rich mantles round their hips. They have a certain free bold look, and perhaps really are courtesans.

The man at the end is holding up, between thumb and forefinger, an egg, showing it to the yellow-haired woman who reclines next to him,

Fig. 13.1.   Tomb of Leopards, Tarquinia.

she who is putting out her left hand as if to touch his breast. He, in his right hand, holds a large wine-dish, for the revel.

The next couple, man and fair-haired woman, are looking round and making the salute with the right hand curved over, in the usual Etruscan gesture. It seems as if they too are saluting the mysterious egg held up by the man at the end; who is, no doubt, the man who has died and whose feast is being celebrated. But in front of the second couple a naked slave with a chaplet on his head is brandishing an empty wine-jug, as if to say he is fetching more wine. Another slave farther down is holding out a curious thing like a little axe, or fan. The last two feasters are rather damaged. One of them is holding up a garland to the other, but not putting it over his head, as they still put a garland over your head, in India, to honour you.

Above the banqueters, in the gable angle, the two great spotted male leopards hang out their tongues and face each other heraldically, lifting a paw, on either side of a little tree. They are the leopards or panthers of the underworld Bacchus, guarding the exits and the entrances of the passion of life.

There is a mystery and a portentiousness in the simple scenes which go deeper than commonplace life. It seems all so gay and light. Yet there is a certain weight, or depth of significance that goes beyond aesthetic beauty.

If one once starts looking, there is much to see. But if one glances merely, there is nothing but a pathetic little room with unimposing, half-obliterated, scratchy little paintings in tempera.

There are many tombs. When we have seen one, up we go, a little bewildered, into the afternoon sun, across a tract of rough, tormented hill, and down again to the underground, like rabbits in a warren. The hilltop is really a warren of tombs. And gradually the underworld of the Etruscans becomes more real than the above day of the afternoon. One begins to live with the painted dancers and feasters and mourners, and to look eagerly for them.

A very lovely dance tomb is the *Tomba del Triclinio*, or *del Convito*, both of which mean: Tomb of the Feast (see Fig. 13.2). In size and

Fig. 13.2. Tomb of the Feast, Tarquinia.

shape this is much the same as the other tombs we have seen. It is a little chamber about fifteen feet by eleven, six feet high at the walls, about eight feet at the centre. It is again a tomb for one person, like nearly all the old painted tombs here. So there is no inner furnishing. Only the farther half of the rock-floor, the pale yellow-white rock, is raised two or three inches, and on one side of this raised part are the four holes where the feet of the sarcophagus stood. For the rest, the tomb has only its painted walls and ceiling.

And how lovely these have been, and still are! The band of dancing figures that go round the room still is bright in colour, fresh, the women in thin spotted dresses of linen muslin and coloured mantles with fine borders, the men merely in a scarf. Widely the bacchic woman throws back her head and curves out her long, strong fingers, wild and yet contained within herself, while the broad-bodied young man turns round to her, lifting his dancing hand to hers till the thumbs all but touch. They are dancing in the open, past little trees, and birds are running, and a little fox-tailed dog is watching something with the naive intensity of the young. Wildly and delightedly dances the next woman, every bit of her, in her soft boots and her bordered mantle, with jewels on her arms; till one remembers the old dictum, that every part of the body and of the *anima* shall know religion, and be in touch with the gods. Toward her comes the young man piping on the double flute, and dancing as he comes. He is clothed only in a fine linen scarf with a border, that hangs over his arms, and his strong legs dance of themselves, so full of life. Yet, too, there is a certain solemn intensity in his face, as he turns to the woman beyond him, who swoops in a bow to him as she vibrates her castanets.

She is drawn fair-skinned, as all the women are, and he is of a dark red colour. That is the convention, in the tombs. But it is more than convention. In the early days men smeared themselves with scarlet when they took on their sacred natures. The Red Indians still do it. When they wish to figure in their sacred and portentous selves they smear their bodies all over with red. That must be why they are called Red Indians. In the past, for all serious or solemn occasions, they rubbed red pigment into their skins. And the same to-day. And to-day, when they wish to put strength into their vision, and to see true, they smear round their eyes with vermilion, rubbing it into the skin. . . .

It is then partly a convention, and partly a symbol, with the Etruscans, to represent their men red in colour, a strong red. Here in the tombs everything is in its sacred or inner-significant aspect. But also the red colour is not so very unnatural. When the Italian to-day goes almost naked on the beach he becomes of a lovely dark ruddy colour, dark as any Indian. And the Etruscans went a good deal naked. The sun painted them with the sacred minimum.

The dancers dance on, the birds run, at the foot of a little tree a rabbit crouches in a bunch, bunched with life. And on the tree hangs a narrow, fringed scarf, like a priest's stole; another symbol.

The end wall has a banqueting scene, rather damaged, but still interesting. We see two separate couches, and a man and a woman on each. The woman this time is dark-haired, so she need not be a courtesan. The Etruscans shared the banqueting bench with their wives; which is more than the Greeks or Romans did, at this period. The classic world thought it indecent for an honest woman to recline as the men did, even at the family table. If the woman appeared at all, she must sit up straight, in a chair.

Here, the women recline calmly with the men, and one shows a bare foot at the end of the dark couch. In front of the *lecti*, the couches, is in each case a little low square table bearing delicate dishes of food for the feasters. But they are not eating. One woman is lifting her hand to her head in a strange salute to the robed piper at the end, the other woman seems with the lifted hand to be saying No! to the charming maid, perhaps a servant, who stands at her side, presumably offering the *alabastron*, or ointment-jar, while the man at the end apparently is holding up an egg. Wreaths hang from the ivy-border above, a boy is bringing a wine-jug, the music goes on, and under the beds a cat is on the prowl, while an alert cock watches him. The silly partridge, however, turns his back, stepping innocently along.

This lovely tomb has a pattern of ivy and ivy berries, the ivy of the underworld Bacchus, along the roof-beam and in a border round the top of the walls. The roof-slopes are chequered in red and black, white, blue, brown and yellow squares. In the gable angle, instead of the heraldic beasts, two naked men are sitting reaching back to the centre of an ivy-covered altar, arm outstretched across the ivy. But one man is almost obliterated. At the foot of the other man, in the tight angle of the roof, is a pigeon, the bird of the soul that coos out of the unseen.

This tomb has been open since 1830, and is still fresh. It is interesting to see, in Fritz Weege's book, *Etruskische Malerei*, a reproduction of an old water-colour drawing of the dancers on the right wall. It is a good drawing, yet, as one looks closer, it is quite often out, both in line and position. These Etruscan paintings, not being in our convention, are very difficult to copy. The picture shows my rabbit all spotted, as if it were some queer cat. And it shows a squirrel in the little tree in front of the piper, and flowers, and many details that have now disappeared.

But it is a good drawing, unlike some that Weege reproduces, which are so Flaxmanized and Greekified; and made according to what our great-grandfathers thought they *ought* to be, as to be really funny, and a warning for ever against thinking how things *ought* to be, when already they are quite perfectly what they are.

We climb up to the world, and pass for a few minutes through the open day. Then down we go again.

Mural Scenes at Bonampak, Chiapas

One of the most notable discoveries of Maya art is that made in 1946 of the painted murals contained in the three rooms of Structure 1 at the Classic site of Bonampak in the state of Chiapas, southern Mexico.

Maya paintings with the degree of realism exhibited at Bonampak are rare, and the more usual expression of both sculptured and painted art is "overburdened with esoteric symbols and had little regard for common occurrences." The Bonampak murals depict lay or semireligious activities.

J. E. S. Thompson, from whose pen the following extract is taken,[2] believes that the murals tell a connected story, since he can identify the same individuals

[2] Karl Ruppert, J. Eric S. Thompson, and Tatiana Proskouriakoff, *Bonampak, Chiapas, Mexico*, Carnegie Institution of Washington, Washington, D.C., 1955, Publication 602, pp. 52–54. By permission of the Carnegie Institution.

in several scenes. The sequence of scenes apparently begins with the preparation for a dance by impersonators of gods of the earth (Room 1), shifts then to
a punitive raid on a small settlement and the capture of prisoners (Room 2),
then portrays the arraignment of the prisoners (Room 2; this is the scene described in the following excerpt), and concludes with the sacrificial ceremony
and dance (Room 3). The principal actors are the head chief (*halach uinic*), his
wife, their daughter (or a second wife?), a child (son?), and three lesser chiefs
(*batabs*).

The illustration shown here is the prisoner arraignment which covers one of
the four walls in Structure 1. However, the reproduction can give no hint of the
original's rich colors, which in this scene number about ten.

The paintings are believed to date from about 800 A.D. in the Goodman-
Martinez-Thompson correlation, or 260 years earlier (540 A.D.) if the alternative Spinden correlation of the Maya and Christian calendars is used. Radiocarbon dating of wooden lintels which bear Maya dates from the Classic Maya
site of Tikal seem to support the Spinden correlation although it is not possible
to affirm positively that the question is settled.

ARRAIGNMENT OF THE PRISONERS

This covers the north wall of Room 2. The scene (see Fig. 13.3) is
laid on and in front of a stepped structure, possibly a squat pyramid but
more probably a long step-terraced platform about 3 m. high. The scene
is out of doors, for blue, to represent the sky, forms the background of
those who stand on the summit of the structure. Satterthwaite calls my
attention to the background being a fairly realistic elevation of a structure resembling the basal platform of Structure R-9 at Piedras Negras.

The most important personages are grouped on the summit of the
structure. Slightly off-center is a personage clad in a jaguar jerkin and
wearing a large jade pectoral; a sweeping panache of long quetzal
feathers attached to his headdress attests to his high rank. I think it can
be fairly assumed that this is the same halach uinic, great chief, whom
we saw watching from his dais the preparations for the ceremony in
Room 1 and whom we have just encountered in the raid. To left and
right of him are three personages wearing jaguar skins and carrying
batons. Two of them wear jaguar heads as helmets; the third has
donned the head of some unidentified animal. It would appear that
these are the same three batabs who were shown in Room 1, first being
attired for the ceremony and, subsequently, as participants in the ceremony. On the flanks are, to the left, five other persons of obvious rank;
to the right, two women and a fat male attendant. The rather imperious
lady presumably is the chief's wife, whom we recognized on the dais in
Room 1. One feels that in our culture she would have been an active
organizer and clubwoman. The second woman supposedly can be equated
with the second woman on the dais; the fat attendant we shall encounter
again in Room 3.

Fig. 13.3. Mural in Room 2, Bonampak.

Seated at the foot of the chief, and looking up to him in an attitude of fear or entreaty, is a naked man whose coarse face and tow-like hair contrast strongly with those of the persons of rank. On the next two steps are seated seven other individuals, whose gross features, lank matted hair, and lack of ornament or clothing except for the simplest loincloth indicate that they are of the same status as the supplicant just noted. Three gaze, presumably in pain or fear, at their hands from which blood drips; a well-clad individual holds the bleeding hand of one of them as though he had just performed the act which caused the bleeding, but unfortunately, his other hand is not visible because of damage to the mural, thereby depriving us of information on the implement used to cause the bleeding. Others hold out their hands as though they awaited with fear and trepidation the same fate.

It is not easy to explain this scene. The bleeding hands do not seem to have been maimed; at least there is no sign that phalanges have been cut off. Moreover, if the person who holds the hand of one of the captives by the wrist has just completed the operation, as seems to be the case, he could hardly have cut off parts of the fingers, since a severing action would require that the captive's hand be placed on the ground or on something solid. There is no evidence that blood is being drawn for ceremonial purposes, since it is not being collected on strips of bark paper or in vessels. As the Maya are not by nature sadists, I do not think that torture of captives is depicted.

These eight men clearly are enemies captured in the raid, for they are of the same physical type as those being captured in the battle scene and they similarly lack ornament and clothing. Moreover, unless it was the convention to represent all enemies as physically repulsive, one must assume that all eight prisoners are peasants, not members of the ruling class.

Throughout Mesoamerica persons of noble blood were sought as sacrificial victims, particularly, it would seem when the victim impersonated a god and so had to be without blemish; prisoners of plebian origin often became the slaves of their captors. However, it is clear that many sacrificial victims were not of rank, for slaves were purchased in large numbers for sacrifice both in Yucatan and on the Mexican plateau, and of the huge quantities of prisoners sacrificed by the Aztec not all could have been persons of importance. Moreover, not a few of the captives depicted on Maya stelae, who presumably were to be sacrificed at the dedicatory ceremonies in connection with the erection of those monuments, appear to be of lowly origin. If the eight are to live, as slaves, it is possible, although hardly probable, that they are being marked in some way, perhaps by scarification. To the best of my knowledge there is no report of slaves being branded in any way.

One is inclined to think that the terror of the eight prisoners is not engendered by fear of the cutting or pricking of their fingers or hands, but may be due to their imminent execution. If, however, they are to be sacrificed, what does the finger bleeding portray? Sahagun, in his description of the ceremonies in the month Panquetzaliztli, records that a short time before the slaves were to be sacrificed each dipped both hands in a bowl of dye either of red ocher or of a blue color and imprinted them on the lintels and house posts of the house of his master. It is just conceivable that the preparations for an analogous ceremony are here depicted, with the imprint of the victim's hand to be made in its own blood. Hand imprints in red paint are not uncommon in Maya temples; the Lacandon believe that red hands were imprinted on a building to mark its completion.

In the middle of the eight captives and with his arm almost touching the foot of the great chief lies a man whose posture is rendered with dignity, realism, and wistful beauty. His closed eye and position together indicate that he is dead or, conceivably has fainted; his features are refined and his hair lacks that towlike quality of the others. Several small gashes on his body seem to represent wounds, although they hardly appear to have been fatal, and there seems to be no sign of blood.

It is hard to surmise what part this handsome man has played in the events. One may, I think, presume that he is one of the enemy. If he died in or immediately after the fight, it is difficult to imagine why his body should have been brought to the scene of this ceremony; if he has just been sacrificed, it is not easy to see how this was done. Moreover, one gets the impression that the events depicted in this scene are not primarily religious, but rather that they are a prelude to the great religious ceremony.

There appears to be a gash below the left breast, but it does not seem to be large enough to have permitted of the removal of the heart. One is mindful of the arrow sacrifice practiced in Yucatan immediately prior to the coming of the Spaniards. That was a late development, and it is almost certain that at the time these murals were painted, the Maya had no knowledge of the bow and arrow. It is probable, however, that the arrow sacrifice derives from an earlier form in which spears were hurled at the victim. The victim on the mural may have been wounded in the genitals, recalling Landa's account of the arrow sacrifice in which he says that at the start of the ceremony the priest wounded the victim in that part. Moreover, it is interesting to note that in a Maya poem on the arrow sacrifice, published with a translation by Barrera Vasquez, the shooters are instructed not to shoot with all their strength but to cause light wounds; the same is true of the Pawnee sacrifice to the morning star. It is, accordingly, possible that this youth has been sacrificially speared, but such an interpretation must be regarded as highly speculative.

At his foot a human head, surrounded by greenery, rests on one of the terraces in a manner strongly reminiscent of the decapitated head of the maize god which rests on the earth symbol on page 34 of Codex Dresden. The green on which the head rests may represent leaves of the wild *Ficus*, the Maya *copo*, which was used to a considerable extent in Maya ceremony. According to Landa, leaves of this tree were strewn on the floor during certain ceremonies. In the Quijada papers it is reported that at a clandestine ceremony at Yaxcaba the victim was sacrificed in front of the idols which had been placed on some leaves of *higuera de infierno*. This is probably the same plant. The same source speaks of the church of Sanahcat being decorated with *copo* leaves for human sacrifice, "which they used to do in their sacrifices of [to] their idols." To the right of this head the wall surface is damaged. The area where the mural has scaled off is perhaps sufficient to have held the body belonging to the head. Conceivably, this is the head of the youth who impersonated the maize god in the dance scene of Room 1. I would hesitate to advance this explanation were it not that decapitation was particularly the fate of impersonators of deities of vegetation and the soil in central Mexico. Completing the scene, various chiefs and attendants to the number of seventeen are ranged on the lower terraces.

The halting interpretation offered for this scene is that it is the preliminary to the great ceremony, which occupies most of the wall space in Room 3. Apparently sacrifices have already been made, as the head resting on the greenery and, apparently, the sprawled body of the young man bear witness. The fate of the group of captives is being pronounced, but whether that is death on the sacrificial stone or slavery is a matter for speculation. For the bleeding of the hands a possible explanation has been offered, but one on which I do not place overmuch confidence, for this is a baffling matter. We may, however, presume with some certainty that the halach uinic and the three batabs are correctly identified in this scene.

A Late Stone Age Mural at Cogul, Spain

Although artistic expression in the form of sculpture and painting must have its origins in very ancient times, it is not until we come to Late or Upper Paleolithic times that we first encounter in quantity the sculptured and painted art of our ancestors (Breuil, n.d.). The true purpose or function of this art is unknown, although it is commonly believed to be magico-religious (cf. Wernert, 1948). We present Breuil and Cabré's account of one of the most ancient known painted ceremonial scenes.[3] It is from the cave site of Cogul in northeastern Spain and belongs to the cave art style which has been called "Spanish Levant."

Maringer and Bandi (1953:114–142) discuss the Spanish Levant cave art at length. This style is different from the Franco-Cantabrian cave art of, for example, Lascaux, Altamira, and Font-de-Gaume, and opinions differ as to whether the northeastern Spanish rock pictures are of Paleolithic date or later—Mesolithic or Neolithic. Maringer and Bandi believe that "the art of the Spanish Levant has no [direct] connexion with the Upper Old Stone Age," and that it may be of Mesolithic date.

A stirring hunt scene in the near-by shelter of Alpera, Spain, of about the same period, is described and illustrated by Breuil (1912).

The painted art of the Paleolithic caves of France and Spain is well presented in various books (e.g., Breuil, n.d.; Maringer and Bandi, 1953), but we can only guess at the reasons which impelled these ancient men to go to the inner recesses of the caves and there paint animals on the walls and ceilings.

Leason (1939) has presented a new view of Paleolithic cave art in which he proposes that dead animals were the chief subject of the artist's paintings. His theory has been criticized, but it is difficult to see many of the painted animals as anything but representations of dead individuals.

[3] H. Breuil and J. Cabré Aguila, "Les peintures rupestres du bassin inférieur de l'Ebre," L'Anthropologie, 1909, vol. 20, pp. 15–19, 21.

The group of nine women dancing around a man which seems to us to need interpretation as a scene of a dance (see Fig. 13.4) is composed of ten well defined persons, arranged as follows: five women at the right and four women at the left of a man in the middle. The latter is much smaller than his neighbors; he is painted in brown, deepening to black; his head is round, and is set on square shoulders, which produce straight

Fig. 13.4.   Rock-painting at Cogul, Spain.

short arms; the trunk is slender and the thin, stiff legs end in feet which are turned toward the right; about each knee is worn an ornament, drawn by two divergent lines, one on each side of the leg, which point downward, this being a schematic design, like the garment at the waist of the bison-hunter; the genital parts are of exaggerated dimensions but are not in a state of erection. To the left of this man whose virility is so clearly delineated, five women are walking away from him. The two furthest away are very plain, of a uniform black, and they huddle closely together. The third is black and red, like the fifth, while the fourth is red only; she is furthermore mutilated because of a scaling off of the rock. Whereas the four nearest are placed almost on a line, this last has her feet situated at the height of the waist of the woman farthest to the right; her legs are bent and her waist is bent forward, as though she were jumping.

The four women on the right are less plain. One may distinguish them as much by the engraving which accompanies the painted features as much as by this: the two closest to the man are black with pale red marks at various places; the two further, in imitation of the ones at the extreme opposite, are black. These four persons are plainly divided into two couples, offering each other their hands. The first one shows several oblique lines radiating from the head in the direction of the man, which evokes a naive representation of the action of blowing or spitting. The second who remains in black is in full face, holding an arm out to her and to the other who is in front of the last group, in a movement of the waist and arms which is graceful and very feminine.

The last two women, the second of which is smaller than the first are making their way rapidly toward the left.

The detail of the reciprocal situation, and the attitudes of these females once known, let us examine the general idea which is presented, and of the slight differences at hand.

The head is a subtriangular spot, with rounded angles; in eight of them this head, in the shape of a bonnet or hood, is not attached to the shoulders, it does not join the body; the second figure (on the left) being the exception, having little black strokes to indicate the neck.

In the third figure, another exception, the head is rounded on top; its base sits directly on the shoulders, without a neck, as though some garment, such as a hood were making the continuity.

The stiff arms are bent harmoniously; the hands are not distinguishable; the two figures on the left seem to have a large swelling at the elbow, due to massive humoral bracelets. The common shape of the bust is a sharp pointed triangle, placed on the extremely slim, narrow waist.

Very pendulous, voluminous breasts ornament the chests of the majority of these women; they are particularly striking on the two at the left; they seem absent in the fourth figure, who is jumping, and smaller, in the last one. Now, one only is shown in profile, hanging in the shape of a pouch (1, 2, 3, 6) or more reduced (8), and now the body is to be seen from the front, and the two breasts are drawn quite small and within the torso, or they may be at the left and right, under each arm (7).

As M. C. Rocafort understood it, one of the most notable qualities of these figures is in their giving some indication of women's clothes of this far distant epoch. It seems that the torso is naked as well as the chest, however much certain peculiarities of the shoulders in the silhouette 3 may indicate to the contrary, as well as the thicker waist of figure 8, and the sort of jacket-lappet which swells lightly in front of the abdomen. In any case the only garment one may be certain of among these silhouettes is their skirt.

This skirt is attached directly to the waist, except for the two figures on the right, where the curves of the body seem to continue as if a garment were draped over it also. It seems to hang down in these two figures, much further than in the others, where it ends a little below the knee; it is true that the legs are too short for the general elongation of the rest of the body, and the knees much too low. The ending of the dress is abrupt and rectangular in two figures, nos. 4 and 6, as with the ox-hunter in the preceding scene; it forms a broken angular line which shows as an arc in figures 2, 3 and 7, and a double arc in figure 1; since in figures 1, 2, 3 and 7 the sides of the skirts, and particularly the back edge, seem more or less to hang, one has the impression on the sides and in back. This "train" is particularly obvious in the three figures at the left. The red and black lines painted on the dress of the third figure should be noted. He certainly seems to be concerned with a dance or some analogous ceremonial where nine "ladies" would encircle a man; one imagines some initiation rite, a dance of the sort that Stow reports intended to celebrate the creative power of Kaang, or it is some Bushman magician personifying God, surrounded by a band of women dancing frenetically who imposes on them, one after the other, the act of procreation.

The scene of the women and the man lifts a little corner of the curtain which covers the social life of these remote populations, and the costumes tell us something of the still unknown fashions in the service of which the Magdalenian couturiers used the fine eyed needles which the Cantabrian caves of the Pyrennes and the Dordogne yielded so long ago to the astonishment of the excavators.

An Engraved Upper Paleolithic Pebble

The following account by Movius and Judson[4] is a description of a small, flattened pebble upon each of whose surfaces a series of outline drawings of animals has been applied. A thoughtful analysis of the piece as a whole leads the authors to conclude that the pebble was used in connection with certain magico-religious rites associated with the hunt.

This is archaeological reporting at its best, since it combines accurate and detailed presentation of facts with a critical review of other data on the subject in order to reach a solid but imaginative conclusion.

The Upper Périgordian culture level at La Colombière is dated by radiocarbon at from 12,000 to 15,000 years old, but Movius believes that these dates are in error and that the age of this level, and therefore of the engraved pebble, is at least 20,000 years.

The engraved pebble, found in the Upper Périgordian horizon at La Colombière in August, 1948, came to light at a depth of 45 cm. below the surface of Deposit D-1 some 40 cm. north of the line between Trenches 18 and 19. The object is 12 cm. long by 8.2 cm. wide, 3.5 cm. thick and of flattened oval section. It was lying with the obverse surface uppermost, and much of the reverse, or lower, surface bore a thin calcareous crust which easily flaked off with the application of a very

---

[4] H. L. Movius, Jr. and Sheldon Judson, *The Rock-Shelter of La Colombière*, American School of Prehistoric Research, Peabody Museum, Harvard University, Cambridge, 1956, Bulletin No. 19, pp. 120–134. By permission of J. O. Brew, Director of the Peabody Museum, Harvard University.

slight amount of pressure. It is composed of a very fine-grained porce-
laneous, or sublithographic, type of Jurassic limestone, believed to be
formed of excessively fine sediments originally accumulated in a lagoon.
It is heavily rolled, and exhibits a smooth, almost polished, surface. One
end is heavily abraded, and the marks of percussion extend part way
along each of the sides, suggesting extensive use as a hammerstone of
some sort. Yet it is very unlikely that the object ever served any such
utilitarian function. Presumably these scars are related to the two breaks
at the opposite end, which are believed to have ritualistic significance.
The photographs and drawings clearly reveal the fact that these fractures
truncate many of the best engravings on the two slightly convex sides
of the pebble. Both of the broken surfaces were partially encrusted with
calcareous material when the object first came to light, demonstrating
that the breaks had definitely occurred in antiquity. Although the surrounding area of the deposits in Trenches 18 and 19 were carefully
searched, there was no trace of the missing pieces.

METHOD OF STUDY

From the outset our objective was to produce photographs and drawings
for publication which depicted as accurately as possible the prehistoric
engravings that appear on the two surfaces of this object. Both chalk
under ordinary lighting and fluorescent powder under infra-red lighting
were tried and abandoned, since it was found that infinitely more satisfactory photographic results could be obtained with carbonate of
manganese carefully rubbed in the engraved lines. This process was suggested by Mr. Rudolph Ruzicka of Concord, Massachusetts, and acted
on under special lighting arrangements by Mr. James Ufford of the Fogg
Art Museum, Harvard University, to both of whom the writer is deeply
grateful for the outstandingly fine results. From these photographs, negative prints were obtained, and these in turn used as the base for tracing
off the outline drawings of each individual animal (Figs. 13.5–13.11), the
original specimen serving as a control in all instances. Admittedly the
facts that (a) the drawings are traced from photographs, and (b) both
surfaces of the pebble are slightly convex, contribute to a certain amount
of distortion, but it is felt that this is so slight as to be practically negligible.

In the drawings all the engravings that we can decipher are reproduced as faithfully as possible. Indeed we have made no attempt
whatsoever to "recreate" or impart our conception of the original "feeling" of the artist into the reproductions. Not only do we feel incompetent
to undertake such a task, but also this would defeat the fundamental
purpose of the present study, which is intended primarily to serve as a
record of the engravings that actually exist on the object in question.
Anyone desiring to pursue further the possible significance of certain
minutiae of detail will find the basic data reproduced in this report for a

study based on this approach. Alternatively, the original object may be consulted at the Musée de l'Ain, Bourg-en-Bresse (Ain). In any case, it is not our intention to attempt an interpretation of highly imaginative combinations of stylized lines (tectiforms and other "magical" signs?), although these will be described in their appropriate context.

DESCRIPTION OF ENGRAVINGS

The engraved pebble found in 1948 certainly testifies to the high artistic attainments and technical ability of certain individual member(s) of

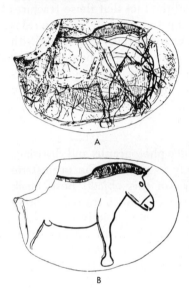

the group of Upper Périgordian hunters who settled at La Colombière. As Mr. Rudolph Ruzicka, one of the most skillful wood engravers now living, pointed out on seeing the object for the first time, the fact that the lines have been produced by a *pushed* stroke, rather than a *pulled* one which lacks control. They are clear-cut and not jagged; the intersections are sharp, and the stroke stays solidly on the line rather than swerving off. In other words, this is the work of a highly experienced artisan who had developed complete control of his technique. He was an exceedingly skillful engraver, and not a beginner in any sense of the word. For this reason, it does not seem likely that the "sketch-book" hypothesis legitimately can be evoked to explain the drawings on the present object.

Fig. 13.5. A: Drawings on the obverse surface of pebble. B: Horse, obverse surface.

Both surfaces exhibit a maze of lines, predominantly of U-shaped section and of inextricable appearance (see Figs. 13.5A and 13.8A). In the entanglement the following outlines have been deciphered:

Obverse Surface (Fig. 13.5A)

(a) An extremely naturalistic male Horse (Fig. 13.5B) with characteristic roached mane and ladder pattern extending down the back. This animal is remarkably expressive, and the facial details are clearly indicated. The forehead is slightly bulging, the mandible strong—almost square—and the lower line of the chest is slightly convex. The significance of the transverse line across the muzzle and the ladder pattern along the back is unknown. The neck is thick, all four legs are shown, and the sex is clearly indicated. The club-like appearance of the hoofs are reminiscent of certain of the Horses on the walls of the Cave of

Lascaux. Unfortunately the rump and tail have been broken off. In general appearance this Horse suggests an animal similar to the living Norwegian Dun.

(*b*) Turning the pebble 180° one can easily discern the very finely drawn outline of a male Reindeer (Fig. 13.6A) with antlers shed and shaded under-belly. The animal's head is lowered to fit the curvature of the pebble in such a way that much of its mandible overlaps the muzzle of the Horse. The nose, mouth, eye and ears are clearly shown, as well as the long hair along the lower side of the neck. The withers are raised in characteristic fashion, but the tail is not shown. All four legs are depicted, but the hind feet have been broken off and the front feet are lost in the superimposed Horse's mane. The fact that this animal is shown hornless suggests that the drawing was executed during the winter months of the year.

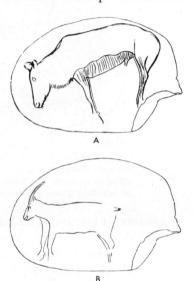

Fig. 13.6. A: Reindeer with antlers shed, obverse surface. B: Ibex, obverse surface.

(*c*) An Ibex (Fig. 13.6B) faces in the same direction as the Reindeer just described. All but one of this animal's feet, which is partially complete, are overlain by the mane and back of the Horse, while the forequarters are in turn surcharged by the head and neck of the Reindeer. Again all four legs are shown, and the details of the head—mouth, nose, eyes, horns and ears—are clearly depicted. In this very realistic drawing the characteristic chunky, rectangular body and short tail of the Ibex are faithfully expressed.

(*d*) An unfinished carnivore—possibly a Bear (Fig. 13.7A)—may be seen just to the rear of the Ibex's head in the area of the Reindeer's neck. The body of this animal is incomplete, with the exception of the neck, single foreleg and partially finished back, indicated by a double line. The line delimiting the animal's muzzle and ear is exceptionally heavy.

(*e*) Turning the pebble so that the Horse is upright two animal outlines may be seen (Fig. 13.7B). Unfortunately the fore-quarters and heads of both these beasts have been broken off. However, when separated out, their silhouettes suggest to us a Cervid-like creature of some sort (Fig. 13.7C) and a headless Bison (Fig. 13.7D). By combining certain lines shown in the area on the left hand side of Fig. 13.7B with the outline of the latter quadruped, the Abbé Breuil has tentatively reconstructed a Woolly Rhinoceros, an interpretation with which we do not agree. In any case, the subsidiary lines shown on the bodies of these two

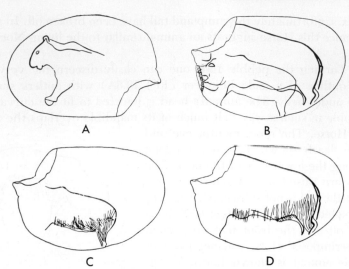

Fig. 13.7. A: Unfinished sketch of carnivore, possibly a Bear, obverse surface. B: Outline drawings of Cervid-like animal and Bison, obverse surface. C: Detail of Cervid-like animal shown in B. D: Detail of headless Bison shown in B.

ruminants (Figs. 13.7C and 13.7D) apparently indicate hair, and in the inextricable maze in the area to the left—just to the rear of the Horse's hind leg—there is another ladder pattern similar to the one extending the length of the animal's back. Although other lines are discernible on this surface of the pebble, we do not feel competent to suggest their possible significance.

Reverse Surface (Fig. 13.8A)

(a) The most outstanding single drawing on the reverse surface of the pebble found by us at La Colombière in 1948 depicts a Woolly Rhinoceros with lowered head, as if the animal were in the act of grazing (Fig. 13.8B). This figure is complete with the exception of the rear legs, which unfortunately have been broken off. Both front feet are shown, and the short hair or wool on the beast's under-belly is clearly indicated. The long, curved main horn and comparatively short rear horn are characteristic, and the eye is correctly placed in relation to the latter, judging by living Rhinoceroses. Both the nostril and small mouth are easily discernible. This is the engraving of a singularly majestic beast, and it should be noted that the lines representing the hair or fleece on the neck, forelegs and massive shoulders have been cleverly arranged so as to suggest shading. As in the case of a finely sculptured figure, this is a thought expressed with greater vigor than is normally found in the case of Upper Palaeolithic engravings and paintings.

(b) In addition there are two incomplete drawings of Woolly Rhinoceroses facing in the same direction as the animal described above (Figs. 13.9A and 13.9B). Part of the back, shoulders, head, two horns, muzzle, nose and eye may be seen in the case of the former, the anterior horn and muzzle being indicated by an especially wide, deep line. The Abbé Breuil feels that the outline shown in Fig. 13.9B, represents the back,

head, eye and trunk of a Mammoth, but this interpretation fails to explain the definitely associated horn, which is clearly the curved main horn of a Rhinoceros and not the tusk of a Mammoth. Therefore, we are inclined to consider both of the drawings reproduced in Fig. 13.9 as unfinished sketches of Rhinoceroses—possibly attempts that were abandoned before the outstandingly fine engravings previously described were achieved.

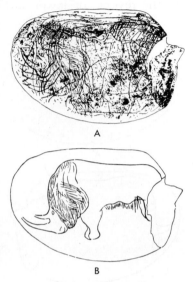

(c) A partially complete second Horse has been surcharged by the drawings of the Rhinoceroses (Fig. 13.10A). The rear quarters of this animal have been broken off, and neither the legs nor the line of the belly are shown. A series of short strokes indicate the line of the neck. The facial details are clearly indicated, the mandible is strong, and the height of the mane, which is suggested by a series of short

Fig. 13.8. A: Drawings on reverse surface of engraved pebble. B: Woolly Rhinoceros, reverse surface.

forward sloping strokes arranged in a broad arc, is not limited. One has the impression that this is a different type of Horse than the one shown on the obverse surface (compare Fig. 13.5B). However, in common with the latter, a serpentine-like ladder pattern, which Breuil calls a "magical serpent," extends along the neck and part way down the back of the animal.

(d) Partially obscured by the complex of Rhinoceroses is a second drawing, this one of a Reindeer in absolute profile (Fig. 13.10B). The antlers, if present, cannot be deciphered; a portion of the line showing the back of the neck and the withers is likewise missing, together with the feet and tail. Only three legs—two rear and one in front—are represented. The eye, indicated by a deep line, is disproportionately large, while the opposite is true of the mouth and nostril. As in the case of the Reindeer on the obverse surface (Fig. 13.6A) this animal's head is lowered as if it were in the act of grazing, and the long hairs on the undersurface of the neck and upper chest region are clearly shown. It is possible that the roughly parallel lines depicted on the lower jaw, throat and upper portion of the neck do not belong to this animal.

(*e*) In the vicinity of the croup of the Horse described above there is an area of diagonal shading (Fig. 13.11A) the significance of which is by no means apparent. As shown in our drawing, there seem to be two independent sets of these lines, one of which—the uppermost one in Fig. 13.11A—is similar to a series of diagonal lines enclosed by an oval line on the reverse or lower surface of Pebble 2. Breuil has suggested the possibility that this complex belongs to a human figure, but he agrees that such an interpretation is exceedingly unlikely.

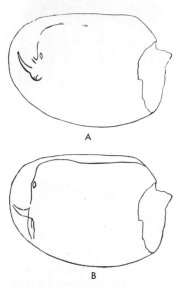

A

B

Fig. 13.9. A: Incomplete drawing of Woolly Rhinoceros, reverse surface. B: Incomplete drawing of Woolly Rhinoceros, reverse surface.

(*f*) Turning the pebble 180° one can discern a partially complete head of a carnivore of some sort (a Felid?) in the upper central portion of the area (Fig. 13.11C). Since we are uncertain with regard to the correct interpretation of this drawing, two possible versions of it are shown. In neither case are the lines strong and sure, indicating either poor technique or the fact that the hunter-artist had never had an opportunity of closely observing his subject.

(*g*) Finally, what is apparently a partially complete Horse, obscured not only by the Rhinoceros but also by the Horse described above, is shown (Fig. 13.11D). The same curious slightly concave muzzle may be noted also in the case of one of the ruminants (possibly a Wild Ox) figured on the obverse surface of Pebble 1.

In addition, the back and head of a fourth Horse may be seen by turning the object 180°. This latter drawing, in which the animal's ears and right eye are indicated, is badly distorted by the curvature of the pebble. Apparently this engraving was never completed; it may have been abandoned since the artist attempted to execute it on an area where it must have been practically impossible to control the engraving tool.

Perhaps the most distinctive single attribute of the drawings on the pebble discovered at La Colombière in 1948 is the fact that their proportion is essentially correct. Furthermore, they are not stiff. Indeed they lack the clumsy awkwardness that characterizes the figures depicted on so many of the contemporary Upper Palaeolithic art objects. Finally, errors are singularly absent, with the exception of the two unfinished Rhinoceroses shown in Fig. 13.9. One may even note incipient attempts at perspective, and also the careful delineation of inner detail. It is at once apparent that the unknown person or persons who produced these drawings knew their models intimately at first hand—a fact which is reflected in the remarkably realistic portrayal of the forms represented. In particular the engravings of the Horse, Reindeer, and Ibex on the obverse, and the large Woolly Rhinoceros on the reverse are so remarkably alive and charged with energy that there is no mistaking the subjects. It may be concluded that these pictures were drawn by a man, or men, who were not only exceedingly skilled engraver(s), but also knew the great animals well—knew the feel of their coats and the tremendous drive of their muscles, as well as the immense danger one faced while hunting them.

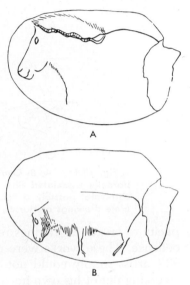

PRESUMED SIGNIFICANCE

In connection with the superimposition of so many animals on two surfaces of a single object that measures only 12 cm. × 8.2 cm. × 3.5 cm., one cannot help wondering if it represents some sort of a "sketch-book" of an Upper Périgordian artist. Now it is very probable that certain drawings of isolated parts of the body—in particular the horns and legs of Cervidae in various Upper Palaeolithic caves of Franco-Cantabria—may be interpreted as sketches, or even as anatomical studies. Furthermore, it is quite likely that many of the engravings of indifferent execution which cannot be deciphered or which only vaguely suggest animal outlines, should be considered as trial or practice pieces. For instance, the majority of the ca. 200 engraved limestone plaques found by Pericot in the Upper Périgordian, or Gravettian, horizon at the Cave of Parpalló, near Gandía (Valéncia), apparently belong in this category. Of the six illustrated in figures 80–85 of Pericot's excavation report, only a Wild Ox whose horns are shown in profile is fairly well done. But as Breuil points out, the rest are extremely mediocre. However, the drawings on the overwhelming majority of the art objects in this series cannot be interpreted and should probably be regarded as testifying to the long hours of practice and training necessary to produce the completed works. For it will at once be apparent to anyone with an artistic background that no single individual(s) could possibly have created so successfully as the unknown person (or persons) who was responsible for the remarkable engravings on the pebble found in 1948 at La Colombière. In other words, he (or they) must have had a wide range of artistic experience in order to have developed the ca-

Fig. 13.10. A: Horse, reverse surface. B: Reindeer, reverse surface.

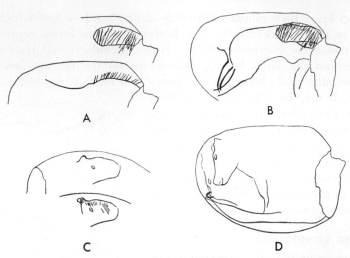

Fig. 13.11. A, B: Oval area of diagonal shading and other apparently associated lines, reverse surface. C: Incomplete head of carnivore, possibly a Felid, reverse surface. D: Two partially complete drawings of Horses, reverse surface.

pacity to create engravings reflecting such a high degree of technical excellence. These works were certainly not produced at the first attempt. The artist simply could not have achieved such outstanding results by "working out of his own head," and for this reason, it is very unlikely that any of the trial or practice pieces will be finished products such as this one.

The foregoing considerations make it seem quite improbable that this particular art object can be interpreted as the "sketch-book" of an Upper Palaeolithic artist, as has been recently claimed by Koppers. This authority states "I have for some time been sceptical of the magical theory to explain the cave paintings. Finds like this [i.e., the engraved pebble found at La Colombière in 1948] seems to be evidence rather of a fundamentally rational kind of artistic activity." In view of this latter concept, it is difficult to understand why Koppers considers that "the 'sketch-book' of La Colombière sheds new light on the art of the Upper Palaeolithic in general," especially if one considers the implications of the following statement, which appears in the next paragraph of the article: "Of course, I do not deny that the art of the Palaeolithic may have served also religious, pseudo-religious or magical purposes." Actually Koppers has published one of the drawings most frequently reproduced in support of the "sketch-book" concept. It depicts a Bison allegedly found in a Late Magdalenian horizon at the La Genière rock-shelter, between Serrières and Merpuis on the left bank of the Ain River, only 8 kilometers upstream from Poncin, and it is almost an exact copy of the famous Magdalenian polychrome painting of a Bison discovered in the early 1900's in the Cave of Font-de-Gaume, near Les Eyzies, Dordogne. But if he had ever made a detailed examination of the original piece, it is unlikely that Koppers, following Kuhn and Abel would have accepted the La Genière Bison as a genuine Upper Palaeolithic art object. For the character of the incised lines by which this drawing has been produced leads one to suspect that they were made by some sort of a metal tool. Finally, the alleged Late Magdalenian assemblage from the La Genière locality, which includes an abundance of microlithic forms, indicates that we are dealing here with some sort of a Sauveterrian or Proto-Azilian occupation, rather than with one dating from the closing stages of Magdalenian times. Such a view is certainly in accord with the evidence of the molluscan fauna, which includes only recent species now living in the region and not a single "cold" form. Thus the writer is in complete agreement with Peyrony who states: "In the interests of science and in the good name of prehistory, it would be better not to talk of this subject [i.e., the La Genière engravings], and to cross them off the list of works of prehistoric art."

As to the La Colombière engravings, however, these must be considered as exemplifying a keen sense of observation and complete mastery of the art of engraving on the part of the individual(s) who created them. Indeed they manifest a very advanced and developed type of creative thinking. For with a minimum number of lines a remarkable realistic series of portrayals of animals as seen in silhouette has been achieved. In certain instances the artist(s) has demonstrated a capacity to dominate his model completely in order to obtain the desired effect. In other words, one is dealing here with true art rather than with a series of experimental sketches or mnemonic devices as a means of representing given forms— further evidence of the fallacy of the "sketch-book" concept. Such a view is also in accord with the evidence furnished by ethnology, since no known group of hunting people living under the conditions of a rigorous and exacting environment have ever been known to indulge in *art for art's sake.* And this was presumably just as true in the Old Stone age as it is today. Although certain gifted members of the group may practice in order to develop their skill, they certainly do not draw merely for the sake of expressing themselves, or creating a beautiful picture, or even making records of the animals they hunted. In other words, art to them was basically a medium of expression for the purpose of propitiating in some manner the spirits of the animal kingdom. The form depicted was what had fundamental significance. If it was well drawn, that depended on the individual endowments and skill of the particular person who executed the engraving, painting, bas-relief or sculpture, as the case may be. For it is patently clear that if certain individuals who lived during Upper Palaeolithic times had not been endowed with a high degree of artistic ability, developed their technical skill to produce drawings, and possessed a true appreciation of aesthetic values, this ceremonial or magico-religious art could not have existed. In other words, the capacity to draw necessarily had to come first in the case of the individual artist. However, it does not by any means follow that the forms which he created in giving expression to this urge were also regarded as works of art (i.e., art as an end in itself) by the other members of his social unit—clan, extended family or tribe. Certainly to these people success in the hunt meant the difference between plenty and starvation, or near-starvation, just as in the case of modern hunting peoples living under comparable environmental conditions. On this basis, therefore, it seems difficult to avoid putting forward the suggestion that, in the eyes of the prehistoric inhabitants of La Colombière, this pebble was probably regarded as a hunting talisman rather than as an art object. There are many hundreds of similar water-worn limestone pebbles strewn about on the floor of the Ain Valley in this region; surely if an Upper Péri-gordian artist had simply wanted to practice reproducing in the form of an outline drawing one of the animals his group was hunting—i.e., art for art's sake—it would be only logical to expect him to select a new pebble and a fresh surface each time he desired to depict a new animal.

Therefore, it is probable that there was some definite reason for super-imposing so many animals on a single pebble, and it is felt that the only plausible explanation is to regard the object as having had importance in connection with certain magico-religious rites associated with the chase. Thus we can imagine that the pebble was initially engraved and used in some sort of hunting ceremony. Since that particular hunt was successful, the object was reengraved and used on subsequent occasion for the same purpose. It possessed magical qualities, or "mana." It is therefore tenta-tively concluded that the primary significance of this very fine object, from point of view of the people who actually lived at La Colombière during the closing stages of the Ice Age, was not the beautiful engravings so care-fully executed on its surfaces, but the fact that it was the medium by which it was possible to commune directly with the spirits of the animal world for the purpose of successfully replenishing the all-important food supply. And having served its purpose in connection with certain particu-lar rites connected with the hunt, it was ceremoniously "killed," as in the case of so many similar objects found in other sites of the same age in West-ern Europe.

Since at La Colombière the drawings under discussion have been exe-cuted on an object small enough to be easily transported, they are cer-tainly very fine expressions of *art mobilier*. But, together with such con-temporary examples of a portable nature as the well-known series of artistically perfect statuettes and low reliefs from various European locali-ties, they cannot be considered utilitarian in the strict sense of the term. In this respect, therefore, they should actually be compared with the wall or cave art group of Franco-Cantabria.

Now almost without exception this cave art is found in places that were perpetually dark, and there even seems to have been a preference on the part of the artists to choose the least accessible corners of the caves. For this reason one is forced to conclude that the pictures were not primarily for decorative purposes. The fact that we are not dealing with art as an end in itself has been very clearly expressed by Breuil and Obermaier with reference to Altamira. These authorities state that this conclusion is even more evident

. . . when we come to the fine engravings, which are hardly visible and generally can only be found with the greatest effort. These pictures, many of very indifferent execution, but sometimes real artistic efforts, certainly owe their existence to the magico-religious idea, especially to the custom of hunting magic, as it is still practised today among living primitive peoples. The fact that in more than one instance . . . arrows or assegais were painted on the animals' bodies agrees with the magic theory, and is undoubtedly a sign of their being spellbound or of symbolic death. . . . Also it seems that certain places or corners in this cave and others must have been considered as especially sacred, and that the spells cast there were especially efficacious. Because of this, although in other parts of the cave there was plenty of available space, the artists repeatedly used the same places, piling their pictures one on the other, like palimpsests, not hesitating to destroy older ones, although they might be of great artistic value. One need not insist further that there may be an influx here of ideas of reproductive magic, or a cult of particular animals—totem animals. All this suggests that caves must then have existed dedicated regularly to a cult, since paintings are not to be found in every cave. . . . In each region, as far as one can see, there were a few places of the same age that can be considered as real "sanctuaries," wherein no doubt Man celebrated ceremonies at which only certain [initiated] individuals might attend.

Although we are dealing with a rock-shelter rather than a cave, and with engraved pebbles and Mammoth bones rather than wall art, the question presents itself: Was La Colombière one of these sacred places in Southeastern France during Upper Périgordian times?

Battle Scenes from Chichen Itza

The great cenote, or sacred well, at Chichen Itza, a major Maya site of the northern peninsula of Yucatan, is about 200 feet in diameter. Seventy feet below its rim stands the water, which is 35 feet deep. At the bottom of the well is about 35 feet of silt. The ancient Maya cast offerings of human beings and precious objects into the cenote. For a most interesting first-hand account of "cenote archaeology" at the site of Dzibilchaltun, in Yucatan, see Marsden (1959).

Between 1904 and 1907 E. H. Thompson dredged the cenote and recovered from it great amounts of material. Thus far only popular accounts of the dredging have been published (Willard, 1926; Schwarz, 1958). Hooton (1940) wrote a most interesting analysis of the skeletal material recovered and S. K. Lothrop has recently published a particularly excellent description of the metals. Among the items of metal are sixteen fairly complete gold disks, the size of saucers or dinner plates, with scenes embossed on the surface. Many of the scenes show battle incidents, the combatants identifiable as Mexican Toltecs, who came from the highland capital at Tula (Hidalgo), and local Maya. The disks were made during the period of Toltec dominance at Chichen Itza in the latter part of the tenth century A.D. and show victorious Toltecs and vanquished Maya.

The following excerpt[5] from Lothrop's monograph deals with three of the embossed gold disks.

Incidentally, the gold value of the cenote metals, computed at the present price of $25.02 per ounce, is about $7000.

DESCRIPTION OF DISKS

Disk B. This disk represents the questioning of two bound prisoners (Fig. 13.12). The chief personage is a bearded Toltec warrior whose rank

Fig. 13.12.   Disk B, showing the Tula-Toltec warrior interrogating Maya captives. Scale 1/1.

is indicated by a mosaic headdress with a bird on the front. There is an arm shield consisting of a band on the upper arm from which hang two furs. The right wrist is adorned with two bracelets of fur and there are

[5] S. K. Lothrop, *Metals from the Cenote of Sacrifice, Chichen Itza, Yucatan,* Memoirs of the Peabody Museum, Harvard University, Cambridge, 1952, vol. 10, no. 2, pp. 45–47, 51–52, 57, 59. By permission of J. O. Brew, Director of the Peabody Museum, Harvard University.

bells on the left leg. Two nose buttons are inserted in the wings of the nose. Two spears and a spear thrower are carried in the hands.

Behind the chief stands an attendant who holds a spear thrower and three spears, bringing the total number to the customary five. He wears bells on the left leg, a mosaic bracelet on the right wrist, a necklace and nose rod of Maya rather than Toltec type. The nature of the headdress and the facial decoration is not clear.

The two prisoners both have their arms bound behind their backs by ropes above the elbows. This was the usual Maya method for securing captives and doubtless caused great pain owing to more or less complete stoppage of circulation of the blood.

Morley has pointed out that captives are shown on stelae at seventeen Maya cities of the Great period and he lists nearly a hundred examples. These he divides into four groups on the basis of the position of the captive in relationship to the principal figure. The prisoner may be (1) behind, (2) a support of, (3) beside or (4) in a panel below the principal figure. These positions seem to be the result of local styles rather than chronological changes, as a single position is dominant at all sites except Cobá where two types are found. In disk B the captives are shown at the same level as the Toltec chief who dominates the scene. This is the most common arrangement in stone. It obviously is not of chronological significance as the dates run from 9.3.0.0.0 to 10.3.0.0.0 (495–889 A.D.).

Both prisoners, to judge by their expressions, are far from happy. They wear typical Maya ornaments, including tubular jade bars on their breasts and nose rods. The standing figure carries a small human statue (?). Behind the knee of the seated captive there is an elaborate plumed back shield which presumably has been ripped off him.

Under the back shield there is a dish containing a human head, perhaps a grim testimonial of what is in store for the prisoners. Tozzer comments on the archaeological occurrence of skulls in bowls. A comparable head and plate, carved in stone, was found in Temple 11 at Copan.

The Sky deity on disk B is a curious assemblage of human head, arms and legs combined with a realistic serpent body. Headdress and gorget are typically Toltec. One arm holds an object which may be interpreted as a rattle with sound scrolls issuing from it. The other arm grasps a spear thrower. Below the face is a speech scroll directed downwards towards the prisoners, which suggests that the deity may be taking part in the interrogation.

The bottom of the disk is lacking, but scrolls at the right indicate that it contained an Earth monster.

As background motives or space fillers four greatly conventionalized serpents' heads are shown. These vary in size and complexity. Similar heads occur in stone carvings at Chichen Itza on buildings of the Toltec period but they are also found on stelae of the Great period at such sites as Copan, Quirigua, Naranjo and Seibal. In addition to the serpent heads there is a glyph, perhaps a name glyph, behind the head of the standing captive.

Looking at the composition as a whole, we may remark that, although no action is suggested except perhaps in the upraised arm of the Sky deity, the scene is tense and emotional. The standing figures lean forward towards each other to stress their earnestness. The seated figure recoils at what is being said. The threatening attitude of the Sky deity dominates the entire picture.

Disks B and C both portray identical subjects: a Toltec chief with his attendant questioning two Maya captives. This raises the question of whether two different artists had been commissioned or ordered to commemorate the same incident in the life of a single chief. There are obvious differences in style and details but there also are parallels which indicate an affirmative answer. These may be listed as follows.

1) The principal insignia of the Toltec chief is his headdress, which is identical on both disks. It consists of a cylindrical band with a bird in front and a domed top to which three feathers are attached.

2) The ear ornaments are the same.

3) The twin bracelets of fur are the same. The bird on the arm in disk C may be a decorative element corresponding to the band and furs in disk B, a so-called arm shield.

4) In each case bells are worn on the calf.

5) In each case one Maya is standing and the other is seated.

6) In each case the standing Maya holds a doll or figurine by the hair.

7) In each case the Maya have been deprived of back shields.

8) The seated Maya has similar leg ornaments in both disks.

9) The Toltec attendant in disk C apparently wears the bar-pendant and back shield belonging to the seated Maya in disk B.

10) The small conventionalized serpent heads used as space fillers on both disks are very similar. They occur on no other disks.

11) The decoration on the back of the Earth monster in disk C corresponds to part of the glyph on the left side of disk B.

In spite of these parallels, however, it should be noted that the Sky deities, Earth monsters and border ornaments are totally unlike.

Disk D. This disk, illustrated in Fig. 13.13, depicts a Toltec chief casting a spear at two retreating Maya warriors. The Toltec wears a beard which falls to his waist. His rank is indicated by a mosaic helmet with a bird on the front. In his left hand he carries two additional spears. Accompanying him is a realistically rendered rattlesnake.

The chief's attendant is clad in a feather tunic with long plumes hanging down the back. He carries a spear thrower but no spears.

Both the Maya wear elaborate plumed headdresses. The left-hand example represents some kind of an animal. The other consists of plumes attached to a basketry base. One warrior carries a spear with a latticed shaft. This feature appears on Toltec bas-reliefs at Chichen Itza and also on Maya stelae of the Great period. The second warrior is unarmed but wears a back shield. He looks backward in an apprehensive manner and raises his hand to ward off the coming attack.

The usual Sky deity has been replaced by a greatly conventionalized serpent which we shall not attempt to analyze. The Earth monster is of

Fig. 13.13. Disk D, showing a Tula-Toltec chief casting a spear at two Maya warriors, who endeavor to escape. Scale 1/1.

the usual type. Border decoration consists of symbols of the planet Venus.

Although disk D is unusually well preserved, it does not rank high in artistic merit. It will be noted that the sky and earth elements are not symmetrically placed, with the result that the central panel is awkwardly shaped. We may also point out that the feet of the Maya and Toltec are not in the same plane, which perhaps denotes that they are not moving in the same direction. The great fault, however, lies in the stiffness of pose which denies vigor to a scene of action. . . .

Disk G. This is an unusual disk both in subject and in workmanship (Fig. 13.14). We feel certain that it could not have been manufactured by the same individual who produced any of the other specimens we illustrate. The subject, an attack by water, is unique in metal although found in frescoes. The composition, with perspective indicated by plac-

Fig. 13.14. Disk G, representing a naval battle. Diameter 6.3 cm.

ing more distant features at higher levels, is characteristic of gold plaques and also is found on frescoes at Chichen Itza. The whole scene is rendered in a smaller technique and in finer detail than occurs on other examples. Furthermore, the greater delicacy with which the Sky deity is depicted, as contrasted with the rest of the disk, raises a suspicion that two different artists may have collaborated.

We may also note that arms, adornments and details of dress are different from those seen on other specimens. There are only a few Toltec characteristics: the spear throwers of the Sky deity and the chief figure in the canoe, the eagle mask of the former and the nose button of the latter. Perhaps then we should interpret the scene as a conflict between two Maya groups, one of which made use of Toltec paraphernalia to a slight extent and presumably fought as Toltec allies. On the other hand, the peculiar perspective, as well as the method of showing water and the fish, are characteristic of frescoes in the Temple of the Warriors which are regarded as typically Tula-Toltec.

Disk G is also unusual although not unique in that it has no Earth monster at the bottom. Instead, the central field is enlarged by extending it to the border pattern. As a result, it contains more subject matter than any other disk. In a circle only 20 centimeters (ca. 8 inches) in diameter there are twelve more or less elaborately dressed individuals, a Sky deity, a two-headed dragon, three rafts, a dug-out canoe, two swimmers and six fish, as well as spears, shields, paddles and the ripples of water.

The glyphs on the border of this disk are unusual in Maya epigraphy as they face not to the left but to the right. It might be argued that this indicates that they were fashioned by some ignorant craftsman who did not understand writing—were they not obviously the work of a master. We think it more probable that the artist, sculptor, featherworker or painter by trade, was unused to working in gold, that he pressed out his inscription from the reverse side of the disk in the manner he normally depicted glyphs, and then was surprised when they appeared backward on the front.

Perspective, in this case, is of a type seen in Chichen Itza frescoes, which do not employ either the linear or aerial perspective we normally use. Each object is pictured in the same scale and as if viewed at eye level. Distance, however, is indicated in two ways: by placing remote objects successively higher in the decorated field and by partly obscuring the more distant by the nearer. The former is a local development but the latter is common to all art portraying more than a single plane.

As for composition, most disks, including disk G, have the decorated area almost completely covered, in many cases by the use of small elements especially introduced for that purpose. The design is cut, however, by a horizontal line along which the major action takes place. This is true of disk G, but the rafts and swimmers below are shown not parallel to the medial base line but diagonal to it. This is the only case in relief at Chichen Itza, apparently, where an attempt has been made to show not only planes of varying distances but also motion in two distinct directions.

The Sky deity, the most elaborately adorned in the series, is pictured against a background of immense scrolls which represent a two-headed dragon with wide-open jaws and protruding tongues. These can be identified by the teeth, seen to the left of the deity's head and to the right of the back plumes. A similar background is shown on a carved slab found in the western court of the acropolis at Copan. The deity is represented as running with outstretched arms and right thigh raised. The pose is one of the most violent represented and perhaps indicates that the god, if not descending to earth, at least is in a hurry to get nearer the action depicted.

The deity wears an eagle mask with open jaws. In the nose there is a nose rod. On the wrists are typical Maya cuffs. Beneath each outstretched arm there is a semi-circular ornament fringed with long plumes which frame an unusually long and slender body. The shoulder and chest are covered by a yoke fringed with beads. The god holds in his left hand two spears. In the right hand is a Toltec spear thrower, held as if it has been just used. Ten spears are shown on the disk, five of which can be attributed by customary count to the standing warrior in the canoe. Did the god hurl the remaining three spears and thus join in the battle?

This sky deity obviously is a Toltec protagonist but, apart from his spears and spear thrower, shoulder yoke, mask and speech scroll, he is shown in Classical Maya style. The semi-circular panels fringed with plumes under the arms contain conventionalized serpent heads which lack the lower jaw. This motive is found on the wings of the Maya deity known as the Moan bird which will be discussed later. Similar symbolism appears on other Tula-Toltec sculpture and in metal at Chichen Itza. A circle surrounding the eye is typical of Tula-Toltec portraits of this divinity.

The principal characters, portrayed across the center of the disk, are five men in a canoe attacking a Maya who is attempting to escape on a raft. Pairs of Mayas are fleeing on two other small rafts and also two individuals are swimming.

The canoe is just large enough to hold five people. There is a distinct gunwale projecting outside the hull. At bow and stern there are platforms with relatively little overhang. The shape of the hull is obscured by water. Similar canoes with greater overhang appear in the Dresden Codex. Three frescoes in the Temple of the Warriors at Chichen Itza show seven canoes which all have bow and stern raised to about double the height of the freeboard amidships. There is an example of this type in the Dresden Codex. Two of the frescoes, however, can definitely be identified as ocean scenes owing to the presence of sting rays. The canoe on disk G then by inference is a type designed for inland waters. We should point out that, although the canoe carries at least two Toltecs, the crew may be Maya and the vessel itself presumably is of Maya workmanship, because a dugout is something one cannot manufacture at a moment's notice in the heat of battle.

The rafts are about half the length of the canoe and are large enough to carry only one or two people. They appear to be made of logs, to which greater buoyancy is given by gourds placed underneath. Rafts supported by gourds were used in Peru.

The paddles used by the occupants of the canoe are shaped like a modern oar. The end of the blade is square and the blade itself tapers to the width of the shaft. The man in the most distant raft holds a paddle of this type in one hand and a circular paddle with a short handle in the other. The circular form also appears on the other two rafts. These paddle types do not occur in the frescoes at Chichen Itza or in the Dresden Codex. In the former, ovate paddles are shown with a split handle attached to the rounded end. In the Codex, the blades are diamond shaped or have rounded ends with either square or rounded shoulders.

The canoe is propelled by a crew of three paddlers, two in the stern and one in the bow. They are dressed alike in ponchos adorned with zig-zag patterns and wear berets surmounted by short rounded feathers. The man in the bow carries a circular shield.

Amidships are two figures, one seated and one standing. The former is largely concealed by a circular shield. He wears an elaborate headdress with long plumes and has an ornament in the shape of a head, perhaps a trophy, on his back. The standing figure also wears a headdress with plumes and a head suspended on his shoulders. He has a nose button, a necklace and some sort of fringed gorget. He has cast two spears at a warrior fleeing on a raft and is in the act of throwing a third. Additional spears have already struck a man on a raft and a swimmer. There is a spear floating on the water and two others are held in the hand. None of the spears have points or feathers such as customarily appear on Toltec weapons but the spear thrower is of Toltec type.

The occupants of the canoe and the Sky deity are given dramatic unity by the presence of speech scrolls. These are shaped like a question mark, tipped forward horizontally. In the case of the man in the bow this is embellished by a second scroll. Evidently both the god and the men are saying the same thing to the fleeing warrior, doubtless a demand to surrender.

This fleeing warrior is in a perilous position. The two spears already cast at him were very near misses and another spear is about to come. The pose, showing the body full-face, the left side of the legs and the right side of the head, is one not easily rendered in low relief but it is adquately portrayed according to our conventions of perspective. The anatomy is in proportion and there is a good impression of flesh and muscle. Both arms are outstretched to hold the paddles out of the water, perhaps as a sign of surrender. At any rate, something is being said to the attackers in the canoe as indicated by a speech scroll.

Maya artists seldom attempted to show the human figure in this strained position but occasional examples occur over a wide area and in various media. Comparable figures, rendered with various degrees of success, may be noted in frescoes at Chichen Itza, Tzulá and Chacmultun, in the Maya Codices, in pottery from Yucatan and the Guatemalan highlands, in Great period [Maya] stone carving and in the frescoes at Bonampak.

Below the warrior and the raft we have described a portion of the disk is missing, but part of two figures are preserved who presumably occupied another raft, as they are shown with round paddles in their hands. The left-hand figure has been struck in the middle of the back by a spear and appears to be bending over in pain. The other is holding up his paddle, perhaps to indicate surrender.

A third raft with two occupants is shown at the bottom of the disk. Both wear ponchos of what appears to be quilted cotton, perhaps a form of body armour. The left-hand figure has a cap, adorned by plumes, which seems to be of the same material. A similar hat is worn by the single warrior on a raft and comparable forms appear on the three paddlers in the canoe.

Behind each of the rafts with two passengers there is a swimmer, perhaps in the water because there was not room on board for three. The upper figure, like one of the occupants of the adjacent raft, has been pierced by a spear. The other, together with the crew of the raft, appears to be making a successful get-away. As for the method of swimming, each individual seems to be using his arms in a different fashion. The right-hand figure may be doing a breast stoke. The other clearly is using his arms alternately in a crawl or "dog paddle." The relaxed fingers of the left hand suggest that it is out of water. The legs evidently are doing a scissors kick.

Little can be said regarding the six fish except that they are of several varieties, presumably fresh water species. With a few exceptions with outstanding characteristics, such as sharks and rays, Maya fish are too conventionalized for identification.

DISCUSSION

The series of disks we have described raises several questions. In the first place, who decorated them? To this the answer is Maya craftsmen working under the orders of Toltec conquerors. Toltec arms, insignia, ornaments, clothing, gods and the physical type are clearly portrayed, but all other details—border patterns, space fillers, Earth monsters, etc.—almost invariably reflect Maya art of the Great period. In other words, except when explicitly directed, the makers of the disks employed their own habitual art forms.

How did one become a gold worker in Yucatan? We do not use the word *smith* because there is no evidence that any Maya ever cast metal. Presumably preliminary training was in painting or the carving of stone or wood. Yet the style of the disks reflects neither the free vigor of the local frescoes nor the stiffness of the bas-reliefs. The answer perhaps is to be found in the statement of Sahagún that Aztec gold beaters had their designs drawn for them on sheet metal of their own manufacture by the featherworkers. The artistry and skill of Aztec featherworkers is fabulous. We have no way of knowing how good a tenth-century Maya was. It seems possible, however, that, when the importation of gold disks to Yucatan started, the local featherworkers were asked to decorate them. This would account for the slight divergence in style between painters, sculptors and metalworkers.

What was the technique of manufacture? Inasmuch as many undecorated disks were found in the Cenote of Sacrifice it seems probable that all examples were imported as plain disks. There is nothing to indicate that the Maya ever learned to hammer gold into sheets. They were able, however, to press designs in sheet metal and to cut it to the desired shape. Pressing a design is a relatively easy process if the sheet is placed on some yielding substance such as leather. We have no knowledge of Maya metal-working tools.

What wars do the disks commemorate? There seem to be two possibilities. One is the conquest of Chichen Itza by Hunac Ceel with the aid of Mexican mercenaries in the katun 8 Ahau which ended in 1204 A.D. This we reject because in the correlation we follow the Initial Series date is 10.19.0.0.0, fifteen katuns after the last-known Initial Series date. We do not believe it possible that the scores of art links with the latter part of baktun 9 which we have pointed out could have survived during the intervening three hundred years. We may add that there is no evidence that the Mexican troops of Hunac Ceel settled permanently in Chichen Itza. On the contrary, we know that it was re-occupied by Itzas within forty years, clearly too short a space to account for the many Toltec buildings.

A second possibility is that the disks commemorate the re-occupation of Chichen Itza and the arrival of Kukulcan in the katun 4 Ahau ending in 987 A.D. or 10.8.0.0.0 in the long count. The difficulty here is that we have no mention of wars at this time except for the conquest of Izamal and Motul in the seventh tun of katun 4 Ahau.

This dating, however, is more satisfactory from the Toltec angle. The disks clearly show the symbolism of Quetzalcoatl-Kukulcan, and details of dress and ornaments correspond closely to the Toltec art of Tula in the Mexican highlands. According to Mexican tradition, Quetzalcoatl-Kukulcan left Tula for Yucatan in the year 947 A.D. . . .

The facts that we have ascertained lead to the conclusion that the battle disks from the Cenote of Sacrifice were made at the beginning of the Tula-Toltec period in Yucatan when the art of the Maya Great period still flourished. In the chronological scheme we follow, they date from the second half of the tenth century A.D.

BIBLIOGRAPHY

ANONYMOUS
1929. "Desert Markings near Ur," *Antiquity,* vol. 3, p. 342, pl. III.

BACHE, CHARLES
1935. "Prehistoric Burials of Tepe Gawra," *Scientific American,* vol. 153, pp. 310–313.

BALL, S. H.
1941. *The Mining of Gems and Ornamental Stones by American Indians,* Smithsonian Institution, Bureau of American Ethnology, Washington, D.C., Bulletin 128, pp. 1–77.

BANK, T. P.
1953. "Ecology of Prehistoric Aleutian Village Sites," *Ecology,* vol. 34, pp. 246–264.

BARTH, F.
1953. *Principles of Social Organization in Southern Kurdistan,* Universitetets Ethnografiske Museum, Oslo, Bulletin 7, pp. 1–146.

BARTOCCINI, R.
n.d. *Les peintures étrusques de Tarquinia,* Bibliothèque des Arts, Paris.

BENNETT, W. C.
1953. *Excavations at Wari, Ayacucho, Peru,* Yale University Publications in Anthropology, no. 49.

BIRD, J. B.
1938. "Antiquity and Migrations of the Early Inhabitants of Patagonia," *Geographical Review,* vol. 28, pp. 250–275.

BIRDSELL, J. B.
1950. "Some Implications of the Genetical Concept of Race in Terms of Spatial Analysis," *Cold Spring Harbor Symposia on Quantitative Biology,* vol. 15, pp. 259–314.
1953. "Some Environmental and Cultural Factors Influencing the Structuring of Australian Aboriginal Population," *American Naturalist,* vol. 87, no. 834, Supplement pp. 171–207.

BOBEK, H.
1954. "Klima und Landschaft Irans in vor- und frühgeschichtlicher Zeit," *Geog. Jahresb. Osterreich,* vol. 25, pp. 1–42.

BORISKOVSKI, P. I.
  1956. *Les habitations paléolithiques sur le territoire de l'U.R.S.S. et leurs parallèles ethnographiques,* Communications de la Délégation Sovietique au V⁰ Congrès International des Sciences Anthropologiques et Ethnologiques [at Philadelphia], Moscow.

BOULE, M., and VALLOIS, H.
  1946. *Les hommes fossiles,* 3rd ed., Paris.

BRADFIELD, W.
  1931. *Cameron Creek Village,* El Palacio Press, Santa Fe.

BRAIDWOOD, R. J.
  1952. "The Near East and the Foundations for Civilization: An Essay in Appraisal of the General Evidence," *Condon Lectures,* Oregon State System of Higher Education, Eugene.
  1956. "Reflections on the Origin of the Village-farming Community," in Saul S. Weinberg (ed.), *The Aegean and the Near East: Studies presented to Hetty Goldman,* Locust Valley, New York: Augustin, pp. 22–31.
  1957. "Jericho and Its Setting in Near Eastern Prehistory," *Antiquity,* vol. 31, pp. 73–81.

BRAINERD, G. W.
  1951. "The Place of Chronological Ordering in Archaeological Analysis," *American Antiquity,* vol. 16, pp. 301–313.

BREUIL, H.
  1912. "Les peintures rupestres d'Espagne," *L'Anthropologie,* vol. 23, pp. 529–562.
  1942–45. "La conquête de la notion de la très haute antiquité de l'homme," *Anthropos,* vols. 38–40, pp. 667–687.
  n.d. *Four Hundred Centuries of Cave Art,* Centre d'Etudes et de Documentation Préhistoriques, Montignac, Dordogne, France.

BROOKS, C. E. P.
  1926. *Climate Through the Ages,* R. V. Coleman, Edinburgh.

BRYAN, K.
  1929. "Flood-water Farming," *The Geographical Review,* vol. 19, pp. 444–456.
  1950. *Flint Quarries—the Sources of Tools and, at the same time, the Factories of the American Indian.* Papers of the Peabody Museum, Harvard University, Cambridge, vol. 17, no. 3.

BUTTLER, W., and HABEREY, W.
  1936. *Die Bandkeramische Ansiedlung bei Koeln-Lindenthal,* Roemisch-germanische Kommission des Deutschen Archaeologischen Instituts zu Frankfurt a.M., Roemisch-germanische Forschungen, Band 11, Walter de Gruyter, Berlin and Leipzig.

BUTZER, K. W.
  1957. "Late Glacial and Postglacial Climatic Variation in the Near East." Erdkund, Arch. f. wissens. Geog., vol. 11, pp. 21–35.

CATON-THOMPSON, G., and GARDNER, E. W.
  1934. *The Desert Fayum,* The Royal Anthropological Institute of Great Britain and Ireland, London.

CHAMBERLAIN, A. F.
1907. "Thomas Jefferson's Ethnological Opinions and Activities," *American Anthropologist*, vol. 9, pp. 499–509.

CHILDE, V. G.
1953. *New Light on the Most Ancient East*, Praeger, New York

CLARK, J. G. D.
1947. *Archaeology and Society*, 2nd ed. rev., Methuen, London.
1952. *Prehistoric Europe: the Economic Basis*, Methuen, London.
1954. *Excavations at Star Carr: An Early Mesolithic Site at Seamer Near Scarborough, Yorkshire*, Cambridge University Press.

COLE, FAY-COOPER, *et al.*
1951. *Kincaid. A Prehistoric Illinois Metropolis*, University of Chicago Publications in Anthropology, Archaeology Series, Chicago.

COLLINS, HENRY B., JR.
1937. *Archeology of St. Lawrence Island, Alaska*, Smithsonian Miscellaneous Collections, Washington, D.C., vol. 96, no. 1.

COLTON, H. S.
1932. "Sunset Crater: the Effect of a Volcanic Eruption on an Ancient Pueblo People," *The Geographic Review*, vol. 22, pp. 582–590.
1946. *The Sinagua: A Summary of the Archaeology of the Region of Flagstaff, Arizona*, Flagstaff.

COOK, S. F.
1946. "A Reconsideration of Shellmounds with Respect to Population and Nutrition," *American Antiquity*, vol. 12, pp. 51–53.
1947. "Survivorship in Aboriginal Populations," *Human Biology*, vol. 19, pp. 83–89.

COON, CARLETON S.
1952. *Cave Explorations in Iran, 1949*, Museum Monographs, University Museum, University of Pennsylvania, Philadelphia.

CRABTREE, D. E.
1939. "Mastodon Bone with Artifacts in California," *American Antiquity*, vol. 5, p. 148.

CRANE, H. R.
1955. "Antiquity of the Sandia Culture: Carbon-14 Measurements," *Science*, vol. 122, pp. 689–690.

CRARY, D. D.
1955. "The Villager," in Sydney Nettleton Fisher (ed.), *Social Forces in the Middle East*, Cornell University Press, Ithaca, pp. 43–59.

CRAWFORD, O. G. S.
1932. "The Dialectical Process in the History of Science," *The Sociological Review*, vol. 24, pp. 165–173.

CUMMINGS, B.
1927. "Ancient Canals of the Casa Grande," *Progressive Arizona*, Tucson, vol. 3, pp. 9–10.
1933. *Cuicuilco and the Archaic Culture of Mexico*, University of Arizona Bulletin, Tucson, vol. 4, no. 8 (Soc. Sci. Bull. no. 4).

DALL, W. H.
1877. *On Succession in the Shell-Heaps of the Aleutian Islands,* Contributions to North American Ethnology, Washington, D.C., vol. 1.
DANIEL, G. E.
1950. *A Hundred Years of Archaeology,* G. Duckworth, London.
DEEVEY, E. S., JR.
1956. "The Human Crop," *Scientific American,* vol. 194 (April), pp. 105–112.
DELOUGAZ, P., and LLOYD, S.
1942. *Pre-Sargonid Temples in the Diyala Region,* Oriental Institute Publications, Chicago, vol. 58.
DIPESO, C.
1958. *The Reeve Ruin of Southeastern Arizona,* The Amerind Foundation, Dragoon, Arizona, Publication no. 8.
DRUCKER, PHILIP
1955. *The Cerro de las Mesas Offering of Jade and Other Materials,* Smithsonian Institution, Bureau of American Ethnology, Washington, D.C., Bulletin 157, pp. 29–68.
DRUCKER, PHILIP, and CONTRERAS, EDUARDO
1953. "Site Patterns in the Eastern Part of Olmec Territory," *Journal of the Washington Academy of Sciences,* Washington, D.C., vol. 43, no. 12 (December), pp. 389–391.
DUBOIS, F.
1897. *Tombouctou la Mystérieuse,* Paris.
EHRICH, R. W.
1954. *Relative Chronologies in Old World Archaeology,* University of Chicago Press, Chicago.
FELTS, W. M.
1942. "A Petrographic Examination of Potsherds from Ancient Troy," *American Journal of Archaeology,* ser. 2, vol. 46, pp. 237–244.
FEWKES, J. W.
1904. *Two Summers' Work in Pueblo Ruins,* Twenty-second Annual Report of Bureau of American Ethnology, Washington, D.C., pt. I, pp. 3–195.
1914. *Archeology of the Lower Mimbres Valley, N.M.,* Smithsonian Miscellaneous Collections, Washington, D.C., vol. 63, no. 10.
FLINT, R. F.
1945. "Chronology and the Pleistocene Epoch," *Quarterly Journal of the Florida Academy of Science,* vol. 8, pp. 1–34.
FORD, JAMES A.
1938. "A Chronological Method Applicable to the Southeast," *American Antiquity,* vol. 3, pp. 260–264.
1949. *Cultural Dating of Prehistoric Sites in Virú Valley, Peru,* American Museum of Natural History, Anthropological Papers, New York, vol. 43, pt. 1.
1951. *Greenhouse: a Troyville-Coles Creek Period Site in Avoyelles Parish, Louisiana,* American Museum of Natural History, Anthropological Papers, New York, vol. 44, pt. 1.
1952. *Measurements of Some Prehistoric Design Developments in the South-*

eastern States, American Museum of Natural History, Anthropological Papers, New York, vol. 44, pt. 3.

FORD, JAMES A., and WILLEY, GORDON K.
1949. *A Surface Survey of the Virú Valley, Peru,* American Museum of Natural History, Anthropological Papers, New York, vol. 43, pt. 1.

FRANKFORT, H.
1950. "Town Planning in Ancient Mesopotamia," *Town Planning Review,* vol. 21, pp. 98–115.

FUJISHIMA, G.
1957. "Considerations for Restoration of Pit-Dwelling Sites at Kurihara Site in Tokyo," in *Kurihara,* College of Arts, St. Paul's University, Tokyo, pp. 11–12.

GABB, W. H.
1881. "On the Topography and Geology of Santo Domingo," *Transactions of the American Philosophical Society,* Philadelphia, n.s., vol. 15, pp. 49–259.

GADD, C. J.
1932. "Seals of Ancient Indian Style Found at Abr," *Proceedings of the British Academy,* vol. 18, pp. 191–210.

GHIRSHMAN, R.
1938. *Fouilles de Sialk près de Kashan, 1933, 1934, 1937,* Musée du Louvre, Départment des Antiquités Orientales, Série Archéologique, Paris, Tome IV, vol. I.

GIFFORD, E. W.
1949. "Early Central California and Anasazi Shell Artifact Types," *American Antiquity,* vol. 15, pp. 156–157.

GLADWIN, H. S.
1957. *A History of the Ancient Southwest,* Bond Wheelright, Portland, Maine.

GLADWIN, N.
1937. "Petrography of Snaketown Pottery," in H. S. Gladwin *et al., Excavations at Snaketown,* Medallion Papers, Gila Pueblo, Arizona, no. 25, chap. 17.

GRIFFIN, J. W.
1955. "Chronology and Dating Processes," *Yearbook of Anthropology,* Wenner-Gren Foundation, New York, pp. 133–147.

HANFMANN, G. M. A.
1951. The Bronze Age in the Near East: a Review Article," *American Journal of Archaeology,* vol. 55, pp. 355–365.

HANSEN, H. P.
1942. *A Pollen Study of Peat Profiles from Lower Klamath Lake of Oregon and California,* Carnegie Institution of Washington, Washington, D.C., Publication 538, pp. 103–114.

HARRINGTON, M. R.
1924. "The Ozark Bluff-Dwellers," *American Anthropologist,* vol. 26, pp. 1–21.
1933. *Gypsum Cave,* Southwest Museum Papers, no. 8.

HAURY, E. W.

1940. *Excavations in the Forestdale Valley, East-Central Arizona*, University of Arizona Bulletin, Tucson, vol. 12, no. 4 (Soc. Sci. Bull. no. 12).

1945. *The Excavation of Los Muertos and Neighboring Ruins in the Salt River Valley, Southern Arizona*, Papers of the Peabody Museum, Harvard University, Cambridge, vol. 24, no. 1.

1947. "A Large Pre-Columbian Copper Bell from the Southwest," *American Antiquity*, vol. 13, pp. 80–82.

1955. "Archaeological Stratigraphy," in *Geochronology*, University of Arizona, Tucson, Physical Science Bulletin no. 2, pp. 123–134.

HAWKES, E. W., and LINTON, R.

1916. *A Pre-Lenape Site in New Jersey*, University of Pennsylvania, University Museum, Anthropological Publications, Philadelphia, vol. 6, no. 3, pp. 49–77.

1917. "A Pre-Lenape Culture in New Jersey," *American Anthropologist*, vol. 19, pp. 487–494.

HAWLEY, FLORENCE

1934. *The Significance of the Dated Prehistory of Chetro Ketl, Chaco Canyon, New Mexico*, University of New Mexico Bulletin, vol. 1, no. 1.

1937. "Reversed Stratigraphy," *American Antiquity*, vol. 2, pp. 297–299.

HEIZER, R. F.

1953. "Long Range Dating in Archeology," *Anthropology Today*, University of Chicago Press, Chicago, pp. 3–24.

1955. "Primitive Man as an Ecologic Factor," *Kroeber Anthropological Society Papers*, Berkeley, no. 13, pp. 1–31.

HEIZER, R. F., and TREGANZA, A. E.

1944. "Mines and Quarries of the Indians of California," *California Journal of Mines and Geology*, vol. 40, pp. 291–359.

HELBAEK, H.

1953. "Archaeology and Agricultural Botany," *Annual Report, Institute of Archaeology*, University of London, pp. 44–59.

HERZ, N., and PRITCHETT, W. K.

1953. "Marble in Attic Epigraphy," *American Journal of Archaeology*, vol. 57, pp. 71–83.

HIBBEN, F. C.

1955. "Specimens from Sandia Cave and Their Possible Significance," *Science*, vol. 122, pp. 688–689.

HILZHEIMER, M.

1941. "Animal Remains from Tell Asmar," *Study of Ancient Oriental Civilization*, University of Chicago, vol. 20, pp. 1–52.

HOLMES, WILLIAM H.

1919. "Introductory, The Lithic Industries," *Handbook of Aboriginal American Antiquities*, Bureau of American Ethnology, Bulletin 60, pt. 1.

HOOTON, E. A.

1920. *Indian Village Site and Cemetery near Madisonville, Ohio*, Papers of the Peabody Museum, Harvard University, Cambridge, vol. 8, no. 1.

1930. *The Indians of Pecos Pueblo*, Yale University Press, New Haven.

1940. "Skeletons from the Cenote of Sacrifice at Chichen Itza," in C. L. Hay *et al.* (eds.), *The Maya and Their Neighbors,* Appleton-Century, New York, pp. 272–280.

HOWELL, DAVID

1940. "Pipestone and Red Shale Artifacts," *American Antiquity,* vol. 16, no. 1, pp. 45–62.

HOWELL, F. C.

1952. "Pleistocene Geology and the Evolution of Classic Neanderthal Man," *Southwestern Journal of Anthropology,* vol. 8, pp. 377–410.

HUNTINGTON, ELLSWORTH

1933. *Civilization and Climate,* Yale University Press, New Haven.

HUTCHINSON, G. E.

1950. *Survey of Contemporary Knowledge of Biochemistry: 3, The Biogeochemistry of Vertebrate Excretion,* American Museum of Natural History, Bulletin, vol. 96.

IVERSEN, J.

1956. "Forest Clearance in the Stone Age," *Scientific American,* vol. 194, pp. 36–41.

JOCHELSON, W.

1925. *Archaeological Investigations in the Aleutian Islands,* Carnegie Institution of Washington, Washington, D.C., Publication 367.

KAY, M.

1955. *Sediments and Subsidence Through Time,* Geological Society of America, Special Paper no. 62, pp. 665–684.

KENDRICK, T. D.

1950. *British Antiquity,* Methuen, London.

KENYON, K. M.

1956. "Jericho and Its Setting in Near Eastern History," *Antiquity,* vol. 30, pp. 184–195.

KIDDER, A. V.

1915. *Pottery of the Pajarito Plateau and of Some Adjacent Regions in New Mexico,* Memoirs of the American Anthropological Association, vol. 2, pt. 6.

KIDDER, A. V., JENNINGS, J. D., and SHOOK, E. M.

1946. *Excavations at Kaminaljuyu, Guatemala,* Carnegie Institution of Washington, Washington, D.C., Publication 561.

KLUCKHOHN, C.

1940. "The Conceptual Structure of Middle American Studies," in C. L. Hay *et al.* (eds.), *The Maya and Their Neighbors,* Appleton-Century, New York, pp. 41–51.

KRIEGER, A. D.

1946. *Culture Complexes and Chronology in Northern Texas with Extension of Puebloan Datings to the Mississippi Valley,* University of Texas Publications, no. 4640.

1947. "The Eastward Extension of Puebloan Datings toward Cultures of the Mississippi Valley," *American Antiquity,* vol. 12, pp. 141–148.

KROEBER, A. L.

1916a. *Zuñi Potsherds,* American Museum of Natural History, Anthropological Papers, New York, vol. 18, pt. 1.

1916b. "Zuñi Culture Sequences," *Proceedings of the National Academy of Sciences*, vol. 2, pp. 42–45.

1939. *Cultural and Natural Areas of Native North America*, University of California Press, Berkeley.

1948. *Anthropology*, Harcourt Brace, New York.

KROEBER, A. L., and STRONG, W. D.

1942. *The Uhle Pottery Collections from Ica*, University of California Publications in American Archaeology and Ethnology, vol. 21, pp. 95–133.

KUBLER, G.

1948. "Towards Absolute Time: Guano Archaeology," in *A Reappraisal of Peruvian Archaeology*, Society for American Archaeology, Memoir no. 4, pp. 29–50.

KULP, L., *et al*.

1951. "Lamont Natural Radiocarbon Measurements, I," *Science*, vol. 114, pp. 565–568.

LADD, J.

1957. "A Stratigraphic Trench at Sitio Conte, Panama," *American Antiquity*, vol. 22, pp. 265–271.

LARTET, E.

1861. "Nouvelle recherches sur la coexistence de l'homme et des grands mammifères fossiles," *Annales des Sciences Naturelles*, ser. 4, vol. 15, pp. 177–253.

LEASON, P. A.

1939. "A New View of the Western European Group of Quaternary Cave Art," *Proceedings of the Prehistoric Society for 1939*, n.s., vol. 5, pp. 51–60.

LEECHMAN, D.

1950. *Aboriginal Tree-Felling*, National Museum of Canada, Bulletin 118.

LEHMANN-HARTLEBEN, K.

1943. "Thomas Jefferson, Archaeologist," *American Journal of Archaeology*, vol. 47, pp. 161–163.

LEISINGER, H.

1953. *Les peintures étrusques de Tarquinia*, Editions Claire-fontaine, Lausanne.

LEROI-GOURHAN, A.

1952. "L'étude des vestiges zoölogiques," in *La Découverte du Passé*, A. Laming, Paris, pp. 123–150.

LOTHROP, S. K.

1928. *The Indians of Tierra del Fuego*, Contributions of the Museum of the American Indian, Heye Foundation, New York, vol. 10.

1937. *Coclé: an Archaeological Study of Central Panama, Part I, Historical Background, Excavations at the Sitio Conte, Artifacts and Ornaments*, Memoirs of the Peabody Museum, Harvard University, Cambridge, vol. 7.

1942. *Cocle: an Archaeological Study of Central Panama, Part II, Pottery of the Sitio Conte and Other Archaeological Sites*, Memoirs of the Peabody Museum, Harvard University, Cambridge, vol. 8.

LUFFKIN, J.
1701. "Part of a Letter from Mr. John Luffkin to the Publisher concerning some Large Bones Lately Found in a Gravel Pit near Colchester," *Proceedings of the Royal Society, Philosophical Transactions,* vol. 22, pp. 924–926.

McCOWN, C. C.
1943. *The Ladder of Progress in Palestine,* Harper, New York.

MacCURDY, G. G.
1924. *Human Origins,* 2 vols., Appleton, New York.

McGREGOR, J. C.
1943. "Burial of an Early American Magician," *Proceedings of American Philosophical Society,* vol. 86, pp. 270–298.

MARINGER, J., and BANDI, H. G.
1953. *Art in the Ice Age,* Praeger, New York.

MARSDEN, L.
1958. "Up from the Well of Time," *National Geographic Magazine,* vol. 115, pp. 110–129.

MASSOULARD, E.
1949. *Préhistoire et protohistoire d'Egypte,* Institut d'Ethnologie, Travaux et Mémoires, Paris, vol. 53.

MATHIASSEN, THERKEL
1936. *The Eskimo Archaeology of Julianehaab District,* Meddelelser om Grønland, Copenhagen, vol. 118, no. 1.

MATSON, F. R.
1955. "Charcoal Concentration from Early Sites for Radiocarbon Dating," *American Antiquity,* vol. 21, pp. 162–169.

MEIGHAN, C.
1955. *Excavation of Isabella Meadows Cave, Monterey County, California,* University of California Archaeological Survey Reports, no. 29 (Paper no. 30), pp. 1–30.

MORRIS, E. H.
1919. *The Aztec Ruin,* American Museum of Natural History, Anthropological Papers, New York, vol. 26, pt. I.
1939. *Archaeological Studies in the La Plata District,* Carnegie Institution of Washington, Washington, D.C., Publication 519.

MOVIUS, H. L.
1950. "A Wooden Spear of Third Interglacial Age from Lower Saxony," *Southwestern Journal of Anthropology,* vol. 6, pp. 139–142.

MÜHLSTEIN, H.
1929. *Die Kunst der Etrusken,* Berlin.

NELSON, N. C.
1917. "Archeology of the Tano District, New Mexico," *Proceedings of Nineteenth International Congress of Americanists,* Washington, D.C., December 1915, pp. 114–118.

NICOLAYSEN, N.
1882. *Langskibet fra Gokstad ved sandefjord,* Christiania.

NIETSCH, H.
1939. *Wald und Siedlung im vorgeschichtlichen Mitteleuropa*, Mannus-Bücherei, Leipzig.

NÜESCH, JAKOB
1902. *Die praehistorische Niederlassung am Schweizerbild bei Schaffhausen. Die Schichten und ihre Einschlusse,* Neue Denkschiften der Allgemeine Schweizerische Gesellschaft fur die Gesammten Naturwissenschaften, vol. 35.

OAKLEY, K. P.
1951. "The Fluorine-dating Method," *Viking Fund Yearbook of Physical Anthropology for 1949,* vol. 5, pp. 44–52.
1955. *Further Contributions to the Solution of the Piltdown Problem,* Bulletin of the British Museum (Natural History), Geology, London, vol. 2, no. 6.
1956. "The Earliest Tool-Makers and the Earliest Fire-Makers," *Antiquity,* vol. 30, pp. 4–9, 102–107.

OLSON, R. L.
1930. *Chumash Prehistory,* University of California Publications in American Archaeology and Ethnology, vol. 28, pp. 1–22.

ORCHARD, W. C.
1925. "Porcupine Quillwork from Lovelock Cave, Nevada," *Indian Notes,* Museum of the American Indian, Heye Foundation, vol. 2, pp. 187–190.

ORSI, P.
1922. "Megara Hyblaea, 1917–1921," *Monumenti Antichi,* R. Accademia Nazionale dei Lincei, Milan, vol. 27, pp. 108–179.

PEPPER, G. H.
1920. *Pueblo Bonito,* American Museum of Natural History, Anthropological Papers, New York, vol. 27.

PETRIE, W. M. F.
1899. "Sequences in Prehistoric Remains," *Journal of the Anthropological Institute of Great Britain and Ireland,* London, vol. 29 (n.s. II), pp. 295–301.
1901. *Diospolis Parva,* Egyptian Exploration Fund Memoirs, London, no. 20.
1904. *Methods and Aims in Archaeology,* New York.

PHILLIPS, P., FORD, J. A., and GRIFFIN, J. B.
1951. *Archaeological Survey in the Lower Mississippi Alluvial Valley, 1940–1947,* Papers of the Peabody Museum, Harvard University, Cambridge, vol. 25.

PIGGOTT, S.
1937. "Prehistory and the Romantic Movement," *Antiquity,* vol. 11, pp. 31–38.

POULSEN, F.
1922. *Etruscan Tomb Paintings,* Oxford.

PRITCHETT, W. K.
1953. "The Attic Stelai, Part I," *Hesperia,* Journal of the American School of Classical Studies at Athens, vol. 22, pp. 225–229.

PUMPELLY, RAPHAEL (ed.)
1908. *Explorations in Turkestan, Expedition of 1904,* Carnegie Institution of Washington, Washington, D.C., Publication 73, vol. 1.

RANDALL-MACIVER, R.
1933. "Archaeology as a Science," *Antiquity,* vol. 7, pp. 5–20.

RANDALL-MACIVER, R., and MACE, M. A.
1902. *El Amrah and Abydos,* Special Publication of the Egypt Exploration Fund, London.

REISNER, G. A.
1908. *The Early Dynastic Cemeteries of Naga-ed-Dêr, Part I,* University of California Publications in Egyptian Archaeology, Leipzig, vol. 2.
1932. *A Provincial Cemetery of the Pyramid Age, Naga-ed-Dêr, Part III,* University of California Publications in Egyptian Archaeology, Oxford, vol. 6.

RICE, T. T.
1957. *The Scythians,* Praeger, New York.

RICKETSON, O. G., and RICKETSON, E. B.
1937. *Uaxactun, Guatemala, Group E, 1926–31,* Carnegie Institution of Washington, Washington, D.C., Publication 477.

RITCHIE, W. A.
1954. *Dutch Hollow, an Early Historic Period Seneca Site in Livingston County, New York,* Research Records of the New York State Archaeological Association, Rochester, vol. 13, no. 1.

ROBINSON, W. S.
1951. "A Method for Chronologically Ordering Archaeological Deposits," *American Antiquity,* vol. 16, pp. 293–301.

ROMANELLI, P.
1951. *Tarquinia,* Rome.

RUSSELL, F.
1908. *The Pima Indians,* Twenty-sixth Annual Report of the Bureau of American Ethnology, Washington, D.C.

SCHAEFFER, C. F.
1948. *Stratigraphie compareé et chronologie de l'Asie Occidentale,* Oxford University Press, London.

SCHENCK, W. E.
1926. *The Emeryville Shellmound: Final Report,* University of California Publications in American Archaeology and Ethnology, vol. 23, pp. 147–282.

SCHWARTZ, D. W.
1956. "Demographic Changes in the Early Periods of Cohonina Prehistory," in *Prehistoric Settlement Patterns in the New World,* Viking Fund Publications in Anthropology, New York, no. 23, pp. 26–31.

SCHWARZ, N.
1958. "Gamble for the Sun God's Gold," *True Magazine,* November, pp. 31–33, 72–78.

SEARS, W. B.
1954. "The Sociopolitical Organization of Pre-Columbian Cultures on the Gulf Coastal Plain," *American Anthropologist,* vol. 56, pp. 339–346.

SHEPARD, A. O.
1942. *Rio Grande Glaze Paint Ware,* Contributions to American Anthropology and History, Carnegie Institution of Washington, Washington, D.C., vol. 7, no. 39.
1948. *Plumbate, a Mesoamerican Trade Ware,* Carnegie Institution of Washington, Washington, D.C., Publication 573.

1956. *Ceramics for the Archaeologist,* Carnegie Institution of Washington, Washington, D.C., Publication 609.

SHORR, P.

1935. "The Genesis of Prehistorical Research," *Isis,* vol. 23, pp. 425–443.

SJØVOLD, T.

1958. "A Royal Viking Burial," *Archaeology,* vol. 11, pp. 190–199.

SMITH, R. E.

1940. "Ceramics of the Peten," in C. L. Hay *et al.* (eds.), *The Maya and Their Neighbors,* Appleton Century, New York, pp. 242–249.

1955. *Ceramic Sequence at Uaxactun, Guatemala,* Middle American Research Institute, Tulane University, New Orleans, Publication No. 20, vol. 1.

SMITH, W.

1952. *Excavations in Big Hawk Valley,* Museum of Northern Arizona, Flagstaff, Arizona, Bulletin 24.

SNOW, C. E.

1948. *Indian Knoll Skeletons,* University of Kentucky Reports in Anthropology, Lexington, vol. 4, no. 3, pt. 2.

SPEISER, E. A.

1935. *Excavations at Tepe Gawra,* Philadelphia, vol. 1.

SPIER, LESLIE

1917. *Outline of Chronology of the Zuñi Ruins,* American Museum of Natural History, Anthropological Papers, New York, vol. 18, pp. 209–231.

1931. "N. C. Nelson's Stratigraphic Technique in the Reconstruction of Prehistoric Sequences in Southwestern America," in S. A. Rice (ed.), *Methods in Social Science,* Chicago, pp. 275–283.

STEKELIS, M., and HAAS, G.

1952. "The Abu Usba Cave," *Israel Exploration Journal,* vol. 2, pp. 15–47.

STEWARD, J. H.

1936. "The Economic and Social Basis of Primitive Bands," in *Essays in Honor of A. L. Kroeber,* University of California Press, Berkeley, pp. 331–350.

1955. *Theory of Culture Change,* University of Illinois Press, Urbana.

STONE, J. F. S.

1949. "A Second Fixed Point in the Chronology of the Harappa Culture," *Antiquity,* vol. 92, pp. 201–205.

STONE, J. F. S., and WALLIS, F. S.

1947. "Second Report of the Sub-Committee of the South-Western Group of Museums and Art Galleries on the Petrological Identification of Stone Axes," *Proceedings of the Prehistoric Society,* Cambridge, n.s., vol. 13, pp. 47–55.

STRONG, W. D.

1947. "Finding the Tomb of a Warrior-God," *National Geographic Magazine,* vol. 91, pp. 453–482.

STRONG, W. D., and EVANS, C., JR.

1952. *Cultural Stratigraphy in the Virú Valley, Northern Peru,* Columbia University Press, New York.

TAYLOR, W. W.

1948. *A Study of Archaeology,* Memoirs of the American Anthropological Association, no. 69.

THOMAS, CYRUS
1894. *Report on the Mound Explorations of the Bureau of Ethnology,* Twelfth Annual Report of the Bureau of American Ethnology, Washington, D.C.
THOMAS, W. L. (ed.)
1956. *Man's Role in Changing the Face of the Earth,* University of Chicago Press, Chicago.
THOMPSON, R. H.
1955. Review of R. E. M. Wheeler, *Archaeology from the Earth,* in *American Antiquity,* vol. 21, pp. 188–189.
THOMSEN, C. J.
1836. *Ledetraad til Nordisk Oldkyndighed,* Copenhagen. (Pub. 1837 as *Leitfaden Zur Nordischen Alterthumskunde,* Copenhagen.)
THOMSON, D. F.
1939. "The Seasonal Factor in Human Culture," *Proceedings of the Prehistoric Society for 1939,* pp. 209–221.
UHLE, M.
1907. *The Emeryville Shellmound,* University of California Publications in American Archaeology and Ethnology, vol. 7, pp. 1–106.
VAILLANT, G. C.
1931. *Excavations at Ticoman,* American Museum of Natural History, Anthropological Papers, vol. 32, pt. 2.
1935. *Excavations at El Arbolillo,* American Museum of Natural History, Anthropological Papers, New York, vol. 35, pt. 2.
VAN BUREN, E. D.
1939. "The Fauna of Ancient Mesopotamia as Represented in Art," *Analecta Orientalia,* vol. 18, pp. 1–113.
WEBB, W. S.
1946. *Indian Knoll,* University of Kentucky Reports in Anthropology, Lexington, vol. 4, no. 3, pt. 1.
WEDEL, WALDO R.
1941. *Archeological Investigations at Buena Vista Lake, Kern County, California,* Smithsonian Institution, Bureau of American Ethnology, Washington, D.C., Bulletin 130.
WEEGE, F.
1931. *Die Malerei der Etrusker,* Halle.
WEINER, J. S.
1955. *The Piltdown Forgery,* Oxford University Press, London.
WEISS, L. E.
1954. "Fabric Analysis of Some Greek Marbles and Its Application to Archeology," *American Journal of Science,* vol. 252, pp. 641–662.
WERNERT, P.
1948. "Les hommes de l'Age de la Pierre: representent-ils les esprits des defunts et des ancêtres?" in M. Garce and R. Mortier (eds.), *Histoire Générale des Religions,* Paris, vol. 1.
WEST, R. G.
1956. "The Quaternary Deposits at Hoxne," *Proceedings of the Prehistoric Society,* n.s., vol. 20, pp. 131–139.

WHEAT, J. B.
  1955. *Mogollon Culture Prior to A.D. 1000,* Memoirs of the Society for American Archaeology, no. 10.
WHEELER, M.
  1947. "Harappa 1946: The Defences and Cemetery R 37," *Ancient India,* no. 3, pp. 59–130.
  1950. *Five Thousand Years of Pakistan: an Archaeological Outline,* Royal India and Pakistan Society, London.
  1954. *Archaeology from the Earth,* Oxford University Press, London.
WILLARD, T. A.
  1926. *The City of the Sacred Well,* New York.
WILLEY, GORDON R.
  1946. "The Virú Valley Program in Northern Peru," *Acta Americana,* vol. 4, no. 4, pp. 224–238.
WILLEY, G. R., and PHILLIPS, P.
  1955. "Method and Theory in American Archeology II: Historical-Developmental Interpretation," *American Anthropologist,* vol. 57, pp. 723–819.
WOODBURY, R. B.
  1954. *Prehistoric Stone Implements from Northeastern Arizona,* Papers of the Peabody Museum, Harvard University, Cambridge, vol. 34.
WOOLLEY, C. L.
  1934. *Ur Excavations,* Publications of the Joint Expedition of the British Museum and the Museum of the University of Pennsylvania to Mesopotamia, vol. II, "The Royal Cemetery."
  1949. *Digging Up the Past,* Pelican Books, Harmondsworth, Middlesex.
WORMINGTON, H. M.
  1957. *Ancient Man in North America,* 4th ed. rev., Denver Museum of Natural History, Popular Series No. 4.
WORSAAE, J. J.
  1849. *Primeval Antiquities of Denmark,* London.
WRIGHT, H. E., JR.
  1952. *The Geological Setting of Four Prehistoric Sites in Northeastern Iraq.* Bulletin of the American Schools of Oriental Research, vol. 128, pp. 11–24.
ZEUNER, F. E.
  1936. "Paleobiology and Climate of the Past," in *Problems of Paleontology,* Moscow, vol. 1, pp. 199–216.
  1952. *Dating the Past: An Introduction to Geochronology,* 3rd ed. rev., Methuen, London.
  1956. "The Radiocarbon Age of Jericho," *Antiquity,* vol. 30, pp. 195–197.

INDEX

Set in Linotype Caledonia
Format by James T. Parker
Manufactured by Kingsport Press, Inc.
Published by HARPER & BROTHERS, New York